Theatre: The Lively Art

TENTH EDITION

EDWIN WILSON
Professor Emeritus
Graduate School and University Center
The City University of New York

ALVIN GOLDFARB
President and Professor Emeritus
Western Illinois University

Mc
Graw
Hill
Education

THEATRE: THE LIVELY ART, TENTH EDITION

Published by McGraw-Hill Education, 2 Penn Plaza, New York, NY 10121. Copyright © 2019 by Edwin Wilson and Alvin Goldfarb. All rights reserved. Printed in the United States of America. Previous editions © 2016, 2012, and 2010. No part of this publication may be reproduced or distributed in any form or by any means, or stored in a database or retrieval system, without the prior written consent of McGraw-Hill Education, including, but not limited to, in any network or other electronic storage or transmission, or broadcast for distance learning.

Some ancillaries, including electronic and print components, may not be available to customers outside the United States.

This book is printed on acid-free paper.

1 2 3 4 5 6 7 8 9 LWI 21 20 19 18

ISBN 978-1-259-91686-1
MHID 1-259-91686-3

Portfolio Manager: *Sarah Remington*
Product Developer: *Beth Tripmacher*
Content Project Managers: *Sandy Wille; Melissa M. Leick*
Buyer: *Sandy Ludovissy*
Design: *Tara McDermott*
Content Licensing Specialist: *Ann Marie Jannette*
Cover Image: *©Sara Krulwich/The New York Times/Redux*
Broadway's Come From Away. *Scenic Design by Beowulf Boritt, Costume Design by Toni-Leslie James, Lighting Design by Howell Binkley, Musical Staging by Kelly Devine, Directed by Christopher Ashley. Cover Photo features (L to R) Lee MacDougall, Rodney Hicks, Chad Kimball, Jenn Colella, Ian Eisendrath, Romano Di Nillo, Caesar Samayoa, Kendra Kassebaum, Nate Lueck, Joel Hatch.*
Compositor: *Aptara®, Inc.*

To Elaine Goldfarb and to the memory of Catherine Wilson

Library of Congress Cataloging-in-Publication Data

Names: Wilson, Edwin, 1927- author. | Goldfarb, Alvin, author.
Title: Theatre: the lively art/Edwin Wilson, Alvin Goldfarb.
Other titles: Theater
Description: Tenth edition. | New York, NY : McGraw-Hill Education, 2019. |
     Includes bibliographical references and index.
Identifiers: LCCN 2017040502| ISBN 9781259916861 (acid-free paper) | ISBN
     1259916863 (acid-free paper)
Subjects: LCSH: Theater. | Theater—History.
Classification: LCC PN2037 .W57 2018 | DDC 792—dc23 LC record available at
https://lccn.loc.gov/2017040502

mheducation.com/highered

Edwin Wilson attended Vanderbilt University, the University of Edinburgh, and Yale University, where he received an MFA and the first Doctor of Fine Arts degree awarded by Yale. He has taught theatre at Vanderbilt, Yale, and, for over 30 years, at Hunter College and the Graduate Center of the City University. Wilson has produced plays on and off Broadway and served one season as the resident director of the Barter Theatre in Abingdon, Virginia. He was the Assistant to the Producer on the Broadway play *Big Fish, Little Fish* directed by John Gielgud, starring Jason Robards, and of the film *Lord of the Flies* directed by Peter Brook. On Broadway, he co-produced *Agatha Sue, I Love You* directed by George Abbott. He also produced a feature film, *The Nashville Sound.* He was the moderator of *Spotlight,* a television interview series on CUNY-TV and PBS, 1989-93, ninety-one half-hour interviews with outstanding actors, actresses, playwrights, directors and producers, broadcast on 200 PBS stations in the United States.

For twenty-two years he was the theatre critic of the *Wall Street Journal.* A long-time member of the New York Drama Critics Circle, he was president of the Circle for several years. He is on the board of the John Golden Fund and served a term as President of the Theatre Development Fund (**TDF**), whose Board he was on for twenty-three years. He has served a number of times on the Tony Nominating Committee and the Pulitzer Prize Drama Jury. He is the also the author or co-author of two other widely used college theatre textbooks in the U.S. The 13th edition of his pioneer book, *The Theater Experience,* was published by McGraw-Hill. The 7th edition of the theatre history textbook, *Living Theatre* (co-authored with Alvin Goldfarb), published previously by McGraw Hill, has been published by W. W. Norton. He is also the editor of *Shaw on Shakespeare,* recently re-issued by Applause Books and a murder mystery, *The Patron Murders,* published by Prospecta Press.

Alvin Goldfarb is President Emeritus and Professor Emeritus of Western Illinois University. Dr. Goldfarb has also served as Provost, Dean of Fine Arts, and Chair of the Department of Theatre at Illinois State University. He holds a Ph.D. in theatre history from the City University of New York and a master's degree from Hunter College.

He is also the co-author of *Living Theatre* as well as co-editor of *The Anthology of Living Theatre* with Edwin Wilson. Dr. Goldfarb is also the co-editor, with Rebecca Rovit, of *Theatrical Performance during the Holocaust: Texts, Documents, Memoirs,* which was a finalist for the National Jewish Book Award. He has published numerous articles and reviews in scholarly journals and anthologies.

Dr. Goldfarb has served as a member of the Illinois Arts Council and president of the Illinois Alliance for Arts Education. He has received service awards from the latter organization as well as from the American College Theatre Festival. Dr. Goldfarb also received an Alumni Achievement Award from the CUNY Graduate Center's Alumni Association, and another Alumni Award from Hunter College, CUNY.

Dr. Goldfarb currently serves as a member and treasurer of Chicago's Joseph Jefferson Theatre Awards Committee, which recognizes excellence in the Chicago theatre, as well as a board member of the Arts Alliance of Illinois.

Contents

PART 2

Creating Theatre: The Playwright   46

(©Geraint Lewis/Alamy Stock
Photo)

(©T. Charles Erickson)

PART 3
Creating Theatre: The Production   104

(©Sara Krulwich/The New York
Times/Redux)

(©Geraint Lewis)

(©Robbie Jack/Corbis Entertainment/Getty Images)

(©blanaru/iStock/Getty Images RF)

PART 4

Global Theatres: Past and Present   252

(©ArenaPal/Topham/The Image Works)

(©Koichi Kamoshida/Getty
Images News/Getty Images)

(©Geraint Lewis)

Contents

(©Nigel Norrington/Camera Press/Redux)

(©Bruce Glikas/FilmMagic/
Getty Images)

(©Craig Schwartz)

Connect: Enhancing the Theatre Experience

Mc Graw Hill Education **connect®**

Several qualities set *Theatre: The Lively Art* apart from other introductory texts. A particularly important element is our emphasis on the audience. All students reading the book are potential theatre-goers, not just during their college years but throughout their lives. We have therefore attempted to make *Theatre: The Lively Art* an ideal one-volume text to prepare students as future audience members. It will give them a grasp of how theatre functions, of how it should be viewed and judged, and of the tradition behind any performance they may attend. In addition to serving as an ideal text for nonmajors, *Theatre: The Lively Art* will also prepare students who wish to continue studies in theatre, as majors, minors, or students from other disciplines who take advanced courses.

MASTERING CONCEPTS

Theatre is not only an art form; it is one of the performing arts. As a result, its quality is elusive because it exists only at the moment when a performance occurs. To study it in a book or classroom is to be one step removed from that immediate experience. This fact is uppermost in the minds of those who teach theatre in a classroom setting. At the same time, the theatre appreciation course can immeasurably enhance an audience's comprehension of theatre. The experience of seeing theatre can be many times more meaningful if audience members understand parts of the theatre, the creative artists and technicians who make it happen, the tradition and historical background from which theatre springs, and the genre.

When students successfully master concepts with McGraw-Hill's Connect, you spend more class time focusing on theatre as a performing art, fostering a greater appreciation for the course, and inspiring students to become life-long audience members. Connect helps students better understand and retain these basic concepts, and allow you to reach your student audience and bring the theatre experience to them. Connect is a highly reliable, easy-to-use homework and learning management solution that embeds learning science and award-winning adaptive tools to improve student results.

Homework & Adaptive Learning

- Contextualized assignments
- SmartBook
- Time-saving tools
- Customized to individual needs

Robust Analytics & Reporting

- Easy-to-read reports
- Individual and class performance data
- Auto grading

Quality Content & Learning Resources

- eBooks available offline
- Custom course content
- Resource library
- Consolidated resources
- Easy course Sharing
- Customized to-do list and calendar
- Lecture capture

Trusted Services & Support

- Seamless LMS integration
- Training
- In-product help and tutorials
- 1:1 or group help

LearnSmart® is an adaptive learning program designed to help students learn faster, study smarter, and retain more knowledge for greater success. Distinguishing what students know  from what they don't, and focusing on concepts they are most likely to forget, LearnSmart continuously adapts to each student's needs by building a personalized learning path. An intelligent adaptive study tool, LearnSmart is proven to strengthen memory recall, keep students in class, and boost grades.

Theatre: The Lively Art now offers two reading experiences for students and instructors: SmartBook® and eBook. Fueled by LearnSmart, SmartBook is the first and only adaptive reading experience currently available. SmartBook creates a personalized reading experience by highlighting the most impactful concepts a student needs to learn at that moment in time. The reading experience continuously adapts by highlighting content based on what the student knows and doesn't know. Real-time reports quickly identify the concepts that require more attention from individual students—or the entire class. eBook provides a simple, elegant reading experience, available for offline reading.

ORGANIZATION OF THE TENTH EDITION

Chapters are again ordered logically to make studying as intuitive as possible. As in previous editions, *Theatre: The Lively Art* can be studied in any order the instructor prefers. We listened to instructors who asked us to improve the overall organization by streamlining some material for easier classroom use.

As in previous editions, we provide discussions of the unique nature of theatre as an art form and highlight the multicultural nature of theatre that today's students will experience. In addition, throughout this edition, we focus on the global

SmartBook

DESIGNED FOR
- Preparing for class
- Practice and study
- Focusing on key topics
- Reports and analytics

SUPPORTS
- Adaptive, personalized learning
- Assignable contents
- Tablet iOS and Android apps

eBook

DESIGNED FOR
- Reading in class
- Reference
- Offline reading
- Accessibility

SUPPORTS
- Simple, elegant reading
- Basic annotations
- Smartphone and tablet via iOS and Android apps

SMARTBOOK™

nature of theatre to give students the groundwork for understanding the wide diversity of theatre today.

In Part 1, Theatre in Today's World, we review theatre in everyday life and the theatre audience. The chapters in this part provide a foundation for studying the elements of theatre in Parts 2 and 3.

In Part 2, Creating Theatre: The Playwright, we introduce students to the person or group creating a script, the dramatic structure, and dramatic characters. We then continue with dramatic genres and investigate point of view in a text as expressed in tragedy, comedy, tragicomedy, and other genres.

In Part 3, Creating Theatre: The Production, we discuss the people and elements that make theatre possible: the actors, the director, the producer, and the designers who together bring the theatre to stunning life. Important too are the theatre spaces where a production occurs. Design and production techniques (in particular lighting, costume, and makeup) have been updated to include the latest advances in technology.

In Part 4, Global Theatres: Past and Present, we offer a survey of theatre history, beginning with Greek theatre and continuing to the present. Chapters 15 and 16 are devoted to theatre of the past one hundred years or so. The forces that came into being just a little more than a century ago—in realism and departures from realism, in acting techniques, in the emergence of the director, and in scene and lighting design—define theatre as it exists today. In these final chapters we cover the contemporary theatre scene around the world and the diverse theatres in the United States, including the LGBT, feminist, African American, Asian American, Native American, and Latino theatres.

Connect: Enhancing the Theatre Experience

FEATURES

Based on feedback from instructors and students, the new Tenth Edition of *Theatre: The Lively Art* offers both time-tested and newly revised text features that help students deepen their understanding and appreciation of the theatrical experience.

URLs to Online Plays Many of the plays referenced in the text that also appear online are highlighted in blue typeface when first mentioned in a chapter. Should you want to read one of these plays, you can refer to the list at the end of the book and find the URL. Titles are listed alphabetically.

Playing Your Part A revised and expanded set of critical thinking questions and experiential exercises has been added to each chapter as part of an extended peda-gogical program. The feature is divided into two categories: ***Playing Your Part: Experiencing Theatre*** and ***Playing Your Part: Thinking About Theatre***. These

PLAYING YOUR PART:
EXPERIENCING THEATRE

1. Have you ever had to pick someone for a team or for a job? How did you go about making your choice? Is that similar to casting in the theatre? Why? Why not?

2. Have one of your classmates read a short speech from a play. Ask her or him to change the pace or rhythm of delivery. What terms or phrases did you use to make this request? Were your directions understood? How did the change in pace or rhythm affect the delivery of the speech and its impact on those listening?

3. Observe how one of your instructors interacts with the class through his or her movement. How does this movement affect the way in which the class material is delivered? Does your observation of this provide you any insight into the importance of stage blocking?

4. Ask if you can attend a technical rehearsal or dress rehearsal at your university theatre. What insights did you gain from attending those rehearsals?

PLAYING YOUR PART:
THINKING ABOUT THEATRE

1. Imagine that while you are watching a production, one performer is overacting badly, to the point that he or she is quite unbelievable. Another performer is listless and has no energy. In each case, to what extent do you think this is the director's fault, and to what extent the performer's failure?

2. If you get bored or impatient when watching a performance, what do you think the director could have done in preparing the production to prevent this from happening?

3. Is it fair to say, as some critics do, when everything "clicks" in a production, that is, when the acting, the scenery and lighting, and the pace of the action all seem to be beautifully coordinated, that the director's hand is "invisible"?

4. If you have read a play this semester (or sometime in the past), what do you think the spine of that play is? What would your directorial concept be if you were directing a production of that play?

questions and exercises not only help students to think critically about what they have read in the chapter, but also help them to connect what they've read to their own experiences. Playing Your Part exercises can be used as homework assignments or to inspire classroom discussion. These sets of questions invite students to engage in experiences relating to the theatre. They may ask students to attend a performance and write about their reactions to it, or to take on the role of playwright by imagining a play about their own lives. These creative activities help students feel the vitality and immediacy of the theatrical experience.

In Focus These boxes help students understand and compare different aspects of theatre, whether in the United States or around the world. Some highlight specific examples of global influence on theatre. Artists discussed include Peter Brook, Josef Svoboda, Julie Taymor, Bertolt Brecht, and Thornton Wilder. Boxes on legendary theatre artists Augusto Boal, Ariane Mnouchkine, and Tadashi Suzuki are also included.

Other In Focus boxes discuss the audience, the playwright, the actor, and the director, each focusing on a unique issue in the contemporary theatre to engage students in discussion and debate.

And some boxes explore the close relationship between theatre and other forms of popular entertainment through the ages, from the mimes and jugglers of ancient Rome to the circuses and vaudeville of the nineteenth century to the rock concerts and theme parks of today.

We have also added new In Focus boxes in every chapter to cover technological developments in theatre (such as discussing technology and the actor) and key issues affecting the contemporary theatre (such as audience etiquette as well as color blind and nontraditional casting).

In addition all of the theatre history chapters now also have new In Focus boxes that help students see the continuing impact of the past on the contemporary theatre. Two examples are the ongoing tradition of theatre festivals and their relationship to the Greek theatre festivals and contemporary religious drama and its relationship to the Middle Ages.

Timelines Timelines are included for each period and country addressed. These timelines have been markedly improved from those in previous editions, with entries much easier to read than before. Each

IN FOCUS: QUESTIONING THE PLAYWRIGHT'S ROLE

Some contemporary commentators have questioned what they refer to as the "centrality" of the playwright and the play. These critics point out that there have been companies whose performers or directors, sometimes with the assistance of audiences, improvise presentations: They create a presentation while actually performing it. There have also been times when texts were developed by performers or by a director who assembled material from various sources. Some theorists argue, therefore, that an "authorless" theatre exists: theatre in which performers create their own works, sometimes using a traditional text only as a jumping-off point.

Theorists who question the centrality of the text also argue that the playwright's importance has been overstated—that a play is simply a suggestion or starting point and that the artists who create a stage presentation are its true "authors." In addition, they hold that each audience member may create his or her own "reading" of a production; in this sense, the spectator is the "author," and any discussion of a play's theme or meaning is inappropriate. It should be pointed out that this argument seems largely a question of semantics.

If a theatre piece is created by a group of performers or by a director, then these people are in effect operating as playwrights. The playwright's function has not been eliminated; it is simply being carried out by someone else.

As for the matter of the "centrality" of the playwright, this argument, too, does not eliminate the necessity of what we are calling the blueprint that every theatre event requires. Whether the blueprint is a text, a script, an idea, a scenario, an improvisation, or anything similar, it is an indispensable element in the process of creating a theatre production. The work of the playwright or other "authors" need not be "central" or predominant to be essential and irreplaceable. Also, the fact remains that throughout the history of both Western and Eastern theatre, the significant role of the playwright has been widely accepted. Whether it is a dramatist like Sophocles, Shakespeare, or Ibsen in the West, or Chikamatsu—an eighteenth-century Japanese dramatist—in the East, both their own contemporaries and later generations have seen their dramatic texts as foundations on which productions are based.

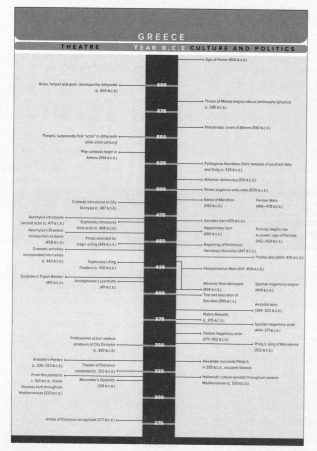

timeline shows landmark events and accomplishments in the social and political arenas on one side and significant theatre events on the other.

Experiencing Theatre History   We present in these boxes narratives of actual events in theatre history, taking the readers back in time so they have a sense of being in the audience at a performance of, say, *Antigone* in Athens in 441 B.C.E., or at the premier of *Hamlet* at the Globe Theatre in London around 1600.

Writing Style   A sense of immediacy and personalization has been a goal in our writing style. We have attempted to write *Theatre: The Lively Art* in the most readable language possible. The book contains a wealth of information presented in a manner that makes it vivid and alive.

Production Photos   As always, the vast majority of the photos in the book are not only in full color but are generously sized to help students see and appreciate the dynamic and dramatic world of the theatre. Also, a number of global theatre productions have been included in this edition. The illustrations we've chosen—both photographs and line drawings—explain and enhance the material in the text.

Experiencing Theatre History
ANTIGONE

Athens, 441 B.C.E. The year is 441 B.C.E. It is a morning in late March in Athens, Greece, and the citizens of Athens are up early, making their way to the Theatre of Dionysus, an open-air theatre on the south side of the Acropolis, the highest hill in Athens. On the Acropolis are several temples, including the Parthenon, a magnificent new temple dedicated to the goddess Athena, which is under construction at this very time.

The Theatre of Dionysus has semicircular seating built into the slope of the hill on the side of the Acropolis. At the foot of the seating area is a flat, circular space—the orchestra—where the actors will perform. Behind the orchestra a temporary stage house has been built,

Dionysia festival, an annual series of events lasting several days. During this festival, all business in Athens—both commercial and governmental—comes to a halt. On the day before the plays, there was a parade through the city, which ended near the theatre at a temple dedicated to the god Dionysus, for whom the festival is named. There, a religious observance was held at the altar.

Today is one of three days of the festival devoted mainly to tragedies. On these days, one playwright will present three tragedies and a satyr play. The three tragedies are sometimes linked to form one long play, called a *trilogy;* but sometimes they are three separate pieces—as they are today.

of a woman, appear in the playing area: They represent Antigone and her sister, Ismene. Antigone tells Ismene that she means to defy their uncle, the king, and give their brother Polynices an honorable burial. Ismene, unlike Antigone, is timid and frightened; she argues that women are too weak to stand up to a king. Besides, Ismene points out, Antigone will be put to death if she is caught. Antigone argues, however, that she will not be subservient to a man, even the king.

When the two female characters leave the stage, a chorus of fifteen men enters. These men represent the elders of the city, and throughout the play—in passages that are sung and danced—they will fulfill several

---

Photo Essays   Students are placed in the audiences of important productions in these pictorial essays to bring to life key elements in the text. These essays provide context for theatre-viewing experiences, while highlighting outstanding performances and designs.

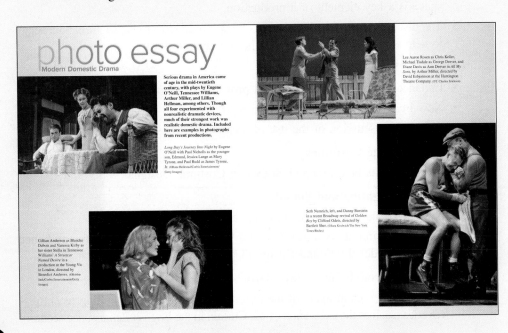

photo essay
Modern Domestic Drama

Serious drama in America came of age in the mid-twentieth century, with plays by Eugene O'Neill, Tennessee Williams, Arthur Miller, and Lillian Hellman, among others. Though all four experimented with nonrealistic dramatic devices, much of their strongest work was realistic domestic drama. Included here are examples in photographs from recent productions.

Long Day's Journey Into Night by Eugene O'Neill with Paul Nicholls as the younger son, Edmund, Jessica Lange as Mary Tyrone, and Paul Rudd as James Tyrone, Jr. (©Ronald Hollard/Corbis Entertainment/ Getty Images)

Lee Aaron Rosen as Chris Keller, Michael Tisdale as George Deever, and Diane Davis as Ann Deever in *All My Sons,* by Arthur Miller, directed by David Esbjornson at the Huntington Theatre Company. (©T. Charles Erickson)

Gillian Anderson as Blanche DuBois and Vanessa Kirby as her sister Stella in Tennessee Williams' *A Streetcar Named Desire* in a production at the Young Vic in London, directed by Benedict Andrews. (©Robbie Jack/Corbis Entertainment/Getty Images)

Seth Numrich, left, and Danny Burstein in a recent Broadway revival of *Golden Boy* by Clifford Odets, directed by Bartlett Sher. (©Sara Krulwich/The New York Times/Redux)

CHAPTER-BY-CHAPTER CHANGES

In addition to the major changes outlined earlier, we have included significant new material throughout the text, including the following:

Chapter 1: Theatre Is Everywhere

- Updated examples of the relationship between theatre and popular entertainments. A new discussion of the theatrical qualities of cosplay.

Chapter 2: The Audience

- New and expanded discussion on "where and how we see theatre." New and expanded discussion of participatory and immersive theatre as well as the history of theatre etiquette.

Chapter 3: Creating the Dramatic Script

- Updated the In Focus box on Writing for Theatre, Film, and Television.

Chapter 4: Theatrical Genres

- New In Focus box on Additional Forms and the Debate over Categorization.

Chapter 5: Acting for the Stage

- More extensive discussion of contemporary acting techniques and actor training.
- New In Focus box on Technology and the Actor.

Chapter 6: The Director and the Producer

- Expanded discussion of the responsibilities of the stage manager and the casting director.
- New In Focus box on Color Blind and Nontraditional Casting.

Chapter 7: Theatre Spaces

- Description of the transformation of the Broadway Imperial Theatre for the musical *Natasha, Pierre, and the Great Comet of 1812* as an example of how space is a key element of a production.
- The discussion of stage direction has been moved to this chapter from "Scenery" to help students better understand the proscenium theatre.

Chapter 8: Scenery

- Enhanced discussion of video and projection design.
- New In Focus box on projection design.
- Enhanced discussion of the use of technology to assist the scene designer.

Chapter 9: Stage Costumes

- New In Focus box on Technology and Costume Design.

Chapter 10: Lighting and Sound

- New In Focus box on Rock Concert and Theatre Lighting.
- New discussion of Assistive Listening Devices for hearing impaired audience members under the Sound Design discussion.

Chapters 11 through 16: Today's Diverse Global Theatre

- Updated coverage in many of the history chapters, particularly citing recent discoveries (such as the excavation of the Curtain in the English Renaissance section).

- Updated examples in the final two chapters, such as references to *Fun Home* and *Hamilton* in the review of musical theatre and multicultural theatre.
- Discussion of additional multicultural theatres and artists in the final chapter.
- In Focus boxes in each chapter that help the students understand the continuing influence of theatre history on our theatre.
- Questions on how to evaluate a production of a historic play as well as how to evaluate a production of a new or contemporary play.

ACKNOWLEDGMENTS

In the preparation of this book, we are indebted to a long list of colleagues whose assistance in providing important insights and material has been invaluable. These include the following: Professor J. Thomas Rimer—Asian Theatre; Professor James V. Hatch—African American Theatre; Professor Sam Leiter—Asian Theatre; Professor Ann Haugo—Native American Theatre. We are grateful to Professor Jeff Entwistle for his important contribution to the chapters on design—scenic, costume, lighting, and sound—and we also thank Professor Laura Pulio for her helpful suggestions on acting. For others whose names we have failed to include, we apologize.

At McGraw-Hill, we wish to express appreciation to the following people: Sarah Remington, brand manager; Art Pomponio, product developer; Kelly Odom, marketing manager; and Sandy Wille and Melissa Leick, content project managers.

Through the years, many instructors have given us helpful comments and suggestions. For their assistance in developing the Tenth Edition of *Theatre: The Lively Art*, we wish to thank the following people:

Daphnie Sicre, Borough of Manhattan Community College
Michael Smith, Ohlone College
Benjamin Haas, Borough of Manhattan Community College
Felecia Harrelson, Borough of Manhattan Community College
Greg McLarty, Wharton County Junior College
David Wolski, Eastern Illinois University
Theresa Layne, Mira Costa College
Caleb Stroman, McLennan Community College
Amy Dunlap, North Greenville University
Michelle Feda, Illinois State University
Rachel Tyson, East Central Community College
Mary Pratt Cooney, Oakland University
Jeremy Peterson, Rowan-Cabarrus Community College
Adam Miecielica, University of Tennessee at Chattanooga
Sam Weakley, Northwest Mississippi Community College
Werner Trieschmann, Pulasko Technical College
Monique Sacay-Bagwell, Lander University
Katherine Kavanagh, Borough of Manhattan Community College
Richard Bristow, Gerogia Highlands College
Carol Lynne Damgen, California State University, San Bernardino
Amanda Labonte, Illinois State University
Sandra Grayson, Mississippi College
Scott Robinson, Central Washington University
Cheryl Hall, University of Alabama at Birmingham

Phyllis W. Seawright, Ph.D., Mississippi College
Claremarie Verheyen, School of Theatre and Dance-University of Houston
Gaye Jeffers, University of Alabama at Birmingham
Stephen Thomas, Tarrant County College Northeast
Shannon Walsh, Louisiana State University
Dr. Lawrence James, Tennessee State University
Michael Detroit, University of Memphis
Rachel Dickson, University of Houston Downtown
Edward Muth, Houston Community College
Lofton L. Durham, Western Michigan University
Courtney Young, University of Houston and Lone Star College
Nicholas Basta, University of North Carolina Wilmington

For the first nine editions of *Theatre: The Lively Art*, the amazing photo expert
and researcher Inge King located and helped us select every photograph. Though
she did not work on this edition, it is impossible to thank her adequately for the
contribution she has made through the years to the continuing success of this
textbook. We are well aware that she has always played an indispensable role in
making its acceptance so widespread and over such a long period of time.

Theatre: The Lively Art

PART

1

Theatre in Today's World

**THE AUDIENCE SALUTES
THE ARTISTS**
The essence of theatre is a live audience in the presence of actors performing a dramatic script. Today, there is more live theatre available to audiences than perhaps at any time in history, with a wide variety of theatre sites and an impressive variety of the types of theatre offered. Central to the theatre experience is the interaction between audience members and live performers. Here we see the audience giving a standing ovation as cast members take their curtain call. (©Eddie Linssen/Alamy Stock Photo)

THEATRE IS EVERYWHERE

As you begin your introductory theatre course, some of you may be asking: Why should I study theatre? For those of you who are theatre majors, you could be asking: Why am I studying theatre? I just want to learn how to be an actor, director, playwright, designer, or to work in production. The answer is knowledge of the basics of theatre is essential to anyone who wishes to pursue a theatre career. For those of you who are not majoring in the subject, this is perhaps an elective for your general education. For you, it should be pointed out that having a general understanding of theatre and its history is important to anyone who has never before gone to live theatre as well as someone who already enjoys attending the theatre and wishes to enhance that experience, an experience that will be with you the rest of your life.

In our textbook we will explain the elements that make up live theatre—acting, directing, design, playwriting, as well as briefly survey its history—but before we turn to specifics we should be aware of two significant facts. One is the longevity and endurance of theatre, and the other is its widespread popularity, the fact that despite the pervasive competition of electronic, digital, and other forms of dramatic entertainment, there is today in the United States more widespread engagement in live theatre than perhaps at any time in its history. To begin with let us explain what we mean by the term "live theatre," and then turn to how various competing media and popular entertainments have borrowed from it and challenged it in the last 100 years.

THEATRE TODAY

Prior to the modern period, for more than 2,000 years in the West and 1,500 years in Asia, the only way audiences could see theatre of any kind was to attend a live performance. Spectators left their homes and went to a space where a theatrical

◀ **THE PERVASIVENESS OF THEATRE**
Symbolic of the far reach of theatre today is the performance of this production of Fous de Bassin, *created by the French company Ilotopie, on the water canals around the Puerto Madero neighborhood as part of the opening of the IX Buenos Aires' International Festival in Argentina in 2013.* (©Natacha Pisarenko/AP Images)

event was taking place where they joined others to watch a production. If people wanted to see a tragedy, with kings and queens, heroes and villains, or a comedy making fun of human foibles, they would have to become audience members to watch a live performance.

Then, after all those centuries, at the beginning of the twentieth century, everything began to change. In rapid succession a series of technological innovations offered alternative ways to hear and observe drama. First, there was radio, and then silent film, and after that, movies with sound. Black-and-white film soon gave way to movies in color and not much later, film was joined by television, first in black and white and after that in color. Film and television now also use 3D technology as well as computerization to create amazingly realistic effects. Today, the computer and a series of hand-held electronic devices, including smartphones and tablets, allow viewers to watch films, television shows, and digitized performances anywhere. With all of these inventions, arriving in quick succession, viewing drama has become much more accessible and much less expensive.

With the development first of radio and silent film, there were predictions that such inventions would sound the death knell of live theatre. Surely, it was argued, with the advent of sound film and television, especially when color came in, live theatre was doomed. Consider what had happened to both film and television: talking pictures eliminated silent film, just as later, color television obliterated black-and-white TV. It seemed likely, therefore, that drama on film and television, and even more, on computers and other digital devices, might well eradicate live theatre.

The term for live theatre that is not observed through an electronic medium is ***nonmediated theatre***. Contrary to the predictions, nonmediated theatre, or *live theatre*, has not only survived but has thrived. In fact, today it is more vibrant, more widespread, and more accessible than at almost any time in history.

Nonmediated or live theatre Theatre that is not observed through an electronic medium.

The Unique Quality of Theatre

In the face of the formidable competition that has arisen from all forms of electronic media, why do we continue to go to the theatre? There are a number of reasons, but the most important single reason can be found in the title of this book. We call theatre the *lively art* not only because it is exciting, suspenseful, and amusing, but also because it is alive in a way that makes it different from every other form of dramatic presentation. It is this live quality of theatre that makes it so durable and so indispensable.

The special nature of theatre becomes more apparent when we contrast the experience of seeing a drama in a theatre with seeing a drama on film or television. In many ways the dramas presented are alike. Both offer a story told in dramatic form—an enactment of scenes by performers who speak and act as if they are the people they represent—and film and television can give us many of the same feelings and experiences that we have when watching a theatre performance. We can learn a great deal about theatre from watching a play on film or television, and the accessibility of film and television means that they have a crucial role in our overall exposure to the depiction of dramatic events and dramatic characters.

Nevertheless, there is a fundamental difference between the two experiences, and we become aware of that difference when we contrast theatre with movies. This contrast does not have to do with technical matters, such as the way films can show outdoor shots made from helicopters, cut instantaneously from one scene to another, or create interplanetary wars or cataclysmic events by using computer-generated special effects. The most significant difference between films and theatre is the *relationship between the performer and the audience.* The experience of being in the presence of the performer is more important to theatre than anything else. No matter how closely a film follows the story of a play, no matter how involved we are with the people on the screen, we are always in the presence of an *image,* never a living person.

We all know the difference between an image of someone and the flesh-and-blood reality. How often do we rehearse a speech we plan to make to someone we love, or fear: We run through the scene in our mind, picturing ourselves talking to the other person—declaring our love, asking for help, asking the boss for a raise. Sometimes we communicate with them via text messages, imagining them in our mind. But when we meet the person face-to-face, it is not the same. We freeze and find ourselves unable to speak; or perhaps our words gush forth incoherently. Seldom does the encounter take place as we planned.

Like films, television seems very close to theatre; sometimes it seems even closer than film. Television programs sometimes begin with words such as "This program comes to you live from Burbank, California." Recent televised musicals have had titles such as *Hairspray Live!* But the word *live* must be qualified. Before television, *live* in the entertainment world meant "in person": not only was the event taking place at that moment; it was taking place in the physical *presence* of the spectators. Usually, the term *live television* still means that an event is taking place at this moment, but "live" television does *not* take place in the presence of all of the viewers. In fact, even if there is a live studio audience, it is generally far removed from the vast majority of the viewing audience, possibly half a world away. In television, like film, we see an image—in the case of TV, on a screen—and we are free to look or not to look, or even to leave the room.

Our fascination with being in the presence of a person is difficult to explain but not difficult to verify, as the popularity of rock stars attests. No matter how often we as fans have seen a favorite star in the movies or heard a rock singer on a CD, computer, tablet, smartphone, or other digital device, we will go to any lengths to see the star in person. In the same way, at one time or another, each of us has braved bad weather and shoving crowds to see celebrities at a parade or a political rally. The same pull of personal contact draws us to the theatre.

At the heart of the theatre experience, therefore, is the performer–audience relationship—the immediate, personal exchange whose chemistry and magic give theatre its special quality. During a stage performance the actresses and actors can hear laughter, can sense silence, and can feel tension. In short, the audience itself can affect, and in subtle ways change, the performance. At the same time, as members of the audience we watch the performers closely, consciously or unconsciously asking ourselves questions: Are the performers convincing in their roles? Have they learned their parts well? Are they talented? Will they do something surprising? Will they make a mistake? At each moment, in every stage performance, we are looking for answers to questions like these. The performers are alive—and so is the very air itself—with the electricity of expectation. It is for this reason that we speak of theatre as the lively art. It is for this reason, as well as a number of others, that we study theatre as an art form.

THE AUDIENCE APPLAUDS
The audience is an integral, indispensable part of any theatre performance. Here, the audience watches a performance of a classical theatre piece in the outdoor theatre of Regents Park in London, England. (©Eric Nathan/VisitBritain/Getty Images)

In the next chapter, we will examine in detail the dynamic of the actor–audience relationship. Before we do so, however, other qualities of live theatre are worth exploring. One, as we've suggested, is the astonishing popularity of live theatre in the face of the competition it faces. Another is the amazing way in which theatre permeates every aspect of our lives, in ways of which we are often not even aware.

The Range and Accessibility of Theatre

One measure of the amazing health of live theatre today is the astounding range of opportunities we have of attending theatre, with locations, not only in the United Sates but throughout the world, presenting a greater variety of theatre offerings perhaps than ever before. For a long time Broadway in New York City was the fountainhead of live theatre in the United States. Though it is still thriving, and Broadway shows, particularly popular musicals, regularly tour to major and mid-size cities throughout America, theatre that originates on Broadway is not as predominant as it once was. Performing arts complexes in all parts of the country that continue to present productions of Broadway shows, in addition, often have other spaces which feature different types of live theatre. These might include 1,000-seat, 500-seat, or 200-seat theatres that offer new plays, revivals, intimate musicals, and other kinds of dramatic entertainment.

As we shall see, in New York, as in other cities throughout the United States and the world, there are also smaller spaces and companies that focus on more cutting edge dramas or experimental works. In addition, we shall also discuss the many theatre companies that focus on underrepresented groups.

At the same time, during the last half-century there has been a burgeoning of what are known as *regional theatres*: permanent, professional, nonprofit theatres that offer a season of first-class productions to their audiences each year. Their association, the League of Resident Theatres, lists a total of 74 such theatres scattered across the country. Added to the above are approximately 120 Shakespeare theatres found in virtually every state in the United States that feature, especially in the summer months, high-quality productions of Shakespeare and the classics as well as modern plays.

Regional theatres
Permanent, professional, nonprofit theatres offering first-class productions to their audiences.

Another important component of today's theatre landscape is the many college and university theatres found in every one of the fifty states, as well as Canada and elsewhere. Many colleges have not one but perhaps two or three theatre spaces in which students and guest artists perform. There might be, for instance, a 500- or 600-seat theatre, a smaller 200-seat theatre with a different configuration, and a 100-seat "black box" for more experimental or intimate productions.

Finally, in every corner of the United States, there are an astonishing 7,000 so-called *community theatres*. These are semiprofessional and experienced amateur groups who present a series of plays each year that appeal to their audiences. It might surprise many of us to learn that these several thousand theatres present roughly 46,000 productions each year to audiences that number in the millions. Obviously, taken together, the total number of theatre events presented each year in the United States is a staggering, almost unbelievable figure.

Community theatres
Semiprofessional and experienced amateur groups that present plays that appeal to their specific audiences.

It is not, however, just the vast range and number of annual productions that is surprising, it is the diversity of offerings. First, there is the rich mixture of traditional theatre from the past with the latest theatre offerings of today. Theatre from the past begins with the Greek theatre, the foundation of all Western theatre, and moves through Shakespeare in the Elizabethan era, the Spanish playwright

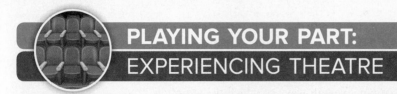
1. Locate as many theatre venues in your area as you can—professional, amateur, college theatres. Also, locate theatres that may be in nearby cities or towns. (The Internet can be helpful in this search.)

2. Find out the size and shape of the theatres you have identified in your area and surrounding area.

3. Learn what kinds of productions each of the theatres presents: musicals, comedies, classics, new plays, and so forth.

4. Make plans to attend a production at one or more of the nearby theatres. (This could be incorporated into a class assignment.)

Site specific theatre
Theatre presented in a nontraditional setting so that the chosen environment helps illuminate the text.

Performance art Most often refers to a solo performance created by the performer but also can be a work that mixes visual arts, dance, film, and/or music.

Lope de Vega from the same era, through the French playwright Molière in the seventeenth century, the great playwrights at the beginning of the modern era—Ibsen, Strindberg and Chekhov—through the outstanding American playwrights of the twentieth century—such as Eugene O'Neill, Arthur Miller, Tennessee Williams, and August Wilson. The works of these playwrights, along with many others, are being offered year in and year out by professional nonprofit, community, and university theatres.

Alongside these plays from the past there is a constant stream of new plays from young playwrights, both in traditional and experimental forms. The latter includes experimental and avant-garde theatre of all kinds. Two such approaches are site-specific theatre and performance art. ***Site-specific theatre*** offers presentations in nontraditional theatre settings, such as warehouses, churches, firehouses, street corners and public parks. The idea is that the unusual locale together with a fresh approach in the material will make audiences conscious in a different way of what they are seeing and experiencing. ***Performance art*** is usually highly individual and presented by only one person but never by more than a small number. The content is usually quite personal, and may be combined with art, dance, film or music. We will discuss both of these forms later in our review of contemporary theatre.

Global and Multicultural Theatre

Two additional types of theatre should be mentioned when we speak of the wide diversity of theatre available to today's audiences. One is *global theatre,* which means theatre not just in the Western tradition, but theatre from around the world. As in the West, there is a rich tradition of theatre in Asia. In India theatre began more than 2,000 years ago, and Chinese theatre, a few centuries after that, while Japanese theatre was established by 800 C.E. In other parts of the world, in Africa, in pre-Columbian Latin America, and in the Native American cultures of North America, there are rich traditions of rituals and ceremonies that have recognizable elements of theatre: costumes; song and dance; and impersonation of people, animals, and divinities.

The various ways in which we see theatrical traditions from different nations and cultures influence one another today were relatively rare prior to 1900. Today we live in a world where such cross-cultural relationships are extremely easy, owing to modern transportation and communication. Thomas Friedman, in his acclaimed book *The World Is Flat,* analyzes how globalization has affected business and

DIVERSE OFFERINGS

Today's theatre offers a wide choice in the places where we see theatre and in the types of theatre we can enjoy. One important aspect involves the many diverse and multicultural theatre experiences that are available. An example would be the scene above from the Bale Folclorico Da Bahia in a performance of *Sacred Heritage* at the Sunset Center in Carmel.

(©Education Images/Universal Images Group/Getty Images)

industry in contemporary society. One can no longer tell whether a product is made by a company in a specific country since most major corporations are multinational. The automobile industry clearly reflects the trend toward industrial globalization, as does the technology industry. A car created today by a Japanese, Korean, or German manufacturer may be fully or partially assembled in the United States. A PC, cell phone, or tablet may be manufactured in China and sold in the United States, but the 24-hour help desk may be located in India. The same is true in today's theatre. Theatre artists cross national boundaries to stage their works with artists of other countries. Popular works tour the world and cross-pollinate other theatrical ventures. International theatre festivals bring artists of various nationalities to interact with those in the host community. In addition, traditional theatrical techniques from differing countries may be fused together to create a unique contemporary work.

People throughout the world are becoming aware of the multiracial and multicultural aspects of our society, as are Americans themselves. In the late nineteenth and the early twentieth centuries, the United States was known as a "melting pot," a term implying that the aim of many foreign-born people who came here was to become assimilated and integrated into the prevailing white, European culture (and we might add, male, as women during this era still had to fight for basic rights, such as the right to vote). In recent decades, however, it has come to be seen that such a homogeneous culture has many biases; as a result, we find a trend to recognize, maintain, and celebrate our differences. This consciousness of diversity has been reflected in theatre. Many organizations have emerged that present productions by and for groups with specific interests including feminism; gay, lesbian, bi-sexual and transgendered points of view; and many others relating to diversity in politics, race, gender, ethnic background, and sexual orientation. Again, we will discuss global and multicultural theatre more fully when we survey our contemporary theatrical landscape.

THEATRE, TELEVISION, AND FILM

Theatre is the fountainhead of all drama in whatever form it appears: film, television, computer, tablet, or theme park. The ancient Greeks, 2,500 years ago, established the categories of tragedy and comedy that are still used today. They also developed dramatic structure, acting, and theatre architecture. Roman domestic comedies are the prototype of every situation comedy we see in the movies or on television. In other words, though we may not be aware of it, each time we see a performance we are taking part in theatre history. Wherever theatre or other media arts occur, their foundation, their roots, are always found in historical forerunners and antecedents.

When audiences watch a performance of a Shakespearean play in an outdoor theatre—for example, at the Shakespeare festival in Ashland, Oregon, or at the Old Globe in San Diego, California—they are not only watching a play by a dramatist who lived 400 years ago but are also sharing in an environment, a configuration of audience and stage space, that goes back much farther to the ancient Greeks.

In the same way, when an audience sees a drama by the French playwright Molière, they are partaking not only of a theatrical tradition that traces its roots to seventeenth-century France, but also of a tradition that goes back to Italian commedia dell'arte, which came to prominence a century earlier. And the theatre space in which it is performed goes back to the proscenium stage, which originated during the Italian Renaissance in the early seventeenth century. Similarly, at a college production of Bertolt Brecht's *The Good Person of Szechwan,* the audience members are not only seeing a play by one of the most innovative playwrights of the twentieth century; they are seeing a play that was strongly influenced by techniques of ancient Asian theatre.

And, as we noted, whenever we watch films or television shows, on whatever electronic device we choose, we are seeing popular works clearly influenced by these traditions, practices, and forms of theatre.

Theatre and Television

The characters of film and television—the heroes, the villains, the victims, the comic figures—all come straight from predecessors in theatre. The way stories are structured—the early scenes, the succession of crises, the withholding and revealing of information—were there first, hundreds of years ago, in the theatre. In other words, the structure, the dynamics, the subject matter of both television and film can be traced directly to antecedents in theatre.

On television, we can see a wide range of dramatic offerings that have a clear counterpart in theatrical prototypes. Daytime soap operas present a variety of domestic crises in family and other relationships. These dramas use many theatrical devices to ensure our continued viewing. A suspenseful moment concludes each segment; heightened music and emotions capture our attention. Recognizable character types—young lovers, difficult parents, doctors, lawyers, and criminals—inhabit the world of the all daytime soap operas.

Nighttime hospital and police shows, as well as earlier popular westerns, present the thrills and suspense of traditional melodrama. The stereotypical characters, including the heroes and villains; the focus on the spectacular and the grotesque; and the neat and happy resolutions are all related, as we shall see, to nineteenth-century melodrama. The popularity of *CSI, Chicago PD, Chicago Fire, The Walking Dead* and *Game of Thrones* is related to their use of traditional characteristics of the suspenseful melodramas staged in the theatres of earlier eras.

Situation comedies depict young as well as middle-age characters in farcical and humorous encounters. These comic television shows have, throughout the history of the medium, focused on domestic situations, language filled with sexual double meaning, physical humor, exaggerated characters, and recognizable situations. Classic situation comedies, such as *I Love Lucy, Will & Grace, Seinfeld, Modern Family, Big Bang Theory, Transparent,* and *Black-ish,* all reflect comic traditions, techniques, characters, and structures developed earlier in theatre.

Popular television variety shows throughout the medium's history have all been influenced by earlier popular theatrical forms that we will discuss later, such as minstrelsy, burlesque, and vaudeville. The long-running format of *Saturday Night Live,* which combines take-offs of serious films or literature, satire of political figures, exaggerated fictional characters, and popular musical acts, is a close replica of vaudeville, a popular theatre form of the early twentieth century.

The NBC network has also televised live stage musicals annually, frequently casting major film, theatre, TV, pop music, and stage stars. To reflect the desire to emulate an actual musical theatre experience, the shows all have *Live* attached at the end of their traditional titles. Those staged for TV productions include: *The Sound of Music* (2013), *Peter Pan* (2014), *Hairspray* (2016), and *Bye, Bye, Birdie* (2017), featuring Jennifer Lopez.

On television, even news documentaries are framed in dramatic terms: a car crash in which a prom queen dies; a spy caught because of an e-mail message; a high government official or corporate officer accused of sexual harassment. Extremely popular reality shows are also staged like theatrical events. Many of the shows focus on highly dramatic situations and turn the real-life individuals into theatrical characters. And we all know that the reality shows are theatrically manipulated to create a sense of dramatic tension, ongoing suspense, and heightened conflict among the participants.

Theatre and Film

Film has been influenced by theatre even more clearly than television has. Movies provide dramatic material of many kinds: science fiction; romantic and domestic comedies; action-packed stories of intrigue; historical epics; and even film versions of classical plays, such as Shakespeare's **Hamlet, Othello,** and **Romeo and Juliet.** And we should note that there is a combination of film and video when we watch movies at home on a DVD, a Blu-ray, or streamed through our smart 4K Ultra HDTV, Blu-ray player, game console, tablet, smartphone, or other device. Various types and categories of theatrical offerings have been appropriated by film. Successful film musicals, such as *Into the Woods* (2014), are movie versions of hugely successful stage musicals. As mentioned earlier, classical and contemporary plays are frequently adapted into movies, such as the Pulitzer Prize winning *Fences.*

In addition, most film genres borrow from past theatrical traditions. For example, popular cinematic melodramas, such as the films based on comic book heroes, reflect the characteristics of the theatrical genre and earlier theatrical innovations. We shall see that the intense interest in creating awe-inspiring special effects was as prevalent in nineteenth-century theatre as it is in twenty-first-century film.

FILM AND THEATRE

From the beginning theatre has had a profound effect on film, as well as on other media. Stories, characters, even dialogue are lifted straight from theatre and put on film. The scene above is from a popular film of 2016, *Fences,* which is based on a play written by August Wilson in which Denzel Washington, seen above, also appeared previously on Broadway. Playing his wife in the film, as she did in the Broadway production, is Viola Davis. (©Joan Marcus)

At the same time, since the inception of commercial film, there has been a great deal of crossover by theatre and film artists. As we shall see, many film stars began their careers in theatre. For that matter, Hollywood frequently raided the New York theatre for actors, directors, and writers during the 1930s, 1940s, and 1950s. Many current film and television stars began their careers in theatre and return to it on occasion; one example is Denzel Washington, who won a Tony Award for a Broadway revival of *Fences* in 2010, which he made into a critically acclaimed film in 2016. And many playwrights, from the earliest days of film and television, write for these media. Sam Shepard, David Mamet, Tony Kushner, Neil LaBute, Theresa Rebecki, Sarah Treem, and Beau Willimon are examples of successful theatre, screenplay, and teleplay authors.

In recent years, many movie and television stars, whose entire careers have been in these media, have performed onstage as an artistic challenge. For example, Daniel Radcliffe, from the *Harry Potter* movies, starred in London and Broadway productions, including the musical *How to Succeed in Business Without Really Trying* (2011), *The Cripple of Inishmann* (2014), *Privacy* (2016), and *Rosencrantz and Guildenstern Are Dead* (2017). In 2013, the film stars Daniel Craig, a recent James Bond, and his wife Rachel Weisz, also a film star, appeared on Broadway in Harold Pinter's *Betrayal;* Craig, along with stage and movie actor David Oyelowo, also starred in *Othello* (2016) off-Broadway. Among other well-known film actors to star in Broadway productions are Tom Hanks, James Franco, and Scarlett Johansson. What attracted audiences to these, and many other examples, were the production's media stars.

And just as film stars are admired for their wealth and status, while at the same time their personal lives are viewed suspiciously—for example, consider the constant attention on their romantic breakups—so, too, were theatrical stars from the earliest times on. This obsession with the lives of stars is reflected today in the popularity of such tabloids and magazines as *Star, National Enquirer,* and *People* as well as Hollywood gossip television shows, including *TMZ;* and in just the same way, there were earlier theatrical publications that reported about the lives of stage personalities.

THEATRE IS EVERYWHERE

The connection between theatre and both television and film probably does not come as a surprise to most people. On the other hand, most of us would no doubt be surprised at the great extent to which theatre permeates and informs so many other aspects of our lives. Think of how often we use theatre as a metaphor to describe an activity in daily life. We say that someone is melodramatic or highly theatrical or acts like a "prima donna." When we don't believe children, we say that they are play-acting. We refer to the battleground on which a war is fought as a "theatre." Clearly, theatre is an activity that we use to describe how we live.

Religious and civic ceremonies and rituals also have theatrical qualities. (We shall see in the chapters "Early Theatres: Greek, Roman, and Medieval" and "Early Theatre: Asian" how the origins of theatre may be connected to religious rituals and ceremonies.) Weddings, funerals, other religious ceremonies as well as family and society celebrations have strong elements of theatre in them. Costumes, a set script, various roles to be played: all of these are similar to counterparts in theatre.

In addition, as we will note in a later chapter, acting is part of our everyday lives. We describe the role-playing we do in our professional and personal spheres as if we were performers on the stage of life. Children and adults imitate behaviors that they admire in the same way that actors and actresses mimic behavior. As we go through our college careers, we play many roles, such as student, friend, romantic partner, organization member, and student government leader. As adults we also play a number of roles: doctor, lawyer, engineer, nurse, parent, teacher, spouse, political figure.

Theatre is incorporated in our lives in other ways. Taken in its broadest sense, it is everywhere around us. A Thanksgiving Day parade, a trial in a courtroom—all of these have recognizable theatrical elements: costumes or uniforms, a formal structure, performers, and spectators. The same is true of such activities as a presidential nominating convention, a Senate hearing, or a White House press conference. Even seemingly spontaneous, unrehearsed events, such as a high-speed automobile chase or a gunman holding hostages in a suburban home, have been imbued with theatrical qualities by the time they are broadcast on television. The person holding the television camera has framed the "shots" showing the

THEATRICAL ELEMENTS IN RITUALS AND CEREMONIES
Weddings, funerals, other religious ceremonies as well as family and society rituals have strong elements of theatre in them. Costumes, a set script, various roles to be played: all of these are similar to counterparts in theatre. Shown here is a wedding ceremony with the bride and groom in appropriate attire, and a presiding official. Often the one officiating is a priest, minister, or rabbi. (©Stewart Cohen/Getty Images RF)

event; and for the evening news, the people who edit and report a segment on a real-life tragedy have taken great care to present the story as a brief drama, with an attention-grabbing opening followed by a suspenseful or shocking revelation and then a closing quotation, perhaps from a relative or neighbor. We even encounter drama in seemingly real-life reports on television: not only the evening news but documentaries and so-called "reality" shows.

Among our popular activities and institutions, rock concerts, amusement parks, museums, sporting events, and digital media all display and rely on strong theatrical components.

Theatre and Rock Music

When we turn from electronic and digital media to live performance, we see that theatre has pervaded and influenced a popular music form with which we are all familiar: rock. Throughout its history, rock has appropriated theatrical elements. The singer and dancer Lady Gaga is a perfect example. Her extravagant outfits and over-the-top visual effects are directly derived from theatrical antecedents, as are her lighting and special effects. The purpose, of course, is to draw attention to the performer. "One of my greatest art works," she has said, "is the art of fame." Her "Monster Ball (2009–2011)" and "ArtRave: The Artpop Ball (2014)" tours were highly staged theatrical events. For that matter, a *New York Times* article describing her Monster Ball performance at Radio City Music Hall was entitled, "For Lady Gaga, Every Concert Is a Drama." The same is true of the highly theatrical performances of many other contemporary pop stars.

Numerous other rock stars have created theatrical characters for their performances. Beginning with Little Richard and Elvis Presley in the 1950s, and continuing with the Beatles in the 1960s, through punk rock, glam rock, rap, hip-hop, and other forms, popular musical performers have used exaggerated characterizations, gender-bending personas, costumes, props, and makeup to create theatrical characterizations. The actual performers were often less recognizable than their stage personae.

The connection between rock performance and theatre is also illustrated by the many rock stars who have acted in films, television, and stage. For example, the hip-hop and rap star Mos Def has appeared on Broadway and in numerous movies.

The popularity of music videos also reflects the integration of theatrical elements into rock and roll. These videos turn many songs into visual, dramatic narratives.

As noted earlier, current rock concerts are also highly theatrical events, using live performers, lights, sound, projections, and properties in ways that are like multi-media presentations. For example, Beyonce's 2016 *Formation* tour incorporated all of these elements almost blurring the distinction between rock concert and theatrical spectacle. Other pop stars such as Justin Timberlake and Christina

THEATRICALITY IN ROCK MUSIC PERFORMANCES
Good examples of the crossover of theatrical elements between the popular arts and traditional theatre are the elaborate, outsize presentations of individual performers and music groups in their live stage presentations. Extravagant costumes, spectacular lighting, sound and scenic effects are the hallmark of these performances. A good example was Lady Gaga's performance at the Super Bowl in 2017. (©Timothy A. Clary/AFP/Getty Images)

Aguilera have staged their concerts like theatre performances, with spectacular lighting effects and gymnastic-like dance routines. Even classic rock groups have added highly visual theatrical elements to their touring shows to appeal to more contemporary fans. Each year, the Grammy Awards becomes a more theatrical event, showcasing incredibly spectacular lighting, costuming, multimedia, and special effects to enhance the show.

Acoustic and less spectacular tours by some well-known rock stars are a reaction against these intensely theatrical concerts and reflect a desire to return the focus to the live performer, stripping away much of the stage effects. We shall see that some contemporary theatrical theorists and experimental artists also argue for diminishing spectacular scenery and using fewer special effects, to reestablish the primacy of live performance.

In the past few years, there has also been a new phenomenon in musical theatre: the use of previously recorded rock and pop music as the score for musicals. The most popular example of such musicals is *Mamma Mia!* (1999), which used the songs of a group from the 1980s, ABBA. Other examples include *All Shook Up* (2005), which used Elvis Presley's hits; *Jersey Boys* (2004), which traced the career of a pop group of the 1960s, the Four Seasons; *Rock of Ages* (2006), which used 1980s rock music; *American Idiot* (2009), adapted from Green Day's concept album; *Motown* (2013), which used the 1960s pop music by African American performers from Detroit; and *Beautiful* (2014), based on the early life and music of Carole King.

Some rock composers have also composed scores for musicals, including Elton John for *Aida* (1998) and *Billy Elliott* (2005), David Bryan, keyboardist for Bon Jovi, for *Memphis* (2009), Bono and Edge of U2 for *Spiderman: Turn Off the Dark* (2011), Cindy Lauper for *Kinky Boots* (2012), and Sarah Bareilles for *Waitress* (2016). We will discuss the influence of rock on the American musical more fully later when we survey the history of this popular theatrical form.

Theatricality in Amusement Parks, Museums, Las Vegas, and Sporting Events

Rock illustrates that we have come to expect theatrical elements as part of our popular entertainments and that theatre is around us in many unexpected venues. Amusement parks like Disney World, Sea World, and Universal Studios incorporate theatrical material; most, for example, present staged productions based on films, which attract huge audiences. The rides at these amusement parks also incorporate theatricality by placing the participant in a theatrical environment and a dramatic situation. Rides based on the *Indiana Jones, Jurassic Park,* and *Harry Potter* films, among many others, allow us, as riders, to be actors in a dramatic plotline, in a space that functions as a kind of stage setting. Disney World has announced plans to build an "immersive" hotel that will allow guests to become part of a *Star Wars* story.

We can also see theatre around us in many other everyday activities. Many restaurants, such as the Rainforest Cafes, have theatrical environments. Shopping centers and specialty stores, such as Niketown and American Girl, contain spaces for performances that highlight specific holiday seasons or product lines.

Museums have recently adopted some of these theatrical techniques to attract visitors. For example, the Abraham Lincoln Presidential Library and Museum in Springfield, Illinois, includes stage presentations, with live actors and high tech special effects, about this famous president as well as about how historians and archivists work. The museum also contains many exhibits that function like stage

LAS VEGAS AS THEATRICAL ENVIRONMENT
Almost the entire central part of Las Vegas, Nevada, is a gigantic stage set. Everything from the pyramids to the Eiffel Tower and New York City is re-produced there. Seen here is a re-creation of a canal in Venice to house shops at the Venetian Hotel, Las Vegas. (©Andreas Sterzing/VISUM/The Image Works)

settings, including a reproduction of the log cabin in which Lincoln originally lived. Many museums now host performances, such as the Museum of Contemporary Art in Chicago and the Walker Center in Minneapolis.

In cities such as Orlando, Florida, dinner theatres present theatrical entertainments based on Roman gladiators, medieval knights, and gangsters of the 1930s. *Medieval Nights* is an extremely popular dinner theatre entertainment in Orlando, New Jersey, and Chicago. Las Vegas is a highly theatricalized environment. Its hotels—such as New York, New York; the Bellagio; Luxor; and Mandelay Bay— are constructed like huge theatrical sets. Lavish stage shows use all the elements of theatre to entertain audiences. Possibly the most spectacular is *KA,* a $165 million production of Cirque du Soleil, staged at the MGM Grand by the avant-garde Canadian director Robert LePage, and which gained notoriety for the death of a performer in 2013. In addition, many performance artists and Broadway musicals have set up companies in Las Vegas. These theatre productions are even modified to meet the time limitations of the traditional Las Vegas stage show.

Contemporary sporting events also integrate significant theatrical elements. Sports arenas, as we will note later, function much like theatre spaces. The introduction of sports teams before the start of competitions is often highly staged, with spectacular sound, lighting, and visual effects. Halftime shows, particularly at championship games such as the Super Bowl, are often huge stage spectacles with musicians, dancers, and special effects. Lady Gaga's 2017 Super Bowl performance, for example, included lighting effects, flying her in, and the use of drones.

THEATRICALITY IN SPORTS EVENTS
Sporting events are often highly theatrical—football, basketball, and baseball, as well as many other sports, have a definite theatrical component. One prime example is the half-time show at the annual Super Bowl. Shown here is the half time show at the Super Bowl in 2017 at which the performer Lady Gaga appeared and which featured stunning lighting and special effects. (©Cal Sport Media/Alamy Stock Photo)

Theatre and Digital Media

At the start of the twenty-first century, digital media are omnipresent, ranging from the computer to the Xbox to the iPad to the multitude of smartphones. One result is the immense popularity of video games and other interactive activities accessed through the Internet, on all of these devices, and which are clearly influenced by theatre. These digital entertainments usually present a theatrical plotline in which we engage. Many of these storylines are based on popular melodramatic premises taken from films, comic books, and other entertainments. Some are based on historical events, such as actual wars and battles; others are fictional tales. Their goal is to make us feel as if we are actors within the universe of the game. The desire to create realistic special effects graphics continues a tradition that began with nineteenth-century stage melodrama, continued into film and television, and now is an engaging element of these digital games.

There are also interactive theatrical role-playing websites on the Internet. These sites all allow us to feel as if we are actors in a theatricalized fantasy world. Even websites that are supposedly realistic chat rooms allow us to play roles as if we are actors in a performance for an unseen audience.

1. Attend a theatre performance. Note the following: (a) What it is like arriving at the theatre, entering the lobby, then entering the theatre itself. (b) As the performance begins, how you become aware of the type of theatre you will see: musical, historical play, modern domestic drama, comedy, or something other than these.

2. As the play gets under way take note of the following:

   a. The scenery: Is it life-like or fantasy? Is it complete or merely suggestive of time and place? Is it beautiful to look at or is it depicting something frightening or strange? Is the stage filled with scenery, or relatively bare? As the play progresses, does the scenery remain constant or are there frequent scene changes?

   b. The lighting: What kind of lighting is there? Is it the lighting of a rock concert or nightclub, or does it seem like the natural lighting of a home or an outdoor park or patio? What are the colors of the lighting? Are the colors appropriate to the situation? Does the lighting change frequently or only rarely?

   c. The acting: Are the performers supposed to be ordinary people, of the type you would recognize from friends, family, or everyday characters on TV? Or are the characters historical people or larger-than-life figures? Is there anything special about the way one or more actors perform? Are they believable and ordinary, or is there something unusual or distinctive?

The term *cosplay* is a contraction of *costume* and *play*. It describes a combination of role-playing, costuming, and social interactions and became a worldwide popular culture phenomenon because of the Internet. Cosplay, which began in the 1990s, refers to people, known as *cosplayers*, dressing up as characters from cartoons, video games, films, television series, and other entertainments.

Often those engaged in cosplay attend large fan conventions for popular television shows, comic book conventions, and cosplay competitions. The combination of online social networks and dedicated websites allows cosplayers to interact virtually and at any time of day or night from across the globe.

Another impact of digital technology is that audiences can attend live broadcast and digitally streamed productions from theatres across their nation and across the globe. The National Theatre, for example, established National Theatre Live, which broadcasts productions via satellite to film houses. Some theatres stream performances to audience members' computers, laptops, tablets or smartphones. Broadway HD was established to allow individuals anywhere to stream Broadway quality shows to their digital devices. But like live television, these streamed events do not place audiences in the presence of the live performers as theatre does.

Although there is an abundance of dramatic materials available in movie houses, on television, on Blu-ray or DVD, streamed digitally into our homes, in amusement parks, at sporting events, in video games, and on the Internet, theatre itself is also a highly diverse and eclectic art form that attracts a wide spectrum of audience members and artists and is, in stark contrast to these others, a truly live, nonmediated art form.

Cosplay A contraction of costume and play that combines role-playing, costuming, and social interactions through the Internet or at conventions.

THEATRE AND THE HUMAN CONDITION

There is one additional, highly significant, but often overlooked reason for us to attend and study theatre. Throughout its history theatre has had a two-fold appeal. One attraction is the sheer excitement or amusement of a theatre event. The other is the unique ability of theatre to incorporate in dramatic material profound, provocative, timeless observations about our human condition. Ideas, moral dilemmas, probing insights—these have long found vivid expression in exceptional plays and exceptional performances. Moreover, in theatre these performances are live, not reproduced on a film, television screen, or digital device.

In Greek and Shakespearean tragedy, and in the works of modern playwrights like Henrik Ibsen, Anton Chekhov, Eugene O'Neill, Tennessee Williams, Arthur Miller, Lorraine Hansberry, and August Wilson, we encounter questions and issues that strike at the very heart of our human existence. In the comedies of the French playwright Molière, we see personal foibles exposed as they have rarely been before or since.

Finally, theatre also differs in significant ways from other types of live entertainment such as performances by rock stars. Rock musicians, for example, make no pretense of offering the same kind of experience as a production by a theatre company. A drama or a piece of performance art has a structure—a beginning, middle, and end—a purpose, a cast of characters, a unique completeness that a concert by a rock artist would never aspire to.

In other words, theatre, which influences so much of the world around us, is an art form with its own characteristics: its own quality, coherence, and integrity.

SUMMARY

1. During the past century live theatre has faced a number of daunting challenges from other dramatic media: films, television, electronic media, etc.

2. Live theatre has been able to meet these challenges not only because of its unique characteristics, but chiefly because it is only in live theatre that the audience is physically present at a performance by live actors.

3. Live theatre today is available in a wide variety of venues: commercial theatre, nonprofit professional theatre, college and university theatre, amateur theatre, children's theatre.

4. There is also a wide range of the types of theatre available today: classic, traditional, experimental, avant-garde.

5. Theatrical elements are part of many other activities in which we engage: religious services, rock concerts, theme parks, sports events.

THE AUDIENCE

2

This chapter is devoted to the role we play as audience members. Before focusing on that role, however, we will examine two important background subjects that will enhance audience participation and awareness. The first is a look at theatre's relationship to the arts in general and to other art forms. The second is knowledge of how a theatre production is conceived, developed, and presented, including a brief examination of the various elements of which a theatre production consists. Though we touch on these elements of theatre here, we will examine them in greater detail in the part "Creating Theatre: The Playwright."

In the second half of the chapter we will focus on the indispensable role the audience plays at a live theatre production. We examine how we, as spectators, might prepare for attending a production and also explore the variety, diversity and range of audiences at various kinds of theatrical presentations. Beyond that, we look at the way in which critics, reviewers, and bloggers can help us become more informed evaluators of a production and how we, as audience members, can develop our own criteria to evaluate our theatre experiences.

WHAT IS ART?

As has often been observed, art is a mirror or reflection of life: an extension or a projection of how we live, think, and feel. Art reveals to us what we treasure and admire, and what we fear most deeply. Art is not only something we find desirable and enjoyable; it is an absolute necessity for human survival.

There are feelings, emotions, and ideas that cannot be expressed in any way other than through art. The beauty of a face or a haunting landscape may be impossible to convey in words, but it can be revealed in a painting; a complex personality can be captured in a novel or a play in a way that reveals the person's

◀ **THE ACTORS MEET THE AUDIENCE**

The essence of the theatre experience is the exchange between performers and audience members. The electricity, the vibrations, the chemistry between the two is at the heart of theatre. Here we see the audience applauding the actors at the conclusion of a 2006 production of Hamlet *at the Guthrie Theatre in Minneapolis.* (©AP Photo/Andy King)

innermost soul; joy or anguish can often be communicated most directly and completely through music, poetry, or drama. Without these modes of expression—that is, without art—human beings would be as impoverished and as helpless as they would be if they tried to live without language.

Characteristics of Art

Visual arts These include painting, sculpture, architecture, and photography.

Performing arts These include theatre, dance, opera, and music, where there are live performers and audience members.

Art can be divided into three categories: *literary, visual,* and *performing.* The literary arts include novels, short stories, and poetry. The **visual arts** include painting, sculpture, architecture, and photography. The **performing arts** are theatre, dance, opera, and music. (Film, another art form, partakes of both the visual and the performing arts.) One characteristic of all art—visual, literary, or performing—traditionally has been that it is selective. As the three categories suggest, different art forms usually focus on certain elements and eliminate others. The visual arts, for example, deal solely with sight and touch—what we can see and feel—and they exclude sound. When we visit an art gallery, there is a hush in the air because the concentration is purely on what the eye observes. Moreover, in the visual arts, a composition is frozen and constant. We value the visual arts partly because they capture subjects—faces, landscapes, a series of colors or shapes—and hold them fast in a painting or a sculpture. We can look at a statue of a Roman soldier from 2,000 years ago, or a Madonna and Child painted 500 years ago, and see exactly the same artifact that its first viewers observed.

Music, on the other hand, concentrates on sound. Although we may watch a violinist playing with a symphony orchestra or observe a soprano singing at a recital, the essence of music is sound. We prove this whenever we close our eyes at a concert, and whenever we listen to recorded music. In both cases, the emphasis is totally on sound. By concentrating on sound, we block out distractions and give our full attention to the music itself. This kind of selectivity is one quality that has traditionally defined each art form.

However, art does not have rules. While we are describing the selectivity of traditional art forms throughout history, experimental artists have often tried to break down the barriers between them. In the contemporary art world, *installations* mix visual, sound, and performative elements. There are concerts that use lights and projections. But these are more the exceptions and also reflect the constant experimentation within all of the arts.

Spatial arts Art forms that exist in space and are created to last over time.

Temporal arts Art forms that exist for only a specific period of time.

Another characteristic of art is its relationship to time or space; thus a second way to differentiate the arts is in temporal and spatial terms. The visual arts are **spatial arts**; they exist in space, which is their primary mode of existence. They occupy a canvas, for instance, or—in the case of architecture—a building. By contrast, music moves through time; it is a **temporal art.** It does not occupy space; musicians performing a symphony exist in space, of course, but the music they perform does not. The music is an unfolding series of sounds, and the duration of the notes and the pauses between notes create a rhythm that is an essential part of music. This, in turn, becomes a time continuum as we move from one note to the next.

Unlike painting and sculpture on the one hand or music on the other, theatre, dance, and opera occupy both time and space. Let's now consider the special characteristics of the performing arts.

Characteristics of the Performing Arts

The performing arts, of which music, theatre, opera, and dance are a part, have several characteristics in common. One is the movement through time described

THE PERMANENCE OF THE VISUAL ARTS
If they are preserved, painting and sculpture—unlike performing arts such as theatre, dance, and music—are permanent and unchanging. An example is this sculpture of the Nike of Samothrace, goddess of victory, on display at the Louvre Museum in Paris, France. The torso enfolded in flowing robes and the outstretched wings appear much as they did when the sculpture was first created on the island of Samothrace in Greece around 200 B.C.E., about 2,200 years ago. (©Crystaltmc/iStock/Getty Images RF)

THE PERFORMING ARTS
Like theatre, opera, and music, dance shares a number of characteristics with these other performing arts. For example, all these arts move through time, they require interpreters as well as creators, and they must be seen live by an audience. In this photo, we see the Kremlin Ballet performing *Swan Lake* in Skopje, Macedonia. (©Boris Grdanoski/AP Images)

above. Another is that they require interpreters as well as creators. A playwright writes a play, but actors and actresses perform it; a composer writes a piece of music that singers and instrumentalists will perform; a choreographer develops a ballet that dancers will interpret.

Another quality shared by the performing arts is that they require an audience. A performance can be recorded on film or tape, but the event itself must be "live," that is, it must occur in one place at one time with both performers and audience present. If a theatre performance is recorded on film or tape without the presence of an audience, it becomes a movie or a television show rather than a theatre experience. To put this distinction another way, when an audience watches a film in a movie theatre, there are no performers onstage; there are only images on a screen.

In addition to the general qualities we have been discussing, each art form has unique qualities and principles that set it apart from other art forms and help us to understand it better. When we know how shapes and designs relate to overall composition, for instance, and how colors contrast with and complement one another, we are in a better position to judge and understand painting. In the same way, we can appreciate theatre much more if we understand how it is created and what elements it consists of.

THE ART OF THEATRE

We now turn our attention to the specific elements and qualities of theatre that make it a unique and lively art.

The Elements of Theatre

When we begin to examine theatre as an art form, we discover that there are certain components common to all theatre. These elements are present whenever a theatre event takes place; without them, an event ceases to be theatre and becomes a different art form and a different experience.

Audience   As we have suggested, a necessary element for theatre is the audience. In fact, the essence of theatre is the interaction between performer and audience. A theatre, dance, or musical event is not complete—one could almost say it does not occur—unless there are people to see and hear it. When we read a play in book form, or listen to recorded music, or even watch a film or television show, what we experience is similar to looking at a painting or reading a poem: it is a private event, not a public one, and the live performance is re-created and imagined rather than experienced firsthand. All the performing arts, including theatre, are like an electrical connection: the connection is not made until positive and negative wires touch and complete the circuit. Performers are half of that connection, and we, as audiences, are the other half.

Performers   Another absolutely essential element for theatre is the performers: people onstage presenting characters in dramatic action. Acting is at the heart of all theatre. One person stands in front of other people and begins to portray a character—to speak and move in ways that convey an image of the character. At this point the magic of theatre has begun: the transformation through which an audience accepts, for a time, that a performer is actually someone else. The character portrayed can be a historical figure, an imaginary figure, or even a self-presentation; still, everyone accepts the notion that it is the character, not the actor or actress, who is speaking.

Acting is a demanding profession. In addition to native talent—the poise and authority needed to appear onstage before others, and the innate ability to create a character convincingly—acting requires considerable craft and skill. Performers must learn to use both voice and body with flexibility and control; they must be able, for example, to make themselves heard in a large theatre even when speaking in a whisper. (This takes extensive physical and vocal training, which we will discuss in more detail later.) Performers must also be able to create believability, or the emotional truth of the characters they portray; that is, the audience must be convinced that the actor or actress is thinking and feeling what the character would think and feel. (This, too, is a difficult task requiring a special kind of training.)

Script or Text   Another element essential to theatre is the *script* or *text*, which could also be called the *blueprint* for a production. The playwright transforms the raw material—the incident, the biographical event, the myth—into a dramatic script, a sequence of events that features characters speaking and interacting with one another. Making this transformation is not easy. It requires intimate knowledge of stage practices, of how to breathe life into characters, of how to build action so that it will hold the interest of the audience and arouse anticipation for what is coming next. In other words, the playwright must create characters and develop a dramatic structure.

The term *text* is used to include any type of theatrical activity presented onstage: for example, all performances created or improvised by performers or directors as well as those created by a playwright. Frequently, the term *text* is all-inclusive, and it is sometimes used in place of *script*. A specific example of

Script (text)   The blueprint for a production, the material staged by the various theatre artists.

Text   Any type of theatrical activity presented onstage: for example, all performances created or improvised by performers or directors rather than a playwright. Frequently, the term *text* is all-inclusive, and it is sometimes used in place of *script*.

a nonliterary theatrical text would be an improvisatory presentation created by actors on a street, in a warehouse, or in a theatre.

Along with structure, a text must have a focus and a point of view. Who and what is the text about? Are we supposed to regard the characters and the events as sad or funny? The person or persons who create the text have the power as well as the responsibility to direct our attention toward certain characters and away from others. We will discover more about how these tasks are accomplished when we look at the nature of a dramatic text.

Director   An additional key element of a theatre production is the work of the *director*: the person who rehearses the performers and coordinates the work of the designers and others to make certain that the production is cohesive as well as exciting. As we will see, the separate role of the director became prominent for the first time in modern theatre, but many of the functions of the director have always been present.

Director The coordinator all of the elements of a production who is responsible for the unifying vision of a production.

Theatre Space   Another necessary element of theatre is the *space* in which performers and audiences come together. It is essential to have a stage, or some equivalent area, where actors and actresses can perform. It is also essential to have a place for audience members to sit or stand. We will discover that there have been several basic configurations of stage spaces and audience seating. Whatever the configuration, however, a stage and a space for the audience must be a part of it. Also, there usually must be a place for the actors and actresses to change costumes, as well as a way for them to enter and exit from the stage. As we shall see, sites for performances may be permanent, temporary, or transformed from spaces not originally intended for theatre.

DESIGN ELEMENTS IN THEATRE
The design elements in theatre include scenery, costume, lighting, and sound. This scene from a production of *Beauty and the Beast* in Paris, France shows vividly the costumes, levels and lighting of a large-scale musical. In such a production all of the visual and aural elements combine to produce the overall effect. (©Kristy Sparow/Getty Images)

Design Elements Closely related to the physical space is another important element: the design aspects of a production. Design includes visual aspects—costumes, lighting, and some form of scenic background—and a nonvisual aspect, sound.

A play can be produced on a bare stage with minimal lighting, and with the performers wearing everyday street clothes. Even in these conditions, however, some attention must be paid to visual elements; there must, for instance, be sufficient illumination for us to see the performers, and clothes worn onstage will take on a special meaning even if they are quite ordinary.

Usually, visual elements are prominent in theatre productions. Costumes, especially, have been a hallmark of theatre from the beginning; and scenery has sometimes become more prominent than the performers. In certain arrangements, visual aspects come to the forefront; in others—such as the arena stage, where the audience surrounds the action—elaborate scenery is impractical if not impossible.

The visual aspects of theatre are particularly interesting to trace through history because their place in theatre production has shifted markedly from time to time. For example, stage lighting changed dramatically when the electric lightbulb came into use at the end of the nineteenth century. In our contemporary theatre, computerization has led to spectacular scenic and lighting effects using projections and videos.

As we noted earlier, a design element that is not visual is sound. This, too, is a modern element that has come into its own with modern technology. Of course, there were always sound effects, such as thunder and wind created by offstage machines; and there was frequently music, especially during certain periods when every intermission was accompanied by orchestral performances. In modern times, though, with digital inventions, there are far more elaborate sound effects; and frequently there are also unobtrusive microphones, sometimes in the general stage area and sometimes worn by the performers.

To sum up, the following are the major elements of theatre:

- Audience
- Performers
- Script or text, with its structure, characters, and point of view
- Director
- Theatre space
- Design aspects: scenery, costume, lighting, and sound

Theatre as a Collaborative Art

It should be clear from what we have said that theatre is a collaborative art. For a theatre event to take place, its various elements must be brought together and coordinated.

The director must stage the play written by the playwright and must share with the playwright an understanding of structure, theme, and style. At the same time, the director must work closely with performers in rehearsing the play, and with the designers of scenery, lights, costumes, and sound, to bring the production to fruition. During performances many elements must be coordinated: the work of actors and actresses along with technical aspects—scene changes, lighting shifts, and sound cues. The people working on these elements are joined, in turn, by a number of collaborators: stage manager, stage carpenters, makeup experts, those who make costumes, and computer lighting experts. In an ensemble piece, where the play is actually composed by a group of actors working with a director, collaboration is more important than ever.

Another essential component in this collaborative enterprise is the business and administrative side of a production or theatre organization. This includes producers and managers, and their staffs—the people who organize and administer press and public relations, advertising, scheduling, fund-raising, and all the details of keeping the theatre running smoothly, including ticket sales, ticket taking, and ushering.

Ultimately, the many elements integrated in a production—text or script, direction, design, and acting, assisted by the technical side and the business side—must be presented to an audience. At that point occurs the final collaboration in any theatre enterprise: the performance itself before spectators. We will be discussing all of these collaborators in the part "Creating Theatre" of our textbook.

THE ROLE OF THE AUDIENCE

If you asked us to list the essential components of what creates a theatre experience, the chances are we would mention several of the elements listed above but might not include the presence of the audience. This is understandable—particularly today, when film and television are so pervasive. In these media, which are so much like theatre in many ways, the "product," as it is sometimes called, stands alone as a finished presentation. When you watch a film at home on a Blu-ray or streamed via the Internet, it has been completed and is in its absolutely final form. The same is true of a film in a movie theatre; when released it might be shown in 1,000 theatres simultaneously across the United States, and it will be exactly the same in each location, time after time. The audience watches but plays no part in what appears on the screen.

Theatre is different. Even when the story and the characters presented are identical—in a film and stage presentation of Shakespeare's *Romeo and Juliet,* for instance—there is the crucial and important difference, namely, that each theatre performance is unique and occurs in the presence of an *audience.* The ramifications of the audience are far-reaching. To begin with, in live theatre the performers have no opportunity to play a scene over or to correct mistakes. Most of us are aware that in creating a film most scenes are filmed a number of times. These repetitions are called "takes," and there may be four, five, or even twenty takes before the director feels that a scene is "right." Moreover, once scenes are filmed, the director decides in the editing room where each scene begins and ends and how scenes are joined together.

In theatre, there is no repeating and no editing. The performers move through a production from beginning to end, and if there is a mishap—if an actor forgets a line, or an unexpected noise occurs offstage—the performers must recover and carry on. The result of all this is that each theatre event is immediate, and unique.

The dynamics and the excitement of being in the presence of a living person are as old as time and have not changed despite the many technological advances of recent years. As we have noted previously, people still wait for hours or stand in the rain to see a rock star or a hip-hop performer in person, although the same performer is readily available on many digital devices. The same is true of film personalities and charismatic political figures—people eagerly throng to see someone "in person." Thousands of people in Chicago lined up in January 2017 in the hopes of getting tickets to hear the farewell speech of outgoing President Barack Obama.

This same chemistry is possible at every stage performance when the actors and actresses and the members of the audience are in the same place at the same time.

There is another aspect in which we, as the audience, play a significant part: the effect that we have on performers. The drama critic Walter Kerr (1913–1996) explained the special relationship between audience and performers at a theatre event:

> It doesn't just mean that we are in the personal presence of performers. It means that they are in our presence, conscious of us, speaking to us, working for and with us until a circuit that is not mechanical becomes established between us, a circuit that is fluid, unpredictable, ever-changing in its impulses, crackling, intimate. Our presence, the way we respond, flows back to the performer and alters what he does, to some degree and sometimes astonishingly so, every single night. We are contenders, making the play and the evening and the emotion together. We are playmates, building a structure.[1]

Or as television, film, and stage actress Kim Cattrall has remarked: "Theatre is immediate, it's alive, you're there with the audience, it can't be done again and again and again and again, it's organic."[2]

In other words, we should always remember that as audience members we have an enormous effect on actors and actresses. They are buoyed up by a responsive audience and discouraged by an unresponsive one. Sometimes, if an audience is not reacting, they might try harder than ever to make contact. This is the case not only with comedy, where laughter is a clear gauge of the audience's response, but also with serious drama. Performers know whether or not spectators are caught up in the action. When audience members are involved in a serious play, they become very quiet; you can sense their fierce concentration. When an audience is not engaged, there may be noticeable coughing or rustling of programs. Reacting to this, actors and actresses will change their performances in subtle but very real ways.

THE AUDIENCE REACTS
The response of the audience affects the performance of the actors, who sense how a play or musical is being received by the spectators. In the scene here the audience at the Globe Theatre in London pays close attention to a performance of *Two Gentlemen of Verona* by William Shakespeare.
(©Gideon Mendel/Getty Images)

[1]Kerr, Walter, "We Call It 'Live Theater,' but Is It?" New York Times, January 2, 1972.
[2]"Kim Catrall," Official London Theatre, January 14, 2005

GAY THEATRE
Among the many diverse theatres that emerged in the last part of the twentieth century was theatre centering on the gay and lesbian experience. Shown here is a scene from *Bent*, a play depicting gay characters during the Holocaust by Martin Sherman in a production at the Trafalgar Studios starring Chris New and Alan Cumming. (©Geraint Lewis/Alamy Stock Photo)

How the Audience Participates

At the heart of the theatre experience, then, is the performer–audience relationship: the immediate, personal exchange; the chemistry and magic that give theatre its special quality. We might ask how the audience becomes involved in a theatre event, aside from sending the performers such obvious signals as laughter, silence, and palpable tension. The answer lies in the power of the imagination.

As audience members, we do not participate physically in a theatre performance, the way we would if we were riding a bicycle, working at a computer, or singing in a chorus. Rather, we participate *vicariously,* through the mind and the heart. The astonishing thing is how powerful these aspects of the human psyche are. Through our imagination, we come to believe in the reality of what we see onstage and to identify with the characters. We feel deep sympathy for those we sense are being treated unjustly, and we suffer with them; we feel hatred for those we consider mean or despicable; we laugh at those we consider foolish.

The events onstage become so real that we often forget who and where we are and enter the imaginary world we see before us. We can be transported to a foreign country, to another century, to an imaginary place—or to the kitchen of people who might be our own neighbors. Some situations in theatre are so vivid and so engrossing that we cry real tears, even though a part of us knows that the events onstage are not actually happening and that the people are only actors and actresses. This experience comes about because of a phenomenon that the English poet and critic Samuel Taylor Coleridge (1772–1834) called the ***willing suspension of disbelief***.

Willing suspension of disbelief The audience's desire to believe in the reality of what is happening onstage.

PLAYING YOUR PART:
EXPERIENCING THEATRE

1. Recall a personal experience with each of three different art forms: *visual* (a painting or a piece of sculpture); *literary* (a poem, a novel, or a biography); the *performing arts* (theatre, a ballet, a musical concert or opera). Describe your experience of encountering each of the three: what you felt, what you thought, what you focused on. Explain how the experience of responding to each one differed from that of seeing or hearing the other two.

2. During a performance you may observe a puppet or group of puppets who appear as real as people we deal with every day. (If you have not seen puppets on stage, you have surely seen them on film or TV.) At the same time, you may see on a bare stage two or three props (a tree, for example, or a throne) and assume you are in a forest or a royal palace. Why do you think during a performance we are able to let our imaginations take over—with a bare stage becoming a forest, or a puppet becoming a person? Is this something we also do in everyday life?

3. While watching a performance you may dissolve into laughter or cry real tears. The whole time, on some level, you know what you are observing is not "real." Does this difference matter? In some sense is the experience real? Is it imaginary? Is it a bit of both? What is the relationship between a theatre experience such as this and an experience in daily life?

4. Imagine two friends viewing the same theatre production. One friend is captivated, feeling that what she saw was genuine and moving, an experience that affected her deeply. The other friend was not moved and felt that the performance was artificial and inauthentic. Why do you think the same performance can elicit two such different reactions?

In other words, we want so much to believe in the reality of what is happening onstage that we willingly put aside all literal and practical considerations in order to enter into the world of the drama.

Another factor that allows us to enter into an imaginative world—even though we are aware that it is separate from everyday reality—is referred to as ***aesthetic distance***. Aesthetic distance is a requirement of virtually all involvement with the arts. It means that the viewer, spectator, or audience member must be in some sense separated from the performance or object—and must be aware that it is a work of art—in order to experience its aesthetic qualities. Paradoxically, once the proper distance is established, the observer can enter into the experience fully and completely.

Aesthetic distance The separation of audience member from the performance or art work to experience its aesthetic qualities.

Throughout theatre history, the power of the audience's mental and emotional participation has manifested itself in both positive and negative ways. Negatively, it has taken the form of censorship—which indicates that those in authority fear the effect theatre can have on audiences. The Greeks of ancient Athens considered certain subjects unfit for drama and banned them. In Rome in the fourth century C.E., in the early days of Christianity, the church had a great deal to do with stopping theatrical activity. In 1642, the Puritans closed the theatres in England. In modern times, there have been many examples of censorship, especially in places like China and various totalitarian countries, where the only drama that can be presented is that which has been approved by the political authorities.

Positively, the power of audience participation can be seen in many ways. To take just one example, many political groups and other groups use theatre as a means of educating people or furthering a cause. In recent times, we have seen theatre representing various groups: feminist theatre, gay theatre, and radical political theatre, for instance. The artists who present such productions feel that the imaginative and symbolic power of theatre will affect their audiences. In sum, our ability as an audience to enter into the world presented onstage is one reason we are always a key factor in any theatre event.

Participatory and Immersive Theatre There are times when observers and audience members actively participate together in a theatre event. In the 1960s, for example, many politically active and socially engaged theatre groups created productions in which spectators were urged to challenge the traditional boundaries between themselves and the performers, instead of viewing the stage action from a separate space. (We will discuss some of these companies, such as the Living Theatre, in the chapters "The Modern Theatre Emerges" and "Today's Diverse Global Theatre.")

In recent years a new phenomenon, *immersive theatre,* has become popular internationally. In immersive theatre, the audience plays an active role in some way, often moving through a performance space, sometimes even choosing where they go within that space and what they see and do. Many immersive productions use transformed, redesigned spaces as well as require the audience member to engage in a complete sensory experience (touch, smell, even taste of foods and drink). The goal is an attempt to personalize the experience for each audience member while still emphasizing the social interaction between small groups in the audience as well as with the performers.

An example of such a work is *Sleep No More* (2003), an adaptation of Shakespeare's *Macbeth,* which the British company Punchdrunk has staged successfully in New York and London. Another group, the Australian theatre company One Step at a Time Like This, also focuses on immersive theatrical experiences. Their production *En Route,* for example, takes individual audience members through city spaces connecting those spaces to theatrical interactions with individual performers along the way.

While there has been a long history of participatory kinds of theatre wherein audience members are asked to take an active role (many of which will be discussed in the part "Global Theatres: Past and Present" of our textbook), the most traditional role of the audience member in the contemporary theatre is as the observer.

Immersive theatre In immersive theatre, the audience plays an active role in some way, often moving through a performance space, sometimes even choosing where they go within that space and what they see and do. Many immersive productions use transformed, redesigned spaces as well as require the audience member to engage in a complete sensory experience.

Makeup of Audiences: Past and Present

As we trace the history of theatre, one thing we will note is that the makeup of audiences has varied from time to time and from place to place. In ancient Greece, for example, a large percentage of an entire city, such as Athens or Epidaurus, would attend the theatre. The same was true of medieval theatre in Western Europe and England; however, when we come to Restoration theatre in England during the late seventeenth century, we find that the audience was often homogeneous, consisting primarily of the upper classes. This affected the kind of writing and acting seen onstage; as a result, Restoration plays still remain less accessible to the general population. In Europe in the nineteenth century, theatre once again came to be a form of art popular with a wide range of people. In various Asian countries, as well, theatre in some eras was only for an elite audience or for the upper classes, but at other times it included audiences from the general population.

As we observed in the chapter "Theatre Is Everywhere," today there is great diversity in both the size and the makeup of those who are present at a theatre event. In a small, intimate theatre, there may be no more than 100 or 200 people attending. On the other hand, at a large city auditorium, there may be 2,000 or 3,000 people, or even more, watching a large-scale musical. This factor will make a difference, both to audience members and to performers. In an intimate space there is more awareness, on the part of everyone, of the interaction between actors and spectators. In a large amphitheatre, a different, less personal relationship exists. In a theatre somewhere in between—a house that seats 800 or 900 people—the relationship will be a mixture of the two.

Aside from the question of size, today there is often a wide variety in the makeup of theatre audiences. Some audiences are homogeneous: the audience members come mostly from similar backgrounds and experiences. A good example would be a performance presented to a group of senior citizens in a retirement village. Other audiences are heterogeneous, such as the spectators at free performances of Shakespeare in an outdoor amphitheatre in a city park.

COLLEGE AND UNIVERSITY THEATRE

A vital segment of theatre in the United States is the many productions mounted by theatre departments in colleges and universities, which often achieve a high degree of professionalism. They also provide excellent training for theatre practitioners, as well as affording audiences first-rate productions. Seen here are (left to right) Danny Pancratz, Nathan Grant, and T. J. Nichols in a production of Molière's *The Miser* at Western Illinois University, directed by Professor Jeannie M. Woods. (Courtesy of Western Illinois University Visual Production Center/Larry Dean, photographer)

More and more today we find audiences that include a mixture of people reflecting the racial, religious, and ethnic diversity of our society: African American, Asian American, Latino and Latina, Native American, feminist, gay, lesbian and transgendered. There is also a wide age range in theatre attendees.

A final word about audience background. No matter the makeup of the spectators at a theatre event, whether homogeneous or heterogeneous, the chemistry of the audience will change from night to night for no apparent reason. At a comedy, for instance, on some nights the audience will laugh at everything; on other nights, audience members may enjoy the show just as much, but they will barely chuckle. It is this kind of variation in response that performers become accustomed to, and that reinforces the spontaneous quality of live theatre.

Where and How We See Theatre

In addition to diversity in the makeup of audiences and in their reactions, as we noted in the chapter "Theatre Is Everywhere," there are many places today where theatre can be seen: Broadway-size theatres, resident professional theatres, small theatres found in cities throughout the world, semiprofessional and amateur community theatres, as well as college and university theatres. In addition there are theatres created from other spaces such as lofts, warehouses, and former churches. Along with those listed above are stages reserved for children's theatre or theatre for youth, focusing on productions for and about young people.

With the abundance of theatre events available, audience members must find ways to select the productions they wish to see and find ways of attending. Today, there are many websites that provide lists of productions currently running in cities around the world, such as *Playbill* (which lists Broadway, off-Broadway, regional and national tours, and London), *Theatremania*, *Theatre in Chicago*, *Theatre Central* (which has international theatre events), and *Talkin' Broadway* (which also lists regional theatres). In addition, most theatre companies across the globe have websites (and apps) announcing the productions they are staging.

Some audience members continue to use traditional ways of selecting a show they wish to attend. Of course, many of us choose shows based on types of works we most enjoy and have experienced in the past: some of us may enjoy musicals, some comedies, and others serious dramas. However, the hope is that we are always open-minded and willing to experience a wide variety of types of theatre works in various types of spaces. Some of us read a favorite and trusted theatre critic or blogger (discussed next). Others may make choices based on "word of mouth" (opinions of friends, relatives, or acquaintances they trust), or others might check online responses.

Once you have chosen a show, there are a variety of ways to purchase tickets for theatres almost anywhere in the world. We should note that there are a few theatre companies built around the concept of **public access theatre**: free admission with requests for donations. But the vast majority of community, commercial, and nonprofit theatres charge for admission.

The most traditional option is to go to the box office. However, you can also purchase tickets online without leaving your residence and then print those tickets. There are centralized online theatre sites and apps, such as Ticketmaster, as well as the websites and apps for specific theatre companies that may offer online ticket purchase options. Such sites do add fees to the face value of the ticket.

There are also discount ticket websites and apps that will help you purchase tickets for some shows at reduced prices, such as *Theatremania, Playbill*, and *Today Tix* (which offers shows across the country and London). In addition, many major cities have centralized discount ticket booths, such as the Theatre Development Fund (TDF) sites in New York, Hottix in Chicago, and London's TKTS booth. In many cases, you can check availability for same-day performance discounts online, and some sites, such as *Hottix*, *Playbill*, and *Theatremania*, allow you to purchase your reduced price tickets online or through their app and print them at home. However, no matter what production you attend, how you choose that production, and how you purchase your admission, you must always remember your responsibilities as an audience member.

Audience Responsibility

Western theatre, particularly since the nineteenth century, has developed certain rules of behavior for audience members—expectations about what audiences do and don't do; however, it should be kept in mind that any given theatre event might have some unique expectations about the audience's behavior.

At a traditional theatre performance, the audience is expected to remain silent for the most part, and not interrupt the performers. Audience members should not talk to each other as if they were at home watching television; they should not send or receive text messages (the light from the handheld screen disturbs audience members and performers), use cell phones, hum or sing along with music, unwrap candy or other food, eat loudly, search through a purse or backpack. Remember that the actors can hear the audience: noises and distracting behavior will have an impact on their concentration and performance. Noise and distractions also affect the experience of other spectators.

Public access theatre
Theatres that have free admission with requests for donations.

Today, audience members at most traditional theatre productions are expected to observe specific rules of behavior, known as **theatre** or **audience etiquette.** We are expected to be silent observers, watching the action on the stage in the dark and engaging through our imaginations and emotions. When attending musicals, we can applaud after a wonderful song is sung or after a choreographed dance number. In a comedy audience members might laugh uproariously at a joke or at a piece of physical action, but after the applause or laughter we are expected to resume our status as silent observers.

This was not always the case. In the Western theatres prior to the nineteenth century, the theatre was truly a popular entertainment and all classes of people attended together. In Shakespeare's time, for example, audience members ate in the theatre, talked back to performers on the stage, and sometimes other entertainments were presented side by side with traditional theatre. At times Shakespeare's great plays appeared in spaces that were near bear-gardens or actually in those arenas that were used for such popular (and brutal) entertainments as bear baiting, in which dogs attacked chained bears.

Historians suggest that rules of social etiquette developed for a variety of reasons. As popular art and the theatre began to separate, and audiences became more stratified by class and economic status, some social critics argue that audience etiquette was a way in which the upper class attempted to exert control over lower classes and create a distinction in the types of theatrical arts each class attended.

Others argue that theatre artists, such as the stars who now traveled the world and playwrights whose works were being staged internationally, wanted their work to be taken more seriously and that audiences respect their artistry through their undivided attention.

Others point to the greater control over stage lighting and the ability to darken the auditorium as another reason that theatre etiquette became normative. And with the development of realistic theatre (which we will discuss in the chapter "The Modern Theatre Emerges"), the audience was expected to view people like themselves through an imaginary fourth wall and not interrupt the illusion of actual life on stage. All of these have led us to our traditional expectation of audience etiquette: an expectation that is questioned today because of changes in our social behavior and in the changing nature of some theatrical performances.

In our 24/7 connected world, should audiences be forced to turn off their cell phones? Because of our rushed and ever more hectic lifestyles, should food and drink be allowed in the theatre because many of us come directly from work? Clearly, there is a different "contract" with the audience for some immersive or participatory theatrical events in contrast to more traditional presentations.

For the most part, however, theatres expect audience members not to text and use their smartphones to tweet or surf the web. In addition, we are seeing some changes that may impact audience etiquette in the future. As we discussed, there are now tweet seats in some sections of the theatre. Many theatres do allow food and drink into the playhouse, asking audience members to be respectful of others as they eat and drink. And some immersive theatre events are using smart devices as a way to guide the audience through the event.

Still, for the most part, texting, not silencing smartphones, or eating and drinking loudly, in the theatre is disconcerting and inappropriate. The London website (and Twitter handle) *Theatre Charter* asks audience members to sign an agreement to behave appropriately in the theatre and explains the concern with distracting behaviors. While we should all observe the expectations of specific theatre productions (and, for the most part, that is to be a polite audience member observing the stage action), it is clear that audience etiquette has changed during the course of theatre history.

Students may be concerned about note-taking because they often will need to make notes in order to remember key elements of the production. An unobtrusive way of taking notes is to jot down only brief phrases or terms that will jog your memory later. Then, you can embellish your notes during the intermission or intermissions, or after the end of the performance.

Theatre (audience) etiquette The specific rules of behavior audience members are expected to observe when attending the theatre.

Of course, traditional audiences are not always absolutely quiet: audiences at comedies laugh, for instance. Audiences at musicals applaud after a song (in fact, they're expected to). On the other hand, audiences at serious plays generally do not applaud until the end of the performance—and even then, an audience may be so stunned or so deeply moved that there will be a moment of silence before the applause begins.

As noted earlier, not all of these traditional expectations may apply at every theatre event. Dinner theatres are one example since the audience may be eating during the presentation. (We might also note that audiences eat during the performance in many traditional Asian theatres, and they may speak back to the stage.) Audiences at some productions are expected to interact with the performers: in some comic presentations, for instance, actors may enter the audience space or actually speak to individual audience members; and in some nontraditional productions, audience members may even be expected to participate in the performance. In the contemporary theatre, there is even, as we noted earlier, a participatory form some critics refer to as *immersive theatre* where individual audience members are actively involved in a fluid, ever changing, and almost voyeuristic experience. We will discuss some of the companies that stage such events in later chapters.

THE AUDIENCE AND THE CRITIC, REVIEWER, AND BLOGGER

Most of us who go to the theatre or the movies, or who watch a television show, are amateur critics. When we say about a performance, "It started off great, but it fizzled," or "The star was terrific, just like someone in real life," or "The woman was OK, but the man overacted," or "The acting was good, but the story was too downbeat for me," we are making a critical judgment. The difference between a critic/reviewer and those of us in the audience is that the former presumably is better informed about the event and has developed a set of critical standards by which to judge it.

The Critic, Reviewer, and Blogger

Critic   Someone who observes a production and then analyzes and comments on it.

A *critic,* loosely defined, is someone who observes theatre and then analyzes and comments on it, and ideally serves as a knowledgeable and highly sensitive audience member. Audiences can learn from critics not only because critics impart information and judgments but also because a critic shares with an audience the point of view of the spectator. Unlike those who create theatre, critics sit out front and watch a performance just as other members of the audience do. Critics generally write serious articles that appear in newspapers, magazines, and books.

Reviewer   A type of critic who reports on a production and gives a brief opinion about whether or not it is worth seeing.

A familiar type of critic is the reviewer. A *reviewer,* who usually works for a newspaper, a magazine, a television station or a professional blog, reports on what has occurred at the theatre. He or she will tell briefly what a theatre event is about, explaining that it is a musical, a comedy, or a serious play and perhaps describing its plot. The reviewer might also offer an opinion about whether or not the event is worth seeing. The reviewer is usually restricted by time, space, or both.

Social Media and the Audience as Critic, Reviewer, and Blogger

Today, in addition to critics and reviewers, whose opinions appear in print or on television, we have a new source of theatre criticism: popular websites and blogs.

Part 1   Theatre in Today's World

Many of these sites, such as *Theatremania.com,* have their own theatre reviewers; other sites may have amateur critics who send in their unsolicited opinions. Some individuals have set up their own websites and blogs for expressing their views about theatre productions.

Opinions about theatre productions also are found on social media sites such as Facebook, Twitter, Snapchat, Instagram, YouTube and even Yelp. Social media allows all of us to function as reviewers and to respond to productions we see. Some theatres request that audience members "like" their Facebook pages in response to productions. Some theatres have set aside specific seats in their theatres, known as "tweet seats." Audience members sitting in these sections can tweet to their Twitter followers their instantaneous reactions to a production, while not distracting other spectators. Some theatres also have personnel backstage who tweet about the show while it is going on.

Another recent development that allows audience members to become part of the critical process is known as *dial testing*, wherein audiences electronically respond to shows that are still being developed. Their responses might then be used to impact the final product. Some theatres use *focus groups* (that is, selected audience members) to provide feedback about a show that is still in development. Often, these methods are used to test reactions to theatre productions that are meant to reach a wide audience and have commercial, box office success. Some theatres e-mail questionnaires to audience members who have attended their productions. Smaller theatres that produce new, cutting edge works would probably not ask potential audience members to respond in these ways.

At times these assessments of a production can be helpful and informative, but a word of caution is in order. A number of self-appointed reviewers may have little or no background in theatre criticism, or, in fact, in theatre itself. They enjoy being part of the wider world of theatre criticism, but may not have the credentials to do so. In other words, these amateur critics may not have the necessary preparation for criticism. In the same way we do not take any or every online review of a product as an expert evaluation, we should do the same when we read responses to theatrical presentations in the various social media.

Preparation for Criticism

The critic/reviewer/blogger should have a thorough background in theatre to make criticism more meaningful to audiences. These commentators should have a full knowledge of theatre history, acting, directing and design. The critic/reviewer/ blogger must be familiar with plays written in various styles and modes and should know the body of work of individual writers. Also, the critic ought to be able to relate what is happening in theatre to what is happening in the other arts and, beyond that, to events in society generally. In addition, the person commenting on theatre should understand the production elements discussed in this book— directing, acting, dramaturgy, and design.

Fact and Opinion in Criticism

In reading the commentary of the reviewer, in print or online, it is important to distinguish between *fact* and *opinion.* Facts may provide helpful information in understanding a play; for example, to know that in Shakespeare's time, men played all the female parts would help explain why a director might make that choice today in assigning actors to their roles. Opinions can also be helpful, but audience members should carefully weigh them against their own knowledge and

BACKGROUND INFORMATION ON PLAYS AND PLAYWRIGHTS
Many times it is helpful for students and audiences to acquire advance
information on a play they are planning to see. A good example would be a drama
by the German playwright Bertolt Brecht, who did not write his plays in the
customary way, but often interrupted the action with a song or a direct address
to the audience. Shown here is a scene from Brecht's *Mother Courage and Her
Children,* translated by Tony Kushner, featuring Fiona Shaw in the title role
in a production at Britain's National Theatre, directed by Deborah Warner.
(©Geraint Lewis/Alamy Stock Photo)

experience. In addition to our professors and instructors, a critic, reviewer or
blogger can often make us aware of information we might not otherwise have
known; for example, by explaining a point that was confusing to the audience or
noting how a particular scene in a play relates to an earlier scene. They might
also offer background material about the playwright, the subject matter of the
play, or the style of the production. Such information can broaden our

Part 1   Theatre in Today's World

understanding and appreciation of a production we are about to see. The more we know about what a playwright is attempting to do and why a playwright arranges scenes in a certain way, the better we will be able to judge the value of a theatre event we attend.

A good example is the German playwright Bertolt Brecht (1898–1956), who lived and wrote in the United States during the 1940s. Brecht wanted to provoke his audiences into thinking about what they were seeing. To do this, he would interrupt a story with a song or a speech by a narrator that commented on the action. His theory was that when a story is stopped in this manner, audience members have an opportunity to consider more carefully what they are seeing and to relate the drama onstage to other aspects of life. If we are not aware that this is Brecht's purpose in interrupting the action, we might conclude that he was simply a careless or inferior playwright. Here, as in similar cases, knowledge of the play or playwright is indispensable to a complete theatre experience.

Critical Criteria

In commenting on a theatre production, a critic, reviewer, or those of us who present our opinions through social media should ask three questions as a guide to arriving at judgments, criteria that will also aid the rest of us to be better informed about a production we have seen and to better explain our reactions to it.

What Is Being Attempted? One of the first questions is: *What is the play, and the production, attempting to do?* This question must be raised both about the script and about the production. Is the play a tragedy meant to raise significant questions and stir deep emotions? Is it a light comedy intended to entertain and provide escape? Is it a political drama arguing for a point of view?

Have the Intentions Been Achieved? A second question is: *How well have the intentions of the playwright been carried out?* If a theatre piece originates with an acting ensemble, or with a director, the question is: *How well have the intentions of the original creators been realized?* A theatre company may be producing an acknowledged masterpiece such as *Hamlet* or *Macbeth,* in which case the question becomes how well the play has been acted, directed, and designed. Have the performers brought Shakespeare's characters to life convincingly and excitingly? Or has the director—perhaps by striving to be too original in approach and staging, without helping us as audience members understand why she or he has done so—distorted Shakespeare's intentions beyond recognition?

In the case of a new script, one must also ask how well the playwright has realized his or her own intentions. If the play is intended to probe deeply into family relationships—parents and children, or husbands and wives—how convincingly and how insightfully has the dramatist accomplished this? If the intention is to entertain, to make the audience laugh, the question to be asked is: Just how funny is the play? Did it succeed in providing entertainment? Was it clever, witty, and full of amusing situations, or did it fall flat?

Was the Attempt Worthwhile? A third question to ask when judging a production falls more into the realm of personal taste and evaluation: *Is the play or production worth doing?* Many critics think that anything that succeeds at giving pleasure and providing entertainment is as worthwhile in its own way as a more serious undertaking. Others, however, do not. In cases like this, readers of criticism and viewers of a performance must make up their own minds.

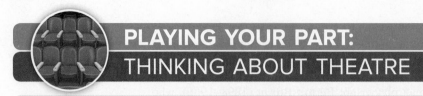

1. When you are attending a theatrical performance, the following are questions for you, as an individual audience member, to consider.

   a. Is the audience a homogeneous group—similar in background and attitude—or a diverse one?

   b. Is the event being presented primarily by and for a particular group—cultural, social, gender, or political? How do you relate to that group?

   c. If it is a serious event, is the audience concentrating and empathizing with what is happening on stage? If the event is comic, is the audience caught up in the amusement and laughter?

2. Read a review online by a *New York Times* or *Chicago Tribune* theatre critic. Which of the critical criteria discussed in this chapter does he or she address? How did the critic help you decide whether you might want to see the production?

3. A theatre critic in New York was so disturbed by an audience member texting throughout a performance that he grabbed the spectator's cell phone and threw it into the aisle of the theatre. A performer stopped a production when a cell phone went off during a key scene and verbally confronted the audience member. Were these responses appropriate? Explain why or why not.

If audience members are aware of these criteria, they not only can note whether critics—in print, on television, or online—address these questions but also can ask the questions for themselves.

The Dramaturg or Literary Manager

Dramaturg The individual who works on literary and historical issues with members of the artistic team mounting a theatre production.

The term ***dramaturg*** (also spelled *dramaturge*) comes from a German word for "dramatic adviser." In Europe, the practice of having a dramaturg, or *literary manager,* attached to a theatre goes back well over a century. In the United States, the role of the dramaturg is relatively new; only in recent years have regional professional groups and other not-for-profit theatres engaged full-time dramaturgs. Among the duties undertaken by a dramaturg are discovering and reading promising new plays, working with playwrights on the development of new scripts, identifying significant plays from the past that may have been overlooked, conducting research on previous productions of classic plays, preparing reports on the history of plays, researching criticism and interpretations of plays from the past, and writing articles for the programs that are distributed when plays are produced.

Just as a good reviewer, critic, or blogger can be helpful to audience members, so too can a perceptive dramaturg. She or he is usually the person who prepares educational material (both in print and online) for students and teachers who attend performances.

The Audience's Relationship to Criticism

As suggested earlier, when we, as audience members, combine awareness of criticism with the theatre event itself, the experience can be greatly enhanced: background information and critical appraisals are added to our own firsthand reactions. There are cautionary notes, however, of which we should be aware. Quite often critic/reviewers state unequivocally that a certain play is extremely well or badly written, beautifully or atrociously performed, and so on. Because these so-called authorities often speak so confidently and because their opinions appear in print or on the Internet, their words have the ring of authority. But as theatergoers, we should not be confused or unduly influenced by them.

In certain large cities—New York City, Chicago, or Los Angeles—where a number of critics and reviewers in various media comment on each production, there is a wide range of opinion. It is not unusual for some critic/reviewers to find a certain play admirable, while others find the same play quite inferior, and still others find a mixture of good and bad. This range of opinion implies that there is no absolute authority among such people, and that we should make up our own minds. If a critic/reviewer, for example, dislikes a certain play because he or she finds it too sentimental and you happen to like that kind of sentiment, you should not be dissuaded from your own preferences. Attending the theatre is a unique, individual experience—it is *your* experience—and you must trust and be guided by your own judgment.

SUMMARY

1. Art forms can be categorized as literary, visual, and performing; theatre is one of the performing arts. All art is selective, and selectivity is one way of distinguishing one art form from another. Art forms may also be distinguished in terms of time and space: the visual arts exist primarily in space; music exists in time rather than space; and theatre (along with dance and opera) exists in both time and space.

2. Important characteristics of the performing arts include the need for interpreters and the need for an audience.

3. The major elements of theatre are audience, performers, text, director, theatre space, and design. Because these elements must be coordinated, theatre is a collaborative art.

4. The audience is a key, indispensable part of theatre.

5. Though the audience participation at a theatre event is vicarious, its involvement is mentally and emotionally active.

6. The critic/reviewer/blogger commenting on theatre can assist the audience in understanding a play and a performance.

Creating Theatre:
The Playwright

THE SCRIPT: BLUEPRINT FOR A PRODUCTION

Every theatre event begins with an idea, an outline, or a concept. Traditionally, the concept originates with the playwright and is developed in his or her script, or blueprint. The script, in turn, is developed into a production by performers, the director, and the designers. Shown here is a scene from *Rosencrantz and Guildenstern* by Tom Stoppard, directed by David Leveaux, with Daniel Radcliffe as Rosencrantz, David Haig as The Player, and Joshua McGuire as Guildenstern. Staged at The Old Vic Theatre in London, this scene clearly reflects the impact actors, directors, and designers have on bringing a text to life on stage.

(©Geraint Lewis/Alamy Stock Photo)

3

CREATING THE
DRAMATIC SCRIPT

A theatre production is a collaboration, not only between the audience and the performers but, as we have noted, among a whole range of people who make it happen: actors, directors, designers, the playwright. All are significant, but like any enterprise, a theatre production must begin somewhere, and in most cases that starting point is the script, also referred to as the *text*.

THE PLAYWRIGHT CREATES THE SCRIPT

The script or the text provides the plan for a production in somewhat the same way that an architect's blueprint provides guidelines for constructing a building. In fact, the script can be looked on as a concept or blueprint. From the beginning, the script or text was the domain of the playwright, also referred to as the dramatist. He or she chose the story to be told; selected the dramatic episodes, including the order in which they were to unfold; and wrote the dialogue for the characters to speak.

While there have been times throughout theatre history that actors, directors, and theatre companies, rather than playwrights or dramatists, have created scripts or outlines for improvised performances, these too are *texts* that serve as blueprints for productions. In this chapter, however, we will focus on the traditional role of the playwright in the theatre.

◀ **THE PLAYWRIGHT CREATES THE CHARACTERS AND THE SCRIPT**

One of the key playwrights ushering in the modern era in theatre was the Norwegian playwright Henrik Ibsen. Shown here is a scene from one of his landmark plays, A Doll's House, *in a new version by Zinnie Harris, directed by Kfir Yefet with Gillian Anderson as Nora and Toby Stephens as her husband Thomas. Presented at the Donmar Warehouse Theatre in London.*

THE PLAYWRITING PROCESS

The playwright has a number of questions to answer and choices to make, involving at least six aspects of a drama. Before we discuss these in detail, however, a word about the writing process is in order. In choosing a subject, developing a structure, or creating characters, the playwright will often work intuitively, sometimes even subconsciously. When the playwright's imagination, for instance, is captured by a certain episode or attracted to certain characters, he or she begins to create a drama. Usually a play evolves rather than being put together in a mechanical fashion.

In past eras, the dramatic structure used and the characters chosen by a playwright were the traditionally accepted practices of a given period and society. Playwrights in ancient Greece, for example, based both their plots and their characters on well-known myths. Throughout theatre history there have been differing established approaches to dramatic structure which we will discuss later in the chapter. In modern times, however, playwrights often begin without a clear plan and only later discover the type of structure and the nature of the characters they have chosen to create.

Following are the six aspects of a script the playwright must address and make choices about.

1. Selecting the specific subject of the play
2. Determining focus
3. Establishing purpose
4. Developing dramatic structure
5. Creating dramatic characters
6. Establishing point of view

In this chapter, we will examine the first five of these aspects. In the following chapter, we will look at the sixth, point of view. Consciously or unconsciously, when a playwright creates a script he or she adopts a point of view toward the story and the material. This viewpoint determines whether the play is a tragedy or comedy, a farce, a melodrama or another category of drama.

SUBJECT

The subject matter of drama is always human beings. In theatre, unlike certain other art forms—music, for instance, or abstract painting—people are invariably at the center. At the same time, a play cannot simply be about "human beings" or "people" in general, or even about "people's concerns," and the first task of the person creating a dramatic text is therefore to decide what aspect of human existence to write about.

Will the drama be based on history—for example, an episode or incident from the Civil War, World War II, or the recent wars in the Middle East? Or will it be based on biography—on the life of Abraham Lincoln, Eleanor Roosevelt, or Martin Luther King Jr.? Another possibility is the dramatization of someone's personal life: confronting some problem of growing up, or facing a personal crisis as an adult. A different possibility would be an imaginary story resembling everyday life or based on a fantasy or nightmare.

FOCUS

Along with selecting a subject to be dramatized, the playwright or dramatist must decide whom and what to focus on. For example, the same playwright can emphasize

EMPHASIS AND POINT OF VIEW

Henrik Ibsen makes it clear that his play *Peer Gynt* is about the title character, who is in virtually every scene. The play itself—which is clearly serious but has numerous comic and tragicomic episodes—ranges over many years and many locations. The character of Peer is always compromising, always running away, and Ibsen shows the consequences of that. In this scene are Mark Rylance (as Peer, wearing the crown), Jim Lichtscheidl, Jonas Goslow, Tyson Forbes, and Richard Ooms. *Peer Gynt,* translated and adapted by Robert Bly from the original by Henrik Ibsen; directed by Tim Carroll; set and costume design by Laura Hopkins; lighting design by Stan Pressner. (©Michal Daniel/Guthrie Theater, Minneapolis)

a particular character trait in one play and a very different trait in another play. This is what the Norwegian playwright Henrik Ibsen often did. In his **Brand**, the leading character is a stark, uncompromising religious man who will sacrifice everything—family, friends, love—for his principles. On the other hand, in Ibsen's *Peer Gynt,* the central character is just the opposite: a man with no principles who is always compromising, always running away.

In determining focus, a playwright may need to decide how to interpret the characters and events of an existing story; in doing this, the playwright may even change the order of events. A good example is the way three tragic dramatists of ancient Greece dealt with the myth of Electra. This myth concerns Electra's revenge on her mother, Clytemnestra, who has murdered Electra's father, Agamemnon, and then married a lover, Aegisthus. In wreaking revenge on Clytemnestra, Electra enlists the help of her brother, Orestes, who has just returned from exile. In **The Libation Bearers** (458 B.C.E.) by Aeschylus, and also in **Electra** (c. 412 B.C.E.) by Euripides, Electra and Orestes first murder Clytemnestra's lover, Aegisthus, and then murder their mother Clytemnestra. This puts emphasis on the horror and aberration of killing one's own mother. But Sophocles saw the story differently. He wanted to emphasize that Electra and Orestes are acting honorably and obeying an order from the gods. He therefore needed to play down the murder of the mother, and so in his version of *Electra* (c. 410 B.C.E.) he reversed the order of the murders: Clytemnestra is killed first, and then the action builds to the righteous murder of Aegisthus.

By means of focus, then, the playwright lets us know whom the play is about—the main character or characters—and how we are to view the characters: whether we are to look at them favorably or unfavorably.

DRAMATIC PURPOSE

Another challenge in creating a script or text is to determine the purpose of a play. A purpose may be casual or unconscious, or quite conscious and deliberate, but every theatre event is intended to serve some purpose.

Throughout theatre history, plays have served different purposes: to entertain, to impart information, to probe the human condition, to provide an escape. Various types of contemporary theatre are frequently presented for a specific sociopolitical purpose: These include feminist theatre, Latino or Latina theatre, and African American theatre. In theatre of this kind, those who create the event are addressing the concerns of a particular constituency.

There is a long tradition as well of theatre as a source of entertainment—similar to modern situation comedies on television and comic films that offer us pleasure and an escape from the cares of everyday life. The comedies of the Roman playwrights Plautus and Terence, written 2,000 years ago, were designed for this sort of entertainment. In the United States, for many years Broadway provided comedies that were written purely for fun and escape from daily life.

There have been times when plays were intended primarily to teach. In the medieval period, prior to the late fifteenth century, very few people could read or write. In order to teach people about the Bible and doctrine, the church encouraged plays that presented religious stories and precepts. Today, political dramatists often write plays specifically to put forward their own opinions and ideas.

At times, the purpose of drama has been to raise philosophical questions or to probe timeless themes, such as why the innocent suffer or why there is so much hatred and violence in the world.

Sometimes a play is intended simply to thrill or frighten us. A horror story or a melodrama is not supposed to make us think or meditate; it is intended to draw us into the action so that we will experience the same fears and apprehensions as the characters and to escape our own worries.

At times a play serves more than one purpose. Satirical comedies may be intended not only to make us laugh, but also to take stabs at hypocrites or charlatans. The works of the French playwright Molière are frequently of this kind: comical, but also revealing human folly. His *Tartuffe*, for instance—about a man who moves into a household falsely posing as a pious cleric—is an indictment of hypocrisy but is also amusing.

Sometimes a playwright may begin working without an exact purpose—the purpose may emerge only as the script goes through several revisions. Before a play goes into production, however, the playwright should know where it is headed. Once the purpose is clear, the director, performers, and designers join the playwright in working to achieve it.

Some contemporary commentators have questioned what they refer to as the "centrality" of the playwright and the play. These critics point out that there have been companies whose performers or directors, sometimes with the assistance of audiences, improvise presentations: They create a presentation while actually performing it. There have also been times when texts were developed by performers or by a director who assembled material from various sources. Some theorists argue, therefore, that an "authorless" theatre exists: theatre in which performers create their own works, sometimes using a traditional text only as a jumping-off point.

Theorists who question the centrality of the text also argue that the playwright's importance has been overstated—that a play is simply a suggestion or starting point and that the artists who create a stage presentation are its true "authors." In addition, they hold that each audience member may create his or her own "reading" of a production; in this sense, the spectator is the "author," and any discussion of a play's theme or meaning is inappropriate. It should be pointed out that this argument seems largely a question of semantics.

If a theatre piece is created by a group of performers or by a director, then these people are in effect operating as playwrights. The playwright's function has not been eliminated; it is simply being carried out by someone else.

As for the matter of the "centrality" of the playwright, this argument, too, does not eliminate the necessity of what we are calling the blueprint that every theatre event requires. Whether the blueprint is a text, a script, an idea, a scenario, an improvisation, or anything similar, it is an indispensable element in the process of creating a theatre production. The work of the playwright or other "authors" need not be "central" or predominant to be essential and irreplaceable. Also, the fact remains that throughout the history of both Western and Eastern theatre, the significant role of the playwright has been widely accepted. Whether it is a dramatist like Sophocles, Shakespeare, or Ibsen in the West, or Chikamatsu—an eighteenth-century Japanese dramatist—in the East, both their own contemporaries and later generations have seen their dramatic texts as foundations on which productions are based.

After subject, focus, and purpose have been decided, two crucial steps in developing a play are creating dramatic structure and creating dramatic characters.

STRUCTURE IN DRAMA

Though it may not be readily apparent, every work of art has some type of structure. When does the action of a play begin? How are the scenes put together? How does the action unfold? What is the high point of the action? Questions like these are related to dramatic structure, but we should note that structure is significant in all art.

As we have said, the structure of a play is analogous to that of a building. In designing a building, an architect plans a skeleton or substructure that will provide inner strength; the architect determines the depth of the foundation, the weight of the support beams, and the stress on the side walls. Similarly, a playwright develops a dramatic structure. The playwright introduces various stresses and strains in the form of conflicts; sets boundaries and outer limits, such as how many characters participate, how long the action lasts, and where it takes place; and calculates dynamics—when tension increases and slackens. Some feminist critics argue that the playwright's gender might also influence structure and that feminist dramas are less linear and less traditional in building dramatic tension.

How do we compare writing for the stage and writing for films or television? Obviously, many writers engage in both, moving from theatre to films or television and back again. Some writers, however, seem to have a natural affinity for one field or the other. There are playwrights who have never attempted to write screenplays or teleplays and never want to. By the same token, there are people who write for films or television who have never been interested in writing plays or musicals for the stage.

Many of the writers who have created shows and written teleplays for cable networks and streaming platforms, which now allow for more developed plots and more adult subject matter, such as Netflix and Amazon Prime, began their careers as playwrights, with some continuing to work in both worlds. *House of Cards, The Affair,* and *The Crown* are just a few examples of streamed television shows created and written by playwrights.

There are also many who write for traditional network television and commercial film. Among the many well-known contemporary playwrights who have written for both the theatre as well as film and/or television are: David Mamet, Sam Shepard, Tony Kushner, Jon Robin Baitz, Theresa Rebeck, Sarah Treem, Adam Rapp, Peter Morgan, and Kenneth Lonergan.

The playwrights who write for film and television give a variety of reasons for moving between media. Some believe that television, in particular the streaming media, allows them the creative freedom to explore more intricate plots and characterizations. Others site both the prestige and greater attention writers for film and television receive. And, of course, there are greater financial rewards in writing for these media since many playwrights cannot make a living writing solely for the live theatre.

Whatever path a writer takes, he or she must meet the requirements we discuss in this chapter: decide on the subject, develop a plot, create the characters, compose the dialogue, and undertake all other necessary steps in creating a completed script. In undertaking these tasks, the writer for film or television must follow a path similar to that of the playwright for the stage, but there are important differences.

The requirements of film, for instance, are not the same as those for the stage. Many scenes in film are action scenes: shots from a helicopter, shots of car crashes, shots of a villain stalking his prey. Such scenes may be described by the writer, but their realization is mostly in the hands of the director and cinematographer. They contain almost no dialogue. As a rule, whatever the storyline, there may be far less dialogue in a film than in a play.

Because of the nature of theatre, as opposed to film or television, the role of the writer is different in other ways. The Dramatists Guild contract, under which most dramas are produced, states unequivocally that no dialogue in a production may be deleted or changed without the permission of the author. By contrast, in films and television two things happen. First, there are often a number of writers on a script. There may be two, three, or more. This means that no one writer has the authority to maintain his or her vision over the material. (We shall see that there have been times in theatre history when plays were also coauthored. For example, we know that some of Shakespeare's works were written with other playwrights.) Second, the writer is unable to prevent changes in the script made by directors, producers, performers, or other writers. Thus in films and television, as compared with theatre, the writer has less control over what happens to his or her words.

Another crossover area for dramatic writers would be opera and musical theatre, in which the playwright would provide the libretto and perhaps the lyrics as well. When working on an opera or musical piece, the dramatist must collaborate with a composer as well as with a director and others.

Buildings vary enormously in size and shape: They can be as diverse as a skyscraper, a cathedral, and a cottage. Engineering requirements vary according to the needs of individual structures: A gymnasium roof must span a vast open area, and this calls for a construction different from that of a sixty-story skyscraper. Plays, too, vary; they can be tightly or loosely constructed, for instance.

The important point is that each play, like each piece of architecture, should have its own internal laws and its own framework, which give it shape, strength, and meaning. Without structure, a building will collapse, and a play will fall apart.

Naturally, structure is manifested differently in theatre and architecture. A play is not a building; it unfolds through time, developing like a living organism. As we experience this development, we become aware of a play's structure because we sense its underlying pattern and rhythm. The repeated impulses of two characters in conflict, the quickening pace and mounting tension of a heated argument—these elements insinuate themselves into our subconscious like a drumbeat. Moment by moment, we see what is happening onstage; but below the surface we sense the structure, the framework of the dramatic action.

Essentials of Dramatic Structure

There are several essentials of dramatic structure. First, the story on which a drama is based must be turned into a plot. Second, the plot involves action. Third, the plot includes conflict. Fourth, a play requires characters who are strongly opposed to one another. Fifth, a reasonable balance is struck between the opposed forces.

Plot   Our first essential of dramatic structure, ***plot***, is the arrangement of events or the selection and order of scenes in a play. The term *plot* can mean a secret scheme or plan. The word is also used to describe the sequence of scenes or events in a novel, but we are speaking here specifically of plot in drama.

A dramatic plot is usually based on a story. Stories are as old as the human race, and today stories form much of the substance of our daily conversation, of newspapers and television, of novels and films. Every medium presents a story in a different form. In theatre, the story must be presented by living actors and actresses on a stage in a limited period of time, and this requires selectivity. Thus the plot of a play differs from a story. A *story* is a full account of an event or series of events, usually in chronological order; a *plot* is a selection and arrangement of scenes from a story for presentation onstage. The plot is what actually happens onstage, not what is talked about.

For example, the story of Abraham Lincoln begins with his birth in a log cabin and continues to the day he is shot at Ford's Theatre in Washington. In developing a plot for a play about Lincoln, however, the playwright must make choices. Will the play include scenes in Springfield, Illinois, where Lincoln served as a lawyer and held his famous debates with Stephen A. Douglas? Or will the entire play take place in Washington after Lincoln has become president? Will there be scenes with Lincoln's wife, Mary Todd; or will all the scenes involve government and military officials? Decisions like these must be made even when a play is based on a fictional story: The plot must be more restricted and structured than the story itself.

Action   A second essential of dramatic structure is ***action***. If we were to construct a "grammar of theatre," the subject would always be human beings—dramatic characters who represent human concerns. In linguistic grammar, every subject needs a verb; similarly, in the grammar of theatre, dramatic characters need a verb—some form of action that defines them. The word *drama* actually derives from a Greek root, the verb *dran,* meaning "to do" or "to act." At its heart, theatre involves action.

Plot   As distinct from story, the patterned arrangement in a drama of events and characters, with incidents selected and arranged for maximum dramatic impact. Also, in Elizabethan theatres, an outline of the play that was posted backstage for the actors.

Action   According to the Greek philosopher Aristotle, a sequence of events linked by cause and effect, with a beginning, middle, and end. Said by Aristotle to be the best way to unify a play. More generally, the central, unifying conflict and movement through a drama.

ACTION: AN ESSENTIAL OF DRAMATIC STRUCTURE
Among the elements required to create a dramatic script is action: the confrontation, the conflicts, the overcoming of obstacles that constitute the events of the drama. In Arthur Miller's *The Crucible*, about the Salem witch hunts in Massachusetts, there are numerous conflicts and complications. Shown here in a production directed by Yael Farber are Richard Armitage as John Proctor, Adrian Schiller as The Reverend John Hale, and Samantha Colley as Abigail Williams. This production was presented at the Old Vic Theatre in London.
(©Geraint Lewis/Alamy Stock Photo)

Conflict Tension between two or more characters that leads to crisis or a climax; a fundamental struggle or imbalance—involving ideologies, actions, personalities, etc.— underlying a play.

Conflict   A third essential of dramatic structure is *conflict*, the collision or opposition of persons or forces in a drama that gives rise to dramatic action. We can perhaps best understand dramatic conflict in terms of everyday experience. People often define themselves by the way they respond to challenges, such as marriage, a job, sudden good fortune, or a serious illness. If they cannot face up to a challenge, that tells us one thing; if they meet it with dignity, even though defeated, that tells us another; if they triumph, that tells us something else. We come to know our family, our friends, and our enemies by being with them over a period of time. We see how they respond to us and to other people, and how they meet crises in their own lives and in ours.

In life, this process can take years—in fact, it continues to unfold for as long as we know a person—but in theatre we have only a few hours. The playwright, therefore, must devise means by which characters will face challenges and be tested in a short time. The American playwright Arthur Miller titled one of his plays *The Crucible* (1953). Literally, a crucible is a vessel in which metal is tested by being exposed to extreme heat. Figuratively, a crucible has come to stand for any severe test of human worth and endurance—a trial by fire. Every play provides a crucible of a sort—a test devised by the playwright to show how the characters behave under stress. Such a test, and the characters' reaction to it, is one way that the meaning of a play is brought out.

Strongly Opposed Forces   A fourth essential of dramatic structure, closely related to conflict, is *strongly opposed forces*. By this we mean that the people in conflict

STRONGLY OPPOSED FORCES
In developing a dramatic structure, a playwright sets powerful forces and characters against one another to provide conflict and dramatic confrontations. A good example is the opposition between Othello (Eamonn Walker) and Iago (Tim McInnerny) in Shakespeare's play *Othello.* The production shown here was directed by Wilson Milam at Shakespeare's Globe in London.
(©Geraint Lewis)

in a play are fiercely determined to achieve their goals; moreover, they are powerful adversaries for one another. The conflicting characters have clear, strong goals or objectives; that is, they have goals they want desperately to achieve, and they will go to any length to achieve them. For example, Macbeth, in the play by Shakespeare, wants to become king; Jean, the servant in August Strindberg's **Miss Julie**, wants to achieve independence; Blanche DuBois, in Tennessee Williams's *A Streetcar Named Desire,* wants to find a haven in the home of her sister. In fighting for their goals, two or more characters find themselves in opposition, and the strength of both sides must be formidable.

A perfect example of two characters bound to clash is found in *A Streetcar Named Desire.* Blanche DuBois is a faded southern belle trying desperately to hold onto her gentility; the crude, aggressive Stanley Kowalski is the chief threat to her stability and her survival. On his side, Stanley, who is insecure about his lack of education and refinement, is provoked almost to the breaking point by Blanche and her superior airs.

One device dramatists often use to establish friction or tension between forces is restricting the characters to members of a single family. Relatives have built-in rivalries and affinities: parents versus children, sisters versus brothers. As members of the same family, moreover, they have no avenue of escape.

Mythology, on which so much drama is based, abounds with familial relationships. Shakespeare frequently set members of one family against each other: Hamlet opposes his mother; King Lear is opposed by his daughters. In modern drama, virtually every writer of note has dealt with close family situations. The American dramatist Eugene O'Neill wrote what many consider his finest play, *Long Day's Journey into Night,* about the four members of his own family.

IN FOCUS: THE GLOBAL INFLUENCES ON THE PLAYWRIGHTS BRECHT AND WILDER

In this chapter we are discussing the work of the playwright. We see in this area, as well as others, the global aspect of theatre today. Two mid-twentieth-century dramatists from the West who were strongly influenced by Asian theatre, and reflect the globalization of contemporary drama, were the German playwright Bertolt Brecht (1889–1956) and American playwright Thornton Wilder (1897–1975).

Brecht, for example, drew from Asian legends and used techniques borrowed from Chinese, Japanese, and Indian theatre. Chinese theatre and literature were to prove particularly important with his *Good Person of Szechuan* (1938–1949) which was set in China, and *The Caucasian Chalk Circle* (1944–1945), based on the Chinese play, *The Story of the Chalk Circle*.

Both Brecht and Wilder had seen Beijing opera and adopted certain features of this dramatic style into their own work. Beijing opera (also called *jingju* and Peking opera) blends song, dance, martial arts, theatre, acrobatics, and dance and uses much symbolism. Beijing opera takes place on an almost bare stage (often with just a table and a few chairs onstage throughout); it uses simple props brought on by stage attendants, and symbolic movements by the actors. For example, an actor walking in a circle around the stage indicates a long journey; a banner with a fish design indicates water, while rolled up on a tray, the same banner would represent a fish.

Brecht used such symbolic props and actions to achieve his alienation or distancing effect, which prevented the audience from identifying emotionally with the drama. In 1935, Brecht saw a performance by the Beijing opera star Mei Lanfang (1894–1961) in Moscow, and the following year wrote his essay "Alienation Effects

Bertolt Brecht
(©Hulton Deutsch/Getty Images)

Thornton Wilder
(©Bettmann/Getty Images)

in Chinese Acting," which noted aspects of Beijing opera conducive to the distancing effect he desired.

Similarly, Wilder had been exposed to Chinese theatre first at an early age, when his father's work took him to Hong Kong and Shanghai; and then as an adult, when he saw Mei Lanfang perform in New York in 1930. Aspects of Beijing opera that Wilder adopted can best be seen in his Pulitzer Prize–winning *Our Town* (1938). In this play, Wilder uses an almost bare stage with just two tables and six chairs positioned by the stage manager (who also acts as a narrator), and other locales are suggested by very simple alterations; in the third act, for example, the cemetery is suggested by just ten or twelve people sitting in chairs.

Both playwrights illustrate the increasing prevalence of global, and specifically Asian, influences in twentieth-century and now current playwriting.

Prepared by Naomi Stubbs, Associate Professor, LaGuardia Community College, CUNY

In plays not directly involving families, the characters are usually still in close proximity. They are fighting for the same turf, the same throne, the same woman or man.

Balance of Forces   A fifth essential of dramatic structure is some sort of *balance* between the opposed forces; that is, the people or forces in conflict must be more or less evenly matched. In almost every case, one side eventually wins, but before this final outcome the opposing forces must be roughly equal in strength and determination.

In most sporting events, there are rules ensuring that the contest will be as equal as possible without coming to a draw, and this notion is equally important in theatre. In sports, fans want their team to win, but they would prefer a close, exciting contest to a one-sided runaway. The struggle, as much as the outcome, is a source of pleasure; and so rules are set up, with handicaps or other devices for equalizing forces. In basketball or football, when one team scores, the other team gets the ball so that it will have a chance to even the score. In theatre, too, a hard-fought and relatively equal contest is usually set up between opposing forces: The vulnerable, artistic Blanche, for example, faces the brutish Stanley.

Sequence in Dramatic Structure

A dramatic structure begins with the all-important opening scene.

Opening Scene   The first scene of a drama starts the action and sets the tone and style for everything that follows. It tells us whether we are going to see a serious or a comic play, and whether the play will deal with affairs of everyday life or with fantasy. The opening scene also sets the action in motion, giving the characters a shove and hurtling them toward their destination.

Providing the characters with a problem or establishing an imbalance of forces compels the characters to respond. Generally, the problem or imbalance has occurred just before the play begins, or it arises immediately after the play opens. In **King Oedipus**, for example, a plague has struck the city just before the opening of the play. In *Hamlet,* "something is rotten in the state of Denmark," and early in the play the ghost of Hamlet's father appears to tell Hamlet that he must seek revenge. At the beginning of **Romeo and Juliet**, the Capulets and the Montagues are at one another's throats in a street fight.

As these examples suggest, in the opening scene the characters are thrust into a situation that provides the starting point for the play.

Obstacles and Complications   Having confronted the initial challenge of the play, the characters then move through a series of steps alternating between achievement and defeat, between hope and despair. The moment they accomplish one goal, something cuts across the play—a new hurdle or challenge is thrown up that they must overcome. These hurdles blocking a character's path—or outside forces that are introduced at an inopportune moment—are known as *obstacles* and *complications*.

Shakespeare's **Hamlet** provides numerous examples of obstacles and complications. Hamlet, suspecting that his uncle, Claudius, has killed his father, seeks revenge; but Claudius, as king, controls the army and other instruments of power. Thus the authority of the throne is one obstacle standing in Hamlet's way.

When Hamlet stages the "play within a play," Claudius's reaction confirms his guilt, and Hamlet's path to revenge seems clear. But on first trying to kill Claudius, Hamlet discovers him at prayer. A complication has been introduced: If Claudius dies while praying, he may go to heaven rather than to hell, and so Hamlet does not kill him.

Later, Hamlet is in his mother's bedroom when he hears a noise behind a curtain. Surely Claudius is lurking there, and Hamlet can kill him instantly. But when Hamlet thrusts his sword through the curtain, he finds that he has killed not Claudius but rather Polonius, who is the father of Ophelia, the young woman Hamlet is supposed to marry. This is another complication: The murder of Polonius

Obstacle   That which delays or prevents the achieving of a goal by a character. An obstacle creates complication and conflict.

Complication   Introduction, in a play, of a new force that creates a new balance of power and entails a delay in reaching the climax.

gives Claudius a pretext for sending Hamlet to England with Rosencrantz and Guildenstern, who carry a letter instructing the king of England to put Hamlet to death.

Hamlet gets out of this trap and returns to Denmark. Now, at last, it seems that he can carry out his revenge. But he discovers that Ophelia has killed herself while he was away; and her brother, Laertes, is seeking revenge on Hamlet. This is still another complication: Hamlet is prevented from killing Claudius because he must also deal with Laertes. In the end, Hamlet does carry out his mission—but only after many interruptions.

Crises and Climaxes   As a result of conflicts, obstacles, and complications, dramatic characters become involved in a series of *crises*. Some crises are less complicated than those in *Hamlet,* some even more complicated. A play builds from one crisis to another; when the first crisis is resolved, the action leads to a second crisis, and so on. The final and most significant crisis is referred to as the *climax*. Sometimes there is a minor climax earlier in a play and a major climax near the conclusion. In the final climax, the issues of the play are resolved—either happily or tragically, depending on the genre.

Often, after the final climax of a drama, there will be a *dénouement*, a French word meaning the untying of the knot or the winding down of the plot.

Two Basic Forms of Structure: Climactic and Episodic

Over the long history of Western theatre, playwrights have usually adopted one or the other of two basic dramatic structures: (1) *climactic, or intensive, structure*; and (2) *episodic, or extensive, structure*. In certain periods, playwrights have combined the two. There are other forms of structure, which we will discuss, but let us consider climactic and episodic structure first.

Climactic Plot Construction   A dramatic form first used in Greece in the fifth century B.C.E. reemerged, somewhat altered, in France in the seventeenth century; in the late nineteenth century and the twentieth century, this same form was adopted in Norway, Sweden, France, and (somewhat later) the United States. This we call *climactic* or *intensive.* We use these terms because in this kind of dramatic construction, all aspects of a play—duration, locale, action, and number of characters—are severely restricted; this results in a contained, or intense, structure, in which little time passes until the climax occurs.

OBSTACLES AND COMPLICATIONS
In developing a dramatic plot, the playwright often incorporates obstacles and complications that impede the movement of the main characters as they attempt to reach their goals. Complications and obstacles also add interest, suspense, and intricacy to the dramatic action. A good example of a play with many obstacles and complications is Shakespeare's *Hamlet.* The scene here shows Hamlet, charged by the ghost of his murdered father to avenge his death, planning to kill the murderer—his uncle, and newly installed king, Claudius. Hamlet cannot carry out the murder, however, for fear that killing Claudius at prayer will send him to heaven. In the scene here from a production at the Open Air Theatre, Damian Lewis plays Hamlet and Paul Freeman plays Claudius. (©Robbie Jack/ Corbis Entertainment/Getty Images)

A good example of climactic structure is found in **Miss Julie** by the Swedish playwright August Strindberg. The play takes place in one space, the kitchen of a home; it focuses on two people, a young woman and a male servant; and it occurs over a brief period, part of one evening. Also, it has a single action: The young woman and the servant, from different social levels, are drawn compulsively into a fatal sexual encounter.

Climactic plots have several distinctive characteristics, which we'll consider one by one.

The plot begins late in the story   The first hallmark of climactic drama is that the plot begins quite late in the story, at a point where the story is near its climax. It focuses on a moment when everything comes to a head, lives fall apart, fate closes in, and there is a final showdown between characters. Because the plot deals with a culmination of events, climactic form is sometimes called *crisis drama,* or *drama of catastrophe.*

King Oedipus by Sophocles offers a good example. When Oedipus is born, it is predicted that he will kill his father and marry his mother; and so his parents, the king and queen of Thebes, order that he be left in the wilderness to die. He is saved, however, and taken to another country where he is raised by another king and queen as their own son. As he grows up, he hears the prophecy about himself, and, assuming that his adoptive parents are his real ones, he leaves home. He goes to Thebes, where he does kill his natural father and marry his mother, not knowing who they are. He becomes king of Thebes, and when a plague strikes the kingdom, he sets out to find the person who has murdered the former king—not knowing that he himself is the guilty party. All this happens *before* the play begins. The drama itself focuses on the single day when the full story emerges.

Whether it is *King Oedipus,* Ibsen's **A Doll's House**, or Tennessee Williams's *Cat on a Hot Tin Roof,* any play in climactic form concentrates on the final hours of a long sequence of events. Because so much has happened before the play begins, details about the past must be provided during the course of the play. In drama, the term for this information is ***exposition***.

The effect of beginning the action near the climax of events is to give a play a very sharp focus and a strong sense of immediacy. In climactic form, everything is concentrated on the showdown, the payoff, the final confrontation.

Scenes, locales, and characters are restricted   Climactic structure is restricted not only in time but also in other ways. For example, it has a limited number of long scenes or acts, or perhaps only one act. Critics in the Renaissance said that a play must have five acts. For much of the nineteenth and twentieth centuries, three acts were standard. Today, the norm is two acts, though the long one-act play, performed without intermission, is also common.

Limited scenes in a play usually entail a restricted locale. All the action in *King Oedipus* takes place in front of the royal palace. **No Exit**, a climactic play by the French writer Jean-Paul Sartre, confines its three characters to one room from which, as the title suggests, there is no escape. Writers like Ibsen and Strindberg also frequently confined their plays to one room, and contemporary plays provide numerous instances of this device.

Climactic dramatic structure also has a limited number of characters. Greek drama generally has four or five principal characters. *King Oedipus* has four:

Crisis   Point within a play when the action reaches an important confrontation or takes a critical turn. In the tradition of the well-made play, a drama includes a series of crises that lead to the final crisis, known as the climax.

Climax   Often defined as the high point in the action or the final and most significant crisis in the action.

Climactic structure   Also referred to as *intensive structure.* Dramatic structure in which there are few scenes, a short time passes, there are few locales, and the action begins chronologically close to the climax.

Episodic structure   Also referred to as *extensive structure.* Dramatic structure in which there are many scenes, taking place over a considerable period of time in a number of locations. Many episodic plays also use such devices as subplots.

Exposition   Imparting of information necessary for an understanding of the story but not covered by the action onstage; events or knowledge from the past, or occurring outside the play, which must be introduced for the audience to understand the characters or plot.

CLIMACTIC STRUCTURE

In climactic structure, everything is restricted: The action occurs in a brief time, in limited locations, and with very few characters involved. Climactic structure was first developed in Western theatre by the Greek dramatists of the fifth century B.C.E. in Athens. In his play *No Exit,* Jean-Paul Sartre offers an excellent example of limited space. He presents three characters involved in an impossible love triangle confined to one room, from which, as the title suggests, there is no escape. Karen MacDonald as Estelle, Will Lebow as Garcin, and Paula Plum as Inez are shown in this scene from a production directed by Jerry Mouawad at the A.R.T. in Boston. (©T. Charles Erickson)

Oedipus, Jocasta, Creon, and Teiresias. French neoclassical drama and many modern plays have the same number of principal characters: four or five.

Construction is tight Construction is tight in a climactic play: Events are arranged in an orderly, compact way, with no loose ends. It is like a chain linked by cause and effect. As in a detective story, A leads to B, B to C, which causes D, leading in turn to E, and so on. This chain of events is unbreakable: Once the action begins, there is no stopping it.

The French playwright Jean Anouilh (1910–1987), in his *Antigone* (1943), compares tragedy to the workings of a machine.

> The spring is wound up tight. It will uncoil itself. That is what is so convenient in tragedy. The least little turn of the wrist will do the job. . . . The rest is automatic. You don't need to lift a finger. The machine is in perfect order; it has been oiled ever since time began and it runs without friction.[1]

[1]Jean Anouilh, *Antigone*, Lewis Galantière (trans. and adaptor), Random House, New York, 1946, p. 36. Copyright 1946 by Random House.

Part 2   Creating Theatre: The Playwright

EPISODIC STRUCTURE: MANY CHARACTERS, PLACES, AND EVENTS
A good example of the typically wide-ranging episodic structure are the plays of William Shakespeare, which are frequently staged today throughout the world. The scene above, which is from a production at London's Globe Theatre, reflects the large number of characters typically found in his episodic plays. (©Steve Vidler/Alamy Stock Photo)

This applies to every play in climactic form. The aim is always to make events so inevitable that there is no escape—at least, not until the very last moment, when a ***deus ex machina*** may intervene to untangle the knot. *Deus ex machina* is Latin for "god from a machine" and comes from ancient Greece and Rome, when a mechanical contraption on the roof of the stage house was used to bring the gods onstage to resolve the action at the end of a play. The term *deus ex machina* has come to stand for any plot contrivance used to resolve a play at the end.

Episodic Plot Construction   When we turn from climactic structure to episodic structure, we find a very clear contrast in almost every respect.

Episodic structure emerged during the Renaissance in England—Shakespeare's plays offer a prime example—and in Spain, in the plays of Lope de Vega and his contemporaries. Later, episodic form was adopted by the German playwrights Goethe and Schiller during the romantic period, in the late eighteenth century and the early nineteenth century. It was also used in the late nineteenth century by the

Deus ex machina
(DEH-oos eks MAH-kih-nah) Literally, "god from a machine," a resolution device in classic Greek drama; hence, intervention of supernatural forces—usually at the last moment—to save the action from its logical conclusion. In modern drama, an arbitrary and coincidental solution.

Norwegian playwright Henrik Ibsen and in the twentieth century by the German playwright Bertolt Brecht. The following are the characteristics of episodic structure.

People, places, and events proliferate   A typical episodic play covers an extended period of time, sometimes many years, and ranges over a number of locations. In one play, we can go anywhere—to a small antechamber, a large banquet hall, the open countryside, a mountaintop.

Short scenes alternate with longer scenes. The large number of characters and scenes in three plays will serve to indicate the expansive nature of episodic drama: Shakespeare's ***Antony and Cleopatra*** has thirty-four characters and more than forty scenes; his ***Julius Caesar*** has thirty-four characters and eighteen scenes; ***The Sheep Well*** by his Spanish contemporary Lope de Vega has twenty-six characters and seventeen scenes.

There may be a parallel plot or a subplot   One technique of episodic drama is the *parallel plot,* or **subplot**. In Shakespeare's ***King Lear***, for example, Lear has three daughters, two evil and one good. The two evil daughters have convinced their father that they are good and that their sister is wicked. In the subplot—a counterpart of the main plot—the Earl of Gloucester has two sons, one loyal and one disloyal; and the disloyal one has deceived his father into thinking that he is the loyal one. Both old men have misjudged their children's true worth, and in the end each is punished for his mistake: Lear is bereft of his kingdom and his sanity; Gloucester loses his eyes. The Gloucester plot parallels and reinforces the Lear plot.

Subplot   Secondary plot that reinforces or runs parallel to the major plot in an episodic play.

Contrast and juxtaposition are used   Another technique of episodic drama is juxtaposition or contrast. Rather than moving in linear fashion, the action alternates between different kinds of elements.

For one thing, as we have noted, short scenes alternate with longer scenes. *King Lear* begins with a short scene between Kent and Gloucester, goes next to a long scene in which Lear divides his kingdom, then returns to a brief scene in which Edmund declares his intention to deceive his father.

Also, public scenes alternate with private scenes. Shakespeare's *Romeo and Juliet* opens with a public scene: a street fight between the Capulet family and the Montague family. This is followed by three private scenes. Then comes a public street scene, followed by a public scene at a masked ball.

In addition, comic scenes often alternate with serious scenes. In ***Macbeth***, just after Macbeth has murdered King Duncan, there is a knock on the door of the castle. This is one of the most serious moments in the play, but the man who goes to open the door is a comic character, a drunken porter, whose speech is a humorous interlude in the grim business of the drama. In *Hamlet,* a gravedigger and his assistant are preparing a grave for Ophelia when Hamlet comes onto the scene. The gravediggers are joking about death; but for Hamlet, who soon learns that the grave is Ophelia's, it is a somber moment.

The overall effect is cumulative   Unlike climactic drama, in which each action follows logically from what precedes it, episodic drama creates an impression of events piling up: a tidal wave of circumstances and emotions sweeping over the characters. Rarely is a character's fate determined by a single letter, a single incident, or a single piece of new knowledge. Time and again, Hamlet has proof that

COMIC SCENES ALTERNATE WITH SERIOUS SCENES
One device possible in episodic drama is the juxtaposition and
alternation of serious and comic scenes. Shakespeare often incorporates
this technique in his plays. In *King Lear,* for example, there is a
character called the Fool who has comic scenes in the midst of a serious
tragedy. Shown here as the Fool is Gleb Podgorodinsky in a production
at the Maly Theatre in Moscow, Russia. (©Stanislav Krasilnikov/TASS/
Getty Images)

Claudius has killed his father, but it is a whole onrush of events—not a single
piece of hard evidence—that eventually leads him to kill Claudius.

Combinations of Climactic and Episodic Construction   There is no rule requiring
a play to be exclusively episodic or exclusively climactic; these forms are not
watertight compartments. It is true that during certain periods one form or the
other has been predominant. And it is not easy to mix the two because each has
its own laws and its own inner logic. In various periods, however, they have been
successfully integrated.

For example, climactic and episodic construction are combined in the comedies of late-seventeenth-century England—the Restoration period. In the late
nineteenth century, the Russian dramatist Anton Chekhov combined elements of
both forms, and in the twentieth century the two forms were frequently integrated.

Other Forms of Dramatic Structure

During the twentieth century and into the twenty-first, new types of dramatic
structure appeared. In some cases, such as ritual structure, the form amounted to
adaptation of an ancient structure for modern use. We will now look briefly at
these variations in dramatic structure, returning to many of them in the part
"Global Theatres: Past and Present," when we study the historical periods in
which they first appeared.

Ritual as Structure   Just as acting is a part of everyday life so is ritual. Basically,
ritual is a repetition or reenactment of some proceeding or transaction that has
acquired special meaning. It may be a simple ritual like singing the national anthem
before a ball game or a deeply religious ritual like the Catholic mass. We all

Ritual   Specifically
ordered ceremonial event,
often religious.

develop ritualistic patterns of behavior in our personal lives, such as following the same routine when we get up in the morning or taking a day off on Sunday. As we shall see, some historians have theorized that theatre grew out of rituals and ritualistic enactments of ancient peoples.

Patterns as Structure   Related to ritual are *patterns* of events. In Samuel Beckett's *Waiting for Godot,* the characters have no personal history, and the play does not build to a climax in the ordinary way. But if Beckett has abandoned many techniques of traditional structure, he has replaced them with something else—a repeated sequence of events containing its own order and logic.

Feminist and Cyclical Structure   A number of feminist commentators have argued that women playwrights employ a unique dramatic structure; they suggest that there is even a new feminist poetics.

According to feminist theorists, female playwrights often write in a cyclical form, one that does not build to a single climax and in which actions are repeated. Instead of a single climax, feminist drama stresses what Professor Sue-Ellen Case calls "contiguity," which is "fragmentary rather than whole" and "interrupted rather than complete." It is frequently open-ended and offers women as subject. Traditional plot is replaced by a serial structure, which is discussed next.

One example is *Fefu and Her Friends*, written and directed by the Cuban-born American dramatist María Irene Fornés (b. 1930). Instead of traditional plot, there is cyclical, physical action; and in place of logical cause and effect, Fornés writes each scene as though it were a new event. There is no hero; the subject of the play is a group of educated women sharing thoughts and ideas.

Not all female dramatists have embraced the new feminist poetics. But increasingly, female playwrights have experimented with dramatic structure and theatrical styles to confront, expose, and rewrite what they see as centuries of male cultural dominance.

Serial Structure   Another kind of structure is a *series* of acts or episodes—individual theatre events—offered as a single presentation. In this case, individual segments are strung together like charms on a bracelet or beads on a necklace. Sometimes a central theme or common thread holds the various parts together; sometimes there is little or no connection between the parts.

One example of serial structure is the musical revue, which has a series of short scenes, songs, and dance numbers. An evening of one-act plays is another example.

Avant-Garde and Experimental Structures   In the second half of the twentieth century, several groups in Europe and the United States experimented with ritual as a dramatic form. These groups included the Polish Laboratory Theatre, the Living Theatre, the Performance Group, and the Wooster Group. One purpose of their experiments was to return to the ritualistic, religious roots of theatre.

From their experiments, these groups developed several significant departures from traditional theatre practice. Among them were (1) interest in *ritual* and *ceremony*; (2) emphasis on *nonverbal and physical theatre,* that is, theatre stressing gestures, body movements, and wordless sounds rather than logical or intelligible language; (3) reliance on *improvisation,* or scenarios developed by performers and directors; (4) stress on the physical *environment* of theatre, including a

COMPARING CLIMACTIC AND EPISODIC FORMS OF STRUCTURE

Climactic	Episodic
1. Plot begins late in the story, toward the very end or climax.	1. Plot begins relatively early in the story and moves through a series of episodes.
2. Covers a short space of time, perhaps a few hours or at most a few days.	2. Covers a longer period of time: weeks, months, and sometimes many years.
3. Contains a few solid, extended scenes, such as three acts with each act comprising one long scene.	3. Has many short, fragmented scenes; sometimes alternates short and long scenes.
4. Occurs in a restricted locale, such as one room or one house.	4. May range over an entire city or even several countries.
5. Number of characters is severely limited—usually no more than six or eight.	5. Has a profusion of characters, sometimes several dozen.
6. Plot is linear and moves in a single line with few subplots or counterplots.	6. Is frequently marked by several threads of action, such as two parallel plots, or scenes of comic relief in a serious play.
7. Line of action proceeds in a cause-and-effect chain. The characters and events are closely linked in a sequence of logical, almost inevitable development.	7. Scenes are juxtaposed to one another. An event may result from several causes, or from no apparent cause, but arises in a network or web of circumstances.

The table above outlines the chief characteristics of climactic and episodic forms and illustrates the differences between them. It is clear that the climactic and episodic forms differ from each other in their fundamental approaches. One emphasizes constriction and compression on all fronts; the other takes a far broader view and aims at a cumulative effect, piling up people, places, and events.

restructuring of the spatial relationship between performers and audience; and (5) stress on each audience member's developing his or her own interpretation of the work being presented.

Segments and Tableaux as Structure   Robert Wilson and Richard Foreman, who will be discussed later, are examples of theatre artists who organize their avant-garde productions into units analogous to the frames of film and television, or to the still-life tableaux of painting or the moving tableaux of dance. Frequently, directors like Foreman and Wilson will use rapid movements—as in silent films—or slow motion. At times, several actions will occur simultaneously. All of these, however, relate both to an image and to a tableaux or frame.

CREATING DRAMATIC CHARACTERS

Along with creating dramatic structure, the playwright must create the characters who carry out the action. In drama, as opposed to a novel or a short story, everything must be transformed into conversation between characters—called *dialogue*—or into action. Literature can rely on passages describing what the characters are thinking and how they react to each other; in theatre, everything must be enacted by the characters.

> **Dialogue** Conversation between characters in a play.

   Though they often seem like real people, dramatic characters are actually created in the imagination of a playwright. By carefully emphasizing certain features of a character's personality and eliminating others, the dramatist can show us in two hours the entire history of a person whom we might need a lifetime to know in the real world. In *A Streetcar Named Desire*, for example, we come to know Blanche DuBois, in all her emotional complexity, better than we know

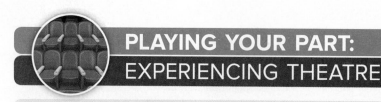

1. If you were to write a play about your life, what would you choose as your opening scene? What would some of your complications be? Would there be a climactic moment?

2. Pick a play you have seen or read. Tell in your own words the story which the play is dramatizing. In the full story, what moments or scenes did the dramatist leave out when turning the story into a drama?

3. After watching a popular film, describe how the opening scene aids in setting the action. Describe one or two of the complications in the film. Can you discuss the film's point of view?

4. Describe the theatrical elements in a religious or family ritual.

people we see every day. As we become intimately acquainted with Blanche, the dramatist reveals to us not only her biography but her mind and soul.

In deciding what to emphasize about a character and how to present the character, a playwright has wide latitude. A stage character can be drawn with a few quick strokes, as a caricaturist sketches a political figure; can be given the surface detail and reality of a photograph; or can be fleshed out with the more interpretive, fully rounded quality of an oil portrait.

Types of Dramatic Characters

Extraordinary Characters Heroes and heroines of most important dramatic works before the modern period are *extraordinary* in some way—that is, "larger than life." Historically, major characters have been kings, queens, generals, members of the nobility, or other figures clearly marked as holding a special place in society.

In addition, extraordinary characters generally represent some extreme of human behavior—men and women at their worst or best. Lady Macbeth is not only a noblewoman; she is one of the most ambitious women ever depicted. In virtually every instance, extraordinary characters are men and women at the breaking point, at the outer limits of human capability and endurance.

For example, the young Greek heroine Antigone and the medieval religious figure Joan of Arc are the epitome of the independent, courageous female, willing to stand up to male authority with strength and dignity. Two heroes from ancient Greece, Prometheus and Oedipus, are men willing to face the worst the gods can throw at them and accept the consequences. Among those qualifying as human beings at their worst is the Greek heroine Medea, who murders her own children.

Comic characters can also be extremes. For instance, the chief character in **Volpone**, by Shakespeare's contemporary, the English comic dramatist Ben Jonson, is an avaricious miser who gets people to present him with expensive gifts because they mistakenly think he will remember them in his will.

Beginning in the eighteenth century, ordinary people took over more and more from royalty and the nobility as the heroes and heroines of drama—a reflection of what was occurring in real life as monarchies became less powerful and

EXTRAORDINARY CHARACTERS
The heroes and heroines of drama of the past—classical tragedies and historical plays—were usually kings, queens, members of the nobility, and military leaders; in other words, figures who by their very positions were exceptional. They may have been evil characters or noble ones, but they stood above the crowd, both because of their positions in society and because of their characteristics. A good example is the title character in Shakespeare's *King Lear,* played here by Frank Gallacher as Lear and Allison Bell as his daughter, Cordelia, at the Melbourne Theatre Company in Australia. (©The AGE/ Fairfax Media/Getty Images)

democracy took hold. Nevertheless, the leading figures of drama continued to be exceptional men and women at their best and worst. The heroine of August Strindberg's *Miss Julie* is a neurotic, obsessive woman at the end of her rope. In *Mother Courage* by Bertolt Brecht, we see a woman who will sacrifice almost anything to survive; she even loses a son by haggling over the price of his release from detention. **The Emperor Jones**, by Eugene O'Neill, shows the downfall of a powerful black man who has made himself the ruler of a Caribbean island.

REPRESENTATIVE OR QUINTESSENTIAL CHARACTERS
In much of modern realistic theatre, the main characters are distinguished not by being extraordinary or larger than life, but by being "representative" of a group or type. Willy Loman, the chief figure in Arthur Miller's *Death of a Salesman*, is just such a character, exemplifying all traveling salesmen pursuing the American dream but often not quite realizing it. Shown here, in a production directed by Gregory Doran at the Royal Shakespeare Company in London, are Antony Sher as Willy and Harriet Walter as his wife Linda. (©Geraint Lewis/Alamy Stock Photo)

Representative characters Characters in a play who embody characteristics that represent an entire group.

Representative or Quintessential Characters Though many characters of modern drama are extraordinary, a new type of main character has emerged—one who is three-dimensional and highly individual but at the same time ordinary. He or she stands apart not by being exceptional but by being typical of a large, important sector of the population. Rather than being "worst," "best," or some other extreme, such characters are notable because they embody the characteristics of an entire group. We can call these characters *representative* or *quintessential*.

A good example of a representative character is Nora Helmer, the heroine of Henrik Ibsen's *A Doll's House*. Though Nora secretly forged a signature to get money that saved the life of her husband when he was very ill, he regards her as spoiled and flighty. All her life, in fact—first by her father and now by her husband—she has been treated as a doll or a plaything, never as a mature, responsible woman. In the last act of the play, Nora rebels: She makes a declaration of independence to her husband, slams the door on him, and walks out. It has been said that Nora's slamming of the door marked the beginning not only of modern drama but of the emancipation of modern women. Nora's demand that she be treated as an equal has made her typical of all housewives who refuse to be regarded as pets. *A Doll's House* was written in 1879, but today—well over a century later—Nora still symbolizes the often inferior position of women.

Another example of a representative character is Willy Loman, in Arthur Miller's *Death of a Salesman.* Willy stands for all salesmen, traveling on "a smile and a shoeshine." He has accepted a false dream: the idea that he can be successful and rich by putting up a good front and being "well liked."

Nora Helmer and Willy Loman are both examples of characters who stand apart from the crowd, not by standing above it but by embodying the attributes of a certain type of ordinary person.

Stock Characters   Many characters in drama are not "complete," not "three-dimensional." Rather, they symbolize and throw into bold relief a particular type of person to the exclusion of virtually everything else. They are called *stock characters*, and although they can be found in almost all kinds of drama, they appear particularly in comedy and melodrama.

Among the most famous examples of stock characters are those in *commedia dell'arte*, a form of comic improvisational theatre that flourished in Italy from the late sixteenth century to the eighteenth century. In commedia dell'arte, there were no scripts; there was only an outline of the action, and the performers supplied the words. There was a set group of stereotypical characters, each one invariably wearing the same costume and displaying the same personality traits. The bragging soldier, called Capitano, always boasted of his courage in a series of fictitious military victories. Pantalone, an elderly merchant, spoke in clichés and chased young women; and a pompous character, Dottore, spouted Latin phrases to impress others with his learning. Among the servant characters, Harlequin was the most popular; both cunning and stupid, he was at the heart of every plot complication.

The familiar figures in situation comedies on television are good examples of stock characters in our own day. The conceited high school boy, the prejudiced father, the harried mother, the dumb blond waitress, the efficient career person, the tough private detective—we can see such stereotypical characters every day on television. We recognize their familiar traits, and their attitudes and actions are always predictable and may reflect biases and prejudices of the times.

Characters with a Dominant Trait   Closely related to stock characters are characters with a *dominant trait*, or *humor.* One aspect of such a character dominates, making for an unbalanced, often comic, personality. Ben Jonson titled two of his plays **Every Man in His Humour** (1616) and **Every Man Out of His Humour** (1616); and he usually named his characters for their single trait or humor. In his play **The Alchemist** (1610), the characters have names like Subtle, Face, Dapper, Surly, Wholesome, and Dame Pliant.

Playwrights of the English Restoration also gave characters names that described their personalities. In **The Way of the World**, by William Congreve, one character is called Fainall, meaning "feign all"; that is, he constantly pretends. Other characters are Petulant, Sir Wilful Witwoud, Waitwell, and Lady Wishfort, the last being a contraction of "wish for it." Molière frequently emphasized the dominant trait of the main character in his titles: **The Miser, The Misanthrope, The Would-Be Gentleman, The Imaginary Invalid**.

Stock character
Character who has one outstanding trait of human behavior to the exclusion of virtually all other attributes. These characters often seem like stereotypes and are most often used in comedy and melodrama.

Commedia dell'arte
(koh-MAY-dee-ah dehl-AHR-teh) Form of comic theatre, originating in sixteenth-century Italy, in which dialogue was improvised around a loose scenario calling for a set of stock characters.

Dominant trait   Found in certain theatrical characters—one paramount trait or tendency that overshadows all others and appears to control the conduct of the character. Examples could include greed, jealousy, anger, and self-importance.

A DOMINANT TRAIT
A favorite character of many comic writers through the ages has been one with a clear, strong trait that overrides all others: jealousy, avarice, miserliness, pomposity, and so forth. A good example is Mrs. Malaprop in *The Rivals* by Richard Brinsley Sheridan. Mrs. Malaprop invariably uses long words in the wrong way, making her an immensely comic figure. Here, she is played by Mary Louise Wilson in a production at the Huntington Theatre.
(©T. Charles Erickson)

Minor characters In a drama, those characters who have small, secondary, or supporting roles. These could include soldiers and servants.

Minor Characters   Characters who play a small part in the overall action are called *minor characters*. Usually, they appear briefly and serve chiefly to further the story or to serve as a foil, that is a contrast, to more important characters.

Narrator or Chorus   Generally, a *narrator* speaks directly to the audience, frequently commenting on the action. The narrator may or may not have a dramatic persona in the same sense as the other characters. In Tennessee Williams's *The Glass Menagerie,* the narrator is also a character in the play; in Thornton Wilder's *Our Town,* the narrator becomes several characters during the course of the action. Greek drama used a *chorus* that commented, in song and dance, on the action of the main plot and reacted to it.

Chorus In ancient Greek drama, a group of performers who sang and danced, sometimes participating in the action but usually simply commenting on it. In modern times, performers in a musical play who sing and dance as a group.

Nonhuman Characters   In many primitive cultures, performers portrayed birds and animals, and this practice has continued to the present. Aristophanes, the Greek comic playwright, used a chorus to play the title parts in his plays ***The Birds*** (414 B.C.E.) and ***The Frogs*** (405 B.C.E.). In the modern era, the absurdist playwright Eugène Ionesco has people turn into animals in *Rhinoceros* (1959). The contemporary American playwright Edward Albee has performers play lizards in *Seascape* (1974).

While authors may create nonhuman characters, however, we should note that their focus is always on drawing parallels with the human experience.

NONHUMAN CHARACTERS

Sometimes characters are nonhuman, although they usually have human characteristics. This tradition goes back at least as far as the comedies of the Greek writer Aristophanes in the fifth century B.C.E. in Greece. Frequently they are animals of some sort. Shown here in a production of Edward Albee's *Seascape*, a play in which several characters are sea creatures, are Paul Gunning, Arden Teresa Lewis, Alan Schack, and Kristin Weigard. The presentation, directed by Charlie Mount, was a Chestnuts Production at Theatre West. (©Thomas Mikusz)

Juxtaposition of Characters

In creating characters, a playwright can use them in combinations that will bring out certain qualities.

One such combination consists of a ***protagonist*** and an ***antagonist***. These terms come from Greek theatre. A *protagonist* is the leading character in a play, the chief or outstanding figure in the action. An *antagonist* is the character who opposes the protagonist. In Shakespeare's **Othello**, for example, the protagonist is Othello and the antagonist is Iago, his chief opponent. Through the interaction and conflict between protagonist and antagonist, the individual qualities of both characters emerge.

Another way to contrast characters is to set them side by side rather than in opposition. Frequently, a dramatist will introduce secondary characters to serve

Protagonist Principal character in a play, the one whom the drama is about.

Antagonist Opponent of the protagonist in a drama.

1. Think of a play or musical you have seen or read where two major characters are in conflict with one another. Describe the two characters and explain the source of their conflict. How does it play out?

2. During the last performance you attended, did the action take place in one locale (one room, for instance) or, instead, in three or four locations? Did the action move frequently, returning at times to a former location? What effect did these elements of location have on your experience of the play?

3. Look at the cast of characters in a Shakespearean play you have seen or read. Place each character in a category: major character; minor character; or a character in between—that is, a character with a clear personality but not a large role. Which characters are in opposition to one another? Which characters in the play dominate in the struggle? Is there a reversal of their fortunes?

4. While you are watching a modern play or drama involving a small group of characters locked in a struggle for dominance or control, how does the action develop? Is one person first in the ascendency and then another? What do shifts of power and control have to do with revealing the personalities of the characters? What do these changes have to do with the meaning of the play?

as *foils* or *counterparts* to the main characters. A foil is a person who stands in contrast to another. In **Hedda Gabler**, by Henrik Ibsen, the main character, Hedda, is destructive and willful, bent on having her own way. Mrs. Elvsted, another character in the play, is Hedda's opposite in almost every regard.

SUMMARY

1. The person or persons creating a dramatic text have a number of tasks and responsibilities, including developing its subject, focus, and purpose.

2. Beyond that, those creating a text must develop a dramatic structure and dramatic characters.

3. Essentials of dramatic structure include plot, conflict, strongly opposed forces, and a reasonable balance between those forces.

4. An opening scene starts the action and sets the tone and style of the play.

5. Then the characters, motivated by objectives or goals, encounter a series of obstacles and complications. The result is a succession of crises leading to the most important crisis, the climax.

6. In the past, playwrights generally used either climactic or episodic structure.

7. In climactic form, all aspects of a play—such as action, duration, and number of characters and locales—are restricted.

8. In episodic form, these aspects are all expanded.

9. At certain times in theatre history, climactic and episodic form have been combined.

10. A playwright or the equivalent must also create characters, using dialogue and action.

11. Playwrights of the past usually presented extraordinary, "larger than life" characters.

12. A modern dramatist is less likely to present elevated characters such as kings and queens, but present-day playwrights still often give us exceptional characters—people at their best or their worst.

13. Today's playwrights might also choose to present ordinary, but representative, characters, typical of a large portion of the population.

14. A playwright may also use stock characters, that is, characters who are easily recognizable as stereotypes.

15. The playwright or whoever creates a text juxtaposes characters to highlight their individual traits—for example, opposing the main character or protagonist with an antagonist or a contrasting character.

Design elements: Playing Your Part box (theatre seats): ©McGraw-Hill Education; In Focus box (spotlight): ©d_gas/Getty Images

THEATRICAL GENRES

4

When we attend a theatre performance, within the first fifteen minutes or so, we sense a tone and a mood that are being communicated. We become aware that those presenting the play—the playwright, the actors, the director—are signaling to the audience that they have adopted a definite point of view and attitude toward what is to follow. For example, in the opening scene of Shakespeare's *Hamlet*, the ghost of Hamlet's father appears to men on guard at the castle. It is an ominous, eerie scene that tells us this will be a serious play, perhaps even a tragedy. On the other hand, at the beginning of Shakespeare's *A Midsummer Night's Dream*, Theseus, the Duke of Athens, says: "Stir up the Athenian youth to merriment, awake the pert and nimble spirit of mirth," a clear sign that this will be a comedy.

TYPES OF DRAMA

In Greece in the fifth century B.C.E., where Western theatre began, the actors wore masks covering their faces when they performed. The Greeks took the idea of the mask to create symbols of the two kinds of plays presented at their dramatic festivals—the mask of tragedy and the mask of comedy—symbols that are still used today. Similarly, in Japan in the fourteenth century C.E., a theatre called nō had become established as the serious form of drama. Alongside nō, however, was a comical, farcical type of drama called kyōgen.

In other words, wherever theatre has appeared, there has been a tendency to divide it into categories or types, often referred to by the French term *genre* (JAHN-ruh). In addition to tragedy and comedy, additional genres have developed: farce, melodrama, tragicomedy, and a number of others.

Genre A French word meaning type or category. In theatre, genre denotes the category into which a play falls: for example, tragedy, comedy, or tragicomedy.

◄ **DRAMATIC GENRE: COMEDY**

Drama is often divided into categories or types, referred to as genres. The Greeks separated tragedy and comedy. To those two genres have been added tragicomedy and others. Shown here are Kristine Nielsen as Mrs. Hardcastle, Jeremy Webb as George Hastings, and Rebecca Brooksher (rear) as Constance Neville in a comedy of wit written by Oliver Goldsmith, She Stoops to Conquer, *which the eighteenth century author called "a laughing comedy." The production was directed by Nicholas Martin at the McCarter Theatre.* (©T. Charles Erickson)

This tendency to divide dramatic works into categories is not confined to theatre. We find it widespread, not only in the arts, but in many aspects of life. Not only those who create theatre adopt different points of view toward events and toward life in general; all of us do. Depending on our perspective, we can see the same subject as funny or sad, take it seriously or laugh at it, make it an object of pity or of ridicule. Just why we look at events from different points of view is difficult to say, but there is no question that we do. The English author Horace Walpole (1717–1797) wrote: "This world is a comedy to those that think, a tragedy to those that feel."[1]

In theatre, this question of viewpoint—looking at people or events from a particular perspective—becomes crucial. Viewpoint is not taken for granted, as it is in everyday life; rather, it is a conscious act on the part of whoever creates the text. To take an example, in most cases death is considered a somber matter; but in his play *Arsenic and Old Lace* (1941), the dramatist Joseph Kesselring (1902–1967) makes it clear that in his play we are to regard death as comic. Kesselring presents two elderly women who kill no fewer than 12 old men by serving them arsenic in glasses of wine. But because the dramatist removes from the play any feeling that the deaths are to be taken seriously, he engenders in the audience the notion that it is all in fun.

Before examining genre, we should note that often a play does not fit neatly into a single category. Those who create a text do not write categories or types of plays; they write individual, unique works—and preoccupation with genre may distract us from the individuality of a play or a production. Still, if we keep these reservations in mind, we will find that it is helpful to understand the traditional genres into which Western dramatic literature has fallen.

TRAGEDY

Serious drama takes a thoughtful, sober attitude toward its subject matter. It puts the spectators in a frame of mind to think about what they are seeing and to become involved with the characters onstage: to love what these characters love, fear what they fear, and suffer what they suffer. The best-known form of serious drama, to which we turn first, is *tragedy*. Other forms of serious theatre are *heroic drama, domestic drama,* and *melodrama*.

Tragedy A serious drama in which there is a downfall of the primary character.

Tragedy asks very basic questions about human existence. Why are people sometimes cruel to one another? Why is the world unjust? Why are men and women called on to endure suffering? What are the limits of human suffering and endurance? In the midst of cruelty and despair, what are the possibilities of human achievement? To what heights of courage, strength, generosity, and integrity can human beings rise? Tragedy assumes that the universe is indifferent to human concerns and often cruel and malevolent. Sometimes the innocent appear to suffer, whereas the evil prosper. In the face of this, some humans are capable of despicable deeds, but others can confront and overcome adversity, attaining a nobility that places them "a little lower than the angels." We can divide tragedy into two basic kinds: traditional and modern. *Traditional tragedy* includes works from several significant periods of the past. *Modern tragedy* generally includes plays from the late nineteenth century to the present day.

[1]Horace Walpole, letter to Anne, Countess of Ossory, August 16, 1776

Traditional Tragedy

Tragic Heroes and Heroines Generally, the hero or heroine of a tragedy is an extraordinary person—a king, a queen, a general, a nobleman or noblewoman—in other words, a person of stature. In Greek drama, Antigone, Electra, Oedipus, Agamemnon, Creon, and Orestes are members of royal families. In the plays of Shakespeare, Hamlet, Claudius, Gertrude, Lear, and Cordelia are also royal; Julius Caesar, Macbeth, and Othello are generals; and others—Ophelia, Romeo, and Juliet—are members of the nobility.

Tragic Circumstances The central figures of the play are caught in a series of tragic circumstances: Oedipus, without realizing it, murders his father and marries his mother; Antigone must choose between death and dishonoring her dead brother; Phaedra falls hopelessly and fatally in love with her stepson, Hippolytus; Othello is completely duped by Iago; and Lear is cast out by the daughters to whom he has given his kingdom. In traditional tragedy, the universe seems determined to trap the hero or heroine in a fateful web and for that character to suffer a tragic fall.

MAJOR CHARACTERS CAUGHT IN A TRAGIC WEB
In traditional tragedy the fall of a hero or heroine has a special significance because of the combination of his or her personality and position. An example of a tragic heroine is the Duchess of Malfi in the play of the same name by John Webster. Despite her title and station in life, the duchess is taunted and destroyed by her evil brothers when she marries someone of a lower social rank. Seen here are Ursina Lardi in the title role and Robert Beyer as Bosola, one of the brothers, in a production at the Schaubuehne Theatre in Berlin, Germany. (©ullstein bild/ullstein bild/Getty Images)

Tragic Irretrievability The situation becomes irretrievable: There is no turning back. The tragic figures are in a situation from which there is no honorable avenue of escape; they must go forward to meet their fate.

Acceptance of Responsibility The hero or heroine accepts responsibility for his or her actions and also shows willingness to suffer and an immense capacity for suffering. Oedipus puts out his own eyes; Antigone faces death with equanimity; Othello kills himself. King Lear suffers immensely, living through personal humiliation, a raging storm on a heath, temporary insanity, and the death of his daughter, and finally confronts his own death. A statement by Edgar in **King Lear** applies to all tragic figures: "Men must endure their going hence even as their coming hither."[2]

Tragic Verse The language of traditional tragedy is verse. Because it deals with lofty and profound ideas—with men and women at the outer limits of their lives—tragedy soars to the heights and descends to the depths of human experience; and many feel that such thoughts and emotions can best be expressed in poetry. Look at Cleopatra's lament on the death of Mark Antony. Her sense of

[2]William Shakespeare, *King Lear* (1606), Act V, Scene 2.

admiration for Antony, and her desolation, could never be conveyed so tellingly in less poetic terms:

> Oh, wither'd is the garland of war,
> The soldier's pole is fall'n! Young boys and girls
> Are level now with men. The odds is gone,
> And there is nothing left remarkable
> Beneath the visiting moon.[3]

These words have even more effect when heard in the theatre spoken by an eloquent actress.

The Effect of Tragedy   When the elements of traditional tragedy are combined, they appear to produce two contradictory reactions simultaneously. One is pessimism: The heroes or heroines are "damned if they do and damned if they don't," and the world is a cruel, uncompromising place, a world of despair. And yet, in even the bleakest tragedy—whether *Hamlet,* **Medea***, Macbeth,* or *King Lear*— there is affirmation. One source of this positive feeling is found in the drama itself. Sophocles, Euripides, Shakespeare, and the French dramatist Jean Racine, although telling us that the world is in chaos and utterly lost, at the same time affirmed just the opposite by creating brilliant, carefully shaped works of art.

There is another positive element, which has to do with the tragic heroes and heroines themselves. They meet their fate with such dignity and such determination that they defy the gods. They say: "Come and get me; throw your worst at me. Whatever happens, I will not surrender my individuality or my dignity." In Aeschylus's play **Prometheus Bound** the title character—who is one of the earliest tragic heroes—says: "On me the tempest falls. It does not make me tremble." In defeat, the men and women of tragedy triumph.

The Greek philosopher Aristotle in *The Poetics* (c. 335 B.C.E.) attempted to describe the effect traditional tragedy had on the audience. He suggested that tragedy arouses pity and fear in the audience and that this genre purges the audience of those emotions. Spectators feel pity for the tragic hero caught in irretrievable circumstances and fear that if characters of noble stature can suffer falls so could they. The purgation of these emotions, however, again reflects a positive outcome of tragedy.

As for the deeper meanings of individual tragedies, there is a vast literature on the subject, and each play has to be looked at and experienced in detail to obtain the full measure of its meaning. Certain tragedies seem to hold so much meaning, to contain so much—in substance and in echoes and reverberations— that one can spend a lifetime studying them.

Modern Tragedy

Tragedies of the modern period—that is, beginning in the late nineteenth century— do not have queens or kings as central figures, and they are written in prose rather than poetry. For these as well as more philosophical reasons, purists argue that modern tragedies are not true tragedies.

In answer to this, it should be pointed out that today we have few kings or queens—either in mythology or, except in certain places like Great Britain, in real life. At the same time, we may ask: Do we not have characters today who can stand

---

[3]William Shakespeare, *Antony and Cleopatra* (1606), Act IV, Scene 5.

Part 2   Creating Theatre: The Playwright

A MODERN TRAGIC FAMILY

In Federico García Lorca's play *The House of Bernarda Alba*, a widow who has grown to hate and distrust men keeps her daughters confined as virtual prisoners in their own home, preventing them from going out. In this production, directed by Elizabeth Huddle at the Madison Repertory Theatre, we see four of the daughters, with the mother in the center. Left to right, the performers are Jamie England, Monica Lyons, Elisabeth Adwin, Margaret Ingraham, and Diane Robinson. (©Zane Williams/Madison Repertory Theatre)

as symbolic figures for important segments of society? Many would answer that we still do. In attempting to create modern tragedy, the question is not whether we view the human condition in the same way as the French did in the seventeenth century or the Greeks did in the fifth century B.C.E.—those two societies did not view life in the same way either—but whether our age allows for a tragic view on its own terms.

The answer seems to be yes. Compared with either the eighteenth or the nineteenth century—ages of enlightenment, progress, and unbounded optimism— our age has its own tragic vision. Modern tragic dramatists probe the same depths and ask the same questions as did their predecessors: Why do men and women suffer? Why do violence and injustice exist? And perhaps most fundamental of all: What is the meaning of our lives?

On this basis, many commentators would argue that writers like Ibsen, Strindberg, García Lorca, O'Neill, Williams, and Miller can lay claim to writing legitimate modern tragedy. The ultimate test of a play is not whether it meets someone's definition of tragedy but what effect it produces in the theatre and how successful it is in standing up to continued scrutiny. Eugene O'Neill's *Long Day's Journey into Night* takes as bleak a look at the human condition, with, at the same time, as compassionate a view of human striving and dignity as it seems possible to take in our day.

HEROIC DRAMA

The term *heroic drama* is not used as commonly as *tragedy* or *comedy,* but there is a wide range of plays for which *heroic drama* seems an appropriate description. We use the term specifically to indicate serious drama of any period that incorporates heroic or noble figures and other features of traditional tragedy—dialogue in verse, extreme situations, and the like—but differs from tragedy in having a happy ending, or in assuming a basically optimistic worldview even when the ending is sad.

Heroic drama Serious but basically optimistic drama written in verse or elevated prose, with noble or heroic characters in extreme situations or unusual adventures.

photo essay
Modern Domestic Drama

Serious drama in America came of age in the mid-twentieth century, with plays by Eugene O'Neill, Tennessee Williams, Arthur Miller, and Lillian Hellman, among others. Though all four experimented with nonrealistic dramatic devices, much of their strongest work was realistic domestic drama. Included here are examples in photographs from recent productions.

Long Day's Journey Into Night by Eugene O'Neill with Paul Nicholls as the younger son, Edmund, Jessica Lange as Mary Tyrone, and Paul Rudd as James Tyrone, Jr. (©Rune Hellestad/Corbis Entertainment/ Getty Images)

Gillian Anderson as Blanche Dubois and Vanessa Kirby as her sister Stella in Tennessee Williams' *A Streetcar Named Desire* in a production at the Young Vic in London, directed by Benedict Andrews. (©Robbie Jack/Corbis Entertainment/Getty Images)

Lee Aaron Rosen as Chris Keller, Michael Tisdale as George Deever, and Diane Davis as Ann Deever in *All My Sons,* by Arthur Miller, directed by David Esbjornson at the Huntington Theatre Company. (©T. Charles Erickson)

Seth Numrich, left, and Danny Burstein in a recent Broadway revival of *Golden Boy* by Clifford Odets, directed by Bartlett Sher. (©Sara Krulwich/The New York Times/Redux)

Several Greek plays ordinarily classified as tragedies are actually closer to heroic drama. In Sophocles's **Electra**, for instance, Electra suffers grievously, but at the end of the play she and her brother Orestes triumph. Another example is **The Cid**, written by Pierre Corneille (1606–1684) in France. It has a hero who leads his men to victory in battle but who is not killed; in the end, he wins a duel against his rival. In the late seventeenth century in England, a form of drama that was called *heroic drama,* or sometimes *heroic tragedy,* was precisely the type about which we are speaking: a serious play with a happy ending for the hero or heroine.

Many Asian plays—from India, China, and Japan—though deviating from the usual Western classifications by including, for example, a great deal of traditional dance and music, bear a close resemblance to heroic drama. Frequently, for example, a hero goes through a series of dangerous adventures, emerging victorious at the end. The vast majority of Asian dramas end happily.

A second type of heroic drama involves the death of the hero or heroine, but the overall effect is not considered tragic. Several of the plays of Johann Wolfgang von Goethe (1749–1832) follow this pattern. (Many of Goethe's plays, along with those of his contemporaries in the late eighteenth century and early nineteenth century, form a subdivision of heroic drama referred to as *romantic drama.* **Romanticism**, a literary movement that took hold in Germany at the time and spread to France and throughout much of Europe, celebrated the spirit of hope, personal freedom, and natural instincts.)

A number of plays in the modern period fall into the category of heroic drama. **Saint Joan**, by George Bernard Shaw, is a good example: Although Joan is burned at the stake, her death is actually a form of triumph. As if that were not enough, Shaw provides an epilogue in which Joan appears alive again.

In the history of theatre, the plays we are discussing as *heroic drama* occupy a large and important niche, cutting across Asian and Western civilizations and across periods from the Greek golden age to the present.

BOURGEOIS OR DOMESTIC DRAMA

With the changes in society that resulted from the rise of the middle class and the shift from kings and queens to more democratic governments, we move from classic tragedy to modern tragedy. In the same way, during the past 150 years heroic drama has largely been replaced by **bourgeois** or **domestic drama**. *Bourgeois* refers to people of the middle or lower middle class rather than the aristocracy, and *domestic* means that the plays often deal with problems of the family or the home rather than great affairs of state. In the Greek, Roman, and Renaissance periods, ordinary people served as main characters only in comedies; they rarely appeared as heroes or heroines of serious plays. Beginning in the eighteenth century, however, as society changed, there was a call for serious drama about men and women with whom members of the audience could identify and who were like themselves.

In England in 1731, George Lillo (1693–1739) wrote **The London Merchant**, a story of a merchant's apprentice who is led astray by a prostitute and betrays his good-hearted employer. This play, like others that came after it, dealt with recognizable people from the daily life of Britain, and audiences welcomed it.

From these beginnings, bourgeois or domestic drama developed through the balance of the eighteenth century and the whole of the nineteenth, until it achieved a place of prominence in the new realistic works of Ibsen, Strindberg, and Chekhov.

Romanticism
Nineteenth-century dramatic movement that imitated the episodic structure of Shakespeare, and thematically focused on the gulf between human beings' spiritual aspirations and physical limitations.

Bourgeois or domestic drama Drama dealing with problems—particularly family problems—of middle- and lower-class characters. There are serious and comic domestic dramas.

DOMESTIC DRAMA OF EVERYDAY LIFE
Domestic drama concerns itself with family problems: parents and children, husbands and wives, growing up, growing old. The characters in it are recognizable people, and it has long been a mainstay of modern drama. Shown here in a recent Broadway revival of Lorraine Hansberry's *A Raisin in the Sun* are Denzel Washington, Sophie Okonedo, Latanya Richardson Jackson, Bryce Clyde Jenkins, and Anika Noni Rose. (©Sara Krulwich/The New York Times/Redux)

In the mid-twentieth century, three major American playwrights of domestic drama emerged: Eugene O'Neill, Arthur Miller, and Tennessee Williams. O'Neill, in such plays as *The Iceman Cometh* and *Long Day's Journey into Night,* probed the depth of his characters' anguish as realistically as any dramatist of modern times. Miller, in *The Crucible* and *Death of a Salesman,* combined the tragic lives of its characters with political and moral investigations. Williams, the most lyrical of the three, in *The Glass Menagerie* and *A Streetcar Named Desire*, explored the limits of human sorrow and endurance.

These three were followed in the decades to come by other important American playwrights such as Lorraine Hansberry, Edward Albee, August Wilson, and Paula Vogel. Problems with society, struggles within a family, dashed hopes, and renewed determination are typical characteristics of domestic drama. When sufficiently penetrating or profound, domestic drama achieves the level of modern tragedy.

In one form or another, bourgeois or domestic drama has become the predominant form of serious drama throughout Europe and the United States during the past hundred years.

MELODRAMA

Melodrama Dramatic
form made popular in the
nineteenth century that
emphasized action and
spectacular effects and also
used music to underscore
the action; it had stock
characters, usually with
clearly defined villains and
heroes.

During the eighteenth and nineteenth centuries, one of the most popular forms of
theatre was *melodrama*. The word, which comes from Greek, means "music
drama" or "song drama." Its modern form was introduced by the French in the
late eighteenth century and applied to plays that had background music of the
kind we hear in movies: ominous chords underscoring a scene of suspense and
lyrical music underscoring a love scene.

Among the effects for which melodrama generally strives is fright or horror. It
has been said that melodrama speaks to the paranoia in all of us: the fear that someone is pursuing us or that disaster is about to overtake us. How often do we have a
sense that others are ganging up on us or a premonition that we have a deadly disease?

Melodrama brings these fears to life; we see people stalked or terrorized, or
innocent victims tortured. Murder mysteries and detective stories are almost invariably
melodramas because they stress suspense, danger, and close brushes with disaster. This
type of melodrama usually ends in one of two ways: Either the victims are maimed
or murdered (in which case our worst paranoid fears are confirmed) or, after a series

SUSPENSION OF NATURAL LAWS IN COMEDY
Frequently in various kinds of comedy, particularly in farce, our natural reaction to events is reordered to achieve a comic
effect, and the audience accepts this. An excellent example is the play *Arsenic and Old Lace* by Joseph Kesselring, in which
two elderly women, who appear to be helpless and harmless, actually murder a number of old men by giving them elderberry
wine laced with poison. Because we have accepted the comic premise of the play, however, we do not condemn their acts, but
we might in a melodrama, but rather become amused. Shown here (left to right) are Nathaniel Fuller (Mr. Witherspoon),
Sally Wingert (Martha Brewster) and Kristine Nielsen (Abby Brewster) in a production at the Guthrie Theater directed by
Joe Dowling. (©Michal Daniel)

of dangerous episodes, they are rescued (in which case the play is like a bad dream from which we awaken to realize that we are safe in bed and everything is all right).

Probably the easiest way to understand melodrama is to look at film and television examples. Among the kinds of popular melodramas we are familiar with are *westerns, science fiction films, horror films, superhero films* and *detective* or *spy films*. All of these emphasize heroes and villains, other stock characters such as sidekicks and love interests, as well as spectacular events and special effects. But the key to the melodramatic form, on stage, and in film and television, is that good is almost always victorious over evil. These characteristics are also present in melodramatic plays.

Still another form of melodrama argues a political or moral issue. Melodrama invariably shows us good characters against bad characters. Therefore, a playwright who wants to make a strong political case will often write a melodrama in which the good characters represent his or her point of view.

Traditional melodrama with its moral outlook, happy ending, stock characters, use of background music, and emphasis on spectacle developed in the nineteenth century. Still, a list of significant melodramas could range over most of theatre history and could include writers from Euripides through Shakespeare and his contemporaries to modern dramatists throughout Europe and the Americas because many types of serious drama, tragic and nontragic, frequently have strong melodramatic elements as well.

Aside from those taking a basically serious point of view, there are two other fundamental approaches to dramatic material. One is *comedy,* with its many forms and variations; the other is a mixture of the serious and the comic, called *tragicomedy.*

COMEDY

People who create **comedy** are not necessarily more frivolous or less concerned with important matters than people who create serious works; they may be extremely serious in their own way. Writers of comedy like Aristophanes, Molière, and George Bernard Shaw cared passionately about human affairs and the problems of men and women. But those with a comic view look at the world differently: with a smile or a deep laugh or an arched eyebrow. Writers like these perceive the follies and excesses of human behavior and develop a keen sense of the ridiculous, with the result that they show us things that make us laugh.

Comedy In general, a play that is light in tone, is concerned with issues that point out the excesses and folly of human behavior, has a happy ending, and is designed to amuse.

It should also be noted that there are many kinds of laughter. They range all the way from mild amusement at a witty saying or a humorous situation to a belly laugh at some wild physical comedy to cruel, derisive laughter. Theatre, which reflects life and society, encompasses comedies that display a similar range, from light comedies to outrageous farces.

Characteristics of Comedy

If we cannot fully explain comedy, we can at least understand some of the principles that make it possible.

Suspension of Natural Laws   One characteristic of most comedy is a temporary suspension of the natural laws of probability, cause and effect, and logic. Actions do not have the consequences they do in real life. In comedy, when a haughty man walking down the street steps on a child's skateboard and goes sprawling on the sidewalk, we do not fear for his safety or wonder if he has any bruises. The focus in comedy is on the man being tripped up and getting his comeuppance.

In burlesque, a comic character can be hit on the backside with a fierce thwack, and we laugh, because we know that it does not hurt anything but his or her pride. At one point in stage history a special stick consisting of two thin slats of wood held closely together was developed to make hitting someone more frightening. The stick was known as a *slapstick*, a name that came to describe all kinds of raucous, physical, knockabout comedy.

Slapstick Type of comedy, or comic business, that relies on ridiculous physical activity—often violent in nature—for its humor.

Prime examples of the suspension of natural laws in comedy are found in film and television cartoons. In animated cartoons, characters are hurled through the air like missiles, are shot full of holes, and are flattened on the sidewalk when they fall from buildings. But they always get up, with little more than a shake of the head. In the audience, there are no thoughts of real injury, of cuts or bruises, because the cause-and-effect chain of everyday life is not operating.

Under these conditions, a significant accident, resulting in physical harm, itself can be viewed as comic. In the 2015 award-winning London backstage comedy *The Play That Goes Wrong*, created by members of the Mischief Theatre Company, a cast member of a disaster-prone fictional production is knocked unconscious but miraculously revives only to find that her replacement, a technician, will not give up the role. We do not really think of the character as being rendered unconscious, and we have none of the feelings one usually has for an accident victim. The idea of suffering and harm has been suspended, and we are free to laugh at the irony and incongruity of the situation.

The Comic Premise

Comic premise Idea or concept in a comedy that turns the accepted notion of things upside down.

The suspension of natural laws in comedy makes possible the development of a *comic premise*. The comic premise is an idea or concept that turns the accepted notion of things upside down and makes this upended notion the basis of a play. The premise can provide thematic and structural unity and can serve as a springboard for comic dialogue, comic characters, and comic situations.

Aristophanes, the Greek satiric dramatist, was a master at developing a comic premise. In **The Clouds**, Aristophanes pictures Socrates as a man who can think only when perched in a basket suspended in midair. In **The Birds**, two ordinary men persuade a chorus of birds to build a city between heaven and earth. The birds comply, calling the place Cloudcuckoo Land, and the two men sprout wings to join them. In another play, **Lysistrata**, Aristophanes has the women of Greece agree to go on a sex strike to end a war: They will not make love to their husbands until the husbands stop fighting and sign a peace treaty with their opponents.

Techniques of Comedy

Incongruity In comedy, incongruity usually refers to a character's inappropriate behavior or actions for a specific circumstance resulting in our laughter.

The suspension of natural laws and the establishment of a comic premise in comedy involve exaggeration and incongruity. *Incongruity* usually refers to a character's inappropriate behavior or actions for a specific circumstance resulting in our laughter. The contradictions that result from these show up in three areas—verbal humor, characterization, and comic situations.

Verbal Humor

Verbal humor can be anything from a pun to the most sophisticated discourse. A *pun*—usually considered the simplest form of wit—is a humorous use of words with the same sound but different meanings. A man who says he is going to start a bakery if he can "raise the dough" is making a pun.

Close to the pun is the *malaprop*—a word that sounds like the right word but actually means something quite different. The term comes from Mrs. Malaprop, a character in **The Rivals** by the English playwright Richard Brinsley Sheridan (1751–1816). Mrs. Malaprop wants to impress everyone with her education and erudition but ends up doing just the opposite because she constantly misuses long

Part 2   Creating Theatre: The Playwright

words. For example, she insists that her daughter is not "illegible" for marriage, meaning that her daughter is not "ineligible," and when asked to explain a situation she says that someone else will provide the "perpendiculars" when she means the "particulars."

A sophisticated form of verbal humor is the *epigram*. Oscar Wilde (1854–1900), a man devoted to verbal humor, often turned accepted values upside down in his epigrams. "I can resist anything except temptation," says one of his characters; and "A man cannot be too careful in the choice of his enemies," says another.[4]

Comedy of Character   In comedy of character the discrepancy or incongruity lies in the way characters see themselves or pretend to be, as opposed to the way they actually are. A good example is a person who pretends to be a doctor—using obscure medicines, hypodermic needles, and Latin jargon—but who is actually a fake. Such a person is the chief character in Molière's ***The Doctor in Spite of Himself***. Another example of incongruity of character is Molière's ***The Would-Be Gentleman***, in which the title character, Monsieur Jourdain, a man of wealth, but without taste or refinement, is determined to learn courtly behavior. He hires a fencing master, a dancing master, and a teacher of literature to teach him these skills, but in every case Jourdain is ridiculed.

Comedy of character is also a basic ingredient of Italian *commedia dell'arte* and all forms of comedy where stock characters, stereotypes, and characters with dominant traits are emphasized.

We can also find examples of comedies of characters today in film and on television. The popular TV show *The Big Bang Theory* focuses on quirky scientists and much of the comedy is created by their unusual exaggerated behaviors and relationships.

VERBAL HUMOR
One key element of comedy is verbal wit. No one was more the master of wit than playwright Oscar Wilde, whose epigrams and clever word play are still quoted today. Shown here is a scene from his play *The Importance of Being Earnest* in a production at the Aldwych Theatre in London featuring Maggie Smith and Richard E. Grant. (©Robbie Jack/Corbis Entertainment/Getty Images)

Plot Complications   Still another way the contradictory or the ludicrous manifests itself in comedy is in plot complications, including coincidences and mistaken identity. A time-honored comic plot is Shakespeare's ***The Comedy of Errors***, based on ***The Menaechmi***, a play of the late third century B.C.E. by the Roman writer Titus Maccius Plautus (c. 254–184 B.C.E.). *The Comedy of Errors* in turn was the basis of a successful American musical comedy, *The Boys from Syracuse*, with songs by Richard Rodgers (1902–1979) and Lorenz Hart (1895–1943). In *The Comedy of Errors*, identical twins and their identical twin servants were

[4]Oscar Wilde, *Lady Windemere's Fan* (1893)

PLOT COMPLICATIONS: A HALLMARK OF FARCE
Frequently used devices of comedy include twists and turns in the plot, mistaken identity, unexpected developments, and ridiculous situations. Michael Frayn's comedy *Noises Off* contains an abundance of these elements. The production shown here was directed by Lindsay Posner in London. (©Geraint Lewis)

separated when young. As the play opens, however, both masters and both servants—unknown to one another—are in one place. The confusion among the twin brothers and the twin servants leads to an endless series of comic encounters.

A classic scene of plot complication occurs in Sheridan's ***The School for Scandal,*** written in 1777. Joseph Surface, the main character in the play, is thought to be an upstanding man but is really a charlatan, whereas Charles, his brother, is mistakenly considered a reprobate. In a famous scene called the "screen scene," both Lady Teazle, a married woman visiting Surface, and her husband, Sir Peter Teazle, are hidden, one behind a screen, one in a closet. When the honest Charles suddenly appears he discovers both of them, exposing their deceptions at a single moment.

Forms of Comedy

Farce A subclass of comedy with emphasis on exaggerated plot complications and with few or no intellectual pretensions.

Comedy takes various forms, depending on the dramatist's intent and on the comic techniques emphasized.

Farce Most plays discussed in the section above on plot complications are *farces*. Farce thrives on exaggeration—not only plot complications but also broad

Part 2 Creating Theatre: The Playwright

1. What recent event in everyday life has been described as a "tragedy"? Would that event meet the traditional definition of tragedy? Does it have the elements of traditional tragedy?

2. Is there a contemporary figure whose life you believe could be dramatized as a "modern tragedy"? Describe.

3. Have you seen a film or television show that could be categorized as "domestic drama"? What are its characteristics that lead you to that categorization?

4. Have you seen a recent film that you would categorize as a "melodrama"? What are its characteristics that lead you to that categorization?

5. Have you seen films or television shows that could be categorized as farce, burlesque, satire, domestic comedy, comedy of manners, comedy of characters?

6. Can you describe any current events that might be dramatized as tragicomedy? Why?

physical humor and stereotyped characters. It has no intellectual pretensions but aims rather at entertainment and provoking laughter. In addition to excessive plot complications, its humor results from ridiculous situations as well as pratfalls and horseplay, not on the verbal wit found in more intellectual forms of comedy. Mock violence, rapid movement, and accelerating pace are hallmarks of farce. Marriage and sex are the objects of fun in *bedroom farce,* but farce can also poke fun at medicine, law, and business.

Burlesque   *Burlesque* also relies on knockabout physical humor, as well as gross exaggerations and, occasionally, vulgarity. Historically, burlesque was a ludicrous imitation of other forms of drama or of an individual play. A recent example is the takeoff of the hit musical *Hamilton,* entitled *Spamilton.* In the United States, the term *burlesque* came to describe a type of variety show featuring low comedy skits and attractive women.

> **Burlesque**   A ludicrous, comic imitation of a dramatic form, play, piece of literature, or other popular entertainment.

Satire   A form related to traditional burlesque, but with more intellectual and moral or political content, is *satire.* Satire uses wit, irony, and exaggeration to attack or expose evil and foolishness. Satire can attack specific figures; for example, the continuously updated and revised revue *Forbidden Broadway* makes fun of the more flamboyant or excessive stars as well as plots and story lines of Broadway musicals. It can also be more inclusive, as in the case of Molière's *Tartuffe*, which ridicules religious hypocrisy generally.

> **Satire**   Comic form, using irony and exaggeration, to attack and expose folly and vice.

Domestic Comedy   The comic equivalent of domestic or bourgeois drama is *domestic comedy.* Usually dealing with family situations, it is found most frequently today in television situation comedies—often called *sitcoms*—which feature members of a family or residents of a neighborhood caught in a series of complicated but amusing situations. Television shows such as *The Simpsons, Modern Family* and *Black-ish* are examples. This type of comedy was once a staple of theatre and can still be found onstage in the frequently revived plays by Neil Simon (b. 1927).

photo essay
Forms of Comedy

Comedy takes a number of forms, depending on whether the emphasis is on verbal wit, plot complications, or the characters' eccentricities. It can range all the way from intellectual comedy, to high comedy (dealing with the upper classes), to domestic comedy (similar to sitcoms on TV), to slapstick farce. Shown here is a variety of types of comedy.

Shown here is Owain Arthur as Francis Henshall in *One Man, Two Guvnors,* a farce by Richard Bean after Goldoni's *The Servant of Two Masters,* in a production directed by Nicholas Hytner at the National Theatre, London. (©Donald Cooper/ PhotoStage)

Shown here are David Shiner, left, and Bill Irwin performing in *Old Hats,* a slapstick comedy they created at the Pershing Square Signature Center, directed by Tina Landau. (©Sara Krulwich/The New York Times/Redux)

COMEDY OF MANNERS

Comedy of manners usually deals with the upper class in a given society. It stresses verbal humor, repartee, and irony. The precursors of modern comedy of manners were the Restoration comedies popular in London in the late seventeenth century. In the nineteenth century, Oscar Wilde was a master of comedy of manners, and in the twentieth century it was Noël Coward. One of Coward's best-known plays is *Private Lives,* about two upper-class couples whose marriages become comically entangled. Seen here in a production at the Guthrie Theater are Tracey Maloney (Sibyl), Kris L. Nelson (Victor), Stephen Pelinski (Elyot), and Veanne Cox (Amanda). (©Michal Daniel)

Comedy of Manners   *Comedy of manners* is concerned with pointing up the foibles and peculiarities of the upper classes. Against a cultivated, sophisticated background, it uses verbal wit to depict the cleverness and expose the social pretensions of its characters. Rather than horseplay, it stresses witty phrases. In comedy of manners, pointed barbs are always at a premium. In England a line of comedies of manners runs from William Wycherley, William Congreve, and Oliver Goldsmith (1730–1774) in the seventeenth and eighteenth centuries to Oscar Wilde in the nineteenth century and Noël Coward (1899–1973) in the twentieth.

Comedy of Ideas   Many of George Bernard Shaw's plays could be put under a special heading, *comedy of ideas*, because Shaw used comic techniques to debate intellectual propositions and to further his own moral and social point of view. Though witty and amusing, Shaw's plays frequently include provocative discussions of controversial social issues. *Mrs. Warren's Profession*, for example, about a woman who runs a house of prostitution, deals with hypocrisy in society and *Arms and the Man* is not only an amusing story of a pompous soldier but also a treatise on war and heroism.

Comedy of manners   Form of comic drama that became popular in the English Restoration, that is set within sophisticated society, while poking fun at its characters' social pretensions, usually through verbal wit.

Comedy of ideas
A comedy in which the humor is based on intellectual and verbal aspects of comedy rather than physical comedy or comedy of character. A drama whose emphasis is on the clash of ideas, as exemplified in the plays of George Bernard Shaw.

In all its forms, comedy remains a way of looking at the world in which basic values are asserted but natural laws are suspended in order to underline human follies and foolishness—sometimes with a rueful look, sometimes with a wry smile, and sometimes with an uproarious laugh.

TRAGICOMEDY

In twentieth-century theatre a new genre came to the forefront—*tragicomedy*. In this section, we examine this form that has proved so important in the modern period.

What Is Tragicomedy?

In the past, comedy has usually been set in opposition to tragedy or serious drama: Serious drama is sad, comedy is funny; serious drama makes people cry, comedy makes them laugh; serious drama arouses anger, comedy brings a smile. True, the comic view of life differs from the serious view, but the two are not always as clearly separated as this polarity suggests. Many comic dramatists are serious people; "I laugh to keep from crying" applies to many comic writers as well as to certain clowns and comedians. A great deal of serious drama contains comic elements. Shakespeare, for instance, included comic characters in several of his serious plays. The drunken porter in *Macbeth*, the gravedigger in *Hamlet*, and Falstaff in *Henry IV, Part 1* are examples.

In medieval plays, comic scenes are interpolated in the basically religious subject matter. One of the best-known of all medieval plays, *The Second Shepherds' Play*, concerns the visit of the shepherds to the manger of the newborn Christ child. While they stop in a field to spend the night, Mak, a comic character, steals a sheep and takes it to his house, where he and his wife pretend that it is their baby. When the shepherds discover what Mak has done, they toss him in a blanket, and after this horseplay the serious part of the story resumes.

The alternation of serious and comic elements is a practice of long standing, particularly in episodic plays; but *tragicomedy* does not refer to plays that shift from serious to comic and back again. It is a view in which one eye looks through a comic lens and the other through a serious lens; and the two points of view are so intermingled as to be one, like food that tastes sweet and sour at the same time. In addition to his basically serious plays and his basically comic plays, Shakespeare wrote others that seem to be a combination of tragedy and comedy, such as *Measure for Measure* and *All's Well That Ends Well*. Because they do not fit neatly into one category or the other, these plays have proved troublesome to critics—so troublesome that they have been officially dubbed *problem plays*.

The "problem," however, arises largely because of difficulty in accepting the tragicomic point of view, for these plays have many of the attributes of the fusion of the tragic and the comic. A sense of comedy pervades these plays, the idea that all will end well and that much of what happens is ludicrous or ridiculous; at the same time, the serious effects of a character's actions are not dismissed. Unlike true comedy, in which a fall on the sidewalk or a temporary danger has no serious consequences, these plays contain actions that appear quite serious. And so we have tragicomedy.

COMBINING TRAGEDY AND COMEDY
Tragicomedy has become more and more prominent in the modern period, and has taken its place alongside traditional tragedy, comedy, and other genres as a major form of our time. In several of Shakespeare's so-called problem plays, comic and serious elements are intermixed in the manner of contemporary tragicomedy. A good example is *All's Well That Ends Well*, which features a strange, almost bizarre, mixture of fairy-tale elements with cynical realism. Shown here is James Garnon as Parolles in a London production at Shakespeare's Globe Theatre, directed by John Dove. (©Geraint Lewis)

Modern Tragicomedy

In the modern period—during the past hundred years or so—tragicomedy has become the primary approach of many of the best playwrights. As suggested in the chapter "The Audience," these writers are not creating in a vacuum; they are part of the world in which they live, and ours is an age that has adopted a tragicomic viewpoint more extensively than most previous ages. As if to keynote this attitude and set the tone, the Danish philosopher Søren Kierkegaard (1813–1855) in 1842 wrote: "Existence itself, the act of existence, is a striving and is both pathetic and comic in the same degree."[5]

The plays of Anton Chekhov, written at the turn of the twentieth century, reflect the spirit described by Kierkegaard. Chekhov called two of his major plays *comedies*; but Stanislavski, who directed them, called them *tragedies*—an indication of the confusion arising from Chekhov's mixture of the serious and the comic.

[5]Terry Pinkard, *German Philosophy 1760–1860: The Legacy of Idealism*, Cambridge University Press, Cambridge, UK, 2002, p. 354.

COMEDIES OF MENACE
Comedies range widely, from the pure entertainment of farce and light comedy to more substantive and probing comedies with a strong serious component. The playwright Harold Pinter calls many of his plays comedies of menace, meaning that they can provoke laughter but also have a deeper, more disturbing, sometimes frightening element. One of Pinter's best-known plays exemplifying this is *The Birthday Party*. Shown here are Timothy West as Goldberg and Nigel Terry as McCann in a production of the play at the Piccadilly Theatre in London. (©PA Images/Alamy Stock Photo)

An example of Chekhov's approach is a scene at the end of the third act of **Uncle Vanya** (1899). The lives of Vanya and his niece, Sonya, have been ruined by Sonya's father, a professor. At the moment where Sonya tells her father how cruel and thoughtless he is, Vanya comes in, waving a pistol in the air, and shoots twice at the professor, but misses both times. There is some doubt that Vanya honestly means to kill the professor and the scene itself is both tragic and comic: The two elements are inextricably joined together.

Theatre of the absurd (discussed below) is an example of modern tragicomedy. It probes deeply into human problems and casts a cold eye on the world, and yet it is also imbued with a comic spirit. The plays of Harold Pinter (1930–2008), a writer associated with theatre of the absurd, have been called *comedies of menace*, a phrase suggesting the idea of a theatre simultaneously terrifying and entertaining.

THEATRE OF THE ABSURD

Theatre of the absurd
Twentieth century plays expressing the dramatists' sense of absurdity and futility of human existence through the dramatic techniques they employ.

After World War II, a new type of theatre emerged in Europe and the United States, which the critic Martin Esslin called *theatre of the absurd*. Although the dramatists whose work falls into this category do not write in identical styles and are not really a "school" of writers, they do have enough in common to be

Part 2 Creating Theatre: The Playwright

THEATRE OF THE ABSURD

Non sequitur, nonsensical language, existential characters, ridiculous situations—these are hallmarks of theatre of the absurd, which can also be viewed as a type of tragicomedy. One example is Eugene Ionesco's *Exit the King.* Shown here, left to right, are Lauren Ambrose (as Queen Marie), Geoffrey Rush (King Berenger), William Sadler (the Doctor, in the background), and Susan Sarandon (Queen Marguerite, the King's wife) in a 2009 Broadway production adapted and directed by Neil Armfield. (©Joan Marcus)

considered together. Esslin took the name for this form of theatre from a quotation in *The Myth of Sisyphus* by the French writer, dramatist, and philosopher Albert Camus (1913–1960). In *The Myth of Sisyphus,* Camus says that in the modern age there is a separation between "man and his life, the actor and his setting," and that this separation "constitutes the feeling of Absurdity."[6]

Plays falling into the category of absurdism convey humanity's sense of alienation and its loss of bearings in an illogical, unjust, and ridiculous world. Although serious, this viewpoint is generally depicted in plays with considerable humor; an ironic note runs through much of theatre of the absurd.

A prime example of theatre of the absurd is Beckett's *Waiting for Godot.* In this play Beckett has given us one of the most telling expressions of loneliness and futility ever written: two tramps on a barren plain waiting every day for a

[6]Albert Camus, *Le Mythe de Sisyphe*, Gallimard, Paris, 1942, p. 18.

TRAGICOMEDY: FUNNY AND SAD AT THE SAME TIME
Several plays by the Russian writer Anton Chekhov could be described as tragicomedies containing elements of both comedy and tragedy, mixed together in a profound way. The scene here is from Chekhov's *Uncle Vanya* with June Watson as Marina, Ken Stott as Vanya, Paul Freeman as Serebryakov and Anna Friel as Yelena. Directed by Lindsay Posner, the production was at the Vaudeville Theatre in London. (©Robbie Jack/Corbis Entertainment/Getty Images)

supreme being called "Godot," who they think will come but who never does. At the same time, they themselves are comic. They wear baggy pants like burlesque comedians, and engage in any number of vaudeville routines. Also, the characters frequently say one thing and do just the opposite. One says to the other, "Well, shall we go?" and the other says, "Yes, let's go." But having said this, they don't move.

Absurdist plays suggest the idea of absurdity both in what they say—that is, their content—and in the way they say it, their form. Their structure, therefore, is a departure from dramatic structures of the past.

Absurdist Plots: Illogicality

Traditional plots in drama proceed in a logical way from a beginning through the development of the plot to a conclusion, an arrangement that suggests an ordered universe. In contrast, many absurdist plays not only proclaim absurdity but also embody it.

Part 2   Creating Theatre: The Playwright

1. A play by Henrik Ibsen, Anton Chekhov, Tennessee Williams, Lorraine Hansberry, or August Wilson might be set in a time fifty years ago or 100 years ago. What do you think it is about these dramas that allow audience members in the twenty-first century to identify strongly with the characters and the situations in the play?

2. Which kind of play do you prefer: a classic tragedy, a serious contemporary drama, a knockabout farce, a comedy, a musical? Can you explain why you prefer one type over the others?

3. Do you favor a play with a strong story line, a tight plot, and unexpected twists and turns? Or do you prefer a looser play that reflects the randomness of everyday life? What do you think attracts you to these characteristics?

An example is *The Bald Soprano* by Eugène Ionesco. The very title of the play turns out to be nonsense; a bald soprano is mentioned once in the play, but with no explanation, and it is clear that the bald soprano has nothing whatever to do with the play as a whole. The absurdity of the piece is manifest the moment the curtain goes up. A typical English couple are sitting in a living room when the clock on the mantle strikes seventeen times; the wife's first words are, "There, it's nine o'clock."

Absurdist Language: Nonsense and Non Sequitur

Events and characters are frequently illogical in theatre of the absurd, and so too is language. *Non sequitur* is a Latin term meaning "it does not follow"; it implies that something does not follow from what has gone before, and it perfectly describes the method of theatre of the absurd. Sentences do not follow in sequence, and words do not mean what we expect them to mean.

An example of the irrationality or debasement of language is found in Beckett's *Waiting for Godot*. The character of Lucky does not speak for most of his time onstage, but at the end of the first act he delivers a long speech consisting of incoherent religious and legalistic jargon. The opening lines offer a small sample:

> Given the existence as uttered forth in the public works of Puncher and Wattmann of a personal God quaquaquaqua with white beard quaquaquaqua outside time without extension who from the heights of divine apathia divine athambia divine aphasia loves us dearly with some exceptions for reasons unknown but time will tell. . . . [7]

Numerous examples of such language appear not only in Ionesco's and Beckett's plays but in plays written by many other absurdist writers.

Absurdist Characters: Existential Beings

A significant feature of absurdist plays is the handling of characters. Not only is there an element of the ridiculous in the characters' actions, but they frequently exemplify an *existential* point of view. In theatre, existentialism suggests that

---

[7]From *Waiting for Godot* by Samuel Beckett. Copyright 1954 by Grove Press; renewed copyright 1982 by Samuel Beckett.

As can be seen in our discussions of tragicomedy and theatre of the absurd, dramas often defy categorization. Plays frequently mix genres and styles. We have noted how Shakespeare wrote plays that did not clearly fit into either tragedy or comedy and some earlier critics referred to them as "problem" plays.

In the late twentieth century, theorists who are referred to as *postmodernists,* and whose concepts we will discuss more fully later, questioned the validity of categorizing dramas by genre. They argued that such categorization led to a hierarchy that was built on sociopolitical and aesthetic biases. Why should tragedy or comedy be privileged over melodrama or domestic drama? Does privileging traditional tragedy over modern tragedy have sociopolitical (and in many cases, gender) implications? Can we really distinguish between any of these genres and do such broad categories even make sense? Do audiences or authors differentiate in this fashion or does each playwright create a unique work and does each audience member have his or her own unique reaction to that work? Is there really a distinction between more popular theatrical forms and entertainments and so-called "high" art?

We can clearly see the problem of trying to categorize drama since the end of the nineteenth century. Throughout this time period there have been many avant-garde and popular theatrical forms that do not neatly fit into any of the categories discussed in this chapter.

Expressionism and surrealism, forms that developed early in the twentieth century, tried to capture the inner workings of the human mind: expressionism presenting drama from the point of view of the protagonist and surrealism trying to mimic the dream and other subconscious states.

The German playwright Bertolt Brecht, between the two World Wars and shortly after World War II, created what he called "epic" theatre, in which audience members were constantly reminded they were in the theatre. Songs broke up the action of his plays and underscored his political messages, and narrators were used to comment on the sociopolitical meaning of the dramatic action.

In the past half-century, many playwrights have written documentary plays based on actual historic events, using testimonies and archival documents as their dramatic material. Since the 1960s, moreover, there have been experimental companies that staged communally created performance pieces that engaged audiences in a variety of ways. As we shall see in the chapter "Today's Diverse Global Theatre," contemporary multicultural, feminist, LGBTQ, and global playwrights, as well as solo performance artists, have experimented with a multitude of styles and forms.

And, of course, over the past 100 years, there have been many popular theatre forms. One example is musical theatre (discussed more fully in the chapter "The Modern Theatre Emerges"), which incorporates plot (referred to as the *book* of a musical), songs, and dance to tell a story. There are also many subcategories of musical theatre.

While we will discuss the development of these and other forms more fully in the final two chapters of our text, the key question that these examples raise is: can we actually categorize plays and are there theatre works that defy categorization?

characters have no personal history and therefore no specific causes for their actions. The two main characters in *Waiting for Godot,* for example, are devoid of biography and personal motivation; we know nothing of their family life or their occupations. They meet every day at a crossroads to wait for Godot, but how long they have been coming there, or what they do when they are not there, remains a mystery.

In addition to the plays of the absurdists, other modern plays also incorporate the tragicomic spirit. In *The Visit,* by Friedrich Dürrenmatt (1921–1990), a Swiss dramatist, a wealthy woman returns to her birthplace, a small, poverty-stricken village. She offers a huge sum of money to the village on the condition that the citizens murder a storekeeper who wronged her when she was young. The townspeople express horror at the idea, but at the same time they begin buying expensive items on credit—some from the man's own store. There is a comic quality to these scenes, but the conclusion is not funny, for the man is eventually murdered by his greedy neighbors.

In tragicomedy, a smile is frequently cynical, a chuckle may be tinged with a threat, and laughter is sometimes bitter. In the past, the attitude that produced these combinations was the exception rather than the rule. In our day, it seems far more prevalent, not to say relevant. As a result, tragicomedy has taken its place as a major form alongside the more traditional approaches.

SUMMARY

1. Tragedy attempts to ask very basic questions about human existence: Why do men and women suffer? Is there justice in the world? What are the limits of human endurance and achievement? Tragedy presupposes an indifferent and sometimes malevolent universe in which the innocent suffer and there is inexplicable cruelty. It also assumes that certain men and women will confront and defy fate, even if they are overcome in the process.

2. Tragedy can be classified as traditional or modern. In traditional tragedy the chief characters are persons of stature—kings, queens, and the nobility. The central figure is caught in a series of tragic circumstances, which are irretrievable. The hero or heroine is willing to fight and die for a cause. The language of the play is verse.

3. Modern tragedy involves ordinary people rather than the nobility, and it is generally written in prose rather than verse. In this modern form, the deeper meanings of tragedy are explored by nonverbal elements and by the cumulative or overall effect of events as well as by verbal means.

4. There are several kinds of nontragic serious plays, the most notable being heroic drama, bourgeois or domestic drama, and melodrama.

5. Heroic drama has many of the same elements as traditional tragedy—it frequently deals with highborn characters and is often in verse. In contrast to tragedy, however, it has a happy ending or an ending in which the death of the main character is considered a triumph, not a defeat.

6. Bourgeois or domestic drama deals with ordinary people, always seriously but not always tragically. It stresses the problems of the middle and lower classes and became a particularly prominent form in the twentieth century.

7. Melodrama features exaggerated characters and events arranged to create horror or suspense or to present a didactic argument for some political, moral, or social point of view.

8. Comedy takes a different approach from serious forms of drama. It sees the humor and incongruity in people and situations. Comic dramatists accept a social and moral order and suspend natural laws (a man falls flat on his face but does not really hurt himself).

9. Comedy is developed by means of several techniques. *Verbal humor* turns words upside down and creates puns, malapropisms, and inversions of meaning. *Comedy of character* creates men and women who take extreme positions, make fools of themselves, or contradict themselves. *Plot complications* create mistaken identity, coincidences, and people who turn up unexpectedly in the wrong house or the wrong bedroom. There are also physical aspects to comedy: slapstick and horseplay.

10. From these techniques, the dramatist fashions various kinds of comedy. For instance, depending on the degree of exaggeration, a comedy can be *farce* or *comedy of manners*; farce features strong physical humor, whereas comedy of manners relies more on verbal wit.

11. Another type of comedy is *domestic comedy,* which deals with ordinary people in familiar situations.

12. Depending on its intent, comedy can be designed to entertain, as with *farce* or *burlesque*; or to correct vices, in which case it becomes *satire*. Many of Shaw's plays represent *comedy of ideas*.

13. Serious and comic elements can be mixed in theatre. Many tragedies have comic relief—humorous scenes and characters interspersed in serious material.

14. Authentic tragicomedy fuses, or synthesizes, two elements—one serious, the other comic. We laugh and cry at the same time. Chekhov, Beckett, Dürrenmatt, and writers of theatre of the absurd use tragicomedy in their plays. Some commentators feel that this is the form most truly characteristic of our time.

Creating Theatre: The Production

THE THEATRE PRODUCTION

Putting a stage production together takes the individual work and coordination of many elements: acting, directing, designing, production. In this section we will examine these elements separately. Shown here is a scene that emphasizes not only acting but the manner in which the director has placed the performers, lighting, scenery and costumes. The production shown here is *An American in Paris* at the Dominion Theatre in London, which was also directed in Paris and on Broadway by Christopher Wheeldon, with sets and costumes by Bob Crowley and lighting by Natasha Katz. (©Robbie Jack/Corbis Entertainment/Getty Images)

5

ACTING FOR THE STAGE

At the heart of the theatre experience is the exchange between actors and the audience. We in the audience observe the performers on stage: their gestures, their movements. And we listen to their words. Actors, in turn, are acutely aware of us in the audience: our presence, our reactions and responses. Previously we have focused on the role of the audience at a performance; in this chapter we examine the art and craft of acting for the stage. Before we turn to the stage actor, however, we should take note of another type of performance in which we are all participants: acting in everyday life, that is, the various roles in our daily lives.

ACTING IN EVERYDAY LIFE

Two examples of acting in daily life are imitation and role playing. The first of these, *imitation*, is found on all levels of society and at all ages. Children, for example, are among the best imitators in the world, and we are often amused by a child who imitates a parent or some other grown-up: a four-year-old, for instance, who puts on a long dress, makeup, and high heels. As we grow older, imitation continues to be a part of our experience: in every class in school, from elementary school through college, there is usually one person—a clever mimic—who imitates the teacher or the principal with great humor, and sometimes with cruelty.

The second type of acting in everyday life we mentioned is *role playing*, which can generally be divided into two categories: social and personal.

Imitation To simulate or copy behavior observed in real life.

Role playing In everyday life, the acting out of a particular role by copying the expected social behavior of that position.

◀ **STAGE ACTING**
To play a character convincingly, an actor must develop both outer techniques and inner emotional resources. This is true whether performing in a classical play or a modern, realistic play. Shown here are Allison Janney and Corey Hawkins in the play Six Degrees of Separation *by John Guare at the Barrymore Theater in New York. In their performances, the actors must convey not only the feelings and emotions of their characters, but also their unique movements, gestures, and vocal qualities.* (©Sara Krulwich/The New York Times/Redux)

Social Roles

Social roles are general roles recognized by society: parent, child, police officer, store clerk, teacher, student, business executive, physician, and so on. Every culture expects certain types of behavior from people who are assigned specific social roles, sometimes resulting in stereotyping or oppressing those individuals. For many years in Western culture, for example, the roles of women as secretaries, teachers, or housewives were considered subordinate to the roles of men and the only ones deemed appropriate for them. Even today when women hold positions similar to those of men in business and the professions, they frequently receive a lower salary for the same job. The women's movement challenged the notion of subservient roles for women. So entrenched was the idea, however, that it took an entire movement to call it into question. (One aspect of this movement was *consciousness raising:* making people aware of sexist social attitudes toward women.) Before changes could begin to be made in the subordinate roles women were forced to play, everyone had to understand that these *were* social roles imposed upon them by the male-dominated society and were clearly unacceptable.

Personal Roles

Aside from social roles, we develop personal roles with our family and friends. For example, some people become braggarts, boasting of their (sometimes imaginary) feats and accomplishments and embellishing the truth to appear more impressive than they are. Others become martyrs, constantly sacrificing for others and letting the world know about it. Still others are conspirators, people who pull their friends aside to establish an air of secrecy whenever they talk. Frequently, two people fall into complementary roles: one dominant and the other submissive, one active and the other passive.

ACTING IN LIFE VERSUS ACTING ON STAGE

Some of the differences between stage acting and acting in daily life are obvious. For one thing, actors and actresses onstage are always being observed. In real life there may be observers, but their presence is not essential to an event. Bystanders on a street corner where an accident has occurred form a kind of audience, but their presence is incidental and unrelated to the accident itself. Onstage, however, the performer is always on display and often in the spotlight.

Acting onstage, too, requires a performer to play roles he or she does not play in life. A scene between a parent and child arguing about money, or between spouses or partners discussing whether or not to have children, is one thing when it is actually occurring in our lives, but something quite different onstage. Generally, the roles we play in life are genuine. A parent who accepts responsibilities toward her or his children does not just play a parent; she or he *is* a parent. A woman who writes novels does not just play a novelist; she *is* one.

In real life, a lawyer knows the law; but onstage, an actor playing the role of a lawyer may not know the difference between jurisprudence and habeas corpus, and probably has never been inside a law school. Playing widely divergent parts or parts outside their personal experience requires actors and actresses to stretch their imagination and ability. For example, a young performer at one time or another might be called on to play parts as dissimilar as the fiery, independent Antigone in the play by Sophocles; the vulnerable, love-struck Juliet in Shakespeare's

REAL-LIFE ROLES SEEN ONSTAGE
Roles onstage are often similar to roles people are called on to play in real life. Cheerleaders at athletic events are a good example. Here we see a scene from *Bring It On: The Musical,* about rival high school cheerleading squads. (©Sara Krulwich/ The New York Times/Redux)

Romeo and Juliet; and the neurotic, obsessed leading character in Strindberg's *Miss Julie.* Beyond playing different roles at different times, performers are even called on at times to *double,* that is, perform several parts in one play.

Another significant difference between acting for the stage and "acting" in life is that dramatic characters are not real people. Any stage character—Joan of Arc, Antigone, Oedipus, Hamlet, Willy Loman—is a symbol or an image of a person. Stage characters are fictions created by dramatists and performers to represent people. They remind us of people—in many cases they seem to *be* these people, but they are not. The task of the performer in attempting to make the characters onstage *appear* to be real requires not only talent but training and discipline as well.

THREE CHALLENGES OF ACTING

Theatre actors and actresses face three major challenges:

1. To make characters believable—inner truth.
2. Physical acting—the use of the voice and body.
3. Synthesis and integration—combining inner and outer skills.

To understand the first two challenges of acting, we will examine them separately. We begin with making characters believable and then turn to the craft of acting—specific physical and vocal techniques required in performance.

Making Characters Believable

One major aspect of the craft of acting is credibility: the ability to make those of us in the audience believe in the characters that appear onstage, to make the characters convincing.

The Development of Realistic Acting   From the mid-seventeenth century on, serious attempts were made to define the craft or technique of credible, natural acting. Such an approach became more important than ever at the end of the nineteenth century, when drama began to depict characters and situations close to everyday life. Three playwrights—Henrik Ibsen of Norway, August Strindberg of Sweden, and Anton Chekhov of Russia—perfected a type of drama that came to be known as ***realism***. This drama was called realistic because it closely resembled what people could identify with and verify from their own experience. In performing plays by these dramatists, not only the spirit of the individual dramatic characters but also the details of their behavior had to conform to what people saw of life around them.

The Stanislavski System: A Technique for Realistic Acting   Before the realistic drama of the late 1800s, individual actresses and actors, through their own talent and genius, had achieved believability onstage, but no one had developed a system whereby it could be taught to others and passed on to future generations. The person who eventually did this most successfully was the Russian actor and director Konstantin Stanislavski. A cofounder of the Moscow Art Theater in Russia and the director of Anton Chekhov's most important plays, Stanislavski was also an actor. By closely observing the work of great performers of his day, and by drawing on his own acting experience, Stanislavski identified and described what these gifted performers did naturally and intuitively. From his observations he compiled and then codified a series of principles and techniques.

We might assume that believable acting is simply a matter of being natural; but Stanislavski discovered first of all that acting realistically onstage is extremely artificial and difficult. He wrote:

> All of our acts, even the simplest, which are so familiar to us in everyday life, become strained when we appear behind the footlights before a public of a thousand people. That is why it is necessary to correct ourselves and learn again how to walk, sit, or lie down. It is essential to reeducate ourselves to look and see, on the stage, to listen and to hear.[1]

To achieve this "reeducation," Stanislavski said, "the actor must first of all believe in everything that takes place onstage, and most of all, he must believe what he himself is doing. And one can only believe in the truth." To give substance to his ideas, Stanislavski developed a series of exercises and techniques for the performer, among them the following.[2]

[1]Konstantin Stanislavsky, *An Actor Prepares*, Theatre Arts, New York, 1948, p. 73.
[2]Konstantin Stanislavsky, *An Actor Prepares*, Theatre Arts, New York, 1948.

Relaxation   When he observed the great actors and actresses of his day, Stanislavski noticed how fluid and lifelike their movements were. They seemed to be in a state of complete freedom and relaxation, letting the behavior of the character come through effortlessly. He concluded that unwanted tension has to be eliminated and that the performer must at all times attain a state of physical and vocal relaxation.

Concentration and observation   Stanislavski also discovered that gifted performers always appeared fully concentrated on some object, person, or event while onstage. Stanislavski referred to the extent or range of concentration as a *circle of attention*. This circle of attention can be compared to a circle of light on a darkened stage. The performer should begin with the idea that it is a small, tight circle including only himself or herself and perhaps one other person or one piece of furniture. When the performer has established a strong circle of attention, he or she can enlarge the circle outward to include the entire stage area. In this way performers will stop worrying about the audience and lose their self-consciousness.

Importance of specifics   One of Stanislavski's techniques was an emphasis on concrete details. A performer should never try to act in general, he said, and should never try to convey a feeling such as fear or love in some vague, amorphous way. In life, Stanislavski said, we express emotions in terms of specifics: an anxious woman twists a handkerchief, an angry boy throws a rock at a trash can, a nervous businessman jangles his keys. Performers must find similar concrete activities. Stanislavski points out how Shakespeare has Lady Macbeth in her sleepwalking scene—at the height of her guilt and emotional upheaval—try to rub blood off her hands.

The performer must also conceive of the situation in which a character exists—what Stanislavski referred to as the *given circumstances*—in terms of specifics. In what kind of space does an event take place: formal, informal, public, domestic? How does it feel? What is the temperature? The lighting? What has gone on just before? What is expected in the moments ahead? Again, these questions must be answered in concrete terms.

Before the twentieth century, the challenges facing performers were dictated by the very specific demands of the type of theatre in which performers appeared. Both classic Greek theatre and traditional Asian theatre stressed formal movement and stylized gestures similar to classical ballet. The chorus in Greek drama both sang and danced its odes, and Asian theatre has always had a significant component of singing and dancing. In addition, Greek performers wore masks and Asian performers often wore richly textured makeup.

In Western theatre, from the time of the Renaissance through the nineteenth century, actions onstage were not intended to replicate the movements or gestures of everyday life. For example, performers would often speak not to the character they were addressing but directly to the audience. In England during the eighteenth and nineteenth centuries, acting alternated between exaggerated and more natural styles. Throughout this period, every generation or so an actor or actress would emerge who was praised for performing in a less grandiose, more down-to-earth way. But exaggerated or not, performance before the twentieth century was more formal and stylized than the acting we are accustomed to today, especially in films and on television.

In Western theatre, from the fifth century B.C.E. in Greece to the middle of the nineteenth century, vocal demands on actors and actresses were greater than they are today. The language of plays was most often poetry; and poetry—with its demanding rhythms, sustained phrases, and exacting meters—required intensive training in order for the performer to speak the lines intelligently and distinctly. There were problems of projection, too. A Greek amphitheatre was an acoustical marvel, but it seated as many as 15,000 spectators in the open air, and throwing the voice to every part of the theatre was no small task.

In Elizabethan England, Christopher Marlowe, a contemporary of Shakespeare, wrote superb blank verse that made severe demands on performers' vocal abilities. One example is found in Marlowe's **The Tragical History of D. Faustus**. Here is a speech by Faustus to Helen of Troy, who has been called back from the dead to be with him:

> O' thou art fairer than the evening's air
> Clad in the beauty of a thousand stars;
> Brighter art thou than flaming Jupiter

> When he appear'd to hapless Semele;
> More lovely than the monarch of the sky
> In wanton Arethusa's azured arms;
> And none but thou shalt be my paramour![3]

These seven lines of verse are a single sentence and, spoken properly, will be delivered as one overall unit, with the meaning carried from one line to the next. How many of us could manage that? A fine classical actor can speak the entire passage as a whole, giving it the necessary resonance and inflection as well. Beyond that, he can stand onstage for two or three hours delivering such lines.

No one would expect an actress or actor today to perform a classical play in the manner in which it was originally presented; such a performance would no doubt seem ludicrous. Besides, we do not know exactly how classical acting looked or sounded. At the same time, it should be clear that any performer today who is appearing in a play from the past must develop a special set of skills and be able to respond successfully to a number of challenges. Not only should an actor have the necessary psychological and emotional tools—a Hamlet, for instance, who must express a wide range of emotions as well as contradictory impulses, or an Ophelia who must play a "mad scene" in which she has lost her mind—but the same actor must also master the necessary physical and vocal techniques. Physically, an actor playing Hamlet would have to move with confidence as well as with the precision of a dancer. He would also be required to climb steps and levels with ease, and since he must engage in sword fighting, he must have mastered fencing techniques.

The Social Status of the Performer

On the subject of historical acting styles, we should also note that through the centuries there has been a wide fluctuation in the social and political position of performers. First, it is important to be aware that in several key periods of theatre history, women were prohibited from performing at all. Two prime examples are the theatre of ancient Greece—the era of the playwrights Aeschylus, Sophocles, and Euripides—and the Elizabethan age, during which Shakespeare and his contemporaries wrote. In both periods women could not even appear onstage. In Roman theatre, women were

[3]Christopher Marlowe, *Doctor Faustus* (1592).

Acting requirements in the past were often different from those of today. Forceful, sometimes exaggerated movements and a powerful voice were two essentials for successful performers. Actors were expected to declaim their lines and strike impressive poses, while wearing elaborate costumes. An example from the late eighteenth century is an actress in the costume for a character in *Athalie* by Jean Racine. (©Historical Picture Archive/Getty Images)

allowed to perform, but only in a lower form of theatre known as *mime*. In Europe, during the Renaissance, acting became more professional, but the social position of actors was still problematic. Women began to appear with acting troupes in Italy and Spain; but in Spain it was required that any actress in a company be a relative (wife, mother, sister) of one of the leaders of the troupe.

The next point to be noted is that frequently in the history of acting, performers were regarded as quite low on the social scale. An early exception was the classical period in Greece. Because theatre presentations were part of a religious festival, actors were treated with dignity. Through most of theatre history, however, this was not the case. An example of the problems faced by actors is the fate of the Frenchman Molière. Though he was one of the most renowned actors and playwrights of his day, France at that time had laws preventing actors from receiving a Christian burial, and thus Molière was buried secretly at night. When women began to appear on

the English stage in the Restoration period, after 1660, they were regarded by some as on a par with courtesans or prostitutes. Other people, however, accepted them into high society, and one actress, Nell Gwynn, was a mistress of the king. During the eighteenth and nineteenth centuries there were a number of famous and celebrated actors and actresses on the European continent, in England, and in the United States. In England, when the actor Henry Irving was knighted in 1895, it was felt that actors had finally arrived socially.

In Asian theatre, performers for many centuries were primarily men, though a curious phenomenon occurred at the beginning of kabuki in Japan. Kabuki began in the early seventeenth century with all-women troupes. Social disruptions arose, however, because of feuds over the sexual services of the women, and in 1629 the shogun forbade performances of women's kabuki. From that point on, kabuki was all-male, as were nō theatre and puppet theatre, bunraku.

Inner truth   An innovative aspect of Stanislavski's work has to do with inner truth, which deals with the internal or subjective world of characters—that is, their thoughts and emotions. The early phases of Stanislavski's research took place while he was also directing the major dramas of Anton Chekhov. Plays like **The Sea Gull** and **The Cherry Orchard** have less to do with external action or what the characters say than with what the characters are feeling and thinking but often do not verbalize. It becomes apparent that Stanislavski's approach would be very beneficial in realizing the inner life of such characters. Stanislavski had several ideas about how to achieve a sense of inner truth, one being the **magic if**. *If* is a word that can transform our thoughts; through it we can imagine ourselves in virtually any situation. *"If* I suddenly became wealthy . . ." *"If* I were vacationing on a Caribbean island . . ." *"If* I had great talent . . ." *"If* that person who insulted me comes near me again . . ." The word *if* becomes a powerful lever for the mind; it can lift us out of ourselves and give us a sense of absolute certainty about imaginary circumstances.

Action on stage: What? Why? How?   Another important principle of Stanislavski's system is that all action onstage must have a purpose. This means that the performer's attention must always be focused on a series of physical actions (also called *psychophysical actions*), linked together by the circumstances of the play. Stanislavski determined these actions by asking three essential questions: What? Why? How? An action is performed, such as opening a letter (the *what*). The letter is opened because someone has said that it contains extremely damaging information about the character (the *why*). The letter is opened anxiously, fearfully (the *how*), because of the calamitous effect it might have on the character.

Through line of a role   According to Stanislavski, in order to develop continuity in a part, the actor or actress should find the **superobjective** of a character. What is it, above all else, that the character wants during the course of the play? What is the character's driving force? If a goal can be established toward which the character strives, it will give the performer an overall objective. From this objective can be developed a *through line* that can be grasped, as a skier on a ski lift grabs a towline and is carried to the top. Another term for through line is *spine*. To help develop the through line, Stanislavski urged performers to divide scenes into units (sometimes called *beats*). In each unit there is an objective, and the intermediate objectives running through a play lead ultimately to the overall objective.

Ensemble playing   Except in one-person shows, performers do not act alone; they interact with other people. Stanislavski was aware that many performers tend to "stop acting," or lose their concentration, when they are not the main characters in a scene or when someone else is talking. This tendency destroys the through line and causes the performer to move into and out of a role. That, in turn, weakens **ensemble playing**—the playing together of all the performers.

Stanislavski and Psychophysical Action   Stanislavski began to develop his technique in the early twentieth century, and at first he emphasized the inner aspects of training; for example, various ways of getting in touch with the performer's unconscious. Beginning around 1917, however, he began to look more and more at purposeful action, or what he called *psychophysical action*. A student at one of his lectures that year took note of the change: "Whereas action previously had been taught as the expression of a previously established 'emotional state,' it is now action itself which predominates and is the key to the psychological."[4] Rather than seeing emotions as leading to action,

Magic if   Stanislavski's acting exercise, which requires the performer to ask, "How would I react *if* I were in this character's position?"

Superobjective   What the character wants above all else during the course of the play.

Ensemble playing   Acting that stresses the total artistic unity of a group performance rather than individual performances.

[4]Jean Benedetti, *Stanislavski*, Routledge, New York, 1988, p. 217.

Stanislavski came to believe that it was the other way around: purposeful action undertaken to fulfill a character's goals was the most direct route to the emotions.

Modern Approaches to Realistic Acting in the United States   In the second half of the twentieth century, there were three broad approaches to actors' training in the United States. Two of these derived from the methods of Stanislavski. In the 1930s and 1940s a number of performers and directors in the United States became greatly interested in the ideas of Stanislavski. One of these, Lee Strasberg, a founder of the Actors Studio in New York City, focused on the inner aspects of Stanislavskian theory. Strasberg emphasized a technique called *emotional recall*, a tool intended to help performers achieve a sense of emotional truth onstage. By recalling sensory impressions of an experience in the past (such as what a room looked like, and the temperature and any prevalent odors in the room), emotions associated with that experience are aroused and can be used as the basis of feelings called for in a role in a play.

> **Emotional recall**
> Stanislavski's exercise, which helps the performer to present realistic emotions. The performer feels a character's emotion by thinking of the conditions surrounding an event in his or her own life that led to a similar emotion.

Though the teachings of Strasberg and his followers were successful with certain performers, other acting teachers, such as Stella Adler (1902–1992) and Sanford Meisner (1905–1997), felt that Strasberg emphasized the inner aspects of acting to the exclusion of everything else. Following the lead of Stanislavski in his later approach with psychophysical action, they balanced the emphasis on inner resources with the inclusion of given circumstances and purposeful action.

Other well-known acting teachers who emphasize approaches to creating realistic performances are: Uta Hagen (1919–2004), Robert Cohen (1938–), Robert Benedetti (1939–), and playwright David Mamet (b. 1947) working with actor William H. Macy (b. 1950).

Hagen, in her book *Respect for Acting,* places a large emphasis on emotional recall and memory in general. She provides a number of exercises that enable the students to pull from past experiences in their own lives as a means of reaching the emotions required within the context of any given role. Hagen's idea is not to allow the student to become overwhelmed by past emotion, but to use it as a springboard into the action of the play.

photo essay

The Actor's Range

In theatre, performers are often called on to play a wide range of diverse parts. Frequently, too, actors portray people unlike themselves. Many performers welcome this challenge. An American actor who has demonstrated tremendous versatility is John Douglas Thompson, shown here in five contrasting roles.

John Douglas Thompson as the lead in Eugene O'Neill's *The Emperor Jones*, Irish Repertory Theatre, 2009.
(©Sara Krulwich/The New York Times/Redux)

John Douglas Thompson as *Richard III* in a production at Shakespeare & Company, Lenox, MA. (©Kevin Sprague/ Studio Two)

Kate Arrington, John Douglas
Thompson, Salvatore Inzerillo in Eugene
O'Neill's *The Iceman Cometh* at the
Goodman Theatre. (©Liz Lauren, Courtesy
Goodman Theatre)

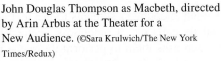

John Douglas Thompson as Macbeth, directed
by Arin Arbus at the Theater for a
New Audience. (©Sara Krulwich/The New York
Times/Redux)

John Douglas Thompson as Othello, Merritt
Janson as Desdemona, directed by Tony
Simotes, Shakespeare & Company,
2008. (©Kevin Sprague/Studio Two)

THE CRAFT OF ACTING: PHYSICAL DEMANDS

Among the many skills involved in becoming a performer are various vocal and physical skills—speaking clearly and distinctly, "projecting" the voice into the auditorium, moving gracefully, and meeting a variety of physical challenges, including sword fights, such as the one shown here. The scene is from a production of Tony Kushner's adaptation of Pierre Corneille's *The Illusion,* at A Noise Within Theatre in Pasadena, CA.

(©Craig Schwartz)

In *Acting One,* Robert Cohen encourages students to use text as an instrument of action. In an exercise that he calls the "Contentless Scene," he has students memorize the same text. He then asks them to perform the scene but changes the given circumstances of the scene each time. The outcome is the obvious realization that the words are not nearly as important as the meaning behind them. And, clearly, without solid given circumstances, actors are simply saying lines instead of using those lines to further the action of the play.

Robert Benedetti in *The Actor at Work* focuses on the actor's body and how performers can use it to help shape character. Using a variety of movement exercises, Benedetti encourages students to explore elements of rhythm, time, weight, intensity, and space through improvisational work. These exercises allow the students to start with the "outside" (physical) aspects of a character's definition. Once the physical form is found, they can then use it to define the character's inner life (emotion).

Playwright David Mamet and actor William H. Macy, in their approach, known as "practical aesthetics," employ elements of Stanislavski and Meisner. Actors analyze a scene to discover what is literally happening as well as what his or her character wants from the others in that scene.

There are, of course, many other teachers and professional schools of acting. For example, Chicago's Steppenwolf Theatre offers acting training, emphasizing their "Chicago style" of realistic performance. The important thing for students of acting is to explore different methods of and approaches to acting, such as those outlined above, and to decide which techniques and types of training—or which combination of these—work best for them. Ultimately each individual actor must develop his or her own methodology.

Physical Acting: Voice and Body

We have been looking at training that helps actors make stage characters truthful and believable. We turn now to a second aspect of actor training: the instruments of the performer, specifically the voice and the body.

Part 3   Creating Theatre: The Production

IN FOCUS: THE PROFESSION OF ACTING AND TECHNOLOGY

The profession of the actor has been impacted in very unique ways by the development of technology. *Backstage*, an online and print magazine that provides information for those working in theatre, film, and other media, published an article entitled "How Has Technology Changed Your Acting Career?"[5] The actors' responses were intriguing and suggest ongoing changes to the profession of the actor.

Many pointed to the ability to access casting sites online from wherever they are living or performing, on any mobile device, in order to request auditions for theatre productions, films, and television series. The opportunity to audition via Skype or FaceTime without having to change geographical location allows the actor to be engaged with the global theatre and media industries. One multilingual performer noted that she was able to act in a production in France while searching for casting opportunities in Los Angeles.

Resumes and headshots can be photoshopped and digitally manipulated so that an actor can, for example, be seen in different costumes or against various backgrounds. These can now be e-mailed or accessed through a performer's website. (Many theatre artists maintain websites that contain links to resumes, photos, and videos.) Actors may create YouTube presentations of auditions and past performances that can be accessed electronically. Actors can also communicate with their fans through Facebook and LinkedIn pages as well as Twitter accounts. (Stars, of course, have staff who sometimes oversee those accounts.)

Even preparing for an audition has changed. Actors can "run their lines" for a monologue with online audio programs and apps. Accents and dialects can be Googled and found on the web. There are digital musical rehearsal apps that allow musical theatre performers to hear and learn their parts via their smartphone, tablet, or computer.

A few theorists and theatre artists have even suggested that actors could be replaced by technology, using 3D images or other digitally created representations. An extreme example is the music-theatre production by German composer Heiner Goebbels, *Stifter's Things* (2008), in which five upside-down, remotely controlled grand pianos that performed and even moved threateningly toward the audience on runners were the only "actors." The production combined light, sound, and recorded text. The question, of course, remains: is this a unique concert, an art installation, or is it theatre without actors?

Still, as one of the actors in the *Backstage* article emphasized, once rehearsals and performances begin, the work of the actor, in most instances, is still "old fashioned" or traditional. Even with all the technology surrounding the actor in the rehearsal room and on stage, the human dynamic between the live actor and the audience is indispensable in any kind of traditional theatre and is why theatre has survived.

[5]http://www.backstage.com/advice-for-actors/professional-tips/how-has-technology-changed-your-acting-career/

Physical elements have always been important in the art of acting. Traditional theatre makes strong demands on the performer's body. In Shakespeare, for instance, performers must frequently run up and down steps or ramps, confront other characters in sword fights, and enact prolonged death scenes. Anyone who has seen an impressive sword fight onstage senses how difficult it must be. A duel, in which the combatants strike quickly at one another—clashing swords continually without hitting each other—resembles a ballet in its precision and grace, and it entails a great deal of physical exertion. Adept physical movement is also required in modern realistic acting. For example, an activity in a modern play analogous to a sword fight would be a headlong fall down a flight of stairs or two people engaged in a knife fight, like the one in Arthur Miller's *A View from the Bridge*.

PERFORMING IN CLASSICS TODAY

Contemporary performers in classic plays must have vocal training to be able to speak and project poetry properly; they must have the physical training necessary to engage in sword fights and other activities; and they must be familiar with the historical eras of the playwrights and of the texts they are to perform. Here we see Stephen Fry as Malvolio and Mark Rylance as Olivia in Shakespeare's *Twelfth Night,* in a Shakespeare's Globe production with an all-male cast directed by Tim Carroll. (©Geraint Lewis)

As to the importance of voice training, because of microphones and sound amplifications, today we have increasingly lost our appreciation of the power of the human voice. But in the past, public speakers from Cicero to Abraham Lincoln stirred men and women with their oratory; and throughout its history, the stage has provided a natural platform for stirring speeches. Beginning with the Greeks and continuing through the Elizabethans, the French and Spanish theatres of the seventeenth century, and other European theatres at the close of the nineteenth century, playwrights wrote magnificent lines that performers, having honed their vocal skills to a fine point, delivered with zest. Any performer today who intends to act in a revival of a traditional play must learn to speak and project stage verse, which requires much the same kind of vocal power and breath control as opera.

In order to develop projection and balance it with credibility, a performer must train and rehearse extensively. For example, an actor or actress might use breathing exercises, controlling the breath from the diaphragm rather than the throat so that vocal reproduction will have power and can be sustained. Many of these exercises are similar to those used by singers. Also, head, neck, and shoulder exercises can be used to relax the muscles in those areas, thus freeing the throat for ease of projection. In the nearby chart we see a group of elementary vocal and body exercises. It must be stressed that these are basic exercises that represent only the earliest beginnings of a true regimen of exercises for the voice and body.

The Actor's Instrument: Voice and Body

Throughout the twentieth century, at the same time that many acting teachers were focusing on the inner life of the actor, another group of teachers and theoreticians were turning to a different aspect, the physical side of performing. This includes

Part 3   Creating Theatre: The Production

IN FOCUS: WARM-UP EXERCISES FOR BODY AND VOICE

To give an indication of the types of exercises performers must undertake during their years of training—and during their careers as professionals—it is interesting to look at some samples of warm-up exercises. The exercises here are designed to relax the body and the voice. The following are typical warm-up exercises for *body* movement:

1. Lie on your back; beginning with the feet, tense and relax each part of the body—knees, thighs, abdomen, chest, neck—moving up to the face. Note the difference in the relaxation of various muscles and of the body generally after the exercise is completed.

2. Stand with feet parallel, approximately as far apart as the width of the shoulders. Lift one foot off the ground and loosen all the joints in the foot, ankle, and knee. Repeat with the other foot off the ground. Put the feet down and move to the hip, spine, arms, neck, etc., loosening all joints.

3. Stand with feet parallel. Allow all tension to drain out of the body through the feet. In the process, bend the knees, straighten the pelvis, and release the lower back.

4. Begin walking in a circle; walk on the outside of the feet, then on the inside, then on the toes, and then on the heels. Notice what this does to the rest of the body. Try changing other parts of the body in a similar fashion and observe the effect on feelings and reactions.

5. Imagine the body filled with either helium or lead. Notice the effect of each of these sensations, both while standing in place and while walking. Do the same with one body part at a time—each arm, each leg, the head, etc.

The following *vocal* exercises free the throat and vocal cords:

1. Standing, begin a lazy, unhurried stretch. Reach with your arms to the ceiling, meanwhile lengthening and widening the whole of your back. Yawn as you take in a deep breath and hum on an exhalation. Release your torso so that it rests down toward your legs. Yawn on another deep breath and hum on an exhalation. On an inhalation, roll up the spine until you are standing with your arms at your sides. Look at something on the ceiling and then at something on the floor; then let your head return to a balance point, so that the neck and shoulder muscles are relaxed.

2. Put your hands on your ribs, take a deep breath, and hum a short tune. Repeat several times. Hum an *m* or *n* up and down the scale. Drop your arms; lift the shoulders an inch and drop them, releasing all tension.

3. Take a deep breath and with the palm of your hand push gently down on your stomach as you exhale. Do this several times. Exhale on sighs and then on vowels.

4. Standing, yawn with your throat and mouth open and be aware of vibrations in the front of your mouth, just behind your front teeth, as you vocalize on the vowels *ee, ei,* and *o.* Take these up and down the scales. Sing a simple song and then say it, and see if you have just as much vibration in your mouth when you are speaking as when you are singing.

5. Using a light, quick tempo, shift to a tongue twister (such as *Peter Piper picked a peck of pickled peppers*). Feel a lively touch of the tongue on the gum ridge on the *t*'s and *d*'s, and a bounce of the back of the tongue on the *k*'s and *g*'s. Feel the bouncing action on the lips on the *p*'s and *b*'s.

Source: Provided by Professor John Sipes of University of Tennessee–Knoxville and Emeritus Professor Barbara F. Acker of Arizona State University.

the freeing and development of the voice and body and combining these with improvisation to create maximum flexibility, relaxation, and imagination in the actor's instrument—his or her voice and body.

There were a number of key figures who contributed to this movement. For example, in the second and third decades of the twentieth century, the Russian director Vsevolod Meyerhold (1874–1942) developed a program called *biomechanics* that emphasized physical exercises and full control of the body, in the manner of circus performers such as acrobats and trapeze artists. In France in the 1920s, Jacques

THE FORMAL GESTURES OF ASIAN THEATRE

In most Asian theatre, acting requires careful, precise, formal gestures. The first example here is a scene from *Journey to the West,* a piece from Beijing (or Peking) opera in China (top). The second example is an actor in a performance of traditional kathakali dance-theatre in India (bottom). Note the poses, the physical requirements, and the dexterity that are required, as well as the elaborate costumes, heavy makeup, and striking headpieces.

(top: ©TAO Images Limited/Alamy Stock Photo; bottom: ©lakhesis/123RF RF)

Copeau (1878–1949) incorporated such disciplines as mime, masks, Italian commedia dell'arte, and Asian acting into his system of training. Beginning in mid-century and continuing for the next fifty years, a Frenchman, Jacques Lecoq (1921–1999), ran an influential school in Paris dedicated to explaining and exploring the physical side of performance. In addition to emphasizing the elements on which Copeau concentrated, Lecoq also incorporated a clown figure in his work.

Along with European influences, there has also been a strong global presence in the new approaches to actor training. A good example is Asian theatre. Stylization and symbolism characterize the acting of the classical theatres of India, China, and Japan. To achieve the absolute control, the concentration, and the mastery of the body and nerves necessary to carry out the stylized movements, performers in the various classical Asian theatres train for years under the supervision of master teachers. Every movement of these performers is prescribed and carefully controlled, combining elements of formal ballet, pantomime, and sign language. Each gesture tells a story and means something quite specific—contributing to a true symbolism of physical movement.

ACTING TRAINING FROM OTHER DISCIPLINES
Actors' training today often involves exercises and other activities from related disciplines such as circus routines, juggling, acrobatics, and Asian martial arts. A good example is tai chi, a refined form of martial arts from China, here being practiced in a park. (©Inge King)

One Asian discipline, not from theatre but from martial arts, which modern acting teachers have found helpful is tai chi chuan, commonly called *tai chi*. Unlike some martial arts, tai chi is not aggressive: it is a graceful, gentle exercise regimen performed widely by men, women, and children in China. It has spread to other countries, where it is sometimes practiced in conjunction with meditation or body awareness. The movements of tai chi are stylized and often seem to be carried out in slow motion. Among other things, tai chi requires concentration and control, both valuable qualities for a performer. The Japanese director Tadashi Suzuki (1939–) developed a training technique, again taken from classical Japanese practices, emphasizing the connection between the feet and the ground underneath. Consciousness of this connection is accomplished by exercises involving "stomping."

An approach to training that originated in the United States and has gained acceptance and wider use in our contemporary theatre is known as *viewpoints theory*. Based on ideas from the avant-garde choreographer Merce Cunningham (1919–2009) and the experimental director Jerzy Grotowski (1933–1999), it combines elements of dance and stage movement with concepts of time and space. The director Anne Bogart (1951–), one of its chief proponents, feels that viewpoints theory provides a new vocabulary for certain elements that have always been significant in performance: spatial relationships onstage, movement, and the notion of time, among others.

In the United States in the twenty-first century the emphasis on physical movement—training in the use of the voice and the body—has become more pronounced and widespread than ever. In the words of author David Bridel in an article in *American Theatre* magazine:

> Body awareness and alignment, mask work, clowning and circus skills, physical characterization, spatial relationships, ensemble work, improvisation, games, mime . . . so many forms of movement training exist today, and so many specialists work in these related fields, that the opportunity to connect the craft of acting with the movement of the body has never been richer.[6]

[6]David Bridel, "In the Beginning Was the Body," *American Theatre*, January, 2011.

Today, no one approach, no one master, no one technique appears to have become universally recognized as the single authority in the field. For that matter, the belief that actors need to study many of these approaches was underscored in the July 7, 2015 *Backstage* article, "7 Movement Techniques All Actors Should Study." Rather, teachers, coaches, and directors draw on a wide variety of sources, including those mentioned above as well as others, to develop their individual approaches to training the voice and body. The field also goes by various names: body movement, physical theatre, and a term favored by many, *physical acting*.

As a way of integrating and unifying various approaches to body and voice training, many acting teachers emphasize a process called *centering*. This is a way of pulling everything together and allowing the performer to eliminate any blocks that impede either the body or the voice. *Centering* involves locating the place—roughly in the middle of the torso—where all the lines of force in the body come together. When performers are able to "center" themselves, they achieve a balance, a freedom, and a flexibility they could rarely find otherwise.

TRAINING FOR MUSICAL THEATRE
Along with the classics and various types of theatre from other nations, the American musical, with its physical and vocal demands, requires extensive training. A prime example is the exuberant dancing by the men in the Broadway musical *Newsies,* choreographed by Christopher Gattelli, directed by Jeff Calhoun, with music by Alan Menken, lyrics by Jack Feldman. (©Sara Krulwich/The New York Times/Redux)

PLAYING YOUR PART:
EXPERIENCING THEATRE

1. Read a speech from Shakespeare aloud in class or to yourself. Why would this speech be difficult for an actor? What are some of the challenges an actor would face in bringing this speech to life?

2. Remember a situation recently that made you happy. Re-create the circumstances in your mind. Where were you? Whom were you with? Can you once again feel the emotions you felt during that situation? Is this similar to an acting exercise developed by Stanislavski?

3. Make a fist. Now make it tighter and tighter. Does it change how you are feeling emotionally? Does this help you understand how an actor might approach developing an emotional moment in a play physically?

4. Analyze why you felt a recent film performance was successful. Describe how the main performer brought his or her character to life.

5. Attend a rehearsal at your university or community theatre. Then attend the final performance. What changes were made between the rehearsal and the performance by one of the actors in the production? Explain how the change affected the performance.

All this should make it clear that to master the many techniques required to play a variety of roles and to be at ease onstage—moving and speaking with authority, purpose, and conviction—performers must undergo arduous training and be genuinely dedicated to their profession.

Training for Special Forms of Theatre

Certain types of theatre and theatre events require special discipline or training. For example, musical theatre obviously requires talent in singing and dancing. Coordination is also important in musical theatre: the members of a chorus must frequently sing and dance in unison. Pantomime is another demanding category of performance: without words or props, a performer must indicate everything by physical suggestion, convincingly lifting an imaginary box or walking against an imaginary wind.

Various forms of modern avant-garde and experimental theatre also require special techniques. A good example is Samuel Beckett's *Happy Days,* in which an actress is buried onstage in a mound of earth up to her waist in the first act, and up to her neck in the second. She must carry on her performance through the entire play while virtually immobile. In some types of avant-garde theatre, the performers become acrobats, make human pyramids, or are used like pieces of furniture. In the theatres of Robert Wilson, Mabou Mines, and similar groups, the elements of story, character, and text are minimized or even eliminated. The stress, rather than being on a narrative or on exploring recognizable characters, is on the visual and ritualistic aspects of theatre, like a series of tableaux or a moving collage.

Stage movement in this approach to theatre is often closely related to dance; thus the performers must have the same discipline, training, and control as dancers. In Wilson's work, performers are frequently called on either to move constantly or to remain perfectly still. In *A Letter to Queen Victoria,* two performers turn continuously in circles like dervishes for long periods of time—perhaps thirty or forty minutes. In other works by Wilson, performers must remain frozen like statues.

Chapter 5 *Acting for the Stage*

125

Synthesis and Integration

The demands made on performers by experimental and avant-garde theatres are only the most recent example of the rigorous, intensive training that acting generally requires. The goal of all this training—both internal and external—is to create for the performer an instrument that is flexible, resourceful, and disciplined. Above all, the actor must bring together the inner approach to acting, the work on truthfulness and believability, with the physical aspects discussed above. He or she must combine inner and outer into one indivisible whole. What is important to remember is that whatever the starting point, the end result must be a synthesis of these two aspects. The inner emotions and feelings and the outer physical and vocal characteristics become one.

Only then will the character be forcefully and convincingly portrayed. This process is termed *integration*. When a performer is approaching a role in a play, the first task is to read and analyze the script. The actress or actor must discover the *superobjective* of the character she or he is playing and put together not only the *spine* of the role but the many smaller moments, each with its own objective and given circumstances. The next challenge is to begin specific work on the role. In taking this step, some performers begin with the *outer* aspects of the character—with

THE SPECIAL DEMANDS OF ACTING

At times performing makes exceedingly strong demands, requiring performers to convey a range and depth of emotions, or to transform themselves in terms of age, mood, and the like. A good example is Samuel Beckett's *Happy Days,* in which the actress playing Winnie—in this case, Fiona Shaw—must perform while buried in a mound of sand up to her waist, and later up to her neck. This production was directed by Deborah Warner at the National Theatre in London in 2006. (©Robbie Jack/ Corbis Entertainment/Getty Images)

Puppetry in its various forms (puppets, marionettes, shadow puppets) has a long and honorable history. Remarkably, it emerged independently in widely separated parts of the world: in Indonesia, in Japan, in sections of Europe, and among Native Americans in the far northwest of what is now the United States.

In whatever form, the puppet figure is the image, reflection, and embodiment of a theatrical character and, therefore, a replacement for the actor. Puppets can run the gamut of emotions. They can be evil, demonic figures; they can be eerie, otherworldly creatures; they can be wildly comic, as in Punch and Judy shows when they biff one another across the head and knock one another down; they can be intensely human, as in the suffering characters in Japanese bunraku. In short, when puppets are onstage, audiences usually experience these silent, nonhuman characters as real people.

It should be noted as well that while puppet or marionette characters are often either comic or tragic figures, they are also frequently employed as advocates for a political point of view. The Bread and Puppet Theatre of San Francisco, founded by Peter Schuman (1934–), features larger-than-life, exaggerated figures made of papier-mâché. This theatre began with protests against the Vietnam War but has continued, often with the figures proceeding down city streets, in protests against all wars, including the Iraq War.

Puppet characters are created and manipulated in various ways. In Indonesia and other parts of Southeast Asia, two kinds of puppets were developed. One kind is rod puppets, so called because the movements of these puppets are controlled by rods attached to the head and limbs and operated by one or more persons, from either above or below. (Though they are most often associated with Southeast Asia, rod puppets, nearly life-size, were developed as well on the island of Sicily in the Mediterranean.) The other type of puppet popular in Southeast Asia—in Java and Bali as well as Indonesia—is the shadow puppet. In this case, silhouette figures, often made of leather, are highlighted on a screen that is lit from behind.

Marionettes are puppets controlled by strings attached to the head, arms, and legs, and operated from above. A unique type of puppet is the *bunraku* puppet from Japan, which will be discussed in more detail later. Originating in the late seventeenth century, it was firmly established by the eighteenth century and has continued to this day. In the early eighteenth century, one of the most famous playwrights of all time, Chikamatsu Monzaemon, wrote masterful plays for *bunraku* theatre. In the case of *bunraku* figures, which today are roughly two-thirds life-size, one man operates the feet, another operates the left hand, and a third controls the face, head, and right hand.

Probably the puppet figures most familiar to Western audiences are hand puppets, operated by a person who has one or two hands inside the puppet itself. Among the immediately recognizable hand puppets are the Muppets, featuring such popular and enduring characters as Kermit the Frog and Miss Piggy. Another example of hand puppets onstage appeared in the successful Broadway production of the musical *Avenue Q* (2003) as well as in the dark comedy *Hand to God* (2011). Remarkable recent examples of puppetry were the horses and other animals created for the play *War Horse* (2007). Puppetry remains, and will continue to remain, a vital art form in its own right, and an important adjunct to live theatre.

Shown here is a rehearsal for the production of *War Horse* at the National Theatre in London. The actors are working with the magnificent, life-sized puppet representing the horse. (©Graeme Robertson/eyevine/Redux)

Avant-garde theatre often requires special training and techniques— acrobatics, tumbling, mime, and special control of voice and body. Here we see Michael C. Hall as Newton and Amy Lennox as Elly in David Bowie's and Enda Walsh's *Lazarus* directed by Ivo van Hove at the Kings Cross Theatre in London, England. (©Robbie Jack/ Corbis Entertainment/ Getty Images)

a walk, a posture, or a peculiar vocal delivery. They get a sense of how the character looks in terms of makeup and other characteristics, such as a mustache or hairstyle. They consider the clothes the character wears and any idiosyncrasies of speech or movement, such as a limp or a swagger. Only then will they move on to the inner aspects of the character: how the character feels; how the character reacts to people and events; what disturbs the character's emotional equilibrium; what fears, hopes, and dreams the character has.

Other performers, by contrast, begin with the *internal* aspects: with the feelings and emotions of the character. These performers delve deeply into the psyche of the character to try to understand and duplicate what the character feels inside. Only after doing this will they go on to develop the outer characteristics. Still other performers work on both aspects—inner and outer—simultaneously. Finally, we must realize that although a competent, well-trained performer may become a successful actress or actor, another ingredient is required in order to electrify an audience as truly memorable stage artists do. This results from intangibles— qualities that cannot be taught in acting schools—that distinguish an acceptable, accomplished actor or actress from one who ignites the stage. *Presence, charisma, personality, star quality*—these are among the terms used to describe a performer who communicates directly and kinetically with the audience. Whatever term one uses, the electricity and excitement of theatre are enhanced immeasurably by performers who possess this indefinable attribute.

EVALUATING PERFORMANCES

As observers, we study the techniques and problems of acting so that we will be able to understand and evelute the performances we see. If a performer is unconvincing in a part, we know that he or she has not mastered a technique for truthful acting. We recognize that a performer who moves awkwardly or cannot be heard clearly has not been properly trained in body movement or vocal projection. We learn to notice how well performers play together: whether they listen to one another and respond appropriately. We also observe how well performers establish and maintain contact with the audience.

1. What is the most convincing performance you've seen, where you felt the actor on stage was really the person being portrayed? What was it about the performance that made it believable? In contrast, what was the least convincing and effective performance you have seen? Explain why this was so.

2. In Shakespearean and other classic plays, the actors often speak in verse. In what way are the various vocal techniques described in this chapter important to actors in preparing to play a role in this kind of play and in the performance itself?

3. Identify a scene in a play in which two, three, or four actors are locked in conflict. What can individual actors do to hold the attention of the audience and make their actions and feelings convincing? How do you think these actors can best prepare for conflict scenes?

4. Read either *Miss Julie* or *A Doll's House*, both of which are available online. What kinds of background information would the actors in these plays need to know? What are the physical attributes actors would need to create for some of the key characters? Choose one scene and one character and discuss what is motivating the character. How might you employ some of Stanislavski's concepts in order to bring the character to life?

NOTE: *A Doll's House* is also available in *Anthology of Living Theatre,* Third Edition, by Edwin Wilson and Alvin Goldfarb.

There are, therefore, some key questions we may ask ourselves about the acting in a production:

1. Were the performers believable, given the requirements of the play? If they were believable, how did they seem to accomplish this? If they were not believable, what occurred to impair or destroy their believability?

2. Identify the performers you considered most successful. Citing specifics from the production, note what they did well: particular gestures, lines, or moments. For example, how did the performer's voice sound? How did she or he interpret the role?

3. If there were performers you did not like, identify them and explain why you did not like them. Give concrete examples to explain why their performances were less successful. (As you discuss this, be sure to separate the performer from the role. For example, you can dislike a character but admire the performance.)

4. Acting is more than a collection of individual performances. The entire company needs to work as a unit (as noted earlier, this is sometimes called ensemble): each member of the cast must not only perform her or his own role but also support the other performers. Discuss how the performers related or failed to relate to one another. Did they listen to each other and respond? Did anyone seem to be "showing off" and ignoring the others?

Before leaving the subject of the performer, we should note that actors and actresses have always held a fascination for audiences. In some cases this is because they portray larger-than-life characters; it can also result from the exceptional talent they bring to their performances. Also, of course, some performers have personal charisma or appeal. Theatre audiences have often responded to stars onstage in the same way that people tend to respond to a rock star or a film star. There is something in these personalities that audiences find immensely attractive or intriguing. Moreover, the personal lives of actors are often of great interest to the public, and some people find it difficult to separate a stage character from the offstage woman or man.

SUMMARY

1. All human beings engage in certain forms of acting; imitation and role playing are excellent examples of acting in everyday life.

2. Acting onstage differs from acting in everyday life, for several reasons—including the fact that a stage actor or actress is always being observed by an audience, and the fact that acting for the stage involves playing roles with which the performer may have no direct experience in life.

3. Historically, stage performances have required exceptional physical and vocal skills: the ability to move with agility and grace and to engage in such actions as sword fights and death scenes; the ability to deal with poetic devices (meter, imagery, alliteration, etc.); the skill to project the voice to the farthest reaches of the theatre space.

4. Acting is a difficult, demanding profession. Despite its glamour, it calls for arduous training and preparation. Looking at what is called for in a role like Hamlet gives some idea of the challenges involved.

5. From the end of the nineteenth century to the present day, many plays have been written in a very realistic, lifelike style. The characters in these plays resemble ordinary people in their dialogue, behavior, etc. Presenting them requires that performers make the characters they portray believable and convincing.

6. A Russian director, Konstantin Stanislavski, developed a system or method of acting to enable performers to believe in the "truth" of what they say and do. His suggestions included applying techniques of relaxation and concentration; dealing with specific objects and feelings (a handkerchief, a glass of water, etc.); using the power of fantasy or imagination (the "magic if") to achieve a sense of inner truth in a role; using psychophysical action; developing a *spine,* or *through line,* which runs through a role from the beginning to the end of a play; and playing together as an ensemble.

7. In the later stages of his work on actor training, Stanislavski moved from an emphasis on internal elements to more external ones—to what he called *psychological action.* Rather than emotion leading to action, he suggested that action leads to emotion.

8. Exercises and tasks have been developed to train performers. These include numerous physical and vocal exercises and techniques taken from other disciplines such as tai chi and the circus. "Centering" is often emphasized as a part of body and voice training.

9. Avant-garde theatre and some other theatres make additional demands on the performer with regard to voice and body training. The voice is sometimes used to emit odd sounds—screams, grunts, and the like. The body must perform feats of acrobatics and gymnastics.

10. The end result must be a synthesis or integration of the inner and outer aspects of acting.

11. Audience members should familiarize themselves with the problems and techniques of acting in order to judge performances properly.

THE DIRECTOR AND THE PRODUCER

6

When we see a theatre performance, our most immediate connection is with the actresses and actors onstage. We begin to identify with the characters they play and absorb the situations in which they find themselves. Behind the performances, however, is the work of another creative person—the *director*. She or he, with the support of the stage manager, rehearses the performers and coordinates their work with that of others, such as the designers, to make certain the event is performed appropriately, intelligently, and excitingly. The director oversees all of the choices made for a production in order to create a unified whole under a unified vision. In this chapter, we will look at the role of the director, and also at the role of the producer or manager—the person who is responsible for the management and business aspects of theatre.

Director In American usage, the person responsible for the overall unity of a production and for coordinating the work of contributing artists. The American director is the equivalent of the British producer and the French *metteur-en-scène* ("meh-TURR ahn SENN").

THE THEATRE DIRECTOR

The director is the person who works most closely with performers in the theatre, guiding them in shaping their performances. When a new play is being presented, the director also works closely with the playwright. The director is responsible, as well, for coordinating other aspects of the production, such as the work of the scene, costume, lighting, and sound designers. The stage manager communicates the breadth of the director's conceptual vision daily with every production area to clarify ongoing production and rehearsal choices.

◀ **THE DIRECTOR SHAPES A PRODUCTION**
The director of a production works closely with the cast and the designers (scenic, costumes, lighting, sound). The director gives shape to the arc of the play or musical, and determines its style, its pace, and the way the actors create their characters and interact with one another. If the production is a new play or musical, the director also collaborates with the playwright and the lyricist and composer. Shown here is director Diane Paulus, on the left, demonstrating a gesture to actor Jeremy Jordan in a scene from Finding Neverland *in a production at the ART theatre in Boston.* (©Boston Globe/Getty Images)

For many of us, as audience members, the director's work on a production is one of the least obvious components. Other elements, such as performers, scenery, and costumes, are onstage and immediately visible to us, and the words of the playwright are heard throughout the performance. But we are often not aware that the way performers speak and move, the way the scenery looks, and the way the lights change colors and intensity often originate with the director. After the playwright, the director is usually the first person to become involved in the creative process of a production, and the choices made by the director at every step along the way have a great deal to do with determining whether the ultimate experience will be satisfactory for us, the members of the audience.

While the playwright incorporates a point of view toward the material dramatized in a script—it may be, for example, a tragedy, a melodrama, or a comedy—it is crucial for the director to understand this point of view and translate it into terms relevant to the production. The director must then make both the playwright's and his or her point of view clear to the performers, designers, and other artists and technicians involved. Although they work together, these artists and technicians must of necessity work on segments of the production rather than the entire enterprise. During rehearsals, for instance, the performers are much too busy working on their own roles and their interactions with each other to worry much about scenery. To take another example, a performer who appears only in the first act of a two-act play has no control over what happens in the second act. The one person who does have an overall perspective is the director. The person who aids in communicating this perspective to everyone involved on a continuing basis is the production stage manager, the only other member of the production team to experience the entire rehearsal process with the director.

Directors get their training in a variety of ways. Many of them begin as actors and actresses and find that they have a talent for working with other people and for coordinating the work of designers as well as performers. Others train in the many academic institutions that have specific programs for directors. These include large universities with theatre as part of a liberal arts focus as well as special conservatories and institutes.

THE TRADITIONAL DIRECTOR

In this chapter we will look at three approaches to directing: traditional, auteur, and postmodern. We begin with the traditional approach, which might also be called a text-based method. The starting point, or the foundation, of the traditional director's work is the script. It might be a well-known play by Shakespeare, Ibsen, or Strindberg, or a more recent work, such as one by Lorraine Hansberry, August Wilson, or Sarah Ruhl. The play might also be a new script by a very young or emerging playwright.

The Director and the Script

For the most part, we experience theatre as a unified event. But, as pointed out before, theatre is a complex art involving not one or two elements but many simultaneously: script, performance, costumes, scenery, lighting, and point of view. These diverse elements—a mixture of the tangible and intangible—must be brought together into an organic whole, and that is the responsibility of the director.

Choosing a Script   Frequently, the director chooses the script to be produced. Generally it is a play to which the director is attracted or for which he or she feels a special affinity. If the director does not actually choose the script but is asked to direct it by a playwright or a producer, he or she must still understand and appreciate the material. The director's attraction to the script and basic understanding of it are important in launching a production. Once the script is chosen, the actual work on the production begins.

If the play is new and has never been tested in production, the director may see problems in the script, which must be corrected before rehearsals begin. The director will have a series of meetings with the playwright to iron out the difficulties ahead of time. The director may feel, for example, that the leading character is not clearly defined, or that a clash of personalities between two characters never reaches a climax. If the playwright agrees with the director's assessment, he or she will revise the manuscript. Generally there is considerable give-and-take between the director and the playwright in these preliminary sessions, as well as during the rehearsal period. The stage manager must maintain well-organized rehearsal documentation of possible script revisions for the playwright and director to discuss outside rehearsals. Ideally, there should be a spirit of cooperation, compromise, and mutual respect in this relationship.

Once the script is selected, the director begins analyzing it and preparing a production. There is no one way a director should go about this: Individual directors adopt their own personal approach. One method of undertaking this task was suggested by the work of the Russian director Konstantin Stanislavski. In this case, an initial step is to determine the *spine* of the play.

The "Spine" of the Play   The spine of the drama, also referred to as the *main action,* is determined by the goal, or the primary objective, of the characters in the play, both collectively and individually. There is nothing magical about the spine: It is a working hypothesis that gives directors a foundation and a through-line on which to base their analysis and their work with the actors.

> **Spine**   Also known as *main action,* the spine is determined by the goal or primary objective of all of the characters in a play, both collectively and individually.

Finding a spine for a play allows the director to understand the action and provides a nerve center from which to develop it. Different directors may find different spines for the same play. With **Hamlet**, for instance, several spines are possible: Much will depend on the period in which the play is produced and on the point of view of the individual director. One spine could be simple revenge; another could be Hamlet's attempt to resolve his inner conflicts; still another could be Hamlet's attempt to locate and expose the duplicity and corruption he senses in Denmark. Such varied interpretations are to be expected and are acceptable as long as the spine chosen remains true to the spirit and action of the play.

The Style of the Production   Once a spine has been found, a second task for a director is to find the *style* in which the play is to be presented. The concept of style in a theatrical production is difficult to explain. It means the *way* a play is presented. When we speak of a "casual style" of clothing, we mean that the clothing is loose and informal; when we speak of a "1960s" style, we mean that it has the look and feel of clothing worn in the that time period. In theatre, one way to consider style is in terms of realism and nonrealism, or as noted elsewhere, sometimes referred to as departures from realism. These two types can also be further subdivided.

For example, there are several types of realism. At one extreme is **naturalism**, a kind of superrealism. The term *naturalism* was originated by several nineteenth-century French writers who wanted a theatre that would show human beings—often in wretched circumstances—as products of heredity and environment. In addition

> **Naturalism**   Attempts to put on stage exact copies of everyday life; sometimes also called "slice of life."

ALLEGORY

The medieval morality play *Everyman* is an excellent example of an allegory, with the title character representing all humankind. In an allegory, characters personify ideas or other worldly characters in order to illustrate an intellectual or moral lesson. Shown here is a rehearsal for *Everyman* with performers Brigitte Grothum, Georg Preusse (in the title role) and Debora Weigert rehearsing a scene in a production of *Everyman* at the Berliner Dom in Berlin. (©Clemens Bilan/Getty Images)

Heightened realism Also known as *selective realism*, refers to plays in which characters and their actions resemble real life but a certain license is allowed for other elements in the play.

to this special use, the term *naturalism* refers more broadly to attempts to put onstage as exact a copy of life as possible, down to the smallest detail. In a naturalistic stage set of a kitchen, for instance, a performer can actually cook a meal on the stove, the toaster makes toast, the faucet produces water, and the light in the refrigerator goes on when the door opens. Characters speak and act as if they had been caught unobserved by a sound camera. In this sense, naturalism is supposed to resemble a documentary film. Naturalism is sometimes called *slice-of-life* drama, suggesting that a section has been taken from life and transferred to the stage.

At the other extreme of realism is **heightened realism**, sometimes referred to as *selective realism*. Here the characters and their activities are intended to resemble life, but a certain license is allowed. The scenery, for example, might be skeletal—that is, incomplete and in outline—although the words and actions of the characters are realistic. Or perhaps a character is allowed a modern version of a soliloquy in an otherwise realistic play. All art calls for selectivity, and heightened realism recognizes the necessity for the artist to make choices and to inject creativity into the process. *Realism* itself occupies the middle ground between naturalism and heightened, or selective, realism; but when it is used as a broad umbrella term, it includes the extremes at each end.

Nonrealism, or departures from realism, can also be divided into types, which might include such forms as fantasy, poetic drama, musical theatre, absurdist theatre, and symbolism. Examples of two well-known types of nonrealism are *allegory* and *expressionism.*

Allegory is the representation of an abstract theme or subject through symbolic characters, actions, or other elements of a production, such as scenery. Good examples are the medieval morality plays, in which characters personify ideas in order to teach an intellectual or moral lesson. In ***Everyman***, performers play parts with names such as Good Deeds, Fellowship, and Worldly Goods. In less direct forms of allegory, a relatively realistic story serves as a parable or lesson. *The Crucible* by Arthur Miller is about the witch hunts in Salem, Massachusetts, in the late seventeenth century; but it can also be regarded as dealing with specific investigations into communism by the United States Congress in the early 1950s that Miller and others considered modern "witch hunts."

Expressionism was at its height in art, literature, and theatre during the first quarter of the twentieth century, but traces of it are still found today, and contemporary plays using its techniques are called *expressionistic.* In simple terms, expressionism gives outward expression to inner feelings. In Elmer Rice's ***The Adding Machine***, when the main character, Mr. Zero, is fired from his job, his feelings are conveyed by having the room spin around in a circle amid a cacophony of shrill sounds, such as loud sirens and whistles.

Deciding on a directorial style for a production involves giving a signature and an imprint to the entire production: the look of the scenery and lights, and the way performers speak and handle their costumes and props. It also involves the rhythm and pace at which the play moves, a subject that is taken up below. When a director arrives at a style for a production, two things are essential: (1) the style should be appropriate for the play, and (2) it should be consistent throughout every aspect of the production.

The Directorial Concept One way for the director to embody the spine in a production and to implement style is to develop a ***directorial concept***. Such a concept derives from a controlling idea, vision, or point of view that the director feels is appropriate to the play. The concept should also create a unified theatrical experience for those of us in the audience.

Concept and period To indicate what is involved for the director in developing a concept, let us begin with period and location. Take, for instance, Shakespeare's play ***The Tempest***. It is set on a faraway, remote island, and an air of mystery is present throughout the play. One director might take a traditional approach and present it as she or he believes it was performed in Shakespeare's day, with appropriate costumes and scenery. Another director might wish to set it in modern times on a secluded island in the Caribbean, with scenery and costumes reflecting a decidedly modern, Latin feeling, including calypso and other native music. A third director might take a *Star Wars* approach, placing the action at some future period in a fictional universe. In this case, performers arrive and depart by intergalactic rocket ships and wear futuristic space outfits. This kind of transposition has been carried out frequently with Greek plays, Elizabethan plays, seventeenth-century French plays, and other dramatic classics.

Concept and central image Another way to implement a directorial concept is to find a *central*, or *controlling*, *image* or *metaphor* for a theatrical production.

Allegory Symbolic representation of abstract themes through characters, action, and other concrete elements of a play.

Expressionism The attempt in drama to depict the subjective state of a character or group of characters through such nonrealistic techniques as distortion, striking images, and poetic language.

Directorial concept Is the controlling idea, vision, or point of view that the director feels is appropriate for the play; it should create a unified theatrical experience for the audience.

IN FOCUS: THE EVOLUTION OF THE DIRECTOR

It is sometimes argued that the theatre director did not exist before 1874, when a German nobleman, George II (1826–1914), duke of Saxe-Meiningen, began to supervise every element of the productions in his theatre—rehearsals, scenic elements, and other aspects, which he coordinated into an integrated whole. It is true that Saxe-Meiningen was one of the first people to emerge as a separate, indispensable member of the theatrical team. Although the title may have been new, however, the *function* of the director had always been present in one way or another, usually in the person of a playwright or an actor.

We know, for example, that the Greek playwright Aeschylus directed his own plays and that the chorus in a Greek play would rehearse under the supervision of a leader for many weeks before a performance. At various times in theatre history, the leading performer or playwright of a company served as a director, though without the title. The French dramatist Molière, for instance, not only was the playwright and the chief actor of his company but also functioned as the director. In Molière's short play ***The Impromptu of Versailles*** he made clear his definite ideas about the way actors and actresses should perform—no doubt the same advice he offered to performers in his company when rehearsing other plays.

When Hamlet gives instructions and advice to the players who perform the play-within-the-play in *Hamlet,* he is functioning as a director. In England after the time of Shakespeare—from the seventeenth century through the nineteenth—there was a long line of *actor-managers* who gave strong leadership to individual theatre companies and performed many of the functions of a director, although they were still not given that title. Among the most famous were Thomas Betterton (1635–1710), David Garrick (1717–1779), Charles Kemble (1775–1854), William Charles Macready (1793–1873), and Henry Irving (1838–1905).

Toward the end of the nineteenth century the term *director* came into common usage and the clearly defined role of the director was fully recognized. Perhaps significantly, the emergence of the director as a separate creative figure coincided with important changes that began to take place in society during the nineteenth century. First, there was a breakdown in established social, religious, and political concepts, resulting in part from the influence of Freud, Darwin, and Marx. Second, there was a marked increase in communication. With the advent of the telegraph, the telephone, photography, motion pictures, and—later—television, various cultures that had remained remote from or unknown to one another were suddenly made aware of each other.

The effect of these changes was to alter the monolithic, ordered view of the world that individual societies had maintained for over 2,000 years prior to that time. By the early twentieth century, societies and nations had become heterogeneous and interconnected. Previously, consistency of style in theatre had been easier to achieve. Within a given society, writers, performers, and spectators were on common ground. For example, the comedies of the English playwrights William Wycherley (1640–1716) and William Congreve (1670–1729), written at the end of the seventeenth century, were aimed at a specific audience—the elite upper class, which relished gossip, clever remarks, and well-turned phrases.

The code of social behavior in this case was well understood by performers and audiences alike, and questions of style in a production hardly arose, because a common approach to style was already present in the fabric of society. The way a man took a pinch of snuff or a lady flung open her fan was so clearly delineated in daily behavior that performers had only to refine and perfect these actions for the stage. Today, however, due to diversity, multiculturalism, and globalization, achieving a unity of style is much more difficult and the director's task, therefore, is that much more important.

An example would be a production of *Hamlet* that envisioned the play in terms of a vast net or spiderweb in which Hamlet is caught. The motif of a net or spiderweb could be carried out on several levels: in the design of the stage set, in the ways the performers relate to one another, and in a host of details relating

THE DIRECTORIAL CONCEPT

At times, directors create an overall image or metaphor in presenting their interpretation of a play. This can serve both to illuminate the text and to give the production unity and cohesion. The South African actor John Kani inspired the Royal Shakespeare Company director Gregory Doran to set Shakespeare's *Julius Caesar* in modern-day Africa with an all-black cast. Kani had referred to the play as "Shakespeare's Africa play" and Nelson Mandela had annotated a copy he read while imprisoned at Robben Island. In this scene we see Paterson Joseph (left) as Brutus and Jeffery Kissoon (right) as Julius Caesar in the RSC production.
(©Geraint Lewis/Alamy Stock Photo)

The English director Peter Brook (b. 1925) presented some of the most memorable productions of the late twentieth and early twenty-first centuries, a number of which drew extensively from the theatrical traditions and source materials of many countries. His major productions include Peter Weiss's *Marat/Sade* (1964), Shakespeare's **A Midsummer Night's Dream** (1970), and his own adaptation of an Indian epic, *The Mahabharata* (1985). His best-known writings include *The Empty Space* (1968), *The Shifting Point* (1987), and *The Open Door* (1993).

As a means of escaping commercial theatre and allowing himself to address the universality of the theatrical experience, Brook founded the International Center for Theatre Research in Paris in 1970. This company was formed of actors from a variety of countries including Algeria, Japan, England, France, America, Spain, and Portugal, with directors from Armenia, England, and Romania and a designer from Switzerland. There was much sharing of ideas and techniques, with the Japanese actor teaching daily classes in nō, for example. Brook's vision was for the actors to learn from each other and to approach a kind of universal theatrical language. A production entitled *Orghast* (1971) first allowed the company to present its experimentation with language. The text was written by Ted Hughes in an invented language influenced heavily by Latin and ancient Greek, and was performed in Iran.

In 1989, Brook's continued interest in identifying a universality of language in theatre was manifest in his production of *The Mahabharata*. The source text for this play was the Indian epic of the same name, which is more than 90,000 verses long, concerns wars between the Pandavas and the Kauravas, and addresses a great number of philosophical questions. Brook's production of this epic text originally took place at the Avignon Festival in France and took a full nine hours to perform. The source text was Indian, the director English, the theatre company French, and the composer Japanese, and the actors were from all over the globe. This production, which toured widely, clearly drew from a large number of different cultures.

Brook continued his onstage exploration of *The Mahabharata* in 2015 in a new work entitled *Battlefield*,

Peter Brook in Paris. (©Julio Donoso/Getty Images)

using just four global actors and a musician along with minimal properties to create a production about the horrific aftermath of war.

Although Brook has been criticized for exploiting and appropriating some of his source material (such as *The Mahabharata,* which he greatly simplified), his work has shown a creative and continued interest in drawing from many different global theatrical traditions. Unlike other directors who have "borrowed" certain aspects of other theatrical traditions, Brook has sought to use them to identify a common theatre language or universality understood by all.

Prepared by Naomi Stubbs, Associate Professor, LaGuardia Community College, CUNY.

to the central image. There might be a huge rope net hanging over the entire stage, for instance, and certain characters could play string games with their fingers. In short, the metaphor of Hamlet's being caught in a net would be emphasized and reinforced on every level.

Concept and purpose The directorial concept should serve the play. The best concept is one that remains true to the spirit and meaning of the script. A director who can translate that spirit and meaning into stage terms in an inspired way will create an exciting theatre experience; however, a director who is too intent on displaying his or her own originality may distort or violate the integrity of the script. For instance, a director might decide to make **Macbeth** into a cowboy play, with Duncan as a sheriff and Macbeth as a deputy who wants to kill the sheriff in order to take the job himself. In this version, Lady Macbeth would be the deputy's wife, whom he had met in a saloon. *Macbeth* could be done this way, but it might also come across as simply a gimmick—a means of calling attention to the director rather than to the script.

In most instances the best directorial concept is a straightforward one deriving from the play itself, not a scheme superimposed from outside.

The Director's Collaborator: The Dramaturg

A person who can be of great assistance to the director is the ***dramaturg*** (sometimes also spelled as dramaturge), or literary manager, whom we mentioned earlier. The duties of the dramaturg are discovering promising new plays, working with playwrights on developing their scripts, identifying significant plays from the past that may have been overlooked, preparing material for teachers whose students will be attending performances, and writing articles for the programs that are distributed at performances. Of particular importance to directors is the work of dramaturgs in conducting research on previous productions of classic plays, as well as researching past criticism and interpretations of these plays. It is easy to see how the work of the dramaturg can be invaluable in assisting the director to arrive at decisions regarding style, approach, and concept.

Dramaturg The individual who works on literary and historical issues with members of the artistic team mounting a theatre production.

THE AUTEUR DIRECTOR AND THE POSTMODERN DIRECTOR

In addition to the traditional director, there are two other types of stage directors: the auteur director and the postmodern director. There are a number of similarities between these two, but we will look at them one at a time, beginning with the auteur director.

The Auteur Director

Auteur is a French word meaning "author." Just after World War II, French critics began using this term to describe certain film directors, who, they said, were really the authors of the films they made. In these films the point of view and the implementation of that point of view came almost entirely from the director, not from a writer. The term has since been applied to a type of stage director as well. We are not speaking here of directors who alter the time or place in which

Auteur French term for author. When used to describe a director it suggests one who makes drastic alterations and transformations to a traditional script.

the action occurs but retain the original script—the playwright's words and the sequence of scenes. We are speaking rather of directors who make more drastic alterations or transformations in the material, taking responsibility for shaping *every* element in the production, including the script.

Interestingly, one of the first and most important auteur directors began his work with a traditional director, Stanislavski, and then went out on his own—the Russian director Vsevolod Meyerhold (1874–1940), who developed a type of theatre in which he controlled all the elements. The script was only one of many aspects that Meyerhold used for his own purposes. He would rewrite or eliminate text in order to present his own vision of the material. Performers, too, were subject to his overall ideas. Often they were called on to perform like circus acrobats or robots. The finished product was frequently exciting and almost always innovative, but it reflected Meyerhold's point of view, strongly imposed on all the elements, not the viewpoint of a writer or anyone else.

Following in Meyerhold's footsteps, many avant-garde directors of the mid-twentieth century, such as Jerzy Grotowski (1933–1999), Richard Foreman (b. 1937), and Robert Wilson (b. 1941), can also be classified as auteur directors. Each in his own way demanded that the text serve his purposes, not the other way around. In some cases, such as many of Wilson's pieces, the text is only fragmentary and is one of the least important elements.

Another recent auteur director is Ivo van Hove (b. 1958), a Belgian-born director who enjoys reinventing the classics. In his *Streetcar Named Desire* (1996),

RICHARD FOREMAN: AUTEUR DIRECTOR
Richard Foreman is one of the foremost auteur directors in today's theatre. Such directors create their own theatre pieces, providing the vision and the interpretation. They serve not only as directors but also as authors, taking elements from many sources and melding them into their own version of what we see onstage. Shown here is a scene from Foreman's *Old-Fashioned Prostitutes (A True Romance)* with Alenka Kraigher, left, and Rocco Sisto at the Public Theater in New York in 2013. (©Karli Cadel/The New York Times/Redux)

Blanche DuBois performs a good part of the play naked in a bathtub; in his staging of Arthur Miller's *A View from the Bridge* (2014), his actors, shoeless and dressed all in casual contemporary clothing, perform on a stripped down rectangular box-like white stage with no props, and with the audience seated on two sides (in the traditional New York Broadway proscenium, bleacher-like seating was set up on the stage).

Other highly regarded auteur directors are Julie Taymor (b. 1952) and Mary Zimmerman (b. 1960).

The Postmodern Director

There is a great deal of overlap between the auteur director and the postmodern director. What is postmodernism? Probably the best way to answer the question is historically. The modern period in drama began in the late nineteenth century with plays like those of Ibsen and Strindberg that broke long-held taboos. The subject matter of their plays included explicit sexual content, social diseases, the subjugation of women, and the hypocrisy of religious figures. The twentieth century, therefore, was the period of *modern drama*.

At mid-century, however, there were people who felt that as advanced as theatre had become, it remained bound by the strictures of the text. In their minds this state of affairs did not properly reflect the chaos, the confusion, and the alienation of the world around us. Two groups especially advanced these ideas: the theoreticians who propounded the doctrine of postmodernism; and a series of stage directors who embodied postmodernism in their work with a radical, rebellious, free-form approach to theatre production.

What are the hallmarks of postmodern production? One, which began with Meyerhold and continued with Grotowski in his "poor theatre," was a taking apart of the text, often called *deconstruction,* in which portions of a text may be altered, deleted, taken out of context, or reassembled.

A second hallmark is the abandonment of a narrative or linear structure in a theatre piece. We have already mentioned (and will discuss more fully later in our survey of modern theatre) that Robert Wilson and Richard Foreman, in his Ontological Hysteric Theatre, both work as auteur and postmodern directors, replacing traditional structure with the use of segments, tableaux, and other nonsequential devices. A third hallmark is unfamiliar, cross-gender, multicultural casting. Lee Breuer (b. 1937) in a Mabou Mines production of *King Lear* recast the title role as a female ranch owner in the southern United States who has difficulty leaving her inheritance to her three "good ole boy" sons. *The Emperor Jones*, a play by Eugene O'Neill (1888–1953), is about the ruler of a Caribbean island who is gradually stripped of his powers. When the Wooster Group produced this play, an actress, Kate Valk, played the ruler, appearing in blackface.

ELIZABETH LeCOMPTE: POSTMODERN DIRECTOR
Elizabeth LeCompte is a postmodern, auteur director who creates her own theatre pieces frequently by reworking classical texts, controlling every aspect of a production and making it her own. Shown here is a scene from her version of Shakespeare's *Hamlet* staged at the Royal Lyceum theatre as a part of the Edinburgh International Festival in 2013. (©Robbie Jack/Corbis Entertainment/Getty Images)

IN FOCUS: MODERN VERSUS POSTMODERN PRODUCTION AESTHETICS

Modern	Postmodern
Organic unity	Interdisciplinary
Single view	No single view can predominate
Single viewer approach	Multiperspective, multifocus
Shared values of audience	Multicultural
Metaphorical or representational	Presentational
Linear	Nonlinear, simultaneous
Closeness	Distance
Time is singularly staged	Multiple time frames are presented simultaneously
Space is unified	Space is fragmented and can be simultaneously conceived

(Prepared by Tom Mikotowicz)

In addition to those discussed above, other postmodern directors include Anne Bogart (b. 1951), working with her SITI organization, Elizabeth LeCompte (b. 1944), working with the Wooster Group, and Simon McBurney (b. 1957). founder of Théâtre de Complicité, and whose most recent work is the one-person *The Encounter (*2015).

THE DIRECTOR AND THE PRODUCTION: THE PHYSICAL PRODUCTION

While developing his or her approach to the play, the director is also working with the designers on the physical production. At the outset—once the director's concept is established—the director confers with the costume, scene, lighting, sound designers, and possibly video designers and projection designers, to give visual and aural shape and substance to the concept. It is the responsibility of designers to provide images and impressions that will carry out the style and ideas of the production. (See the chapters on the various design elements.)

During the preproduction and rehearsal period, the director meets with the designers to make certain that their work is on schedule and keeping pace with the rehearsals. Obviously, the preparation of these elements must begin long before the actual performance, just as rehearsals must, so that everything will be ready on time for the performance itself. Any number of problems can arise with the physical elements of a production. For example, the appropriate props may not be available, a costume may not fit a performer, or scene changes may be too slow. Early planning will allow time to solve these problems.

THE DIRECTOR'S WORK WITH THE PERFORMERS

Casting

Now we come to the director's work with the performers. Along with choosing and developing a script and settling questions of concept, style, and the physical production, the director also casts the play. In theatre, **casting** means fitting performers into roles; the term *casting* is derived from the phrase "casting a mold." Generally speaking, directors attempt to put performers into the roles for which their personalities and physical characteristics are best suited. A young actress will play Juliet in **Romeo and Juliet**, a middle-aged or elderly actor with a deep voice will play *King Lear,* and so on. When a performer closely resembles in real life the character to be enacted, this is known as *typecasting.* There are times, however, when a director will deliberately put someone in a role who does not appear to be right for the part. This is frequently done for comic or satiric purposes and is called *casting against type.* For example, a sinister-looking actor might be called on to play an angelic part.

Casting Fitting performers into roles.

In the modern American theatre, performers frequently *audition* for parts in a play, and the director casts from those performers who audition. In an audition, actors and actresses read scenes from a play or perform portions of the script to give the director an indication of how they talk and move, and how they would interpret a part. From this the director determines whether or not a performer is right for a given role.

Historically, casting was rarely done by audition, because theatrical companies were more permanent. In Shakespeare's time, and in Molière's, as well as in Asian theatre, certain people in a theatrical troupe always played certain parts: One person would play heroic roles while another always played clowns. Today each production begins with a fresh cast, frequently chosen through an audition process, though stars are sometimes pre-cast in commercial productions. A theatre company and/or director may also employ a *casting director* who is responsible for helping to identify actors appropriate for roles in a production.

From our standpoint as members of the audience, it is important to be aware of casting and the difference it can make to the effectiveness of a production. Perhaps an actor or actress is just right for the part he or she is playing. On the other hand, sometimes the wrong performer is chosen for a part: The voice may not be right, or the gestures or facial expressions may be stilted or inappropriate for the character. One way to test the appropriateness of casting is to imagine a different kind of actor or actress in a part while watching a performance.

Rehearsals

Once a play is cast, the director supervises all the rehearsals. He or she listens to and watches the performers as they go through their lines and begin to move about the stage. Different directors work in different ways during the early phases of rehearsal. Some directors *block* a play in advance, giving precise instructions to the performers. The term **blocking** means deciding when and where performers move and position themselves on the stage. Other directors let the actors and actresses find their own movements, their own vocal interpretations, and their own relationships. And of course, there are directors who do a bit of both.

Blocking Pattern and arrangement of performers' movements onstage with respect to each other and to the stage space, usually set by the director.

At the beginning of the rehearsal process the director often has the cast sit around a table, while reading through the script and discussing individual scenes as well as the play in general. After this, the director may break down the script

IN FOCUS: COLOR BLIND AND NONTRADITIONAL CASTING

While there have been many significant African American, Latino/a, and Asian stage performers, there is continuing recognition that there are limited opportunities for actors and actresses from underrepresented groups in the theatres around the United States (and in other countries). In order to address this issue, there have been productions employing what was originally referred to as *color blind casting*, or what many now refer to more inclusively as *nontraditional casting*, in which roles are cast by directors without considering a performer's ethnicity, gender, transgender identity, or disability.

Nontraditional casting, for example, has been frequently employed in productions of Shakespeare across the globe as well as in other classic dramas. Some actual examples include: all female productions of Shakespeare; an all Asian American cast playing the Jewish family in the 1930s drama *Awake and Sing;* an African American cast performing Tennessee Williams's *Cat on a Hot Tin Roof;* and a transgender performer playing a female character in Thornton Wilder's *The Matchmaker.* The acclaimed musical *Hamilton* (2015), which has African American and Latino actors portraying many of the Caucasian founders of the United States, including those playing Alexander Hamilton, George Washington, and Thomas Jefferson, is another example.

Yet, directors still rarely cast performers of color, as well as women, in multi-racial and gender-bending productions of contemporary texts. For that matter, many performers from underrepresented groups point out that "whitewashing," having Caucasian actors play other races such as a white actor playing the Latino lead in *In the Heights* or the Asians in the musicals *The King and I, Flower Drum Song*, and *Miss Saigon*, is still too common and undercuts even those limited opportunities for performers of color.

Some underrepresented theatre artists (including the playwright August Wilson), however, have argued that nontraditional casting undermines the ongoing need to present the voices of marginalized populations and that there will be fewer dramas dealing with their social and political concerns. Instead, performers who are cast in these nontraditional roles are often forced to erase their ethnic identities and not fully express them. Katori Hall, who disapproved of what she considered the inappropriate "color blind" casting of a white student actor as Martin Luther King Jr. in her play *The Mountaintop*, also questioned the nontraditional casting of *Hamilton*, echoing August Wilson's arguments: "And though I applaud *Hamilton* for its use of race-revolutionary casting, let us not forget that brown bodies are still being used to further mythologize and perpetuate the narratives of dead white men, historically and currently the most privileged group in American society."[1]

[1]Viagas, Robert, "Playwright Katori Hall Expresses Rage Over "Revisionist Casting" of Mountaintop With White Dr. Martin Luther King," *Playbill*, November 9, 2015

into segments or scenes, which will be rehearsed separately. Some scenes will involve only a few people; others, as in a Shakespearean play, may be crowd scenes. At a certain point, the actors will be expected to be "off book," meaning that they have memorized their lines. Gradually, scenes are put together, and an entire act is played without stopping. After that, individual scenes are refined, and then there is a run-through, when the play is performed straight through without stopping.

Also, some directors want the actors to become thoroughly familiar with the script while they remain seated. Others wish to get the play "on its feet" as soon as possible, meaning that the actors are moving about the rehearsal hall early in the process. Regardless of the director's approach to staging, the production stage manager keeps detailed notes of all the actors' movements and actions to help maintain consistency during rehearsals.

Throughout the rehearsal period, the director must make certain that the actors and actresses are realizing the intention of the playwright—that they are making sense of the script and bringing out its meaning. Also, the director must ensure that the performers are working well together—that they are listening to one another and beginning to play as an ensemble. The director must be aware of performers' needs, knowing when to encourage them and when to challenge or criticize them. The director must understand their personal problems and help them overcome such obstacles as insecurity about a role or fear of failure.

The Director as the Audience's Eye

One could say that there are two people in theatre who stand in for us, the audience, serving as surrogate or substitute spectators. One, the critic or reviewer (discussed earlier), does his or her work after the event; the other, the director, does his or her work before it. In preparing a theatrical production, the director acts as the eye of the audience. During rehearsals, only the director sees the production from our point of view. For this reason, the director must help the performers to show the audience—us—exactly what they intend to show. If one performer hides another at an important moment, if a crucial gesture is not visible, if an actor makes an awkward movement, if an actress cannot be heard when she delivers an emotional speech, the director points it out.

USING STAGE AREAS PROPERLY
One responsibility of the director is to make appropriate use of stage areas to create clarity, balance, and the proper emphasis in the visual picture on stage. The scene here is from Chekhov's *The Cherry Orchard*, in a production at the Huntington Theatre. Note how the director Nicholas Martin has arranged the performers so that Kate Burton as Madame Ranevskaya in light grey costume, the leading figure in the play, stands out in front of the other actors who surround her expertly positioned.
(©T. Charles Erickson)

Also, the director underscores the meaning of specific scenes through *visual composition* and *stage pictures,* that is, through the physical arrangement of performers onstage. The spatial relationships of performers convey information about characters. For example, important characters are frequently placed on a level above other characters—on a platform, say, or a flight of stairs. Another spatial device is to place an important character alone in one area of the stage while grouping other characters in another area. This causes our eye to give special attention to the character standing alone. Also, if two characters are opposed to each other, they should be placed in positions of physical confrontation onstage. Visual composition is more crucial in a play with a large cast, such as a Shakespearean production, than in a play with only two or three characters.

Certain areas onstage can assume special significance. A fireplace, with its implication of warmth, can become an area to which a character returns for comfort and reassurance. A door opening onto a garden can serve as a place where characters go when they want to renew their spirits or relieve a hemmed-in feeling. By guiding performers to make the best use of stage space, the director helps them communicate important visual images to us—images consistent with the overall meaning of the play.

It is important to note, too, that directors must adjust their notions of blocking and visual composition to different types of stages, discussed in our chapter on stage spaces: the arena stage, the thrust stage, and the proscenium stage. Each of these calls for different approaches to the performers' movements and to the audience's sight lines.

Movement, Pace, and Rhythm

The director gives shape and structure to a play in two ways: in *space,* as was just described, and in *time.* Since a production occurs through time, it is important for the director to see that the *movement, pace,* and *rhythm* of the play are appropriate. If a play moves too quickly, if we miss words and do not understand what is going on, that is usually the director's fault. The director must determine whether there is too little or too much time between speeches and whether a performer moves across the stage too slowly or too quickly. The director must also attempt to control the pace and rhythm within a scene and the rhythm between scenes.

One of the most common faults of directors is not establishing a clear rhythm in a production. At a performance we are often impatient to see what is coming next, and the director must see to it that the movement from moment to moment and scene to scene has enough thrust and drive to maintain our interest. Variety is also important. If a play moves ahead at only one pace, whether slow or fast, we will become fatigued simply by the monotony of that pace. Rhythm within scenes and between scenes works on us subliminally, but its effects are very real. It enters our psyche as we watch a performance and thus contributes to our overall response.

It must be borne in mind as well that although pace, rhythm, and overall effect are initially the responsibility of the director, ultimately they become the performers' responsibility. Once a performance begins, the actors and actresses are onstage and the director is not. In cinema, pace and rhythm can be determined in the editing room; in theatre, by contrast, they are in the hands of the performers. Then, too, the audience's reaction will vary from night to night, and that will also alter pace and rhythm. The director must therefore instill in the performers such a strong sense of inner rhythm that they develop an internal clock that tells them the pace at which they should play.

Part 3 Creating Theatre: The Production

Technical Rehearsal

Just before public performances begin, a ***technical rehearsal*** is held. The performers are onstage in their costumes and all of the production elements are in place: scenery, props, lighting, sound, and, in some instances, videos and projections for the first time. There is a *run-through* of the show from beginning to end, with all the props and scene, lighting, and other technical changes.

The stagehands may move scenery, the crew handles the needed props, lighting technicians use computer controls to dim and raise lights as well as control other lighting effects, technicians may also run a sound board and control intricate videos and projections that change settings and environments. The backstage crew, under the supervision of the stage manager, must coordinate its work with that of the performers.

Let us say that one scene ends in a garden, and the next scene opens in a library. When the performers leave the garden set, the lighting fades, and the scenery and furniture may be removed, which can be done either by stagehands or using stage machinery, such as a revolving stage, or an elevator stage, or even through lighting, projection, and video changes. Then, the scenery for the library must be brought onstage, again either by stagehands or employing stage technology. The books and other props may actually be put in place as part of the new setting or again possibly represented by projections. Next, the performers for the new scene in the library take their places as the lighting comes up.

Extensive rehearsals are required to ensure that all these changes occur smoothly, especially when there is the use of complex computer-controlled sets, lights, projections, and videos. Any mishap on the part of the technical crew, or the performers, would affect the illusion and destroy the aesthetic effect of the complex scene change.

Technical rehearsal A rehearsal that focuses on running through the production with scenery, props, lighting, costumes and sound for the first time.

Dress Rehearsal

Just after the technical rehearsal, but before the first preview or tryout with an audience, the director will hold a ***dress rehearsal***. The purpose of the dress rehearsal is to put all the elements together: the full involvement of the performers as well as the technical components. The dress rehearsal is performed as if an audience were present, with no stops or interruptions and with full lights, scenery, costumes, and sound. Sometimes a few people are invited—friends of the director or cast members—to provide a token audience.

One function of the dress rehearsal is to give everyone concerned—cast, crew, and director—a sense of what the finished performance will be like. The dress rehearsal also allows for any last-minute changes before the first performance in front of a full audience.

Dress rehearsal The first full performances of a production before performances for the public.

Previews

Once the technical rehearsals and the dress rehearsal are completed and remaining problems are solved, the next step is a performance in front of an audience. We have stressed from the beginning the importance of performer-audience interaction and the fact that no play is complete until it is actually enacted for an audience. It is crucial, therefore, for a production to be tried out before a group of spectators. What has gone before, in terms of rehearsals and other elements, must now meet the test of combining harmoniously in front of an audience.

TECHNICAL REHEARSAL

Before performances begin, a technical rehearsal is held. All the technical aspects—scenery, lighting, sound, costumes, props—are employed in the same sequence and manner as in performance. This is in order to see that everything is in proper working order and is coordinated. Shown here is a rehearsal at the Guthrie Theater in Minneapolis for a production of *When We Are Married,* directed by John Miller-Stephany. Note the tables on which computers are being used by sound, light, and scenic designers to check out the running order and the coordination of all the elements. The set was designed by Frank Hallinan. (©T. Charles Erickson)

Previews Tryout performances of a production before an audience, preceding the official "opening" performance.

For this purpose there is most often (but not always) a period of *previews*— also called *tryouts*—when the director and the performers discover which parts of the play are successful and which are not. Frequently, for example, the director and performers find that one part of the play is moving too slowly; they know this because the audience members become restless and begin to cough or stir. Sometimes, in a comedy, there is a great deal of laughter where little was expected, and the performers and the director must adjust to this. In this preview period the audiences become genuine collaborators in shaping the play. After several performances in front of an audience, the director and the performers get the "feel" of the audience and know whether or not the play is ready.

Part 3   Creating Theatre: The Production

1. Have you ever had to pick someone for a team or for a job? How did you go about making your choice? Is that similar to casting in the theatre? Why? Why not?

2. Have one of your classmates read a short speech from a play. Ask her or him to change the pace or rhythm of delivery. What terms or phrases did you use to make this request? Were your directions understood? How did the change in pace or rhythm affect the delivery of the speech and its impact on those listening?

3. Observe how one of your instructors interacts with the class through his or her movement. How does this movement affect the way in which the class material is delivered? Does your observation of this provide you any insight into the importance of stage blocking?

4. Ask if you can attend a technical rehearsal or dress rehearsal at your university theatre. What insights did you gain from attending those rehearsals?

The Director's Collaborator: The Stage Manager

Another key collaborator of the director, especially during the rehearsal process and then during the run of the show, is the stage manager. During the rehearsal process the stage manager works as the right-hand person to the director, doing such tasks as taking notes, keeping track of blocking, noting decisions about visual elements, communicating with all of the designers, make sure everyone is aware of rehearsal schedules, and keeping daily reports and logs. Throughout the final stages of preparing the production, for example, the stage manager continues to give detailed notes to all actors to ensure consistency in dialogue and movement.

Once the play has opened and the director is no longer present at every performance, it is the stage manager's responsibility to maintain the consistency of the director's vision. Among her or his responsibilities are to make sure that actors stay true to the director's interpretation and that all technical cues are called on time during the run of the show. If understudies should go on for missing actors, it is the stage manager's responsibility to make sure they are prepared. If a performer in a long running show is replaced, it is often the stage manager's responsibility to work with the replacement to make sure she or he works within the confines of the director's vision.

The responsibilities of the stage manager vary depending on the type of theatre in which they are working and from director to director. In commercial theatre it is important to realize that stage managers and actors are members of the same union, Actors' Equity Association (AEA), reflecting the close work stage managers do with performers.

THE DIRECTOR'S POWER AND RESPONSIBILITY

Any artistic event must have a unity not encountered in real life. We expect the parts to be brought together so that the total effect will enlighten us, move us, or amuse us. In theatre, the director—who has a voice in so many areas of a production—is in a unique position to bring this about. This power, however, is a double-edged sword. If a director gets too carried away with one idea, for example, or lets the scene designer create scenery that overpowers the performers, the experience for the audience will be unsatisfactory or incomplete. If, on the other hand, the director has a strong point of view—one that is appropriate for the theatre piece and illuminates the script—and if all the parts fit and are consistent with one another, the experience will be meaningful and exciting, and at times even unforgettable.

For an idea of the director's full range of responsibilities, see the following chart "Duties of a Director."

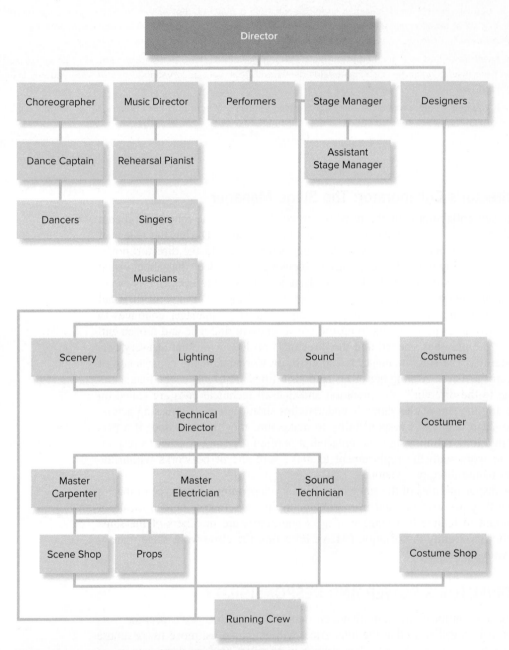

DUTIES OF A DIRECTOR IN A THEATRE PRODUCTION
Once a director has decided on a script (and has worked with the playwright, if it is a new play), he or she must organize the entire artistic side of the production. This chart indicates the many people that the director must work with and the many elements that must be coordinated.

1. Imagine that while you are watching a production, one performer is overacting badly, to the point that he or she is quite unbelievable. Another performer is listless and has no energy. In each case, to what extent do you think this is the director's fault, and to what extent the performer's failure?

2. If you get bored or impatient when watching a performance, what do you think the director could have done in preparing the production to prevent this from happening?

3. Is it fair to say, as some critics do, when everything "clicks" in a production, that is, when the acting, the scenery and lighting, and the pace of the action all seem to be beautifully coordinated, that the director's hand is "invisible"?

4. If you have read a play this semester (or sometime in the past), what do you think the spine of that play is? What would your directorial concept be if you were directing a production of that play?

THE PRODUCER OR MANAGING DIRECTOR

As spectators, we naturally focus on the event onstage rather than on what happens behind the scenes. But no production would ever be performed for the public without a business component. Here, too, the coordination of elements is crucial, and the person chiefly responsible, known as the ***producer*** in the commercial theatre, or ***managing director*** in the noncommercial theatre, is the behind-the-scenes counterpart of the director.

The Commercial Producer

In a commercial theatre venture, the producer has many responsibilities. (See the nearby chart.) In general, the producer oversees the entire business and publicity side of the production and has the following duties:

1. Raising money to finance the production.
2. Securing rights to the script.
3. Dealing with the agents for the playwright, director, and performers.
4. Hiring the director, performers, designers, and stage crews.
5. Dealing with theatrical unions.
6. Renting the theatre space.
7. Supervising the work of those running the theatre: in the box office, auditorium, and business office.
8. Supervising the advertising.
9. Overseeing the budget and the week-to-week financial management of the production.

It is clear that the responsibilities of the commercial producer range far and wide. They require business acumen, organizational ability, aesthetic judgment, marketing know-how, and an ability to work with people. The producer in commercial theatre must have the artistic sensibility to choose the right script and hire the right

Producer   In American usage, the person responsible for the business side of a production, including raising the necessary money. (In British usage, a producer for many years was the equivalent of an American director.)

Managing director   In nonprofit theatre organizations, the individual who controls resources and expenditures.

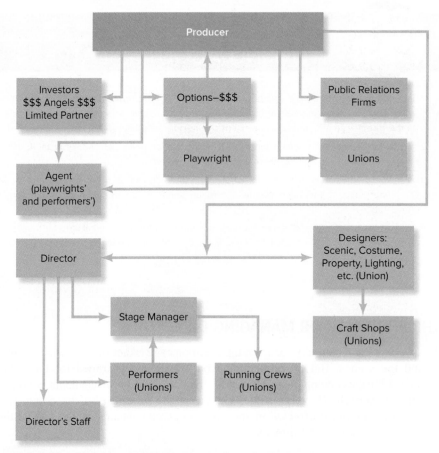

RESPONSIBILITIES OF THE COMMERCIAL THEATRE PRODUCER
When a commercial theatre production is mounted, the person responsible for organizing the full range of nonartistic activities is the producer. This chart shows the producer at the top and indicates the people the producer must deal with and the numerous elements he or she must coordinate.

director, but at the same time must be able to raise capital as well as oversee all financial and business operations in a production.

Noncommercial Theatres

In a nonprofit theatre the person with many of the same responsibilities as the producer is called the *executive director* or *managing director*.

Administrative Organization of a Nonprofit Theatre Most nonprofit theatres—including theatres in smaller urban centers as well as the large noncommercial theatres in major cities like New York, Chicago, and Los Angeles—are organized with a board of directors, an artistic director, and an executive or managing director. The board is responsible for selecting both the artistic and the managing director. The board is also responsible for overseeing the financial affairs of the theatre, for fundraising, for long-range planning, and the like. To carry out some of these tasks, the board frequently delegates authority to an executive committee.

The artistic director is responsible for all creative and artistic activities. He or she selects the plays that will constitute the season and chooses directors, designers, and other creative personnel. Frequently, the artistic director also directs one or more plays during the season.

Responsibilities of a Noncommercial Managing Director   The managing director in a noncommercial theatre is, in many respects, the counterpart of a producer in commercial theatre. In both a commercial production and the running of a nonprofit theatre organization, the tasks of the person in charge of administration are many and complex.

The managing director is responsible for the maintenance of the theatre building, including the dressing rooms, the scene and costume shops, the public facilities, and the lobby. The managing director is also responsible for the budget, making certain that the production stays within established limits. The budget includes salaries for the director, designers, performers, and stage crews, as well as expenditures for scenery, costumes, and music. Again, an artistic element enters the picture. Some artistic decisions—such as whether a costume needs to be replaced or scenery needs to be altered—affect costs. The managing director must find additional sources of money or must determine that a change is important enough artistically to justify taking funds away from another item in the budget. In other words, she or he must work very closely with the director and the designers in balancing artistic and financial needs.

The managing director, often with additional staff members, is also responsible for publicity. The audience members would never get to the theatre if they did not know when and where a play was being presented. The managing director must work with staff to advertise the production and decide whether the advertisements and information should be placed in daily newspapers, magazines, on radio, on television, or in social media (such as Facebook, Twitter, and Instagram).

A host of other responsibilities come under the supervision of the managing director and his or her staff: Tickets must be ordered, the box office must be maintained, and plans must be made ahead of time for how tickets are to be sold. Securing ushers, printing programs, and maintaining the auditorium—usually called the *front of the house*—are also the responsibility of the managing director's staff.

Front of the house
Portion of a theatre reserved for the audience; sometimes called simply the *house*.

Once again, plans must be made well in advance. In many theatre organizations, an entire season—the plays that will be produced, the personnel who will be in charge, and the supplies that will be required—is planned a year ahead of time. It should be clear that coordination and cooperation are as important in this area as they are for the production onstage. (For the organization of a nonprofit theatre company, see the nearby chart.)

The Producer and Director's Collaborator: The Production Manager

In some nonprofit theatres, a production manager is employed to serve as a liaison between the design artists and technical staff and the director and producer or managing director. The production manager oversees the budgets for all of the design and technical areas, sets deadlines for completion, and makes sure that those deadlines are met. Should there be delays, possible

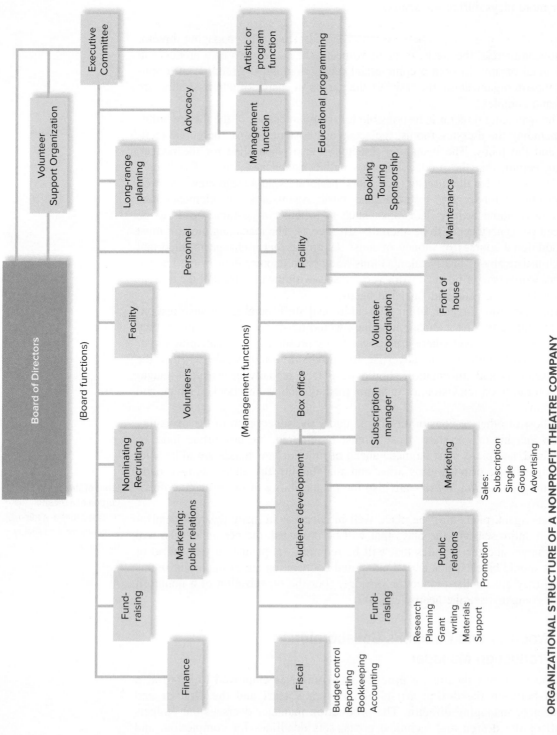

ORGANIZATIONAL STRUCTURE OF A NONPROFIT THEATRE COMPANY

A nonprofit theatre is a complex institution, with many facets. This chart shows the various activities that must be organized for the successful management of such a theatre.

budget overruns, or other behind-the-scenes problems, the production manager will attempt to resolve the issues as well as communicate with the director and/or the producer to make sure that those issues do not impact the artistic quality of the production or its financial well being. The responsibilities of the production manager may vary from theatre to theatre, depending on budgets and size of operations. If there is not a specifically designated production manager, then someone within the artistic or administrative staff will take on these duties.

COMPLETING THE PICTURE: PLAYWRIGHT, DIRECTOR, AND PRODUCER

A theatre presentation can be compared to a mosaic consisting of many brightly colored pieces of stone that fit together to form a complete picture. The playwright puts the words and ideas together; the performers bring them to life; the designers provide the visual and aural environment; the director integrates the artistic elements; the producer or managing director coordinates the business side of a production. The separate pieces in the mosaic must become parts of an artistic whole, providing us with a complete theatre experience.

Evaluating Directing

While watching a production or experiencing a performance, we do not have time to pause and analyze every aspect of the production, from the acting and the script to the visual and aural elements. There is even less time, perhaps, to analyze the work of the director. But the topics covered in this chapter should give us, as audience members, some idea of what might or might not be the responsibility of the director: when the director might be at fault for a failure, or, on the other side, when he or she should be given credit for the successful unfolding of a theatrical event.

There are some key questions we might ask to determine whether the director was successful after we attend a production:

1. Did all the elements of the production seem to be unified and to fit together seamlessly? How was this reflected, in particular, in the visual elements— the scenery, costumes, and lighting; or in the sound, video, or projection design?
2. How did the director move the actors around onstage? Were there any moments when you felt that such movement was particularly effective or ineffective? Were entrances and exits smooth?
3. Did the pace or rhythm of the production seem right for the type of play you are attending? Did it drag or move swiftly? Did one scene follow another quickly, or were there long pauses or interruptions?
4. Did there seem to be a unifying idea or concept behind the production? If so, how was it reflected in the production? How were we, as audience members, able to see it embodied in the production? Was it reflected in striking images or in the way the actors developed their performances? (Evaluating a directorial concept can be one of the most difficult aspects of a production for us to judge, even for those of us who are very experienced theatergoers.)

1. The term *director* did not come into general use until the end of the nineteenth century. Certain functions of the director, however—organizing the production, instilling discipline in the performers, and setting a tone for the production—have been carried out since the beginning of theatre by someone in authority.

2. The director's duties became more crucial in the twentieth century. Because of the fragmentation of society and the many styles and cultures that now exist side by side, it is necessary for someone to impose a point of view and a single vision on individual productions.

3. The director has many responsibilities: working with the playwright if the script is a new work; evolving a concept or approach to the script; developing the visual side of the production with the designers; holding auditions and casting roles; working with the performers to develop their individual roles in rehearsals; ensuring that stage action communicates the meaning of the play; establishing appropriate pace and rhythm in the movement of the scenes; establishing the dynamics of the production as a whole; and supervising the technical and preview rehearsals.

4. *Auteur* directors demand that a text serve their own purposes, rather than shaping their purposes to serve the text. *Postmodern* directors often "deconstruct" a text or rearrange elements to create a theatre piece.

5. Because the director has such wide-ranging power and responsibilities, he or she can distort a production and create an imbalance of elements or an inappropriate emphasis. The director is responsible for a sense of proportion and order in the production.

6. The producer or manager of a production is responsible for the business aspects: maintaining the theatre, arranging publicity, handling finances, as well as managing the ticket sales, budgets, and ushers.

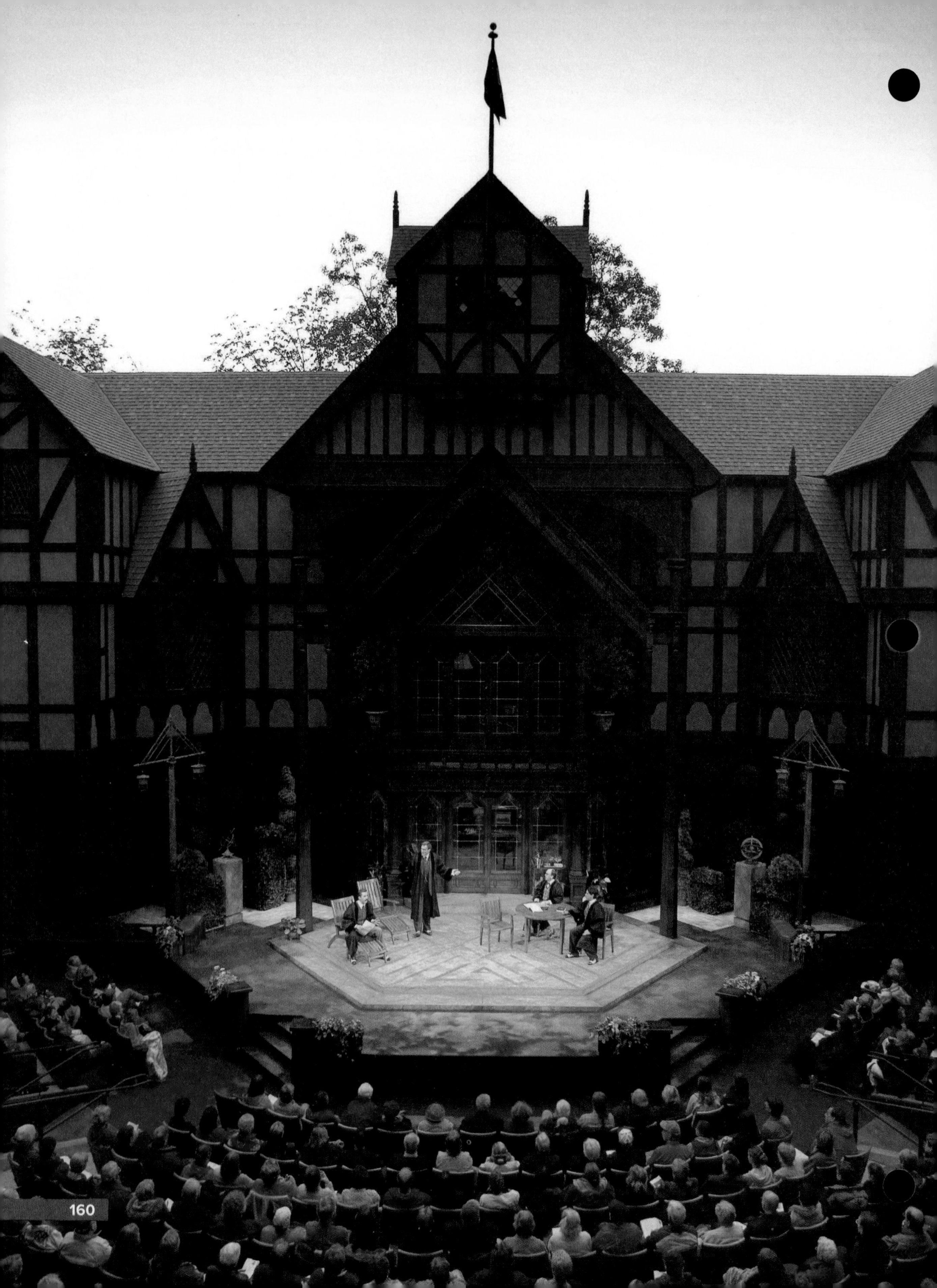

THEATRE SPACES

7

When we attend the theatre, our experience begins in advance. Sometimes we read or hear reports of the play online or in print; we anticipate seeing a particular actress or actor or a specific type of production; we buy tickets and make plans with friends to attend; and before the performance, we gather outside the theatre space with other members of the audience.

CREATING THE ENVIRONMENT

When we arrive inside a theatre building or other space for a performance, we immediately take in the environment in which the event will occur. The atmosphere inside the space for a production has a great deal to do with our mood in approaching a performance, not only creating expectations about the event but conditioning the experience once it gets under way. As spectators, we have one feeling if we come into a formal setting, such as a picture-frame stage surrounded by carved gilt figures, with crystal chandeliers and red plush seats in the auditorium. We have quite a different feeling if we come into an old warehouse converted for a performance, with bare brick walls, and a stage in the middle of the floor surrounded by folding chairs.

For many years people took the physical arrangement of theatres for granted. This was particularly true in the period when all houses were facsimiles of the Broadway theatre, with its proscenium, or picture-frame, stage. Since the 1950s, however, not only have people been exposed to other types of theatres; they have also become more aware of the importance of environment. Many experimental groups have deliberately made awareness of the environment a part of the experience. And even in the commercial Broadway theatre there have been experiments with transforming the environment.

An example of such a production is *Natasha, Pierre, & the Great Comet of 1812*. This musical, based on a section of Leo Tolstoy's novel *War and Peace*,

◄ **STAGE SPACES: AN OUTDOOR THRUST STAGE**

The Allen Pavilion at the Oregon Shakespeare Festival is a 1,200-seat theatre with an Elizabethan thrust stage. With the audience on three sides, this is one of the oldest and most popular configurations for a theatre performance space. The production shown here is Shakespeare's Love's Labour's Lost, *directed by Kenneth Albers.* (©T. Charles Erickson)

was first produced in a 99-seat off-Broadway house and then to accommodate even larger audiences in a tent in Manhattan's Meatpacking district. (The use of a tent reflects how theatre spaces can be created anywhere.) In 2016, the play opened at the Imperial Theatre, a Broadway playhouse that can seat over 1,400 audience members.

In order to transform this traditional proscenium arch theatre into an immersive space that feels like a nineteenth-century Russian supper club, set designer Mimi Lien added red velvet curtains surrounding the entire audience area. In addition, portraits line all the walls of the theatre; a wooden curving road goes through the middle of the orchestra bringing actors into the midst of audience members and brilliant chandeliers come down from the ceiling engulfing the audience. Staircases lead from the traditional orchestra level to the upper seating area for audience members; tables and chairs replace five rows of seats usually used for spectators (the only physical change in the theatre), with ramps and the curving road being built on existing seats. In the center of the Imperial Theatre there is a constructed oval that again thrusts the performance into the audience.

What was the goal of transforming this traditional Broadway theatre for *Natasha, Pierre, & the Great Comet of 1812?* Director Rachel Chavkin, when she describes the reaction of an audience member, indicates that the goal is to immerse the audience, to integrate them into the world of the production to become part of the action, blurring the distinction between performance and spectator space. The director explained: "A woman walked in the theatre one day… and she was like, 'Where's the stage?' The answer is: There isn't one. Or it's everywhere, which is the joy of it."[1] Designer Lien says the Imperial was transformed so that the experience begins from the moment the audience enters: "Then you come inside, and I really wanted that moment of stepping inside to be impactful," she says. "This feeling of a warm, lush, opulent cocoon-like space was really important to us, and so we have hung onto that every step of the way."[2]

The feeling we have about the atmosphere of a theatre building as we enter the space has always been an important element in the experience. In the past, spectators may not have been conscious of it, but they were affected by it nevertheless. Today, with the many varieties of theatre experience available to us, the first thing we should become aware of is the environment in which an event takes place: whether it is large or small, indoors or outdoors, formal or informal, familiar or unfamiliar.

At times scenic designers are able to alter the architecture of a theatre space to create a new arrangement or configuration, as we explained was done for *Natasha, Pierre & the Great Comet of 1812.* If the auditorium space is too large for a specific production, balconies might be blocked off, or the rear of the orchestra might be closed in some manner. Also, the decor can be altered: bright colors, banners, and bright lighting could create a festive atmosphere in a space that is ordinarily formal and subdued. The first thing for us, as audience members, is to note the general characteristics of the space: Is it formal or informal? Is it large or small? Next, is the question of the configuration of stage and audience seating.

Proscenium ("pro-SEEN-ee-um") Arch or frame surrounding the stage opening in a box or picture stage.

Arena Stage entirely surrounded by the audience; also known as *circle theatre* or *theatre-in-the-round.*

Thrust stage Stage space that thrusts into the audience space; a stage surrounded on three sides by audience seating.

Black box A theatre space that is open, flexible, and adaptable, usually without fixed seating. The stage-audience configuration can be rearranged to suit the individual requirements of a given production, making it both economical and particularly well suited to experimental work.

Fourth wall Convention, in a proscenium-arch theatre, that the audience is looking into a room through an invisible fourth wall.

[1]Gioia, Michael, "How The Great Comet Transformed the Imperial Theatre Into an Immersive Russian Supper Club," Playbill, December 1, 2016.
[2]"Mimi Lien on the Set Design of 'The Great Comet of 1812'" interview conducted and edited by Victoria Myers, *The Interval,* January 4, 2017.

THEATRE SPACES

A consideration of environment leads directly to an examination of the various forms and styles of theatre buildings, including the arrangements of audience seating. Throughout theatre history, there have been five basic stage arrangements, each with its own advantages and disadvantages, each suited to certain types of plays and certain types of productions, and each providing the audience with a somewhat different experience. The five are (1) the *proscenium*, or picture-frame, stage; (2) the *arena*, or circle, stage; (3) the *thrust* stage with three-quarters seating;[3] (4) *created* and *found* stage spaces; and (5) all-purpose or *"black box"* theatre spaces, out of which a version of any one of the other four can be created.

Proscenium or Picture-Frame Stage: History and Characteristics

Perhaps the most familiar type of stage is the proscenium (pro-SEEN-ee-um), or picture-frame, stage. Broadway-style theatres, which for many years were models for theatres throughout the country, have proscenium stages.

The term *proscenium* comes from *proscenium arch,* the frame that separates the stage from the auditorium and that was first introduced in Italy during the Renaissance in the seventeenth century. Today this frame is not an arch but a rectangle. As the term *picture-frame stage* suggests, it resembles a large frame through which the audience looks at the stage. Another term for this type of stage is *fourth wall*, from the idea of the proscenium opening as a transparent glass wall through which the audience looks at the other three walls of a room.

Because the action takes place largely behind the proscenium opening, or frame, the seats in the auditorium all face in the same direction, toward the stage, just as seats in a movie theatre face the screen. The auditorium itself—the *house*, or *front of the house*, as it is called—is slanted downward from the back to the stage. (In theatre usage, the slant of an auditorium or stage floor is called a *rake*.) The stage is raised several feet above the auditorium floor, to aid visibility. There is usually a balcony (sometimes two balconies) protruding about halfway over the main floor. The main floor, incidentally, is called (in American usage) the *orchestra*. (In ancient Greek theatre, the orchestra was the circular acting area at the base of the hillside amphitheatre, but in modern usage it is the main floor of the theatre, where the audience sits.) In certain theatres, as well as concert halls and opera houses that have the proscenium arrangement, there are horseshoe-shaped tiers, or *boxes*, which ring the auditorium for several floors above the orchestra.

The popularity of the proscenium stage on Broadway and throughout the United States in the nineteenth century and the early twentieth century was partly due to its wide acceptance throughout Europe. Beginning in the

[3]Material on the proscenium, arena, and thrust stages was suggested by a booklet prepared by Dr. Mary Henderson for the educational division of Lincoln Center for the Performing Arts.

Front of the house Portion of a theatre reserved for the audience; sometimes called simply the *house.*

Rake (1) To position scenery on a slant or at an angle other than parallel or perpendicular to the curtain line. (2) An upward slope of the stage floor away from the audience.

Orchestra A circular playing space in ancient Greek theatres; in modern times, the ground-floor seating in a theatre auditorium.

Box Small private compartment for a group of spectators built into the walls of traditional proscenium-arch and other theatres.

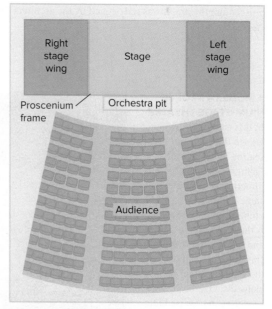

PROSCENIUM THEATRE
The audience faces in one direction, toward an enclosed stage encased by a picture-frame opening. Scene changes and performers' entrances and exits are made behind the proscenium opening, out of sight of the audience.

THE PROSCENIUM THEATRE

The traditional proscenium theatre resembles a movie theatre in terms of audience seating: All the seats face in one direction, toward the stage. The frame of the stage is like a picture frame, and behind the frame are all the elements of the visual production such as scenery, painted drops, pieces that move across the stage, platforms, steps, perhaps the interior of a room or several rooms. The theatre shown here, the Bolton Theatre at the Cleveland Play House, is an excellent example of a proscenium theatre. It was redesigned by the architect Philip Johnson and renovated in 1983. (©Photo by Paul Tepley/Courtesy of Cleveland Play House)

A MODERN PROSCE-NIUM-STAGE THEATRE

In this cutaway drawing we see the audience seating at the left, all facing in the one direction, toward the stage. Behind the orchestra pit in the center is the apron on the stage; and then the proscenium frame, behind which are the flats and other scenic elements. Overhead, scenery can be raised into the fly loft above the stage area.

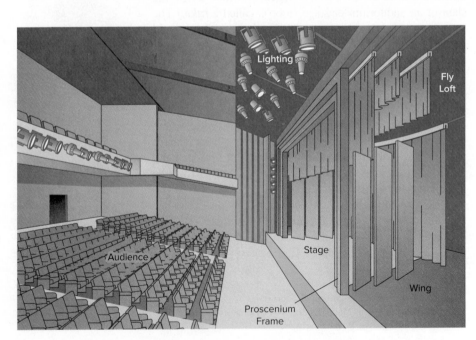

A BIBIENA SET FOR A FORMAL PROSCENIUM THEATRE

The standard theatre throughout Europe and the United States from the eighteenth century to the early twentieth century was a formal proscenium space. The audience sat in a downstairs orchestra, in balconies, and in side boxes facing an ornate picture-frame stage. Impressive scenery and other visual effects were created and changed behind the curtain that covers the proscenium opening. In the eighteenth century, the Bibiena family from Italy created scene designs on a grand scale for such theatres throughout Europe. They painted backdrops with vistas that seemed to disappear into the far distance. This scene is by Giuseppe di Bibiena (1696–1757). (©akg-images/Newscom)

late seventeenth century, the proscenium theatre was adopted in every European country. For the next two centuries in Europe both the mechanics of stage machinery and the artistry of scene painting improved steadily allowing designers to create extraordinary stage pictures.

An Italian, Giacomo Torelli (1608–1678), developed methods of moving scenery on and off stage felicitously, and throughout the eighteenth century, members of one family, the Bibiena family, dominated the art of scene painting. The Bibiena sets usually consisted of vast halls, palaces, or gardens with towering columns and arches that framed spacious corridors or hallways, which disappeared into an endless series of vistas as far as the eye could see. At times during this period, audiences, as well as scene designers and technicians, became so carried away with spectacle that the visual aspects were emphasized to the exclusion of everything else, including the script and the acting.

Although there have been many changes in theatre production, and today we have a wide variety of production approaches, we are still attracted to ingenious displays of visual effects in proscenium theatres. This is especially true of large musicals such as *The Phantom of the Opera, The Lion King, Wicked, Aladdin,* and *Charlie and the Chocolate Factory.* Because the machinery and the workings of scene changes can be concealed behind a proscenium opening, this type of stage offers a perfect arrangement for spectacle.

There are other advantages to the proscenium stage. Realistic scenery—a living room, an office, a kitchen—looks good behind a proscenium frame; the scene designer can create the illusion of a genuine, complete room more easily with a proscenium stage than with any other. Also, the strong central focus provided by the frame rivets the attention of the audience. There are times, too, when we want the detachment, the distancing, that a proscenium provides.

There are disadvantages as well, however. As we have seen, the proscenium stage creates a temptation to get carried away with visual pyrotechnics. In addition,

STAGE AREAS
Various parts of the stage are given specific designations. Near the audience is *downstage:* away from the audience is *upstage. Right* and *left* are from the performers' point of view, not the audience's. Everything out of sight of the audience is *offstage.* Using this scheme, everyone working in the theatre can carefully pinpoint stage areas.

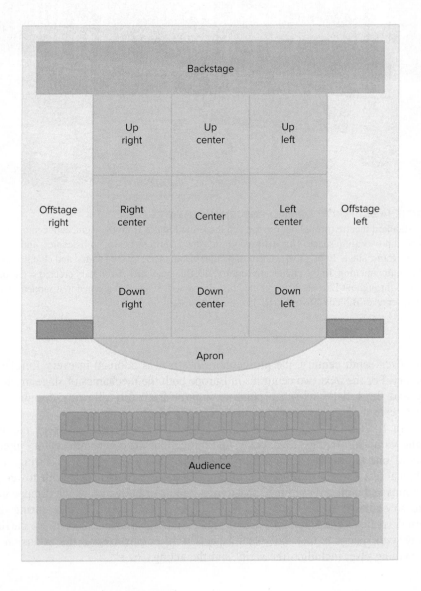

Part 3   Creating Theatre: The Production

For large-scale productions the proscenium theatre is ideal. The scenery and other elements can be hidden above, behind, and around the stage, and then moved into the main stage area, as if by magic. Costumes can be displayed at their finest. In addition, the scale of the scenic effects can be extensive and sometimes electrifying. The scene shown here is from the hip-hop influenced *Aladdin* by Joel Horwood in a production at the Lyric Hammersmith theatre in London. (©Elliott Franks/eyevine/Redux)

a proscenium stage tends to be remote and formal. Some of us, as spectators, prefer the intimacy and informality—the experience of being close to the action—found in the arena and thrust theatres.

Physical Layout: The Proscenium Arch To designate areas of the stage, usually in a proscenium theatre, scene designers, directors, performers, and technicians use terminology peculiar to theatre. *Stage right* and *stage left* mean the right side and the left side of the stage, respectively, as seen from the position of a performer facing the audience. (In other words, when we, as spectators, in the auditorium look at the stage, the area to their left is known as right stage and the area to their right as left stage.)

The area nearest to us, the audience, is known as *downstage*; farthest away from us is *upstage*. The designations downstage and upstage come from the eighteenth and nineteenth centuries, when the stage was *raked,* that is, sloped downward from front to back. As a result of this downward slope, the performer farthest away from the audience was higher, or "up," and could be seen better. Also, performers downstage from, or below, an upstage performer would be forced to turn their backs on the audience when addressing her or him. This is the origin of the expression "to upstage" someone. Today, the term is used whenever one performer grabs the spotlight from everyone else or calls attention to himself or herself by any means whatever. At first, however, it meant simply that one performer was in a better position than the others because she or he was standing further back on the raked stage and, therefore, was higher.

Stage right Right side of the stage from the point of view of a performer facing the audience.

Stage left Left side of the stage from the point of view of a performer facing the audience.

Downstage Front of the stage, toward the audience.

Upstage At or toward the back of the stage, away from the front edge of the stage.

Rake (1) To position scenery on a slant or at an angle other than parallel or perpendicular to the curtain line. (2) An upward slope of the stage floor away from the audience.

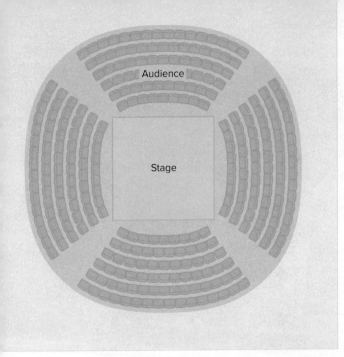

PLAN OF AN ARENA STAGE

The audience sits on four sides or in a circle surrounding the stage. Entrances and exits are made through the aisles or through tunnels underneath the aisles. A feeling of intimacy is achieved because the audience is close to the action and encloses it.

Arena Stage: History and Characteristics

To some of us, proscenium theatres, decorated in gold and red plush, look more like temples of art than theatres. We prefer a more informal, intimate theatre environment. A movement in this direction began in the United States just after World War II, when a number of theatre practitioners decided to break away from the formality of proscenium theatres. This was part of an overall desire to bring many aspects of theatre closer to everyday life: acting styles, the subject matter of plays, the manner of presentation, and the shape of the theatre space. One form this reaction took was the *arena stage*—a return to one of the most ancient stage arrangements.

From as far back as we have records, we know that tribal ceremonies and rituals, in all parts of the world, have been held in some form of circle space. For example, many scholars believe that the ancient Greek theatre evolved from an arena form. In an arena theatre (also called *circle theatre* or *theatre-in-the-round*) there is a playing space in the center of a square or circle, with seats for spectators all around it. The arrangement is similar to that in sports arenas featuring boxing or basketball. The stage may be a raised area a few feet off the main floor, with seats rising from the floor level; or it may be on the floor itself, with seats raised on levels around it. When seating is close to the stage, there is usually some kind of demarcation indicating the boundaries of the playing area.

One advantage of the arena theatre is that it offers more intimacy than the ordinary proscenium. With the performers in the center, even in a larger theatre, we can be closer to them. If the same number of people attends an arena event and a proscenium event, at least half of those at the arena will be nearer the action: Someone who would have been in the twelfth row in a proscenium theatre will be in the sixth row in an arena theatre. Besides, with this proximity to the stage, the arena theatre has another advantage: There is no frame or barrier to separate the performers from us.

Beyond these considerations, in the arena arrangement there is an unconscious communion, basic to human behavior, which comes when people form a circle—from the embrace of two of us to a circle for children's games to a larger gathering where we form an enclosure around a fire or an altar. It is no coincidence that virtually all of the earliest forms of theatre were "in the round."

A practical advantage of the arena theatre is economy. All you need for this kind of theatre is a large room: You designate a playing space, arrange rows of seats around the sides, and hang lights on pipes above, and you have a theatre. Elaborate scenery is impossible because it would block the view of large parts of the audience. A few pieces of furniture, with perhaps a lamp or sign hung from the ceiling, are all you need to indicate where a scene takes place. Many low-budget groups have found that they can build a workable and even attractive theatre-in-the-round when a proscenium theatre would be out of the question. These two factors—intimacy and economy—no doubt explain why arena theatre is one of the oldest stage forms, as well as one still very much in use today.

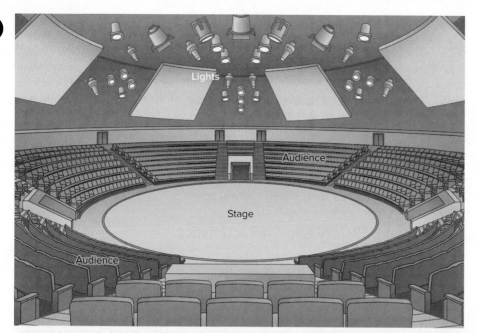

The arena theatre attempts to capture the immediacy of primitive theatre. It uses the barest essentials of stage scenery but the full resources of contemporary stage lighting.

ARENA STAGE

With an arena stage, also referred to as a circle stage or theatre-in-the-round, the audience surrounds the stage area on all sides. In addition to aisles for audience members to enter, there are passages that the performers use to enter and leave the stage. One effect of the arena stage is to create a close rapport between actors and audience. Seen here is the renovated Fichandler Stage at the Arena Stage in Washington, D.C. (©Photo by Nic Lehoux/Courtesy of Bing Thom Architects)

In spite of its long history, however, and its resurgence in recent years, the arena stage has often been eclipsed by other forms. One reason is that its design, while allowing for intimacy, also dictates a certain austerity. As we noted before, it is impossible to have elaborate scenery because that would block the view of many spectators. Also, the performers must make all their entrances and exits along aisles that run through the audience, and they can sometimes be seen before and after they are supposed to appear onstage. The arena's lack of adaptability in this respect may explain why some of the circle theatres that opened twenty or thirty years ago have since closed. A number survive, however, and continue to do well. Among the best-known are the Arena Stage in Washington, D.C., and Circle in the Square in New York City. In addition, throughout this country there are a number of *tent theatres* in arena form where musical revivals and concerts are given.

Thrust Stage: History and Characteristics

Falling between the proscenium and the arena is a third type of theatre: the *thrust stage* with three-quarters seating. In one form or another, this U-shape arrangement has been the most widely used of all stage spaces. In the basic arrangement for this type of theatre, we sit on three sides, or in a semicircle, enclosing a stage, which protrudes into the center. At the back of the playing area is some form of **stage house** providing for the entrances and exits of the performers as well as for scene changes. The thrust stage combines some of the best features of the other two stage types: the sense of intimacy and the "wraparound" feeling of the arena, and the focused stage placed against a single background found in the proscenium.

The thrust stage was developed by the classical Greeks for their tragedies and comedies. They adapted the circle used for tribal rituals and other ceremonies—the circle called the *orchestra*—by locating it at the base of a curving hillside. The slope of the hill formed a natural amphitheatre for the spectators. At the rear of the orchestra circle, opposite the hillside, was placed a stage house, which had formal doors through which characters made their entrances and exits and served as a background for the action. The stage house also provided a place for the actors to change their costumes. The largest Greek theatres seated 15,000 or more spectators.

Stage house Stage floor and the space around it to the side walls, as well as the space above it up to the grid.

THRUST STAGE WITH THREE-QUARTERS SEATING
The stage is surrounded on three sides by the audience. Sometimes seating is a semicircle. Entrances and exits are made from the sides and backstage. Spectators surround the action, but scene changes and other stage effects are still possible.

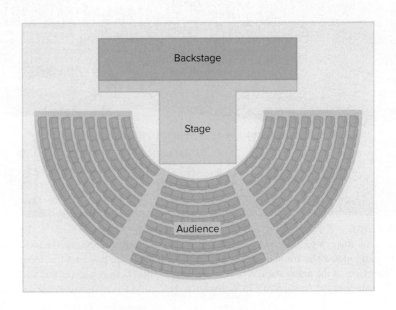

Backstage

Stage

Audience

Part 3   Creating Theatre: The Production

PLAYING YOUR PART:
EXPERIENCING THEATRE

1. Rearrange your classroom seating into proscenium, arena, and thrust configurations. Read a speech aloud from a play or a paragraph from a novel to the class in each of these configurations. How is your presentation affected by the arrangement of the space?

2. Visit a gym or sports arena on your campus. What is the configuration of the space? How does it relate to a theatre environment? What type of popular entertainment might be staged there?

3. Find an outdoor space on your campus that might be used for theatre. What type of presentation would you stage there? Why?

A MODERN THRUST STAGE
The thrust stage, with a stage area extending into audience seating that surrounds it on three sides, is one of the oldest arrangements, having been used by the Greeks and by the Elizabethans in the time of Shakespeare. It has been revived successfully in the modern period and is widely used in Europe and the United States. A good example is the recently renovated Mark Taper Forum in Los Angeles. (©Craig Schwartz)

The Performance Group, which, for example, led spectators one at a time into its adaptation of the Greek tragedy *The Bacchae, Dionysus in 69*, is typical in this regard. It presented its productions in a large garage converted into an open theatre space. At various places in the garage, scaffolding and ledges were built for audience seating. The Performance Group, like other modern avant-garde companies, owed a great debt to a Frenchman, Antonin Artaud (1896–1948), one of the first

SITE-SPECIFIC THEATRE: CREATED AND FOUND SPACE

Shown here are two examples of site-specific theatre. In the first, a formal garden in the Aberglasney Gardens in Wales is the the site of a performance by young actors dressed in black and white using the garden space as their stage.

The second example shows the Polish theatre company Biuro Podrozy in a production of *Macbeth,* using its trademark stilts on a street, at the Edinburgh Fringe Festival in Edinburgh, Scotland.

(top: ©Keith Morris/Alamy Stock Photo; bottom: ©Jeff J Mitchell/Getty Images)

theatre people to examine in depth the questions raised by the avant-garde. An actor and director who wrote a series of articles and essays about theatre, Artaud was brilliant but inconsistent (he spent several periods of his life in mental institutions). Many of Artaud's ideas, however, were to prove prophetic: Notions he put forward in the 1920s and 1930s, considered impossible or impractical at the time, have since become common practice among experimental theatre groups. Among his proposals was one on the physical theatre:

> We abolish the stage and auditorium and replace them by a single site, without partition or barrier of any kind, which will become the theater of the action. A direct communication will be reestablished between the spectator and the spectacle, between the actor and the spectator, from the fact that the spectator, placed in the middle of the action, is engulfed and physically affected by it. This envelopment results, in part, from the very configuration of the room itself. Thus, abandoning the architecture of present-day theaters, we shall take some hangar or barn which we shall have reconstructed according to processes which have culminated in the architecture of certain churches or holy places, and of certain temples in Tibet.[4]

Some of Artaud's ideas were put into practice when the movement to explore new concepts became widespread. In the generation after Artaud, Jerzy Grotowski included the physical arrangements of stage space in his experiments. Not only Grotowski but others in the avant-garde movement developed theatre space in a variety of ways.

Nontheatre Buildings   Artaud mentioned a barn or hangar for performances. In recent years virtually all kinds of structures have been used: lofts, warehouses, fire stations, basements, churches, breweries, and gymnasiums. This practice should not be confused with the conversion of unusual spaces to full-scale theatres, which has numerous precedents in the past; historically, indoor tennis courts, palace ballrooms, and monastery dining halls have been converted into theatres. We are, instead, describing here the use of nontheatre structures as they are, with their original architectural elements intact, and carving out special areas for acting and viewing—as with the garage used by the Performance Group. In our contemporary theatre, ***site-specific companies*** are theatre groups that create productions for specific nontheatre locations. For example, the English company Punchdrunk staged *Sleep No More,* an adaptation of Shakespeare's *Macbeth*, in three abandoned warehouses in Manhattan with the audiences moving through various spaces, supposedly in a 1930s hotel, created in them.

Site-specific companies   Theatre groups that create productions for specific nontheatre locations.

Adapted Spaces   One frequent practice was using or creating a space to fit a play, rather than (as is normally the case) making the play fit the space. Grotowski, in particular, pursued the notion of finding a different, appropriate configuration for each production. In Grotowski's production of the Doctor Faustus story, for example, the theatre was filled with two long tables at which spectators sat as if they were guests at a banquet hosted by Faustus. The action took place at the heads of the tables and even on the tabletops. For his production of *The Constant Prince,* a fence was built around the playing area, and the audience sat behind the fence, looking over it like spectators at a bullfight. In recent decades there have been similar attempts to deal with theatre spaces in many parts of Europe and the United States.

[4]Artaud, Antonin, "The Theater and Its Double," Grove, New York, 1958, pp. 96–97.

AN ISLAND FOR SITE-SPECIFIC THEATRE

In the Netherlands there is a festival, known as the Oerol Festival, in which for ten days in June an entire island, Terschelling, is used by a variety of theatre companies to present their pieces. Groups set up in all kinds of places on the island—taverns, barns, tents, and garages, and on beaches—to offer their productions. Shown here on a beach is a production entitled *Salted,* written and directed by Judith de Rijke and produced by Tryater of Holland, which brought together young artists from various regions to celebrate the linguistic diversity of Europe. (©Sake Elzinga)

Street Theatre   One development—which was actually a return to practices in medieval Europe—is theatre held outdoors in nontraditional settings. A good example is *street theatre.* Generally, street theatre is of three types: (1) plays from the standard repertoire presented in the streets; (2) *neighborhood theatre,* in which an original play deals with problems and aspirations of a specific population of a city, such as Puerto Ricans, African Americans, or Italians; and (3) *guerrilla theatre,* aggressive, politically oriented theatre produced by an activist group in the streets in an attempt to persuade us to become more politically involved, such as street presentations during the Occupy Wall Street movement in 2012.

Whatever the form, the important point for our purposes is that these productions take place not in theatre buildings but in places like streets, parks, hospitals, jails, and bus stations.

In these productions, theatre is brought to those of us who might not otherwise see it. Also, audiences in such unusual settings are challenged to rethink what theatre is all about. On the other hand, there are inherent disadvantages to impromptu productions in the streets or other "found spaces": The audience must be caught on the run, and there is rarely time for more than a sketch or vignette. Nor are there facilities for presenting a fully developed work—but often that is not the purpose of these undertakings in the first place.

Multifocus Environments   An approach that sometimes accompanies these unusual arrangements is ***multifocus theatre***. In simple terms, this means not only that there is more than one playing area, such as the four corners of the room (as Artaud suggested in one article), but also that something is going on in several

Multifocus theatre An environment in which there is more than one playing area.

of them simultaneously. This is somewhat like a three-ring circus, where we see an activity in each ring and must either concentrate on one or divide our attention among two or three.

There are several theories behind the idea of multifocus theatre. One is that a multifocus event is more like everyday life; if you stand on a street corner, there is activity all around you—in the four directions of the streets, in the buildings above—not just in one spot. You select which area you will observe, or perhaps you watch several areas at one time. The argument is that in theatre, you should have the same choice. In multifocus productions no single space or activity is supposed to be more important than any other. We either take in several impressions at once and synthesize them in our own mind or select one item as most

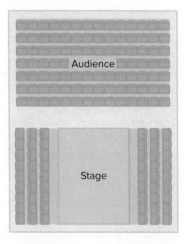
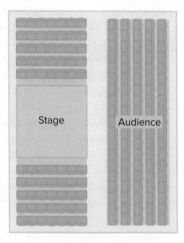
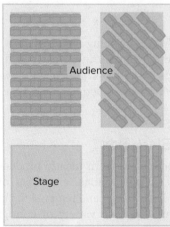
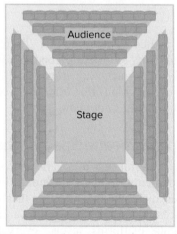

THE MULTIPURPOSE OR "BLACK BOX" THEATRE
A popular type of modern theatre is the multipurpose space, sometimes called a "black box." It consists of an open space with perhaps a pipe grid on the ceiling from which lighting and sound instruments can be suspended. A stage platform can be positioned at any place in the space, and movable chairs for spectators can be placed around the playing area. The diagrams suggest some of the possibilities of stage arrangements in a multipurpose theatre.

Many spaces used for live popular entertainments are reminiscent of theatre environments. Arenas used for sports, circuses, and rock concerts are configured much like theatrical spaces discussed in this chapter. Madison Square Garden in New York, Soldier Field in Chicago, the Rose Bowl in Pasadena, California, and university sports arenas are all large spaces that primarily house sporting events but are also used for rock concerts and other popular spectacles. Madison Square Garden, for example, has housed circuses, elaborate rock concerts, and music award ceremonies. This means that an arena like the Garden is often equipped with the most innovative technology for lighting, stage, and sound effects.

Spectacular performance spaces for magicians, circuses, concerts, and stage extravaganzas are found in all of the major hotels in Las Vegas. There is live entertainment also presented in fairgrounds and amusement parks across our country.

These spaces for popular performances are most often configured in the round, with spectators surrounding the events. Some are configured three-quarters round. The reason is to maximize the number of audience members as well as to create an electrifying interactive entertainment. With these configurations, we, as spectators, are also able to watch and possibly influence each other's reactions.

Such popular performance spaces are usually extremely large, much larger than environments created exclusively for theatre. For example, the Rose Bowl accommodates over 90,000 fans for football games. Even a comparatively small collegiate athletic facility, Western Hall on the Western Illinois University campus, can accommodate approximately 5,000 spectators.

The relationship between spaces for popular entertainments and theatrical environments is complex. Throughout theatre history, the same spaces were used for popular arts and for theatrical performances. Modern theatre artists have experimented with staging dramatic performances within spaces created for concerts and circuses.

For that matter, the performance qualities of sports, the circus, and rock concerts underscore their shared heritage with the theatrical arts. It is not surprising, then, that their spaces are also similar and often multipurpose.

arresting and concentrate on that. There is no such thing as the "best seat in the house"; all seats are equally good, because the activity in all parts of the theatre is equally important. Sometimes multifocus theatre is joined with *multimedia theatre*—presentations that offer some combination of acting, films, video, dance, music, slides, and light show.

All-Purpose Theatre Spaces: The Black Box

Because of the interest in a variety of spaces in modern theatre production, and the requirements of many different kinds of productions, a number of theatre complexes, including many college theatre departments and regional theatres, have built spaces that can be adapted to an almost infinite variety of configurations. Seats, lights, platforms, levels—every aspect of such a theatre is flexible and movable.

In this kind of space the designers can create a proscenium, a thrust, an arena, or some combination of these, but the designers can also create corner stages, island stages, and multifocus arrangements with playing areas in several parts of the studio. This space is sometimes referred to as a *black box* because it is often an empty rectangular space into which various audience seating and stage arrangements can be introduced.

PLAYING YOUR PART:
THINKING ABOUT THEATRE

1. As discussed in this chapter, there are five major types of stage spaces: proscenium, arena, thrust, found space, and black box. What do you think are the advantages and disadvantages of each? On which type of stage space would you prefer to watch a performance?

2. Using information from this chapter, explain which type of stage space you would feel is best suited for the following productions: a large-scale musical, an intimate personal drama, a Shakespearean drama, and a play of political protest.

3. The size of theatre spaces can range from fewer than 100 spectators to more than 3,000. What do you consider an ideal-sized theatre for the following types of productions: a musical, a Shakespearean play, a modern family drama? Suggest the ideal number of audience seats for each and the shape and size of the ideal stage space for each.

SPECIAL REQUIREMENTS OF THEATRE ENVIRONMENTS

Simply assigning a theatre to a category does not adequately describe the environment; we must also take into account a number of other variables. Two theatres may be of the same type and still be quite different in size, atmosphere, and setting. The experience in a small off-off-Broadway-type thrust theatre will be far different from that in a thrust theatre several times larger, such as the Guthrie in Minneapolis. The experience in a 99-seat arena theatre at a university would be quite different than in the 886-seat arena playhouse used for musicals at the suburban Chicago Marriott Lincolnshire. Also, one theatre may be indoors and another of the same type outdoors.

There are other factors that architects, producers, and designers must take into account, one of which is the human scale. No matter what the configuration, the performer is the basic scale by which everything is measured in theatre. Theatre architects as well as scenic and lighting designers must always keep this in mind, and we should be aware of it as well. When the theatre environment and the stage space violate this human scale in some way, problems are created for performers and us.

There is also the question of appropriateness. By *appropriateness* we mean the relationship of a stage space to a play or production. A large-scale musical requires a full stage—usually a proscenium stage—and a large auditorium from which we can get the full effect of the spectacle. However, an intimate, small cast family drama with its intense personal confrontations might require a small playing area so that we are close enough to the action to make a connection with the characters onstage.

Rather than being limited to one type of building and one type of stage, we are fortunate today in having a full range of environments in which to experience theatre. Taken all in all, whether single-focus or multifocus, indoors or outdoors, the recent innovations in theatre milieus have added new alternatives, rich in possibilities, to the traditional settings for theatrical productions. They have also called attention to the importance of environment in our total theatre experience.

Evaluating the Theatre Space

While we do not often think about evaluating the use of theatre space for a production, it is an element that can impact audience engagement and the work of the theatre artists. When we attend a theatre production, there are key questions we should ask ourselves as we interact with the environment used for staging:

1. What type of theater was it? How large or small? How opulent or elaborate? How simple or modern? What type of stage did it have: proscenium, thrust, arena, or some other type? Was it a found space? How did the area for the actors relate to the audience seating?
2. What was the size and shape of the playing space? Were any modifications made to a pre-existing space?
3. What sort of atmosphere did the space suggest? How was that atmosphere created?
4. Did the space seem to meet the needs of the play (such as special performance requirements or technical requirements)? Did it affect the production, and if so, how?
5. Did the space seem appropriate for the type of play you were seeing (an intimate family drama, a spectacular musical, a classical tragedy, a work by Shakespeare, etc.)?

SUMMARY

1. The atmosphere and environment of the theatre space play a large part in setting the tone of an event.
2. Experimental theatre groups in recent years have deliberately made spectators aware of the environment.
3. Throughout theatre history there have been five basic stage and auditorium arrangements: proscenium, arena, thrust, created or found space, and all-purpose or "black box" spaces.
4. The proscenium theatre features a picture-frame stage, in which the audience faces directly toward the stage and looks through the proscenium opening at the "picture." The proscenium stage aids illusion: Placing a room of a house behind the proscenium, for example, allows the scene designer to create an extremely realistic set. This type of stage also allows elaborate scene shifts and visual displays because it generally has a large backstage area and a fly loft. It also creates a distancing effect, which works to the advantage of certain types of drama. At the same time, however, the proscenium frame sets up a barrier between the performers and the audience.
5. The arena or circle stage places the playing area in the center with the audience seated in a circle or square around it. This offers an economical way to produce theatre and an opportunity for great intimacy between performers and spectators, but it cannot offer full visual displays in terms of scenery and scene changes.
6. The thrust stage with three-quarters seating is a platform stage with seating on three sides. Entrances and exits are made at the rear, and there is an opportunity for a certain amount of scenery. This form combines some of the scenic features of the proscenium theatre with the intimacy of the arena stage.

7. Created or found space takes several forms: use of nontheatre buildings, adaptation of a given space to fit individual productions, use of outdoor settings, street theatre, multifocus environments, and all-purpose spaces.

8. The theatre space referred to as a *black box* is an open, adaptable space that can be configured into a variety of stage-audience arrangements, providing for maximum flexibility and economy.

9. Size and location (indoors or outdoors, etc.), along with the shape and character of a theatre building, affect the environment.

8

SCENERY

When we attend a theatre production, we first encounter the environment—the look and size of the space. Is it large or small, formal or informal? Then, as the presentation begins, we become aware of the performers and the roles they are playing. as well as the story that begins to unfold.

But along with these elements, which we immediately notice, there are other design factors that impact how we experience a production: the scenery (possibly including video and projections), costumes, lighting, and sound. In their own way, these are indispensable elements of the theatre experience.

THE AUDIENCE'S VIEW

As we begin to take in the visual elements of a performance, we should look for specifics. Is the scenery realistic, resembling a recognizable kitchen, bedroom, or office? Or is the scenery abstract: shapes, steps, levels, platforms on a relatively bare stage? Is it futuristic or dreamlike? What about the costumes? Are they like everyday clothes, or do they suggest some period: ancient Rome, the American Revolution, the Civil War, the 1920s, the 1960s? Are the costumes fanciful, like Halloween outfits, or do they resemble clothes from daily life: judges' robes, police uniforms, physicians' outfits?

As for lighting, is it what we would expect in a normal setting, coming from sunlight outdoors, or lamps indoors? Or perhaps the lighting is abstract and arbitrary: beams of light cutting through the darkness, special lighting illuminating one part of the stage while the rest is dark. We must also take sound into account. Are there arbitrary sounds: a music track, specials effects such as sudden eruptions of synthetic noises? Or is the sound realistic: sirens for ambulances, thunder for a storm?

◀ **SCENE DESIGN PROVIDES THE VISUAL ENVIRONMENT**

For a production of The Railway Children *at the Kings Cross Theatre in London, the designer, Joanna Scotcher, has created an arresting image of a sunken railroad track on stage with a young woman (played by Serena Manteghi) fleeing an oncoming locomotive spewing steam. The play was written by Mike Kenny, based on the book by E. Nesbit, and directed by Damian Cruden.* (©Geraint Lewis)

In all these areas, we should be conscious of the visual and aural signals that are being sent continuously. As for who prepares these signals, they are the designers and all the technicians and others who work with them.

THE SCENE DESIGNER

The scene designer creates the visual world in which a play unfolds. Together with the playwright and the director, the scene designer determines whether a scene is realistic or in the realm of fantasy. He or she decides on the colors, shapes, and visual style that the spectators view and the actors inhabit. The set indicates the kind of world we are in—outdoors or indoors; an affluent environment or a humble one; a time period long ago, today, or in the future. When different locales are called for—in a play with an episodic structure, for instance—the scene designer must ensure that we move smoothly and quickly from one locale to another.

Designers and lead technicians in their respective areas must deal with practical as well as aesthetic considerations. A scene designer must know in which direction a door should open onstage and how high each tread should be on a flight of stairs. A lighting designer must know exactly how many feet above a performer's head a particular light should be placed and whether it requires a 500- or 750-watt lamp. A costume designer must know how much material it takes to make a certain kind of dress and how to "build" clothes so that performers can wear them with confidence and have freedom of movement. A sound designer must know about acoustics, be familiar with echoes, and understand electronic sound systems.

As in other elements of theatre, symbols play a large role in design. A single item onstage can suggest an entire room—a bookcase, for instance, suggests a professor's office or a library; a stained-glass window suspended in midair suggests a church or synagogue. A stage filled with a bright yellow-orange glow suggests a cheerful sunny day, whereas a single shaft of pale blue light suggests moonlight or an eerie graveyard at night. How designers deal with the aesthetic and practical requirements of the stage will be clearer when we examine the subject in detail: scene design in this chapter, costumes and lighting and sound in the following chapters.

A BRIEF HISTORY OF STAGE DESIGN

At the beginning of both western and Asian theatre there was little of what we now call scene design. The stage itself was the background for the action. In Greek theatre, for instance, the facade of the stage house usually represented a palace or some other imposing edifice. In medieval theatre, "mansions" were set up in town squares. These were small set pieces representing such things as Noah's ark, the whale that swallowed Jonah, and the manger in which Christ was born.

The Elizabethan and Spanish theatres of the Renaissance had bare stages in which the facade of the stage house functioned as the background for the action, just as it had in Greece. In Elizabethan England and Spain, set pieces as well as furniture such as thrones were used, but there was still little scenery as we know it. More elaborate settings began to appear along with the proscenium theatres in Italy and later in France and England in the seventeenth and eighteenth centuries. These were the theatres (described in our chapter "Theatre Spaces") where designers such as the Bibiena family came to the forefront.

Since then, theatre has experienced improved stage machinery (that is, the means by which scenery is shifted) as well as increasing realism in depicting scenes; also, the use of videos and projections and the use of computers to assist in creating designs. This growing emphasis on mechanization, technology, and realism has been the basis of much modern stage scenery.

SCENIC DESIGN TODAY

We are accustomed to "stage settings" in everyday life; but as with other elements in theatre, there is an important difference between interior decoration in real life and set designs for the stage. For example, the stage designer must deal with scale: the relationship of the performer in the set to his or her surroundings. This must in turn correspond to the scale of settings we experience in the world outside the theatre. The scale in a stage set may be different from that of a living room or a courtroom in real life. Robert Edmond Jones, who is often considered the most outstanding American scene designer of the first half of the twentieth century, put it in these terms:

> A good scene should be, not a picture, but an image. Scene-designing is not what most people imagine it is—a branch of interior decorating. There is no more reason for a room on a stage to be a reproduction of an actual room than for an actor who plays the part of Napoleon to be Napoleon or for an actor who plays Death in the old morality play to be dead. Everything that is actual must undergo a strange metamorphosis, a kind of seachange, before it can become truth in the theater.[1]

A stage set signals an atmosphere to us in the same way as a room in real life, but the scene designer must go a step further. As has been pointed out many times, theatre is not life: It resembles life. It has, as Jones suggests, both an opportunity and an obligation to be more than mere reproduction.

The special nature of scenery and other elements of scene design will be clearer when we examine the objectives and functions of scene design.

The Scene Designer's Objectives

In preparing scenery for a stage production, a scene designer has the following objectives:

1. Help set the tone and style of the production.
2. Establish the locale and period in which the play takes place.
3. Develop a design concept consistent with the director's concept.
4. Provide a central image or metaphor, where appropriate.
5. Ensure that scenery is coordinated with other production elements.
6. Solve practical design problems.

Establishing Tone and Style   A stage setting can help establish the mood, style, and meaning of a play. In the arts, style refers to the manner in which a work is done: how scenery looks, how a playwright uses language or exaggerates dramatic elements, how performers portray characters. (A realistic acting style, for example, resembles the way people behave in everyday life; in contrast, the lofty quality of traditional tragedy calls for formal, larger-than-life movements and gestures.)

[1]Robert Edmond Jones, *The Dramatic Imagination,* Theatre Arts, New York, 1941, p. 25.

SCENERY: AN ENVIRONMENT FOR A PLAY

Scenery provides the visual world in which a performance takes place. It indicates whether a play is realistic, expressionistic, or fantastic and where the action takes place: inside a home, at various locations, in some exterior setting; and also whether the story occurs in a past era or at the present time. For *The Curious Incident of the Dog in the Night-Time*, the scene designer, Bunny Christie, created a visual environment filled with mathematical formulas, equations, diagrams—some indicated in silhouette others in falling papers covered with formulas—to indicate the world in which the main character, Christopher Boone, exists. The production shown here at the National Theatre in London was directed by Marianne Elliott. Christopher was played by Graham Butler. (©Geraint Lewis/Alamy Stock Photo)

A slapstick farce might call for a design style involving comic, exaggerated scenery, like a cartoon; and perhaps for outrageous colors, such as bright reds and oranges. Such scenery would match the acting, which would also be exaggerated, with lots of physical comedy—people tripping over carpets, opening the wrong doors, and so forth. A satire would call for a comment in the design, like the twist

MOOD AND STYLE

The designers should establish the mood, tone, and style of a production, a challenge which is accomplished with architectural shapes, colors, fabrics, furniture, and other elements. Note here the sage setting of the facade of a house with projections of ominous lighting on a rear screen and the stage floor. (©Chris Selby/Alamy Stock Photo)

in the lines of a caricature in a political cartoon. A serious play would call for less exaggerated or less comic scenery.

As an illustration of what is called for in scene design, let us consider two plays by the Spanish playwright Federico García Lorca. His **Blood Wedding** is the story of a young bride-to-be who runs away with a former lover on the day she is to be married. The two flee to a forest. In the forest, allegorical figures of the Moon and a Beggar Woman, who represents Death, seem to echo the fierce emotional struggle taking place within the characters who are torn between duty to their families and passion for each other. For this part of the play, the scenery and costumes must have the same sense of mystery, of the unreal, which rules the characters. The forest should not have real trees but should represent the thicket of emotions in which the man and woman are entangled; the costumes of the Moon and the Beggar Woman should not be realistic but should suggest the forces that endanger the lovers.

Another play by García Lorca, **The House of Bernarda Alba**, is a contrast in style: It has no fantasy or fantastic characters. This play concerns a woman and her five daughters. The mother has grown to hate and distrust men, and so she locks up her house, like a closed convent, preventing her daughters from going out. From a design point of view, it is important to convey the closed-in, cloistered feeling of the house in which the daughters are held as virtual prisoners. The walls of the house and its furniture should all have solid reality, creating an atmosphere that will convey a sense of entrapment.

Scene design is especially important in indicating to us whether a play is realistic or departs from realism. **Realism** in theatre means that everything connected

Realism Broadly, an attempt to present onstage people, places, and events corresponding to those in everyday life.

REALISTIC AND NONREALISTIC SCENERY

Generally, realism and nonrealism call for different design elements, underscoring the difference in style between these two types of theatre. Here (top), we see an extremely realistic set, designed by James Noone for a production of William Inge's *Bus Stop* at the Huntington Theatre, directed by Nicholas Martin. Lighting design: Philip Rosenberg; costume design: Miranda Hoffman. The bottom scene is a surrealistic landscape designed by the avant-garde director Robert Wilson for his rock opera *POEtry,* about Edgar Allan Poe. There is no attempt to portray reality; rather, there is a surrealistic presentation of images and ideas. (top: ©T. Charles Erickson; bottom: ©Hermann and Clärchen Baus)

with a production conforms to our observation of the world around us. This includes the way characters speak and behave, the clothes they wear, the events that occur in the play, and the physical environment. Characters presented in a living room or a bar, for example, will look and act as we expect people in those settings to look and act.

On the other hand, *nonrealism*, or *departures from realism,* means all types of theatre that depart from observable reality. A musical in which characters sing and dance is nonrealistic because we do not ordinarily go around singing and dancing in public places. A play like Shakespeare's **Macbeth** is unrealistic because it has witches and ghosts—two types of creatures not encountered in our everyday existence. Also, the language of the play is poetry, and there are soliloquies in which characters speak thoughts out loud—again, these are elements that depart from the reality we see in our daily lives. Nonrealistic elements are, of course, highly theatrical and can increase our pleasure and excitement. Moreover, they often indicate a deeper reality than we see on the surface. Thus "departures from realism" does not imply that something is not genuine or not true; it simply means that something is a departure from what we see in the world around us.

The terms, then, are simply ways of categorizing aspects of theatre and are not mutually exclusive; they can be a helpful starting point in evaluating scene design, because scenery can quickly signal to an audience the type of world we are viewing.

Establishing Locale and Period   Whether realistic or not, a stage set should tell us where and when the play takes place. Is the locale a bar? A bedroom? A courtroom? A palace? A forest? The set should also indicate the time period. A kitchen with old-fashioned utensils and no electric appliances sets the play in the past. An early radio and an icebox might tell us that the period is the 1920s. A spaceship or the landscape of a faraway planet would suggest that the play is set in the future.

In addition to indicating time and place, the setting can also tell us what kinds of characters a play is about. For example, the characters may be neat and formal or lazy and sloppy. They may be kings and queens or members of an ordinary suburban family. The scenery should suggest these things immediately.

Developing a Design Concept   In order to convey information, the scene designer frequently develops a *design concept*. Such a concept should be arrived at in consultation with the director and should complement the directorial concept, as discussed previously. The design concept is a unifying idea carried out visually. For García Lorca's *The House of Bernarda Alba*, for example, such a concept would be a claustrophobic setting that sets the tone for the entire play.

A strong design concept is particularly important when the time and place of a play have been shifted. Modern stage designs for Shakespeare's **A Midsummer Night's Dream** illustrate this point. In most productions, this play is performed in a palace and a forest, as suggested by the text. But the director Peter Brook, in his landmark production, wanted to give the play a clean, spare look so that the audience would see its contemporary implications. Accordingly, the scene designer, Sally Jacobs (1932–), fashioned a single set consisting of three bare white walls, rather like the walls of a gymnasium. This single set was used as the background for all the scenes in the play, giving visual unity to the production and also creating a modern, somewhat abstract atmosphere. As part of the action, trapezes were lowered onto the stage at various times, and in some scenes the performers actually played their parts suspended in midair.

Nonrealism   Also known as *departures from realism,* means all types of theatre that depart from observable reality.

SCENE DESIGN SETS THE TONE

Good scene design sets the tone and style of a production, letting the audience know where and when the action takes place and whether the play is a tragedy, a comedy, or some other type of drama. Also, it harmonizes with other elements of the production—script, acting, and direction—to create a unified whole. The scene designer Patrick Carl created this rural Russian setting for Chekhov's *The Three Sisters,* directed by Joe Dowling at the Guthrie Theater. The costumes are by Paul Tazewell. (©T. Charles Erickson)

A more recent example of a distinctive design concept was that of director Diane Paulus, scene designer Scott Pask, and other members of the design team to create on stage the world of a circus for a Broadway revival of the musical *Pippin* in 2013. To accomplish this, acrobats, high wire performers, jugglers and a host of other circus artists were incorporated into the production.

Providing a Central Image or Metaphor   The design concept is closely related to the idea of a central image or metaphor. Stage design not only must be consistent with the play; it should have its own integrity. The elements of the design—lines, shapes, and colors—should add up to a complete visual universe for the play. Often, therefore, the designer tries to develop a central image or metaphor. In a 2013 production of *The Color Purple*, designed by John Doyle, who was also the director, the set was an abstract recreation of a single room, a wooden house, with a number of straight-back chairs hanging on the back wall as the central image. Company members would take chairs from the wall and create various spaces that represented the constant change of environment as the lead character went on her journey.

Coordinating Scenery with the Whole   Because scenic elements have such strong symbolic value and are so important to the overall effect of a production, the designer needs to provide scenery consistent with the playwright's intent and the

A CENTRAL DESIGN IMAGE

For a production of the musical *The Color Purple*, director and designer John Doyle created a central design concept consisting of a bare wooden wall on which chairs were hung. To create different locales and scenes, performers would take chairs off the wall and place them on stage. They could thus indicate a wide variety of spaces in a very novel and economic way. Based on the novel by Alice Walker, the book was by Marsha Norman and the music by Brenda Russell. Shown here in the role of Harpo is Adebayo Bolaji. (©Geraint Lewis/Alamy Stock Photo)

director's concept. If the text and acting are highly stylized, the setting should be stylized too. If the text and acting are realistic, the setting should also be realistic, rather than, say, a fantastic or overpowering spectacle. As with other elements, the setting should contribute to the overall effect of a production.

Solving Practical Design Problems   Finally, the scene designer must deal with practical problems of design. Many of these involve physical elements of stage design, to which we'll now turn.

Elements of Scene Design

Five Elements of Scene Design   As the scene designer proceeds, he or she makes use of the following elements:

1. *Line*, the outline or silhouette of elements onstage; for example, predominantly curved lines versus sharply angular lines.

2. *Mass*, the overall bulk or weight of scenic elements; for example, a series of high, heavy platforms or fortress walls versus a bare stage or a stage with only a single tree on it.

3. *Composition*, the balance and arrangement of elements; the way elements are arranged; for example, mostly to one side of the stage, in a vertical or horizontal configuration, or equally distributed onstage.

4. *Texture*, the "feel" projected by surfaces and fabrics; for example, the slickness of chrome or glass versus the roughness of brick or burlap.

5. *Color*, the shadings and contrasts of color combinations.

The designer will use these elements to affect us, in conjunction with the action and other aspects of the production.

Physical Layout: The Playing Area   A playing area must, obviously, fit into a certain stage space and accommodate the performers. A designer cannot plan a gigantic stage setting for a theatre where the proscenium opening is only twenty feet wide and the stage is no more than fifteen feet deep. By the same token, to design a small room in the midst of a forty-foot stage opening might be ludicrous.

The designer must also take into account the physical layout of the stage space. If a performer must leave by a door on the right side of the stage and return a few moments later by a door on the left, the designer must obviously provide space for crossing behind the scenery. If performers need to change costumes quickly offstage, the scene designer must make certain that there is room offstage for changing. If there is to be a sword fight, the actors must have space in which to make their turns, to advance and retreat.

> **Ground plan**   A blueprint or floor plan of the stage indicating the placement of scenery, furniture, doors and windows, and the various levels of the stage, as well as the walls of rooms, platforms, etc.

Any type of physical movement requires a certain amount of space, and the scene designer must allow for this in his or her ground plan. A ***ground plan*** is a floor plan outlining the various levels on the stage and indicating the placement of all scenery, furniture, doors, windows, and so on. The designer, working in conjunction with the director, is chiefly responsible for ensuring a practical ground plan.

How doors open and close, where a sofa is placed, at what angle steps will lead to a second floor— all these are important. Performers must be able to execute stairs easily and to sit in such a way that the audience can readily see them, and they must have enough space to interact with each other naturally and convincingly. If a performer opens a door onstage and is immediately blocked from the view of the audience, this is obviously an error on the part of the scene designer.

Materials and Machinery of Scene Design   There are some long-used materials and machinery for scene design that continue to be

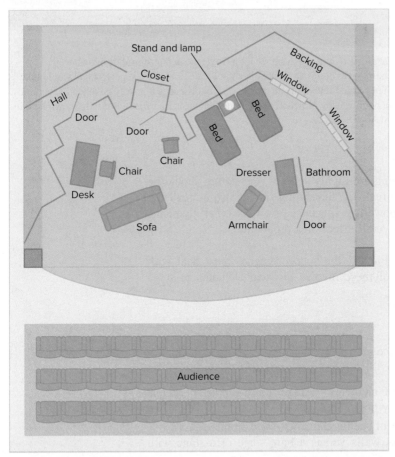

GROUND PLAN
To aid the director, performers, and stage technicians, the designer draws a ground plan, or blueprint of the stage, showing the exact locations of furniture, walls, windows, doors, and other scenic elements.

IN FOCUS: THE TECHNOLOGICAL INNOVATIONS OF THE GLOBAL DESIGNER JOSEF SVOBODA

The Czech scene designer Josef Svoboda (1920–2002) developed a number of significant techniques in stage design, which have since been adopted and utilized by designers in countries around the globe. Svoboda's work centered on his understanding of the kinetic stage and scenography. The term *kinetic stage* refers to his belief that the set should not function independently of the actors, but rather should develop and adapt as a performance progresses. *Scenography* was what he called his art, conveying the sense that he created a whole physical space, not just designs on paper intended for the back of the stage. His experiments with these ideas led to many significant concepts in modern stage design, most notably the *polyekran*, *diapolyekran,* and *laterna magika*.

Polyekran literally means multiscreen and was the practice, devised by Svoboda, of using multiple screens

at multiple angles and heights. Although real people and objects were projected, the aim was to convince the spectators not that they were looking at the real object, but rather that they were looking at a projection, or a collage of projections. A later development of this technique was *diapolyekran*, which employed whole walls of small, square screens making up a composite image. The wall of screens could be used to present one unified image, cubist images, or a collage.

Laterna magika, the best-known of his innovations, used screens in conjunction with actors; the actors were part of the film, and the film was part of the action. The projections used in this form were not simply for decoration, or for communicating images independent of the action; rather, the projections and action functioned together, creating a new manner of performance.

These developments were introduced to the global community in 1958 at the Brussels World's Fair, where they instantly commanded attention from the wider theatrical community. Svoboda had been the chief designer at the National Theatre in Prague at the time of the World's Fair, and a showcase of the work of the theatre was displayed to the global audience, winning him three medals.

What was seen as ingenious in 1958 was quickly adopted and adapted by numerous practitioners in many countries, and the effect of these means of design can still be witnessed in contemporary theatre, in performance art, and on Broadway, as well as at rock concerts and sporting events. This incorporation of screens and projections as well as video into onstage action has infiltrated the world of the theatre to the extent that it has become one of the conventional tools of theatre design worldwide.

Prepared by Naomi Stubbs, Associate Professor LaGuardia College, CUNY.

(©Michael Krumphanzl/AFP/Newscom)

used even in our increasingly technologically advanced theatre world. In creating a stage set, a designer begins with the stage floor. At times, trapdoors are set into the floor; through them, performers can enter or leave the stage. For some productions, tracks or slots are set into the stage floor, and set pieces or wagons are brought onstage in these tracks. A **wagon** is a low platform set on wheels.

Wagon Low platform mounted on wheels or casters by means of which scenery is moved on and offstage.

SPECIAL SCENIC EFFECTS: THE SCRIM

Scene designers use various materials and devices to achieve their effects. One popular scenic element is the scrim, which can be transparent when light comes from behind it and opaque when light comes from the front. It is especially effective for scenes of memory and fantasy. Shown here is the use of a scrim in the Broadway musical *An American in Paris*. (©Nigel Norrington/Camera Press/Redux)

SCENIC PROJECTIONS

An increasingly popular scenic resource is projections: rear-screen and front-screen projections, produced on an opaque surface or on a scrim. Projections allow rapid changes of locale, panoramic views, and abstract designs. Shown here is a scene from a production of *The Curious Incident of the Dog in the Night-Time* at the National Theatre in London, with video designed by Finn Ross. Note the letters highlighted and silhouetted on the walls around the main character Christopher Boone, played by Graham Butler. (©Geraint Lewis/Alamy Stock Photo)

SPECIAL EFFECTS

All manner of stage spectacle, from the eerie to the comic, come under the heading of special effects. An ancient tradition in the theatre, these effects can include fog, ghosts, and swords that appear to run through victims. The play *Thirty Nine Steps* calls for fog when we see the characters, Pamela (Jennifer Ferrin) and Hannay (Charles Edwards) running for their lives, hoping to escape danger by climbing up a ladder. The play, which had its American premiere with the Huntington Theatre Company, is based on the Alfred Hitchcock film of the same name. The scenic and costume designer was Peter McKintosh. (©T. Charles Erickson)

Wagon stages are brought onstage electronically using computer assistance or by stagehands hidden behind them. This type of scene change is frequently used in musical theatre. Another device used along the stage floor is a *treadmill*, which can carry performers, furniture, or props from one side of the stage to the other. Sometimes the stage floor includes a ***turntable***—a circle, set into the floor, which is rotated mechanically or electronically to bring one set into view as another disappears.

Formerly, equipment such as turntables, wagons, and treadmills would be moved mechanically or by hand. In recent years, however, these operations have been computerized. Complicated scene changes can be controlled by computer so that they take place efficiently and simultaneously. Computers can also control the turning and shifting of scenic elements. In addition, safety features are built into the new computerized equipment. When performers are on a moving treadmill, for example, light beams or pressure-sensitive plates can detect a malfunction and shut the system down before anyone is hurt.

Instead of coming from the sides, scenery can be dropped from the ***fly loft***; *to fly* is the term used when scenery is raised into the area above the stage, out of sight of the audience.

From floor level, ramps and platforms can be built to any height desired. To create walls or divisions of other kinds, for many years the most commonly used element was the ***flat***, so named because it is a single flat unit, consisting of canvas stretched on a wood frame. The side of the flat facing the audience was painted to look like a solid wall, and flats used connected together were made to look like a complete room.

Today scene designers and shop technicians have turned increasingly to the *hard flat*, sometimes called a *movie* or *Hollywood flat*; it consists of a thin, solid material, called *lauan*, mounted on a wooden or hollow metal frame. A hard flat can be painted, and three-dimensional plastic moldings can be attached to it, creating cornices, chair rails, and other interesting features. Other vertical units are cutouts—small pieces made like flats or cut out of plywood. These too can be painted.

A special type of scenery is the ***scrim***—a gauze or cloth screen. A scrim can be painted like a regular flat; however, the wide mesh of the cloth allows light to pass through. When light shines on a scrim from the front—that is, from our point of view in the audience—it is reflected off the painted surface, and the scrim appears to be a solid surface. When light comes from behind, the scrim becomes transparent and, as audience members, we can see performers and scenery behind it. Scrims are particularly effective in scenes where ghosts appear or when eerie

Turntable A circle set into the floor of a stage, which is rotated mechanically or electronically to bring one set into view as another disappears.

Fly loft Space above the stage where scenery may be lifted out of sight by ropes and pulleys.

Flat A scenic unit consisting of canvas stretched on a wooden frame often used with similar units to create a set.

Scrim Thin, open-weave fabric which is nearly transparent when lit from behind and opaque when lit from the front.

IN FOCUS: NEW DESIGN MATERIALS: VIDEO AND PROJECTION DESIGN

Video design and projection design are burgeoning areas of stage design. While early on, video and projection design consisted of integrating film and static images onto the stage of live theatre events, with the advent of greater computer control, the introduction of tablets and other hand-held devices, high definition video, more sophisticated projection technology, and digital downloads, designers in these areas have become more significant contributors to the creation of an overall stage design, not just special effects. In some instances, they have become equal partners with the set designer.

The design process itself has changed owing to the development of 3D animation software in which the set design can be manipulated and presented without the need to create a series of traditional models. Projection mapping allows projection to be designed and viewed on a computer and then projected on various three-dimensional objects of varying sizes on stage, not just on a two-dimensional surface as was true in the past.

But even more significantly, the designs themselves incorporate these new technologies. Today, enhanced projectors, 3D projections, and high-definition video can be employed to create on stage, for example, avatars that seem to interact with live actors. Actors can walk through projections or become part of a projection, creating magical effects. Entire sets can be replaced by high-tech videos and projections. Gaming technology allows live actors to initiate moments of special effects on stage themselves.

Some critics worry that the emphasis on technology in design is an ultimately unsuccessful attempt by theatre artists to compete with film and television and unfortunately undercuts what theatre does best: creating live interaction between the actor and the audience. However, others point out that throughout theatre history, all the way back to the Greeks and Romans, there have been experiments with special effects and new technologies. Our theatre will continue to explore the ways in which the innovations of this digital age can be incorporated in live performances.

effects are desired. Scrims are also useful in memory plays or plays with flashbacks: The audience sees the scene in the present in front of the scrim; then, as the lights in front fade and the lights behind come up, a scene with a cloudy, translucent quality appears through the gauzelike scrim, indicating a scene taking place in someone's memory or in the past.

Another scenic device is *screen projection*. An image can be projected on a screen either from in front—as in an ordinary movie theatre—or from behind. The advantage of projection from behind is that the performers will not be in the beam of light, and thus there will be no shadows or silhouettes. And today, projections can be projected onto three dimensional objects and manipulated through the use of computers.

Obviously, projections offer many advantages: images can change with the rapidity of cinema, and vast scenes can be presented onstage in a way that would otherwise require tremendously elaborate scene painting. Two recent productions that used projections extensively and successfully in London and then on Broadway were *War Horse* and *The Curious Incident of the Dog in the Night-Time*.

The use of video and projection has led to scene designers either becoming proficient with the new technology (since in some instances, video and projections literally replace scenery) or with video and projection designers being employed as part of the design team.

1. Think about your residence hall room or your home as a set design. What does it reveal about you? Why?

2. Set your classroom up as a proscenium theatre, with the audience facing in one direction. Using stage directions (stage right, stage left, upstage, downstage), direct a classmate around the stage area.

3. If a designer was going to create a play with you as a character, what props would be most central to representing you on stage?

4. Watch a recent film that employs significant special effects. Why are such special effects so popular? Is there any way that the same effects could be created in the theatre?

5. Visit your university or community theatre scene shop. What types of equipment are found in the shop? Is there a set under construction? Ask if there are drawings, elevations, or ground plans that you might review.

6. Visit a technical rehearsal at your university or community theatre. Ask if you can walk around the setting prior to or after the rehearsal. What elements make up the set? Is any machinery being employed for set changes?

In recent years, many avant-garde artists have also incorporated video screens and video projections into production design, frequently to draw stark parallels or contrasts between the live performance and something captured on video.

Special Effects   Scrims and projections bring us to a consideration of special effects. These are effects of scenery, lighting, sound, and props that seem unusual or even miraculous. (The term ***prop*** comes from the word property; it refers to any object that will be used onstage but is not a permanent part of the scenery or costumes. Props are such things as smartphones, lamps, mirrors, computers, walking sticks, umbrellas, and fans.) Special effects include fog, ghosts, knives or swords that appear to stab victims, walls and windows that fall apart, and so forth.

Prop   Properties; objects that are used by performers onstage or are necessary to complete a set.

Today, films and television—because of their technical capabilities—have very realistic special effects, like burning buildings and exploding cars. Also, computers can create the world of dinosaurs, supernatural universes, or all forms of catastrophes.

However, the use of special effects onstage is almost as old as theatre itself. From the Greeks on, theatre has tried to create the illusion of the miraculous or extraordinary. With the enhanced use of technology, along with all of the ways in which new media can be employed, theatrical productions frequently incorporate sophisticated effects.

An example of the use of an onstage special effect occurs in the internationally popular musical *The Phantom of the Opera*, when a huge chandelier falls from the top of the auditorium onto the stage. In the musical *Matilda* (2010), a child seemingly writes on a chalkboard using her eyes. Unbeknownst to the audience, the chalkboard is plastic and has the letters projected on it from a screen behind it.

We will see, in a later discussion, that there are also many special effects using lighting and sound.

The Process of Scene Design

In meeting the objectives described above, how does the scene designer proceed? Although every designer has his or her own method, usually the same general pattern is followed.

STEPS IN THE SCENE DESIGN PROCESS

In designing a production, the scenic, costume, lighting, and sound designers look closely at the script and work cooperatively with the director and with one another. Scene designers often make sketches, computer-generated designs, and models in preparing for the scenic aspect of a production. Here we see three stages in the scene design for the musical *In the Heights,* which originated off-Broadway at the 37 Arts Theatre in New York and later moved to Broadway. The scene designer Anna Louizos carefully scouted out the Washington Heights neighborhood in Manhattan where the play takes place and made many rough pencil sketches, one of which is shown here at the top. The second photo shows one of various set models she built and the bottom photo shows the completed set with actors onstage. (Upper left and right: ©Anna Louizos; Bottom: ©Sara Krulwich/The New York Times/Redux)

The designer reads the script and develops ideas about scene designs and a design concept. He or she may even make a few rough sketches to illustrate thoughts about the designs. Meanwhile, the director also has ideas about the scenery. These ideas may vary considerably, depending on the director: They may be vague, or they may be an exact picture of what the scenery should look like.

Director and designer meet for a preliminary conference to exchange ideas about the design. During these discussions, they will develop and discuss questions of style, a visual concept for the production, and the needs of the performers.

Next, the designer develops preliminary sketches, called *thumbnail sketches*, and rough plans to provide a basis for further discussions about the scenic elements.

As the designer proceeds, he or she attempts to fill out the visual concept with sketches, drawings, models, and the like. Sometimes the designer will bring the director sketches showing several possible ideas, each emphasizing different elements to achieve different results.

When the director and the designer have decided on an idea and a rough design, the designer will make a more complete sketch, usually in color, called a ***rendering***. If the director approves of the rendering, the designer will make a small-scale three-dimensional model that the director can use to help stage the show. There are two types of models. One shows only the location of the platform and walls, with perhaps some light detail drawn in; it is usually all white. The other is a complete, finished model: Everything is duplicated as fully as possible, including color and perhaps moldings and texture.

Rendering A complete drawing of a set, usually in color.

Today, designers increasingly use computers and computer graphics to develop not only ground plans but also their renderings, thumbnail sketches, and three-dimensional models of what a set will look like. Computerized design, known technically as ***computer-assisted design (CAD)***, is very flexible. The designer can make instantaneous changes in what appears on the screen and can easily indicate to the director and others alternative plans and features of a stage set. Not only ground plans but also the three-dimensional look of a set can be instantaneously rearranged to let both director and designer see what various configurations would look like. In this way, the scene can be shown in three dimensions; it can also be looked at from various perspectives: from the right or left, from above, from the front.

Computer-assisted design (CAD) Designs created by computer. All features of a set design, including ground plans, elevations, and walls, can be indicated by computer, and variations and alternations can be easily created and displayed.

These digital renderings and models can be created and shared on tablets and other hand-held devices as well as on computers. Designs can be sent immediately to directors and other collaborators via e-mail or on the "digital cloud."

THE SCENE DESIGNER'S COLLABORATORS AND THE PRODUCTION PROCESS

As with every element of theatre, there is a collaborative aspect to scene design: In addition to the director, there are a number of other important people with whom the scene designer works. In fact, any scene design would be little more than a creative idea without the input of the following collaborators: technical directors, property designers, scenic charge artists, stage managers, design assistants, and skilled technicians working in every one of these areas, often with expanded new technologies. These scenic collaborators are essential at every level of production, from university theatre to regional professional theatre to Broadway.

A few definitions are in order. The ***technical director*** is responsible for solving overall technical problems; he or she is in charge of scheduling, constructing

Technical director Staff member responsible for scheduling, construction, and installation of all equipment; he or she is responsible for guaranteeing that designs are executed according to the designer's specifications.

and painting scenery, and in general making certain that all designs are executed as conceived by the scene designer. The *property designer* creates and executes all props; this work may include building special pieces of furniture, finding or devising magical equipment, and selecting items such as lamps and other accessories. *Scenic charge artists* are responsible for seeing that sets are built and painted according to the specifications of the scene designer. In the case of painting the set, the person in charge is referred to as the *paint charge artist.* As noted earlier in this chapter, projection design is becoming a more common feature of the scenic environment, also requiring additional skilled technicians to bring the world of the play to life.

Realizing the design typically begins with drafting (predominantly with CAD these days, including the use of tablets and other hand-held digital devices) all production ground plans, also known as floor plans, which are detailed layouts of each scenic location drafted within the context of a specific theatre space. Drawings that show all exact scenic details from the point of view of the audience are known as *designer/front elevations.* The drafting of the designer/front elevations is completed either by the scene designer or by various design assistants. These drawings are then used to construct accurate scenic models or perspective renderings that are useful visual tools for anyone involved in the production. Once they have been given final approval by the director, the floor plans are delivered to the stage manager, who will tape on the floor of the rehearsal spaces an accurate, full-scale version of all platforms, ramps, staircases, and entrances and exits to be used by the director and the actors in rehearsal.

The use of CAD (which, as noted, includes the use of hand-held digital devices as well as computers) is now commonplace to create almost all of these representations of settings since designers and their associates, assistants and collaborators are now using advanced CAD skills. The flexibility of CAD allows designers to make changes very quickly and to share designs electronically with all collaborators. Designs can be sent via e-mail, by placing them in the "digital cloud," or viewed on tablets or other hand-held devices. Such technological flexibility in the design process, along with the use of projection and video technology, have made all forms of computer-assisted design the norm in almost all theatres today.

The technical director uses the floor plans to determine where all the construction elements will go, as well as to determine backstage escapes for actors. The technical director then completes construction drawings for all those floor plan elements. The technical director also converts the complete set of designer/front elevations into a complete set of rear elevations or working drawings for construction purposes. Without this critical engineering and drafting step, the scenery could never be built accurately or safely. The technical director and scenic designer work together in much the same way an engineer will work with an architect in completing the blueprints to plan construction of a building.

The visual world of many production designs is so complex that a property designer typically works as an essential collaborator with the scenic designer. The property area is also broken down into areas: (1) functional props used by actors, and (2) set dressing, which fills out the visual stage reality. Once the scene designer has approved all of the property designer's research, solutions, and drawings, those are also forwarded to the technical director to be worked into the construction schedule. It is also frequently the property designer who completes the mechanical special effects used in theatrical production.

1. What production that you have attended had the most elaborate scenery and special effects? What effect did these visual elements have on you? Were you captivated by the visual elements or did you think they were overdone?

2. What production that you have seen had the least amount of scenery and visual effects? Did you miss seeing an elaborate scene design or did you enjoy using your imagination to create the setting in your mind?

3. Have you seen a production that has many changes of setting? How efficiently and effectively were the scene changes carried out? What types of stage machinery was employed to create smooth transitions?

4. It is often argued that film and television can employ more realistic scenery and special effects than the theatre. Is there any way in which theatrical scenery and special effects compete with those in the media?

Owing to developments in computer and electronic technology, special effect solutions are frequently crafted by projection designers as well. Although not many productions utilize the intense level of scenic projection noted previously, projection technology solutions are finding their way into many production designs for special visual effects requiring the presence of yet another essential scenic collaborator.

The scene designer and his or her assistants also complete a full series of paint elevations that are delivered to the scenic charge artist who works with a group of scenic artists in completing the painting of the actual scenery. Paint charge and scenic artists require both talent and technique, for instance, to create the feeling of rare old wood in a library, or of bricks, or of a glossy, elegant surface in an expensive living room.

In commercial theatre, construction drawings and paint elevations are sent to scenic houses separate from the theatre that specialize in both construction and painting. In regional theatres and university settings there are typically support spaces and support staff for scenic, property, painting, and costume construction on-site. In these settings the entire production team is typically present at all times, allowing for convenient tracking of the construction and painting process. In Broadway and other professional producing theatres without technical support spaces and staff, it is necessary for the designer or the assistant designers (or both) to visit the scenic houses and paint studios to check on progress and to assure consistency with the original design intent.

When the time comes for technical rehearsals, dress rehearsals, and the actual performances after the official opening, a production requires backstage leadership by the stage management team. The members of this team call all the cues for lights, sound, projections, scenic shifts, and actors' entrances. An entire crew of stagehands will work together to coordinate every change, no matter how small, in the visual world of the play. These changes may involve a fly crew for flown scenery, a shift crew for either automated or manual shifting of entire settings, and a property crew for any preparation or movement of furniture and properties onstage or off. Meanwhile a crew of dressers, whose work will be covered in more detail in the next chapter, will work backstage with the actors helping them prepare for the upcoming scene. As noted earlier in our discussion of directing, once a production moves beyond opening night, it is controlled by the stage manager, who is also responsible for maintaining the director's artistic intent as well as maintaining consistency in cue placement and the visual world of the play.

Designing a Total Environment

Sometimes a designer goes beyond scenery and special effects to design an entire theatre space, rearranging the seating for spectators and determining the relationship of the stage area to the audience. For instance, in an open space such as a gymnasium or warehouse, a designer might build an entire theatre, including the seats or stands for the audience and the designated acting areas. In this case, the designer considers the size and shape of the space, the texture and nature of the building materials, the atmosphere of the space, and the needs of the play itself. This is also true of multifocus theatre.

Even in Broadway theatres some designers change the architecture of the theatre space in creating the world of the play; we noted, in the previous chapter, that a current example is *Natasha, Pierre & the Great Comet of 1812*. Another example, was that when the rock musical *Bloody, Bloody Andrew Jackson* transferred to Broadway in 2010, the design for that production extended into the audience area.

A slight twist on the idea of creating a total environment was employed in the musical *Once* (2012). The bar used as the set was also used during intermission to serve refreshments to audience members, thereby blurring the distinction between the auditorium and the playing space.

Evaluating Scene Design

After we attend a production, there are many questions we should ask ourselves as we try to evaluate the scene design and its success in supporting the play presented. Among those questions are:

1. What information was conveyed by the scenery about time, place, characters, and situation? How was this information conveyed to you?
2. What was the overall atmosphere of the setting? How was that atmosphere created?
3. Did any colors dominate the design? How did colors affect your impression of the theater event?
4. Was the setting a specific place, or was it no recognizable or real locale? Did that choice seem appropriate for the play?
5. If the setting was realistic, how effectively did it reproduce what the place would actually look like?
6. Were there symbolic elements in the scenery? If so, what were they? How did they relate to the play?
7. Were there many scene changes? Were they handled effectively? Could you tell how they were done?
8. Were projections or video used in the production? If so what was their function: to create scenery, for special effects, for both? Did you feel the use of these media was appropriate? Why or why not?
9. Were there any special effects? Were you able to ascertain how they were done?

We have been examining the work of the scene designer. We turn in the next chapter to someone whose work is closely related: the costume designer.

SUMMARY

1. We encounter forms of scene design in everyday life: in the carefully planned decor of a restaurant, in a hotel lobby, or in a decorated apartment.

2. Scene design for the stage differs from interior decorating in that it creates an environment and an atmosphere that is not complete until occupied by performers and that is able to meet the practical needs of the script.

3. In addition to creating an environment, the scene designer has the following objectives: to set tone and style, distinguish realism from nonrealism, establish time and place, develop a design concept, provide a central design metaphor, coordinate scenery with other elements, and deal with practical considerations.

4. As in other aspects of theatre, in scene design there has been more and more crossover, and interaction, between theatre design and design for many types of popular entertainment.

5. In practical terms the scene designer must deal with the limits of the stage space and the offstage area. For example, ramps must not be inclined too steeply, and platforms must provide an adequate playing area for the performers. In short, the stage designer must know the practical considerations of stage usage and stage carpentry, as well as the materials available, in order to achieve desired effects. Close work with the technical director allows the scene designer to push the limits of construction in creating a unique visual world while maintaining a safe environment for performers.

6. In theatrical productions that stress visual elements over the play or the acting, the scene design must constantly engage and entrance the spectator.

7. Special effects are elements of scenery, lighting, costumes, props, or sound that appear highly unusual or miraculous. Technical expertise is required to develop them properly.

8. Elements of design include line, mass, composition, texture, color, rhythm, and movement.

9. The scene designer works closely with the director and other designers and creates a series of drawings (sketches and renderings) and models of what the final stage picture will look like.

10. In dealing with created or found space, the designer must plan the entire environment: the audience area as well as the stage area.

11. The technical director, with his or her staff, supervises the construction of scenery, special effects, and the like, in order to meet the designer's specifications.

12. A scenic charge artist and additional scenic artists must translate the look shown in models, renderings, and paint elevations into the full-scale version of the design.

13. Working with the technical director and the scenic charge artist are the property designer and the paint charge artist.

STAGE COSTUMES

9

Clothes have often indicated or signaled a number of things regarding the wearer, including the following:

- Position and status
- Gender identity
- Occupation
- Relative flamboyance or modesty
- Degree of independence or regimentation
- Whether one is dressed for work or leisure, for a routine event or a special occasion

As soon as we see what clothing people are wearing, we receive messages about them and form impressions of them. We instantaneously relate those messages and impressions to our past experience and our preconceptions, and we make judgments, including value judgments. Even if we have never before laid eyes on someone, we feel we know a great deal when we first see what he or she is wearing.

COSTUMES FOR THE STAGE

In theatre, clothes send us signals similar to those in everyday life, but as with the other elements of theatre, there are significant differences between the costumes of everyday life and theatrical costumes. Stage costumes often communicate the same information as ordinary clothes with regard to gender identity, position, and occupation; but onstage this information is magnified because every element in theatre is a focus of attention. Also, costumes on a stage must meet other requirements not normally imposed in everyday life. These requirements will be clearer after we look at the objectives of costume design.

◀ **STAGE COSTUMES: AESTHETIC, SYMBOLIC, AND SUITED TO THE CHARACTER**
In addition to being stylish and beautiful, costumes can convey a wealth of information to the audience. Seen here in a stylish, lavish costume of clearly expensive materials is actress Olivia Llewellyn in a production of Les Liaisons Dangereuses *at the Playhouse Theatre in London directed by Tim Fywell.* (©Robbie Jack/Corbis Entertainment/Getty Images)

Objectives of Costume Design

Stage costumes should meet the following seven requirements:

1. Help establish the style of a production.
2. Indicate the historical period of a play and the locale in which it occurs.
3. Indicate the nature of individual characters or groups in a play—their stations in life, their occupations, their personalities.
4. Show relationships among characters—separating major characters from minor ones, contrasting one group with another.
5. Where appropriate, symbolically convey the significance of individual characters or the theme of the play.
6. Meet the needs of individual performers, making it possible for a performer to move freely in a costume, perhaps to dance or engage in a sword fight, and (when required) to change quickly from one costume to another.
7. Be consistent with the production as a whole, especially other visual elements.

The Process of Costume Design

In order to achieve these objectives, the costume designer goes through a process similar to that of the scene designer. He or she reads the script, taking particular note of the characters: their age, gender identity, physical qualities, and special traits, as well as their roles in the play.

Early in the process, the costume designer also meets with the director and other designers to discuss the "look" that the show will have and how the various elements will be coordinated. The costume designer may make preliminary sketches, or use computer-assisted design, to show the director and other designers. These may include not only suggestions about style (for example, historical, modern, futuristic) but also ideas for colors and fabrics. Once agreed upon, these designs will move from sketches to renderings (which again may be done by hand or on computers or hand-held devices) of what the costumes will look like in their final form. Swatches of material may be attached to these designs, indicating the texture and color of the fabrics to be used.

As part of this process, the costume designer will meet with the members of the cast, measuring each performer and making certain that the costumes will be workable and appropriate for the individual actresses and actors.

The following sections discuss how the various objectives of costume design are realized by the designer in this process.

Setting Tone and Style   Along with scenery and lighting, costumes should inform us about the style of a play. For a production set in outer space, for instance, the costumes would be futuristic. For a Restoration comedy, the costumes could be quite elegant, with elaborate gowns for the women and lace at the men's collars and cuffs. For a tragedy, the clothes might be formal and dignified—seeing them, we would know immediately that the play itself was serious.

Indicating Time and Place   Costumes indicate the period and location of a play: whether it is historical or modern, whether it is set in a foreign country or the United States, and so on. A play might take place in ancient Egypt, in seventeenth-century Spain, or in modern Africa. Costumes should tell us when and where the action occurs.

For most historical plays, the director and the costume designer have a range of choices, depending on the directorial concept. For a production of Shakespeare's *Julius Caesar,* for instance, the costumes could indicate the ancient Roman period when Caesar actually lived; in this case, the costumes would include Roman togas and soldiers' helmets. Or the costumes could be Elizabethan. We know that in Shakespeare's day costumes were heightened versions of the English clothes worn at the time, regardless of the period in which a play was set. As a third option, the designer could create costumes for an entirely different period, even our own day—with the men in business suits, modern military uniforms, and perhaps even tuxedos. Whatever the choice, the historical period should be clearly indicated by the costumes.

A Girl   Dumas   Benoit

Cyrano de Bergerac Eleonora Duse Sarah Bernhardt
costume for Coquelin

COSTUME DESIGN: THE PROCESS
Costume designers often make preliminary sketches of costumes as they begin to design a production. Shown here are sketches for *The Ladies of the Camellias* by the costume designer Jess Goldstein for a production at the Yale Repertory Theatre. (©Jess Goldstein)

Identifying Status and Personality   Like clothing in everyday life, costumes can tell us whether people are from the aristocracy or the working class, whether they are blue-collar workers or professionals. But in theatre, these signals should usually be clear and unmistakable. For example, in real life a woman in a long white coat could be a doctor, a laboratory technician, or a hairdresser. A costume onstage must indicate the occupation exactly—by giving the doctor a stethoscope, for instance.

Costumes also tell us about the personalities of characters: A flamboyant person could be dressed in flashy colors; a shy, retiring person might wear subdued clothing.

Costumes also indicate age. This is particularly helpful when an older performer is playing a young person, or vice versa. A young person playing an older character, for instance, can wear padding or a beard.

Indicating Relationships among Characters   Characters in a play can be set apart by the way they are costumed. Major characters, for example, will be dressed differently from minor characters. Frequently, the costume designer will distinguish the major characters by dressing them in distinctive colors, in sharp contrast to the other characters. Consider, for instance, Shaw's *Saint Joan,* a play about Joan of Arc. Obviously, Joan should stand out from the soldiers surrounding her. Therefore, her costume might be bright blue while their costumes are steel gray. In another play of Shaw's, *Caesar and Cleopatra,* Cleopatra should stand out from her servants and soldiers.

photo essay
Stage Costumes Make a Strong Visual Statement

On these pages are three examples of striking costumes. Costume designers, using colors, fabric, intricate cuts and shapes of cloth, accessories, and other elements, create a special look for each production. The costumes must fit the actor and allow for easy movement, as well as be visually appealing. They must also be appropriate for the play, and communicate to the audience the period and the social status and the financial level of the characters wearing the costumes.

Seen in the first photo are John Scherer (Hysterium) and Beth McVey (Domina) in vividly colorful costumes designed by Matthew Hemesath for *A Funny Thing Happened On The Way To The Forum*, at the Papermill Playhouse. (©T Charles Erickson)

For this African-themed production of Shakespeare's *The Tempest* directed by Janice Honeyman at the Royal Shakespeare Company in collaboration with the Baxter Theatre Centre of Cape Town, South Africa, Illka Louw designed the spectacular scenery and costumes worn by Antony Sher as Prospero and Atandwa Kani as Ariel. (©Geraint Lewis)

Deborah Hay (Celimene) sinks to the floor in exasperation in Chicago Shakespeare Theater's *The School for Lies,* adapted from Molière's *The Misanthrope.* Directed by CST Artistic Director Barbara Gaines, written by David Ives, with hilarious costumes designed by Susan E. Mickey. (©Liz Lauren)

COSTUMES INDICATE SOCIAL RELATIONSHIPS
Along with their many other properties, costumes can signal the relationships and contrasts among characters in a production. Not only can costumes indicate the time period when a drama takes place, and the locale where it occurs, but they can and should indicate occupations and relative social positions. Who, for example, is a laborer or tradesman and who is a professional businessperson? In this scene from August Wilson's *Radio Golf* at the Goodman Theatre, we see John Earl Jelks as Sterling Johnson and Hassan El-Amin as Harmond Wilks in costumes designed by Susan Hilferty. The man on the right is a succcessful businessman; the man on the left is a laborer. (©Peter Wynn Thompson/Courtesy of the Goodman Theatre)

Costumes underline important divisions between groups. In **Romeo and Juliet,** the two feuding families, the Montagues and the Capulets, would be costumed in different colors. In a modern counterpart of *Romeo and Juliet,* the musical *West Side Story,* the two gangs are dressed in contrasting colors: The Jets might be in various shades of pink, purple, and lavender; the Sharks in shades of green, yellow, and lemon.

Creating Symbolic and Nonhuman Characters   In many plays, special costumes are called for to denote abstract ideas or give shape to fantastic creatures. Here the costume designer must develop an outfit that conveys the appropriate imaginative and symbolic qualities. In **Macbeth,** for instance, how does one clothe the witches or the ghost of Banquo? For the musical *The Lion King,* the director Julie Taymor, who was also the costume designer, used puppets, masks, and other devices to create outfits for numerous animal characters, such as lions, tigers, giraffes, and elephants.

Meeting Performers' Needs   Virtually every aspect of theatre has practical as well as aesthetic requirements, and costume design is no exception. No matter

THE COSTUME DESIGNER MEETS PERFORMERS' NEEDS
Costume designer Stefano Nicolao, a prodigious designer for theatre and film, works in his Venice studio on the creation of an elegant gown for a performer who is standing at a mirror. (©Reuters/Alamy Stock Photo)

how attractive or how symbolic, stage costumes must work for the performers. A long, flowing gown may look beautiful, but if it is too long and the performer wearing it trips walking down a flight of steps, the designer has overlooked an important practical consideration. If performers are required to duel or engage in hand-to-hand combat, their costumes must stand up to this wear and tear, and their arms and legs must have freedom of movement. If they are to dance, they must be able to turn, leap, and move freely.

Quick costume changes are also frequently called for in theatre. Tear-away seams and special fasteners are used so that one costume can be ripped off quickly and another put on (often with the assistance of dressers). On Broadway and in national touring productions it is also necessary to make costumes for more than one performer for the same role, although this is not typically the case in shorter runs in regional or university theatre productions.

Unlike scenery, which stays in place until it is moved, a costume is always in motion, moving as the performer moves. This provides an opportunity for the designer to develop grace and rhythm in the way a costume looks as it moves across the stage, but with that goes the great responsibility of making the costume workable for the performer.

Each of these specific costuming needs points to the absolute importance of skilled *stitchers* (technicians who sew all the costumes) and *drapers* (technicians who pattern, pin, and drape the fabric to fit individual actors perfectly) in a costume shop.

At times it is important for the costume designer to work closely with individual performers, who must know how to use the accessories and costumes provided for them. This is particularly true for historical costumes that re-create elements unique to that time period; such costumes often require the performer to work closely with the director and the costume designer and frequently with a movement specialist as well.

Stitchers The technicians who sew all of the costumes for a production.

Drapers Technicians who pattern, pin, and drape the fabric to fit the actors in a production perfectly.

Maintaining Consistency   Finally, costumes must be consistent with the entire production—especially with the various other visual elements. A realistic production set in the home of everyday people calls for down-to-earth costumes. A highly stylized production requires costumes designed with flair and imagination.

The Costume Designer at Work

The Costume Designer's Responsibilities   As noted earlier, the person who puts all these ideas into effect is the costume designer. Every production requires someone who takes responsibility for the costumes. This is true whether the costumes are *pulled* or *built*.

Pull   To choose a costume from an inventory owned by a theatre company or costume warehouse.

Pulling is a term used when costumes are rented (or maintained in an extensive costume collection in, for example, a university or regional theatre) and the designer goes to a costume house or storeroom and selects outfits that are appropriate for the production. The designer must already know about period, style, and the other matters discussed above. He or she must also have the measurements of all the performers for whom costumes are to be pulled. Seldom will pulled or rented costumes fit perfectly, and it is the responsibility of stitchers, often with tailoring experience, to complete the necessary alterations.

Build   To create a costume from scratch in a costume shop.

When costumes are *built*, they are created in a costume shop under the direction of the shop supervisor, who works closely with a costume designer in much the same way the technical director and scene designer work together. Before making a costume out of expensive fabrics, well-staffed costume shops will make *muslin mock-ups* of the costumes first, and those are then fitted to the actor. Next, the mock-ups are taken apart and used as patterns for the actual costume fabric.

In these shops, costumes are built in two different ways. Some are drafted as flat patterns based on the performer's measurements, and some are draped. Draping involves pinning and tucking the fabric directly to a dress form of the proper size and marking the fabric while it is on the dress form, in preparation for stitching, detailed finish work, and closures.

Today, technology has also made it possible to create mock-ups on a computer and cutting and draping can be completed with computer assistance.

The Costume Designer's Resources   Among the elements a costume designer works with are (as discussed below) (1) line, shape, and silhouette; (2) color; (3) fabric; and (as discussed later) (4) accessories.

Line   Of prime importance is the cut or line of the clothing. Do the lines of an outfit flow, or are they sharp and jagged? Does the clothing follow the lines of the body, or is there some element of exaggeration, such as shoulder pads or a bustle at the back of a dress? The outline or silhouette of a costume has always been significant. There is a strong visual contrast, for instance, between the line of an Egyptian female garment, flowing smoothly from shoulder to floor, and that of an empire gown of the early nineteenth century in Europe, which featured a horizontal line high above the waist, just below the breasts, with a line flowing from below the bosom to the feet. The silhouettes of these two styles would stand in marked contrast to a female outfit in the United States during the early 1930s: a short outfit with a prominent belt or sash cutting horizontally across the hips.

Undergarments are an aspect of costume design often overlooked by audiences. For female costumes, one example is the hoopskirt. In *The King and I,* a musical of 1951 that was revived at Lincoln Center in New York in 2015, Anna, an English schoolteacher in Siam, wears dresses with hoop skirts several feet in diameter,

One of the most active costume designers of recent times is William Ivey Long. Like many costume designers, he often sketches the costumes of the characters in the play, indicating the style of the clothes, the fabrics, the colors, and the silhouette. Long developed a collage board for all the characters in the "grand finale" of the musical *Hairspray*, not only sketching the costumes themselves but—below the sketches—adding swatches of fabric indicating colors and other qualities of the fabrics. Shown here are several of the costumes taken from the full cast of the finale, giving an indication of how the final costumes were developed. (Courtesy of William Ivey Long Studios)

which were in fashion in England in the mid-nineteenth century, the time of the play.

Other undergarments include bustles, which exaggerate the lines in the rear; and corsets, which can greatly alter posture and appearance. For example, some corsets pull in the waist and cause the wearer to stand very straight. But in the first decade of the twentieth century, women in society often bent forward because they wore a curved corset that forced them to thrust their shoulders and upper body forward.

Shown here is famed designer William Ivey Long in front of a display of his costume sketches for *The Lost Colony*, the nation's longest running historical drama, presented annually on Roanoke Island, on the outer banks of North Carolina. (©Chris Curry/AP Images)

COSTUMES CONVEY A MESSAGE
Costume designers for musicals, fantasies, and historical plays have the opportunity to create costumes that are highly decorative as well as eye-catching but also tell a story. In the musical *Hamilton,* non-traditionally cast contemporary performers wear elaborate costumes from the Revolutionary period in American history, thus presenting an interesting juxtaposition of time and events. Shown here are two stars of the original production Lin-Manuel Miranda (also the author) and actress Phillipa Soo, with costume design by Paul Tazewell. (©Theo Wargo/Getty Images)

A costume designer will be aware of the importance of undergarments and will use them to create the appropriate silhouette and line. During the nineteenth century there were times when men wore corsets to achieve the fashionable posture of the day.

Color A second important resource for costume designers is color. Earlier, we saw that leading characters can be dressed in a color that contrasts with the colors worn by other characters, and that characters from one family can be dressed in colors different from those of a rival family. Color also suggests mood: bright, warm colors for a happy mood; dark, somber colors for a more serious mood.

Beyond these applications, however, color can indicate changes in character and changes in mood. Near the beginning of Eugene O'Neill's *Mourning Becomes Electra,* General Manon, who has recently returned from the Civil War, dies, and his wife and daughter wear dark mourning clothes. Lavinia, the daughter, knows that her mother was involved in her father's death, and she and her brother conspire to murder the mother. Once they have done so, Lavinia adopts characteristics of her mother, and as an important symbol of this transformation, she puts on brightly colored clothes of the same shades her mother had worn when she was young.

Fabric Fabric is a third tool of the costume designer. In one sense, this is the costume designer's medium, for it is in fabric that silhouette and color are displayed. Just as important as those qualities are the texture and bulk of the fabric. What is its reflective quality? Does it have a sheen that reflects light? Or is it rough, so that it absorbs light? How does it drape on the wearer? Does it fall lightly to the floor and outline physical features, or does it hide them? Does it wrinkle naturally, or is it smooth? Ornamentation and trim can also be used. Fringe, lace, ruffles, feathers, beads—all these add to the attractiveness and individuality of a costume.

Beyond its inherent qualities, fabric has symbolic values. For example, burlap and other roughly textured cloths suggest people of the earth or of modest means. Silks and satins, on the other hand, suggest elegance and refinement—perhaps even royalty.

The connotations of fabrics may change with passing years. Two or three generations ago, blue denim was used only for work clothes, worn by laborers or by cowboys who rode horseback on a ranch. Today, denim is the fabric of choice in informal clothes for people of all incomes and all ages.

Using the combined resources of line, color, fabric, and trims, the costume designer arrives at individual outfits, which tell us a great deal about the characters who wear them and convey important visual signals about the style and meaning of the play as a whole.

The Costume Designer's Collaborators Once again, it is important to recognize that a number of collaborators aid in the process of costume design. Remember

IN FOCUS: TECHNOLOGY AND COSTUME DESIGN

As in the practice of scene design, costume designers also have had their work transformed by new technologies.

Costume research is now more easily done through the Web. Designers can review historical costumes by browsing museum sites through the Internet. Photographs and images of people in period clothing can be found through web browser searches. Newspapers and magazines from different time periods are also accessible.

Designers can use software to create their sketches on their computers or tablets. Designers who still sketch by hand can also scan and save their drawings digitally, as well as manipulate them in this fashion. This also makes all of their designs mobile so that they can have them on their laptop or hand-held device. In addition, designs can be e-mailed or shared through the "cloud." (This is also true for set design sketches.)

Technology has also affected the types of fabrics available and the ways in which designers and their collaborators work with them. Computers can now be used to assist in cutting and embroidering of costume materials and technology has allowed the production of fabrics that in the past might have been too expensive to use or too difficult to re-create. And laser cutting can allow for easier construction of very intricate designs.

Technology has also impacted costume designs that require ornamentation and special effects. 3D printing can be used to create hats, helmets, and other ornamental elements. A character who needs lights in his costume, such as in the Disney musical *Beauty and the Beast*, can have LED lights embedded in what he is wearing and the actor can control them with an unseen small switch. Fiber optics can be sewn into a fabric to create a costume that can be illuminated.

There are many other cutting edge costume technologies that are still being explored, including robotics (in which there are mechanized, computer controlled elements by the performer wearing the costume) and "intelligent" costumes that allow off-stage personnel to communicate with the costumes via a wireless network in order to create special effects.

that the costume shop supervisor is the lead costume technician, and there are other very specific job responsibilities in a typical costume shop.

Often young professionals, beginning a career, will start as buyers for professional shops that have copies of the designers' renderings. They will scour garment districts to find fabrics that best match the designer's renderings. After fabric comes back to the shop and the muslin mock-ups are made, it will go to a cutter-draper. A costume designer's "first hand" (see below) will often build the initial costume and complete the fitting with the designer and the actor.

It is important to note that the stage manager is typically responsible for scheduling all actors' fittings to work out times that coordinate with rehearsals and also the designer's shop schedule. Once the fitting has been completed, the costume will proceed to the costume designer's *first hand,* or a lead stitcher, who completes the detailed sewing. Once construction is completed, in cases where costumes should not look brand-new, they are turned over to design assistants for the purpose of ***distressing***, to make them look weathered and worn.

Distressing Making a costume look weathered or worn.

When costumes are completed and ready for dress rehearsals and performances, they become the responsibility of the wardrobe supervisor, who makes all decisions related to costume organization and preparation in the theatre. The wardrobe crew's responsibilities begin with backstage preparation before every performance and end when the laundry is completed following every performance. In an elaborate production, there are numerous dressers from the wardrobe crew assigned to actors, especially lead actors, during rehearsals and performances. There are other areas of specialty, and artisans integral to costume design, discussed in the next section.

RELATED ELEMENTS OF COSTUME DESIGN

Makeup

A part of costume is makeup—the application of cosmetics (paints, powders, and rouges) to the face and body. With regard to age and any other special facial features, an important function of makeup is to help the performer personify and embody a character.

Theatrical makeup used to be more popular than it is today. In a modern small theatre, performers playing realistic parts will often go without makeup of any consequence, in which case, they can handle their own makeup. Anything beyond the most simple makeup, however, demands an accomplished makeup designer to plan specifically what makeup performers will wear. Historical figures are frequently incorporated into realistic plays and may demand extensive use of extremely realistic prosthetic makeup. An example on Broadway was William Gibson's one-woman play *Golda's Balcony*. Nine prosthetic noses, cast in foam latex, were required each week for the show's star who played Israeli prime minister Golda Meir.

Makeup has a long and important history in theatre, and sometimes it is a necessity—one good example being makeup to highlight facial features that would not otherwise be visible in a large theatre. Even in a smaller theatre, bright lights tend to wash out cheekbones, eyebrows, and other facial features.

Makeup is often essential because the age of a character differs from that of the performer. Suppose that a nineteen-year-old performer is playing a sixty-year-old character. Through the use of makeup—a little gray in the hair or simulated wrinkles on the face—the appropriate age can be suggested. Another situation calling for makeup to indicate age is a play in which the characters grow older during the course of the action. The musical *I Do! I Do!* with book and lyrics by Tom Jones and music by Harvey Schmidt is based on the play *The Fourposter* by

 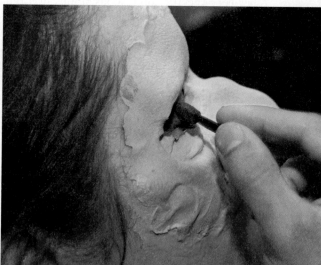

MAKEUP: CHANGING A FACE OR CREATING A NEW ONE

Makeup is an ancient theatre tradition. Makeup can highlight features of the face or parts of the body that might be washed out under the glare of stage lights. Makeup can also be used to alter the appearance of the face altogether. In the first photograph, makeup artist Suhyun Kang applies Day of the Dead makeup on actress Morwynna Cambridge for a performance mounted in London. The second photo shows a makeup artist altering the skin and eyes of a performer who is to play a witch. (left: ©Terence Mendoza/Alamy Stock Photo; right: ©Paul Wood/Alamy Stock Photo)

Jan de Hartog. In the musical, a husband and wife are shown in scenes covering many years in their married life, from the time when they are first married until they are quite old. In order to convey the passing years and their advancing age, the actress and actor must use makeup extensively.

Makeup is also a necessity for fantastic or other nonrealistic creatures. Douglas Turner Ward (b. 1930), a black playwright, wrote *Day of Absence* to be performed by black actors in whiteface. The implications of this effect are many, not the least being the reversal of the nineteenth-century minstrel performances in which white actors wore blackface to create stereotypical and racist depictions of African Americans.

Ward was not the first to put black actors in whiteface; French dramatist Jean Genet had part of the cast of his play *The Blacks* wear white masks.

A popular musical on Broadway and on tour, Stephen Schwartz's *Wicked* portrays a green witch named Elphaba, from birth until she becomes better known as the Wicked Witch of the West. Perhaps even more amazing in *Wicked* is the makeup on the numerous flying monkeys in the production.

Asian theatre frequently relies on heavy makeup. For instance, Japanese *kabuki*, a highly stylized theatre, uses completely nonrealistic makeup. The main characters must apply a base of white covering the entire face, over which bold patterns of red, blue, black, and brown are painted. The colors and patterns are symbolic of the character. In Chinese theatre, too, the colors of makeup are symbolic: All white suggests treachery, black means fierce integrity, red means loyalty, green indicates demons, while yellow stands for hidden cunning.

When using makeup, the human face becomes almost like a canvas for a painting. The features of the face may be heightened or exaggerated, or symbolic aspects of the face may be emphasized. In either case, makeup serves as an additional tool for the performer in creating an image of the character.

Hairstyles and Wigs

Another important component of costume design includes hairstyles and wigs. When costume designers create their renderings, they include characters' hairstyles as a part of the design, which will later require a hair and wig specialist as a part of the crew.

For women, hairstyles can sometimes denote period and social class. In the middle of the nineteenth century, for example, women often wore ringlets. A few decades later, in the 1890s, women wore their hair piled on top of the head in a pompadour referred to as the Gibson girl look. In the 1920s, women wore their hair marcelled, a hairstyle with waves made by a heated curling iron, sometimes slicked down close to the head. In the modern period, women wear their hair in more natural styles. But again there is tremendous variety—some women have short, curly hair; others have long hair, perhaps even down to the waist. The musical *Hairspray* featured young women in the bouffant hairdos of the 1960s.

For men, too, hairstyles are significant and sometimes symbolic. A military brush cut, an Elvis Presley–style pompadour, and a ponytail each point to a certain lifestyle, but each may be interpreted in several ways.

Audiences would actually be surprised to know how often wigs are used in theatrical productions. They may not even recognize a performer outside the theatre, because such a complete visual transformation can be accomplished with the use of wigs made from real hair. For a production, hair designers fashion the wigs in the shop before dress rehearsals. A hair and wig specialist is also required backstage to care for the wigs throughout the performance process to keep the hair looking exactly as the designer envisioned it.

One of the most amazing uses of a wig on Broadway was the extraordinary design by Paul Huntley for *Jekyll and Hyde the Musical*: The actor could manipulate the character's wig instantaneously, allowing him to shift back and forth between Jekyll and Hyde within the same song.

Masks

Masks appear to be as old as theatre, having been used in ancient Greek theatre and in the drama developed by primitive tribes. In one sense, the mask is an

1. How might what you are wearing today reveal your personality, your station in life, your character? What would lead someone to make those observations?

2. If you were a character in a play, what costume would you design for yourself to tell us the most about you? What are the key elements? Why?

3. Have you ever commented on a friend's makeup, hair, or accessories? What did your comments suggest about how you characterized your friend due to these "costume" elements?

4. Find photos of famous film stars in publications or on-line. What does the clothing they are wearing tell you about them? Why?

5. Visit the costume shop of your university or community theatre. Are there costumes available to be pulled? Are there renderings of costumes that are under construction? What types of equipment can you find in the shop?

WIGS AND HAIRSTYLES

Hairstyle indicates social status and other facts about a character; it provides information about when and where a play is taking place. Beyond that, hairstyles and wigs can make a comment. Shown here is a scene from Rodgers & Hammerstein's *Cinderella*. The actors are Harriet Harris, standing, as Cinderella's stepmother, with, from left, Laura Osnes as Cinderella, and Ann Harada and Marla Mindelle, who play the stepsisters, wearing elaborate wigs in hairstyles that exaggerate the norm even for the period. The hair and wig designs are by veteran Broadway designer Paul Huntley. (©Sara Krulwich/The New York Times/Redux)

photo essay

Masks are as old as theatre—they were part of ancient Greek theatre and early Asian theatre, and of ceremonial costumes in Africa and elsewhere. Masks can have a variety of uses: They can be highly decorative, but they can also convey the character and temperament of the actor wearing them. Here we see a variety of masks in old and new plays.

Khon dancers during the Phimai festival in Thailand. Khon is a traditional Thai masked dance-drama based on stories from the national epic, the *Ramakian*. (©Andrew Watson/Getty Images)

The Asaro "mud men" from the Asaro Valley in Papua New Guinea's eastern highlands are known for the ghoulish clay masks they use in many rituals. Here they perform for visitors at the Australian Museum in Sydney in 2016. (©PETER PARKS/Getty Images)

Venetian carnival masks are worn by actors in Shakespeare's *The Merchant of Venice,* a production by the Habima National Theatre, in Hebrew, at Shakespeare's Globe in London, as part of the World Shakespeare Festival, 2012. (©Tristram Kenton/Lebrecht Music & Arts/The Image Works)

Tristano (Pedro Pascal) and Don Bertolino Fortunato (Dick Latessa) perform the commedia play, *Pulcinella Goes to Hell*, in the Huntington Theatre Company's production of *The Miracle at Naples*, by David Grimm, directed by Peter DuBois, with costumes and masks designed by Anita Yavich. (©T Charles Erickson)

extension of the performer—a face on top of a face. Theatre masks remind us, first of all, that we are in a theatre, that the action going on before our eyes is not real in a literal sense but is a symbolic or an artistic presentation. For another thing, masks allow a face to be frozen in one expression: a look of horror, perhaps, which we see throughout a production. Masks can also make a face larger than life, and they can create stereotypes, in which one particular feature—for example, cunning or haughtiness—is emphasized to the exclusion of everything else.

Masks offer other symbolic possibilities. In his play **The Great God Brown**, Eugene O'Neill calls for the performers at certain times to hold masks in front of their faces. When the masks are in place, the characters present a facade to the public, withholding their true selves. When the masks are down, the characters reveal their inner feelings.

Neutral masks are also frequently used in actors' training, to prompt them to use more dynamic physical movement without the benefit of facial expression to express character. More often today, audiences will see half masks, like those used in the *commedia dell'arte* of the Italian Renaissance, as these allow for stylized character expressions but also give the actor more freedom to speak clearly and effectively.

Characters' mask designs are also incorporated into the costume renderings and are typically built by a makeup or crafts specialist in the costume shop.

Millinery, Accessories, and Crafts

A number of the seven objectives of costume design noted at the beginning of this chapter are actually achieved through the design and use of accessories to the costumes. Accessories include items such as hats, walking sticks, jewelry, purses, and parasols. All these items instantly refer to various historical periods and also make visual statements about character and locale. Virtually every major costume shop will have a technician who specializes in millinery and crafts. Each of these pieces must be carefully designed and constructed to connect visually to the costumes and to other areas of design. It is hard to imagine a production of Shakespeare's **A Midsummer Night's Dream** without some kind of delightful donkey's headpiece or mask made specifically for the character Bottom. Theatre design and execution in all areas, including millinery, accessories, and craft, rely heavily on extensive details to make the visual world of the play compelling for audiences.

COORDINATION OF THE WHOLE

Actors and actresses would have great difficulty creating a part without costumes and accessories, and in some cases without makeup or a mask. These elements help the performer define his or her role and are so closely related to the performer that we sometimes lose sight of them as separate entities. At the same time, costumes, makeup, hairstyles, and masks must be integrated with other aspects of a production, and each demands special technical skills in order to complete the visual design.

For example, these elements are essential in carrying out a point of view in a production. Masks, for instance, are clearly nonrealistic and signal to the audience that the character wearing the mask and the play itself are also likely to be

1. Think back to the last play or film you attended. How did the costume designer use color, fabric, and/or other elements to set up visual coordination and contrast among the characters?

2. Watch a historical film, like Steven Spielberg's *Lincoln*. Are there any unique accessories employed to help establish time period? What about the hairstyles? Are wigs used?

3. How are Halloween masks like theatre masks? How are they different?

4. If you have been required to read a play this semester, how might you use color and line to define one of the leading characters?

nonrealistic. Costumes suggest whether a play is comic or serious, a wild farce or a stark tragedy. Costumes, makeup, hairstyles, and masks must also be coordinated with scenery and lighting. The wrong kind of lighting can wash out or discolor costumes and makeup. It would be self-defeating, too, if scenery were in one mood or style and the costumes in another. Ideally, these elements should support and reinforce one another, and spectators should be aware of how essential it is for them to work together.

Evaluating Costume Design

There are key questions we should ask ourselves about costume design after we attend a production. By doing so, we can then assess how successful we believe the costume designer was in helping support the director's concept, the actors, and the other designers. Among these questions are:

1. What information was conveyed by the costumes about time, place, characters, and situation? How was this information conveyed to you?

2. What was the period of the costumes? What was the style? Were the costumes from a period other than the period in which the play was written or originally set? If so, how did this affect the production? Why do you think this choice was made?

3. How was color used to give you clues to the personalities of the characters and the relationships between them?

4. Did each character's costume or costumes seem appropriate for his or her personality, social status, occupation, etc.? Why or why not?

5. Did the costumes help you understand conflicts, differing social groups, and interpersonal relationships? If so, how?

6. Were makeup, wigs, unique hairstyles, masks, millinery, ornamentation, and/or special effects used with the costuming? How integrated were these elements into the overall design? Did these elements help you better understand the characters and the play?

SUMMARY

1. The clothes we wear in daily life are a form of costume. They indicate station in life, occupation, and a sense of formality or informality.

2. Onstage, costumes—like clothes in real life—convey information about the people wearing them; more than that, these costumes are chosen consciously and are designed to give the audience important information.

3. The objectives of costume design are to set tone and style, indicate time and place, characterize individuals and groups, underline personal relationships, create symbolic outfits when appropriate, meet the practical needs of performers, and coordinate with the total production.

4. The designer works with the following elements: line and shape, color, fabric, and accessories.

5. Costumes can be pulled or built. When they are pulled, they are drawn from a preexisting costume collection. Building costumes means creating the complete costume: sewing and constructing the outfit in a costume shop.

6. Those working with a costume designer include a first hand (or lead stitcher) and other assistants.

7. Makeup and hairstyles are also important to the appearance of the performers and are part of the designer's concern.

8. Where called for, masks, too, are under the direction of the costume designer.

9. Often, costume, makeup, and wig assistants work with actors during a performance.

LIGHTING AND SOUND

Like scenery, costumes, and other elements of theatre, stage lighting and sound have counterparts in everyday life. For example, in real life the basic function of lighting is, of course, illumination—to allow us to see at night and indoors. But there are also many theatrical uses of light in daily life. Advertising signs often have neon lights or brightly colored bulbs. Restaurants feature soft lights, candles, and background music to help establish mood and atmosphere.

With the explosion of such handheld devices as digital music players and smartphones, all of us carry our own sound tracks each day. In our homes, we put spotlights on special parts of a room, such as a dining-room table. Also, in our homes we frequently use a rheostat so that we can dim lights to create a mood. What home does not have projected images available through a flat-screen HD television or the ability to change digital images in picture frames? And today some of us can control all of the lighting and sound throughout our residence with our computers, tablets, or smartphones.

STAGE LIGHTING

Lighting was historically the last element of visual design to be incorporated into theatre production—and, ironically, it is perhaps the most advanced in terms of equipment, technology, and techniques. Most of the advances have occurred in the past 100 years. Before we look at theatre lighting today, it will be helpful to have a short historical view of its development.

A Brief History of Stage Lighting

For the first 2,000 years of its recorded history, theatre was held mostly outdoors during the day. A primary reason was the need for illumination. The sun, after

◀ *Startling, evocative lighting is the setting and background to this contemporary dance piece entitled* Listen to Your Heart! *Note the cloud effect in the background and the way it absorbs and reflects light, establishing a mood for the performance. Lighting and sound are indispensable, effective ingredients of any stage presentation.* (©blanaru/iStock/Getty Images RF)

all, is an excellent source of light. Since sophisticated lighting was unavailable, playwrights used imagination—the handiest tool available—to suggest nighttime or shifts in lighting. Performers brought on torches, or a candle, as Lady Macbeth does, to indicate night. Playwrights also used language to indicate lighting.

In *The Merchant of Venice*, Shakespeare has Lorenzo say, "How sweet the moonlight sleeps upon this bank"; this is not just a pretty line of poetry but also serves to remind us that it is nighttime. The same is true of the eloquent passage when Romeo tells Juliet that he must leave because dawn is breaking.

> Look, love, what envious streaks
> Do lace the severing clouds in yonder East:
> Night's candles are burnt out, and jocund day
> Stands tiptoe on the misty mountain tops.

Around 1600 C.E., theatre began to move indoors. Candles and oil lamps were used for illumination, and the chief refinements were more sophisticated uses of these basic elements, such as those achieved in the 1770s by David Garrick, the actor-manager of the Drury Lane Theatre in London, and Philippe Jacques DeLoutherbourg (1740–1812), a French designer whom Garrick brought to the Drury Lane. DeLoutherbourg, for example, installed lighting above the stage and used gauze curtains and silk screens to achieve subtle effects with color. In 1785 an instrument known as the Argand lamp (after its inventor, Aimé Argand of Geneva) was introduced. It made use of a glass chimney and a cylindrical wick to create a steadier, brighter light.

Not until 1803, however, when a theatre in London installed gaslights, was there a genuine advance in stage lighting. With gas, which was the principal source of illumination during the nineteenth century, lighting was more easily controlled and managed. Lighting intensity, for example, could be raised or lowered. Its effectiveness, however, remained limited. In addition, the open flames of gas and other earlier lighting systems posed a constant threat of fire. Through the years there were several tragic and costly fires in theatres, both in Europe and in the United States.

In 1879 Thomas Edison invented the incandescent lamp (the electric light-bulb), and the era of imaginative lighting for the theatre began. Not only are incandescent lamps safe, but they can also be controlled. Brightness or intensity can be increased or decreased: The same lighting instrument will produce the bright light of noonday or the dim light of dusk. Also, by putting a colored film over the light or by other means, color can be controlled.

Beyond the power and versatility of electric light, there have been numerous other advances in controls and equipment over the past fifty years. Lighting instruments have been continually refined to become more powerful, as well as more subtle, and to throw a more concentrated, sharply defined beam. Also, lighting has lent itself more successfully than other theatre elements to miniaturization and computerization.

When applied to lighting, technological developments have allowed for increasingly complex and sophisticated controls. For a large college theatre production, 200 to 300 lighting instruments may be hung around and above the stage, whereas for a large Broadway musical, there may be 800 or many more. (The Broadway musical *Wicked*, for example, uses 650 instruments.) Each of these instruments can be hooked up to a central computer board, and light settings can be stored in the computer. By pushing a single button, an operator can, in a split second, bring about a shift in literally dozens of instruments, changing, for example, focus, color, and intensity. The resulting flexibility and control are remarkable tools for achieving stage effects.

Objectives and Functions of Lighting Design

Adolphe Appia (1862–1928), a Swiss scene designer, was one of the first to see the vast artistic possibilities of light in the theatre. He wrote: "Light is to the production what music is to the score: the expressive element in opposition to the literal signs; and, like music, light can express only what belongs to the inner essence of all vision's vision." Norman Bel Geddes (1893–1958), an imaginative American designer who was a follower of Appia, put it in these words: "Good lighting adds space, depth, mood, mystery, parody, contrast, change of emotion, intimacy, fear." Edward Gordon Craig (1872–1966), an innovative British designer, spoke of "painting with light." The lighting designer can indeed paint with light, but far more can be done. On the deepest sensual and symbolic level, the lighting designer can convey to us something of the feeling, and even the substance, of a play.

It is intriguing that today's leading lighting designers still speak of the artistic potential and aesthetics of light in precisely the same way as these early innovators did. In a sense the art of lighting has not changed, but the innovation continues, and the technology has exploded in the last twenty years. In fact, the most serious problem in lighting for the theatre today is to prevent the technology from taking over the aesthetics of the design, which is where the greatest distinction exists between contemporary lighting technicians and earlier lighting designers.

The following are the primary functions and objectives of stage lighting:

1. Provide visibility.
2. Reveal shapes and forms.
3. Provide a focus onstage and create visual compositions.
4. Assist in creating mood and reinforcing style.
5. Help establish time and place.
6. Establish a rhythm of visual movement.
7. Reinforce a central visual image, establish visual information, or both.

An experienced lighting designer will be capable of accomplishing all these functions simultaneously and will emphasize various objectives at various times during a production to help maintain a strong physical and emotional connection between audience members and the world of the play on stage.

Visibility   On the practical side, the chief function of lighting is illumination or visibility. We must be able, first and foremost, to see the performers' faces and their actions onstage. Occasionally, lighting designers, carried away with atmospheric possibilities, will make a scene so dark that we can hardly see what is happening. Mood is important, but seeing the performers is obviously even more important. It is true that unless you can see the actors and actresses, the lighting designer has not carried out his or her assignment; however, the accomplished designer will establish a balance that allows for visibility while meeting other design objectives effectively.

Shape and Form   The lighting designer must enhance the visual world of the play by revealing the objects in that world as interestingly as possible. Lighting objects from the front, with lights above the audience illuminating the stage, visually washes out all three-dimensional objects onstage, making them look flat and uninteresting. The designer must therefore enhance the actors and other visual elements of the world of the play with lighting and color from the side, top, and behind.

Focus and Composition   In photography, the term *focus* means adjustment of the lens of a camera so that the picture recorded on the film is sharp and clear. In theatre lighting, *focus* refers to the fact that beams of light are aimed at—focused on—a particular area. In stage action the director and lighting designer collaborate in creating a continually moving visual composition that always keeps the audience focused on the central action of the play. This kind of collaboration and compositional focus also allows a character to slip into position without those of us in the audience ever realizing how he got there until it is time to reveal him. Careful focus of light is integral to successful visuals onstage. Adjacent lighting and acting areas must be overlapped in focus to allow actors to move across the stage without going into and out of the edges of light beams. At the same time, the designer must control the *spill* of the light in front of and behind the actor so that it will not distract us as we watch the action of the play.

By means of focus and changes in light cues the lighting designer and director keep the audience focused on the essential action. These compositions or *looks* can vary from turning the stage into one large area to creating small, isolated areas all intended to take the audience on an interesting visual journey through the world of the play.

Mood and Style   Theatre, as a collaborative art form by definition, combines all areas of a production to establish the mood and world of the play. Once that predominant mood is established for an audience, the individual production areas can manipulate mood throughout the play, especially through lighting and sound. A production can also effectively manipulate our reaction. For example, early in a play we may see two or three romantic moments when the stage is filled with blue moonlight; then, in a later scene the look may seem the same until the action starts and we realize that the mood has changed to a cold, dark, evil situation. Action, scenery, and words, in conjunction with light, tell us exactly what the mood is. Experienced playwrights and designers know how we can be manipulated and will often take advantage of our expectations to make our journey more interesting.

In terms of style, lighting can indicate whether a play is realistic or nonrealistic. In a realistic play, the lighting will simulate the effect of ordinary sources—table lamps, say, and outside sunlight. In a nonrealistic production or a highly theatrical musical, the designer can be more imaginative: Shafts of light can cut through the dark, sculpturing performers onstage; a glowing red light can convey a scene of damnation; a ghostly green light can cast a spell over a nightmare scene; a hard-edged spotlight can let the audience members know that what they are now seeing is not a realistic moment in a character's life.

Time and Place   By its color, shade, and intensity, lighting can suggest the time of day, giving us the pale light of dawn, the bright light of midday, the vivid colors of sunset, or the muted light of evening. Lighting can also indicate the season of the year, because the sun strikes objects at very different angles in winter and summer. Lighting can also suggest place, by showing indoor or outdoor light. In this manner, lighting helps reinforce the story being told.

Rhythm   Since changes in light occur on a time continuum, they establish a rhythm running through a production. It is absolutely imperative that the seemingly simple lighting changes from scene to scene help establish the kind of

LIGHTING CREATES MOOD AND STYLE
Along with scenery and costumes, lighting is a key element in creating the mood and style of a production. Shown here is a scene where light criss-crosses the stage creating abstract shapes and illuminating the performers, as well as projecting colors that contrast the top section with that below. The scene is from a production of *Eurydice* by Sarah Ruhl, directed by Geoff Elliott at A Noise Within. The lighting was designed by Meghan Gray. (©Craig Schwartz)

rhythm and timing that the director needs for us to be drawn into the action. Abrupt, staccato changes with stark blackouts might unsettle us if that is called for, and languid, slow fades and gradual cross-fades can allow us a more thoughtful transition between scenes. Does the designer fade out the previous scene slowly while the next scene is beginning, thus prompting us to think about the connection? Or does the designer make the lights fade in very slowly, prompting us to ask what is to come and pulling our attention in? Either way these changes in rhythm have an effect on our interaction with and understanding of the world of the play.

photo essay
The Many Uses of Stage Lighting

Stage lighting can be used for many purposes: to illuminate, to highlight characters or stage areas, to create mood.

In this scene, lighting designer Justin Townsend has used lights to highlight the couple in the center (Dashiell Eaves and Amanda Quaid) and also the single figure at the right (Eisa Davis) in a different color and mood. The lights above add framing and atmosphere. The play is Kirsten Greenidge's *Luck of the Irish* directed by Rebecca Taichman. (©Sara Krulwich/The New York Times/Redux)

A scene from a production of *Desire Under the Elms* by Eugene O'Neill, directed by Dámaso Rodriguez at A Noise Within, in Pasadena, California, shows a skillful use of local front lighting: The oil lamp illuminates Abbie (Monette Magrath). Lighting by James P. Taylor; costumes by Julie Keen. (©Craig Schwartz)

In *Jesus Christ Superstar,* an Andrew Lloyd Webber musical directed by Des McAnuff, lighting designer Howell Binkley has used down lighting and back lighting to isolate and highlight actor Paul Nolan in the title role. (©Sara Krulwich/The New York Times/ Redux)

Lighting designer Elizabeth Harper has used lighting to create a crimson sky in the dust bowl area of the Midwest in a production of *The Grapes of Wrath* by John Steinbeck, adapted by Frank Galati, directed by Michael Michetti at A Noise Within. Note the effective use of the light to silhouette the silent actors. (©Craig Schwartz)

Since many lighting changes are coordinated with scene changes and changes in other production elements, it is a challenge for the lighting designer to make artistic choices that will support the director's vision, whether a change is pragmatic or solely aesthetic. Either way the importance of this synchronization is recognized by directors and designers, who take great care to ensure the proper changes—"choreographing" shifts in light and scenery like dancers' movements.

Reinforcement of the Central Image   Lighting—like scenery, costumes, and all other elements—must be consistent with the overall style and mood of a production. Over the past thirty years there has been a dramatic change in the style of writing plays. Long, extended scenes taking place in a single location are less and less common. Today's audiences are most accustomed to film and television editing, and to shorter scenes with multiple locations. Most of our contemporary plays tend to be written in a style that also cuts frequently from location to location; the actors may be on a bare stage with only the most essential props or suggested props to support the action. These kinds of changes in writing style prompt the lighting designer to provide more visual information than ever before about place and locale to allow for such simple staging. The wrong choices in lighting can distort or even destroy the effect of a play. At the same time, because lighting is the most flexible and the most atmospheric visual element of theatre, it can aid enormously in creating our theatre experience.

The Lighting Designer

The person responsible for creating, installing, and setting controls for stage lighting is the lighting designer and his or her collaborators. It is important for the lighting designer to have a background in the technical and mechanical aspects of lighting as well as a broad, creative visual imagination. The ability to translate words and actions and feelings into color, direction, and intensity comes only after much training and experience.

The Process of Lighting Design   In creating the lighting design for a production, the lighting designer first reads the script and begins to form some rough ideas and develop some feelings about the play. He or she meets with the director and other designers to discuss visual concepts. The lighting designer receives from the set designer copies of all the scenery plans and usually consults with the costume designer to learn the shape and color of the costumes.

The lighting designer will do a great deal of visual research and will also see one or perhaps several rehearsals to get the feel of the production, to see the exact location of various pieces of furniture and stage business, and to consult with the director about possible effects. Following this, the lighting designer draws a plan called a *light plot*. This includes the location and color of each lighting instrument. Also indicated is the kind of instrument called for and the area of the stage on which it is focused. When lighting instruments are moved into the theatre and hung (that is, placed on pipes and other supports), the designer supervises the focusing.

During technical rehearsals, the lighting designer works with the director to establish light cues; that is, instructions about when the lights go on and off. The designer also sets the length of time for light changes and the levels of intensity on the computer-controlled light board, which sends a digital signal to the actual dimmers to adjust the lighting instrument levels. (The actual dimmers, which allow lighting intensities to be changed smoothly and at varying rates, are located in a remote off-stage location.)

Properties of Stage Lighting   When working on the design for a production, the lighting designer knows what controllable properties of light will achieve the objectives discussed above. The lighting designer can manipulate four different properties of light for any visual change onstage: intensity, color, distribution, and movement.

Intensity   The first property of light is brightness, or intensity. Intensity can be controlled (as noted above) by devices called dimmers, which make the lights brighter or darker. A dimmer is an electric or electronic device that can vary the amount of power going to the lights. This makes it possible for a scene at night to take place in very little light and a daylight scene to take place in bright light. Since the advent of computer control systems, lighting intensities can be set at any level between 1 percent and 100 percent of full, as opposed to levels 1 through 10 on older manual controls.

Color   The second property of light is color. Color is a very powerful part of lighting, and theatre lights can very easily be changed to one of several hundred colors simply by placing colored material in slots at the front of the lighting instruments. This material is usually called a gel—short for gelatin, of which it was originally made. Today, however, these color filters are generally made of plastic, such as Mylar, or acetate.

Also in recent years, color *scrollers* have been introduced. These devices typically make it possible to change up to fifteen colors for each lighting, and the scrollers are also programmed into each light cue along with intensity and timing. Color is often mixed so that the strong tones of one shade will not dominate, since such dominance would give an unnatural appearance. Colors are most often selected to support choices made by the scenic and costume designers while still including sufficient dramatic color to support the varied action of the play. Quite often scenes will call for special effects; we expect stark shadows and strange colors, for example, when Hamlet confronts the ghost of his father.

Distribution   The third property of light that the lighting designer can use is distribution: the position and type of lighting instrument being used and the angle at which the light strikes the performers onstage. (Another term for this property could be *direction,* that is, the source from which the light comes, the type of instrument used, and the points on the stage at which a light beam is aimed.) In earlier days, footlights—a row of lights across the front of the stage floor—were used, primarily because this was almost the only location from which to light the front of the performers. However, footlights, which were below the performers, had the disadvantage of casting ghostly shadows on their faces. Footlights also created a kind of barrier between performers and audience. With the development of more powerful, versatile lights, footlights have been eliminated and they are now used only when a production is trying to re-create the look and style of a classic play of the eighteenth or nineteenth century.

Today, most lighting hits the stage from above, coming from instruments in front of the stage and at the sides. The vertical angle of light beams from the *front of the house* is typically close to 45 degrees; this is an excellent angle for lighting the actor's face without creating harmful shadows, and it also gives a sense of sunlight or an overhead light source found in most locations.

There are a wide variety of lighting instruments available today, both conventional instruments and automated moving light fixtures. They all have distinctive features, and each instrument is selected for the quality of light and the design

THE USE OF COLOR IN LIGHTING

One of the prime elements in stage lighting is color: It can alter and transform a stage set, changing and establishing different moods. Here we see the same set from *The Underpants* by Carl Sternheim, adapted by Steve Martin, presented at the Alley Theatre, Houston. Note the stark white of the first photograph and the pink and purple hue of the second, contrasting the mood and the tone from one visual picture to another. All this is done with light. The director was Scott Schwartz, with lighting design by Pat Collins, costume design by David C. Woolard, and set design by Anna Louizos.

(both: ©T Charles Erickson)

options it allows. What visual qualities or "texture" does the light produce on stage? Is it a single shaft of light, like a single beam of moonlight through the trees or a spotlight in a nightclub?

Or is the light in a pattern, such as dappled sunlight through the leaves of trees in a forest? Are the edges of the light sharp, or soft and diffused? In conventional ellipsoidal lighting instruments, light can be shaped by special shutters that close in at the edges (very few moving lights even have that capability). All these are additional tools for the designer.

Movement   The last property of light the designer can work with is movement, and in fact this is where the lighting design comes to life. On one level, the eye is carried from place to place by the shifting focus of lights: follow spots moving from one person or one area to another, automated lights changing directions, a performer carrying a candle or flashlight across the stage. The subtlest and often the most effective kind of movement of light comes with shifting the audience's focus when lights go down in one area and come up in another. Lighting cross-fades like this can shift the focus from location to location and from color to color, but even within single scenes a good lighting design will force the audience members to change their focus without even realizing it. Also, time of day, sun-sets, and so on can help provide visual information for the audience.

For an example of how these properties function, consider the lighting for a production of **Hamlet**. To emphasize this play's eerie, tragic quality, with its murders and graveyard scene, the lighting would generally be cool rather than warm, but it could also have a slash of red cutting through the otherwise cool light. As for angles, if the production took place on a proscenium stage, there would be more dramatic downlighting and backlighting to give the characters a sculptured, occasionally unreal quality. In terms of movement, the lights would change each time there was a shift in locale, or a low-angle special could come on diagonally from behind the ghost of Hamlet's father. This would give a rhythm of movement throughout the play and would also focus the audience's attention on particular areas of the stage as well as support the thematic elements of the play.

The Lighting Designer's Resources
Among the resources of the lighting designer are various kinds of lighting instruments and other kinds of technical and electronic equipment.

Types of Stage Lights   Most stage lights have three main elements: a lamp that is the source of the light, a reflector, and a lens through which the beams pass. The two basic categories of lighting fixtures are conventional lighting instruments and automated or moving light fixtures. Conventional lights are fixed instruments with a single focus and design purpose. Intelligent moving light fixtures are able to alter focus, change color, project multiple patterns, rotate the patterns at varying speeds, change the size of the beam, and give a sharp or diffused focus.

Examples of common conventional lights are the ellipsoidal reflector spotlights, Fresnel spotlights, strip/cyc/flood/border lights, PAR floodlights, and followspots:

1. *Ellipsoidal reflector spotlight or ERS.* This is the most widely used conventional fixture. It creates a bright, hard-edged spot. However, the edge can be softened with focus adjustment or with a different fusion filter. Lenses of different focal lengths allow for eight different standard-size beams depending on the distance from the theatre's hanging positions to the stage; this instrument is, therefore, useful from almost any position in the theatre. Clearly, it is the "workhorse" of contemporary lighting practice. It also has a special *gobo* slot for pattern projection. A *followspot* is another typically hard-edged spotlight controlled by an operator that is designed to follow the leading performer across the stage. Originally, this type of light was created by igniting the mineral lime in front of a reflector in the back end of a long metal tube. The chemical reaction created a bright but slightly green light, which led to the common expression for someone who likes attention as "liking to be in the limelight."

Philips Selecon Pacific 2350 Ellipsoidal.
(Courtesy of Philips Selecon)

Philips Selecon Rama Fresnel.
(Courtesy of Philips Selecon)

2. *Soft-edged spotlights.* The most popular soft-edged spotlight is the Fresnel (pronounced "fruh-NEL"). It is a high-wattage spot, and the Fresnel lens helps dissipate the heat, but it can create only a soft-edged beam of light that can be focused down to a small spot or flooded to cover a larger stage area. The lens is named for Auguste Fresnel, who designed, for lighthouses, the first lenses that would not crack with intense heating and cooling. The concentric rings he cut into the lens allowed the lens to function properly while preventing the buildup of heat from cracking the lens after the light was turned off. Many lighting designers use this instrument for toplighting and backlighting and to cover a large stage area with a wash of color. The Fresnel is generally used in positions near the stage—behind the proscenium opening, or mounted close to the action on an arena or thrust stage. Another common soft-edged lighting instrument is the parabolic aluminized reflector (PAR), which emits an oval beam. *Barn doors,* with flaps that can cut off an edge of the beam, and *color changers/scrollers,* which increase the options from one color to fifteen colors on a single instrument, are common accessories used on both PARs and Fresnels.

3. *Floodlights, strip lights, and border lights.* These lights bathe a section of the stage or scenery in a smooth, diffused wash of light. Floodlights are used, singly or in groups, to provide general illumination for the stage or scenery. The light from floods can be blended in acting areas, or used to "tone" settings and costumes. They are most often used to illuminate cycloramas at the rear of the stage, or ground rows along the floor of the stage.

Philips Selecon Hui Flood.
(Courtesy of Philips Selecon)

Vari*Lite VL6 spot luminaire.
(Courtesy of Philips Vari-Lite)

4. *Automated or moving light (also referred to as intelligent fixtures).* The moving light is the newest and most versatile instrument of the group, although there are still only a few moving lights with an independent shutter function that can be focused in a theatre like an ellipsoidal spotlight. Automated light fixtures are able to alter focus, change color using dichroic—or two-beam—color mixing, project multiple patterns, rotate the patterns at varying speeds, change the size of the beam, and give a sharp or diffused focus. One moving light fixture used as a special can replace numerous conventional fixtures. Most contemporary lighting designers use a combination of both types of instruments. Automated fixtures are particularly useful in elaborate musical productions and are widely used in rock concerts.

Lighting Controls Lighting design is clearly the most technologically developed element of theatre. We have already considered some of the advances in this area in terms of lighting instruments. These fixtures can now be hung all over a performance space and aimed at every part of the stage. In addition, one person sitting at a console can control the elements of these lighting instruments. New technologies have also prompted a great deal of change in the design of control systems, which now allow for remarkable computer-controlled lighting along with the ability to employ traditional methods of cue changes. Lighting control systems are extremely expensive, so the change to systems that continue to evolve technologically happens only gradually for most theatre operations.

Lighting changes—or ***cues***, as they are called—are usually arranged ahead of time. Sometimes, in a complicated production (a musical, say, or a Shakespearean play), there will be from 75 to 150 or more light cues. A cue can range from a *blackout* (in which all the lights are shut off at once), to a *fade* (the lights dim slowly, changing the scene from brighter to darker), to a *cross-fade* (one set of lights comes down while another comes up) or a split cross-fade (the lights that are coming up are on a different fade count from the lights that are coming down). Thanks to computerized control, the split cross-fade is the most common.

Although light board programming is complicated and somewhat time-consuming the actual running of a show has become a fairly simple task because of well-designed computer control systems. The most critical aspect of the lighting design is the ability of the stage manager to fully understand the pacing and design aesthetic in calling the lighting and sound cues. Even the process of calling cues has been simplified in some ways by technology. In lighting for dance or for large-scale musicals it is critical to merge the lighting and sound cues. Through the use of new digital sound technology a computer-controlled sound program can interface with a computer light board and both light and sound cues can be run simultaneously with one tap of the keyboard space bar.

For instance, Strindberg's ***A Dream Play*** has numerous and complex scene changes—like a dream, as the title implies—in which one scene fades into another before our eyes. At one point in the play, a young woman, called the Daughter, sits at an organ in a church. In Strindberg's words, "The stage darkens as the Daughter rises and approaches the Lawyer. By means of lighting the organ is transformed into a wall of a grotto. The sea seeps in between basal pillars with a harmony of waves and wind." At the light cue for this change, a button is pushed, and all the lights creating the majesty of the church fade as the lights creating the

Cues Any prearranged signal—such as the last words in a speech, a piece of business, or any action or lighting change—that indicates to a performer or stage manager that it is time to proceed to the next line or action.

IN FOCUS: ROCK CONCERT AND THEATRE LIGHTING

As we mentioned in the chapter "Theatre Is Everywhere," rock music and theatre have strong connections. One of those connections is the influence theatre has had on rock concert lighting design and vice versa.

In the early days of touring rock performers, particularly in the 1950s and 1960s, many of the designers for their concerts were theatre trained and had the same aesthetic goals as theatre lighting design: clear illumination, mood, and slight changes of color. This was particularly true because available lighting instruments had to be hung in multi-use spaces on pre-existing grids and put up and taken down quickly.

Beginning in the 1970s, with the development of computer-assisted technology and new lighting technology, rock concerts began to become performance events with lighting design becoming almost another on-stage performer. Lighting designers for rock concerts used cutting edge computer-assisted controls, new software and lighter materials to create poles for hanging multiple instruments as well as lighter instruments, more

intense floodlights for color, intelligent instruments that could move, and the use of projections and media.

A recent example of rock performance using cutting edge technology to create lighting effects was Lady Gaga's 2017 Super Bowl performance. Besides the intricate light plot that employed 84 intelligent Philips Vari-Lites, 300 Intel Shooting Star drones flew over Lady Gaga during her opening number creating a mechanized and computer-controlled light show. The drones were outfitted with colored LEDs and the unmanned aerial vehicles (UAVs) were remotely controlled in order to create stunning images including the American flag.

Many of the technological innovations used to create spectacular lighting designs for rock musicians were later incorporated into large-scale commercial productions. For example, some Broadway rock and juke box musicals have re-created the visual aesthetic of rock concerts. *Natasha, Pierre, and the Great Comet of 1812*, which opened on Broadway in 2016, uses spectacular lighting that frequently mimics a rock concert.

---

grotto come up. In many ways stage lighting technology has finally started to catch up with, and serve, the creative ideas that artists like Strindberg and Appia had at the start of the twentieth century.

The Lighting Designer's Collaborators   As in every aspect of theatre, in lighting too there is collaboration. Those who work with the lighting designer include assistant designers and people who help create the light plot, as well as a master electrician responsible for the preparation, hanging, and focusing of the lights and all accessories (often, if not always, electricians must climb on catwalks and ladders to remote areas above, behind, and in front of the stage). One of the newer jobs is that of the moving light programmer. Until the advent of moving lights, programming light cues had always fallen to either the lighting designer or the lead associate designer. More recently, however, the complexity of programming has grown exponentially with automated fixtures and other digital accessories, thus requiring another technical specialty.

Large-scale musical productions, for example, are often so complex that even calling all the cues is impossible for one person to do. For that reason, all followspot cues (usually three or four followspots in a design) are typically called by the lead spot operator. In the concert industry, this gets even more complex, as there are usually a minimum of eight followspots and often as many as sixteen or more on a major tour of a rock musical production in addition to almost unimaginably complex moving light packages.

SOUND IN THE THEATRE

Scenery, costumes, and lighting can all be described as the visual elements of theatre. Another major design element is sound. In recent years, sound has become an increasingly important aspect of theatre, with its own artistry, technology, and designers.

In 2007, the Tony Awards voted to include sound design as a category beginning with the 2008 awards. However, in 2014, the Tony Administration Committee eliminated the category. Even though the committee stated it could give a special award to a production with extraordinary sound design, there was great protest by many members of the profession reflecting how significant sound design has become in so many Broadway productions; the committee, therefore, reinstated the award for both a play and a musical for the 2017–18 season. In other cities, sound design is recognized as a separate theatre awards category; for example, Chicago's Joseph Jefferson Award Committee recognizes sound design in Equity and non-Equity productions.

Sound Reproduction: Advantages and Disadvantages

Amplification   In the past few decades, sound reproduction has become increasingly prominent in theatre. For some audience members, it has sometimes proved to be controversial as well. The intense amplification at popular music concerts along with the availability of inexpensive personal audio systems—now in digital formats—are just two of the reasons we now expect widespread sound reproduction in the theatre. As a result, large musicals, whether presented in Broadway houses or in spacious performing art centers across the country, are now extensively amplified. Most of us, accustomed to amplified sound in many other settings, take such amplification for granted.

Some critics charge, however, that amplification in theatre is sometimes overdone, with the sound too loud, as well as too mechanical and artificial. In opera the objections are even stronger. In today's theatre, those continuing to oppose amplification appear to be "purists" who want a return to past theatrical practice. It may be difficult for us in the early twenty-first century to imagine, but the great American musicals of the 1940s and the 1950s—by composers like Rodgers and Hammerstein, Cole Porter, and Irving Berlin—were all produced without any sound amplification whatsoever. Today, however, electronic amplification is a way of life in theatre, and sound design has become an indispensable part of any production.

We are speaking here of larger spaces: college or university theatres of approximately 400 or 500 seats, and professional theatres that might range from 800 to 2,000 seats. The issue of amplification is less pressing in smaller venues: in "black boxes," for example, or fringe theatres in lofts, warehouses, or storefronts, that seat perhaps 100 spectators. In such spaces, sound amplification is likely to be less used. (It should be noted, however, with the advent of less expensive computer-assisted sound design, such theatres may still have intricate sound effects for their productions.)

Sound Effects   Aside from the argument about the volume or pervasiveness of voice amplification, we should recognize that sound has always been an important, and necessary, component of theatre production. One aspect of this is sound effects. In earlier years—for several centuries, in fact—various devices were developed to create such sounds.

THE SIGNIFICANCE OF SOUND

There are times when sound takes over in a production. Of course, in most musical productions, all the voices, as well as the instruments of the orchestra, are enhanced by sound equipment. But in many productions there are certain moments when sound is crucial. An example is the scene shown here from a production of *Uncle Vanya* by Anton Chekhov. Derek Jacobi, as Vanya, fires a gun at a professor he finds unbearable. The gunshot goes astray (perhaps on purpose), but the sound of the firing is central to the scene, underscoring Vanya's rage. Sound design was by David Van Teighem. (©Sara Krulwich/The New York Times/Redux)

Historically, for example, a wooden drum made from slats was used to produce the sound of wind. The drum was usually two or three feet in diameter, and covered with a muslin cloth. When the drum was turned, by means of a handle, it made a noise like howling wind. Thunder was suggested by hanging a large, thick metal sheet backstage and gently shaking it. For the sound of a door slamming, a miniature door or even a full-size door in a frame was placed just off-stage and opened and shut. Two hinged pieces of wood slammed shut also simulated the sound of a closing door.

A gunshot sound could also be created with these hinged pieces of wood, as well as by firing a gun loaded with blank cartridges. Live ammunition could not be used safely onstage. In some states, blank guns were (and still are) illegal. As we shall see, recorded sound, now easily digitized, makes this issue irrelevant in the contemporary theatre.

Today, of course, the developments in computer technology and digitization, which support sound design and its playback on stage, are extensive. There are many programs available on the Internet for free download as well, so it is not difficult to get started using simple sound programs. Most often these same programs have more advanced and complex capabilities that are available for purchase. You can record and play back a myriad of sound cues; if you want to interface those sound cues through a lighting control board or projection system, for creation and alteration, then you may use sophisticated software packages such as Pro Tools, Final Cut Pro, or Garage Band. Also available are SFX and CueLab computer playback systems.

The Sound Designer

The person responsible for arranging and orchestrating all the aural aspects of a production is the sound designer. Like his or her counterparts in visual design, the sound designer begins by reading the script, noting all the places where sound might be needed. For a large-scale musical, the designer also decides on the number and type of microphones to be used, the placement of speakers throughout the theatre, and all other aspects of sound reproduction.

After reading the script, the sound designer consults with the director to determine the exact nature of the sound requirements, including sound effects and amplification. The designer then sets about preparing the full range of components that constitute sound for a production. Encompassing anything from preshow and intermission music to any and all microphones to special prerecorded sound effects to preshow announcements about cell phones to live voice-overs, sound is an essential component of every theatre production.

Understanding Sound Reproduction and Sound Reinforcement

One way to classify sound design is as *sound reproduction* and *sound reinforcement*. Sound *reproduction* is the use of motivated or environmental sounds. **Motivated sounds** would be, for instance, the noise of a car crunching on gravel, a car motor turning off, and a door slamming—a sequence that would announce the arrival of a character at a house where a scene is taking place. Motivated sounds, then, are those called for by the script. **Environmental sounds** are noises of everyday life that help create verisimilitude in a production: street traffic in a city, crickets in the country, loud rock music coming from a stereo in a college dormitory. Such sounds are usually heard as background.

Motivated sound Sounds called for by the script.

Environmental sounds Noises of everyday life that help create a sense of reality in a production.

Sound effects are one form of sound reproduction. A sound effect can be defined as any sound produced by mechanical or human means to create for us a noise or sound associated with the play. Today, as we noted previously, sound effects are most often digitally downloaded to computers. Virtually every sound imaginable—from birds singing to dogs barking to jet planes flying—is available for digital downloading from the Internet, not only for expensive commercial, professional productions but also for small noncommercial companies, college, university, and community theatres.

Sound *reinforcement* is the amplification of sounds produced by a performer or a musical instrument. With the growth of electronics and computerization in music, more and more instruments have been amplified. At any rock concert, you can see wires coming out of the basses and guitars. In an orchestra pit in a theatre, the quieter acoustic instruments such as the guitar are miked to achieve a balance of sound with the louder instruments. In today's Broadway theatres it is not unusual to have some members of the orchestra in a separate room in another part of the building with a television monitor showing the conductor. In most cases, the audience would never know about this seating arrangement. The total sound can overwhelm a singer, especially one who has not been trained—as opera singers are—to project the voice into the farther reaches of a theatre. As a result, we have body mikes on the performers.

Reinforcement The amplification of sounds produced by a performer or a musical instrument.

1. How do you use lighting in your room or home for different circumstances? How do you change the lighting for those occasions? How is this similar to what is done in the theatre?

2. What sound technology do you use in your everyday life? How might this also be employed in the theatre?

3. If someone asked, "What is the soundtrack for your life?" what would your response be? How does that sound reflect who you are? How is that similar to the use of sound accompanying the production of a play?

4. On a sunny day, observe how the light shines through the leaves of a tree on your campus or near your home. What mood does the light evoke in you? Why? How?

5. What is the lighting like in your favorite restaurant? What mood does it evoke in you? Why? How?

6. Watch a film and discuss how the sound enhances the film. How is underscoring used?

7. Attend a technical rehearsal at your university or community theatre. Observe the light changes. Do you see who is operating the light and sound boards? Can you identify any of the lighting instruments and where they are hung in the theatre? Ask if you may see the computer boards that operate lighting and sound.

At first, a body mike was a small microphone attached in some way to the performer's clothing. A wire ran from the mike to a small radio transmitter concealed on the performer; from the transmitter, the sound was sent to an off-stage listening device that fed it into a central sound-control system. In today's large musical productions, the microphone worn by a performer is frequently a small instrument, hardly larger than a piece of wire, worn over one ear alongside the temple or placed elsewhere near the performer's head, that carries the sound to the body transmitters.

It is now very common in large musical theatre playhouses for performers to wear this very tiny, almost unnoticeable microphone around the ear; it is also most commonly used by rock performers in concerts. Head microphones are used so that they will be as close as possible to the performer's mouth and at a constant distance away from it. (How many of us attending a musical realize that the tap dancers are frequently wearing wireless microphones near their feet, inside their dance tights?)

Still another kind of sound that must be added to the final mix is musical or other *underscoring,* which one hears between scenes or acts, and sometimes during spoken sections of a performance, to add emphasis or create mood.

Sound Technology

Microphones and Loudspeakers   In preparing the sound for a production, the designers and engineers not only must assemble all the necessary sounds but also must be certain that the appropriate microphones are used correctly and must place the speakers effectively onstage and in the auditorium.

Several types of microphones are used. A *shotgun mike* is highly directional and is aimed from a distance at a specific area. A *general mike* picks up sounds in the general area toward which it is aimed. A *body mike,* as we described above, is a wireless microphone attached to a performer's body or clothing. Microphones not worn by performers are placed in various locations. One position is alongside the downstage edge of the stage. Another position is hanging in the air above the stage. Any type of microphone must be hooked up to an amplifier that increases the electronic energy of the sound and sends it through the speakers.

The placement of loudspeakers is both an art and a science. It is necessary to determine the correct speakers for the size and shape of the theatre, and to position them so that they carry sound clearly and evenly into the auditorium—to the upper reaches of the balcony, to the side seats, and to areas underneath the balcony as well as the first few rows in the orchestra. Also, live sound from the performers must reach the sides and back of the theatre at the same time that it reaches those of us seated in the front. One problem in this regard is that sound travels much more slowly than light.

The speed of sound is only 1,100 feet per second—which means that for those of us seated at the back of a large theatre, sound from a speaker at the rear of the auditorium will be heard before the human voice from the stage. Developments in digital electronics have led to devices that process, sample, and synthesize sound for various effects, including delaying the electronic sound so that it arrives through a loudspeaker at the same time as the much slower live sound.

Sound Recordings   The process of assembling sound recordings is similar for professional and nonprofessional productions. First, a list is made of all sound required. This list is usually developed by the sound designer in consultation with the director, and possibly with a composer: For a show with a great deal of sound or music, there may be both a sound designer and a music composer.

Once the list is drawn up, a master recording is made and the sounds are arranged in their order of appearance in the script. This process is called *editing* and is now done with computer assistance. In addition, sound designers and music composers can also have their digital sounds and new music captured on their tablets, smart devices, or stored online, so that they can share with the director and other collaborators.

When the production moves into the theatre, there is a technical rehearsal without performers, during which each sound cue is listened to and the volume is set. When rehearsals with the performers start in the theatre, more changes will be made. Depending on the action and the timing of scenes, some cues will be too loud and others too soft; some will have to be made shorter and others made longer.

During an actual performance of a production using sound reinforcement, an operator must sit at a complex sound console *mixing* sound or, as is becoming the norm, use a computerized playback system such as SFX or CueLab. In this way the operator blends all elements from the many microphones and from the master sound recording—so that there is a smooth, seamless blend of sound. Also, the operator must make certain not only that all sound is in balance but also that sound does not intrude on the performance or call attention to itself, away from the stage and the performers.

New Technologies in Sound   As with lighting, in recent years we have seen frequent advances and breakthroughs in sound equipment and technology. The new body microphones and tiny head microphones as well as a device that delays the delivery of electronic sound have already been mentioned. There are other developments as well.

Analog reel-to-reel tape decks, which were standard, have given way to digital technology such as direct playback from a computer's hard drive. Sound is now recorded and edited at digital audio workstations, housed on personal computers as well as on tablets and even smartphones. Such stations allow easier editing of sound, more complex effects, and higher-quality sound. Digital playback systems allow very easy and precise cueing of shows, as well as greatly improved sound quality.

New sound technology has also improved the theatre experience for audience members with hearing issues through Assistive Listening Devices (ALD). An ALD consists of a small wireless radio receiver and either an independent earpiece or an earpiece compatible with certain hearing aids. ALDs transmit amplified sound from the stage through a sophisticated set of tiny microphones. These devices allow those audience members who need assistance to hear the dialogue spoken by performers, sound effects, as well as songs and music. The ALDs also eliminate a significant amount of the ambient noise thereby enhancing the hearing experience. (Of course, some theatres may also offer captioned and/or signed performances for those audience members with profound hearing loss.)

SPECIAL EFFECTS IN LIGHTING AND SOUND

As in scene design, some effects of lighting and sound, separately or in combination, can seem unusual or even miraculous and add to the magic of live theatre.

There are several special lighting effects that can be used to create interesting visual pictures. One simple effect is to position a source of light near the stage floor and shine the light on the performers from below. This creates shadows under the eyes and chin and gives performers' faces a ghostly or horrifying quality. Another common special effect is ultraviolet light, a very dark blue light that causes phosphorus to glow; when the stage is very dark, or completely dark, costumes or scenery that have been painted with a special phosphorus paint will "light up."

The effect of slow motion—where the performers seem to be moving in jerks— is created by a strobe light, a very powerful, bright gas-discharge light that flashes at rapid intervals. As we saw earlier, technological advances in lighting have made it possible to create even more spectacular effects and to enhance these effects as well.

There are also a number of special sound effects. Sometimes speakers are placed completely around the audience so that the sound can move from side to side. Echoes can be created by a machine that causes reverberations in sound waves. Expanding audio technology also allows for more complex sound effects. Computerized noises and electronic music can be used to create special sounds for various situations, and digitization gives instantaneous access to any element of the sound design. Also, with computerized synthesizers, a few musicians can now replace a large orchestra.

Lighting and sound, therefore, like scenery and costumes, are means to an end: They implement the artistic and aesthetic aspects of a production. The colors, shapes, and lines of lighting and the qualities of sound design interact with other elements of theatre and contribute to the overall experience.

Evaluating Lighting and Sound Design

As with the other design elements, there are key questions we should ask ourselves as we try to determine how successful the lighting and sound designers were in supporting the production we have attended. These include:

1. What information was conveyed by the lighting about time, place, characters, and situation? How was this information conveyed to you?
2. Describe the mood of the lighting. How was color and intensity used to affect your mood? What other characteristics of light were used to affect mood? Was the lighting appropriate for the mood of each scene? Why or why not?

PLAYING YOUR PART:
THINKING ABOUT THEATRE

1. During the last play you attended, what did you notice about the lighting? Were there lighting instruments throughout the theatre aimed at the stage? When the performance began, where did the beams of light appear to come from?

2. During that same production, what colors were created on the stage by lighting? Did you think the colors were appropriate for the production? How did the color of the lights affect your overall experience?

3. Again, during that same production, were you able to spot sound speakers? Where were they located? During the performance, did you notice if microphones were attached to the actors? Do you think there were microphones elsewhere on stage? Can you speculate as to where they were?

3. Was the lighting realistic or nonrealistic? What was the direction of the light? Did it seem to come from a natural source, or was it artificial? Did this choice seem appropriate for the text?

4. Were the performers properly lit? Could their faces be seen?

5. Were light changes made slowly or quickly? How did this affect the play? Did it seem right for the type of play you attended?

6. Were there any lighting special effects? What were they? How were they used to support the play?

7. Were sound effects used in the production? How did they help support your understanding of the play?

8. Were the sound effects realistic or nonrealistic?

9. Were the performers amplified? Was that a distraction or did it seem well integrated into the production?

10. Was there original music? How did it help set the mood or help you better understand the action of the play?

SUMMARY

1. Stage lighting, like other elements of theatre, has a counterpart in the lighting of homes, restaurants, and other environments in our everyday life.

2. Lighting was historically the last visual element to be fully developed for the stage but is today the most technically sophisticated. Once the incandescent electric lamp was introduced, it was possible to achieve almost total control of the color, intensity, and timing of lights. Lighting controls have also benefited from computerization, with extensive light shifts being controlled by an operator at a computerized console.

3. Lighting design is intended to provide illumination onstage, to establish time and place, to help set the mood and style of a production, to focus the action, and to establish a rhythm of visual movement.

4. Lighting should be consistent with all other elements.

Chapter 10 *Lighting and Sound*

249

5. The lighting designer uses a variety of instruments, colored gels, special accessories, and advanced dimmer controls as well as computerized control consoles to achieve effects. Electronic developments and computers have greatly increased the flexibility and control of lighting instruments and equipment.

6. Sound is taking its place alongside scenery, costumes, and lighting as a key design element.

7. Rapid advances in technology allow for sophisticated delivery in a theatre of both sound reproduction—sound effects and such—and sound reinforcement of both musical instruments and the human voice.

8. The sound designer and engineer must (a) prepare the sound track, (b) place microphones and speakers appropriately, and (c) mix recorded and live sounds during the performance to achieve the desired effects.

PART 4

Global Theatres: Past and Present

GLOBAL THEATRES

In this part of our book we explore global theatres of the past and of today. The two are inextricably linked: Contemporary theatre around the world builds on theatre from the past in both the Western and Asian traditions. This is a scene from *A Funny Thing Happened on the Way to the Forum,* staged at the Papermill Playhouse in New Jersey in 2011. The musical is an adaptation of ancient Roman comedy and shows the continuing influence of that form into our time.

(©T. Charles Erickson)

11

EARLY THEATRES: GREEK, ROMAN, AND MEDIEVAL

The ancient civilizations of Greece and Rome have had a profound impact on Western civilization. Their innovations in the arts, architecture, culture, science, philosophy, law, engineering, and government shaped much of later thought and practice in the Western world. The theatres of Greece and Rome laid the foundations of many traditions of today's Western theatre. The theatre of the Middle Ages was the bridge between these eras and the Renaissance. Before turning to these three remarkable eras, however, we should first briefly discuss some of the possible origins of theatre.

ORIGINS OF THEATRE

No one knows exactly how theatre began, or where or when it originated. We do know, however, that the impulse to create theatre is universal among humans.

Two elements of theatre are storytelling and imitation. These, along with other elements, are an important part of religious observances and rituals—formal, repeated ceremonies—in cultures around the world. An example is found in ancient Egypt, where there was an elaborate ritual concerning the god Osiris. Osiris became a ruler of Egypt, married his sister Isis, was murdered by his brother, and was eventually avenged and resurrected. The ceremony retelling the story of Osiris was performed over a period of nearly 2,000 years, from around 2500 B.C.E. to 550 B.C.E., at a sacred place called Abydos.

◀ **THE BEGINNING OF WESTERN THEATRE**

Western theatre began with Greek and Roman theatre and, after a hiatus of many centuries, continued with medieval theatre. The early Greek theatre is well known for its tragedies by Aeschylus, Sophocles, and Euripides. Seen here is a scene from Oedipus at Colonus *by Sophocles in a production at the National Theatre in London, directed by Peter Hall. The production featured Alan Howard, shown above, playing the title role of Oedipus.* (©ArenaPal/Topham/The Image Works)

ORIGINS OF THEATRE
Most ritual ceremonies—whether in Africa, for instance, or among Native Americans, or in southeast Asia—have a strong theatrical component. This includes masks, costumes, repeated phrases, music, and dancing. Here, in Mali, West Africa, teetering on stilts, masked Dogon dancers in a traditional ceremony imitate a long-legged waterbird. (©Jon Arnold Images Ltd/Alamy Stock Photo)

Another recurring theatrical element is costuming. Throughout central and western Africa, for example, striking and imaginative costumes and masks are used in a variety of ceremonies. Among the Kuba people in Zaire, there is a dance that marks the initiation into manhood. The central figure in this ceremony is the Woot, a mythical hero who wears an enormous headdress and a mask made of feathers, plumes, shells, and beads.

In certain societies, rituals, religious ceremonies, imitation, and storytelling have been combined and transformed into theatrical events. In Western culture, the first place where this occurred was ancient Greece.

GREECE

Background: The Golden Age

There are times in history when many forces come together to create a remarkable age. Such a time was the fifth century B.C.E. in Athens, Greece, when there were outstanding achievements in politics, philosophy, science, and the arts, including theatre. This era has come to be known as the *classical period* and also as the *Golden Age* of Greece.

Greece was then a collection of independent city-states, and Athens—the most important—is credited with being the birthplace of democracy (although only male citizens had a voice in politics and government). Greek philosophers, such as Socrates and Plato, tried to explain the world around them; Herodotus transformed history from a simple account of events into a social science. Also, a number of important mathematical and scientific discoveries were made; for instance, the Greek mathematician Pythagoras formulated a theorem that remains one of the cornerstones of geometry; and Hippocrates formulated an oath for physicians that is the one still taken today. Greek sculpture from this period is treasured in museums around the world, and buildings such as the Parthenon—the temple that sits atop the Acropolis in Athens—remain models for architects.

Theatre and Culture: Greek Theatre Emerges

Of particular importance to Greek theatre were the ceremonies honoring Dionysus—the god of wine, fertility, and revelry. Later, Greek drama was presented in honor of Dionysus, and most (though not all) historians believe that Greek drama originated out of the dithyrambic chorus, a group of fifty men who sang and danced a hymn praising Dionysus.

A performer named Thespis is customarily credited with transforming these songs into drama in the sixth century B.C.E. by stepping out of the **chorus** and becoming an actor. He moved from simply reciting a story to impersonating a character and engaging in dialogue with members of the chorus. The contribution of Thespis is reflected in the term **thespian**, which is often used as a synonym for "stage performer."

Theatre and Religion   Greek theatre was intimately bound up with Greek religion, which was based on worship of a group of gods. Annual festivals were held in honor of the gods, and theatre became a central feature of certain Greek festivals. In Athens, a spring festival called the **City Dionysia** (SIT-ee digh-eh-NIGH-see-uh), honoring the god Dionysus, incorporated tragic drama in 534 B.C.E. and comedy about 487 B.C.E. This festival lasted several days, including three days

Chorus   In ancient Greek drama, a group of performers who sang and danced, sometimes participating in the action but usually simply commenting on it. In modern times, performers in a musical play who sing and dance as a group.

Thespian   Synonym for "performer"; from Thespis, who is said to have been the first actor in ancient Greek theatre.

City Dionysia   The most important Greek festival in honor of the god Dionysus, and the first to include drama.

GREEK THEATRE AND RELIGION

Throughout its history theatre has often had a close association with religion. This is true of both Western and Eastern theatre. The Greek and Roman theatres were often linked to religious festivals, and an important segment of medieval theatre dealt directly with religious subjects. The chief Greek theatre festival honored the god Dionysus, who was the subject of a play by Euripides called *Bacchai* (also known as *The Bacchae*). The scene here is from a production of the play by the Royal National Theatre in London. The performers, left to right, are William Houston (Agave), Greg Hicks (Dionysus), and David Ryall (Cadmus).

(©Donald Cooper/Photostage)

Satyr play   One of the three types of classical Greek drama, usually a ribald takeoff on Greek mythology and history that included a chorus of satyrs, mythological creatures who were half-man and half-goat. On festival days in Athens, it was presented as the final play following three tragedies.

Choregus   Wealthy person who financed a playwright's works at an ancient Greek dramatic festival.

devoted to tragedies, and had time set aside for five comedies. *Satyr plays* were also performed; they were satiric versions of Greek history and mythology and featured a chorus of half-man and half-goats, known as satyrs. A few days after the festival, awards were given, the festival operation was reviewed by a representative body, and people who had behaved improperly or disrespectfully were judged and penalized.

Since theatre was a religious and civic event, the organization of dramatic presentations was undertaken by the government. Eleven months before a festival, an appointed official of the city-state would choose the plays to be presented and would appoint a *choregus* (ko-REE-guhs)—the equivalent of a modern-day producer—for each of the selected playwrights. In the early days of Greek dramatic festivals, the tragic playwrights themselves functioned as directors. A playwright would choose the actors and supervise the production, working with the chorus and conferring with the actors about their roles.

Theatre and Myth   What kind of stories were told in the plays written for the festivals? Where did the writers find these stories? The answer, in most cases, is Greek myths.

A *myth* is a story or legend handed down from generation to generation. In every culture, certain myths have a strong hold because they seem to sum up a view of human relationships and try to explain the problems, catastrophes, and opportunities life presents to individuals. Greece had a multitude of myths, which furnished the stories for Greek drama.

The tradition of theatre festivals continues throughout the world. Unlike the Greek festivals, these are not connected to religious events or ceremonies but instead often highlight new or classical works, frequently incorporate a variety of art forms, including theatre, music, and the visual arts, and are staged over an extended period of time. Some of the most well-known festivals, which include or focus on theatre, are Spoleto in Charleston, South Carolina, Edinburgh Theatre Festival in Scotland, and Avignon Festival in France.

There are many festivals that revolve around specific playwrights such as Shakespeare and George Bernard Shaw or that present cutting edge works by theatre artists from across the world. Shakespeare festivals, which present plays by the Bard as well as other classical authors, for example, are held each summer in many states, including Oregon, Colorado, Utah and Illinois. The Stratford Festival in Canada presents Shakespearean works, musicals, and contemporary dramas in multiple spaces every summer.

Contemporary scholars debate the impact of these festivals on our contemporary theatre. Some point out that they introduce audiences to artists from across the globe as well as to avant-garde works and lead to a vital artistic cross-fertilization in our global, postcolonial society. Others argue that the festivals lead to commercialization, homogeneity, and the appropriation (almost the stealing of) unique theatrical traditions of other cultures.

Still, the popularity of these festivals reflects the continuing tradition of bringing various theatrical (and sometimes other) events together in a way that began in Classical Greece. These modern versions are also an attempt to remind audiences of the centrality of theatre in our lives and its ability to establish a sense of community.

Greek Tragedy

The most admired form of drama at the Greek festivals was *tragedy*. Approximately 900 tragedies were produced in Athens during the fifth century B.C.E., of which thirty-one have survived—all by three dramatists: Aeschylus, Sophocles, and Euripides.

Tragedy A serious drama in which there is a downfall of the primary character.

Tragic Dramatists: Aeschylus, Sophocles, and Euripides   Aeschylus (525–456 B.C.E.) is considered the first important Greek dramatist and therefore the first important Western dramatist. He began writing at a time when a theatre presentation would be performed by a large chorus of fifty men and a single actor. In his own dramas, however, Aeschylus called for a second actor, who could play different parts when he put on different masks. This made possible a true dramatic exchange between characters and was the start of drama as we know it. (It should be noted that all performers were men; women's roles were played by men.) In another innovation, Aeschylus reduced the size of the chorus to twelve, making it more manageable.

The dramas of Aeschylus dealt with noble families and lofty themes and were praised for their lyric poetry as well as their dramatic structure and intellectual content. He was the acknowledged master of the *trilogy*—three tragedies that make up a single unit. The best-known of his trilogies is the **Oresteia** (458 B.C.E.): the saga of Agamemnon, a hero of the Trojan war who, when he returns home, is murdered by his wife, Clytemnestra. She in turn is killed by their children, Electra and Orestes.

Trilogy In classical Greece, three tragedies written by the same playwright and presented on a single day; they were connected by a story or thematic concerns.

Sophocles (c. 496–406 B.C.E.), who lived through most of the fifth century B.C.E., built on the dramatic form that Aeschylus had begun. He raised the number in the chorus to fifteen, where it was to remain. More important, he realized that an additional third actor—who, again, might play several parts—would allow enormous flexibility. Because each actor, by wearing different masks in turn, could play two or three parts, the use of three actors meant that a play could have seven or eight characters.

With this newfound flexibility, Sophocles became particularly adept at dramatic construction, introducing characters and information skillfully and building swiftly to a climax. (We will see a good example when we look more closely at **King Oedipus**, which is also called **Oedipus Rex** and **Oedipus the King** in differing translations.)

The third great dramatist of the period, Euripides (c. 484–406 B.C.E.), was more of a rebel and has always been considered the most "modern" of the three. This results from several factors: sympathetic portrayal of female characters, increased realism, mixture of tragedy with melodrama and comedy, and skeptical treatment of the gods.

Tragic Structure   Let's look now at the structure of Greek tragedy, and at the plot of one tragedy—*King Oedipus*—in particular.

Pattern and Plot in Greek Tragedy   Though there are variations among the surviving thirty-one plays of the three great dramatists, the structure in most of them follows the same pattern. First comes the opening scene, after which the chorus enters. This is followed by an episode between characters; then comes the first choral song. From that point on, there is an alternation between character episodes and choral songs until the final episode, which is followed by the exit of all the characters and the chorus.

The chorus was a key—and unique—element of Greek drama, never again being used in the same way. The characters portrayed by the chorus usually represented ordinary citizens, and they had several functions. First, they reacted the way people in the audience might react and thus became surrogates for the audience. They were a group with which the audience members could identify. Second, the chorus often gave background information necessary for an understanding of the plot. Third, the chorus represented a moderate balance between the extreme behaviors of the principal characters. Fourth, the chorus frequently offered philosophical observations and drew conclusions about what had happened in the play. It is important to note that the choral passages were sung and danced, though we do not know what the music sounded like or how the movements were choreographed.

Whether representing men or women, chorus members were always male—as were all performers in Greek theatre.

The Plot of King Oedipus   In the chapter "Creating the Dramatic Script", we discussed two basic plot arrangements developed in Western drama: climactic and episodic construction. Climactic structure, like so much else in theatre, got its start in Greek drama, and Sophocles's play *King Oedipus* (c. 430 B.C.E.) is a good example.

The story of Oedipus begins long before the opening of the play, when Oedipus—the son of King Laius and Queen Jocasta of Thebes—is born. When he is an infant, it is prophesied that he will kill his father and marry his mother,

THE GREEK CHORUS
The chorus in classical Greek theatre served many functions. It provided exposition, narrated the action, interacted with the other actors, and added spectacle. Shown here is a production of *Medea* by Euripides with Helen McCrory as Medea, surrounded by the chorus of women. The production was directed by Carrie Cracknell at the National Theatre in London.
(©Marilyn Kingwill/Arenapal/The Image Works)

and so he is left on a mountaintop to die. A shepherd saves him, however, and takes him to Corinth, where he is raised by the king and queen of Corinth as their own son.

When Oedipus grows up, he learns of the oracle that prophesied that he would kill his parents. Thinking that the king and queen of Corinth are his true parents, he flees Corinth and heads for Thebes. As he approaches Thebes, he encounters, at a crossroads, a man whom he kills in a fight, not realizing that the man is his natural father, the king of Thebes. Oedipus proceeds on to Thebes and, after correctly answering the riddle of the Sphinx, he becomes king; he also marries the queen, Jocasta, not realizing that she is his mother. After a time, a plague hits Thebes.

This is when the play begins. The action takes place on one day in one place: in front of the palace at Thebes. After the play opens, there is an

KING OEDIPUS

In Sophocles's *King Oedipus*—one of the most famous Greek tragedies—Oedipus becomes king of Thebes after unknowingly killing his father and marrying his mother. Upon learning what he has done, Oedipus puts out his eyes. According to Aristotle, *King Oedipus* represents the quintessential Greek tragedy. In this scene we see Russian actor Viktor Dobronravov as Oedipus in a production staged by director Rimas Tuminas at the Vakhtangov Theatre. The production was a joint project of the Vakhtangov Theatre and the National Theatre of Greece in Athens and was staged as part of the Russia and Greece cross-cultural year. (©Vyacheslav Prokofyev/TASS/Getty Images)

alternation of choral sections and episodes. The plot has many twists and turns as well as ups and downs for the characters. First, it is revealed that an oracle has said that the plague will not be lifted until the murderer of the former king is found and punished. Oedipus, not knowing that he himself is the murderer, vows to find the guilty party. After that, Jocasta says Oedipus should ignore the oracle because it stated that her husband, the king, would be killed by his son, but he was killed at a crossroads. Then Oedipus says he killed a man at a crossroads. Next, a messenger arrives from Corinth saying that the king there is dead. Jocasta points out that this proves that Oedipus did not kill his father because the father died while Oedipus was away. But then the messenger reveals that the king of Corinth was not the real father of Oedipus, and so forth, until the final revelations and conclusion—when Oedipus puts out his eyes and Jocasta kills herself.

Thematically, *King Oedipus* raises questions that have provoked philosophical discussions for centuries: questions about fate, pride, and the ironic nature of human events.

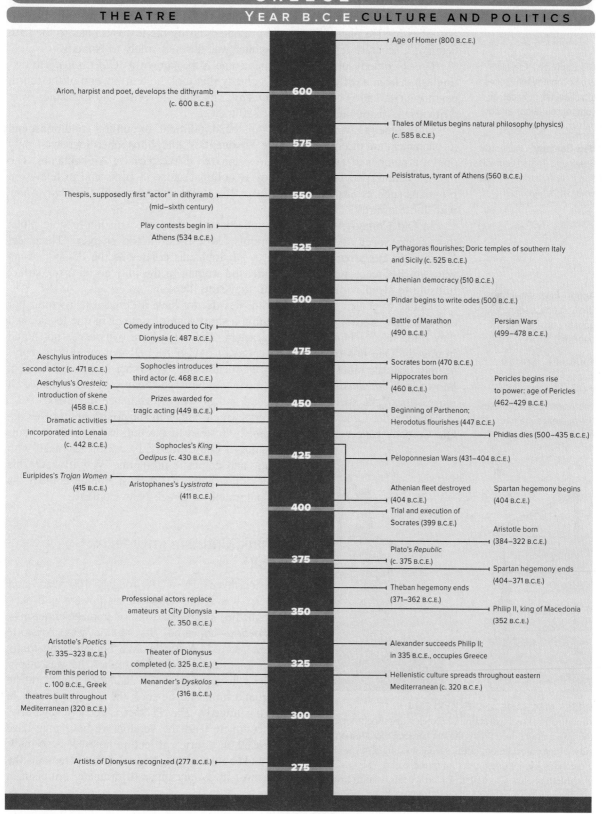

Age of Homer (800 B.C.E.)

600

Arion, harpist and poet, develops the dithyramb (c. 600 B.C.E.)

575

Thales of Miletus begins natural philosophy (physics) (c. 585 B.C.E.)

Peisistratus, tyrant of Athens (560 B.C.E.)

550

Thespis, supposedly first "actor" in dithyramb (mid–sixth century)

Play contests begin in Athens (534 B.C.E.)

525

Pythagoras flourishes; Doric temples of southern Italy and Sicily (c. 525 B.C.E.)

Athenian democracy (510 B.C.E.)

500

Pindar begins to write odes (500 B.C.E.)

Comedy introduced to City Dionysia (c. 487 B.C.E.)

Battle of Marathon (490 B.C.E.) Persian Wars (499–478 B.C.E.)

475

Aeschylus introduces second actor (c. 471 B.C.E.)

Sophocles introduces third actor (c. 468 B.C.E.)

Socrates born (470 B.C.E.)

Aeschylus's *Oresteia*; introduction of skene (458 B.C.E.)

Prizes awarded for tragic acting (449 B.C.E.)

Hippocrates born (460 B.C.E.) Pericles begins rise to power: age of Pericles (462–429 B.C.E.)

450

Dramatic activities incorporated into Lenaia (c. 442 B.C.E.)

Beginning of Parthenon; Herodotus flourishes (447 B.C.E.)

Phidias dies (500–435 B.C.E.)

Sophocles's *King Oedipus* (c. 430 B.C.E.)

425

Peloponnesian Wars (431–404 B.C.E.)

Euripides's *Trojan Women* (415 B.C.E.)

Aristophanes's *Lysistrata* (411 B.C.E.)

Athenian fleet destroyed (404 B.C.E.) Spartan hegemony begins (404 B.C.E.)

400

Trial and execution of Socrates (399 B.C.E.)

Aristotle born (384–322 B.C.E.)

Plato's *Republic* (c. 375 B.C.E.)

375

Spartan hegemony ends (404–371 B.C.E.)

Theban hegemony ends (371–362 B.C.E.)

Professional actors replace amateurs at City Dionysia (c. 350 B.C.E.)

350

Philip II, king of Macedonia (352 B.C.E.)

Aristotle's *Poetics* (c. 335–323 B.C.E.)

Theater of Dionysus completed (c. 325 B.C.E.)

Alexander succeeds Philip II; in 335 B.C.E., occupies Greece

325

From this period to c. 100 B.C.E., Greek theatres built throughout Mediterranean (320 B.C.E.)

Menander's *Dyskolos* (316 B.C.E.)

Hellenistic culture spreads throughout eastern Mediterranean (c. 320 B.C.E.)

300

Artists of Dionysus recognized (277 B.C.E.)

275

Greek Comedy

As we've noted, part of the seven-day City Dionysia was devoted to comedy, and comedies by five playwrights were presented during the festival. Later in the fifth century, a separate festival in the winter was devoted solely to comedy.

Greek comedy of this period has come to be known as **Old Comedy** to distinguish it from a different kind of comedy that took hold at the end of the fourth century B.C.E. and is called **New Comedy**. The only surviving Old Comedies were written by Aristophanes (c. 448–c. 380 B.C.E.).

Old Comedy always makes fun of social, political, or cultural conditions, and its characters are often recognizable personalities; the philosopher Socrates is only one of a number of prominent figures satirized in the plays of Aristophanes. The modern counterpart of Old Comedy is political satire in films and in television programs such as *Saturday Night Live, The Colbert Report,* and *The Daily Show* with Jon Stewart.

In Old Comedy, the satire is underlined by fantastic and improbable plots; this is an aspect of the comic premise, discussed in the chapter "Theatrical Genres." In **Lysistrata**, for instance, Aristophanes condemns the Peloponnesian war, which Greece was then fighting; the women in the play go on a sex strike, refusing to sleep with the men until they stop the war.

Unlike tragedies, most Old Comedies do not have a climactic structure. For example, they do not take place within a short span of time or in one locale, and they often have a large cast of characters. They also have two scenes not found in tragedy. One is a debate, called an **agon** (AG-ohn), between two forces representing opposite sides of a political or social issue. The other is a choral section, known as a **parabasis** (puh-RAB-uh-sihs), addressed directly to the audience; it makes fun of the spectators in general and of specific audience members.

During the Greek Hellenistic era, which began in the fourth century B.C.E., Old Comedy gave way to New Comedy. Instead of the political, social, and cultural satire of Old Comedy, New Comedy dealt with romantic and domestic problems. We will study this kind of drama when we look at Roman comedy—a direct outgrowth of Greek New Comedy.

Dramatic Criticism in Greece: Aristotle

In the fourth century B.C.E., roughly 100 years after Sophocles was at the height of his powers as a playwright, the first significant work of dramatic criticism—*The Poetics*—appeared. Its author was Aristotle (384–322 B.C.E.). Aristotle, like Socrates and Plato, was an important Greek philosopher; he was also a scientist who described and cataloged the world he saw around him, and he took the same approach in analyzing tragedy. *The Poetics* is loosely organized and incomplete, and the version we have may have been based on a series of lecture notes. It is so intelligent and so penetrating, however, that it remains the single most important piece of dramatic criticism in existence.

Old Comedy Classical Greek comedy that pokes fun at social, political, or cultural conditions and at particular figures.

New Comedy Hellenistic Greek and Roman comedies that deal with romantic and domestic situations.

Agon In classical Greek Old Comedy, a scene with a debate between the two opposing forces in a play.

Parabasis Scene in classical Greek Old Comedy in which the chorus directly addresses the audience members and makes fun of them.

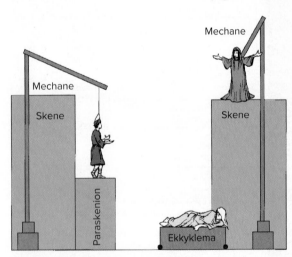

GREEK MECHANE AND EKKYKLEMA
A conjectural reconstruction of Greek stage machinery. On the left, a crane used for flying in characters located on a side wing (paraskenion) of the scene building. On the right, a mechane higher up on the roof of the skene. The ekkyklema below was a platform on wheels used to bring out characters from inside the building.

ザ

Athens, 441 B.C.E. The year is 441 B.C.E. It is a morning in late March in Athens, Greece, and the citizens of Athens are up early, making their way to the Theatre of Dionysus, an open-air theatre on the south side of the Acropolis, the highest hill in Athens. On the Acropolis are several temples, including the Parthenon, a magnificent new temple dedicated to the goddess Athena, which is under construction at this very time.

The Theatre of Dionysus has semicircular seating built into the slope of the hill on the side of the Acropolis. At the foot of the seating area is a flat, circular space—the orchestra—where the actors will perform. Behind the orchestra a temporary stage house has been built, from which the performers will make entrances and exits. The facade of the stage house for the performance today represents the temple at Thebes, where the action will take place.

Priests of various religious orders are sitting in special seats at the edge of the circle opposite the stage house. Other dignitaries, such as civic and military officials, are arranged around them in the first few rows; above them sit both citizens and slaves. No one—not even those sitting in the top row—will have any trouble hearing the performers; the acoustics are so good that a whisper by an actor in the orchestra will carry to the upper reaches of the amphitheatre.

The plays performed for the citizens of Athens are part of the City Dionysia festival, an annual series of events lasting several days. During this festival, all business in Athens—both commercial and governmental—comes to a halt. On the day before the plays, there was a parade through the city, which ended near the theatre at a temple dedicated to the god Dionysus, for whom the festival is named. There, a religious observance was held at the altar.

Today is one of three days of the festival devoted mainly to tragedies. On these days, one playwright will present three tragedies and a satyr play. The three tragedies are sometimes linked to form one long play, called a *trilogy;* but sometimes they are three separate pieces—as they are today.

The play about to begin is **Antigone** by Sophocles. Its subject comes from a familiar myth: Antigone is the daughter of King Oedipus. After her father's death, her two brothers, Eteocles and Polynices, fight a war against each other to see who will become king of Thebes; during the war, they kill each other. Antigone's uncle, Creon, then becomes king of Thebes. Creon blames Polynices for the conflict and issues an edict that Polynices is not to be given an honorable burial. Antigone decides to defy Creon's order and bury Polynices. The audience members know this myth well and are curious to see how Sophocles—one of their favorite dramatists—will deal with it.

As the play begins, two actors, each wearing the mask and costume of a woman, appear in the playing area: They represent Antigone and her sister, Ismene. Antigone tells Ismene that she means to defy their uncle, the king, and give their brother Polynices an honorable burial. Ismene, unlike Antigone, is timid and frightened; she argues that women are too weak to stand up to a king. Besides, Ismene points out, Antigone will be put to death if she is caught. Antigone argues, however, that she will not be subservient to a man, even the king.

When the two female characters leave the stage, a chorus of fifteen men enters. These men represent the elders of the city, and throughout the play—in passages that are sung and danced—they will fulfill several functions: providing background information, raising philosophical questions, and urging the principal figures to show restraint. The choral sections alternate with scenes of confrontation between Antigone, Creon, and the other main characters.

As the play continues, Antigone attempts to bury Polynices, but she is caught and brought before the king. In their confrontation, Antigone defies Creon. She is sentenced to death and put into a cave to die. By the end of the play, not only is Antigone dead; so too are Creon's wife and son, who have killed themselves. In the final scene, we see Creon standing alone, wearing his tragic mask, bereft of all those whom he held dear.

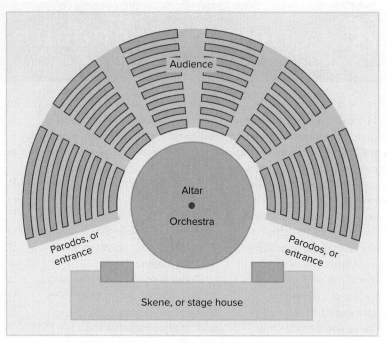

GROUND PLAN OF A TYPICAL GREEK THEATRE
The theatres of ancient Greece were set into hillsides, which made natural amphitheatres. At the base of the seating area was a circular space (orchestra) in which the chorus performed; at the center of the orchestra was an altar (thymele). Behind the orchestra was a temporary stage house (skene), at each side of which was a corridor (parodos) for entrances and exits.

Amphitheatres Large oval, circular, or semicircular outdoor theatre with rising tiers of seats around an open playing area; also, an exceptionally large indoor auditorium.

Orchestra A circular playing space in ancient Greek theatres; in modern times, the ground-floor seating in a theatre auditorium.

Skene Classical Greek and Hellenistic scene house.

Parodos In classical Greek drama, the scene in which the chorus enters. Also, the entranceway for the chorus in Greek theatre.

Theatron Where the audience sat in an ancient Greek theatre.

In *The Poetics* Aristotle describes six elements of drama: (1) plot (arrangement of dramatic incidents), (2) character (people represented in the play), (3) thought or theme (ideas explored), (4) language (dialogue and poetry), (5) music, and (6) spectacle (scenery and other visual elements). These correspond roughly to the elements of theatre we explore in the chapters "Creating the Dramatic Script" through "Lighting and Sound," except that Aristotle does not include the performers. Tragedy, Aristotle suggests, deals with the reversals in fortune and eventual downfall of a royal figure.

Theatre Production in Greece

Greek drama, as we have noted, was staged in *amphitheatres*, which were cut out of the side of a hill and probably held between 15,000 and 17,000 spectators. At the base of the hillside was a circular playing area called the *orchestra* (recent excavations suggest that the earliest orchestra may have been rectangular or trapezoidal). Behind the playing area was a scene house, known as the *skene*. The chorus made its entrances and exits on each side of the scene house through an aisle called a *parodos* (PAR-uh-dohs). This is the first recorded example of the thrust stage, discussed in the chapter "Theatre Spaces." The standard scenic setting for Greek tragedy was a palace, which was represented by the *skene*, and simple devices were used to indicate locales and to move characters on- and offstage. The audience sat in the *theatron*. During the classical period the hillside

Part 4 Global Theatres: Past and Present

theatron probably had temporary wooden bleachers, but these were replaced by stone seats during the later Hellenistic era.

All the characters in Greek drama, male and female, were portrayed by men. The performers, particularly the chorus members, had to be accomplished at singing and dancing as well as vocal projection. The actors may have been paid, and after 449 B.C.E. an acting contest was introduced.

The major element in Greek costuming was the mask, worn by all performers. The mask covered the entire head and included hairstyle and distinctive facial features such as a beard. Masks indicated the emotional state of the characters and also made it possible for male actors to play female characters.

Music and dance were always important elements of classical Greek theatre. By the time of Euripedes, it is believed that music was used, as in today's films, almost throughout a presentation. Dance also reflected the type of play for which it was created.

Later Greek Theatre

In the two centuries after Aristotle—referred to as the *Hellenistic Age*—there were several developments in Greek theatre.

The period of great original drama was over, and revivals of plays from the past were increasingly presented. As original drama became less important, there was a shift of focus to acting and the actor. The theatre of this period saw the introduction of enlarged masks, exaggerated headdresses, and platform shoes that made the performers taller. Also, larger, more permanent stages were built, and these too directed more attention toward the actors. Emblematic of this new status for performers was the creation in 277 B.C.E. of a guild known as the Artists of Dionysus, which was the ancient equivalent of today's Actors Equity Association.

Theatre buildings proliferated throughout the Hellenistic world. We know of at least forty theatres built during this period from Asia Minor in the east to Italy in the west, many of them still standing. These were permanent structures, with both the seating area and the stage house built of stone, in contrast to the less permanent wooden structures of earlier times.

Theatre continued to flourish in Greece long after the second century B.C.E., but it was no longer purely Greek theatre—it was influenced by the omnipresent Roman civilization.

ROME

Background: Rome and Its Civilization

As ancient Greece declined in power and importance, another civilization began to emerge in Europe on the Italian peninsula. Its center was the city of Rome, from which it took its name. While Greece is noted for its creativity and imagination, Rome is recognized more for its practical achievements: law, engineering, and military conquest. And just as these achievements were more down to earth than those of Greece, so too was Roman theatre. Instead of high-minded tragedy, it focused on comedy and other popular entertainments, comparable to our movies, television, and rock concerts.

Rome was founded, according to legend, around 750 B.C.E., and for more than 200 years it was ruled by kings. Around 500 B.C.E. the kings were overthrown, and a republic—which was to last nearly 500 years—was established.

ROME

THEATRE	YEAR B.C.E.–C.E.	CULTURE AND POLITICS

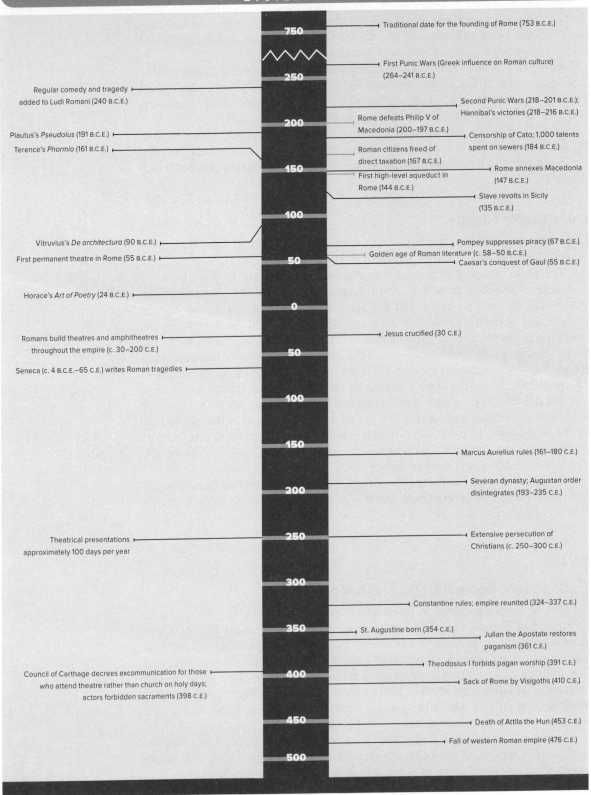

750 — Traditional date for the founding of Rome (753 B.C.E.)

250 — First Punic Wars (Greek influence on Roman culture) (264–241 B.C.E.)

Regular comedy and tragedy added to Ludi Romani (240 B.C.E.)

200 — Second Punic Wars (218–201 B.C.E.); Hannibal's victories (218–216 B.C.E.)

Rome defeats Philip V of Macedonia (200–197 B.C.E.)

Plautus's *Pseudolus* (191 B.C.E.) — Censorship of Cato; 1,000 talents spent on sewers (184 B.C.E.)

Terence's *Phormio* (161 B.C.E.)

Roman citizens freed of direct taxation (167 B.C.E.)

150 — Rome annexes Macedonia (147 B.C.E.)

First high-level aqueduct in Rome (144 B.C.E.)

Slave revolts in Sicily (135 B.C.E.)

100

Vitruvius's *De architectura* (90 B.C.E.) — Pompey suppresses piracy (67 B.C.E.)

Golden age of Roman literature (c. 58–50 B.C.E.)

First permanent theatre in Rome (55 B.C.E.) — Caesar's conquest of Gaul (55 B.C.E.)

50

Horace's *Art of Poetry* (24 B.C.E.)

0

Romans build theatres and amphitheatres throughout the empire (c. 30–200 C.E.) — Jesus crucified (30 C.E.)

50

Seneca (c. 4 B.C.E.–65 C.E.) writes Roman tragedies

100

150 — Marcus Aurelius rules (161–180 C.E.)

200 — Severan dynasty; Augustan order disintegrates (193–235 C.E.)

250 — Extensive persecution of Christians (c. 250–300 C.E.)

Theatrical presentations approximately 100 days per year

300

Constantine rules; empire reunited (324–337 C.E.)

350 — St. Augustine born (354 C.E.)

Julian the Apostate restores paganism (361 C.E.)

Theodosius I forbids pagan worship (391 C.E.)

Council of Carthage decrees excommunication for those who attend theatre rather than church on holy days; actors forbidden sacraments (398 C.E.)

400 — Sack of Rome by Visigoths (410 C.E.)

450 — Death of Attila the Hun (453 C.E.)

Fall of western Roman empire (476 C.E.)

500

POPULAR ENTERTAINMENTS IN ROME
The Romans constructed large arenas for the presentation of popular entertainments, including gladiator battles, chariot races, and animal battles. Seen here is the Roman Colosseum, an amphitheatre originally built in 70 to 82 C.E., that still stands today and has undergone a recent renovation. It was the scene of many spectacular events, including bloody combats. (©Jennifer Barrow/123RF RF)

During the third century B.C.E., Rome engaged in a lengthy conflict with Carthage known as the Punic Wars and finally emerged victorious. As a result, Rome controlled large parts of the central and western Mediterranean. It was at this period of conquest that Rome also came into contact with Greece and saw first-hand Greek art and culture, including theatre.

During the first century B.C.E., the Roman republic began to show signs of serious strain in attempting to govern so vast an area. In the midst of general turmoil, Julius Caesar made himself dictator. He was subsequently assassinated by a group led by Brutus, who in turn was defeated in battle by Mark Antony and Octavius. The republic could not survive these shocks, and in 27 B.C.E. Rome became an empire with one supreme ruler. This form of government continued for several centuries, during which most of the civilized Western world was unified under Roman rule.

Roman laws dealing with property, marriage, and inheritance have continued to influence Western civilization to the present day; in addition, the Romans were great engineers and architects, building important aqueducts and roadways. Religion was also of utmost importance to the Romans, who worshipped gods that were counterparts of the Greek deities, as well as a large number of other divinities.

Theatre and Culture in Rome

When the Romans turned to theatre, they were strongly influenced by the Greeks, just as they were in sculpture and architecture. They borrowed freely from Greek theatre—particularly Greek New Comedy, from which they developed their own form of popular comedy. We should note that the Romans' popular entertainments were also influenced by Etruria, a civilization northwest of Rome that flourished from 650 to 450 B.C.E.

In 240 B.C.E., a festival called the **Ludi Romani**, dedicated to the god Jupiter (the Roman counterpart of Zeus), became the first major Roman festival to incorporate theatre. Five more official festivals eventually incorporated theatre; in addition, an increasing number of days were set aside for minor festivals and theatrical activities.

Ludi Romani A festival dedicated to the god Jupiter which was the first major Roman festival to incorporate theatre.

Popular Entertainment in Rome

Throughout theatre history, all civilizations have developed popular entertainments, which appeal to all levels of society, and require no educational, social, or cultural sophistication to appreciate them. Many popular entertainments are theatrical in nature, using live performers. Some historians say that twenty-first-century American culture, with its highly developed popular entertainments—television, film, rock concerts, athletic competitions, and other less sophisticated dramatic arts—is much like Roman culture. The reason for this is that many Roman entertainments correspond to modern ones. The Romans, for example, greatly enjoyed chariot racing, equestrian performances, acrobatics, wrestling, prizefighting, and gladiatorial combats—though the gladiatorial combats were not simulated but actual battles to the death.

To house these spectacles, the Romans constructed special buildings, counterparts to our modern football and baseball stadiums. The Circus Maximus in Rome, first laid out in 600 B.C.E. for chariot races and frequently remodeled thereafter, eventually seated more than 60,000 spectators. The most renowned amphitheatre constructed by the Romans was the Colosseum, built around 80 C.E.

The Romans also developed popular entertainments that were more closely connected to theatre. Roman mime, like Greek mime, included gymnastics, juggling, songs, and dances. Short comedic skits, which were often sexually suggestive, were also presented. A unique Roman stage presentation was **pantomime**, which used a single dancer, a chorus, and musical accompanists and was somewhat akin to modern ballet; its performers were often sponsored by emperors and members of the nobility.

Pantomime Originally a Roman entertainment in which a narrative was sung by a chorus while the story was acted out by dancers. Now used loosely to cover any form of presentation that relies on dance, gesture, and physical movement without dialogue or speech.

Roman Comedy: Plautus and Terence

Although theatre and drama existed in Rome for nearly seven centuries, the works of only three playwrights survive: the comedies of Plautus and Terence and the tragedies of Seneca.

Plautus (c. 254–184 B.C.E.), who based almost all his comedies on Greek New Comedy, dealt exclusively with domestic situations, particularly the trials

Some of the amphitheatres of Roman times continue to be used today as tourist attractions and for the staging of popular concerts. Two examples are the Colosseum and the Circus Maximus.

The Colosseum, built to house many of the Romans' popular entertainments, is now an extremely popular modern tourist attraction. However, the space we visit today has been damaged by earthquakes, and some of the structure was dismantled during the Middle Ages. Nevertheless, the Colosseum continues to be used in contemporary times for special events, including occasional performances.

Pope Benedict XVI first employed the space to stage the Stations of the Cross for Good Friday in 2009, a tradition continued by Pope Francis. In 2011, a restoration of the space was proposed using private and public funds. There have been controversial suggestions for using the renovated arena, including soccer games and rock concerts, and while these proposals were rejected, the exterior restoration and cleaning was completed by the summer of 2016. A plan to create a modern floor, to replace the no longer extant one, and for the presentation of large-scale cultural events is slated for completion in 2018. The primary aim now is to enhance the Colosseum's appeal as a tourist attraction.

Like the Colosseum, other Roman arenas have housed contemporary entertainments. Operas, for example, are staged in the amphitheater in Verona. The Circus Maximus is used today as a public park and for popular entertainments. In 2014, the rock group the Rolling Stones staged a concert there. In 2016, Bruce Springsteen performed at the Circus Maximus. In addition, this ancient arena has been used to host public celebrations, such as those held for victorious Italian soccer teams.

and tribulations of romance. His characters are recognizable, recurring stock types, the most popular being the parasite who lives off others and is motivated mainly by sensuality. Courtesans, lovers, and overbearing parents were also favorite characters. Most of the dialogue was meant to be sung. Plautus's comedies are farces, and they use such farcical techniques as mistaken identity. A good example of mistaken identity is found in **The Menaechmi**, which is also called **The Menaechmus Brothers** or **The Twin Menaechmi** in differing translations.

The Roman comic writer who followed Plautus was Terence (c. 185–159 B.C.E.). Although Terence's plots are as complicated as those of Plautus, his style is more literary and less exaggerated. Terence's **Phormio** (161 B.C.E.) dramatizes the attempts of two cousins to overcome their fathers' objections to their lovers. The plot complications and stock characters are similar to those found in *The Menaechmi,* but *Phormio* is less farcical and slapstick and gives more emphasis to verbal wit. Also, whereas much of Plautus's dialogue was meant to be sung, most of Terence's dialogue was spoken.

Roman Tragedy: Seneca

The most notable tragic dramatist of the Roman period was Seneca (c. 4 B.C.E.–65 C.E.). Seneca's plays appear to be similar to Greek tragedies but in fact are quite distinct. His chorus is not integral to the dramatic action; and—unlike Greek dramatists, who banished violence from the stage—Seneca emphasizes onstage stabbings, murders, and suicides. In addition, supernatural beings often appear in the dramatic action.

ROMAN COMEDY
Roman comedy, which was based on Greek New Comedy, stressed domestic travails presented humorously. Roman comedy has been the basis for comedy running through the entire Western tradition, right up to the point of today's television situation comedies. One of the most popular adaptations of ancient Roman comedy is the musical *A Funny Thing Happened on the Way to the Forum* with music and lyrics by Stephen Sondheim. The scene here is from a production at the Paper Mill Playhouse in New Jersey, with Paul C. Vogt as Pseudolus (center), the lead character. (©T Charles Erickson)

Although his plays were probably not performed for large public audiences, Seneca had a noteworthy influence on later authors, particularly Shakespeare. *Hamlet*—which has much onstage violence and includes a supernatural character (the ghost of Hamlet's father)—is often described as influenced by Senecan revenge tragedy.

Dramatic Criticism in Rome: Horace

Like Roman drama, Roman dramatic criticism was based on the work of others, especially Aristotle. Horace (65–8 B.C.E.), sometimes called the "Roman Aristotle," outlined his theory of correct dramatic technique in *Ars Poetica (The Art of Poetry)*. Horace argued that tragedy and comedy must be distinct genres, or types, of drama, and that tragedy should deal with royalty, whereas comedy should depict common people. He also stressed that drama should not just entertain but also teach a lesson.

Rome, 184 B.C.E. It is 184 B.C.E., and many of the inhabitants of the city of Rome are on their way to attend performances at a spring festival in honor of Jupiter. Their mood today is happy and ebullient, because they are about to see a comedy by Plautus, whose plot twists and comic invention have made his works favorites with everyone.

The Romans are heading toward a large, temporary wooden theatre building, seating several thousand, that has been erected next to a temple of Jupiter. All theatre productions in Rome now take place during religious festivals, and all the theatres are near temples. A Roman theatre—unlike the Greek theatres in the lands Rome has conquered—is a single unit, built on level ground, with the stage house attached directly to the ends of a semicircular audience area. In front of the stage house is a long platform stage; and in front of that is a half-circle surrounded by the audience.

The group converging on the theatre consists of people from all walks of life. Plautus himself has remarked that a Roman audience is a genuine mixture: In addition to well-to-do middle- and upper-class citizens, it includes government officials and their wives; children with nurses; prostitutes; slaves—in short, virtually every social group. Because this is a state festival, admission is free.

Magistrates of the state have received a grant to produce today's plays and have engaged acting troupes to present individual plays. Each troupe is under the direction of a manager, and one of these managers has bought from Plautus a play called *The Menaechmi* and has arranged for the costumes, music, and other production elements.

As the Romans enter the theatre, they see two doors onstage: One opens on the house of Menaechmus of Epidamnus (the Greek city in which Plautus has set his play); the other is the door to the house of Erotium, a woman with whom Menaechmus is having a love affair that he is trying to keep secret from his wife. The stage represents the street in front of the two houses; at one end is an exit to the port, and at the other end is an exit to the center of town.

An actor comes onstage to deliver a prologue. He asks the audience members to pay careful attention to what Plautus has to say, and then he outlines the background of the story: how the Menaechmi twins were separated when they were infants and how the twin who grew up in Syracuse is just now returning to try to find his long-lost brother. As in many of Plautus's plays, most of the dialogue is sung, somewhat like the musical numbers in contemporary musical comedies.

When the play opens, Menaechmus is shown to be the despair of his jealous wife. He confides to "Sponge," a parasite, that he has stolen his wife's dress, hiding it under his own clothes—and is going to give it to his mistress, Erotium. At Erotium's house he suggests that in return for the dress, she invite them to dinner. Menaechmus exits.

Meanwhile, the twin from Syracuse has arrived with his slave, Messenio. His master gives Messenio a purse full of money for safekeeping. At that point, Erotium steps out of her house and, mistaking the Syracuse twin for Menaechmus, makes advances to him, by which he is totally confused. Not knowing he is a twin, she is equally confused by his odd behavior. Meanwhile, the two servants of the twins are constantly confused with one another as well.

Finally, the Syracuse twin does enter the house of Erotium to have dinner, and later leaves with the dress that his twin brother Menaechmus had previously given her. Menaechmus comes back just in time to have his wife demand that he return her dress. He goes to Erotium to retrieve the dress, only to be told by her that she has already given it to him. In short, he is rebuffed by both his wife and his mistress.

The play continues like this, with the two brothers constantly being confused for one another by everyone, including the wife, the mistress, the father, and the two servants. Confusion and slapstick comedy abound until the end of the play, when everything is resolved.

Although we focus on the great dramas and comedies created during the Greek and Roman eras, we should not forget that there was a strong tradition of popular entertainment during these time periods. The types of popular arts that flourished during these eras were to have a great influence on popular culture through our own times.

During the classical and Hellenistic Greek eras, we know that there were traveling mimes who performed throughout the Greek world. Historians believe that mime may have developed in the fifth and fourth centuries B.C.E., but there is a great deal of debate over how to define the form. Greek mime is often described as dealing with domestic and sexual situations in a popular and highly bawdy manner, though it may have first been a form that parodied mythological figures and stories.

Mimes sometimes performed by themselves, but by the Hellenistic era they were usually organized into troupes. Mime was never introduced into the festivals and was seen as a lower form of theatrical art. Women eventually were performers in mime troupes, and frequently the actors in this type of popular entertainment, especially in the Hellenistic era, appeared without masks. In order to survive economically, mime troupes traveled extensively. For that reason, it is often argued that Greek mime performers influenced the development of Roman theatre and popular entertainments.

Roman theatre had great competition in the popular arts that were available to the Roman public. Mime troupes continued to perform in Roman times. The Romans also developed a form referred to as *pantomime,* in which a single male dancer interpreted classical literature, sometimes accompanied by a chorus that chanted and by musicians.

But the Romans also organized even greater spectacles. As we have noted, they created huge circuses,

GLADIATOR BATTLES
Shown here is a Roman mosaic depicting a gladiator battling a leopard. Such battles between human combatants and animals were extremely popular, particularly during the Roman empire. (©Fratelli Alinari IDEA S.p.A./Getty Images)

stadiums, and amphitheatres for popular arts. Some of the circuses, for example, had tracks for chariot races. Stadiums held animal battles, battles between gladiators, and fights between humans and animals; the Circus Maximus and the Colosseum were erected for just such events.

In modern times, we can see many similarities to the popular arts of Greece and Rome. Stand-up comedians and small troupes of improvisatory comics entertain us regularly in events that are very reminiscent of the early mimes. Sports arenas, indoors and outdoors, house gladiator-like battles, such as football and boxing. And many of these events are highly theatrical, mixing pregame, halftime, and postgame performances into already highly theatricalized sports.

Theatre Production in Rome

Roman production practices differed slightly from those of Greece. Roman festivals were under the jurisdiction of a local government official who hired an acting troupe. The **dominus,** or head, of a troupe—who was usually the leading actor—made financial arrangements, bought dramas from playwrights, hired musicians, and obtained costumes. Acting companies had at least six members,

Dominus   Leader of a Roman acting troupe.

all male; and the Romans ignored the three-actor rule of Greek theatre. Roman acting technique emphasized detailed pantomime and broad physical gestures, necessitated by the size of Roman theatres; it also stressed beautiful vocal delivery. The Romans admired performers who specialized in one type of role and refined the characterizations of stock figures. Facial expression was unimportant since full linen head masks were worn; only mime performers appeared without masks.

As we've seen, Roman theatres were based on Greek models. The Romans did not construct a permanent theatre until 55 B.C.E. Thus there were no permanent spaces for presenting the works of Plautus and Terence, the best-known Roman playwrights. Instead, elaborate temporary wooden structures, probably similar to the later permanent ones, were erected.

A Roman theatre had the same three units as a Greek theatre: (1) a semicircular, sloped seating area; (2) an orchestra; and (3) a stage house, called the *scaena* (SKAY-nah). The Roman structures, however, were different from classical Greek theatres in that they were freestanding buildings with the tiered audience section connected to the stage house to form a single unit. The sloped, semicircular audience seating area was often larger than its Greek counterpart; with seating capacity ranging from 8,000 to 25,000.

Scaena Stage house in a Roman theatre.

The Roman orchestra, which was semicircular (rather than circular as in Greek theatres), was rarely used for staging; rather, it was used for seating government officials or, in some theatres, was flooded for sea battles.

In front of the stage house was a large raised stage about 5 feet high whose area varied from approximately 100 feet by 20 feet to 300 feet by 40 feet. The stage house itself was a unique feature of the Roman theatre structure. Two or three stories high, it was used for storage and dressing space, and a roof extended from the scene building over the stage to protect the actors from the weather. Two side wings connected the stage house to the audience area. The facade of the stage house—the *scaena frons*—was elaborate and ornate, with statuary, columns, recesses, and three to five doorways.

There were also passageways, *vomitoria,* that came out from under the seating area, and which led to the orchestra and stage; they could be used by actors for entrances and exits. Because of its emphasis on the raised stage and the facade behind it, the Roman theatre moved to a point somewhere between the thrust stage of the Greek theatre and later proscenium stages.

Vomitoria These were passageways in Roman theatres that came out from under the seating area, and which led to the orchestra and stage; they could be used by actors for entrances and exits.

Decline of Roman Theatre

In the fourth century C.E., it was clear that the Roman Empire was beginning to fall apart. In 330, Emperor Constantine established two capitals for the empire: Rome in the west and Constantinople in the east. From that point on, the center of gravity shifted to Constantinople, and the city of Rome became less and less important.

The downfall of Rome was marked in 476 C.E. by the unseating of the western Roman emperor by a barbarian ruler. It had probably been caused by the disintegration of the Roman administrative structure and the sacking of Roman cities by northern invaders; but in any case the fall of the empire also meant the end of western Roman theatre.

Another important factor in the decline of Roman theatre was the rise of Christianity. From the outset, the Christian church was opposed to theatre because of the connection between theatre and pagan religions and because the church

THE ROMAN THEATRE AT ORANGE

The Romans built theatres throughout their empire, which circled the Mediterranean Sea. One of the best-preserved, built in the first or second century C.E., is at Orange in France, near the center of town. Note the semicircular orchestra, the large stage area, and the stage house at the back, with its ornate facade with niches for statues and other adornments. (©Jose Antonio Moreno/age fotostock Spain, S.L./Alamy Stock Photo RF)

GROUND PLAN OF A TYPICAL ROMAN THEATRE

Roman theatres, in contrast to Greek theatres, were freestanding structures—all one building—with the stone stage house connected to the seating area, known as the cavea. The orchestra was a semicircle instead of a full circle as in Greek theatres. The stage was long and wide, and the stage house was several stories high with an elaborate facade.

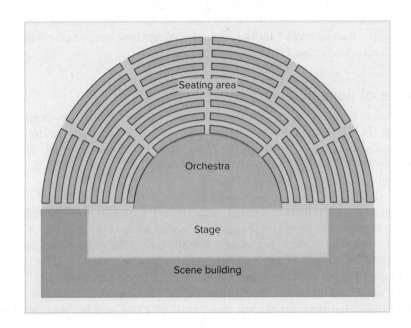

Seating area

Orchestra

Stage

Scene building

fathers felt that evil characters portrayed onstage taught immorality to audiences. In addition, the sexual content of Roman entertainments offended church leaders. As a result, the church issued various edicts condemning theatre and in 398 C.E. decreed that anyone who went to the theatre rather than to church on holy days would be excommunicated.

THE MIDDLE AGES

Background: Medieval Europe

The period from 500 to 1500 C.E. in Western history is known as the Middle Ages or the medieval era. The first 500 years are referred to as the early Middle Ages, and the next 500 years as the later Middle Ages.

At the start of the early Middle Ages in Europe, following invasions from the north and the dissolution of Roman civilization, cities were abandoned and life throughout southern and western Europe became largely agricultural. The nobility controlled local areas, where most people worked as vassals. Gradually, several hundred years after the fall of the Roman Empire, towns began to emerge, and with them trade and crafts. Learning also slowly revived. The strongest force during this period was the Roman Catholic Church, which dominated not only religion but education and frequently politics as well.

We should also note that theatrical activity did continue in the eastern Roman Empire, known as Byzantium, until 1453, when the region was conquered by the Islamic Turks. The theatre of Byzantium was reminiscent of theatre during the Roman Empire. The Hippodrome, a large arena in Constantinople, was the Byzantine equivalent of the Circus Maximus or the Colosseum, and popular entertainments like those of Rome flourished in the east. One contribution of the Byzantine Empire to the continuity of theatre consists of these popular presentations; another important contribution lies in the fact that Byzantium was the preserver of the manuscripts of classical Greek drama: The plays of Aeschylus, Sophocles, and Euripides and the criticism of Aristotle were saved. When the eastern Roman Empire fell in 1453, these manuscripts were transferred to the Western world and became part of the rediscovery that influenced the Renaissance.

Theatre and Culture in the Middle Ages

During the early part of the Middle Ages, there were some scattered traces of theatrical activity, mostly based on the popular entertainments of Greece and Rome—traveling jugglers, minstrels, and mimes. In the late tenth century a nun in a convent in Germany, Hrosvitha of Gandersheim (c. 935–1001), wrote religious plays based on the dramas of the Roman writer Terence. Though her plays were probably not produced, it is still remarkable that she created drama almost in a vacuum. (Hrosvitha's work has been reexamined more fully by feminist critics.)

Essentially, though, theatre had to be reborn in the West during the latter part of the Middle Ages. Interestingly, key elements of the new theatre first appeared in the church, which had suppressed theatre several hundred years earlier. In certain portions of the church service, priests or members of the choir chanted the lines of characters from the Bible. Gradually these small segments, which were delivered in Latin, were enlarged and became short dramas—known as *liturgical dramas*—enacted in the church.

Liturgical dramas Early medieval church drama, written in Latin and dealing with biblical stories.

Also, during this early period of the Middle Ages, a German nun named Hildegard von Bingen (1098–1179) wrote short musical plays that were probably performed in her convent. Hildegard wrote liturgical songs that were accompanied by texts. These dramatic musical pieces honored saints and the Virgin Mary and were written for performance on religious days. Hildegard also created a play in Latin, *Ordo Virtutum (Play of Virtues),* that seems to foreshadow the later vernacular morality plays.

Later in the Middle Ages, ***vernacular drama*** developed. The language of these later plays was not Latin but the everyday speech of the people. Like the brief church plays, vernacular dramas dealt with biblical stories and other religious stories. Vernacular dramas, however, were more elaborate and were usually presented as a series of one-act dramas. Also, they were presented not inside churches but in town squares or other parts of cities. Historians continue to debate whether vernacular drama evolved from liturgical drama or developed independently.

Vernacular drama Drama from the Middle Ages performed in the everyday speech of the people and presented in town squares or other parts of cities.

Mystery plays Also called *cycle plays.* Short dramas of the Middle Ages based on events of the Old and New Testaments and often organized into historical cycles.

Morality plays Medieval drama designed to teach a lesson. The characters were often allegorical and represented virtues or faults.

Medieval Drama: Mystery and Morality Plays

Two types of religious vernacular plays were popular in the medieval period. **Mystery plays** or *cycle plays* dramatized a series of biblical religious events that could stretch from Adam and Eve in the Garden of Eden, Noah and the flood, and Abraham and Isaac to the stories of Christ in the New Testament as well as the lives of the saints. **Morality plays** such as **Everyman** (c. 1500) used allegorical characters and religious themes to teach a moral lesson. Virtually all the plays were short—the equivalent of a one-act play today—and mystery plays were often strung together to form a series, known as a *cycle.*

The best-known mystery play is **The Second Shepherds' Play**, produced in England in the late fourteenth century. It concerns three shepherds who, according to the Bible, went to visit the Christ child just after his birth in a manger. The first section of the drama comically depicts the stealing of a sheep from the shepherds by a rogue, Mak. When the three shepherds search for the missing sheep in Mak's home, his wife Gil pretends that the sheep is her newborn child. When the shepherds return a second time to offer gifts to Mak's "child," they discover that the infant is the stolen sheep, and they proceed to toss Mak in a blanket. In the second section of the play, the shepherds are called by an angel to visit the newborn Christ child, to whom they also bring gifts.

The Second Shepherds' Play illustrates most of the standard dramatic techniques of medieval cycle plays. One technique is to take things out of their actual time period. Though this is a Bible story, the shepherds are not biblical characters but people of the Middle Ages who complain about their lords and feudal conditions. And even though

MYSTERY PLAYS

The mystery plays depicted scenes from the Bible, both the Old Testament and the New Testament. These plays were frequently presented in a cycle, a series of short dramas each of which dramatized an episode from the Bible. They were strung together over several hours or several days. The play *Noah* comes from the Wakefield mystery play cycle. The scene here shows Daniel Thorndike playing Noah and staged at the Mermaid Theatre. (©Hulton Deutsch/Getty Images)

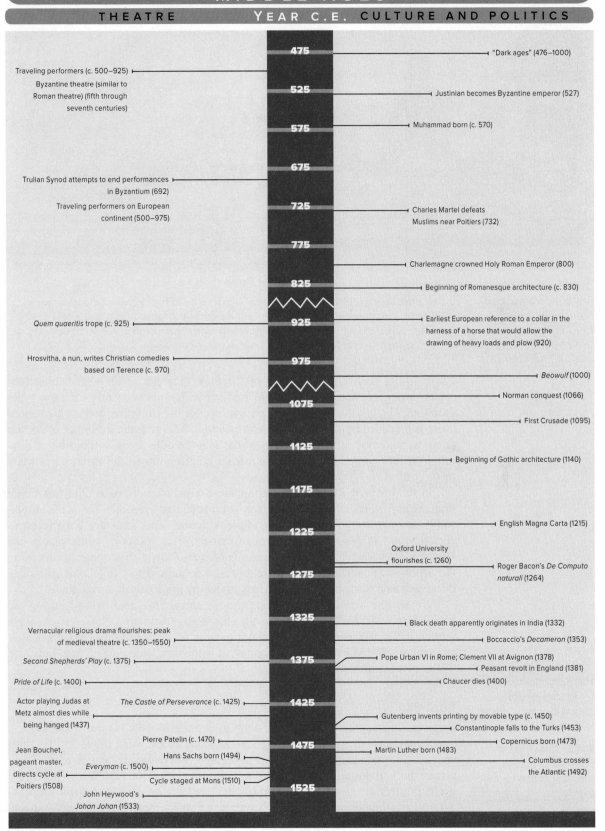

MIDDLE AGES

THEATRE	YEAR C.E.	CULTURE AND POLITICS

475
"Dark ages" (476–1000)

Traveling performers (c. 500–925)

Byzantine theatre (similar to Roman theatre) (fifth through seventh centuries)

525
Justinian becomes Byzantine emperor (527)

575
Muhammad born (c. 570)

675

Trulian Synod attempts to end performances in Byzantium (692)

Traveling performers on European continent (500–975)

725
Charles Martel defeats Muslims near Poitiers (732)

775

Charlemagne crowned Holy Roman Emperor (800)

825
Beginning of Romanesque architecture (c. 830)

Quem quaeritis trope (c. 925)

925
Earliest European reference to a collar in the harness of a horse that would allow the drawing of heavy loads and plow (920)

Hrosvitha, a nun, writes Christian comedies based on Terence (c. 970)

975

Beowulf (1000)

Norman conquest (1066)

1075
First Crusade (1095)

1125
Beginning of Gothic architecture (1140)

1175

1225
English Magna Carta (1215)

Oxford University flourishes (c. 1260)

1275
Roger Bacon's *De Computo naturali* (1264)

1325
Black death apparently originates in India (1332)

Vernacular religious drama flourishes: peak of medieval theatre (c. 1350–1550)

Boccaccio's *Decameron* (1353)

Second Shepherds' Play (c. 1375)

1375
Pope Urban VI in Rome; Clement VII at Avignon (1378)

Peasant revolt in England (1381)

Pride of Life (c. 1400)
Chaucer dies (1400)

Actor playing Judas at Metz almost dies while being hanged (1437)

The Castle of Perseverance (c. 1425)

1425
Gutenberg invents printing by movable type (c. 1450)

Constantinople falls to the Turks (1453)

Pierre Patelin (c. 1470)

1475
Copernicus born (1473)

Jean Bouchet, pageant master, directs cycle at Poitiers (1508)

Hans Sachs born (1494)

Martin Luther born (1483)

Everyman (c. 1500)

Columbus crosses the Atlantic (1492)

Cycle staged at Mons (1510)

John Heywood's *Johan Johan* (1533)

1525

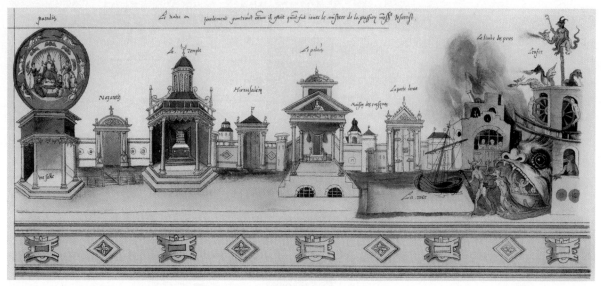

OUTDOOR STAGES AT VALENCIENNES
A popular form of medieval staging, especially on the European continent, was a series of stage areas set alongside each other. In the one at Valenciennes, France, shown here in a color rendering of the original stage set, the action would move from one area to the next. At the far left is heaven or paradise, at the right is hell with a hell mouth out of which devils came. In between are other "mansions" representing various locales. (©Falkenstein Foto/Alamy Stock Photo)

Christ is not born until the close of the play, they pray to him and to various saints throughout the initial section. Another technique is to mix different types of drama. Though the play dramatizes the birth of the Christian savior, this serious event is preceded by an extended comic section, reflecting the influence of secular farce on medieval religious drama. In the later Middle Ages, a tradition of non-religious folk comedies made a significant contribution to the theatrical activity of the period.

In the chapter "Creating the Dramatic Script," we discussed the two major dramatic structures of Western theatre—climactic and episodic. The seeds of episodic form are found in medieval religious drama. This structure has numerous episodes and is expansive rather than restrictive in terms of time, place, and numbers of characters. In *The Second Shepherds' Play,* a forerunner of this form, the action shifts abruptly from a field to Mak's hut and to Christ's manger some distance away; also, comic and serious elements are freely intermingled.

We should mention that *secular* theatre and drama also existed during the Middle Ages. In France and Germany, for example, many popular farces were written and performed. They are a continuation of the tradition of popular entertainment discussed earlier in this chapter. It is medieval religious drama, however, which is most remembered today.

Medieval Theatre Production

Large-scale productions of mystery plays took place in what is now Spain, France, the Netherlands, Belgium, and England. In some cases, most often on the continent of Europe, stages were set up in a large town square, behind which were placed the individual scenic units—the ***mansions***—one for each of the plays in a cycle. In other cases, particularly in England and Spain, portable ***wagon stages***—whose appearance and mode of operation are still debated by scholars—moved

Mansions Individual scenic units used for the staging of religious dramas in the Middle Ages.

Wagon stages Low platform mounted on wheels or casters by means of which scenery is moved on- and offstage.

IN FOCUS: CONTEMPORARY PASSION PLAYS

As we noted, mystery plays dealt with Biblical stories from the Old and New Testament, dramatizing from the Creation through the Crucifixion of Christ. Passion plays, contemporary versions of the mystery plays that depict the life of Christ, continue to be staged for large audiences in many parts of the world. Two long-running examples are the Oberammergau Passion play and the American Passion Play.

The Oberammergau play was first staged in Bavaria (now part of Germany) in 1634 after the community members of Oberammergau promised that they would stage a play about the life of Christ regularly if they were spared from the bubonic plague.

The German passion play is now presented only in years ending in "0." The next performances, therefore, are scheduled for 2020. In 2010, over a hundred performances were given, employing 2,000 performers, musicians, and stage technicians from the local community. The current version of the drama, staged in an open-air theatre, employs materials from scripts that were written in the fifteenth and sixteenth centuries and juxtaposes scenes from the Old Testament with the passion of Christ.

Debate rages over whether the play's portrayal of Jewish characters and Jewish Biblical tales is anti-Semitic. In medieval cycle plays dealing with the life of Christ, Jews were often presented negatively. In addition, Jewish Old Testament stories were Christianized. The same is true of the Oberammergau Passion Play.

In the United States, the American Passion Play, staged indoors in Bloomington, Illinois, celebrated its 94th consecutive season in 2017 and is the longest running passion play in the country. (However, its producers have announced that financial difficulties threaten its future.) The play, set in 30 C.E., traces Christ's life from his Sermon on the Mount to his resurrection and ascension. All the performers are nonprofessionals, much like their medieval counterparts in the cycle plays.

---

through towns and stopped at points along the way to present one of the plays. (We should note that a few historians even question whether the wagons actually stopped to present the plays at different points or simply paraded through the town to one central location.)

The performers, who prepared for a few weeks for their roles, were amateurs. Only men performed in England, but women were performers in some continental European countries. Craft guilds—silversmiths, leather workers, carpenters, and so forth—or laypeople who belonged to religious organizations were responsible for producing individual plays, which were presented as part of annual festivals. In some cases, individual plays were assigned to appropriate guilds: *The Last Supper* to the baker's guild; the Noah play to the shipbuilder's guild; and *The Visit of the Magi* to the goldsmiths. Frequently, they provided their own costumes, which for the most part were contemporary dress rather than historically accurate clothing. Sometimes these presentations became extremely prolonged and elaborate; a series of plays presented in Valenciennes, France, in 1547 lasted for twenty-five days.

Music also played a significant role, with some dramas including choruses and others featuring songs performed by an individual or group of actors. This is another reason why vocal ability was admired in the amateur players. Professional musicians provided accompaniment.

Because of the complexity of cycle plays, there developed, both on the continent and in England, a practice of having one person organize and oversee production. In England, there are records of a ***pageant master,*** who supervised the mounting of plays on wagons. This might include advance preparations—both for the wagons and for the rehearsals of plays to be presented on them—and the logistics of seeing that the plays unfolded on schedule.

Pageant master During the Middle Ages, one who supervised the mounting of mystery plays.

1501, Mons The year is 1501. In a large town square in Mons—in the area that will much later become Belgium—a row of small stage houses called mansions has been erected. They serve as the setting for a series, or cycle, of plays based on the Old and New Testaments: dramatized Bible stories that move from the Creation to the Crucifixion. In the biblical plays at Mons this year, about 150 actors will perform 350 roles. They have held forty-eight rehearsals, and it will take four days to present all the plays in the cycle.

The mansions set up across the stage area are changed to suit whatever play is being performed. More than sixty different mansions—representing the Garden of Eden, the manger in Bethlehem, the temple where Christ drove out the money changers, and so forth—will be used during these four days. At each end of the stage area are two permanent mansions, symbolic of the opposing sides in this great religious drama: One is heaven and the other hell. Hell is represented by the large mouth of a monster, out of which devils and smoke pour forth at appropriate moments.

This kind of religious drama is the chief theatrical presentation in the medieval period. It takes forms that vary in theatrical setting and in staging, but in both England and continental Europe, it is widespread and popular. The church encourages it because most people cannot read or write, and this is an excellent way for them to become familiar with stories from the Bible. The only other form of entertainment in this era is traveling troupes of jugglers, singers, dancers, and mimes. They go from place to place, performing brief dramatic sketches along with musicals and other pieces.

A good percentage of the people who live in Mons and the surrounding areas are present at the four-day cycle of religious plays. They represent a cross section of the community. The spectators either sit in temporary wooden bleachers or stand in the town square, trying to get the best possible view of the acting area and the various "mansions" from which the action of each episode begins.

The audience members have already seen dramas about Adam and Eve and about Cain slaying his brother Abel; now they will see a play about Noah, who is commanded by God to build an ark to save his family and the animals from the flood.

In the play, Noah is warned by God that it will rain for forty days and forty nights, and that he must build an ark into which he will take his family and two animals of every kind. As Noah begins building, his neighbors make fun of him, and his shrewish wife argues with him. The wife does not want to go aboard the ark; she feels that Noah is foolish. She chides and criticizes her husband, and it is only when the rain begins to fall that she agrees to board the ark.

The spectators enjoy this comic interaction, but the moment they are waiting for is the deluge of rain, which is expected to be spectacular. At last the moment arrives, and the audience is not disappointed. On the roofs of houses behind the stage area, water has been stored in wine barrels and men are standing by, waiting for a signal to open the barrels. Now the signal is given, and the deluge begins: torrents of water fall onto the stage. The audience is completely in awe; enough water has been stored to provide a steady rain for five minutes. Water rises all around, but Noah, his family, and his animals are safe in the ark. Soon after, a dove comes, indicating that Noah can leave the ark.

During the remaining days of the cycle of plays, the spectators will see a continuing series of biblical stories, which trace episodes from both the Old Testament and the New Testament, including many events from the life of Christ. When the entire cycle has concluded, audience members will recall many highlights, but none, perhaps, more spectacular than the sensational flood in the play about Noah and his family.

Platform stage Elevated stage with no proscenium.

To accommodate the abrupt changes in location that characterized the plots of mystery plays, medieval theatres used a neutral *platform stage,* set up either in a town square or on one of the wagon stages. This platform was not a specific locale, like a palace in Greek drama, but an unidentified space that could become whatever was designated. If the performers or the script indicated that a scene was set in a field, the platform instantaneously became a field; if it was supposed

PAGEANT WAGONS

One form of staging for medieval religious plays was the pageant wagon, which could be rolled into a town or a nearby field. The wagon—or wagons—served as a stage, contained scenery, and had a backstage area for costume changes. We do not know exactly how a pageant wagon worked, but shown here are two suggestions or speculations. Above is a hand-colored woodcut of the performance of a mystery play on a pageant wagon in Coventry, England, at the height of medieval theatre. The wagon has a platform with a cloth covering its lower part (from which characters could emerge). The drawing below shows a cutaway view of two wagons; one serves as a stage platform while the other, behind it, provides a place for scenery, changing costumes, and hiding special effects. (©North Wind Picture Archives)

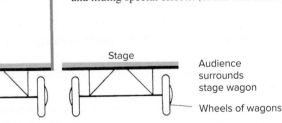

Side view of possible arrangement of medieval pageant wagon behind a second wagon

1. Imagine yourself at the first production of *Oedipus the King*. Describe the theatre space in which the production is staged. Was there scenery onstage? What part does the chorus play in the production?

2. The Greeks observed a *three-actor rule* in classical tragedy. What does this mean? How would three actors play all of the roles in a tragedy that you have read?

3. Watch a skit on *Saturday Night Live*. In what way is that skit similar to Classical Greek Old Comedy?

4. Some historians believe that in ancient Rome, popular entertainments were more prevalent than Roman theatre. Others suggest that the popular and theatrical forms were interrelated. Which of these opinions seems to be true about our own times? Name several forms of popular entertainment today. Do these performances overshadow dramatic presentations, or do they exist side by side?

5. Describe the key similarities and differences between the classical Greek and Roman theatres both in architecture and in dramatic content.

6. Religion played a central role in the theatre of the Middle Ages. Do you believe there is any relationship between theatre and religion today? Support your answer based on what you learned in the chapter and your own experience.

7. Medieval theatre was frequently performed outdoors. Does this tradition survive today? Identify and describe three examples.

to be a ship at sea, it became a ship. This freedom of movement, based on the imagination, later became the basis of theatrical techniques perfected by Renaissance playwrights in Spain and England.

Toward the end of the Middle Ages, there was a gradual decline of religious theatre. One reason was a weakening of the church, culminating in the Protestant Reformation; a second reason was that the secular qualities of drama finally overcame the religious material.

Evaluating a Production of an Historic Play

As a theatre audience member, you might be asked to attend a production of a play from one of the historical periods we have just discussed or will discuss in the next chapters. To help you better evaluate the production of a play from a past era, here are some questions you might ask yourself:

1. From which period is the play?

2. Why do you think the director chose this specific play? Was the director trying to draw contemporary parallels through the historical plot?

3. Did the subject matter of the play seem to reflect on contemporary issues?

4. Were there any unique conventions (chorus, poetic language)? How were they handled?

5. Did the actors seem comfortable with the language and the historical circumstances of the play?

6. Were the designers (scenery, costume, lighting) trying to re-create the historical period in which the play was written or were the visual elements from a different period?

7. If there were updates to the play (e.g. changes in time period, language), did they seem appropriate? Why or why not?

8. Was there an attempt to reproduce the original space the play was performed in and, if so, was it successful?

9. Do you feel contemporary audiences can relate to the subject matter and characters of the historical play? Why or why not?

SUMMARY

1. The impulse to create theatre is universal. Elements of theatre exist in rituals and ceremonies in Africa, Asia, Europe, and wherever human society develops.

2. Greek theatre set the stage for all future Western theatre with the tragedies of Aeschylus, Sophocles and Euripides, which were written using the intensive or climactic plot structure, as well as with the comedies of Aristophanes.

3. Classical Greek theatre buildings were large outdoor spaces built into hillsides, which accommodated audiences attending religious festivals.

4. In the Classical Greek theatre, all the performers were male and the chorus was an integral element of the presentations.

5. During the Hellenistic era, New Comedy, which was concerned with domestic and romantic situations, prepared the way for almost all later popular comedy.

6. The Romans borrowed many of the Greek theatre conventions but emphasized domestic and romantic comedies, as in the plays of Plautus and Terence.

7. The tragedies of Seneca are noteworthy for their influence on later playwrights.

8. The Romans also developed various popular entertainments and built huge arenas to accommodate presentations.

9. Roman theatres were also outdoors but completely man-made. All of the structural elements were connected and the most significant element was a large raised stage with an ornate façade.

10. In Europe, during the period from 500 to 1000 C.E.—the early Middle Ages— minstrels kept the theatrical tradition alive.

11. Later in the Middle Ages, theatre was reborn primarily through the influence of the Roman Catholic Church and through dramatic interpolations, written in Latin, which were added to religious services.

12. In the fourteenth century, plays in everyday language dramatizing Biblical stories, known as mystery plays, were staged outdoors by amateurs. These plays established the basis for the episodic or extensive plot structure.

12

EARLY THEATRE: ASIAN

For 1,000 years, from approximately 350 to 1350 C.E., there was no organized theatre in the West. But on the continent of Asia, thousands of miles away, theatre had begun to emerge. The development of theatre began in India more than 2,000 years ago, and theatre later became well established in China while formal theatre was still moribund in the West. Theatre in Japan followed not long after. These traditions of Asian theatre, established centuries ago, continue to the present day.

THE THEATRES OF ASIA: BACKGROUND

The people who created theatre in Asia knew nothing of the theatres of Greece or Rome. In the chapter "Early Theatres: Greek, Roman, and Medieval," we mentioned the universal tendency toward theatre; and except where theatre is expressly forbidden by religious or other laws, it is likely to emerge in any civilization. This was true in India, China, and Japan—the countries we will focus on in this chapter—and also in other Asian countries, such as Indonesia.

Each of the Asian theatres is unique, but these theatres also have aspects in common that set them apart from Western theatre. To mention two: They rely much more on dance than Western theatre does (in many instances, Asian theatrical presentations could be called *dance dramas*), and they more heavily emphasize symbolism. All the great Asian traditions—including those of India, China, and Japan—have created and sustained one form or another of what has been described

◀ **NŌ: CLASSIC JAPANESE THEATRE**

Theatre began to develop in various parts of the world many years ago. In India, China, and other parts of the Asian continent, theatre emerged between 350 B.C.E. and 1350 C.E. It developed initially in India and China. In Japan, it appeared first during the fourteenth century. One of the three major classic forms of Japanese theatre is nō. Shown here is a scene from a recent performance in Tokyo of a nō play. Nō as well as kabuki and bunraku are classic theatrical forms that have been kept alive in Japan for many centuries. (©Koichi Kamoshida/Getty Images News/Getty Images)

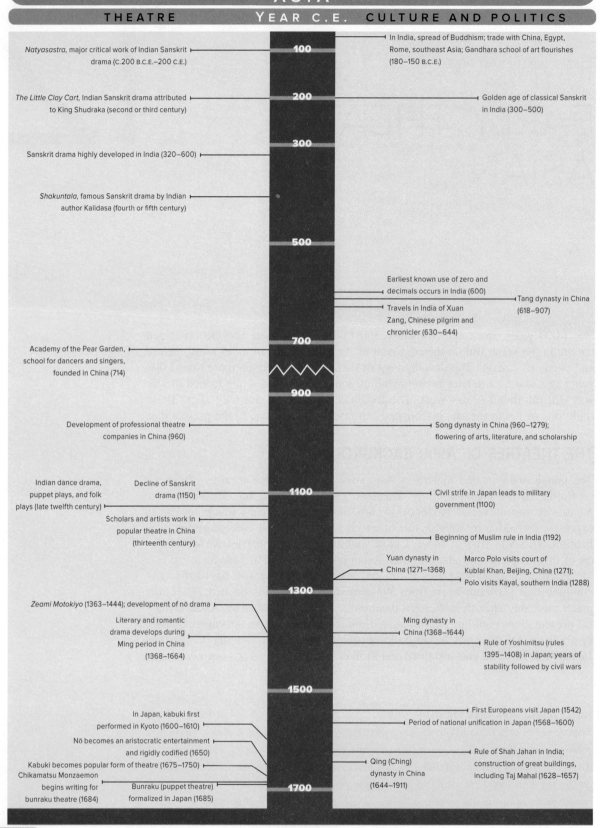

ASIA

THEATRE	YEAR C.E.	CULTURE AND POLITICS

100 — In India, spread of Buddhism; trade with China, Egypt, Rome, southeast Asia; Gandhara school of art flourishes (180–150 B.C.E.)

Natyasastra, major critical work of Indian Sanskrit drama (C.200 B.C.E.–200 C.E.)

200 — Golden age of classical Sanskrit in India (300–500)

The Little Clay Cart, Indian Sanskrit drama attributed to King Shudraka (second or third century)

300

Sanskrit drama highly developed in India (320–600)

Shakuntala, famous Sanskrit drama by Indian author Kalidasa (fourth or fifth century)

500

Earliest known use of zero and decimals occurs in India (600)

Tang dynasty in China (618–907)

Travels in India of Xuan Zang, Chinese pilgrim and chronicler (630–644)

700

Academy of the Pear Garden, school for dancers and singers, founded in China (714)

900

Development of professional theatre companies in China (960)

Song dynasty in China (960–1279); flowering of arts, literature, and scholarship

1100

Indian dance drama, puppet plays, and folk plays (late twelfth century)

Decline of Sanskrit drama (1150)

Civil strife in Japan leads to military government (1100)

Scholars and artists work in popular theatre in China (thirteenth century)

Beginning of Muslim rule in India (1192)

Yuan dynasty in China (1271–1368)

Marco Polo visits court of Kublai Khan, Beijing, China (1271); Polo visits Kayal, southern India (1288)

1300

Zeami Motokiyo (1363–1444); development of nō drama

Literary and romantic drama develops during Ming period in China (1368–1664)

Ming dynasty in China (1368–1644)

Rule of Yoshimitsu (rules 1395–1408) in Japan; years of stability followed by civil wars

1500

First Europeans visit Japan (1542)

Period of national unification in Japan (1568–1600)

In Japan, kabuki first performed in Kyoto (1600–1610)

Nō becomes an aristocratic entertainment and rigidly codified (1650)

Rule of Shah Jahan in India; construction of great buildings, including Taj Mahal (1628–1657)

Kabuki becomes popular form of theatre (1675–1750)

Chikamatsu Monzaemon begins writing for bunraku theatre (1684)

Bunraku (puppet theatre) formalized in Japan (1685)

Qing (Ching) dynasty in China (1644–1911)

1700

as *total theatre*. In this type of theatre there is a synthesis or integration of elements—acting, mime, dancing, music, and text—more complete than in traditional Western theatre. Though each of the Asian theatrical traditions is unique and self-contained, all have qualities that may seem familiar to Westerners who have been exposed to opera in which a colorful blending of ideas, art, and technique is crucial.

One reason why this kind of synthesis developed in Asia and found continued support lies in the fact that the religious roots of theatre are still kept alive there. Each of the three Asian traditions on which we will focus—Indian, Chinese, and Japanese—reached a high point of artistic excellence at a time when religion and philosophy were central in its culture. This level of excellence has kept the focus of traditional theatre at least allied to religion and philosophy, even when society itself changed and became modernized.

We can speculate on the antecedents of theatre in India, China, and Japan, but the actual origins of theatre in each culture remain obscure. The high point, however, usually occurred when writers of poetic and intellectual ability began to create a dramatic tradition in which the text assumed a central place.

What remained in later years was usually the words rather than the production style; this is, of course, partially explained by the fact that anything written, such as a script, has some permanence, whereas a performance is ephemeral. Thus, little is known of early performance practices in China or India. Japan, on the other hand, is unique in having preserved many of the ancient techniques of acting, dancing, and singing. Still, in all three theatres the ancient traditions—interpreted and reinterpreted as these cultures developed and changed—have continued to color and shape many later experiments.

INDIAN THEATRE

Indian history has been characterized as a succession of immigrations into the Indian subcontinent. Early traces of civilization there go back to 3000 B.C.E. The Aryans, who came into southern India 1,000 years later, left behind works in Sanskrit that constitute the basis of the great Indian literary traditions. Scholars believe that by 1000 B.C.E., certain fundamental aspects of Indian civilization were already established; one of these is the caste system under which people are classified by heredity: A person must remain in the caste to which he or she is born, and people are forbidden to change occupations.

Around 400 B.C.E., Buddhism, which had its origins in India, reached a peak of development, and soon it became a major force throughout eastern and central Asia. Based on the ideas of Gautama Buddha (c. 563–483 B.C.E.), Buddhism teaches that suffering is inherent in life but that human beings can be liberated from suffering by mental and moral self-purification. King Asoka, who ruled in India about 240 B.C.E., managed to unite the whole nation under Buddhist rule, but a period of disorder and confusion followed until the Gupta dynasty began to unite the nation again around 320 C.E.

It was at this time that another important thread in Indian history, Hindu culture, entered a golden age; and it was during the following centuries that the great Sanskrit dramas were written and performed. Hinduism stresses the belief that soul or spirit is the essence of life; that the goal of all people is to achieve oneness with the supreme world-soul, known as *Brahman*; and that the things of this life do not exist in the same way as Brahman, which is eternal, infinite, and indescribable.

Sanskrit Drama

What remains from the tradition of the Indian Golden Age is a group of plays written in Sanskrit, the language of the noble classes, to be performed in various court circles. There are between fifty and sixty plays that can be reliably assigned to this period, and the greatest of them are among the finest works of classical Indian literature.

We have been provided a great insight into this early Indian theatre by a remarkable document called the *Natyasastra* (translated as *The Study of Theatre* or *The Art of Theatre*). The *Natyasastra* has been attributed to Bharata Muni but may well be by someone else, possibly by several people. Written sometime during the 400-year period between 200 B.C.E. and 200 C.E., it describes the mythological origin of theatre in India and also presents important material about the nature of Indian drama; it even includes a description of the theatre space in which performances took place.

Rasa As defined in the *Natyasastra*, quality or flavor that characterizes a dramatic situation.

In the course of this complex treatise, the author defines a quality called **rasa**, or flavor, which permits spectators to surrender themselves to a dramatic situation corresponding to some powerful feeling that they themselves possess. Theatre can thus serve as a means toward enlightenment; art becomes a way to move toward metaphysics and the divine.

The *Natyasastra* also serves as a kind of encyclopedia of theatrical practice. In an abstract way, every element of the complex ancient theatre is treated, from gesture and posture to music, dance, voice, and so forth. Types of characters and categories of plays are discussed, and all this specific information is related in turn to a series of metaphysical principles, which, although perhaps difficult for the modern reader to grasp, are nevertheless challenging, even humbling, to read.

From comments in a book entitled *Mahabhasya* (*Great Commentary*), some scholars believe that the main elements of Sanskrit drama, as described in the *Natyasastra,* were in place by 140 B.C.E. However, this is speculative and has not yet been proved. The earliest plays that survive, from the first and second centuries C.E., were written by Asvaghosa.

As we have noted, these plays were written in Sanskrit, the classical language of the nobility, though some of the lover characters in the later plays speak a hybrid of Sanskrit and local dialect. Thus the plays had little following among the general public, who could not understand them. The plays usually drew on themes from Indian epic literature.

From what we know, the most productive playwright of classical India was Bhasa, who may have lived around the second or third century C.E. Thirteen surviving plays have been attributed to him, but it is not certain they are all his. Among the best-known plays of this general era is **The Little Clay Cart**, attributed to King Sudraka, although his identity and dates have not been clearly established. He is thought by many (though there is much disagreement) to have lived as late as the fifth century C.E. *The Little Clay Cart* concerns the love between a ruined merchant and a courtesan; its style is enlivened and enriched by politics and humor. The most famous Sanskrit play, however, comes from the fourth or fifth century. This is **Shakuntala**, which is usually considered the finest classical Indian drama and whose author, Kalidasa, is the greatest of the playwrights from the classic period.

Kalidasa   Though *Shakuntala* is an acknowledged masterpiece of Indian drama, almost nothing is known about its author, Kalidasa. Many scholars have attempted to establish his date of birth and to learn some details of his life, but they have had little success. Recent studies have placed his writings between

KATHAKALI: INDIAN DANCE DRAMA

Much of Asian theatre includes a large element of dance. A prime example is kathakali, a dramatic form found in southwestern India. In kathakali, stories of strong passions, the furies of gods, and the loves and hates of extraordinary human beings are told in dance and mime. Notice the makeup and highly stylized costumes and headdresses on these dancers in a recent performance in Kerala, South India. (©Hideo Haga/The Image Works)

the late fourth and mid-fifth century. There is no doubt, however, that *Shakuntala* is a masterwork of Sanskrit drama. In seven acts, the play recounts the romance of King Dushyanta and Shakuntala, the foster daughter of a hermit, who secretly marry and are then subjected to a long separation brought about by the curse of an irate sage. After many trials, the lovers are reunited and the king finally meets his son and heir.

Shakuntala, which is subtitled *The Recovered Ring,* has story elements such as a secret marriage, forgetfulness caused by a curse, and a magic ring. It also has ideas from Indian philosophy, religion, aesthetics, and psychology. Like all Sanskrit drama, it has both serious and comic elements and includes a large number of locations and characters. It also includes supernatural elements. In addition, *Shakuntala* has a recognition scene in which the lovers confirm their identity through signs; this recognition through signs bears some resemblance to scenes in classic Greek tragedy.

While *Shakuntala* follows traditional patterns of Sanskrit drama, it is set apart by Kalidasa's delicate lyricism. Kalidasa wrote several poems that mingle love, nature imagery, and religion. He also wrote two other plays: *Malavike and Agnimitra,* a courtly comedy about a king's love for one of the palace serving women, and *Vikrama and Urvashi,* a heroic mythological drama focusing on the love of a king and a nymph.

Later Indian Drama

Sanskrit drama—both the plays themselves and dramatic criticism—had faded by the end of the ninth century. By the twelfth century, the Arabs had begun to invade India, and in 1206 they established the sultanate of Delhi. With this series of invasions, the Hindu Sanskrit tradition disappeared. Under Islamic rule, theatrical activities were not encouraged and the old ways of performing were no longer maintained among educated people.

However, folk dramas in the many vernacular languages of India had always been popular, and the continued performances of such works, while they may not have achieved a very high artistic level, helped to keep certain traditions alive. Many of these folk plays have continued to the present day. They used the same traditional epic materials as Sanskrit dramas, but most of them were created by dramatists whose names are now unknown, and the scripts—assuming that these dramas were written down—have not been preserved. Folk plays were extremely eclectic and emphasized spectacle rather than metaphysical profundity.

Also popular with the public were dance dramas that took up aspects of Indian myths. In the performance of such dramas, movement, rather than the spoken word, was strongly emphasized. These and other developments in later Indian theatre, including a well-known dance-drama form called *kathakali,* will be discussed in detail later.

How Was Indian Drama Staged?

Although we do not know exactly how plays were performed, we learn from the *Natyasastra* that each early troupe presenting Sanskrit theatre had a leader, the *sudtradhara,* who was the chief actor and also managed all others involved in production. Men were the main performers, but women played important roles too. Acting in this type of theatre was a skill that combined voice, body, emotions, costume, and makeup in an integrated whole.

The typical theatre in which Sanskrit drama was performed was ninety-six feet long and forty-eight feet wide, divided equally into stage and auditorium, and its seating capacity was probably between 200 and 500. There were four pillars in the auditorium—colored white, yellow, red, or blue—indicating where members of different castes were to sit. A curtain divided the stage into two parts: one part for the action and the other for dressing rooms and a behind-the-scenes area. The few records available from the later period of Sanskrit drama indicate that most performances were given by troupes invited to the courts of the nobility, and performing spaces were arranged in courtyards and similar areas.

Scenery was evidently not used, although elaborate costumes probably were. Dance, symbolic gestures, and music played an important part in the productions; but again, we have no specific information about performance practices. The plays often make use of fixed characters, such as a narrator and a clown; once again, there are no details concerning how these performers appeared onstage.

CHINESE THEATRE

The civilization of China can be traced back to at least 2000 B.C.E., when a unified culture spread over large parts of the area that is now the People's Republic of China. The Shang Dynasty represents the first period that can be authenticated through artifacts and documents. The period following the Shang Dynasty was a turbulent era known as the Zhou Dynasty. The dates of both dynasties are somewhat disputed. Traditionally, the Shang was thought to have been from 1766 to 1122 B.C.E., but some scholars suggest either 1600 or 1523 to 1028 B.C.E. The Zhou Dynasty was dated from 1122 to 256 B.C.E., but alternative dates have been offered: 1027 to 256 B.C.E. In any event, during the later Zhou Dynasty, Confucius, Lao-tzu, and Mencius—three of the greatest Chinese philosophers—lived and wrote. They formed part of the general background of religions, philosophies, and religious practices out of which later Chinese theatre developed.

Confucianism was based on the teachings of Confucius (551–479 B.C.E.), whose ideas about the perfectibility of human beings were never wholly embraced in his lifetime but were widely adopted by later generations. Confucianism emphasized the responsibility of one individual or group to others: a ruler to his subjects, family members to one another, friends to friends. Taoism began in the sixth century B.C.E. with the teachings of Lao-tzu (born c. 604 B.C.E.), who believed in the importance of the *tao,* or path. Taoism stresses simplicity, patience, and nature's harmony; following the tao, the path of the cosmos, leads to self-realization. A key element in the philosophy of Mencius (c. 371–288 B.C.E.) is that all people are good. Their innate moral sense can be cultivated, or it can be perverted by an unfavorable environment.

Another movement that was to influence the development of theatre, in China as well as in other societies, was *shamanism,* whose rituals combined costume, song, dance, and gesture. Shamans were spiritual leaders who were thought to have magical powers to communicate with the dead and to ward off evil spirits. Buddhism, too, found its way from India to China and was added to the religious thought and practice of the time.

In terms of political developments, by 200 B.C.E. the centralized imperial system had been developed, and China was provided with a central government that continued to remain effective through many long periods of stability down to modern times.

Early Theatre in China

The early development of theatre in China—as with many other forms of Chinese art—was linked to the patronage of the imperial court. Popular forms of theatre may also have flourished, though no records of early folk performances survive. Records of court entertainments, however, go back as far as the fifth century B.C.E., and such diverse activities as skits, pantomimes, juggling, singing, and dancing are frequently mentioned in ancient chronicles.

The court of the emperors during the Tang period (618–906 C.E.) was one of the high points of human culture. At this time there was a kind of actors' training institute in the capital; it was called the Pear Garden and had been founded in 714. Details of activities and performances at the Pear Garden have not been preserved, but it firmly established a tradition of training theatrical performers. Comic skits, puppet shows, and storytelling were popular during the Tang period.

In the Song Dynasty (960–1279), which preceded the coming of the Mongols, various court entertainments contributed to the development of what

EARLY CHINESE THEATRE

This illustration depicts a Chinese theatre set up for a festival. Note the covered stage on which the performers appear, and the audience members able to stand on three sides of the stage. (©Culture Club/Hulton Archive/Getty Images)

Sheng Male characters in popular twelfth century Chinese drama.

Dan Female characters in the popular twelfth century Chinese drama.

Jing Characters with painted faces in popular twelfth century Chinese drama.

Chou Clown characters in popular twelfth century Chinese drama.

are known as *variety plays*. In addition to court records, there are other documents recording the existence of traveling theatrical troupes, some permanent playhouses, and theatrical activity that involved not only actors, dancers, and singers but also shadow puppets and marionettes. Low comedy was popular as well, and its effect must have been something like our vaudeville.

A form that emerged in the province of Zhejiang, possibly in the early twelfth century, was called *nanxi*, which means "southern drama," after the region where it developed. Indications are that at this time four types of characters were predominant in Chinese theatre: the ***sheng***, or male character; the ***dan***, or female character; the ***jing***, or painted face; and the ***chou***, or clown. These were to remain staples of Chinese theatre in subsequent works.

As urban areas developed during the Song dynasty, theatres began to be built in designated locations to house these popular forms. In the twelfth century, one such entertainment area contained fifty distinct theatres of varying sizes.

A significant synthesis of art and popular tradition was to come in the dramas of the Yuan period, which followed the Song.

Theatre in the Yuan Dynasty

The Yuan Dynasty (1279–1368) was well known in the West through the writings of the Italian explorer Marco Polo. The ruler at this time was not a Chinese emperor but a Mongol, Kublai Khan, whose grandfather Genghis Khan had come down from the north to conquer China.

Although they tolerated many Chinese customs, the Mongols nevertheless dismantled much of the traditional bureaucracy. Ironically, this turned out to be an important impetus for the development of Chinese theatre. Earlier, the highly educated literati—literary intellectuals—had composed essays and poetry of the highest quality but had disdained plays as beneath their dignity. With the coming of the Mongols, many of the literati were no longer employed by the government and took up literary and theatrical work to make a living. In this way, high art and the popular theatrical tradition met. Because the complex mixture of cultural influences produced such a rich outpouring during the Yuan Dynasty, scholars have compared its theatre to that of Greece in the fifth century B.C.E. and to that of Elizabethan England.

The form of drama perfected in the Yuan Dynasty, often referred to as *zaju*, usually had four acts or—perhaps more accurately since these plays used a great deal of music—four song sequences. Rather than writing specifically for the dramas, playwrights composed their texts to suit the rhythms and meters of popular music already known to the audience. Usually the protagonist sang all the music in any act. Unfortunately, none of the music has survived.

The poetic content of these plays was considered the central factor in their success. Because of their lyrical nature, these dramas had only a few characters and avoided subplots and other complications. Accounts from the Yuan period tell us that topics chosen by the playwrights ranged from love and romance to religion and history, domestic and social themes, crimes and lawsuits, and bandit heroes.

Important Plays from the Yuan Period Though we do not know exactly how many plays were produced during the Yuan period, there are records indicating that more than 500 dramatists were writing at this time; and we know the titles of some 700 plays, of which 168 survive.

Perhaps the most famous of the plays surviving from this period is *The Romance of the Western Chamber,* actually a cycle of plays, by Wang Shifu, who wrote in the late thirteenth century. These dramas chronicle the trials of two lovers—a handsome young student and a lovely girl of good family—who have been models for thousands of imitations down to the present century. The plays contain a certain amount of adventure and a good deal of superlative poetry.

Another popular play that has survived is *The Orphan of Chao,* which deals with vengeance, sacrifice, and loyalty. *The Orphan of Chao* was one of the first Chinese plays known in the West, as a version of it was translated into French in 1735 and was adapted for the French stage by the philosopher Voltaire.

Another popular Yuan drama, *The Circle of Chalk,* is an excellent example of the lawsuit-and-trial genre in which a clever, Solomon-like judge frees an innocent person accused of a crime. When the twentieth-century German playwright Bertolt Brecht saw a version of this play (it had been freely adapted and translated into German), he was so intrigued with the theme that he created his own version: *The Caucasian Chalk Circle.*

One of the most prolific and respected playwrights of the Yuan period was Guan Hanquing (c. 1245–1322), who is credited with writing 65 plays, 14 of which survive. One of his best known, and frequently adapted by later writers, is *Snow in Midsummer,* also known as *The Injustice to Dou E.*

Theatre Production in the Yuan Period Despite the fact that many Yuan texts survive and have been admired down to the present day, relatively little is known about how they were performed. Contemporary spectators left few records of their reactions, perhaps because theatregoing was regarded as beneath the notice of highly educated people. Nevertheless, in recent years careful scholarship has managed to piece together a certain amount of information on theatre presentations.

Professional actors and actresses performed in Yuan dramas, and on occasion both would play male and female roles. Some of the actresses performed for private entertainments at the palace, and stories of their affairs in high society were as eagerly sought out as stories about the activities of today's film and television stars. The performers were organized into troupes, some of which were run by women.

Only meager information remains about the theatres used for these performances. Evidently, there was a bare stage with two doors on each side at the rear, and a painted cloth hanging between the doors. (This arrangement is shown in a wall hanging from northwestern China painted about 1324.) Most stages seem to have been built for outdoor use and were not roofed over. Curtains and such properties as swords and fans were used, but there is no evidence of any scenery. Much of the color of performances came from elaborate costumes. Some of the stylized robes, which are illustrated in artworks of the time, resemble those in modern Peking (or Beijing) opera. Makeup was also important and was evidently applied heavily in a stylized manner.

Theatre in the Ming Dynasty

By the end of the Yuan period, the level of accomplishment in theatre was very high and drama had become firmly established as a respectable art form. With the overthrow of the Mongols, however, and the establishment of the Ming Dynasty (1368–1644), a Chinese emperor was restored to the throne. At this point, the traditional patterns of social behavior were restored; highly educated scholars were still able to write plays, but they tended to confine their efforts more and more to dramas that would please the elite. The theatre tended to become ornate and artificial; it lost contact with the broad mass of the public, which had originally supported it.

What had been an active theatre in the Yuan Dynasty, responsive to general audiences, now became a kind of literary drama that emphasized poetry and was averse to sustained or powerful dramatic action. The structure of Ming plays often became far more complex than that of Yuan plays. Also, only one actor had sung in each act of a Yuan play, but several actors were now permitted to sing during an act, and the instrumental accompaniments became very elaborate.

One of the earliest and best plays written in this expanded form is *Lute Song* by Gao Ming (c. 1301–1370), dealing with questions of family loyalty in a woman whose husband has abandoned her for political reasons. *Lute Song* contains strong characterizations and beautiful poetry and has been popular ever since its composition; this story of a faithful wife even reached Broadway in a musical theatre version, also called *Lute Song,* written for Mary Martin in 1946.

GROUND PLAN OF A TRADITIONAL CHINESE THEATRE
Diagrammed here is the arrangement for seating in Chinese theatres for the period from the seventeenth through the nineteenth centuries. Before that, performances were held in teahouses; when permanent theatres were built, tables with chairs around them were retained in the section nearest the stage. Women and commoners sat at the sides and back.

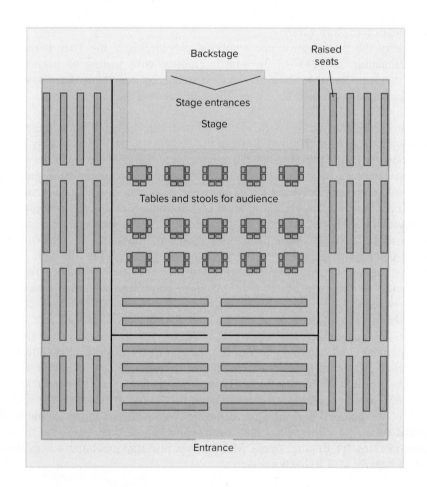

Backstage

Raised seats

Stage entrances

Stage

Tables and stools for audience

Entrance

Attempts to create drama of distinction during the Ming dynasty culminated in the works of Li Yu, a scholar who failed his examinations and became instead a playwright, theatre critic, and impresario.

Li Yu   Li Yu (1611–c. 1685), China's first important drama theorist, believed that a playwright should write clearly, with a mass audience in mind, and should be well versed in practical stage knowledge. These conclusions were based on his own experience as a popular playwright. His writings on theatre—in which he dealt with such matters as plot construction, dialogue, music, and versification—are among the most important in the history of Chinese dramatic criticism.

As a playwright, Li Yu wrote plays for entertainment and placed little emphasis on the poetic songs that other playwrights favored. Instead, he developed well-made situation comedies with intricate plots and sophisticated dialogue. Rather than borrow his material from standard literary sources, Li created original plots based on the lives of common people. He was particularly skilled at writing strong characters for his young female performers. Most of his notable plays, including *Ordained by Heaven, Be Circumspect in Conjugal Relationships,* and *The Error of the Kite,* revolve around romantic themes.

At the end of the Ming Dynasty, theatre, which was patronized almost entirely by the rich, began to lose any real contact with the larger public, and its vitality seeped away. Events in Chinese theatre following the Ming dynasty and into the modern period will be covered in later chapters.

JAPANESE THEATRE

Although the civilization of Japan is younger than that of China, the Japanese heritage is long and complex. The origins of the Japanese people are obscure, but anthropologists have found artifacts suggesting migrations from such diverse areas as Siberia, Korea, south China, and southeast Asia. We know that by the fifth century C.E. the southern portions of Japan were consolidated and a series of capitals were established in the vicinity of present-day Kyoto. At the time, the Japanese followed a religion called Shinto, or the Way of the Gods, closely allied to nature and spirit worship.

With the growing influence on the Japanese aristocracy of the Tang Dynasty in China (618–906 C.E.), Buddhism, a religion that was more sophisticated than Shinto in both ritual and doctrine, became a prevailing influence, first in court circles and then in the country as a whole. Influences from both Shinto and Buddhism were strong in the development of theatre in Japan.

Early Theatre in Japan

The earliest recorded theatrical activities in Japan are the court entertainments of the Heian period (794–1195 C.E.). These entertainments were influenced by Chinese models, but that is the only link—a very remote one—between the two traditions. Later, similar kinds of performances formed part of annual Shinto and Buddhist ceremonies. These were usually of a popular nature and included juggling, skits, dancing, and the like.

The first great period in Japanese theatre occurred in the fourteenth century, not long after similar developments in China. The sudden and remarkable development of *nō* (it is also spelled *noh*)—one of the three principal forms of traditional Japanese theatre—came about when popular stage traditions were combined with serious scholarly pursuits.

Nō   Rigidly traditional form of Japanese drama combining music, dance, and lyrics.

Nō

In the fourteenth century in Japan, there were a number of roving troupes of actors who performed in a variety of styles; some of their presentations were simply popular entertainment, but some aspired to art. One of the more artistic troupes was directed by the actor Kan'ami (1333–1384), who was also a playwright. A typical, well-known play by Kan'ami is **Sotoba Komachi (Komachi at the Stupa)**, which was based on a familiar legend of the time. In this legend, Komachi, a beautiful but cruel woman, is pursued by a man named Shii no Shōshō. She tells him that he must call on her for 100 nights in a row, and for 99 nights he comes, in all kinds of weather. But on the hundredth night he dies.

At the beginning of the play, two priests enter, discussing the virtues of following Buddha. They then come upon an old woman—the leading actor in the mask and wig of Komachi in old age. She says that she was once beautiful but has grown old and lost her beauty. She argues with the priests about religion and then reveals who she is. She recounts the story of what she did to Shōshō.

A presentation by Kan'ami's troupe was seen by the shogun Ashikaga Yoshimitsu (1358–1408), a man of wealth, prestige, and enormous enthusiasm for the arts. Fascinated by what he saw, he arranged for Kan'ami's son, Zeami, who was then twelve years old, to have a court education in order to improve the quality of his art.

When Zeami succeeded his father as head of the troupe, it remained attached to the shogun's court in Kyoto. With a patron of this caliber, Zeami was freed from financial problems and could devote himself to all aspects of theatre: writing plays, training actors, and constantly refining his own acting style, whose outlines had been inherited from his gifted father.

Zeami Motokiyo   More than 500 years after his death, Zeami Motokiyo (1363–1443) is still considered the most important figure in the history of Japanese nō theatre. A gifted actor, Zeami brought new prestige to nō, and his plays remain an important part of its repertoire. He was most influential, however, as a theorist; in his writings, he established the aesthetic and philosophical basis of nō. Zeami became the director of his father's troupe when Kan'ami died in 1384. He continued to improve nō, borrowing elements of other, earlier, forms of dance drama. His 200 plays, 124 of which remain in the active nō repertory, incorporated his innovations; one of his best known plays is *Atsumori*.

Zeami also began writing on the theory and philosophy of nō, presenting ideas that were heavily influenced by his study of Zen. In his several volumes of theoretical works, Zeami developed the concept of *yūgen,* the mysterious inner heart or spirit behind outward form. Yūgen is the aim of nō performances; another definition of it might be philosophical and physical gracefulness.

Characteristics of Nō Theatre   Under Zeami's direction, nō became the dominant form of serious theatre in his generation, and it remained dominant well past 1600 until it was supplanted in the popular taste by bunraku and kabuki.

Nō, as perfected by Zeami, was and is a remarkably successful synthesis of various theatrical forms into a single, total experience. Nō actors (there were no actresses in Zeami's theatre) trained from childhood and became adept at singing, acting, dancing, and mime. The plays they performed were remarkably sophisticated in language and content and were all constructed around a definite series of organizational principles based on musical, psychological, and mimetic—or imitative—movements, which change gradually from a slow to a fast tempo. Many of the greatest nō plays were written by Zeami himself.

The stories considered appropriate for nō plays were often from literary or historical sources. One important source was a famous novel of Heian court life, Lady Murasaki's *Tale of Genji,* written around 1000. Another important source was *The Tale of the Heike,* a chronicle of the devastating civil wars that destroyed the power of the aristocracy in Japan at the end of the Heian period in 1185. Nō characters were generally based on literary or historical figures already familiar to the audience. A nō play reveals some working out of passions felt by a character, who often appears as a ghost or spirit.

The major roles in nō are the **shite** (SHEE-tay), or main character, who is often masked; the **waki,** a supporting character; and the **tsure,** an accompanying role. There may be various smaller parts as well, including a **kyōgen** (kee-OH-gehn), or comic character.

The occasional comic elements in nō eventually developed as a separate form called *kyōgen.* Kyōgen plays, which use a good deal of folk humor and slapstick, are still performed and appreciated today.

The Kyōgen are usually performed without special costumes, masks, or wigs, except when a nō play is being parodied, in which case the appropriate nō mask is used. Parody and satire are common in Kyōgen, and no subject is sacrosanct or exempt from being treated comically. A feudal lord, monk, or friar can be the main figure; so might a drunken or stupid servant, a braggart, a shrew, or a gallant.

Producing Nō Theatre   The elegance, mystery, and beauty of nō have fascinated the Japanese since the time of Zeami, and the nō tradition, passed on from teacher to disciple, has been carried on to this day. In most of the larger Japanese cities, nō can be seen in excellent performances by troupes whose traditions go back to the fourteenth century—a remarkable legacy.

Even the nō stage has remained roughly the same since the time of Zeami and his immediate successors. There is a bridge, called the **hashigakari** (ha-shee-gah-KAH-ree), which leads from the actors' room offstage to the stage. The bridge is normally about twenty feet long. The main playing space to which it leads is about eighteen feet square; it is roofed and has a ceremonial pine tree painted on the rear wall. At the back of the playing space is a narrow section for four musicians who accompany the play on flute, small hand drum, large hand drum, and stick drum. Nō theatres were originally outdoors, and the audience sat on three sides of the stage. The modern nō theatre is built inside a larger shell as though it were a giant stage set itself, and the audience sits on two sides.

The temple roof above the stage is supported by four columns or pillars, each of which serves a definite purpose in the staging. In addition to the actors and musicians, in nō there is a chorus of ten men who serve as a very rough

NŌ PERFORMANCE TODAY
Traditional nō theatre is still performed in Japan and other parts of the world, and its stylized acting, minimalist settings, ornate costumes, and distinctive masks are still used. Shown here is Terukazu Mizukami performing in a nō play *Hagoromo (The Feather Robe)* at the Iohji Temple in Fukushima, Japan in 2004. (©Jun Sato/Getty Images)

Shite   Major role in nō.

Waki   Supporting role in nō.

Tsure   Accompanying role in nō.

Kyōgen   Comic role in nō.

Hashigakari   Bridge in nō theatre on which the performers make their entrance from the dressing area to the platform stage.

1413, Kitano Temple, Japan The year is 1413. In Japan, at the Kitano temple, a platform stage, with a floor of polished wood, has been set up. There is also a wooden walkway, or bridge, on which actors can move to the stage from a dressing room set up in one of the temple buildings. The spectators are on three sides of this platform stage.

The actor performing today is Zeami. He is fifty years old and has been under the patronage of the shogun of Japan since he was twelve. Zeami's father, Kan'ami, was a renowned actor before him, and Zeami has carried his father's art to even greater heights. He has studied different acting styles, perfected his own technique, trained other actors, and written plays for them to perform.

The theatre he has fashioned from all this is called *nō*; it has elements of opera, pantomime, and formal, stylized dance. In nō theatre, the main character, who wears a beautifully carved, hand-painted wooden mask, recites his or her adventures to the constant accompaniment of several onstage musicians. Toward the end of the play, the chief actor will perform a ritualistic dance that includes symbolic gestures of the head and hands and stomps of the feet on the wooden floor.

The crowd is gathered today for a special reason. Usually, Zeami performs only in a restricted theatre space for the shogun and members of his court, or at a temple for a select audience. But here at the Kitano temple, performances will go on for seven days and will be open to everyone; as one later commentator will explain: "All were admitted, rich and poor, old and young alike."

As with all nō performances, several plays will be presented each day. The play the audience awaits now, *Sotoba Komachi*, was written by Zeami's father. In it, Zeami portrays a woman. (As in ancient Greek theatre, all the performers in nō are men.) The legend of Komachi is as well known to the audience as the story of Antigone was to the Greeks. Komachi, a beautiful but cruel woman, is pursued by a man named Shii no Shōshō. She tells him that he must call on her for 100 nights in a row, and for 99 nights he comes in all kinds of weather. But on the hundredth night he dies. On that night a snowstorm is raging and he falls, exhausted, to die on her doorstep.

When the play begins, we see two priests enter. As they discuss the virtues of following Buddha, they come upon an old woman. This is Zeami in the mask and wig of Komachi in old age. She is a wretched woman approaching her hundredth birthday. Komachi tells how she was once beautiful but has lost her beauty and grown old. She argues with the priests about religion and then reveals who she is. She recounts the story of what she did to Shōshō.

As the play progresses, the audience watches Zeami's performance with rapt attention. At one point, his character becomes possessed: The spirit of Shōshō takes over Komachi, and Zeami acts this out in pantomime to a musical accompaniment. At times, he acts out Komachi's part while her lines are chanted by a chorus of ten or twelve men sitting at the side of the stage. At another point, Komachi is dressed as Shōshō and becomes him, feeling his death agony. Zeami performs this sequence as a mesmerizing, frightening dance. At the end of the play, the spirit of Shōshō leaves Komachi, and she prays to Buddha for guidance and for a peaceful life in the hereafter.

The audience members, who have heard a great deal about Zeami but have never before seen him perform, watch in awe. Throughout, he plays the various parts with astounding grace, subtlety, and understatement, developed through years of training and performance. The segments when he lets go—as in Shōshō's death agony—are all the more effective because of their contrast with the measured quality of the rest. For the audience, the play is a revelation of how moving a theatrical performance can be—an experience unlike any they have had before.

equivalent of the chorus in Greek theatre. Nō actors move in a highly stylized fashion that involves important elements of both dance and pantomime. During the performance of a nō text, the actors alternate sections of chanting with a kind of heightened speech that might best be compared to recitative, sung dialogue in Western opera. The costumes made for nō are usually of great elegance, and the masks worn by the shite are among the most beautiful, subtle, and effective created for any theatre.

Bunraku

Nō remained the most popular theatrical form of theatre during Japan's medieval period. During the sixteenth century, civil wars and other disturbances caused political disarray of increasing gravity until a general, Tokugawa Ieyasu, unified the country in 1600. All through the long Tokugawa period (1600–1868), which bears his family name, Japan was unified and at peace, but this calm was purchased at a price. Alarmed at the political maneuvering of Japan's growing number of Christians, who had been converted by European missionaries, the Tokugawa family outlawed Christianity and cut Japan off from any extensive contact with either China or Europe until the middle of the nineteenth century.

Peace did bring a rapid development of commerce and trade that led to increasingly sophisticated urban life. As the merchant class grew, its members' wealth and their increasing leisure time allowed them to patronize various entertainments. The aristocracy and the Tokugawa family continued to support nō as a kind of private state theatre, but the merchants supported theatrical arts that more closely mirrored their own world. These entertainments flourished in large cities, such as Osaka, Kyoto, and Edo (now Tokyo).

Before we turn to puppet theatre—bunraku—and to the later kabuki, it is worth noting that both forms of theatre can be understood more fully if one takes into account certain tenets of neo-Confucianism. These tenets form the basis of rigid codes of behavior regarding such matters as sacrifice, loyalty, and revenge as found in the class system and the samurai code of the warrior aristocracy of Japan. These strict codes of behavior, in turn, are reflected in the theatrical presentations of bunraku and kabuki.

Of the new popular forms of theatre that developed in Japanese cities, puppet theatre was the first. Since the nineteenth century, this puppet theatre has been called **bunraku** (buhn-RAH-koo), a name that derives from a famous puppeteer. It developed in a most unusual way. One widespread form of entertainment in the medieval period was the art of the chanter—who, with his *biwa* (a kind of large lute), would travel around the countryside intoning chronicles of wars and tales of romantic heroes and heroines. Between 1570 and 1600 the *samisen,* a three-stringed instrument something like a banjo, replaced the biwa as the chief instrument accompanying the chanter. By around 1600, it became customary to add to these performances, as a kind of extra attraction, companies of puppeteers who

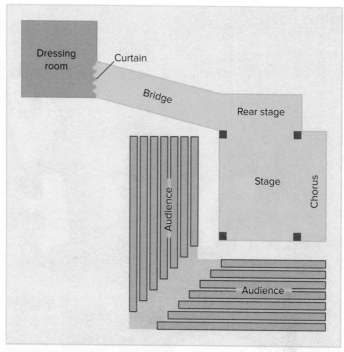

GROUND PLAN OF A TRADITIONAL NŌ THEATRE
Nō theatre of Japan—a stylized theatre originally for the upper classes—began nearly 600 years ago. It was performed outdoors; a ramp at the left led from a dressing room to the wooden platform stage. Spectators sat on two sides of the stage, to the left and in front.

Bunraku Japanese puppet theatre.

JAPANESE BUNRAKU: PUPPET THEATRE
Bunraku—puppet theatre—became a popular form in Japan in the 1600s. In bunraku, unlike traditional Western puppet theatre, the puppeteers are in full view of the audience and are almost always dressed in black. Often, the story is delivered by a chanter, with the puppets dramatizing the action. Because the puppets are very complex, there is usually more than one puppeteer controlling each of them, as is the case in the photo shown here. (©Kyodo/AP Images)

Jōruri In Japanese puppet theatre, chanted text.

would act out the stories, "illustrating" the chanter's music. The introduction of the samisen and the puppeteers made possible the development of bunraku.

The chanted texts are called *jōruri* (joh-ROO-ree) after the name of a popular female character in one of the recited tales. The chanters, down to the present day, have been regarded with the kind of awe reserved for opera singers in the West. The chanters perform all the voices in a play, as well as the narration, and set the general mood. Originally, they also wrote their own scripts. Eventually, however, it became customary to ask someone else to write the text.

In bunraku, the puppets representing important characters are manipulated by three people: one for the legs, one for the left arm, and the chief handler for the head and right arm. The chief handler is often dressed in an elaborate, gorgeous costume, but the other handlers are dressed in black and are assumed to be invisible. The puppets, which today are approximately two-thirds life-size, were originally smaller. Bunraku reached its characteristic form in the 1730s when it became a three-man form. Before that, a significant step in its development was taken in 1685, when the writer Chikamatsu began to collaborate with Takemoto Gidayu, the outstanding bunraku chanter of the day. The first and undoubtedly the best of the bunraku writers, Chikamatsu contributed enormously to the transformation of this popular form into a vehicle for great art.

Chikamatsu Monzaemon   Chikamatsu Monzaemon (1653–1725) was born to a provincial samurai family in 1653 and became the first important Japanese dramatist since the great period of nō drama 300 years earlier. His family apparently had literary interests; in 1671, they published a collection of haiku poetry that included some pieces by the future dramatist.

Chikamatsu did not begin to write plays until the age of thirty, but thereafter he was a prolific writer. His best-known dramas were written for the puppet theatre, bunraku. He is one of the world's only major dramatists to write primarily for that form. He also wrote for kabuki theatre (discussed below), and many of his puppet plays were later adapted for kabuki.

As a playwright, Chikamatsu used his knowledge of Japanese life to create vivid, detailed, and accurate pictures of his society. His history or heroic plays are loosely constructed stories about the nobility; they sometimes feature military pageantry and supernatural apparitions. In his domestic dramas he explored the problems of the middle and lower classes; many of these plays are based on actual events. Often, his domestic plays deal with unhappy lovers, who may even be driven to suicide by the problems they face. Both Chikamatsu's history plays and his domestic plays are known for the beauty of his poetry, which elevates the incidents and the characters.

Western critics have compared Chikamatsu to both Shakespeare and Marlowe because of the quality of his verse and his knowledge of society. His most famous history play is *The Battles of Coxinga* (1715). His notable domestic dramas include *The Love Suicides at Sonezaki* (1703), *The Uprooted Pine* (1718), *The Courier for Hell* (1711), *The Woman Killer and the Hell of Oil* (1721), and *The Love Suicides at Amijima* (1721).

Chikamatsu spoke of maintaining in his dramas "what lies in the slender margin between the real and the unreal," and this quality, plus his remarkable ability as a poet, has kept his plays popular. His emphasis on ordinary people, too, not only was new to the Japanese stage but also foreshadowed later developments in European theatre.

Kabuki

In the early seventeenth century a new form of Japanese theatre, **kabuki**, had emerged. Combining elements of nō, bunraku, and folk theatre, kabuki became the most popular form of theatre in Japan throughout the seventeenth century despite challenges and other vicissitudes. It has remained a part of the theatre scene in Japan in the centuries between and is still performed today.

Kabuki   Form of popular Japanese theatre combining music, dance, and dramatic scenes.

Origins of Kabuki: Okuni of Izumo   According to Japanese legend, credit for developing kabuki, the most popular form of traditional Japanese theatre, belongs to a Shinto priestess, Okuni of Izumo (born in the late sixteenth century). Though little is known of her life or of the circumstances that led to the development of kabuki, tradition holds that in 1603 this priestess began kabuki by dancing on a temporary stage set up in the dry bed of the Kamo River in Kyoto.

Probably, Okuni's early dances were of Buddhist origin and had been secularized by being intermingled with folk dances. It is said that Nagoya Sanzaemon, a samurai warrior who is believed to have been Okuni's lover, taught her adaptations of dances from nō, the samurai-sponsored drama of the period. She might have used nō dances as well as elements of popular dances, but no detailed descriptions of her performances survive.

ORIGINS OF KABUKI: OKUNI OF IZUMO

One branch of the classic Japanese theatre is kabuki, which is supposed to have originated with the performer Okuni. In this drawing, from a 17th century Japanese scroll, Okuni (center) is seen dancing in a Shinto temple in Kyoto. (©bpk, Berlin/Art Resource)

That her dances were popular, however, is shown by the fact that she and her troupe toured Japan in 1603. Okuni used a stage similar to the nō stage for the performances of her group. In 1607 she performed for the shogun. The kabuki developed by Okuni became so popular that in 1616—only a few years after she had begun her performances—there were seven licensed kabuki theatres in Kyoto.

Development of Kabuki Dance was the basis of early kabuki performances, and the musical dance-dramas that developed revolved around stories that were romantic and often erotic. As a composite entertainment appealing to townspeople, kabuki was seen by some authorities as an unsettling influence on the rigid social and artistic structure.

A fascinating series of events occurred in the early days of kabuki related to social concerns and problems of gender and sex. Originally, most of the performers were women; but when social disruptions arose because of feuds over the sexual services of the women, the authorities intervened, and in 1629 women's kabuki was banned. Thereafter, young boys performed kabuki; but eventually it was felt that they, too, as sexual targets of older men in the audience, were causing problems of social and class conflicts, and so in 1652 the authorities also banned boys' troupes.

In addition to concerns about sexual relationships between performers and audience members, the authorities also worried about the mingling of different classes and improper displays by samurai at kabuki performances. After 1652, therefore, men's troupes, in which sexual glamour was deemphasized, became the rule—a custom that remains to the present day. Though the men's troupes were heavily regulated, kabuki flourished in the following centuries and the eroticism that had marked kabuki in the early days was reintroduced. Part of this is due to the necessary development of the art of female impersonation by the male performers.

Kabuki was greatly indebted to the plays and performance of puppet theatre, including scenes in which actors imitated puppets' movements. At least half of the current kabuki repertoire was adapted from puppet theatre. Both kabuki and the puppets were less formal and distant than nō, which remained largely the theatre of the samurai class. Still, many samurai—despite official restrictions on their doing so—secretly attended kabuki, whose action, spectacle, and rhetoric they preferred to the solemnities of nō.

As kabuki itself became popular, the playwright Chikamatsu tried writing for troupes of kabuki actors and wrote off and on for kabuki for many years. Eventually, however, he abandoned the attempt because these performers, it is assumed, unlike chanters, tended to change his lines. Kabuki actors founded dynasties, many of

KABUKI PERFORMANCE TODAY
Seen here is a kabuki actor performing *Fuji Musume* (*Wisteria Maiden*). Today, all roles in kabuki are performed by men; most of the actors are descended from generations of kabuki performers and train for years. Note the heavy, stylized makeup, which covers the entire face; the ornate costume; and the highly theatrical wig. The costumes, makeup, gestures, and stage configuration are part of a long-standing tradition. (©Universal Images Grou/AGE Fotostock)

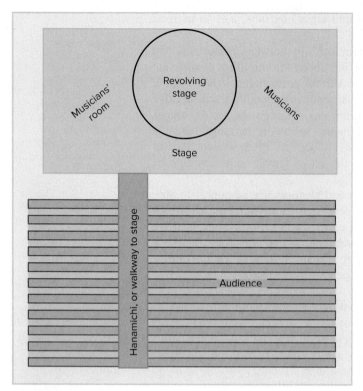

Within the diagram:

Musicians' room

Revolving stage

Musicians

Stage

Hanamichi, or walkway to stage

Audience

A KABUKI THEATRE

Kabuki, a 400-year-old Japanese theatre, is performed today in elaborate spaces with staging devices that include onstage turntables for shifting scenery. As shown in this ground plan, the stage covers the entire front of the theatre and is approached by a ramp—the hanamichi—on which performers make dramatic entrances and exits.

Onnagata In Japanese kabuki, women's roles played by men.

Hanamichi In kabuki theatre, a bridge running from behind the audience (toward the left side of the audience) to the stage. Performers can enter on the hanamichi; important scenes may also be played on it.

them still active. A kabuki dynasty that lasted through twelve generations was founded by Ichikawa Danjuro (1660–1704), who became known as Danjuro I and who began a bravura acting style known as *aragato*. Many actors came to fame in *Chushingura* or *The Forty-Seven Rōnin,* a frequently revived play originally written for puppets. It is perhaps Japan's most popular history play. The play is based on an actual historical incident in which a provincial lord was provoked into an act of violence and forced to commit ritual suicide. It traces the vendetta or revenge of the forty-seven retainers who are left behind and is a remarkable blend of adventure, pathos, and romance. Ghost stories, too, were popular dramas in the kabuki repertoire.

Producing Kabuki Kabuki actors are trained from childhood in vocal technique, dancing, acting, and physical versatility. The male actors who play women's parts—these actors are called **onnagata**—are particularly skillful at imitating the essence of a feminine personality through stylized gestures and attitudes. Costumes and makeup in kabuki are elegant and gorgeous, although they may often be strikingly gritty and realistic. The effect of an actor's performance is frequently quite theatrical and a bit larger than life. Again, however, it must be emphasized that, for all its theatricality, kabuki actually expresses a wide range of styles, from the fantastical to the realistic.

The stage used for kabuki performances underwent various changes during the history of this art, but the fundamental arrangement was reached in the mid-nineteenth century and then altered somewhat after 1853, when Japan was opened to the West. The stage is wide and has a relatively low proscenium. Musicians—sometimes onstage, sometimes offstage—generally accompany the stage action. Kabuki features elaborate and beautiful scenic effects, including the revolving stage, which was developed in Japan before it was used in the West. Another device used in kabuki is the **hanamichi** (hah-nah-MEE-chee), or "flower way," a raised narrow platform connecting the rear of the auditorium with the stage. Actors often make entrances and exits on the hanamichi and occasionally perform short scenes there as well.

Some kabuki plays use a second or temporary hanamichi down the aisle on the audience's opposite side. The stage is also well equipped with large and small elevator traps, used to lift actors in tableaux as well as spectacular settings, which come into view as the audience watches. There is even a small trap on the hanamichi that allows supernatural characters to emerge (or disappear) in the midst of the audience.

In the first decade after World War II, kabuki struggled since many of the theatres were destroyed and there was a general rejection of past forms by the defeated Japanese population. However, a number of innovative directors and popular actors helped resuscitate the classical theatre. Today, unlike many other classical theatres, kabuki remains extremely popular with audiences throughout Japan, with its star actors highly recognized and also appearing in other roles on television and in film.

There are also significant kabuki theatres still staging traditional productions in Tokyo, Kyoto, and Osaka as well as smaller companies throughout the country.

Japanese kabuki troupes frequently undertake tours across the world, playing in major cities in Asia, Europe, and the Americas.

Kabuki has also influenced Western theatre practice with many of its unique characteristics employed by innovative directors. There have been productions of canonical Western works, including plays by Shakespeare, which have employed the theatrical conventions of the kabuki theatre. In addition, kabuki theatre troupes have been established in countries outside of Japan in an attempt to preserve this tradition throughout our global society.

SOUTHEAST ASIA: SHADOW PLAYS

Though we have focused on theatre in India, China, and Japan, it is important to remember that considerable theatre activity has occurred in other parts of Asia, such as Korea and the southeastern countries of Myanmar (Burma), Cambodia, Laos, Indonesia, Malaysia, Thailand, and Vietnam. Though each of these southeastern nations has its own theatrical history and tradition, all of them share certain characteristics. Most of their theatrical styles were influenced by the theatre of India and in some instances by that of China. In virtually every one of these countries we note the influence of two epics from India, the *Ramayana* and the *Mahabharata.* These stories and others are almost always performed as dance drama, classical dance, or puppet theatre. As is true in other Asian countries, theatrical presentations combine dance, song, movement, and recited text with elaborate costumes. It is worth noting that most of these countries do not even have a word in their language that denotes a dramatic form that is only written or spoken.

One type of theatrical activity that came to prominence in southeast Asia in the eleventh century is particularly significant. This was the ***shadow play***, which is widely performed in Thailand, Malaysia, and Indonesia. It appears to have been developed most fully in Java, an Indonesian island. ***Wayang*** (WHY-young) is the term that usually refers to Indonesian puppet theatre but is also used sometimes to refer to live dance performances.

The best known form of a shadow play uses flat puppets made of leather. These figures are intricately carved to create patterns of light and shadow when their image is projected on a screen. The puppets are manipulated by sticks attached to the head, the arms, and other parts of the body. The person manipulating the puppets also narrates the drama and speaks the dialogue of the characters. Shadow plays usually take place at night—sometimes they last all night long—and are accompanied by music and sound effects. In various places, other theatrical forms have been developed from shadow puppets. One variation uses three-dimensional doll puppets; another uses human performers wearing masks.

Shadow play A play performed widely in Thailand, Malaysia, and Indonesia involving intricately carved flat leather puppets that create patterns of light and shadow when their image is projected on a screen.

Wayang Term usually referring to Indonesian shadow plays but sometimes used for live dance performances.

PLAYING YOUR PART:
THINKING ABOUT THEATRE

1. Describe the origins of Asian theatres. How are they similar to the origins of the Western theatres discussed earlier?

2. Asian theatre is often referred to as total theatre because of its mixture of drama, music, and dance. What are some examples of total theatre in today's Western theatre?

3. Many of the Asian theatres employ puppets. Are puppets popular in today's theatre? How is the use of puppets today different from the use of puppets in the traditional Asian theatres?

4. Many of the Asian theatres employ men to play female roles. What are your thoughts about this convention? Identify contemporary examples of men playing women in film, television, or the theatre.

5. Some of the Asian theatres evolved into entertainment for the elite members of their societies. Name at least three examples of entertainment today that appeal primarily to a specific group of individuals.

SHADOW PUPPETS

A longtime theatrical tradition in southeast Asia is shadow puppets. Shadow play or shadow puppetry is an ancient form of storytelling and entertainment using opaque, often articulated figures in front of an illuminated backdrop to create the illusion of moving images. It is thought to have originated in China during the Song Dynasty (960–1127), and later spread to southeast Asia, particularly Indonesia, Malaysia, and Thailand. At present, more than twenty countries are known to have shadow show troupes. The figures are manipulated by puppeteers holding sticks attached to the puppets, which themselves are intricately carved flat figures, made of leather, that create patterns of light and shadow when projected on a screen. Above are examples of Javanese shadow puppets. (©jatmika jati/Shutterstock.com RF)

SUMMARY

1. The traditional theatres of Asia originated from religious ceremonies and concepts.

2. Most of these theatres are highly theatrical and stylized and fuse acting, mime, dance, music, and text.

3. In India in the fourth and fifth centuries C.E., a theatre of a very high order—Sanskrit drama—came to full flower. Its origins and dramatic rules were outlined in a revealing document call the *Natyasastra*.

4. In China, an acting school called the Pear Garden flourished in the early eighth century and professional theatre companies flourished in the tenth century.

5. The first significant Chinese theatre from which we have surviving manuscripts emerged during the Yuan Dynasty from 1271 to 1368. During the succeeding Ming Dynasty, from 1368 to 1644, theatre became more "literary" and less in touch with ordinary people.

6. In Japan, the first important theatre form was nō, which emerged in the fourteenth and fifteenth centuries and is still performed today.

7. Bunraku—puppet theatre—came on the scene in Japan in the seventeenth century followed closely by kabuki. Both bunraku and kabuki are still performed in Japan today.

8. Like most Asian theatres, nō, kabuki, and bunraku are complex forms; to understand them, audiences need to be aware of their intricate conventions.

9. Considerable theatrical activity has also taken place elsewhere in Asia; one example is the shadow plays performed in Thailand, Malaysia, and Indonesia.

RENAISSANCE THEATRES

13

Renaissance is a term that means rebirth; it refers to an awakening of the arts and learning in the Western world, which occurred during the period stretching roughly from the late fourteenth through the early seventeenth century. The center of activity was Italy, which at this time was made up of a group of independent city-states. The Renaissance was also prevalent a short time later in England, Spain, and France. During the Renaissance, theatre blossomed in these countries. Before we discuss the theatrical innovations of this time period, however, let us first examine social and cultural changes.

THE RENAISSANCE: BACKGROUND

European politics changed markedly during the Renaissance. There was a rise of kings and princes, and merchants became key economic figures. As these people's wealth increased, they had leisure time to fill and also became eager to display their fortunes; consequently, they often hired artists to create lavish works for them.

Renaissance art is noticeably different from medieval art. During the Middle Ages, painting and sculpture had religious subjects. Renaissance artists, on the other hand, treated their subjects as human beings with whom we can identify. A good example is the statue of David by the Italian sculptor Michelangelo: The figure of David looks like a real person, not an otherworldly religious image. Painting also became more realistic through the use of oils and perspective, a technique that gives the illusion of three-dimensional depth on a flat canvas. In Renaissance literature, the major movement was *humanism,* which imitated the Greeks and Romans and

◀ **THE THEATRE OF SHAKESPEARE**

In the West, the Renaissance saw a resurgence of theatre, beginning in Italy and moving through various countries of Europe and in England. An example of the vibrancy of this period is the plays of William Shakespeare, a leading English Renaissance dramatist, which continue to be immensely popular. There are frequent productions of his plays, and many have been adapted into films. Seen here is a scene from Shakespeare's The Comedy of Errors *at the Globe in London directed by Blanche McIntyre.* (©Geraint Lewis)

focused on human beings rather than the gods. The printing press, which appeared in Europe in the 1450s, made this literature available to great numbers of people.

The Renaissance was also a period of exploration and invention. Discoveries in North and South America brought new wealth to Europe; at the same time, scientific advances revolutionized Western ideas about of the position of humanity in the universe. For example, the Italian astronomer Galileo argued that the sun, not the earth, is the center of the solar system.

The Renaissance also saw remarkable developments in theatre, especially in Italy, England, Spain, and France.

THE ITALIAN RENAISSANCE

As we noted, during the Renaissance European culture advanced dramatically, and the first center of cultural activity was Italy. At that time, Italy (like Classical Greece, upon which much of its art was based) was not a unified nation but a group of individual city-states.

Renaissance art flourished there, with such artists as Leonardo da Vinci (1452–1519) and Michelangelo (1475–1564) creating renowned works during this era. Many innovative painting techniques, such as perspective, were introduced.

Italian Renaissance scientists, such as the artist Leonardo, who was a brilliant scientist also, and Galileo (1565–1642), made discoveries that supported the Renaissance's focus on humanism. Italians also led the way in the Age of Discovery, with explorers such as Columbus (c. 1451–1506) and Amerigo Vespucci (1454–1512), opening up routes to the Americas.

And just as Italian Renaissance art, politics, and culture were influenced by the Classical Greeks, so, too, we shall see, was the theatre.

Commedia Dell'arte and Other Forms of Italian Renaissance Theatre

Italy, which led the way in Renaissance painting and sculpture, also saw radical transformations in its theatre between 1550 and 1650. These were chiefly in improvisational theatre, acting, dramatic criticism, theatre architecture, and scene design. The written drama of the Italian Renaissance is less significant: Much of it was modeled after Greek and Roman plays and presented at academies or at the homes of wealthy patrons, and almost none of it left a lasting mark. Two other dramatic forms that were developed in the Renaissance and were influenced by classical subject matter and dramatic techniques were intermezzi and pastorals.

Intermezzi were short pieces depicting mythological tales; they were presented between the acts of full-length plays and were often thematically related to the full-length works they accompanied. Intermezzi often required spectacular scenic effects. Although popular in the 1500s, this form disappeared in the 1600s.

The Italians also imitated Greek satyr plays—short, ribald comic pieces that had been presented as a follow-up to Greek tragedies—in a form they called a *pastoral*. The subject matter of a Renaissance pastoral is romance; the characters are usually shepherds and mythological creatures. Unlike Greek satyr plays, the Italian pastorals are not overtly bawdy or sexual. These pastorals usually deal with lovers who are threatened and often at odds with each other; while the action is serious, the endings are happy.

A third form developed during this period which, unlike the intermezzi and the pastoral, was to be of important and lasting value. This was *opera*, invented

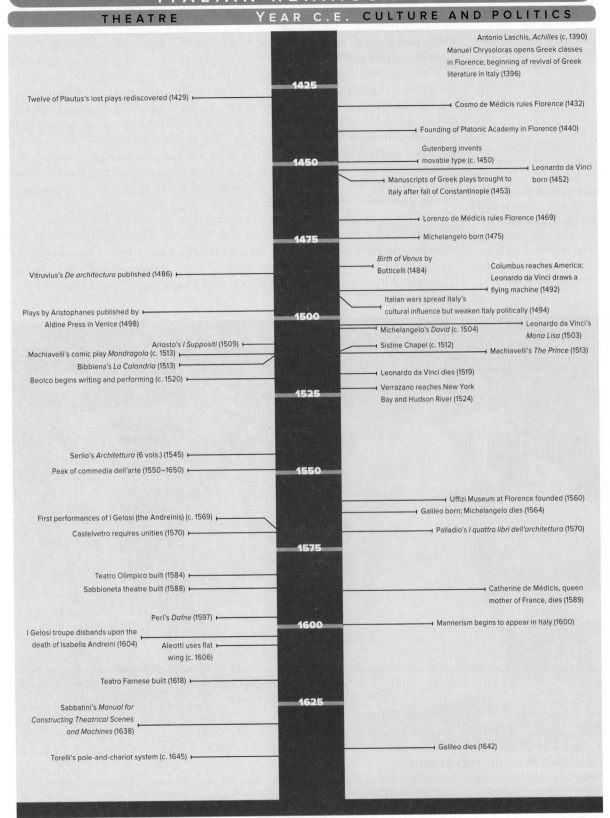

ITALIAN RENAISSANCE

| THEATRE | YEAR C.E. | CULTURE AND POLITICS |

Antonio Laschis, *Achilles* (c. 1390)

Manuel Chrysoloras opens Greek classes in Florence; beginning of revival of Greek literature in Italy (1396)

1425

Twelve of Plautus's lost plays rediscovered (1429)

Cosmo de Médicis rules Florence (1432)

Founding of Platonic Academy in Florence (1440)

1450

Gutenberg invents movable type (c. 1450)

Leonardo da Vinci born (1452)

Manuscripts of Greek plays brought to Italy after fall of Constantinople (1453)

Lorenzo de Médicis rules Florence (1469)

1475

Michelangelo born (1475)

Birth of Venus by Botticelli (1484)

Columbus reaches America; Leonardo da Vinci draws a flying machine (1492)

Vitruvius's *De architectura* published (1486)

Italian wars spread Italy's cultural influence but weaken Italy politically (1494)

Plays by Aristophanes published by Aldine Press in Venice (1498)

1500

Michelangelo's *David* (c. 1504)

Leonardo da Vinci's *Mona Lisa* (1503)

Ariosto's *I Suppositi* (1509)

Sistine Chapel (c. 1512)

Machiavelli's *The Prince* (1513)

Machiavelli's comic play *Mandragola* (c. 1513)

Bibbiena's *La Calandria* (1513)

Leonardo da Vinci dies (1519)

Beolco begins writing and performing (c. 1520)

Verrazano reaches New York Bay and Hudson River (1524)

1525

Serlio's *Architettura* (6 vols.) (1545)

Peak of commedia dell'arte (1550–1650)

1550

Uffizi Museum at Florence founded (1560)

First performances of I Gelosi (the Andreinis) (c. 1569)

Galileo born; Michelangelo dies (1564)

Castelvetro requires unities (1570)

Palladio's *I quattro libri dell'architettura* (1570)

1575

Teatro Olimpico built (1584)

Sabbioneta theatre built (1588)

Catherine de Médicis, queen mother of France, dies (1589)

Peri's *Dafne* (1597)

Mannerism begins to appear in Italy (1600)

1600

I Gelosi troupe disbands upon the death of Isabella Andreini (1604)

Aleotti uses flat wing (c. 1606)

Teatro Farnese built (1618)

1625

Sabbatini's *Manual for Constructing Theatrical Scenes and Machines* (1638)

Galileo dies (1642)

Torelli's pole-and-chariot system (c. 1645)

by people in Italy who believed they were recreating the Greek tragic style, which had fused music with drama. Opera is the only Italian Renaissance theatrical form that has survived. It can be defined as a drama set entirely to music. Every part is sung, including not only solos, arias, duets, trios, and quartets, but also the transitional sections between them known as *recitatives*. Having begun in Florence, Italy, around 1600, opera spread to other parts of Italy during the seventeenth century. After that, for three centuries, from 1600 to 1900, it spread not only throughout Italy, but throughout Europe, including France, Germany, and England. For all of its dramatic qualities, however, opera has always been considered more a part of music than theatre. This is because in opera the emphasis is always on the musical components: the composer, the singers, and the orchestra. However, opera has influenced modern musical theatre; some recent musicals use sung-through dialogue and many significant contemporary theatre directors have staged operas.

Commedia dell'arte An Italian Renaissance form of popular theatre that was highly improvisational, used stock characters, masks, and was staged by traveling professional performers.

Returning to the theatre itself, we repeat that the Italian Renaissance is not distinguished for its written drama. It did, however, originate a significant and immensely popular form of improvisational theatre, closely related to many of our popular performance and comic forms today. This was ***commedia dell'arte***—comedy of professional artists. Commedia dell'arte flourished in Italy from 1550 to 1750.

COMMEDIA DELL'ARTE PERFORMERS
One of the most famous family troupes of commedia dell'arte, the improvisational Italian theatre, was known as I Gelosi. Performers from the troupe are seen here with the leading actress, Isabella Andreini, in the center. (©Photo12)

In commedia, performers had no set text; they invented words and actions as they went along. *Scenarios*—short plot outlines without dialogue—were written by company members.

Commedia companies, usually consisting of ten performers (seven men and three women), were traveling troupes; the most successful companies were often organized by families. Commedia companies were adaptable: They could perform in town squares, in theatre spaces, in the homes of wealthy merchants, or at court.

Commedia performers played the same stock characters throughout most of their careers. Among the popular comic personages were a lecherous, miserly old Venetian man, Pantalone; a foolish scholar, Dottore; a cowardly, braggart soldier, Capitano; and sometimes foolish servants known as *zanni* (ZAH-nee), of whom Arlecchino, or Harlequin, was the most popular. Commedia scenarios also included serious young lovers. All commedia characters used standard *lazzi* (LAHT-zee)—repeated bits of comic business, usually physical, and sometimes bawdy and obscene.

Commedia characters wore traditional costumes, such as Harlequin's patchwork jacket and Dottore's academic robes. A significant addition to Harlequin's costume was the *slapstick*, a wooden sword used in comic fight scenes; today, we still use the term *slapstick* for comedies emphasizing physical horseplay. Masks, usually covering part of the face, were a significant element of commedia costumes. The young lovers, however, did not wear masks.

Zanni Comic male servants in Italian commedia dell'arte.

Lazzi Comic pieces of business used repeatedly by characters in Italian commedia dell'arte.

Slapstick A type of comedy or comic business that relies on exaggerated or ludicrous physical activity for its humor.

Italian Dramatic Rules: The Neoclassical Ideals

In terms of drama, critics rather than playwrights proved influential in the Italian Renaissance. Italian critics formulated dramatic rules—known as the *neoclassical ideals*—that were to dominate dramatic theory through much of Europe for nearly 200 years.

One overriding concern of the neoclassicists was *verisimilitude,* by which they meant that drama should be "true to life." Their verisimilitude, however, was not the kind of realism we find in modern drama. Though the neoclassicists insisted that these dramas be recognizable and verifiable from real life, nevertheless they permitted stock dramatic situations and stock characters.

Another concern of the neoclassicists—in fact, their most famous mandate—was their insistence on three *unities*: unity of time, place, and action. The unities grew out of the desire for verisimilitude. Unity of time required that the dramatic action in a play should not exceed twenty-four hours. Unity of place restricted the action of a play to one locale. Unity of action required that there be only one central story involving a relatively small group of characters; this meant that there could be no subplots. The three unities are often mistakenly attributed to Aristotle, though in fact he had suggested only one unity: the unity of action.

The neoclassicists interpreted genre very narrowly. For many of them, tragedy dealt with royalty, comedy with common people; tragedy must end sadly and comedy happily; and the two genres must never be mixed.

The function of all drama, the neoclassic critics insisted, was to teach moral lessons. Also, they held that characters must be morally acceptable to the audience.

There were numerous other rules. Onstage violence was forbidden, for instance; and the neoclassicists banished the chorus and supernatural characters. They were also opposed to the *soliloquy*—a monologue through which a character reveals thoughts by speaking them aloud.

Neoclassical ideals Rules developed by critics during the Italian Renaissance, supposedly based on the writings of Aristotle.

Unities Term referring to the preference that a play's plot occur within one day (unity of time), in one place (unity of place), and with no action irrelevant to the plot (unity of action).

The historical significance of commedia dell'arte is seen in its influence on later theatre practitioners. Its stock characters—which seem to have evolved from figures in ancient mime, from the plays of Plautus and Terence, and from medieval farces—were further refined by later playwrights. The miserly merchant Pantalone, for instance, is the ancestor of the avaricious Harpagon in the late-seventeenth-century French play *The Miser* by Molière, and the comic servant Pulcinella evolved into Punch in the English Punch and Judy puppet shows.

Possibly the most important influence of the commedia del'arte can be seen in the contemporary development of improvisational theatre. In the United States, early vaudeville comics during the late nineteenth and early twentieth centuries frequently improvised stage routines. As noted earlier, comparisons can also be drawn between commedia performers and many of the classic early twentieth-century film comics—including Charlie Chaplin, Laurel and Hardy, the Marx Brothers, Abbott and Costello, and the Three Stooges. The zany films of the Marx Brothers, who began their careers in vaudeville, for example, used many techniques reminiscent of commedia. Groucho, Harpo, and Chico portrayed the same kinds of characters, with only slight deviations, in all their movies; that is, they created stock characters. Groucho was an unsuccessful, pedantic gigolo; Harpo was a lecherous, musically inclined mute; Chico was a scheming immigrant. Some of their action and dialogue—to the chagrin of their screenwriters—was improvised. Also, the Marx Brothers used standard lazzi and stock costumes. Groucho walked with a stoop and toyed with a cigar; Harpo always wore a long trench coat, carried a horn, and mimed messages. Audiences enjoyed seeing repetitions of these characters' wildly comic business as they became involved in different complicated situations.

From the 1960s through the present there have been many significant improvisatory troupes and performers. One of the most famous is Second City in Chicago (which now also has a location in Toronto), which opened in 1959. Second City has produced many leading comic stars, including a number of whom have appeared on the long running TV series *Saturday Night Live.*

Second City performers create sketches from improvisations that then become set scenarios, much like in commedia dell'arte. In addition, they may request ideas from audience members to create skits, but again use frequently repeated circumstances and character types to aid in their improvisations. The same is true for *Saturday Night Live,* where certain character types, circumstances, and situations are used to assist in the creation of sketches by the writers and performers.

The improvisatory nature of commedia influenced many avant-garde twentieth-century theatre companies, including the politically oriented San Francisco Mime Troupe, popular in the 1960s and 1970s and still performing today, and the Living Theatre; and contemporary performers such as Bill Irwin (b. 1950) and David Shiner (b. 1953), who brought their commedia-like clowning to Broadway and off-Broadway several times, most notably in *Fool Moon* (1993) and *Old Hats* (2013). We will discuss many of these troupes and performers later in our textbook.

While there were significant differences among the various Italian critics, they were all highly *prescriptive*, telling authors how to write in order to create great drama. The rules of the neoclassical critics were to have particular influence on playwrights in France during the seventeenth century.

Theatre Production in Italy

A particularly significant contribution of the Italian Renaissance was made by architects who revolutionized theatre construction. Two specific buildings illustrate the gradual development of Italian theatre architecture, and fortunately both are still standing.

Experiencing Theatre History
COMMEDIA DELL'ARTE

1500s, Rome The time is the late 1500s; the place is a town square in Rome. Set up in the square is a wooden platform stage with a backdrop at the rear. This backdrop, or curtain, not only forms the scenic background of the action on the platform but also provides a hidden space in which the performers can adjust their costumes and from which they can make their entrances and exits.

A crowd is beginning to gather, and people are trying to get the best position to see the performance that is about to begin. In front of the stage, people are already standing several rows deep; at the sides the audience members push closer, but they won't be facing the stage directly. As the spectators look around, they can see that the audience represents a cross section of Roman citizens.

There is great anticipation in the air because the performers are members of one of the best-known theatre companies in Italy—a troupe called *I Gelosi*, led by Francesco and Isabella Andreini. The ten members of the company have perfected commedia dell'arte, a form of improvisational comedy that has become the most popular type of theatre in Italy.

Commedia is different from many other kinds of theatre. There is no script in the usual sense. There is an outline of the action—the characters portrayed in a scene, what happens, how the scene develops—but the dialogue is not written out. The lines the characters speak are not provided. The performers, therefore, improvise their speeches—that is, they make the dialogue up as they go along. This, plus the fact that the movements also are improvised, adds a great air of immediacy to the production. It is most challenging to the performers, and this makes the presentation all the more exciting for those now assembled to watch.

Soon the performance is under way, and the fun begins. The story is partly about an actress who is pursued by every man—unmarried or married—in town, and partly about the adulterous intrigues of her pursuers' wives. There are insults, cases of mistaken identity, and plans gone wrong, and people's misbehavior is exposed.

The characters are stock figures: an old Venetian merchant, a foolish pedant, a cowardly braggart soldier, comic servants, and young lovers. All the characters except the lovers wear masks, most of which are half masks covering the upper part of the face. Each character wears a costume that makes him or her easily recognizable: the pedant, for instance, wears academic robes; the captain wears a uniform; the young lovers are fashionably dressed. One source of great pleasure in watching the performance is seeing the pompous, self-important characters get their comeuppance during the course of the action.

The servants are a special delight. They are known as *zanni* and are usually of two types. The first, called Buffetto and various other names, is a clever, domineering intriguer who motivates the plot through various schemes. The other, even better known, is Arlecchino, or Harlequin. He wears a patchwork outfit of many colors, is given to pratfalls, and is often the victim of knockdown physical humor. Frequently, the servants outwit their masters and help the young lovers get together.

One plot twist operates around the notion that older characters attempt to thwart the desires of the young lovers, and it is only at the conclusion that the lovers achieve their objective.

The spectators crowded around the platform, knowing that the performers are improvising, are amazed at how quick on their feet the performers are and how readily they respond to the dialogue thrown at them.

The interaction of the performers is very physical. In one scene, a master beats a servant with a stick, which is hinged with a flap to make an exaggerated sound when it hits the servant's backside. In another scene, a soldier challenges a lover to a duel and becomes hopelessly entangled with his own sword; at times his sword sticks out from between his legs, taking on a sexual connotation. The more entangled he becomes, the louder the audience laughs.

At the end of the play, as they make their way home, audience members talk among themselves, sometimes laughing out loud as they recall highlights of the performance.

TEATRO OLIMPICO

Completed in 1584, the Teatro Olimpico in Vicenza, Italy, is the oldest surviving theatre from the Renaissance. The stage attempted to duplicate the facade of the Roman scene house and had five alleyways leading off it. Down each alleyway, small models of buildings were created to give the illusion of disappearing perspective. This photo shows the ornate facade, a holdover from Roman theatres, with the five stage openings, two on each side of the large central one, with miniature representations of increasingly smaller buildings. (©Dennis Marsico/Corbis/VCG/Getty Images)

The oldest surviving theatre built during the Italian Renaissance—the Teatro Olimpico in Vicenza, completed in 1584—was designed as a miniature indoor Roman theatre. Its auditorium, accommodating approximately 3,000 spectators, had curved benches connected to the *scaena,* or stage house; this arrangement created a semicircular *orchestra.* There was a raised stage, about seventy feet wide by eighteen feet deep, in front of the scaena. The ornate facade of the scene house, patterned after the Roman scaena frons, was designed to look like a street. There were five openings in the facade—three in the back wall and one on each side. Behind each opening was an alleyway or street scene that seemed to disappear in the distance. To achieve an effect of depth, in each alleyway there were three-dimensional buildings—houses and shops—that decreased in size as they were positioned farther and farther away from the opening onstage.

The most renowned theatre building of the Italian Renaissance was the Teatro Farnese in Parma, completed in 1618, extensively damaged during World War II, and then almost completely reconstructed. The Farnese had a typical court, or academic, theatre auditorium, with raised horseshoe seating that accommodated about 3,500 spectators. What was revolutionary in the Teatro Farnese was its *proscenium-arch* stage. Despite the term *arch,* a proscenium opening is usually a rectangular frame. Realistic scenery can be placed much more effectively behind such a frame than in any other type of theatre; thus the proscenium arch, along with Renaissance innovations in scene design, became an impetus for greater theatrical realism. (See the chapter "Theatre Spaces" for a fuller discussion of the proscenium-arch theatre.)

When we move from the stage to the auditorium, we find that the major changes occurred in the public opera houses of Venice. These were proscenium-arch houses, but—unlike court or academy theatres—they were commercial ventures that needed as many paying customers as possible; thus, they required

TEATRO FARNESE

Completed in 1618, the Teatro Farnese was the first theatre with a proscenium arch—the opening behind which scenery and stage machinery are concealed. The auditorium is horseshoe shaped, and the orchestra is a semicircle placed between the audience and the stage. (©Ruggero Vanni/Getty Images)

a larger audience area. Opera houses were therefore designed with "pit, boxes, and galleries," which had already been used in France, England, and Spain. It was their combination of a "pit, box, and gallery" auditorium with a proscenium-arch stage that made the Venetian opera houses innovative. This kind of proscenium-arch theatre with pit, box, and gallery seating would later become the standard theatre space throughout the Western world and would remain so for more than 300 years.

The *pit*, in which audience members stood, was an open area on the house floor extending to the side and back walls. Built into the walls were tiers of seating. The lower tiers were usually the most expensive; they were divided into separate private *boxes* and were frequented by the upper classes. The upper tiers, which were called *galleries*, had open bench seating. The pit—a raucous area where the spectators ate, talked, and moved around—and the galleries were the least expensive accommodations.

Advances in scene design during the Italian Renaissance were no less impressive than architectural innovations. *Perspective* drawing, which creates an illusion of depth and which had become an important feature of Renaissance art, was introduced into theatre.

The earliest painted-perspective scenery was not easy to shift; as a result, by the early 1600s flat wings were used to create painted-perspective settings. In this arrangement, a series of individual wings on each side of the stage, parallel to

Pit Floor of the house in Renaissance theatres. It was originally a standing area; by the end of the eighteenth century, backless benches were added in most countries.

Box Small private compartment for a group of spectators built into the walls of traditional proscenium-arch and other theatres.

Gallery In theatre buildings, the undivided seating area cut into the walls of the building.

Perspective Illusion of depth in painting, introduced into scene design during the Italian Renaissance.

A DESIGN BY TORELLI

Giacomo Torelli, a master scene designer during the Italian Renaissance, continued the use of painted perspective scenery; he also improved scene shifting by inventing the pole-and-chariot system for wings and shutters. The setting shown here was designed for *Jealous Venus,* an opera by Niccolò Bartolini, performed at the Teatro Novissimo in Venice in 1643. It would have been created from wings and shutters, with some three-dimensional ornamentation, and shifted by the pole-and-chariot method. Torelli's work was so highly esteemed that he was invited to France to design for the court. (©Giacomo Torelli/Getty Images)

Groove system   System in which tracks on the stage floor and above the stage allowed for the smooth movement of flat wings onto and off the stage; usually there were a series of grooves at each stage position.

Pole-and-chariot system
A mechanized means of changing scenery that was developed in the Italian Renaissance. Flats were attached to poles and wheels which were shifted by means of ropes, pulleys, and a single winch.

the audience, were placed in a progression from the front to the back of the stage and enclosed at the very back by two shutters that met in the middle. The final element in these perspective settings was provided by overhead borders—strips across the top of the stage that completed the picture.

The method of scene shifting used with settings of this kind is often referred to as the *groove system* because the wings and shutters were placed in parallel grooves on and above the stage floor. The major problem with this system was coordinating the removal of the flat wings by scene shifters at each groove position. This problem was solved with an innovative scene-changing system developed by Giacomo Torelli (1608–1678) and known as the *pole-and-chariot system*. Poles attached to the flats continued below the stage floor, where they were connected to wheels ("chariots") in tracks. In this way, the flats could be moved offstage smoothly; by connecting a series of ropes and pulleys, the entire set could be removed by turning a single winch. The pole-and-chariot system was adopted and used throughout much of the world for more than two centuries. The focus on illusion and spectacular scene shifts continues in our contemporary theatre.

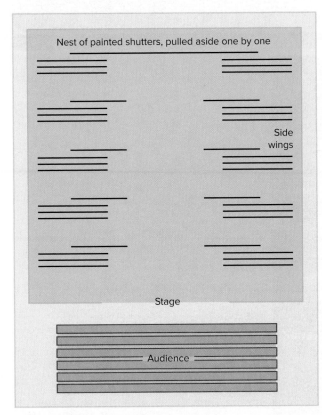

Nest of painted shutters, pulled aside one by one

Side wings

Stage

Audience

GROOVE SYSTEM OF SCENE CHANGES
During the Italian Renaissance, the groove method of shifting scenery was perfected. Along the sides of the stage, in parallel lines, scenery was set in sections. At the back, two shutters met in the middle. Together, these pieces formed a complete stage picture. When one set of side wings and back shutters was pulled aside, a different stage picture was revealed.

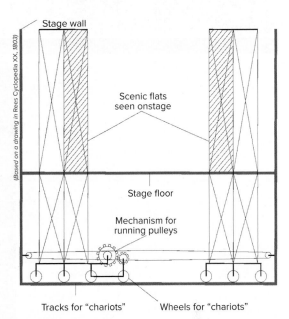

Stage wall

Scenic flats seen onstage

(Based on a drawing in Rees Cyclopedia XX, 1803)

Stage floor

Mechanism for running pulleys

Tracks for "chariots"   Wheels for "chariots"

POLE-AND-CHARIOT SYSTEM
This method of changing wings and back shutters was developed by Torelli. When a series of wheels and pulleys below the level of the stage—attached on frameworks to the scenery above—were shifted, the scene changed automatically. Because the mechanisms were interconnected, scene shifts could be smooth and simultaneous.

ENGLAND

Background: Elizabethan England

The English Renaissance is often called the *Elizabethan* period because its major political figure was Elizabeth I, who reigned for forty-five years from 1558 to 1603. Throughout the English Renaissance, explorations abroad were undertaken, and language and literature flourished. The English were intrigued by language—Queen Elizabeth herself was an amateur linguist—and at the heart of the English Renaissance in literature and the arts was theatre.

Elizabethan Drama

Christopher Marlowe and the "Mighty Line"   One of the most important of the Elizabethan playwrights was Christopher Marlowe (1564–1593), who advanced the art of dramatic structure and contributed a gallery of interesting characters to English drama; he also perfected another element that was to prove central to later Elizabethan plays: dramatic poetry. Critics speak of Marlowe's "mighty

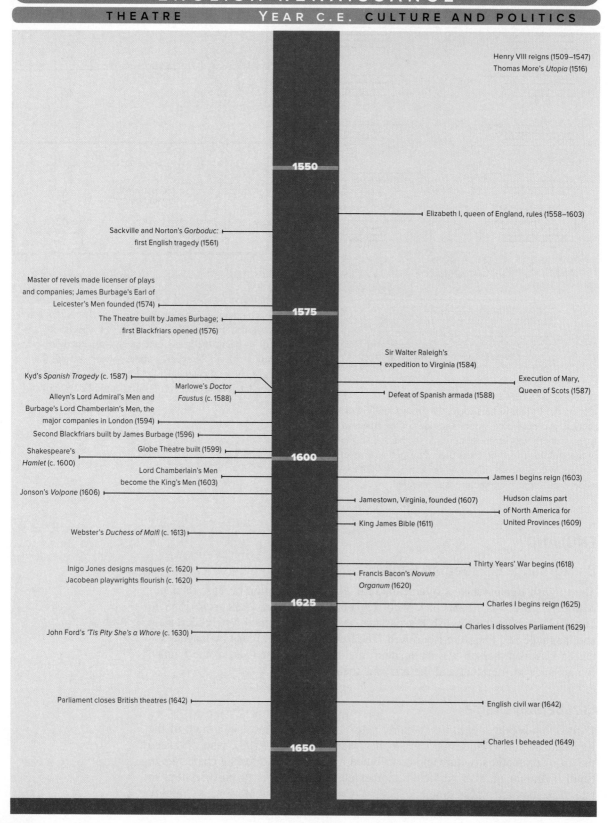

Henry VIII reigns (1509–1547)

Thomas More's *Utopia* (1516)

1550

Elizabeth I, queen of England, rules (1558–1603)

Sackville and Norton's *Gorboduc:* first English tragedy (1561)

Master of revels made licenser of plays and companies; James Burbage's Earl of Leicester's Men founded (1574)

1575

The Theatre built by James Burbage; first Blackfriars opened (1576)

Sir Walter Raleigh's expedition to Virginia (1584)

Kyd's *Spanish Tragedy* (c. 1587)

Marlowe's *Doctor Faustus* (c. 1588)

Execution of Mary, Queen of Scots (1587)

Alleyn's Lord Admiral's Men and Burbage's Lord Chamberlain's Men, the major companies in London (1594)

Defeat of Spanish armada (1588)

Second Blackfriars built by James Burbage (1596)

Shakespeare's *Hamlet* (c. 1600)

Globe Theatre built (1599)

1600

Lord Chamberlain's Men become the King's Men (1603)

James I begins reign (1603)

Jonson's *Volpone* (1606)

Jamestown, Virginia, founded (1607)

Hudson claims part of North America for United Provinces (1609)

King James Bible (1611)

Webster's *Duchess of Malfi* (c. 1613)

Inigo Jones designs masques (c. 1620)

Thirty Years' War begins (1618)

Jacobean playwrights flourish (c. 1620)

Francis Bacon's *Novum Organum* (1620)

1625

Charles I begins reign (1625)

Charles I dissolves Parliament (1629)

John Ford's *'Tis Pity She's a Whore* (c. 1630)

Parliament closes British theatres (1642)

English civil war (1642)

1650

Charles I beheaded (1649)

line," by which they mean the power of his dramatic verse. The meter of this verse is iambic pentameter, which has five beats to a line, with two syllables to each beat and the accent on the second beat. In Marlowe's hands, dramatic verse in iambic pentameter developed strength, subtlety, and suppleness, as well as great lyric beauty.

Marlowe wrote several important plays, including *The Tragical History of Doctor Faustus* (c. 1588), *Tamburlaine, Parts 1 and 2* (c. 1587), and *Edward II* (c. 1592), but his promising career as a dramatist was unfortunately cut short when he was stabbed to death in a tavern brawl in 1593 at the age of twenty-nine in 1593.

William Shakespeare: A Playwright for the Ages William Shakespeare (1564–1616) appeared on the theatre scene around 1590, just after Marlowe had made his debut. Shakespeare was a native of Stratford-upon-Avon (a town about eighty-five miles northwest of London); his father was a prosperous glove maker and town alderman, and his mother—Mary Arden—was the daughter of a prominent landowner and farmer. Shakespeare was educated in Stratford; he then married Anne Hathaway, who was several years older than he and who bore him three children.

At some point after the third child was born, Shakespeare left his family and went to London, where he worked first as an actor and shortly after that as a playwright. As a dramatist, he worked with elements that had been established in early Elizabethan drama—Senecan dramatic devices; the platform stage; powerful dramatic verse; source material from English history, Roman history and drama, and Italian literature; and the episodic plot structure that had its roots in medieval theatre. He fused these elements into one of the most impressive groups of plays ever created.

Shakespeare was an expert in many aspects of theatre. As an actor and a member of a dramatic company, the Lord Chamberlain's Men (which was London's leading troupe), he understood the technical and business elements of theatre.

TWO PLAYWRIGHTS OF THE ELIZABETHAN ERA Christopher Marlowe (left) and William Shakespeare (right) are the most renowned playwrights of an era that produced many great dramatists. (Marlowe: ©Hulton Archive/Getty Images; Shakespeare: ©DavidBukach/ Getty Images RF)

MEMORABLE CHARACTERS IN SHAKESPEARE
Shakespeare's plays are filled with a number of memorable, major characters, from tragic figures such as Hamlet and Macbeth to comic ones like Falstaff. Shown here is Benedict Cumberbatch as Hamlet in a production directed by Lyndsey Turner at London's Barbican Centre in 2015. (Johan Persson/ArenaPal/The Image Works)

As a writer, he excelled in several genres, including tragedy, comedy, and history. His tragedies include *Romeo and Juliet* (1595), *Julius Caesar* (1599), *Hamlet* (1601), *Othello* (1604), *Macbeth* (1605–1606), and *King Lear* (1605–1606). His comedies include *The Comedy of Errors* (1592), *A Midsummer Night's Dream* (1595), *As You Like It* (1599), and *Twelfth Night* (1601). Among his well-known histories are *Richard III* (1592–1593); *Henry IV, Parts 1 and 2* (1597–1598); and *Henry V* (1599). Like other Elizabethan authors, he also sometimes wrote with collaborators. For example, in 2016, the New Oxford Shakespeare credited Christopher Marlowe with coauthoring the three *Henry VI* plays previously credited solely to Shakespeare.

His verse, especially the power of his metaphors and the music of his language, is extraordinary; and his characters are so well-rounded and carefully detailed that they often seem like living people. He was also a master of plot construction, notably episodic plot structure—which, as we have seen, stands alongside climactic structure as one of the two main forms that have been predominant throughout the history of Western theatre.

The Globe Theatre, where his plays were produced, burned in 1613; after that, Shakespeare retired to Stratford and became one of its leading citizens. He died three years later.

1600, London It is early afternoon on a day around the year 1600. In London, England, people from many parts of the city are gathering along the north bank of the Thames River to be carried by boat across to its south bank. There is a special excitement in the air because most of those crossing the Thames are headed for the Globe Theatre to see the first public performance of a new play by William Shakespeare called *Hamlet.*

The Globe is one of the newest and finest playhouses serving London. The reason it is on the other side of the Thames, outside city limits, is that officials in London have forbidden theatrical performances inside the city. The first permanent theatres in England have been built to the north of London or across the Thames to the south, outside the jurisdiction of city officials.

When the spectators arrive at the theatre—more than 2,000 people all together—they can pay a penny at the main door to get in, or they can use another entrance for the more expensive accommodations. Those who use the main door move into a central courtyard, open to the sky, where they will stand during the performance around three sides of a platform stage at one end of the courtyard. Those who can afford to pay more enter one of three levels of covered gallery seats surrounding the stage and courtyard on three

sides. By paying even more, the nobility can sit on cushioned seats in boxes next to the stage. Food and drink—apples, nuts, water, ale—are being sold throughout the playhouse.

As the audience gathers, there is a great deal of conversation about the play. Some audience members already know something about *Hamlet;* they are familiar with earlier versions of the story, and they know that *Hamlet* will be a revenge play—one of their favorite types of drama. There is keen interest, too, because *Hamlet* is by William Shakespeare, a favorite playwright; and its star is Richard Burbage, who is considered by many people the finest actor in England.

At two o'clock, the play begins. Two sentinels standing watch on the parapet of a castle appear onstage, soon to be joined by Horatio, a friend of Hamlet's; the three men discuss a ghost that has been appearing every night. All of a sudden, the ghost is there: It is the ghost of Hamlet's father, and it is played by Shakespeare himself, who is also an actor with the company. Horatio and the sentinels are frightened; the ghost stays briefly and then disappears.

The scene shifts to the interior of the castle: King Claudius enters. He is the brother of Hamlet's father, the dead king, and he has married Hamlet's mother, Queen Gertrude. Onstage, too, are the other principals of the play, including Hamlet, who is

dressed in black and stands apart from the others.

The action of the play is full of twists and turns. In the next scene, Hamlet himself sees the ghost of his father, who says that Hamlet must avenge his murder at the hands of his brother, Claudius. Hamlet later has a group of strolling players present a drama that proves Claudius did murder Hamlet's father. In a later scene, Hamlet thrusts his sword through a curtain in his mother's bedroom, thinking that Claudius is hiding behind it, but the person concealed there turns out to be someone else.

As the plot continues to unfold, the audience is enthralled—all the way to the end, when almost everyone is killed: Hamlet and Laertes in a duel, Gertrude by poisoning, Claudius by stabbing. Throughout the play, the audience enjoys not only the action and suspense but also the memorable lines and speeches. Several times Hamlet stands alone onstage delivering a soliloquy.

On the way back across the Thames, after the play is over, and all evening, the audience members will continue to discuss *Hamlet.* They would like to see it again because there is more to it than they were able to take in at one viewing; they want to live through it once more to feel the thrill of the action and to sort out their thoughts about what it means.

IN FOCUS: SHAKESPEARE: 400 YEARS LATER

The continued admiration for the works of William Shakespeare is evident in the many theatres and festivals across the world dedicated to producing his plays. These include both semi-professional and professional companies, some of which do only the works by the great Elizabethan author as well as others that do other notable works in addition to those by the Bard. Among the most notable are England's Royal Shakespeare Company and the Globe Theatre (discussed later), Canada's Stratford Festival, and in the United States, the New York Shakespeare Festival, the Oregon Shakespeare Festival, the Utah Shakespeare Festival, and the Chicago Shakespeare Theatre.

But two remarkable projects undertaken to commemorate the 450th anniversary of Shakespeare's birth and the 400th anniversary of his death reflect his continued impact. On April 23, 2014, the current Globe Theate in London organized a tour of Hamlet, directed by artistic director Dominic Dromgoole, to mark the anniversary of the author's birth and scheduled to tour every country in the world. The company staged performances of Shakespeare's classic work in refugee camps, such as in 2015 for those escaping war-ravaged Syria, in order to perform for peoples whose countries were inaccessible.

In 2016, to mark the 400th anniversary of Shakespeare's death, the Chicago Shakespeare Theatre scheduled a year-long festival of international companies, including the Royal Shakespeare Company, China's Shanghai Peking Opera, and the Pushkin Theatre of Moscow, visiting the city and presenting about 100 productions and other arts events that would attract half a million audience members. Not only theatre productions but also ballets, such as Hamburg Ballet's *Othello,* operas, and concerts based on Shakespeare's works would be presented. Museum and art exhibitions, and even leading chefs and restaurants, found innovative ways to be involved in the festival.

These two events, along with the continuing popularity of Shakespeare Festivals, clearly reflect how this Elizabethan author continues to inspire the imaginations of contemporary theatre artists and their audiences.

Elizabethan Theatre Production

Public theatres Outdoor theatres in Elizabethan England.

Public or Outdoor Theatres   The plays of Shakespeare, Marlowe, and their contemporaries were performed primarily in *public theatres*. Between the 1560s and 1642, at least nine open-air public theatres were built just outside the city of London. They were located just outside the city limits to avoid government restrictions. All levels of society attended productions at the public theatres. The most famous public theatre was the Globe because it was the home of Shakespeare's plays.

Elizabethan playhouses flourished 400 years ago. By a strange coincidence, within the last twenty years, the sites of four of these theatres have been rediscovered and excavated: the Rose (1587), the Globe (1599), The Theatre (1576), and the Curtain (1577). These discoveries have aided our understanding of the size, shape, and configurations of the original theatres. For example, the ongoing excavation of the Curtain revealed, in 2016, that its shape was rectangular rather than circular as previously assumed. The excavation also yielded information on food consumed by audiences.

Also, in 1997, a replica of the Globe Theatre opened near the site of the original Globe, and performances are staged there each summer. This theatre provides opportunities to experiment with many of the staging conventions of the era.

The stage of a public theatre—a raised platform surrounded on three sides by the audience—was closer to a contemporary thrust stage than to a proscenium

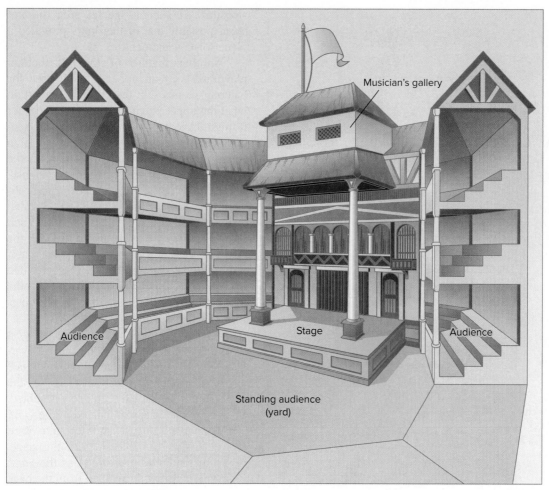

Musician's gallery

Audience

Stage

Audience

Standing audience
(yard)

AN ELIZABETHAN PLAYHOUSE
This drawing shows the kind of stage on which the plays of Shakespeare and his contemporaries were first presented. A platform stage juts into an open courtyard, with spectators standing on three sides. Three levels of enclosed seats rise above the courtyard. There are doors at the rear of the stage for entrances and exits and an upper level for balcony scenes.

stage. This platform stage was a neutral playing area that could become many different places in quick succession: a room in a palace, a bedroom, a street, a battlefield. When one group of characters left the stage and another group entered, this generally signaled a change of scene. Sometimes the characters announced where they were; at other times, the location was apparent from the action.

In the stage floor were trapdoors. Behind the raised platform was the stage house, known as the ***tiring house***. This three-story building served as a place for changing costumes as well as for storing properties and set pieces. The stage house was also the basic scenic piece in an Elizabethan public theatre.

There is a great deal of debate over the configuration of the tiring house, but it is usually argued that the first level had two doorways, one on each side; and that entrances and exits through these doors indicated scene changes. For plays with scenes in which characters were concealed, there was probably an inner stage on the first level, either as part of the tiring house or within a freestanding

Tiring house   The stage house in the Elizabethan theatre used for scenic background, changing costumes, and storing properties and scenic pieces.

structure. If such a special area did not exist, possibly one of the doors provided a place for concealment.

Another feature of the Elizabethan playhouse was an upper playing area for balcony scenes. No one knows for certain what the upper playing area looked like, but it might have been an inner area on the second level of the tiring house or part of a freestanding structure at the rear of the stage. The third level of the stage house, referred to as the *musicians' gallery,* probably housed the musicians who provided accompaniment for the plays. A roof, which protected the stage, extended out from the stage house. In some theatres it was supported by pillars; in others, it was suspended from the back. A flag was flown from the top of the stage house on days when a performance was taking place.

As noted earlier, excavations suggest that the exact shape of public theatres varied. It is estimated that their audience capacity was between 1,500 and 3,000—the larger number is now more widely accepted. Spectators were accommodated in the *yard, boxes,* and *galleries.* On the ground floor, in front of, and on the sides of the stage, was the standing area, known as the *yard,* the front half of which sloped from the back to the stage. The lower-class audience members who stood in the yard were known as *groundlings.* The galleries were usually three tiers of seating ranged on three sides around the stage. One tier was divided into boxes known as *lords' rooms* because they were frequented by the wealthy; the undivided tiers were equipped with bench seating. Spectators—even those at the back wall of the galleries—were never very far from the actors.

Recent excavations indicate that audiences ate such foods as grapes, figs, blackberries, raspberries, plums, cold chicken, and oysters, as well as drank water, ale, and wine in the public theatres. Some of the foods and drinks were sold in the playhouses and in nearby taphouses. Spectators no doubt decided to limit how much they ate or drank since the only toilet facilities were buckets or the nearby river.

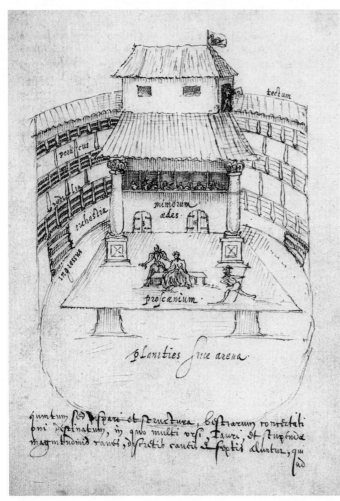

THE SWAN THEATRE

This drawing of an Elizabethan playhouse is a copy of a sketch made by a Dutch visitor to London in 1596. While the sketch shows the platform stage, tiring house, and galleries, controversial questions remain. Is the sketch complete? If so, where is the space for concealed characters? Who are the people in the gallery? Is this a rehearsal or a performance? (©University Library, Utrecht, Ms. 842, fol. 132r)

Private theatres Indoor Elizabethan theatres.

Private Theatres Elizabethan ***private theatres*** were indoor spaces, lit by candles and high windows. The term *private* in this context often causes confusion because today it would imply that certain classes were excluded. In Elizabethan England, however, private theatres were open to the general public, though they were usually smaller (seating about 600 to 750 spectators) and therefore more expensive than public theatres.

The pit of a private theatre, which faced the stage in only one direction, had backless benches. The platform stage extended to the side walls, with galleries and boxes facing the stage on three sides.

Again, there is much debate over the configuration of private theatres. In 2014, a replica of an indoor private theatre, like those used for Shakespeare's late plays, opened in London next door to the replica of the Globe Theatre. That theatre, not modeled after any specific private English Renaissance playhouse, is based on drawings originally thought to be from the era but now believed to have been drawn around 1660.

Scenery and Costumes in Elizabethan Theatres

The Elizabethans did not use painted scenery in their public or private theatres, and the stage space did not represent a specific locale. Instead, the extensive, episodic nature of Elizabethan drama required scenes to be changed rapidly. Sometimes actors coming onstage would bring out minimal properties, such as a throne, to suggest a locale.

Costuming followed the conventions and traditions of medieval English theatre. While their dramas exhibit a great deal of historical and geographical variety, the Elizabethans were not overly concerned with accuracy; most costumes were simply contemporary clothing, reflective of the social classes being depicted.

English Actors and Acting Companies

Throughout the English Renaissance, the monarchy exerted considerable legal control over theatre, and the number of acting companies was restricted by law.

Elizabethan acting companies—each of which had approximately twenty-five members—were organized on a **sharing plan**. There were three categories of personnel in a company: *shareholders, hirelings,* and *apprentices.* Shareholders, the elite members of the company, received a percentage of the troupe's profits as payment. Hirelings were actors contracted for a specific period of time and for a specific salary, and they usually played minor roles. Apprentices—young performers training for the profession—were assigned to shareholders. There were no female performers; women's roles were played by boys or men. Since the plays had many characters, doubling of roles was common.

What style of acting was used by the Elizabethans continues to be debated, particularly how realistic it was; that is, how close to the speech and gestures of everyday life. Many of the conventions of the period, such as dramatic verse, seem to suggest a departure from realistic style.

An English company would rarely perform the same play on two consecutive days, and each company had to be able to revive plays on very short notice. Thus the primary concern was not so much a carefully realized production as expert

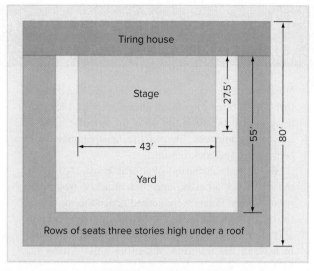

GROUND PLAN OF THE FORTUNE THEATRE
The only English Renaissance theatre for which we have a number of specific dimensions is the Fortune. From the builder's contract we know the size of the stage, the standing pit, the audience seating area, and the theatre building itself. The building was square; the backstage area ran along one side; the stage was rectangular; and the audience—both standing and sitting—was on three sides.

Sharing plan The business organization of Elizabethan acting companies. The elite members of the company, shareholders received a percentage of the troupe's profits.

When we review the history of English Renaissance theatre, we often forget that Shakespeare and his contemporaries had to battle with the popular arts for London's audiences. Two of the most popular were bearbaiting and cockfighting.

Bearbaiting consisted of a bear being chained in the middle of an arena and then attacked by trained mastiff dogs. Points were scored depending on where the dogs struck the bear. The entertainment was probably developed out of the Roman animal entertainments and the tradition of baiting bulls during the Middle Ages.

In the 1500s, bearbaiting became a commercial entertainment in London. Up until 1574, there were two baiting rings in that city. During Shakespeare's time, there was one extremely popular arena: the Bear Garden. The Bear Garden was allowed to present bearbaiting on Sundays, when the theatres were closed. Sunday attendance was so great that in 1583, parts of the building collapsed because of the large number of spectators.

Shakespeare comments on the popularity and theatricality of bearbaiting in his comedy *The Merry Wives of Windsor* (published in 1602). The comedic character Slender comments about how much he loves the sport of bearbaiting and the audience's admiration for the great bear Sackerson:

I love the sport well, but I shall as soon quarrel at it as any man in England. You are afraid if you see the bear loose, are you not? . . . I have seen Sackerson loose twenty times, and have taken him by the chain; but I warrant you, the women have so cried and shrieked at it, that it passed.[1]

This form of entertainment remained popular through the English Restoration and was not made illegal until 1835.

The Cockpit, also known as the Phoenix, was opened in 1609 as an indoor space to house cockfights, another animal entertainment. Spectators would watch and bet on cocks, which were trained to fight with each other. The Cockpit became one of the best-known private, or indoor, theatres in the late English Renaissance after it was remodeled in 1616.

The popularity of cockfighting continued into the eighteenth-century English world. For that matter, the sport was popular in the early American colonies. George Washington, in his diaries, comments on attending cockfights in the new world.

Given the great competition for audiences, it is clear that the stage fights, violence, and slapstick comedy that abound in English Renaissance drama were techniques used to combat the popularity of these other forms of entertainment.

[1]William Shakespeare, *The Merry Wives of Windsor* (1602).

delivery of lines. Actors were provided with *sides,* which contained only their own lines and cues rather than the full script, and improvisation must have been used frequently. *Plots*—outlines of the dramatic action of the various plays—were posted backstage so that performers could refresh their memories during performances. Rehearsals were run by playwrights or leading actors; and since rehearsal time was minimal, the prompter (who stood just offstage) became an indispensable part of the productions.

Theatre after Elizabeth's Reign

After Elizabeth I died in 1603, the great Elizabethan dramatists, including Shakespeare and Ben Jonson (1572–1637), continued to write plays. Ben Jonson's comic masterpiece *Volpone,* for example, was staged in 1606. In contrast to Shakespeare, Jonson championed a more literary approach to drama.

James I succeeded Elizabeth; his reign of England, from 1603 till his death in 1625, is known as the *Jacobean* period. **The Duchess of Malfi** (c. 1613–1614), by John Webster (c. 1580–c. 1630), is probably the most renowned Jacobean

POPULAR ARTS IN SHAKESPEARE'S TIME
Bearbaiting was a popular entertainment during Shakespeare's lifetime. Arenas were constructed for this form of entertainment in which bears were attacked by trained dogs. Remarkably, bearbaiting continued to attract audiences in the early nineteenth century. Shown here is an illustration of bearbaiting in Westminster, London, in the 1820s.
(©Hulton Deutsch/Getty Images)

tragedy. These later tragedies were usually very melodramatic and emphasized violence and spectacle.

Another development in English drama in the early 1600s was a mixing of serious and comic elements. Such plays generally had many of the qualities of tragedy but ended happily. Francis Beaumont (c. 1584–1616) and John Fletcher (1579–1625), two playwrights who often collaborated with each other, excelled at this form.

An elaborate type of entertainment featured at court during the reign of James I and his successor Charles I, and not found in either public or private theatres, was the *masque*. Masques were ornate, professionally staged, mythological allegories intended to praise the monarch; they were embellished by music and dance, and they frequently used amateur performers from the court. In the first decade of the seventeenth century, Inigo Jones (1573–1652), a designer who had studied in Italy, began to introduce the Italian style of theatre architecture and scene design into English court masques.

James I was succeeded by Charles I in 1625; his reign is referred to as the Caroline era. Though Charles I was not deposed—and beheaded—until 1649, the

THE DUCHESS OF MALFI

The most important writer of the Jacobean period was John Webster. His drama *The Duchess of Malfi* is a passionate study of love, incest, and political intrigue in the Renaissance and contains violence, horror, grotesque comedy, and lyrical poetry. Shown here are David Dawson and Gemma Arterton at the Sam Wanamaker Playhouse in London in 2014 in a production directed by Dominic Dromgoole. In the play, two brothers, one of them shown here, persecute the duchess and ultimately murder her and her two children. (©Karwai Tang/WireImage/Getty Images)

English Renaissance ended in 1642. By then, a civil war had begun between supporters of Charles I and the Puritan-backed Parliament. The Puritans were vehemently opposed to theatre; they believed that playgoing was an inappropriate way to spend one's leisure time and that theatre was a den of iniquity, teaching immorality. In 1642, the Puritans outlawed all theatrical activity.

SPAIN

Background: The Spanish Golden Age

The period from about 1550 to 1650 is known as the Spanish Golden Age. During this rich period, Spain, which had a formidable navy, became a leading world power, primarily because of its exploration and conquest of the New World. Spain also remained a devoutly Catholic nation in the face of the Protestant Reformation, which had swept much of the rest of Europe. In order to keep Spain Catholic, the

THEATRE FLOURISHES IN SPAIN'S GOLDEN AGE
During the late sixteenth century and the early seventeenth century, Spain enjoyed an outpouring of masterworks in the arts, as well as accomplishments in many other fields. Among the well-known plays of the period is Calderón's play *Life Is a Dream,* about a king's son who is kept in prison by his father until he comes of age because it is feared he will be too dangerous and unruly. Shown here is a recent production of the play staged by Miracle Theatre at the Trebah Amphitheatre in Cornwall, England. (©G Scammell/Alamy Stock Photo)

church instituted the Inquisition, a type of court that punished any seeming religious heresy. During this period a popular theatre, which incorporated both religious and popular secular forms, flourished.

Spanish Drama

Spain was one of England's chief rivals in the late sixteenth century and the early seventeenth. At the same time that the two nations competed with each other, there were many similarities in their theatres. One important difference, however, is that the Spaniards—unlike the English—adopted the techniques of medieval religious drama and continued to produce religious dramas throughout their golden age and beyond: until 1765, in fact.

Secular drama, which flourished between 1550 and 1700, developed in Spain side by side with religious drama and was created by the same artists. Full-length secular plays, known as *comedias* (koh-MAY-dee-ahs), usually dealt with themes of love and honor; the leading characters were often minor members of the nobility. Comedias were written in three acts, and like English Renaissance plays, they were extensive or episodic in form. Comedias mix serious and comic subject

Comedia Full-length (three-act) nonreligious play of the Spanish Golden Age.

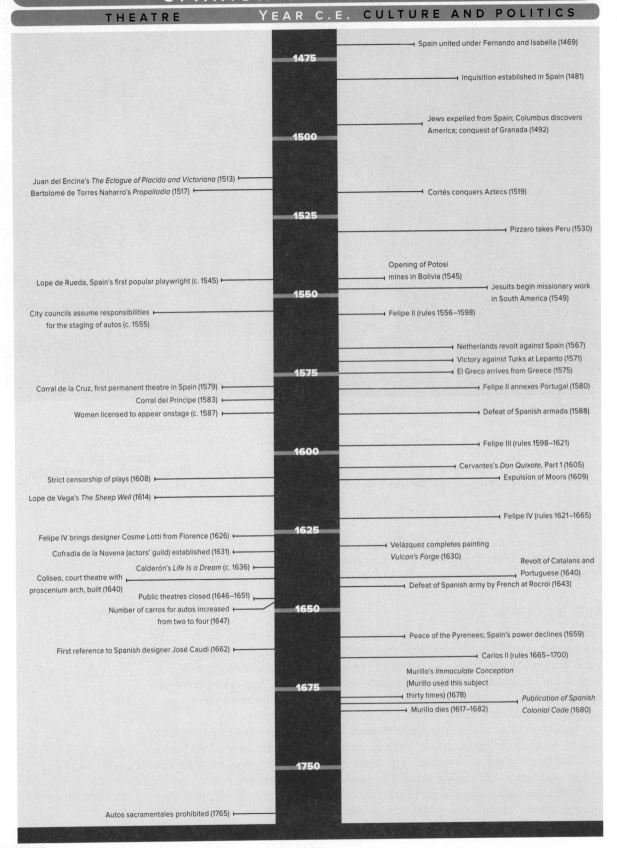

SPANISH GOLDEN AGE

THEATRE	YEAR C.E.	CULTURE AND POLITICS

1475

Spain united under Fernando and Isabella (1469)

Inquisition established in Spain (1481)

Jews expelled from Spain; Columbus discovers America; conquest of Granada (1492)

1500

Juan del Encina's *The Eclogue of Placida and Victoriana* (1513)
Bartolomé de Torres Naharro's *Propalladia* (1517)

Cortés conquers Aztecs (1519)

1525

Pizzaro takes Peru (1530)

Lope de Rueda, Spain's first popular playwright (c. 1545)

Opening of Potosí mines in Bolivia (1545)

Jesuits begin missionary work in South America (1549)

1550

City councils assume responsibilities for the staging of autos (c. 1555)

Felipe II (rules 1556–1598)

Netherlands revolt against Spain (1567)
Victory against Turks at Lepanto (1571)

1575

El Greco arrives from Greece (1575)

Corral de la Cruz, first permanent theatre in Spain (1579)
Corral del Principe (1583)
Women licensed to appear onstage (c. 1587)

Felipe II annexes Portugal (1580)

Defeat of Spanish armada (1588)

1600

Felipe III (rules 1598–1621)

Cervantes's *Don Quixote*, Part 1 (1605)

Strict censorship of plays (1608)

Expulsion of Moors (1609)

Lope de Vega's *The Sheep Well* (1614)

Felipe IV (rules 1621–1665)

1625

Felipe IV brings designer Cosme Lotti from Florence (1626)
Cofradia de la Novena (actors' guild) established (1631)

Velázquez completes painting *Vulcan's Forge* (1630)

Calderón's *Life Is a Dream* (c. 1636)

Revolt of Catalans and Portuguese (1640)

Coliseo, court theatre with proscenium arch, built (1640)

Defeat of Spanish army by French at Rocroi (1643)

Public theatres closed (1646–1651)
Number of carros for autos increased from two to four (1647)

1650

Peace of the Pyrenees; Spain's power declines (1659)

First reference to Spanish designer José Caudi (1662)

Carlos II (rules 1665–1700)

Murillo's *Immaculate Conception* (Murillo used this subject thirty times) (1678)

Murillo dies (1617–1682)

Publication of Spanish Colonial Code (1680)

1675

1750

Autos sacramentales prohibited (1765)

1620, Madrid It is four o'clock on a lovely spring afternoon in 1620. In Spain, a new full-length play by the Spanish playwright Félix Lope de Vega is about to be performed at the Corral del Principe, one of two public theatres in Madrid. The audience has paid two entrance fees, one to the company presenting the play and the second to a charity supporting the city's hospital. The fee to the charity is one reason why government and church officials allow theatre in Madrid.

As the audience gathers inside the corral, there is great excitement about the performance that will soon begin. Those standing in the patio are a bit noisy. Many of the spectators have bought nuts, fruit, and spiced honey from the *alojero* (refreshment stand). People in the pit are jostling for the best vantage point; people in the galleries are exchanging pleasantries, speaking to friends, and looking around the theatre to see who is here this afternoon.

The audience is particularly excited to attend a new play by Lope de Vega. Some years ago, in 1609, Lope argued, in an essay titled "The New Art of Writing Plays in This Age," that the most important measure of success in theatre is the

audience's enjoyment. He has certainly passed his own test for he is the most popular playwright of the day. The play about to be seen, *The King, the Greatest Alcalde,* promises to be filled with thrilling episodes.

Now the performance begins. First, before the actual play, there is a comic prologue. Then comes the play itself. It is a comedia; in Spain, this is the term for any full-length nonreligious play, serious or comic. *The King, the Greatest Alcalde* is serious, but it also has comic elements. It is about a farmer who promises his daughter Elvira to a peasant, Sancho. Sancho seeks approval for the marriage from his lord, Don Tello. Don Tello agrees, but when he sees Elvira, he wants her for himself. He postpones the wedding and kidnaps Elvira. As the play unfolds, it seems to have all the ingredients of a sparkling drama: a clash between peasants and the nobility, a wronged peasant, a kidnapping, a beautiful maiden in distress. The boisterous spectators in the pit are especially vocal in responding to each twist and turn of the plot and to the mixture of comedy and suspense, but the entire audience finds itself caught up in the story.

The actors and actresses in the theatre company play fifteen speaking roles and some nonspeaking parts, and the audience responds enthusiastically to the performances. Though the play has thirteen scenes in different locations, all the action takes place on the platform stage. It is easy to follow the action because—through a combination of dialogue and properties, such as a throne—the playwright and the performers let the spectators know exactly where they are in every scene. The scenes are divided into three acts; during intermissions between the acts, the spectators are also entertained by short comic pieces and musical interludes.

As the play continues, Sancho appeals to the king to help him regain Elvira from Don Tello; after several complications, the king arrives in disguise. When the king discovers that Don Tello has forcibly seduced Elvira, he orders Don Tello to marry her and then has him executed so that Elvira will be honorably widowed and can marry Sancho. At this conclusion, everyone in the audience—in the galleries as well as the pit—is pleased that justice has been done.

matter and are very similar to modern melodrama. Thus if Spanish plays of the golden age are very close to Elizabethan drama in their dramatic form, they seem closer in their subject matter to the swashbuckling films of the 1940s, romantic novels, and television soap operas.

Besides full-length plays, the Spaniards developed many popular, short, farcical forms. A short farce of this kind would be presented on the same program with a comedia.

The major playwrights of this period were Lope de Vega (1562–1635) and Calderón de la Barca (1600–1681). Lope de Vega was born within a year of Shakespeare and was a remarkable playwright—one of the most prolific dramatists of all time. He is said to have written 1,500 plays (although 800 is a more realistic

THE CLASSIC SPANISH STAGE
The corrales were outdoor courtyard theatres used for the presentation of secular drama during the Spanish Golden Age. These playhouses were similar to the public theatres of the English Renaissance. A corral uncovered accidentally in Almagro, Spain, in 1955 is shown here. A theatre festival is staged in this space every year. (Courtesy of the Festival Internacional de Teatro Clásico de Almagro. Photographer: Guillermo Casas)

figure); 470 of them survive, one of the best-known being **The Sheep Well** (c. 1614). One of Calderón's most famous plays is ***Life Is a Dream*** (c. 1636).

There were also a number of female playwrights in Spain during the seventeenth century, though most of their works were not produced. However, recent scholarship has shown that these women wrote texts subverting many of the traditions of the comedias and calling into question the traditional views of gender roles, love and honor, and political authority. Female playwrights of the Spanish Golden Age whose works have received significant scholarly attention are Angela de Azevedo, Ana Caro Mallén de Soto, Leonor de la Cueva y Silva, Feliciana Enríquez de Guzmán, María de Zayas y Sotomayor, and Sor Juana Inés de la Cruz.

Theatre Production in Spain

The Corrales Nonreligious plays by writers like Lope de Vega and Calderón were staged in public theatres known as ***corrales*** (the plural of *corral*). Corrales were constructed in existing courtyards; like Elizabethan public theatres, they were open-air spaces with galleries and boxes protected by a roof. These courtyard theatres were temporary at first but later became permanent spaces. The two most famous were both in Madrid: the Corral de la Cruz (1579) and the Corral del Principe (1583).

Corral Theatre of the Spanish Golden Age, usually located in the courtyard of a series of adjoining buildings.

Part 4 Global Theatres: Past and Present

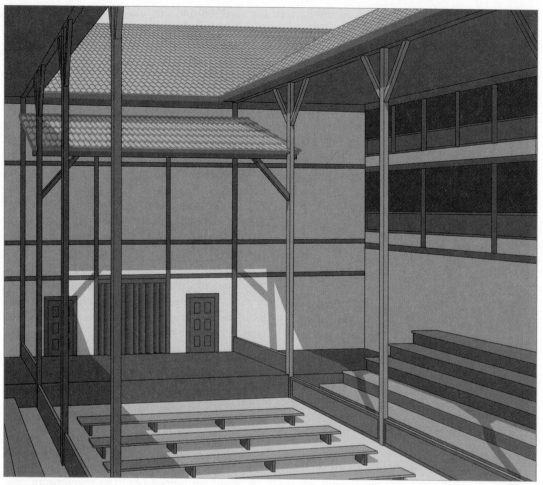

A SPANISH CORRAL
This illustration is based on John J. Allen's research on the Corral del Principe in Madrid. Note the various elements of the corral: the yard (patio), the seating areas (boxes and galleries), and the platform stage with the tiring house behind it. Note also that in front of the yard there were benches or stools and that seats are set up at the side of stage. In addition, notice how similar the face of the building behind the stage was to the facade of the Elizabethan tiring house.

The stage in a corral was a platform erected opposite the entrance to the yard. Access to the yard was usually through a street building; there were also several entranceways for other seating areas. The yard floor or *patio* was primarily an area for standing and, like the pit of an Elizabethan public theatre, was a raucous area. At the front of the yard, near the stage, a row of stools—later, a few benches—were set up, separated from the rest of the yard by a railing.

In the back wall opposite the stage, above the main entranceway in the yard, was a gallery for unaccompanied women known as the ***cazuela*** (cah-zoo-EHL-ah); it had its own separate entrance and was carefully guarded to prevent men from entering. Above the cazuela, there was a row of boxes for local government officials; above these boxes was a larger gallery for the clergy. Along the side walls of the yard were elevated benches and above them windows, protected by grills, from which a play could be viewed. On the next level were boxes that extended out from the buildings around the courtyard. A fourth floor had cramped boxes

Cazuela Gallery above the tavern in the back wall of the theatres of the Spanish Golden Age; the area where unescorted women sat.

with low ceilings. At the back of the yard, on one side of the main entrance, was a refreshments box, the *alojero,* from which food and drinks were sold.

A corral held about 2,000 spectators: 1,000 places for men, 350 for women, and the rest reserved boxes and other accommodations for government officials and the clergy.

Scenic conventions in Spain were similar to those in England. A two-story facade behind the platform stage was the basic scenic construction; a curtain, props, and flats might be used in conjunction with this facade. There were three openings for entrances, exits, and scenes of concealment, as well as an upper playing area. The facade, therefore, served the same function as the Elizabethan tiring house. Spoken dialogue was also used to indicate locale.

Spanish Acting Companies In Spain during the golden age, acting troupes consisted of sixteen to twenty performers. Unlike Elizabethan companies, these Spanish companies included women. In many places on the European continent—in contrast to England—women had been allowed to act in medieval religious drama, and the inclusion of women in Spanish companies during the Renaissance was an outgrowth of this custom. The church, though, did not support the use of female performers; as a result, the Spanish government was forced to impose stringent restrictions on women working in the theatre—for instance, only a woman who was married or otherwise related to an actor in a troupe could be employed. Most Spanish acting troupes were *compañías de partes* (cahm-pa-NYEE-ahs day PAHR-teh)—sharing companies, like those of Elizabethan England. Some companies, however, were organized by a manager who contracted performers for a specific period of time.

FRANCE

Background: France in the Seventeenth Century

Renaissance theatre did not reach its zenith in France until the seventeenth century, later than in Italy, England, or Spain. This was partly due to a religious civil war taking place in France between Catholics and Protestants, a war that was finally brought to an end in 1594 when Henry IV formulated the Edict of Nantes, which offered religious tolerance to Catholics and Protestants. With religious and political stability established in the seventeenth century, French society was able to flourish under Louis XIV, who ruled from 1643 to 1715. Among France's significant accomplishments during this period was exploration of the new world, particularly in Canada and the Louisiana Territory of the United States.

During this period, French society was greatly influenced by the innovations of the Italian Renaissance. As we shall see, French theatre in the seventeenth century adopted and adapted many of the Italian theatrical innovations.

French Neoclassical Drama

The most important seventeenth-century French dramatists were Molière, noted for his comedies; and two authors known for tragedy: Pierre Corneille and Jean Racine.

Among all the French neoclassical playwrights, the one who exerts the most influence on modern theatre is Molière (Jean-Baptiste Poquelin; 1622–1673). Molière was not only a dramatist but also an actor and the leader of a theatrical troupe. His first theatre venture in Paris was a failure, and so he

LE BOURGEOIS GENTILHOMME

One of Molière's most popular works is *Le Bourgeois Gentilhomme (The Bourgeois Gentleman)* about a self-important man who puts on airs, attempting to move into the upper class. He takes lessons of all kinds—dancing, fencing, reading—but in each case makes a fool of himself without realizing it. Shown here is a scene from the play as staged by the Theatre National de Nice. (©SYSPEO/SIPA/Newscom)

toured the provinces for twelve years, learning firsthand the techniques of theatre and perfecting his craft as a dramatist. He then returned to establish himself as France's leading actor-manager and playwright, specializing in comedies of character.

Molière's work was strongly influenced by Italian commedia dell'arte. In plays like **Tartuffe** (1664), **The Misanthrope** (1666), **The Miser** (1668), and **The Imaginary Invalid** (1673), he creates exaggerated character types and makes fun of their eccentricities. The title character in *The Miser,* for example, is a man so greedy and so possessive of his money that he becomes paranoid when he thinks anyone knows where he has hidden it; in protecting his treasure, he even turns against his children. Molière was a master of slapstick as well as more subtle kinds of comedy, and he frequently used a *deus ex machina* to resolve his contrived plots.

Pierre Corneille (1606–1684) began his career writing comedies but soon turned to tragedy. His play **The Cid**, which opened in 1636, became a huge success. It aroused opposition from intellectuals because it did not follow the neoclassic rules established by Italian critics; despite this, it remained enormously popular and was presented frequently not only in France but in other European countries. Corneille, however, stopped writing plays for four years.

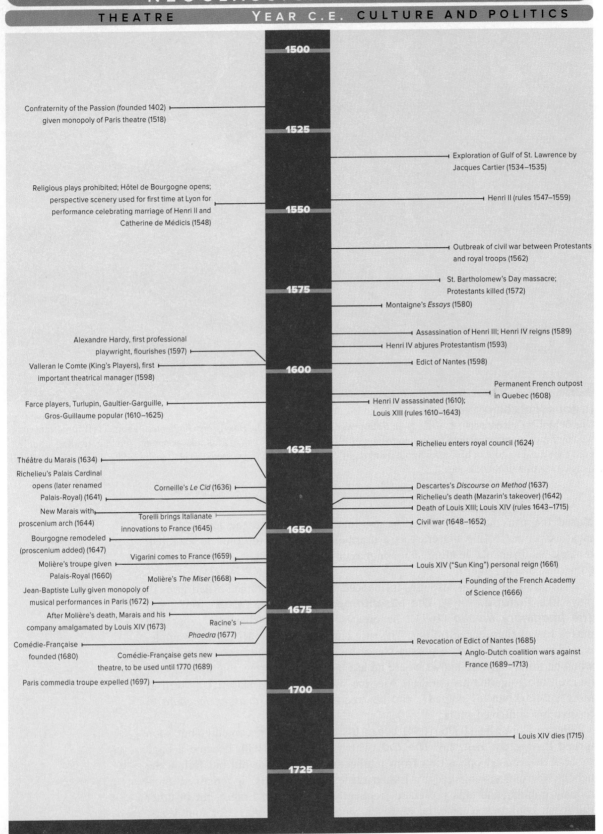

1500

Confraternity of the Passion (founded 1402) given monopoly of Paris theatre (1518)

1525

Exploration of Gulf of St. Lawrence by Jacques Cartier (1534–1535)

Religious plays prohibited; Hôtel de Bourgogne opens; perspective scenery used for first time at Lyon for performance celebrating marriage of Henri II and Catherine de Médicis (1548)

Henri II (rules 1547–1559)

1550

Outbreak of civil war between Protestants and royal troops (1562)

1575

St. Bartholomew's Day massacre; Protestants killed (1572)

Montaigne's *Essays* (1580)

Alexandre Hardy, first professional playwright, flourishes (1597)

Assassination of Henri III; Henri IV reigns (1589)

Henri IV abjures Protestantism (1593)

Valleran le Comte (King's Players), first important theatrical manager (1598)

Edict of Nantes (1598)

1600

Permanent French outpost in Quebec (1608)

Farce players, Turlupin, Gaultier-Garguille, Gros-Guillaume popular (1610–1625)

Henri IV assassinated (1610); Louis XIII (rules 1610–1643)

Richelieu enters royal council (1624)

1625

Théâtre du Marais (1634)

Richelieu's Palais Cardinal opens (later renamed Palais-Royal) (1641)

Corneille's *Le Cid* (1636)

Descartes's *Discourse on Method* (1637)

Richelieu's death (Mazarin's takeover) (1642)

New Marais with proscenium arch (1644)

Death of Louis XIII; Louis XIV (rules 1643–1715)

Torelli brings Italianate innovations to France (1645)

Civil war (1648–1652)

Bourgogne remodeled (proscenium added) (1647)

1650

Vigarini comes to France (1659)

Molière's troupe given Palais-Royal (1660)

Louis XIV ("Sun King") personal reign (1661)

Molière's *The Miser* (1668)

Founding of the French Academy of Science (1666)

Jean-Baptiste Lully given monopoly of musical performances in Paris (1672)

After Molière's death, Marais and his company amalgamated by Louis XIV (1673)

Racine's *Phaedra* (1677)

1675

Comédie-Française founded (1680)

Revocation of Edict of Nantes (1685)

Comédie-Française gets new theatre, to be used until 1770 (1689)

Anglo-Dutch coalition wars against France (1689–1713)

Paris commedia troupe expelled (1697)

1700

Louis XIV dies (1715)

1725

Because of the controversy, when he resumed playwriting, he adhered more closely to the neoclassical rules.

Jean Racine (1639–1699) was the other great writer of tragedy in seventeenth-century France. Unlike Corneille, he was comfortable with the neoclassic rules from the start; all of Racine's tragedies adhere to these rules.

One of Racine's best-known tragedies, **Phaedra** (1677), is based on a play by Euripides. In Racine's version, Phaedra, queen to King Theseus, falls in love with her stepson, Hippolytus. Upon hearing that Theseus has died, she admits her love to Hippolytus, who reacts with disgust. When Phaedra discovers that Theseus is not dead, she allows her maid to spread the rumor that it was Hippolytus who made amorous advances to Phaedra, rather than the other way around. Hearing the rumor and believing it, Theseus invokes a god to kill his son Hippolytus, after which a heartbroken Phaedra takes poison—before she dies, however, she reveals the truth.

Racine's *Phaedra* is a perfect example of climactic plot structure: It has only a few characters, and the action takes place in one place at one time. Furthermore, Racine's masterful handling of poetry and emotion established a model to be followed in France for the next three centuries.

Theatre Production in France

The French were probably the first Europeans after the Romans to construct a permanent theatre building. This was the Hôtel de Bourgogne, completed in 1548. The Bourgogne was built by the Confraternity of the Passion, a religious order that had been granted a monopoly for the presentation of religious drama in Paris. When religious drama was outlawed—in the same year that the Bourgogne was completed—the Confraternity rented its space to touring companies.

The Hôtel de Bourgogne, a long, narrow building with a platform stage at one end, was

PHAEDRA

Racine's *Phèdre* (also known as *Phaedra* in other translations) is probably the best-known neoclassical tragedy. It is the story of a queen who falls in love with her stepson, with the result that everyone involved—including these two, as well as Phaedra's husband—meets a tragic end. Shown here is Helen Mirren, in the title role, with Dominic Cooper as her stepson, Hippolytus, in a version by Ted Hughes directed by Nicholas Hytner at London's National Theatre. (©Geraint Lewis)

the sole permanent indoor theatre building in Paris for nearly a century until the Théâtre du Marais opened in 1634. The Marais was a converted indoor tennis court. Such indoor courts were long and narrow—like the Bourgogne—and had galleries for spectators (court tennis was a popular sport); thus they could be transformed into theatres very easily.

1669, Paris The date is February 9, 1669. At the Palais-Royal theatre in Paris, France, spectators are eagerly awaiting a performance of *Tartuffe*, written by France's best-known comic playwright and actor, Molière.

Tartuffe has already been the cause of an enormous controversy. Molière first read it four years ago to King Louis XIV at his palace at Versailles; the king liked it, but before it could be presented publicly, it provoked an uproar. The reason is its subject matter. The title character of the play, Tartuffe, is a religious hypocrite. He pretends to be very pious and wears clothing that looks like a religious habit, but he is actually interested in acquiring money and seducing women. He has come to live in the house of Orgon, a wealthy man who has been completely taken in by Tartuffe's false piety.

The people who oppose the presentation of *Tartuffe* include a number of religious figures (one of them is the archbishop of Paris) who say that it is an attack on religion. Molière, however, insists that his play is not an attack on religion but rather an attack on people who hide behind religion and exploit it.

The audience is aware that until now the opposition has been successful in keeping *Tartuffe* out of theatres; the king did not dare authorize its presentation as long as the forces against it were so strong. So far, the play has been presented only once, in the summer of 1667, and then for only one night. The king was out of the country at that time, and in his absence the religious authorities had it closed down. Now, however, *Tartuffe* has finally been given royal approval, and today's performance is to be its official public unveiling.

The Palais-Royal theatre, where Molière's troupe performs, is a rectangular space with a stage at one end and galleries on three sides around it. It accommodates almost 1,500 people: 300 stand in a "pit" in front of the stage, about 700 sit in a raised amphitheatre behind the pit, about 330 sit in the galleries, 70 stand at the very back, and 50 wealthy nobles sit on the sides of the stage itself. Having spectators onstage is customary in French theatres but makes things very difficult for the performers.

The stage is fitted with wings and shutters, like Italian Renaissance theatres, and scenery can be changed with a pole-and-chariot system. For *Tartuffe*, however, there will be no scene changes: The entire action takes place in the drawing room of Orgon's house.

Well aware of all the scandal and debate, the audience feels a rush of anticipation as this performance of *Tartuffe* begins. Once it is under way, though, the spectators realize that the controversial figure of Tartuffe does not even make an appearance for two full acts. Rather, it is the figure of Orgon, played by Molière himself, on whom they first concentrate. The spectators see that Orgon is thoroughly duped and pays no attention to the members of his family when they tell him how dishonest and disreputable Tartuffe is.

Finally, in the third act, Tartuffe makes his entrance. He is challenged by Orgon's family, but Orgon remains loyal to him. Only when Orgon learns for himself the awful truth about Tartuffe does he realize his error. This occurs in a scene in which Orgon, hiding under a table, hears Tartuffe try to seduce his wife. The wife has led Tartuffe on, and he exposes himself as a genuine scoundrel. As the audience members watch the scene, they think it is one of the funniest they have ever seen.

Orgon's discovery of Tartuffe's true nature seems to come too late: At this point, Orgon has already handed his house and his fortune over to Tartuffe, disinheriting his own children. At the end of the play, though, the king intervenes. This is the same Louis XIV who in real life has intervened on Molière's behalf so that the play can be presented.

A few weeks from now, both king and playwright will be vindicated: *Tartuffe* will be performed twenty-eight times in a row—an unprecedented number—and will show every sign of becoming a classic comedy.

The Italian influence on French theatre architecture became evident in 1641, when Cardinal Richelieu, a leading political figure, erected the Palais Cardinal, renamed the Palais-Royal after his death. This is the theatre that Molière's troupe eventually used. The Palais Cardinal was the first proscenium-arch theatre in

France and also had Italian-style machinery to shift scenery. Following the construction of Richelieu's theatre, the Théâtre du Marais and the Hôtel de Bourgogne were remodeled in the 1640s into proscenium-arch theatres. Painted-perspective wing-and-shutter scenery—shifted by the pole-and-chariot system—was used in the two remodeled theatres.

Early French proscenium-arch theatre buildings differed slightly from those of the Italian Renaissance; in the back wall opposite the stage was an *amphithéâtre*, an undivided gallery with inexpensive bleacherlike seating. In both the Marais and the Bourgogne, there was probably a small upper stage, raised thirteen feet above the main stage and used for special effects such as flying. At the close of the seventeenth century, upper-class audience members were frequently seated onstage.

In the 1650s, Louis XIV's interest in ballet brought this form of entertainment back into prominence at court. To satisfy the royal taste for elaborate ballets and to prepare for Louis's marriage, a new court theatre was built, known as the Salle des Machines ("Hall of Machines"). It was completed in 1660 and was the largest playhouse in Europe: 52 feet wide and 232 feet long. The auditorium took up only 92 feet of the 232-foot length, leaving 140 feet for the stage and its machinery. The backstage equipment included one piece of machinery on which the entire royal family and all their attendants—more than 100 people—could be "flown" into the space above the stage. Because of its unsatisfactory acoustics, its size (especially backstage), and the expense of producing spectacles, the Salle des Machines was rarely used after 1670.

Another major theatre building of the French neoclassical period was the Comédie-Française, which housed the national theatre. The French national theatre had been founded by Louis XIV in 1680, but the company did not move into

Amphithéâtre An undivided gallery with inexpensive bleacherlike seating in the back wall at the French neoclassical theatre.

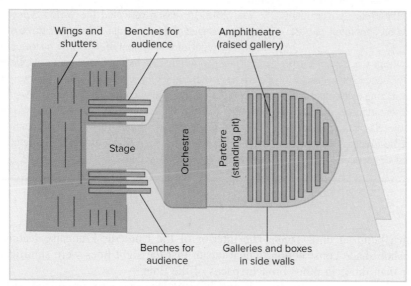

Wings and shutters

Benches for audience

Amphitheatre (raised gallery)

Stage

Orchestra

Parterre (standing pit)

Benches for audience

Galleries and boxes in side walls

GROUND PLAN OF THE COMÉDIE-FRANÇAISE
The French national theatre company performed in this playhouse for eighty-one years, beginning in 1689. The theatre had a proscenium-arch stage with machinery for scene shifts, and a horseshoe-shaped auditorium for improved sight lines. The parterre was where audience members stood; the amphitheatre contained bleacherlike seating.

IN FOCUS: COMÉDIE-FRANÇAISE'S LONG HISTORY

As noted, the Comédie-Française has had a long history that continues into the present. Today, the French national theatre has over 3,000 dramas in its repertoire and performs in three different spaces in Paris: the theatre at the Palais Royal, which was opened in 1799, renovated and made larger in the nineteenth-century, and rebuilt in 1900 following a fire; the Théâtre du Vieux-Colombier (founded in 1913 by the French director Jacques Copeau, who is discussed later), and Studio-Théâtre.

The history of the Comédie-Française since its inception has been, at times, tumultuous. During the French Revolution the company broke into opposing groups: those who supported the monarchy and those who wanted a republic. Many of the actors were imprisoned. By 1799, the company was reunited.

Under Napoleon, the company signed new agreements outlining its relationship with the government. In 1830, the company saw a riot due to the presentation at the Comédie-Française of the romantic play *Hernani* by Victor Hugo, which broke from the theatre's classical traditions. By the mid-nineteenth century, the Comédie-Française's repertoire was again primarily classical works. Also, in 1860, the French government began determining who was to be appointed the theatre's chief administrator.

The twentieth century saw both the expansion of the theatre into additional performance spaces as well an ongoing debate over modern staging techniques and, particularly after 1968, the presentation of more contemporary drama along with the classical repertoire. From 1946 to 1960, the Comédie-Française operated the Odeón Theatre, which had opened originally in 1792. In 1990, a renovated Théâtre du Vieux-Colombier became part of the national theatre and its Studio-Théâtre opened in 1996 in order to support more contemporary work. In addition, since the 1960s, the Comédie-Française has been administered by actors chosen from within the permanent company or respected figures from the French theatre, including from outside of Paris.

In 2013, the Comédie Française space at the Palais-Royal was reopened after a year of renovation. The theatre today seats 800 audience members. (The chair in which Moliére died on stage remains in the theatre.) Visitors to the theatre can see statues of the famous actresses Mademoiselle Mars (1779–1847) and Rachel (1821–1858) as well as the playwrights Moliére, Racine, and Beaumarchais.

The company, still organized as it originally was under the sharing plan for actors, presently has 450 employees, including 62 *sociétaires*, who are the shareholders in the company and selected from the *pensionnaires*, performers who are paid a salary. The Ministry of Culture appoints the theatre's chief administrator.

The 2015–16 season reflected the varied types of plays now staged at the Comédie-Française's three theatres. The repertoire consisted of works by historically important playwrights, including Shakespeare, Molière, Marivaux, the eighteenth-century Italian playwright Carlo Goldoni, the nineteenth-century realist August Strindberg, the twentieth-century Spanish playwright Federico Garcia Lorca, and the twentieth-century British playwright Edward Bond, as well as more contemporary French playwrights.

its own building until 1689. The interior of the Comédie-Française featured a horseshoe-shape construction, which meant that the sight lines were significantly better than those in other French spaces of the time.

Acting companies in French neoclassical theatres were organized under a sharing plan and had women members who could become shareholders. Rehearsals were supervised by the playwright or a leading performer or both, but troupes spent little time on rehearsals. Once a play was introduced, the troupe was expected to be able to revive it at a moment's notice, and the bill at theatres was changed daily.

1. Describe the physical theatre spaces (stage configuration, scenery, audience seating) employed in each of the following eras: (a) the Italian Renaissance; (b) the English Renaissance; (c) the Spanish Golden Age; (d) the French neoclassical. What are the advantages and disadvantages of each type?

2. Describe the type of drama featured (the structure and content of dramatic scripts) in each of the eras mentioned in the first item above.

3. While Shakespeare's plays are considered to be classics, identify at least three similarities between his works and popular contemporary film and television.

4. Molière authored comedies that focused on exaggerated comic types and their eccentricities. Identify and describe at least three examples of popular films and television shows that also focus on these types of characters and their eccentric behavior.

SUMMARY

1. During the Italian Renaissance, the neoclassical rules for drama were formulated.

2. Commedia dell'arte developed as a popular theatre, based on stock characters, repeated pieces of comic business, and recognizable characters.

3. Painted perspective scenery, which could be changed easily, and the proscenium arch theatre were both introduced, leading to greater verisimilitude—the quality of being true to life—in theatre.

4. During the English Renaissance, the great plays of Shakespeare and his contemporaries were staged.

5. Outdoor public and indoor private theatres accommodated these episodic-form dramas through the use of an unlocalized platform stage and a flexible tiring—or stage—house. Poetic language also set the action.

6. In Spain during its golden age, the secular dramas of Lope de Vega and Calderón de la Barca were performed in corrales, theatres built in courtyards.

7. Corrales used many of the same staging conventions as Elizabethan theatres.

8. In French neoclassical theatre, the tragic dramas of Corneille and Racine and the comedies of character by Molière were clearly patterned after traditions established in the Italian Renaissance.

9. French theatre architecture and design were also based on Italian models.

Design elements: Playing Your Part box (theatre seats): ©McGraw-Hill Education; In Focus box (spotlight): ©d_gas/Getty Images

THEATRES FROM THE RESTORATION THROUGH ROMANTICISM

The period from 1660 to 1875 saw radical transformations in Western society. Revolutions and nationalism led to changes in governments and the establishment of new nations. Mechanization and new technology transformed work, the workplace, and economic classes. Innovations in modes of transportation made travel easier, both within nations and internationally. Theatre mirrored the social, political, and economic issues of the times, and it too was transformed. In this chapter, we will examine the theatre of England in the late seventeenth century as well as developments in global theatre in the eighteenth and nineteenth centuries.

THE ENGLISH RESTORATION

Background: England in the Seventeenth Century

After a bitter civil war lasting from 1642 to 1649, Charles I of England was removed from the throne by the Puritans and beheaded. For the next eleven years, England was a Commonwealth eventually governed by Oliver Cromwell with a Parliament that had been purged of all his opponents.

◀ **EIGHTEENTH-CENTURY ENGLISH COMEDY**

She Stoops to Conquer, by playwright Oliver Goldsmith, is an example of eighteenth-century comedy of manners in which audiences were made to laugh at their own foibles, excesses, and eccentricities. Shown here are Katherine Kelly as Kate Hardcastle and Steve Pemberton as Mr. Hardcastle in a recent production of the play at London's National Theatre directed by Jamie Lloyd. (©Nigel Norrington/Camera Press/Redux)

When Cromwell died in 1658, his son was unable to keep control of the government; and in 1660 Charles II, who had been living in exile in France, was invited by a newly elected Parliament to return and rule England. The monarchy was thus restored, and this period in English history—usually dated from 1660 through 1700—is therefore called the *Restoration.*

During the period of the Commonwealth, many members of the English nobility had been exiles in France; when the English monarchy returned, these people took back with them the theatrical practices they had seen in France.

Restoration Drama: Comedies of Manners

The theatres that reopened in England represented a fusion of Elizabethan, Italian, and French stage conventions. This gave a unique flavor to every aspect of Restoration theatre: texts, theatre buildings, and set designs.

Comedies of manners
Form of comic drama satirizing social conventions that became popular in seventeenth-century France and the English Restoration, and which emphasized a cultivated or sophisticated atmosphere and witty dialogue.

The best-known Restoration comedies, many of which were influenced by the French dramatist Molière, are referred to as **comedies of manners**. They poked fun at the social conventions of the upper class of the time and satirized the preoccupation of English aristocrats with reputation: Most of the upper-class characters in these plays are disreputable. Emphasizing witty dialogue and filled with sexual intrigue and innuendo, the plays took an amoral attitude toward human behavior, including sex. Audiences consisted primarily of members of the nobility and the upper class, the same people whom the playwrights were satirizing.

In their dramatic structure, Restoration comedies combine features of Elizabethan theatre and the neoclassical theatre of Italy and France. For example, in **The Country Wife** by William Wycherley (1640–1715), the action is far more unified than in a Shakespearean play, with fewer scene shifts. But it does move from place to place, involves many characters, and even has a subplot. The characters in Wycherley's play are stock types with names that usually describe their distinctive personality traits. Fidget and Squeamish are nervous about their reputations; Pinchwife is a man who doesn't want his wife pinched by other men; and Sparkish is a fop who mistakenly believes himself to be a real "spark," witty and fashionable.

Other types of Restoration comedies included *comedies of humors* and *comedies of intrigue*. Comedies of humors followed the tradition of Ben Jonson in which characters have one trait overshadowing all others. Comedies of intrigue featured daring exploits of romance and adventure and had complicated plots. One of the most successful writers of this type of comedy was a woman, Aphra Behn (1640–1689), whose most famous play is **The Rover** (1677).

Another well-known comic playwright of the Restoration is William Congreve (1670–1729). Congreve's **The Way of the World** (1700) is often considered a bridge between Restoration comedy and the later, more traditional morality of eighteenth-century English sentimental comedy. In eighteenth-century English comedy, as we will see, the sinful are punished and the virtuous are rewarded. Like Restoration comedy, *The Way of the World* has a number of characters involved in adulterous affairs, as well as the traditional stock characters; but its two young lovers, Mirabell and Millamant, are united, while the wicked characters, Fainall and Marwood, are punished.

Following the lead of Aphra Behn, female playwrights emerged at this time. The London season of 1695–1696 saw productions by seven female dramatists. Three women, known as the "female wits," were active in the period that marked

Part 4   Global Theatres: Past and Present

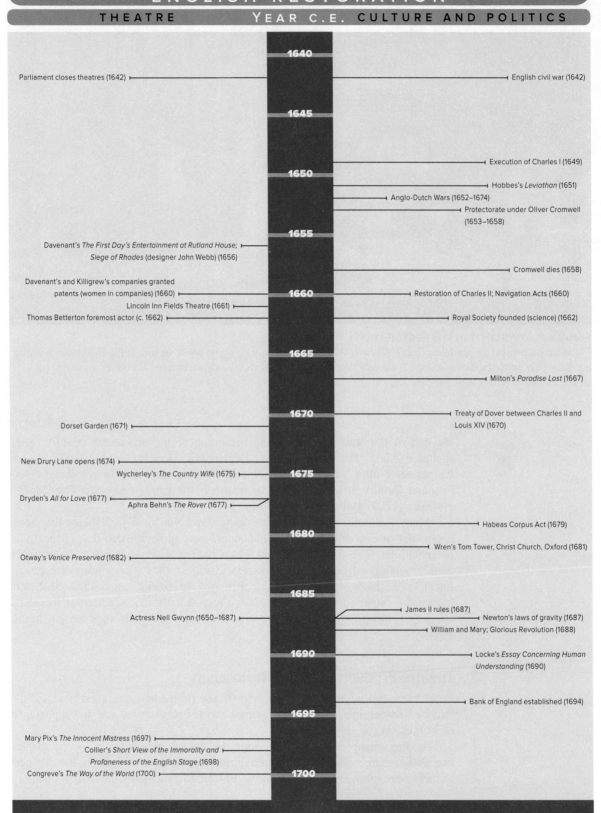

ENGLISH RESTORATION

| THEATRE | YEAR C.E. | CULTURE AND POLITICS |

1640

Parliament closes theatres (1642) ⊢ — English civil war (1642)

1645

— Execution of Charles I (1649)

1650

— Hobbes's *Leviathan* (1651)

Anglo-Dutch Wars (1652–1674)

Protectorate under Oliver Cromwell (1653–1658)

1655

Davenant's *The First Day's Entertainment at Rutland House; Siege of Rhodes* (designer John Webb) (1656)

— Cromwell dies (1658)

Davenant's and Killigrew's companies granted patents (women in companies) (1660)

1660 — Restoration of Charles II; Navigation Acts (1660)

Lincoln Inn Fields Theatre (1661)

Thomas Betterton foremost actor (c. 1662)

— Royal Society founded (science) (1662)

1665

— Milton's *Paradise Lost* (1667)

1670 — Treaty of Dover between Charles II and Louis XIV (1670)

Dorset Garden (1671)

New Drury Lane opens (1674)

Wycherley's *The Country Wife* (1675) **1675**

Dryden's *All for Love* (1677)

Aphra Behn's *The Rover* (1677)

— Habeas Corpus Act (1679)

1680

Otway's *Venice Preserved* (1682)

— Wren's Tom Tower, Christ Church, Oxford (1681)

1685

— James II rules (1687)

Actress Nell Gwynn (1650–1687)

— Newton's laws of gravity (1687)

— William and Mary; Glorious Revolution (1688)

1690 — Locke's *Essay Concerning Human Understanding* (1690)

— Bank of England established (1694)

1695

Mary Pix's *The Innocent Mistress* (1697)

Collier's *Short View of the Immorality and Profaneness of the English Stage* (1698)

Congreve's *The Way of the World* (1700) **1700**

FEMALE PLAYWRIGHTS IN THE RESTORATION

There were a number of significant female playwrights during the Restoration. Among them was Aphra Behn, whose works are frequently revived today. Seen here is a production of her most famous comedy of intrigue, *The Rover,* as staged at Illinois State University. (©Peter Guither)

the end of the Restoration and the beginning of the eighteenth century. They included Mary Pix (1666–1706), Delarivière Manley (c. 1663–1724), and Catherine Trotter (1679–1749). Another transitional female playwright was Susanna Centlivre, (c. 1667–1723), whose best-known works are **The Stolen Heiress** (1702) and **The Busy Body** (1709).

Many Restoration comedies, including *The Country Wife,* indicate that audiences of that era, unlike today's audiences, were quite spirited during theatrical presentations. The fop Sparkish in *The Country Wife* describes how audience members bought fruit from the "orange wenches" (some of whom were prostitutes), spoke back to the performers, arranged assignations, and attended theatre to be seen rather than to see the play. These extratheatrical activities increased attacks on theatre by religious leaders, who were generally opposed to theatre anyway.

Theatre Production in the Restoration

Performers and Acting Companies   In theatre production, the most obvious difference between the English Renaissance and the Restoration was the appearance of women on the English stage.

Another change was that in London the sharing plan followed by companies like Shakespeare's almost disappeared during the Restoration. Instead, London performers were hired for a specific period of time at a set salary. In order to increase

RESTORATION DRAMA: COMEDIES OF MANNERS
During the period of the English Restoration, beginning in 1660, the most popular plays were comedies that satirized the upper classes—their gossip, emphasis on dress and decorum, infidelity, sexuality, and conspiracies. In the scene here from William Congreve's *The Way of the World,* Claire Price plays Mrs. Millamant and J. Stone-Fewings plays Mirabell in a production directed by Rachel Kavanaugh at the Chichester Festival. Restoration comedy of manners put a premium on language (including sexual double meanings). (©Nigel Norrington/Camera Press/Redux)

the set wage, an actor or actress was provided with a yearly *benefit,* a performance of a play from which he or she kept all the profits. The benefit system was used in English theatre from the Restoration through the nineteenth century.

The Restoration also saw the emergence of theatrical entrepreneurs who were often part owners of theatre buildings and companies. The rise of the entrepreneur as a powerful theatrical force was, of course, a step in the development of modern theatre business with its independent theatre owners and producers.

Government and Theatre   When English theatre was restored in 1660, Charles II issued patents to two entrepreneurs, William Davenant and Thomas Killigrew (1612–1683), which in effect gave them a monopoly on presenting theatre in London.

By the early eighteenth century, this monopoly would become unenforceable, however; and in 1737 Parliament was to pass the Licensing Act, a new attempt to regulate London theatre. Under this act, only two theatres—Drury Lane and Covent Garden—were authorized to present drama for "gain, hire, or reward," and the lord chamberlain became responsible for licensing plays.

Theatre Architecture   During the Restoration, there were three theatres of note in London: Drury Lane (1663); Lincoln Inn Fields (1661), a converted tennis court; and Dorset Garden (1671). Though the interiors of these theatres were distinct, all three showed a unique fusion of Italian and Elizabethan features.

All Restoration theatres were indoor proscenium-arch buildings. The area for the audience was divided into pit, boxes, and galleries and had a total seating capacity of about 650. The pit, which had backless benches to accommodate spectators, was raked—or slanted—for better sight lines.

DRURY LANE THEATRE
This reconstruction of the Drury Lane Theatre in the Restoration period shows Christopher Wren's design for the Theatre Royal, Drury Lane, 1674. Note the pit for the audience and the two doors on each side of the stage. (From Richard Leacroft, in *The Theatre,* Methuen & Co., 1958. p. 34)

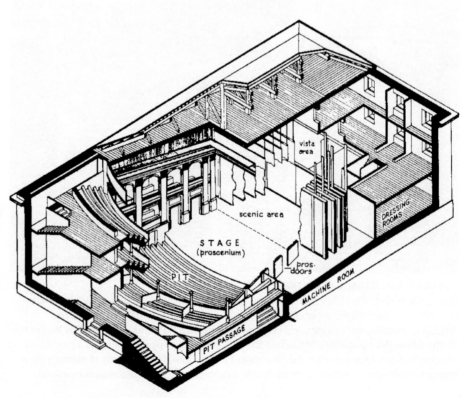

The origins of the Drury Lane Theatre—a theatre that still exists in London today—go back to the patent Charles II granted to Thomas Killigrew in 1662 early in the Restoration. The first Drury Lane was built in 1663. After being rebuilt a number of times in the eighteenth century, often due to fires, Drury Lane was again rebuilt in 1812. This is the theatre that continues to house productions today and has had a significant history over the last century.

Drury Lane, from the mid-twentieth century till today, houses large-scale musicals. For example, the original London productions of *Oklahoma*, *My Fair Lady*, and *Miss Saigon* premiered here. The renowned British musical theatre composer Andrew Lloyd Weber, who in 2013 undertook a renovation of the theatre's public spaces in order to restore them to the original architectural style, currently owns the theatre.

Today's Drury Lane Theatre is on the same site as the original playhouse built during the Restoration and is the oldest site in London to continuously house a theatre. Drury Lane is said to have a ghost: an eighteenth-century gentleman in cloak and riding boots who appears in the upper circle only at matinees when the house is full.

The Restoration stage was highly unusual in that it was divided into two equal halves by the proscenium arch. In the seventeenth century, only English theatres had this extended apron, and most historians believe that it was a vestige of the Elizabethan platform stage. The deep apron was a major performance area in Restoration theatres; the upstage area housed the scenery. The entire stage was raked to improve the spectators' sight lines.

Another unique element of the Restoration stage was the proscenium doors, with balconies above them. On each side of the stage there were two proscenium doors leading onto the forestage. These doors were used for exits and entrances and for concealment scenes—scenes in which one character listens from out of sight, a popular device in Restoration comedy. The balconies above these doorways could be used for balcony and window scenes.

Scenery, Lighting, and Costumes   Restoration scenery and lighting also illustrate a fusion of Italian and English stage practices. The basic scenic components were wings, shutters, which were sometimes replaced by rolled backdrops, and borders for masking. The English rarely used the pole-and-chariot system for scene changes; instead, they used the groove system. Throughout the Restoration, companies kept collections of stock sets, painted in perspective; these were reused frequently, partly because it was expensive to have new scenery painted.

Because Restoration theatres were indoors, lighting was a major concern. During the late seventeenth century, theatre performances were normally given in the afternoon so that the windows could provide some natural lighting. Candles were the source of artificial light; these were placed in chandeliers above the stage and the audience, and also in brackets attached to the fronts of the boxes. The stage and audience area were always lit, and footlights—candles on the floor along the front of the stage—were also used.

Restoration costuming followed the traditions of the English Renaissance and the French neoclassical era: Contemporary clothing was used rather than historically accurate costuming.

1675, London, England

It is a raw, overcast day in January 1675, and two young men—members of the nobility—have set forth to the theatre in London. They are making their way to the new Drury Lane Theatre. Another theatre once stood at the site of the Drury Lane, but it burned in 1672; the new theatre, designed by the architect Christopher Wren and erected on the same spot, opened only a year ago, in 1674.

The play they will see is a new one by William Wycherley called *The Country Wife*. They anticipate that they will hear witty, rapier-like exchanges between the characters, and doubtless many double entendres: clever lines that operate on two levels, one ordinary and the other decidedly sexual.

It is just after two o'clock in the afternoon. The play will not begin until 3:30, but the young men want to arrive at the theatre early—to talk to their acquaintances, to flirt with the attractive young women who sell oranges and other things to eat, and even to go backstage to try to see the actresses. As they arrive at the playhouse, the young men join a carefree, pleasure-loving crowd.

The new Drury Lane—a building 58 feet wide by 140 feet long—seats 650 people, some in a pit facing the stage, others in boxes and galleries along the sides and back. Its stage is a platform about 34 feet deep; the front half of the stage is open, and the back half—framed by a proscenium—contains the scenic elements.

When the performance begins, the first person onstage is an actor named Charles Hart, who delivers a prologue; then the play itself starts. Hart plays a character called Horner, who spreads the rumor that he has been rendered impotent by a venereal disease he contracted while abroad. Horner's doctor, Quack, substantiates the rumor, and Horner uses this "cover story" to gain access to his acquaintances' wives; because of his supposed condition, the husbands will regard him as no threat. The wife he most desires is Margery Pinchwife, a naive woman whose husband usually keeps her locked away in the country and tries to disguise her as a boy when they are in town. Coming upon Pinchwife and the disguised Margery in the street, Horner realizes that the "boy" is a woman in a man's clothing and takes advantage of the situation to make amorous advances, hugging and kissing her in front of her husband, who can do nothing. During the course of the dramatic action, a subplot develops: Horner's friend Harcourt steals Pinchwife's sister Alithea away from her intended husband, Sparkish.

The young male spectators are particularly taken with Elizabeth Bowtell, who plays Margery. In France and Spain, women have appeared onstage for some time; but England forbade actresses until 1660—only a few years ago—and seeing them now is a novelty that strongly appeals to the men in the audience. Moreover, ever since women have been allowed to perform onstage in England, a favorite dramatic device is to have a woman dress as a man; parts that require this kind of cross-dressing are called *breeches roles*. Seeing a woman's legs—which are usually hidden under wide skirts—has a strong sexual fascination.

The audience is also titillated by the sexual references, especially by a scene which is to become famous—the "china closet" scene. In this scene, Horner and Lady Fidget are in a room offstage while Lady Fidget's husband is onstage listening to their conversation. Horner and Lady Fidget are supposed to be examining Horner's collection of china, but the audience soon realizes that though Horner is speaking about china, he is actually making love to Lady Fidget while her husband stands by in ignorance. Then another woman, Mrs. Squeamish, arrives, and she too asks to see Horner's china. When Horner tells Mrs. Squeamish he has no more, the audience knows that china has become a code word for sex and that Horner is unable at that moment to make love.

At the conclusion of the play, Horner's scheme has been successful: He has made love not only to Margery but to the other wives as well.

THE EIGHTEENTH CENTURY

Background: A More Complex World

Throughout Europe, the eighteenth century was a time of transition. As the world was slowly transformed into a global community, homogeneous, self-contained societies began to disappear. Increased manufacturing and international trade affected populations worldwide. The major eighteenth-century mercantile powers were England and France, and decisions made in these two nations directly affected people in such places as North America, India, and Africa. One effect on Africa was a marked increase in the slave trade.

Because of the growth in trade, western Europe prospered more than ever before. Profits from colonial trade filtered down to the emerging middle class, which included merchants and others in commercial enterprises and which now became a social as well as a political force.

There were so many new developments in learning and philosophy that the eighteenth century is called the *Age of Enlightenment.* Two major political and social upheavals, the American Revolution (1775–1783) and the French Revolution (1789–1799), were based on ideals of the Enlightenment. Unfortunately, the ideals of the French Revolution were compromised by the Reign of Terror; instead of liberty, equality, and fraternity, the French in 1799 wound up with Napoléon.

Much of the new knowledge that characterized this era had practical applications. Inventions of the late eighteenth century facilitated the Industrial Revolution in the nineteenth century. The flying shuttle, the spinning jenny, and the cotton gin revolutionized the textile industry; James Watt's improved steam engine revolutionized manufacturing and transportation.

Baroque Eighteenth-century art and music that emphasized ornamentation.

In the arts of the late seventeenth century and early eighteenth century, the predominant style was **baroque**. Baroque painters emphasized detail, color, and ornamentation to create a more total visual illusion. Renowned baroque composers achieved unity of mood and continuity of line, but their music—like baroque painting—was filled with movement and action.

The complexity of eighteenth-century society was mirrored in an extremely complex theatre that crossed many national boundaries and saw the rise of many new theatrical forms.

Eighteenth-Century Drama: New Dramatic Forms

The eighteenth century did not produce outstanding drama; rather, this was a time when new dramatic forms, with lasting influences, began to appear.

In terms of genre, for instance, many eighteenth-century plays deviated from traditional definitions

SENTIMENTAL COMEDY

In the eighteenth century in England a type of comedy emerged that was much less amoral than Restoration comedy. Called sentimental comedy, it satirized social pretensions but upheld middle-class values. A good example of the form is *The Rivals* by Richard Brinsley Sheridan. Shown here in a production at the Huntington Theatre are Cheryl Lynn Bowers (as Lydia Languish) and Scott Ferrara (as Captain Jack Absolute). (©T. Charles Erickson)

of tragedy and comedy. The *drame* (DRAHM), a new French form, was a serious play that did not fit the neoclassical definition of tragedy. ***Bourgeois (middle-class) tragedy*** and ***domestic tragedy*** are eighteenth-century examples of drame. Bourgeois and domestic tragedies ignored the neoclassical requirement that the chief characters be kings, queens, or nobles; their new tragic heroes and heroines were members of the emerging middle class. These plays were frequently sentimental and melodramatic, and they usually reflected eighteenth-century middle-class morality with the virtuous being rewarded and the wicked punished. By the close of the century, such melodrama was being written in France, Germany, and England.

The English and the French originated additional dramatic forms during this period. In England these included the satirical ***ballad opera***, which employed popular music and was popularized by the success of ***The Beggar's Opera*** (1728) by John Gay (1685–1732), as well as *sentimental comedy*. Sentimental comedy of eighteenth-century England, like Restoration comedy, was comedy of manners, except that it reaffirmed middle-class morality. The major examples of this later form are ***The Rivals*** (1775) and ***The School for Scandal*** (1777), by Richard Brinsley Sheridan (1751–1816). In the emerging American theatre, ***The Contrast*** (1787) by Royall Tyler (1757–1826) was patterned after Sheridan's sentimental comedies.

There were opponents of sentimental comedy; the best-known was the English dramatist Oliver Goldsmith (c. 1730–1774), who wrote two plays: ***The Good Natur'd Man*** (1768) and ***She Stoops to Conquer*** (1773). Goldsmith advocated "laughing comedy," which would force audiences to laugh at their own eccentricities and absurdities.

In the late eighteenth century, many German playwrights revolted against the neoclassical ideals. The playwright and critic Gotthold Ephraim Lessing (1729–1781), for example, was a leader in the *Sturm und Drang* (S*torm and Stress*) movement, in which dramatists patterned their works on Shakespeare's extensive episodic structure, his mixture of genres, and his onstage violence. "Storm and Stress"—which included such plays as ***Goetz von Berlichingen*** (1773) by Johann Wolfgang von Goethe (1749–1832) and ***The Robbers*** (1782) by Friedrich Schiller (1759–1805)—was the forerunner of nineteenth-century Romanticism.

In Italy during the mid-eighteenth century, there was a struggle between the playwrights Carlo Goldoni (1707–1793) and Carlo Gozzi (1720–1806) over what direction commedia dell'arte should take: Goldoni wanted to make it less artificial, while Gozzi wanted to make it even more fantastic.

Theatre Production in the Eighteenth Century

Government and Theatre   In certain countries—such as England, France, and the independent German states—the eighteenth century was marked by governmental attempts to regulate theatre. We noted earlier that in 1737 the English Parliament issued the Licensing Act, which restricted the presentation of drama in London to the Drury Lane and Covent Garden theatres and made the lord chamberlain responsible for licensing plays. Frequently, however, ingenious theatrical entrepreneurs found ways to outwit the government and get around its restrictions.

In eighteenth-century France, the government restricted what types of plays could be produced and granted monopolies to certain theatres: The Opera, the Comédie Française (the home of nonmusical drama), and the Comédie Italienne (the home of commedia dell'arte and, later, of comic opera) were the three major

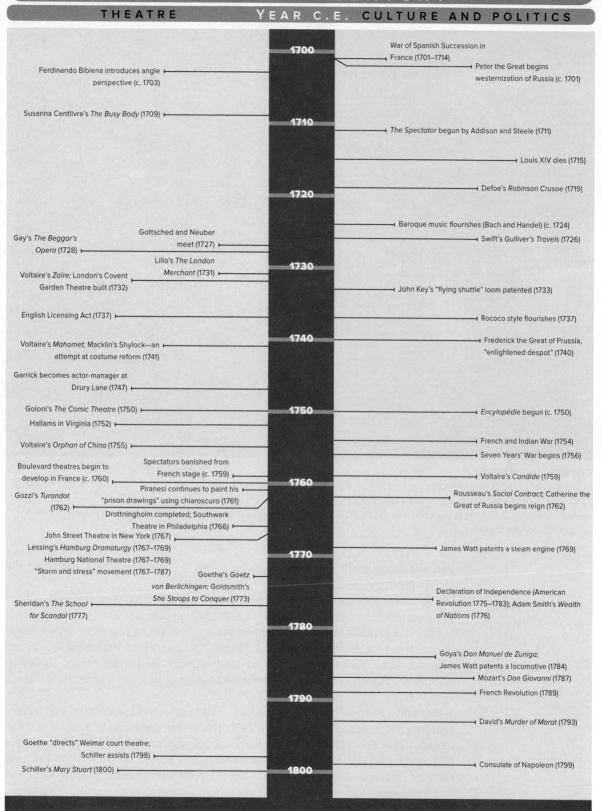

EIGHTEENTH CENTURY

| THEATRE | YEAR C.E. | CULTURE AND POLITICS |

1700

War of Spanish Succession in France (1701–1714)

Peter the Great begins westernization of Russia (c. 1701)

Ferdinando Bibiena introduces angle perspective (c. 1703)

Susanna Centlivre's *The Busy Body* (1709)

1710

The Spectator begun by Addison and Steele (1711)

Louis XIV dies (1715)

1720

Defoe's *Robinson Crusoe* (1719)

Baroque music flourishes (Bach and Handel) (c. 1724)

Gay's *The Beggar's Opera* (1728)

Gottsched and Neuber meet (1727)

Swift's *Gulliver's Travels* (1726)

Lillo's *The London Merchant* (1731)

1730

Voltaire's *Zaïre*; London's Covent Garden Theatre built (1732)

John Key's "flying shuttle" loom patented (1733)

English Licensing Act (1737)

Rococo style flourishes (1737)

1740

Voltaire's *Mahomet*; Macklin's Shylock—an attempt at costume reform (1741)

Frederick the Great of Prussia, "enlightened despot" (1740)

Garrick becomes actor-manager at Drury Lane (1747)

Goloni's *The Comic Theatre* (1750)

1750

Encylopédie begun (c. 1750)

Hallams in Virginia (1752)

Voltaire's *Orphan of China* (1755)

French and Indian War (1754)

Seven Years' War begins (1756)

Boulevard theatres begin to develop in France (c. 1760)

Spectators banished from French stage (c. 1759)

Voltaire's *Candide* (1759)

1760

Piranesi continues to paint his "prison drawings" using chiaroscuro (1761)

Gozzi's *Turandot* (1762)

Rousseau's *Social Contract*; Catherine the Great of Russia begins reign (1762)

Drottningholm completed; Southwark Theatre in Philadelphia (1766)

John Street Theatre in New York (1767)

Lessing's *Hamburg Dramaturgy* (1767–1769)

Hamburg National Theatre (1767–1769)

"Storm and stress" movement (1767–1787)

1770

James Watt patents a steam engine (1769)

Goethe's *Goetz von Berlichingen*; Goldsmith's *She Stoops to Conquer* (1773)

Sheridan's *The School for Scandal* (1777)

Declaration of Independence (American Revolution 1775–1783); Adam Smith's *Wealth of Nations* (1776)

1780

Goya's *Don Manuel de Zuniga*; James Watt patents a locomotive (1784)

Mozart's *Don Giovanni* (1787)

1790

French Revolution (1789)

David's *Murder of Marat* (1793)

Goethe "directs" Weimar court theatre; Schiller assists (1798)

Schiller's *Mary Stuart* (1800)

1800

Consulate of Napoleon (1799)

Chapter 14 *Theatres from the Restoration Through Romanticism*

GOLDONI VERSUS GOZZI

In the middle of the eighteenth century, two Italian dramatists, Carlo Goldoni and Carlo Gozzi, took different approaches in adapting Italian commedia dell'arte to a more modern form. Goldoni wanted drama to be more realistic; Gozzi wanted it to be more fanciful. Seen here is a scene from Goldoni's *La Locandiera* (*The Mistress of the Inn*) presented in Lyon, France. (©JACQUES MORELL/Getty Images)

Parisian theatres. In 1791, the leaders of the French Revolution abolished the earlier theatrical restrictions.

In Germany, government intervention in theatre was of a somewhat more positive nature. Eighteenth-century Germany was not unified but consisted of several independent states, and German theatre became an important artistic force in the last part of the century. Subsidized theatres were organized in several German states; and this practice provided stability for theatre artists, though it also meant that the government could wield control over the content of plays.

Eighteenth-Century Theatre Architecture The basic configuration of eighteenth-century continental theatres followed the Italian Renaissance tradition; but to accommodate the new middle-class audiences, both continental and English theatres became larger. The interiors were usually egg-shaped to improve sight lines. In England, playhouses moved more toward the continental model: The apron shrank to about twelve feet, and the area behind the proscenium became much deeper.

Drottningholm, built on the island of Lovön, served as a summer palace for the Swedish royal family and, when rebuilt in the eighteenth century, was modeled on the French palace of Versailles. However, financial limitations resulted in the Swedish royal residence being much less ornate.

An earlier theatre at the summer palace of Drottningholm served as a performance space for a French acting troupe between 1754 and 1762; when that playhouse burned down, Queen Louisa Ulrika (1720–1782), whose husband was King Adolf Frederick and her son later King Gustav III, had a new theatre built for summer performances. The Drottningholm theatre that opened in 1766 is still in use today.

The auditorium of the Swedish palace theatre is shaped like a T and the proscenium stage is exceptionally deep in order to create illusion through painted perspective scenery and the scene shifting accomplished by the pole-and-chariot system. This original system is still in use today and can shift scenery in as little as six seconds.

Much of the theatre's eighteenth-century special effects and sound technology are also usable today, including a wave machine that simulates a rough sea, thunder machine, and a flying chair that allows for the appearance of gods or other supernatural beings. In addition, the theatre can employ some of the original lighting positions for candles.

In 1921, Swedish theatre historian Agnes Beijer (1888–1975) rediscovered the theatre, which had become a storage facility after it was closed down in 1792 following the assassination of King Gustav III, who had hired an acting company for the summer theatre and had written and staged performances there. Following the rediscovery, the theatre was renovated to include electric lights, which mimic the effects of candle lighting, new ropes for the pulley systems, and reproductions of some of the eighteenth-century backdrops so as not to damage the originals.

Although the theatre reopened in 1922, it was initially used for limited performances until the early 1950s when it became the summer home of the Royal Swedish Opera and the Royal Swedish Ballet. Today, performances in the 400-seat theatre often make use of original eighteenth-century musical instruments or replicas of them as well as some of the original stage technology in order to stage operas from the period by such composers as Franz Joseph Haydn (1732–1809), George Frederick Handel (1685–1759), Christoph Willibald Gluck (1714–1787), and Wolfgang Amadeus Mozart (1756–1791).

Visitors can also tour the theatre (as well as other parts of the summer palace, including its extensive gardens), which is one of the United Nations' World Heritage sites.

Throughout Europe—in such countries as Germany, Russia, and Sweden—theatre buildings proliferated during the eighteenth century. One of the most significant theatre buildings of this period is Drottningholm in Sweden, erected in 1766 outside Stockholm. Drottningholm was boarded up in the 1790s and remained closed until the twentieth century, when it was reopened. Today tourists there can explore a perfect working example of an eighteenth-century theatre.

In the United States, during the colonial era and after the American Revolution, permanent theatres were constructed following the English model.

Scenery, Lighting, and Costumes   In the eighteenth century, as in the Renaissance, Italy was the birthplace of many scenic innovations. For nearly 100 years, from 1690 to 1787, the most influential Italian designers and theatre architects of the period were the Bibienas—an extended family that included several generations of designers. One innovation by the Bibienas was *angle* or *multipoint perspective*. Previously, the painted sets used during the Italian Renaissance pulled the eye to a central vanishing point and appeared to be totally framed and enclosed by the

Angle perspective   Also known as multipoint perspective, painted settings that pull the eye to multiple vanishing points.

THE THEATRE AT DROTTNINGHOLM, SWEDEN
This theatre still has the same sets and stage machinery that were used when it was built as a court playhouse in the eighteenth century. It is an excellent example of an Italianate proscenium theatre with the pole-and-chariot system for changing scenery. Below, contemporary stagehands use its pole-and-chariot system to execute a scene change. (©Joerg Modrow/laif/Redux)

(Courtesy of Drottningholms Slottsteater)

proscenium arch. In the Bibienas' designs, the eye was attracted to various vanishing points, and the set seemed to extend beyond the proscenium. Typically, the Bibienas' designs were grandiose, lavish, and ornate.

Elsewhere, Italian influence was pervasive in eighteenth-century scene design. Most continental theatres used wing-and-shutter settings, painted in perspective and shifted by Torelli's pole-and-chariot mechanism. Additional elements occasionally incorporated into the painted designs included the following: (1) borders at the top; (2) *ground rows* (cutouts along the stage floor); (3) large scenic cutouts, such as painted trees; (4) rolled backdrops; and (5) *act drops*—curtains at the front of the stage.

A few historians have argued that sometime between the Renaissance and the eighteenth century, Italian designers also introduced the *box set* in which flats are used to create three sides of a room onstage. We will look at the development of the box set more closely when we discuss nineteenth-century theatre.

There were also experiments with stage lighting in the late 1700s, including attempts to mask lighting sources, to use silk screens for coloring, and to replace candles with oil lamps and other sources. These lighting sources were not easily controlled, however, and the auditorium as well as the stage had to remain lit.

Unlike scenery and lighting, theatrical costuming remained underdeveloped throughout most of the eighteenth century. Actors and actresses believed that the chief criterion for a costume was to show the performer off to the best advantage. Daring theatre artists throughout Europe experimented with historically accurate costuming, but their attempts rarely resulted in the kind of historical reconstructions we see today.

SET DESIGN BY ONE OF THE BIBIENAS
During the eighteenth century, one family dominated scene design in Europe: the Bibiena family, whose second, third, and fourth generations carried on the tradition begun by Giovanni Bibiena. The Bibienas also designed ornate theatre interiors. Shown here is the Margravial Opera House in Bayreuth, Germany, designed by Giuseppe Galli Bibiena (1696-1757) and his son Carlo of Bologna. Built between 1744 and 1748, it is one of the surviving Baroque buildings in Europe. The stage design is typical of the family's work, with its vast scale, ornateness, and elegance, and its perspective vistas disappearing in several directions. (©Erich Lessing/Art Resource)

Acting in the Eighteenth Century   If many of the plays of the eighteenth century were not noteworthy, the performers often were. This was an age that glorified star performers. All across Europe, successful actors and actresses developed dedicated followings.

The predominant approach to acting in the eighteenth century was *bombastic,* emphasizing the performer's oratorical skills. More often than not, performers addressed their lines to the audience rather than the character to whom they were supposed to be speaking. Standardized patterns of stage movement were necessary because rehearsal time was limited and bills were changed frequently.

In the midst of these conventional practices, however, there were some innovators. Among those who rebelled against the bombastic, conventionalized style were the English actors Charles Macklin (c. 1700–1797) and David Garrick (1717–1779). Macklin and Garrick rejected formal declamation, stereotyped patterns of stage movement, and singsong delivery of verse.

The Emergence of the Director   In terms of the future, possibly the most significant development during the eighteenth century was the first emergence of the modern director. Before then, playwrights or leading performers normally doubled as directors of stage business, and actual directing was minimal; furthermore, little time was spent on preparing a production in rehearsal. What was missing in theatre was someone to oversee and unify stage productions, assist performers, and ensure the appropriateness of visual elements. Two eighteenth-century figures are often considered the forerunners of the modern stage director: the English actor David Garrick and the German playwright, poet, and novelist Johann Wolfgang von Goethe.

Régisseur   Continental European term for a theatre director; it often denotes a dictatorial director.

Between 1747 and 1776, David Garrick was a partner in the management of the Drury Lane Theatre and was therefore responsible for all major artistic decisions. He championed a more natural style of acting and argued for careful development of characters' individual traits as well as for thorough preparation and research. In contrast to the usual eighteenth-century custom, Garrick's rehearsals were quite extended. Garrick was also a strict disciplinarian: He required his performers to be on time, know their lines, and act—not simply recite—during rehearsals. As part of his reform of stage practices, Garrick also no longer allowed audience members to sit on the stage.

Goethe, unlike Garrick, was not restricted by commercialism and was not an actor in the company he directed. In 1775, Goethe—by then a famous author—was invited to oversee the court theatre at Weimar in Germany. Initially, Goethe did not take his theatre duties seriously, but by the 1790s he had become enthusiastic about the theatre and had become a *régisseur* (ray-zhee-SUHR), or dictatorial director. (*Régisseur* is the French term for director.)

Goethe rehearsed for long periods and expected his performers to work as an ensemble. He established rules for stage movement and vocal technique, and he also set rules for his performers' behavior in their personal lives. He even laid down rules for the conduct of his audiences; the only appropriate audience reactions, he insisted, were applause and withholding applause.

Goethe did not advocate a completely natural style of acting; he believed, for instance, that performers should speak facing the audience rather than each other. He used routine blocking patterns, although he did emphasize careful stage composition. Goethe oversaw settings and costumes and believed in historical accuracy.

EIGHTEENTH-CENTURY STAR: DAVID GARRICK
The eighteenth century was an era of great stars, some of whom paid close attention to details of performance and costuming to achieve a greater sense of reality. David Garrick was both an outstanding example of this approach to acting and also a strong manager of his theatre company. In the portrait here (by Nathaniel Dance) he is shown in the title role in Shakespeare's *Richard III*. (©Stratford Town Council, Stratford-upon-Avon)

1784, Paris, France It is a brisk spring day in May 1784. In Paris, the Comédie Française is giving a performance in its new theatre building, which opened two years ago. With great expectations, Parisians depart early so that they can arrive at the theatre before the starting time, 5:30. Tonight they are to see Beaumarchais's new play, *The Marriage of Figaro*.

The Comédie-Française is noted not only for traditional neoclassical drama but also for new drama by French authors. At this performance, there will be dance presentations between the acts of the play and also a short, comic afterpiece following *The Marriage of Figaro*. Not since *Tartuffe* has there been such controversy over a play.

The Marriage of Figaro—set in Spain—is about an older man's attempt to seduce a servant girl, and its key character is a comic servant; Beaumarchais introduced his characters several years ago in *The Barber of Seville*. The real point of *The Marriage of Figaro* is social and political satire, and it is this that is controversial. Because of the controversy, the king, Louis XVI, has refused to give his permission for its production. Despite this, it has been performed continuously since its opening in April and is clearly a success. People who were present on the opening night have reported that the theatre was filled hours beforehand and that some of the audience members had brought food with them so that they would not have to risk losing their seats by leaving the theatre to eat.

As the spectators enter the theatre, they are struck by its size and beauty. Remarkably, everyone in the audience now has a place to sit. In earlier French theatres, the pit in front of the stage had no seats, and people in that area stood during performances; in fact, people in the old seatless pits would move about and socialize. The new seats are controversial—Parisians enjoyed the social ambience of the old pit, and one of the leading playwrights of the day, Louis Sébastian Mercier, has publicly criticized the addition of benches. The audience area is egg-shaped; this configuration, at least, will be welcome, making it easier for everyone in the audience to see the action onstage. Like older theatres, the new Comédie-Française has three rows of boxes with a row of galleries above those. Spectators who cannot afford the more expensive sections take their place in the pit, sitting on the new benches.

When the curtain rises, the spectators are impressed at once by the stage, which is large and very deep. However, it has a smaller apron than the company's previous theatres had: The actors and actresses must all perform behind the proscenium arch. The scenery is painted and will be changed by wings and shutters. As the play begins, the spectators are very excited because they are seeing performers they have heard much about.

The plot of *The Marriage of Figaro* is full of intrigue, unexpected twists, and great comic moments. Figaro, the servant, is engaged to marry Suzanne, who is also a servant; but his master, Count Almaviva, wants to sleep with her himself. The count has been unfaithful to his wife, and the audience watches with great enjoyment the various complications that develop as he tries to conquer another woman but is thwarted. At the end of the play, the count is exposed in his plotting and is humiliated; he pledges fidelity to his wife, and Figaro and Suzanne are brought together.

As the Parisians walk home, they relive many of the comic moments in the play. Yet they also understand why this seemingly simple, farcical work has caused such a political furor. It is the master who is ridiculed and frustrated: Despite his social rank, his machinations are futile and his clever servants outwit him. Clearly, Beaumarchais is questioning the social structure of France. Some people are saying that this play threatens society with the same kind of revolution that has taken place in the new world. Are these people right? Was the king right to be concerned about the political implications of this comedy? These questions remain long after the evening at the Comédie-Française.

David Garrick is often cited as one of the earliest directors in the theatre. It is, of course, pointed out that he functioned not only as a director but also as an actor as well as playwright and theatre manager. While we shall see that there were many actor-managers, who often took on directorial responsibilities in the nineteenth century, historians most often focus on the artists who eventually functioned solely as directors beginning in the late 1800s. However, the tradition of the lead actor who also functions as a director continued through the twentieth century into our contemporary theatre of the twenty-first century.

Many twentieth-century actors were renowned for their directorial abilities. In the American theatre, for example, Orson Welles (1915–1985) served both as actor and director for the Federal Theatre Project and the Mercury Theatre in the 1930s and 1940s, both of which we discuss later. Welles also co-wrote, directed, and produced (much like David Garrick did in the eighteenth-century theatre) the renowned film *Citizen Kane* (1941).

British theatre in the twentieth and twenty-first centuries has seen a significant number of actor-directors. Laurence Olivier (1907–1989) was not only known for the direction of plays and films but was co-director of the Old Vic Theatre in the 1940s and the original founding artistic director of the Royal National Theatre from 1963 to 1973. Among contemporary British actor-directors are Kenneth Branagh (b. 1960), who is also known for his film directing as well as screenwriting and often compared to Olivier; Jonathan Kent (b. 1946); Ian McDiarmid (b. 1944); Mark Rylance (b. 1960); Simon McBurney (b. 1957); Maria Aitken (b. 1945); and Fiona Shaw (b. 1958). The award-winning Australian film actress Cate Blanchett (b. 1969) served as the co-artistic director of the Sydney Theatre Company and has directed productions there.

We should note that many other contemporary film actors, besides those we have already mentioned, also direct. Among the most well known are George Clooney (b. 1961), Woody Allen (b. 1935), Clint Eastwood (b. 1930), Ben Affleck (b. 1972), and Jodie Foster (b. 1962).

David Garrick's influence as an actor who also was an innovative director is mirrored in the careers of these well-known performers who also have had an impact on theatre history through their work as directors.

THE NINETEENTH CENTURY

Background: A Time of Social Change

Major social changes took place in the period from 1800 to 1875, including the Industrial Revolution, which involved technological advances such as steam power, expanded means of transportation, and new modes of communication. Another major development was the rise of nationalism, colonialism, and revolts against colonial oppression.

There was also intellectual ferment. Two especially significant theoretical works were Charles Darwin's *On the Origin of Species* (1859) and Karl Marx's *Das Kapital (Capital;* 1867). Darwin's work, which dealt with evolution by natural selection, led to the questioning of traditional religious concepts; Marx's work questioned the capitalist system, which was the driving economic force of the Industrial Revolution.

These societal transformations had a major impact on the nature of theatre. Nineteenth-century theatre built on the innovations of the eighteenth century and paved the way for modern theatre.

IN FOCUS: NINETEENTH-CENTURY POPULAR THEATRICAL ARTS

As we have noted, it is hard to distinguish between the popular entertainments of the nineteenth century and the theatre of that era. Many of the popular forms were presented in theatres, and many traditional dramas were adopted for spaces that usually held mass audience entertainments.

The nineteenth century saw an explosion of museums, music halls, and circuses. The American who was world-renowned for his ability to draw mass audiences was P. (Phineas) T. (Taylor) Barnum (1810–1891), who in 1841 opened the American Museum in which he exhibited human curiosities and also staged concerts and plays, including many temperance melodramas. Later, in the early 1870s, Barnum was also instrumental in developing the three-ring circus as we know it today. But even before Barnum, there were circus rings that housed clowns, equestrian performances, trained animal acts, and pantomimes. In the early nineteenth century, dramas staged on horseback were presented in many of these spaces.

The music halls of England served food and drink and had a small platform stage for popular song and dance presentations. A master of ceremonies moved the show along, providing comic interludes. By the end of the 1800s, these early music halls evolved into theatrical spaces dedicated exclusively to the presentation of these musical performances.

The nineteenth century also saw the development of many other forms of popular entertainments, including wild west shows, vaudeville, and minstrelsy. Wild west shows (or exhibitions), popular in the last quarter of the nineteenth century, presented heroic figures of the west

POPULAR ARTS

During the nineteenth century, a number of highly theatrical popular entertainments developed. Among those was the circus. The American entrepreneur P. T. Barnum was a significant innovator in developing the circus as we know it today. Seen here are female trapeze artists, performing in 1890. (Source: Library of Congress Prints and Photographs Division [LC-USZC4-2091])

as well as Native Americans, most often to audiences in the eastern United States who had little real contact with that world.

Minstrel shows were variety shows that featured white performers wearing blackface, and caricaturing African Americans. Later in the nineteenth century, there were African American minstrel troupes. Vaudeville was a series of variety acts—music, sketches, juggling, animal acts—that made up an evening's entertainment.

The intertwining of the popular arts and theatre made the two almost indistinguishable. Furthermore, many of the popular forms that developed in the nineteenth century continue to have an impact on our performance arts. For example, the well-known Canadian circus troupe Cirque du Soleil stages productions that break the boundaries between popular art and theatre. Television has incorporated the tradition of vaudeville and variety.

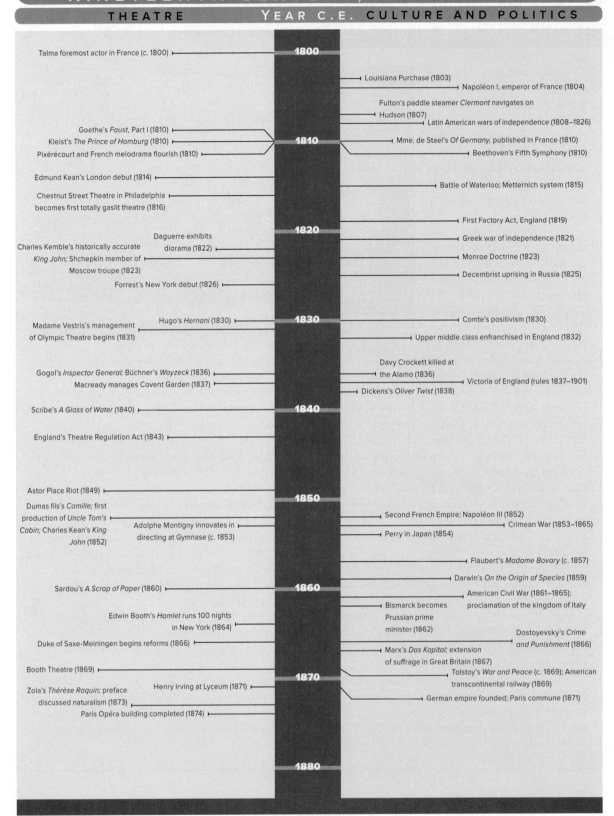

Talma foremost actor in France (c. 1800)

1800

Louisiana Purchase (1803)

Napoléon I, emperor of France (1804)

Fulton's paddle steamer *Clermont* navigates on Hudson (1807)

Latin American wars of independence (1808–1826)

Goethe's *Faust*, Part I (1810)

Kleist's *The Prince of Homburg* (1810)

Pixérécourt and French melodrama flourish (1810)

1810

Mme. de Stael's *Of Germany*, published in France (1810)

Beethoven's Fifth Symphony (1810)

Edmund Kean's London debut (1814)

Chestnut Street Theatre in Philadelphia becomes first totally gaslit theatre (1816)

Battle of Waterloo; Metternich system (1815)

1820

First Factory Act, England (1819)

Daguerre exhibits diorama (1822)

Charles Kemble's historically accurate *King John*; Shchepkin member of Moscow troupe (1823)

Greek war of independence (1821)

Monroe Doctrine (1823)

Forrest's New York debut (1826)

Decembrist uprising in Russia (1825)

1830

Hugo's *Hernani* (1830)

Comte's positivism (1830)

Madame Vestris's management of Olympic Theatre begins (1831)

Upper middle class enfranchised in England (1832)

Gogol's *Inspector General*; Büchner's *Woyzeck* (1836)

Macready manages Covent Garden (1837)

Davy Crockett killed at the Alamo (1836)

Victoria of England (rules 1837–1901)

Dickens's *Oliver Twist* (1838)

Scribe's *A Glass of Water* (1840)

1840

England's Theatre Regulation Act (1843)

Astor Place Riot (1849)

1850

Dumas fils's *Camille*; first production of *Uncle Tom's Cabin*; Charles Kean's *King John* (1852)

Adolphe Montigny innovates in directing at Gymnase (c. 1853)

Second French Empire; Napoléon III (1852)

Crimean War (1853–1865)

Perry in Japan (1854)

Flaubert's *Madame Bovary* (c. 1857)

Darwin's *On the Origin of Species* (1859)

Sardou's *A Scrap of Paper* (1860)

1860

American Civil War (1861–1865); proclamation of the kingdom of Italy

Edwin Booth's *Hamlet* runs 100 nights in New York (1864)

Bismarck becomes Prussian prime minister (1862)

Duke of Saxe-Meiningen begins reforms (1866)

Dostoyevsky's *Crime and Punishment* (1866)

Marx's *Das Kapital*; extension of suffrage in Great Britain (1867)

Booth Theatre (1869)

1870

Tolstoy's *War and Peace* (c. 1869); American transcontinental railway (1869)

Zola's *Thérèse Raquin*; preface discussed naturalism (1873)

Henry Irving at Lyceum (1871)

German empire founded; Paris commune (1871)

Paris Opéra building completed (1874)

1880

Theatre in Nineteenth-Century Life

Before examining specific transformations in drama and production techniques during the nineteenth century, we should look at the unique place theatre held at that time. Between 1800 and 1875, the dramatic arts exploded. The working and middle classes who filled the fast-growing cities demanded theatre; it was a passion, a fad, and also a seeming necessity for these new audiences. Nineteenth-century theatre, therefore, was a true popular entertainment that attracted huge numbers of spectators and helped audiences to forget—momentarily, at least—the cares and drudgery of daily life.

Nonliterary forms of entertainment also attracted the masses. The American public, for example, supported such popular arts as the *minstrel show, burlesque, variety, the circus, wild west shows,* and *medicine shows.* Throughout the nineteenth century, concert halls, saloons, and playhouses presented collections of entertainments—including songs, dances, acrobatics, and animal acts—on one bill; these developed into the popular variety and vaudeville presentations at the turn of the century and in the early twentieth century. The renowned popularizer of the circus, P. T. Barnum (1810–1891), merits special mention. Barnum developed the art of spectacular advertising to attract audiences to his entertainments; when he became involved with the circus in the 1850s, he advertised it as the "greatest show on earth." The wide variety of attractions to which audiences responded in the nineteenth century is a prime example of the tradition of popular entertainments of which we have spoken in earlier chapters.

The increase in numbers of spectators and types of entertainments resulted in the construction of more and larger playhouses throughout the Western world. With improvements in rail transportation, the dramatic arts were also brought to new places and new audiences.

The passion that audiences felt for theatre helps to explain several infamous theatre riots. One of these episodes, the "Old Price Riots," took place when London's Covent Garden Theatre was remodeled in 1809 and prices for admission were raised by the actor-manager John Philip Kemble (1757–1823). Another theatre riot took place in Paris in 1830, when *Hernani* by Victor Hugo (1802–1885) premiered at the Comédie Française. Some audience members were upset by the play's break from the neoclassical form.

The most violent of the nineteenth-century riots occurred outside New York's Astor Place Theatre in lower Manhattan and grew out of rivalry between the English star William Charles Macready (1793–1873) and the American star Edwin Forrest (1806–1872). Forrest, who was noted for his portrayals of melodramatic heroes, had made an unsuccessful English tour; he blamed its failure on Macready, whose performance style was more subtle and realistic. When Macready appeared at the Astor Place Theatre on May 8, 1849, Forrest's working-class fans prevented the performance.

Macready was persuaded by his aristocratic admirers to appear again two nights later on May 10, but this performance brought out a mob of 15,000 who assembled outside the playhouse and began to attack it. The infantry was called out to disperse the mob, and by the time the riot ended, twenty-two people had been killed.

The popularity of theatre between 1800 and 1875 has not been equaled in modern times. Partial parallels could be drawn to movies and television, which present similar kinds of entertainment, attract mass audiences, and feature popular stars. Still, the passion of nineteenth-century audiences has rarely been aroused by other forms of entertainment. In our own time, the only equivalent might be the emotional intensity of audiences at rock concerts or at professional sports events.

ASTOR PLACE RIOT PAINTED BY C. M. JENKES
This riot, which happened in New York in 1849, was a result of nationalistic fervor and the passionate involvement of theatre audiences. It broke out when working-class fans of the American star Edwin Forrest attacked the theatre in which the English actor William Charles Macready, who had supposedly insulted Forrest, was performing. (Source: Library of Congress Prints and Photographs Division [LC-USZC2-2532])

The Astor Place Riot and the subject matter of much popular drama also reflected growing nationalism. For example, Anna Cora Mowatt, one of America's first significant female playwrights, wrote a comedy of manners, *Fashion* (1845), that depicted the values of hardworking America as more honest than the social pretensions of Europe. The character Adam Trueman in *Fashion* was a descendant of an earlier popular stock figure in American melodramas and comedies—the "stage Yankee," a representative of diligent, unpretentious, rural America.

Nineteenth-Century Dramatic Forms

Two major forms of drama that came to the fore between 1800 and 1875 were Romanticism and melodrama.

Romanticism   *Romanticism,* influenced by the German storm and stress movement, was a revolutionary literary trend of the first half of the nineteenth century. The most noted Romantic dramas of the period were Goethe's **Faust** (**Part 1**, 1808 and **Part 2**, 1831) and Victor Hugo's **Hernani** (1830).

The Romantics rejected all artistic rules, believing that genius creates its own rules. Since many of the Romantics adopted Shakespeare's structural techniques, their plays were episodic and epic in scope; but unlike Shakespeare, they were often more interested in creating dramatic mood and atmosphere than in developing believable plots or depth of character. The Romantic hero was frequently a social outcast—a bandit, for example—who sought justice, knowledge, and truth.

GOETHE'S FAUST
The greatest nineteenth-century Romantic drama was Goethe's *Faust,* which is written in two parts. It follows the pattern of episodic Shakespearean drama and deals with the temptation of Faust by Mephistopheles. Shown here is German actor Lutz Salzmann as Faust at the Deutsches Nationaltheater and Staatskapelle in Weimar, Germany in 2016. (©Martin Schutt/ EPA/Redux)

Melodrama   Another dramatic form that came to the forefront in the nineteenth century was melodrama. As was discussed in the chapter "Theatrical Genres," *melodrama* literally means "song drama" or "music drama"—a reference to the background music that accompanied these plays.

In nineteenth-century melodrama, the emphasis was on surface effects, such as those evoking suspense, fear, nostalgia, and other strong emotions in the audience. The conflict between good and evil was clearly established: Melodramatic heroes and heroines stood in sharp contrast to villains, and the audiences sympathized with the good characters and despised the bad ones. Virtue was always victorious.

To hold the audience's interest, melodramas had suspenseful plots with a climactic moment at the end of each act (the modern equivalent would be a television drama that has a car crash or a sudden confrontation just before a commercial break). Since melodrama is primarily an escapist form, visual spectacle and special effects were important.

The Well-Made Play   Many popular melodramas of the nineteenth century had a structure described by the term ***well-made play***. Characteristic of such plays were tightly constructed cause-and-effect development, and action revolving around a secret known to the audience but not to the characters. The opening scenes carefully spell out the necessary background information, or *exposition*. Throughout the play, the dramatic action is clearly foreshadowed, and each act builds to a climax. In the

Well-made play   Tightly constructed plays with cause and effect development and actions revolving around a secret. Every act ends with a climactic moment with the plot carefully resolved.

MELODRAMA

A type of drama that came to prominence in the nineteenth century was the *well-made play.* The term means a play that was carefully constructed and featured unity of action and often unity of time and place as well. It incorporated a tightly managed plot with a strong cause-and-effect sequence of events. The well-made play is particularly well suited to melodrama, a genre that also came to prominence in the nineteenth century and continues into the twenty-first century. In melodrama, the emphasis is on suspense and excitement, with good and bad characters clearly delineated. Stephen Sondheim's musical *Sweeney Todd* is based on a 19th century melodrama. The two main characters are Sweeney, a barber, and Mrs. Lovett, his partner. In the story, Sweeney kills victims and turns their bodies over to Mrs. Lovett to make into meat pies. Shown here are Jeremy Secomb and Siobhan McCarthy in a 2017 production of the musical at the Barrow Street Theater in New York. Directed by Bill Buckhurst, this production immersed the audience within the melodramatic action. (©Sara Krulwich/The New York Times/Redux)

major scene, known as the *obligatory scene,* the opposed characters confront each other in a showdown. The plot is carefully resolved so that there are no loose ends.

The two most famous writers of well-made plays were both French: Eugène Scribe (1791–1861) and Victorien Sardou (1831–1908).

Theatre Production in the Nineteenth Century

Performers and Acting   Even more than the eighteenth century, the nineteenth century was an era of great stars; performers throughout the world were idolized by the audiences who flocked to see them. Some of these performers amassed— and frequently lost—fortunes, and a number of them were not only national but global figures.

During the nineteenth century, the traditional *repertory company,* a troupe of actors and actresses performing together for a set period of time in a number of plays, gradually disappeared. As transportation improved, not only stars but full productions—known as *combination companies*—began to tour, replacing the local repertory troupes. At about the same time, the long run became more common: Popular plays might run for more than 100 consecutive performances.

Most performers of the period acted in the classical, Romantic, and melodramatic styles. Many, however, moved toward modern realism. Among such more realistic performers were the American Edwin Booth (1833–1893) and the Italian Eleonora Duse (1858–1924).

Nineteenth-Century Developments in Directing The art of directing, pioneered by David Garrick and Johann Wolfgang von Goethe in the eighteenth century, was refined and developed in the nineteenth century by many actor-managers, including a significant number of women.

The goal of innovative nineteenth-century directors was to create a unified stage picture, particularly by allotting more time for rehearsal and paying more attention to production details. Many of them also experimented with historical accuracy in scenery and costuming.

In England and the United States, numerous performer-managers took great interest and care in creating stage productions. On the European continent, a number of people significantly developed the art of directing, including two Germans—the opera composer Richard Wagner (1813–1883) and George II (1826–1914), Duke of Saxe-Meiningen—who were not actors within their companies and thus were closer to our modern idea of the director.

Wagner's concept of a totally unified artwork—the **Gesamtkunstwerk** (guh-Zahmt-Koonst-verk)—controlled by one person influenced twentieth-century theories of "total theatre" and directing. Wagner believed that an opera, which is made up of many musical and theatrical elements, needs a controlling figure to unify it. At his Bayreuth Festspielhaus, he put this theory into practice, becoming its *régisseur*, or director. Wagner's innovations for increasing stage illusion are particularly important. Musicians were forbidden to tune their

EDWIN BOOTH
An outstanding actor of the nineteenth century was Edwin Booth, famous for his portrayal of Hamlet, shown here, and other Shakespearean characters, as well as for building his own theatre. As a performer, he was renowned for depth of character, grace, and freedom from mannerisms. In an age of stage posturing, he took a more natural approach to his roles.
(©Bettmann/Getty Images)

ELEONORA DUSE: PORTRAIT BY E. GORDIGIANI
Duse was the great Italian actress of the late nineteenth century and early twentieth century. She was known for her more realistic acting style, and the English playwright George Bernard Shaw considered her a greater performer than her rival, Sarah Bernhardt. (©DEA Picture Library/Getty Images)

Gesamtkunstwerk
Richard Wagner's theory of a totally unified theatrical work of art.

instruments in the orchestra pit, and audiences were not supposed to applaud during the course of a presentation. Wagner is also often credited with being the first director to extinguish the house lights in order to focus the audience's attention on the stage.

In 1866, the duke of Saxe-Meiningen—a small state in northwestern Germany—took control of his court theatre; and between 1874 and 1890 he made the Meiningen Players the most renowned company in the world and revolutionized stage production. He rehearsed for extensive periods of time, refusing to open a show until he believed it was ready. He was opposed to the star system and employed mostly young performers. His productions were especially famous for intricately planned crowd scenes and were also admired for their historically accurate settings and costumes. Because his company toured frequently to other countries, the duke's theatrical innovations became well known throughout Europe.

Nineteenth-Century Theatre Architecture

Between 1800 and mid-century, many playhouses, with the traditional proscenium arch and "pit, box, and gallery" arrangement, were enlarged to meet the demands of the expanding lower-class urban audiences. By the 1860s, however, there was a shift away from the construction of huge theatres.

In the United States, the Booth Theatre, completed in 1869 for the renowned American Shakespearean actor Edwin Booth, is often cited as the first modern theatre in New York City. Instead of a pit and galleries, it had a modern orchestra area and balconies, and the seats were individual armchairs. The stage in Booth's theatre was revolutionary: It was not raked, and it had no grooves. Rather, scenery could be raised from the basement by elevators or dropped in (flown in) from above, and scenic pieces were often supported by braces.

Another innovative nineteenth-century theatre building, the Bayreuth Festspielhaus, built for Richard Wagner, opened in 1876. Wagner wanted seating that would not emphasize class distinctions, and so his theatre had 1,300 individual seats in thirty raked rows, forming a fan-shaped auditorium. Audiences exited at the ends of the rows, an arrangement known as *continental seating.*

Scenery, Costumes, and Lighting

Eighteenth-century experiments with realistic devices and conventions in scenery and costuming were carried even further in the nineteenth century. Historical accuracy in sets and costumes became more common with the increasing availability of works of historical research. This new knowledge about the past—combined with the fascination with antiquity that characterized the nineteenth century—led various theatre artists, including the Duke of Saxe-Meiningen, to mount historically accurate productions.

Wing-and-shutter settings shifted by pole-and-chariot or groove systems gradually disappeared during the nineteenth century. The most significant alternative was the *box set,* an arrangement in which flats are cleated together at angles—rather than set up parallel to the audience—to form the walls of a three-dimensional room. As noted previously, the box set may have been introduced as early as the Renaissance, but it was in the nineteenth century that box sets revolutionized scene design.

During this same period, the technology of the Industrial Revolution was introduced into theatre. New means of scene shifting were developed: By the close

The Bayreuth Festspielhaus, designed for and by the composer Richard Wagner, opened on August 13, 1876 with his *Das Rheingold*. In attendance at the premiere production were such notable figures as the philosopher Friedrich Nietzche, the composers Anton Bruckner, Peter Tchaikovsky, and Franz Liszt, as well as Kaiser Wilhelm.

Under the management of the composer until his death and later by members of his family, the Festspielhaus has housed a summer festival that continues to this day. When Wagner died in 1883, his second wife Cosima Wagner (1837–1930), the daughter of Liszt, administered the festival and announced that Wagner's final ten operas would be the festival's repertoire. She also began the tradition of employing internationally renowned conductors. In addition, she made sure that the operas were staged just as they had been in initial Bayreuth productions.

When Cosima retired in 1906, Wagner's son Siegfried (1869–1930) managed the festival. After he died, his British-born wife Winifred Wagner (1897–1980), who was an active supporter of the Nazis and Adolf Hitler, took control. Under the Third Reich, the Nazi Party oversaw the theatre and festival and, surprisingly, allowed changes in the production style of Wagner's operas.

While much of Bayreuth suffered significant damage from Allied bombings during World War II, the Festspielhaus was not damaged. Winifred, however, was not allowed to resume control of the summer festival due to her collaboration with the Nazis. Instead, her two sons, Wieland (1917–1966) and Wolfgang (1919–2010) took over administration of the festival.

Wieland's staging of his grandfather's operas was highly controversial because he broke with the original traditions and instead directed more minimalist and theatrical productions. After Wieland died in 1966, Wolfgang, who was not as innovative a director, took sole control. In the early 1970s, under the supervision of a new board, the festival began to hire international directors to create more contemporary interpretations of the Wagnerian operas. Among those who staged acclaimed productions were Patrice Chéreau (French, 1944–2013), Peter Hall (English, b. 1930) and Heiner Müller (German, 1929–1995).

After Wolfgang retired in 2008, the festival board appointed his daughters, Eva Wagner-Pasquier (b. 1945) and Katharina Wagner (b. 1978), Eva's half-sister, as the new administrators. In 2012, a major renovation of the deteriorating Festspielhaus was completed with support from the German and Bavarian governments. The festival's website currently announces summer productions through 2020.

of the century, the *elevator stage* (which allows sections of a stage floor, or even the entire floor, to be raised or lowered) and the *revolving stage* were perfected. The latter is a large turntable on which scenery is placed; as it moves, one set turns out of sight and another is brought into view.

Nineteenth-century technology also revolutionized stage lighting. In 1816, Philadelphia's Chestnut Street Theatre became the world's first playhouse to be completely gaslit. Gaslight allowed control of the intensity of lighting in all parts of the theatre; and by the middle of the century, the *gas table*—the equivalent of a modern dimmer board—enabled one stagehand to control all the stage lighting.

Thomas Edison's incandescent lamp, invented in 1879, further revolutionized stage lighting. Electricity, of course, is the most flexible, most controllable, and safest form of theatre lighting. By 1881, London's Savoy Theatre was using incandescent lighting, though some other playhouse may actually have used it earlier.

NINETEENTH-CENTURY THEATRE ARCHITECTURE

Significant changes took place in theatre architecture during the 1800s. This illustration of Covent Garden in London (top) shows a typical "pit, box, and gallery" theatre of the era. The photograph of Wagner's Bayreuth Festspielhaus (right), however, shows that by 1876 significant transformations were occurring. Wagner's theatre is much more like a modern proscenium theatre, with comfortable seating in the orchestra area, a small balcony, and a sunken orchestra pit. (top ©Heritage Images/Getty Images; right ©ArenaPal/Topham/The Image Works)

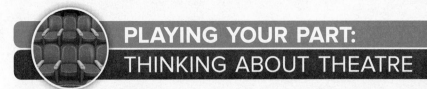

1. Restoration and eighteenth-century sentimental comedy focus on sexual intrigue and the moral weaknesses of human beings. Identify at least three contemporary films or television shows that employ the same subject matter. Explain the similarities in your answer.

2. How was the proscenium-arch theatre of the Restoration different from a proscenium-arch theatre on your campus?

3. What new elements were introduced by eighteenth-century designers to aid in enhancing the illusion of reality in scene design?

4. Why was the emergence of the director in the eighteenth century so significant?

5. List and describe present-day examples of nineteenth-century popular entertainments.

6. Explain why a film or television show you have seen recently might be categorized as melodrama.

7. How is a romantic film or television show today different from a nineteenth-century drama of the Romantic era? Describe any similarities.

SUMMARY

1. The theatre of the English Restoration combined aspects of English and continental Renaissance theatre.

2. Restoration drama had elements of both Elizabethan theatre and the French theatre of Molière.

3. The Restoration stage also had native and continental elements: Its modified proscenium came from French and Italian practice, but its elongated apron came from Elizabethan theatres.

4. In the eighteenth century, there were many attempts throughout Europe to break away from the Italianate tradition.

5. Theatres were still constructed as proscenium-arch spaces, but their shapes and sizes changed.

6. Revolutionary authors—especially the storm and stress dramatists of the late 1700s—abandoned the neoclassical ideals.

7. Many new genres that ignored the Italian Renaissance rules were developed, including bawdy Restoration comedy, sentimental comedy, middle-class tragedy, drame, and ballad opera.

8. There were also attempts in the 1700s to develop unity in production; these included some primitive experiments with historical accuracy and—especially notably—the directorial controls instituted by David Garrick and Johann Wolfgang von Goethe.

9. The nineteenth century was the bridge to our modern era.

10. Comfortable modern proscenium-arch theatres, such as Booth's theatre and the Bayreuth Festspielhaus, were built.

11. Principles of modern directing were developed and were clearly manifested in the work of the Duke of Saxe-Meiningen.

12. Historical accuracy in costuming and settings as well as expanded use of the box set added to theatrical illusionism.

13. Theatre was also affected by technological advances, such as gas lighting.

Design elements: Playing Your Part box (theatre seats): ©McGraw-Hill Education; In Focus box (spotlight): ©d_gas/Getty Images

15

THE MODERN THEATRE EMERGES

In the modern era, usually defined as 1875 to the present, the arts have, as always, mirrored changes occurring in society. In theatre, these developments have been reflected in a great diversity of types of theatre as theatre has become increasingly global, eclectic, and experimental. Avant-garde theatre appears alongside more conventional theatre, and new plays are produced while classics from the past also enjoy great popularity. In this chapter, we will focus mainly on the years 1875 to 1975.

In the theatre of the modern era, five major strands stand out. The first strand is realism; the second is departures from realism; the third strand is known as eclecticism, movements and artists who combine the various trends or are able to work across the boundaries of these trends; the fourth is a continuation of traditional and popular theatres from the past—comedies, tragedies, melodramas, and spectacular extravaganzas that nineteenth-century audiences applauded; the fifth strand is multiculturalism and globalization. During the period of 1875 to 1975, theatre practitioners in various parts of the world—Asia (China, India, Japan, Indonesia), Africa, Europe, the United States, Central and South America—became increasingly aware of the theatrical activities and practices in other places. Often, they adopted the techniques and theatrical innovations of these other cultures. In this chapter we will examine how these five approaches developed in the modern theatre.

◀ **THE MODERN THEATRE EMERGES**
Between 1875 and the 1950s what is known as the Modern Theatre came to full flower, with both realism and departures from realism. A work that has become a contemporary classic is Waiting for Godot, *written by Samuel Beckett. Absurdist playwrights focused on the ridiculous aspects of twentieth-century life and used absurd language, characters, and situations to dramatize their point of view. Shown here are Patrick Stewart as Vladimir and Ian McKellen as Estragon in a 2009 London production that came to Broadway in 2013 and was directed by Sean Mathias.* (©Bruce Glikas/FilmMagic/Getty Images)

REALISM AND THE MODERN ERA

Background: The Modern Era

Modern theatre in the West began with the plays of three dramatists: the Norwegian Henrik Ibsen; the Swede August Strindberg; and the Russian Anton Chekhov. Their works also reflect the period in which they were written—the modern era, which began in the late nineteenth century and continues to this day. Their plays ushered in the techniques and the outlook that characterized Western theatre throughout most of the twentieth century.

In the mid-nineteenth century, profound changes began to occur in religion, philosophy, psychology, and economics. In 1859, Charles Darwin published *On the Origin of Species,* which challenged the concept that human beings are special and created by God in his own image. In 1867, Karl Marx's *Das Kapital* questioned the fundamentals of capitalism. In 1900, Sigmund Freud's *Interpretation of Dreams* suggested that we are not in complete control of our actions or even our thoughts. In 1905, Albert Einstein presented the first part of his theory of relativity, which stated that many aspects of the universe that we consider fixed and immutable are subject to variation and change. One result of this series of intellectual, religious, and moral challenges was that societies that had been unified now became fragmented.

Along with fragmentation, the first half of the twentieth century was marked by tremendous unrest, in both Europe and Asia. This era of unrest was ushered in by World War I, which lasted from 1914 to 1918 and resulted in 8.5 million deaths. Unrest also contributed to the Russian Revolution of 1917, which led to the establishment of the Soviet government. When World War I ended, it was hoped that peace would come to the Western world, but severe economic problems developed in Europe and the United States that led to the emergence of totalitarianism in Europe and the rule of fascist dictators such as Benito Mussolini in Italy, Adolf Hitler in Germany, and Francisco Franco in Spain.

The extremes of fascism were frighteningly illustrated by Hitler's Nazi Germany, in which individual liberty was suppressed and millions of Jews, Roma (inappropriately referred to as gypsies), and others were exterminated in concentration camps. Hitler's government murdered 6 million Jews and millions of others. Similar abuses occurred in other totalitarian states, including the Soviet Union, where Joseph Stalin (who ruled the country from 1928 until 1951) sent millions to their deaths in slave-labor camps.

After World War II, which began in 1939 and ended in 1945 with the defeat of Germany and Italy in Europe and of Japan in Asia, there was again hope for peace. The period after World war II was different from the period after World War I. For one thing, the atom bomb—which had been dropped on two cities in Japan at the close of World War II—and later the hydrogen bomb had been developed. These weapons were potentially so deadly that a stalemate developed between the United States and the Soviet Union which came to be called the cold war and which lasted for decades, not ending until the Soviet Union was dissolved at the end of 1991.

The end of World War II did not mean the end of military conflicts. From 1945 to the present, there have been numerous other wars, including the Korean War, the Israeli-Arab conflicts in the Middle East, the Vietnam War, a Soviet-led war in Afghanistan, the Persian Gulf War, the Bosnian-Serb War in the former Yugoslavia, the Rwandan civil war in Africa, and the wars in Afghanistan, Iraq, and Syria. There was also a great deal of social unrest, including civil rights

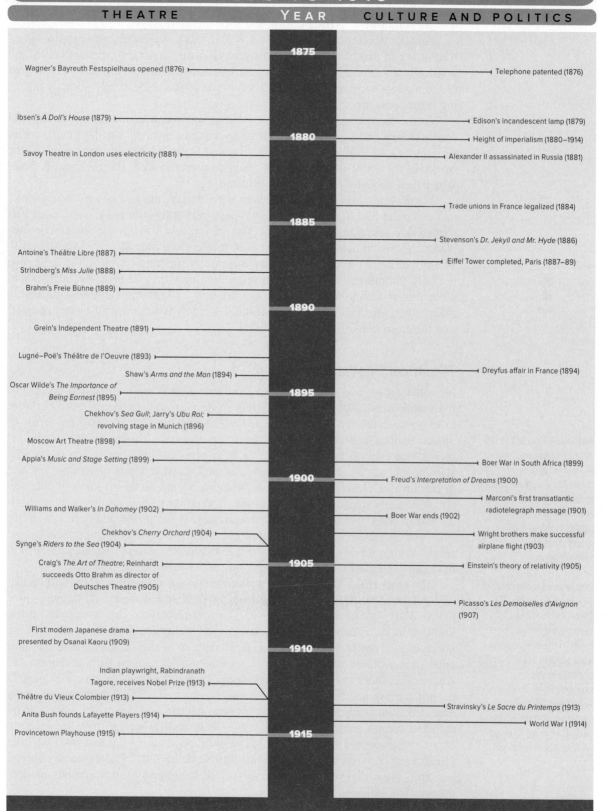

1875 TO 1915

THEATRE	YEAR	CULTURE AND POLITICS

Wagner's Bayreuth Festspielhaus opened (1876) — Telephone patented (1876)

1875

Ibsen's *A Doll's House* (1879) — Edison's incandescent lamp (1879)

1880

Height of imperialism (1880–1914)

Savoy Theatre in London uses electricity (1881) — Alexander II assassinated in Russia (1881)

Trade unions in France legalized (1884)

1885

Stevenson's *Dr. Jekyll and Mr. Hyde* (1886)

Antoine's Théâtre Libre (1887) — Eiffel Tower completed, Paris (1887–89)

Strindberg's *Miss Julie* (1888)

Brahm's Freie Bühne (1889)

1890

Grein's Independent Theatre (1891)

Lugné–Poë's Théâtre de l'Oeuvre (1893)

Shaw's *Arms and the Man* (1894) — Dreyfus affair in France (1894)

Oscar Wilde's *The Importance of Being Earnest* (1895)

1895

Chekhov's *Sea Gull*; Jarry's *Ubu Roi*; revolving stage in Munich (1896)

Moscow Art Theatre (1898)

Appia's *Music and Stage Setting* (1899) — Boer War in South Africa (1899)

1900

Freud's *Interpretation of Dreams* (1900)

Marconi's first transatlantic radiotelegraph message (1901)

Williams and Walker's *In Dahomey* (1902)

Boer War ends (1902)

Chekhov's *Cherry Orchard* (1904)

Synge's *Riders to the Sea* (1904)

Wright brothers make successful airplane flight (1903)

Craig's *The Art of Theatre*; Reinhardt succeeds Otto Brahm as director of Deutsches Theatre (1905)

1905

Einstein's theory of relativity (1905)

Picasso's *Les Demoiselles d'Avignon* (1907)

First modern Japanese drama presented by Osanai Kaoru (1909)

1910

Indian playwright, Rabindranath Tagore, receives Nobel Prize (1913)

Théâtre du Vieux Colombier (1913)

Anita Bush founds Lafayette Players (1914) — Stravinsky's *Le Sacre du Printemps* (1913)

World War I (1914)

Provincetown Playhouse (1915)

1915

movements by underrepresented groups such as African Americans, women, and gays and lesbians. Also, there were wars of independence and civil wars throughout the continent of Africa during much of this period.

Another development after World War II was a striking increase in the industrial power of two of the defeated nations: Germany and Japan. Economically and politically, the world became more interdependent, with developments in one part of the world—such as environmental pollution or the price of oil—directly affecting other areas around the globe.

At the same time, tremendous problems remained: economic inequality and conflicts between rich and poor in many nations, assaults on the environment, persistent racial prejudice, and starvation and homelessness in many parts of the world. In the midst of this turmoil, theatre recovered from the ravages of World War II just as many parts of the world did.

Meanwhile, inventions continued at a rapid pace: nuclear power, for example, and computer and digital technology, which revolutionized many aspects of life, particularly communication. Earlier, this period saw the development of jet airplanes, television, and many advances in medical science. Moreover, in the post–World War II era there was a startling increase in communication across the globe, not only through radio but through television, movies, and then the Internet and other digital technologies. It was against this background (and also reflecting many other worldwide developments that we will touch on in the next chapter) that theatre became increasingly global.

Theatrical Realism

Realism One of the five strands of theatre in the modern era, realism conveys everything onstage to resemble observable, everyday life to promote a strong sense of audience recognition and identification.

As noted above, two major strands of modern theatre are realism and departures from realism, each addressing a different world view in the modern era. The desire to re-create everyday life on stage led to the development of two new forms of drama: realism and naturalism. In theatre, *realism* has a specific connotation. It means that everything on-stage is made to resemble observable, everyday life. How people speak, dress, and behave, as well as what kinds of rooms they live in conform as closely as possible to what we in the audience know is the way people actually speak, dress, act, and live. The power of realism lies in its credibility and in the sense of identification it creates. If we in the audience can verify from our own experience and observation the way people are acting onstage, we relate strongly to what we are observing. Realistic theatre is so effective that it has been a predominant form throughout the modern period.

Departures from realism To overcome perceived limitations of realistic theatre, this strand of modern theatre departs from realism via nonrealistic or antirealistic presentations. It often uses symbolism, nonlinear narrative, dream imagery, and other ways to avoid realistic representation.

The other major movement we call ***departures from realism***. This will be discussed later in this chapter, but a few points should be noted here. At the same time that realism was becoming pervasive, there were playwrights who found it too limiting. In fact, many devices that have served well throughout theatre history are not realistic: They include poetry (a characteristic of Shakespearean drama and most other drama before recent centuries), supernatural characters such as ghosts and witches (like those in *Macbeth*), songs, fantasies, and dream sequences. Such devices do not correspond to our experience of everyday life and hence are generally excluded from realism. The division between realism and departures from realism therefore creates something of a dilemma: With realism we can have strong audience recognition and identification; but we need departures from realism if we want to use a whole range of poetic and imaginative devices that make theatre richer.

Still, these divisions are a useful way of beginning to examine our modern theatre. We will look first at realism.

IBSEN'S REALISTIC DRAMA
The Norwegian dramatist Henrik Ibsen was a pioneer in developing modern realistic drama. Along with playwrights such as August Strindberg, he revolutionized the theatre of the late nineteenth century by dealing with taboo subject matter in a manner that mirrored everyday life. Much of their work was controversial and could not be produced in commercial theatres. This is a scene from one of Ibsen's landmark plays, *An Enemy of the People,* in an updated version by Christopher Hampton at the Chichester Festival Theatre in England. Hugh Bonneville played Dr. Tomas Stockmann and William Gaminara was Peter Stockmann. (©Elliott Franks/eyevine/Redux)

Realistic Playwrights

Henrik Ibsen   The Norwegian playwright Henrik Ibsen (1828–1906) is often considered the founder of modern realistic drama. It should be noted, however, that Ibsen wrote nonrealistic works at certain times in his career: As a young man he created romantic dramas, and near the end of his life (as discussed later) he experimented with abstract symbolist drama. He is best known, however, for his realistic works—plays such as **A Doll's House** (1879), **Ghosts** (1881), and **Hedda Gabler** (1890).

As a realistic playwright, Ibsen sought to convince his audiences that the stage action in his dramas represented everyday life. But he went further than that: He felt that drama should tackle subjects that had previously been taboo onstage—economic injustice, the sexual double standard of men and women, unhappy marriages, venereal disease, and religious hypocrisy. In his plays he refused to make simple moral judgments or resolve the dramatic action neatly. Not surprisingly, Ibsen and other realists met a great deal of opposition in producing their plays and were constantly plagued by censorship.

August Strindberg   A second major figure ushering in the era of modern realism was the Swedish playwright August Strindberg (1849–1912). Strindberg, who was twenty years younger than Ibsen, took realism another step in plays like *The Father* (1887) and *Miss Julie* (1888): He personalized and intensified Ibsen's realism. Instead of focusing on people in a social context, Strindberg concentrated on individuals at war with themselves and with each other. In both *The Father* and *Miss Julie,* there is a war between the sexes: Men and women vie with each other and attempt to dominate one another. In the end, one of them is destroyed—the man in *The Father* and the woman in *Miss Julie.* Also, Strindberg's characters are subject to the neuroses and anxieties that characterized so much of twentieth-century life. In fact, Strindberg took realistic drama closer to naturalism, a type of realism we will discuss shortly.

Anton Chekhov   The third significant playwright in the birth of modern realism is the Russian Anton Chekhov (1860–1904), whose play *The Sea Gull* (1896) was at first a failure but was later successfully revived by the Moscow Art Theatre. He wrote three other major plays: *Uncle Vanya* (1899), *The Three Sisters* (1900), and *The Cherry Orchard* (1904).

Chekhov's realism moved away from melodramatic elements such as the suicides in Ibsen's *Hedda Gabler* and Strindberg's *Miss Julie.* He also dealt with a full gallery of characters—often twelve or fourteen rather than five or six—and he orchestrated his characters in such a way that their stories overlapped and echoed one another. Chekhov also developed a blend of tragedy and comedy, employing a genre—often referred to as tragicomedy, discussed in the chapter "Theatrical Genres"—that has characterized much of modern drama.

Naturalism

Naturalism is a form of theatre that developed alongside the realism of Ibsen, Strindberg, and Chekhov; it can be seen as a subdivision of realism or an extreme form of realism. The naturalistic movement began in France in the nineteenth century and spread to other European countries. In *naturalism*, everything onstage—characters, language, properties, settings, costumes—should seem to have been lifted directly from everyday life. Dramatic action should never seem contrived but rather should look like a "slice of life."

Many of the naturalists believed that the most appropriate subject matter for drama was the lower class, and they frequently focused on the sordid and seamy aspects of society in order to confront audiences with social problems and instigate reforms. The most famous naturalistic theorist and playwright was the French author Émile Zola (1840–1902).

The naturalists' extreme position of absolutism in form and subject matter ultimately prevented their movement from being more influential and realism was seen as a more viable theatrical form.

Producers of Realism: Independent Theatres

At the time when they were first written, realistic and naturalistic works were seen by the mainstream as too controversial for production; in England, for example, the Lord Chamberlain refused to allow many of these works to be performed. In order to overcome this problem, a number of independent theatres were established throughout Europe. They were exempted from government censorship

AUGUST STRINDBERG
Along with Ibsen, the Swedish dramatist August Strindberg was a pioneer in developing modern realistic drama. These playwrights revolutionized the theatre of the late nineteenth century by dealing with taboo subject matter in a manner that mirrored everyday life. As already noted, much of their work was controversial and could not be produced in state or commercial theatres. (©Hulton Deutsch/ Getty Images)

Naturalism   Special form of realism developed in Europe in the late nineteenth century; it was not carefully plotted or constructed but was meant to present a "slice of life."

THE CHERRY ORCHARD BY ANTON CHEKHOV
The Russian dramatist Anton Chekhov created a type of modern realistic drama that has
had a profound influence on subsequent dramatists. Subtle, low-key, it avoided melodramatic
elements but probed deeply and movingly into the hearts and souls of the characters he
depicted. His final masterpiece was *The Cherry Orchard,* in which the main character,
Madame Ranevskaya, unable to adjust to modern times, loses the family home and her precious
cherry orchard. In this scene we see the cast, with Zoë Wanamaker, seated left, as Ranevskaya,
in a production at London's National Theatre, directed by Howard Davies. (©Geraint Lewis)

because they were organized as subscription companies, with theatregoers being
treated like members of a private club.

The best-known of these independent theatres were the Théâtre Libre (Free
Theatre), founded in Paris in 1887 by André Antoine (1858–1943); the Freie
Bühne (Free Stage), founded in Germany in 1889 by Otto Brahm (1856–1912);
and the Independent Theatre, founded in London in 1891 by J. T. Grein (1862–
1935). In 1892, the year after its founding, the Independent Theatre introduced
the Irish-born realistic playwright George Bernard Shaw (1856–1950) to the
London public by producing his first play, **Widowers' Houses**. Shaw's plays
dealt with the sociopolitical and economic issues of late nineteenth- and early
twentieth-century English society.

Possibly the most influential of the late-nineteenth-century theatres dedicated to realism was the Moscow Art Theatre, which mounted a landmark production of *The Sea Gull* as well as Chekhov's other major plays. Founded in
1898 by Konstantin Stanislavski (1863–1938) and Vladimir Nemirovich-
Danchenko (1858–1943), it continues to produce drama today. In addition to
giving the world an important theatre, the Moscow Art Theatre provided the
first systematic approach to realistic acting; that of Stanislavski, discussed in
detail in the chapter on acting, which formed the basis for most realistic acting
in the twentieth century.

During the early decades of the twentieth century—after the initial objections
and censorship had eased—realistic plays began to be presented commercially in

NATURALISM

An extreme form of realism is naturalism, which attempts to put onstage an unflinching, almost documentary version of people and events as they are encountered in real life. An early example is *Thérèse Raquin* (1873), a drama by Émile Zola. In the preface to this play, Zola stated the tenets of naturalism. Here we see Ben Daniels as Laurent and Charlotte Emmerson as Thérèse in a London production. (©Geraint Lewis)

both Europe and the United States. In the United States, however, for a long time, small, independent groups like those that developed in France, Germany, and England produced these plays. The Provincetown Playhouse, the Neighborhood Playhouse, and the Washington Square Players, all founded in 1915 as alternatives to commercial theatre, often presented experimental, nonrealistic work; they also offered a haven for controversial or unknown realistic drama. The Provincetown Playhouse, in particular, supported the early work of the playwright Eugene O'Neill (1888–1953).

In terms of realism, the most important producing group in the United States between World War I and World War II was the Group Theatre, a noncommercial company in New York's Broadway district. Its founding members were Lee Strasberg (1901–1982), Cheryl Crawford (1902–1986), and Harold Clurman (1901–1980); and its acting company included a number of performers who became well known in movies as well as on the stage. Its resident playwright was Clifford Odets (1906–1963), whose plays include *Awake and Sing* (1935) and *Golden Boy* (1937). The Group Theatre disbanded in 1941, but its influence on realistic acting, directing, and playwriting continued for many years.

Experiencing Theatre History

THE SEA GULL

1898, Moscow It is the evening of December 17, 1898, and the Moscow Art Theatre is about to give its first performance of *The Sea Gull* by the Russian playwright Anton Chekhov. Backstage, the actors and actresses are nervous—so nervous that just before the curtain is to rise, most of them have taken valerian drops, a tranquilizer. Konstantin Stanislavski, the director of the play, who is also playing the role of Trigorin—a bored commercial writer—finds it difficult to control a twitch in his leg.

The reason for their anxiety is easy to understand. The author, Anton Chekhov, who trained to be a doctor, is one of the best-known short-story writers in Russia. So far, however, his dramatic work has not met with the same approval as his stories. In fact, when *The Sea Gull* was first produced two years ago in Saint Petersburg, the performance was a fiasco, not because of the play but because the company presenting it had not rehearsed and had produced it very badly. So devastated was Chekhov by the experience that after the performance he left the theatre in despair and swore never again to write plays or even to let *The Sea Gull* be performed.

One reason why the company in Saint Petersburg failed to give a decent performance of *The Sea Gull* is that the play was quite different from anything they were accustomed to. It takes place on a Russian country estate and is about

two generations of actresses and writers. The leading female character, Madame Akardina, is a vain, self-absorbed actress. Her son Treplev, an idealistic young writer, is in love with Nina, a young woman who aspires to be an actress. Akardina's lover, Trigorin, with whom Nina falls in love, is a successful writer but dissatisfied with his life. (This is the character Stanislavski is now playing in Moscow in 1898.)

A number of other people are also involved with these four main characters, and one of the unusual aspects of the play is that the characters' lives are all closely intertwined. This orchestration of a group of characters is unlike previous nineteenth-century dramas. Another unusual aspect is an absence of melodramatic confrontations and developments, such as the murders, suicides, and sudden plot twists that had been staples of most nineteenth-century theatre. Rather, the action is subtle, modulated, and true to life.

Interestingly, the same lifelike qualities that have confused so many people have attracted a playwright and producer named Vladimir Nemirovich-Danchenko—a cofounder, with Stanislavski, of the Moscow Art Theatre. Nemirovich-Danchenko and Stanislavski want their theatre to be different from others, and Nemirovich-Danchenko feels that *The Sea Gull* is just the kind of play that will set it apart. However, when he first asked Chekhov to let

the Moscow Art Theatre present this play, Chekhov adamantly refused, because of the debacle in Saint Petersburg. It has taken all of Nemirovich-Danchenko's powers of persuasion to win Chekhov's consent.

All this explains why there is so much at stake tonight in Moscow, as Act I of *The Sea Gull* begins. Chekhov himself is so worried about the outcome that he is not even here; he is far away, in Yalta—partly because of ill health, it is true, but also because of his nervousness.

Now the performers are halfway through Act I, but they cannot tell how the audience is responding. When the act ends, they are greeted by a monumental silence. Fearing failure, the actress Olga Knipper (who will later become Chekhov's wife) fights desperately to keep from breaking into hysterical sobs. Then, all of a sudden, the silence is broken; the audience breaks into thunderous, tumultuous applause. In the words of an eyewitness: "Like the bursting of a dam, like an exploding bomb, a sudden deafening eruption of applause broke out." The applause goes on and on, and Stanislavski dances a jig. The same reaction will greet the next three acts.

Both Chekhov and the Moscow Art Theatre have triumphed, and a new chapter in modern theatre has begun. So significant is this event that a century later the symbol on the curtain of the Moscow Art Theatre will still be a sea gull.

THE GROUP THEATRE'S *AWAKE AND SING*
Clifford Odets's play, first produced in 1935, is an example of a realistic social drama dealing with American concerns of the 1930s. It is an intense family drama set in a Bronx apartment during the Depression, and it required the realistic acting for which the Group Theatre was noted. Seen here is a 1971 revival directed by Vivian Matalon for the Hampstead Theatre Club in London. The actors include Patience Collier as Bessie and Harold Kasket as Jacob. (©ArenaPal/Topham/The Image Works)

During the Depression of the 1930s, President Franklin Delano Roosevelt established the Works Progress Administration (WPA), which organized governmentally subsidized agencies to put the unemployed back to work. The Federal Theatre Project, producing both realistic and highly theatrical productions and headed by Hallie Flanagan Davis (1890–1969), a college professor, supported theatrical ventures throughout the United States and helped revitalize interest in theatre outside New York City. The Federal Theatre also assisted aspiring African American theatres and artists, supporting, for example, an all-black production of **Macbeth** directed by Orson Welles (1915–1985) under the auspices of the Negro Theatre Project. For political reasons the government discontinued funding the project in 1939.

Realism in the Twentieth Century

Playwrights in many countries throughout the twentieth century continued the realistic drama initiated by Ibsen, Strindberg, and Chekhov. In Europe, for example, two Irish playwrights who had a strong impact on realism were John Millington Synge (1871–1909), in plays like *Riders to the Sea* (1904); and Sean O'Casey (1884–1964), in such works as *Juno and the Paycock* (1924) and *The Plough and the Stars* (1926).

THE REALISM OF IRISH PLAYWRIGHTS
Among the important realistic playwrights in Ireland who emerged between the two world wars was Sean O'Casey. O'Casey carefully reconstructs Irish life and concerns in such plays as *Juno and the Paycock*. Shown here from left to right are: J. Smith-Cameron, Ed Malone and Ciaran O'Reilly in a production at the Irish Repertory Theatre in New York. (© Ruby Washington/The New York Times/Redux)

In the United States, Eugene O'Neill wrote a number of realistic plays early in his career, including **Anna Christie** (1921) and **Desire Under the Elms** (1924). After writing experimental plays through much of the 1920s and 1930s, O'Neill later returned to realism and wrote what many consider his finest plays: *The Iceman Cometh* (1939), *A Moon for the Misbegotten* (1947), and *Long Day's Journey into Night* (produced in 1957). Another well-known realistic playwright of the 1930s and 1940s was Lillian Hellman (1905–1984).

Between 1945 and 1975, many playwrights continued to refine the realistic form. Two important American writers in this category were Tennessee Williams (1911–1983) and Arthur Miller (1915–2005). Williams's important realistic plays include *A Streetcar Named Desire* (1947) and *Cat on a Hot Tin Roof* (1954)—both of which won the Pulitzer Prize—and *The Night of the Iguana* (1961). Miller's realistic works include *All My Sons* (1947) and *A View from the Bridge* (1955).

Some critics suggest that Miller and Williams wrote in a form known as *selective realism*—a type of realism that heightens certain details of action, scenery, and dialogue while omitting others. For example, in Miller's *Death of a Salesman* (1949), the playwright highlights selected elements of the world of the main character, Willy Loman—elements that symbolize his downfall. Moreover, scenes in Willy's mind and scenes from the past are interspersed with scenes in the present. Tennessee Williams combines the theatrical device of a narrator with realistic scenes in his play *The Glass Menagerie* (1945).

REALISTIC THEATRE CONTINUES
In the second half of the twentieth century, realism continued to be a major form of drama by Western playwrights. A good example is the work of Arthur Miller. Some of his plays could be classified as "selective realism," but others were realistic in the traditional sense. A good example is *The Price,* which was revived by the Roundabout Theatre Company at the American Airlines Theater in New York in 2017 with Tony Shalhoub, Mark Ruffalo and Jessica Hecht in the cast. (©Sara Krulwich/The New York Times/Redux)

Throughout the twentieth century, the end of realism was pronounced periodically, but the form has continued with great vigor to the present day. In 1962, another American writer, Edward Albee (1928–2016), joined the list of important realists with his play *Who's Afraid of Virginia Woolf?* (1962). Albee's style was highly enigmatic, however, and some of his plays—such as *Three Tall Women* (1991); *The Play about the Baby* (1998); and *The Goat, or Who Is Sylvia?* (2002)—combine techniques from realism and departures from realism.

In England in the 1950s, a group of anti-establishment playwrights known collectively as the angry young men dealt with the dissolving British empire, class conflict, and political disillusionment. Most of the dramas by the "angry young men" are in the traditional realistic form, slightly modified. The most famous of these plays was *Look Back in Anger* (1956) by John Osborne (1929–1994).

DEPARTURES FROM REALISM

In spite of its substantial impact on our contemporary theatre, as well as on film and television, theatrical realism is often seen as having serious limitations. For example, realistic drama excludes a number of effective, long-standing theatrical devices, such as music, dance, symbolism, poetry, fantasy, and the supernatural. Some authors argue that

theatre can never truly be realistic, that the conventions of the art are always apparent. From the outset of realism, then, there have been strong countermovements.

In discussing these ***departures from realism***, we will look at the following: early antirealist playwrights; symbolism; antirealist designers; Russian theatricalism; expressionism; futurism; surrealism; theatre of cruelty; epic theatre; and absurdism. In addition we will discuss other nontraditional approaches including happenings, multimedia, environmental theatre, and poor theatre.

Departures from realism
To overcome perceived limitations of realistic theatre, this strand of modern theatre departs from realism via nonrealistic or antirealistic presentations. It often uses symbolism, nonlinear narrative, dream imagery, and other ways to avoid realistic representation.

Departures from Realism—Playwrights: Ibsen, Strindberg, and Wedekind

As we noted earlier in this chapter, Ibsen and Strindberg are remembered most for their realistic plays, but late in their careers they moved away from realism. In plays such as *The Master Builder* (1892) and *When We Dead Awaken* (1899), Ibsen adopted many of the tenets of symbolism, discussed below; and August Strindberg's later antirealistic dramas, such as **A Dream Play** (1902) and **The Ghost Sonata** (1907), have been especially influential. As its title indicates, *A Dream Play* evokes the world of dreams.

As Strindberg says in his explanatory note to *A Dream Play,* the events of the play are dramatized in "the disconnected but apparently logical form of a dream. Everything can happen; everything is possible and likely."

The German dramatist Frank Benjamin Wedekind (1864–1918), in such plays as **Spring's Awakening** (1891), combined symbolist and grotesque elements with realistic—sometimes controversial—subject matter. This particular play was the basis for a successful 2007 musical version.

Symbolism

The leading antirealistic movement between 1880 and 1910 was ***symbolism***. Its major proponents were French, but it influenced playwrights and practitioners in

Symbolism Movement of the late nineteenth century and early twentieth century that sought to express inner truth rather than represent life realistically.

DEPARTURES FROM REALISM: STRINDBERG

Toward the end of his career, August Strindberg wrote plays that departed from the realistic style. These dramas were forerunners of many avant-garde texts of the later twentieth century. Strindberg's *A Dream Play* uses the structure of a dream to break many of the conventions of realistic drama. Seen here are Angus Wright, Mark Arends, and Anastasia Hille, in a new version of the play by Caryl Churchill, directed by Katie Mitchell and staged at the Royal National Theatre in London. (©Geraint Lewis)

many other countries. The symbolists believed that drama should present not mundane, day-to-day activities but the mystery of being and the infinite qualities of the human spirit. They called for poetic theatre in which symbolic images rather than concrete actions would be the basic means of communicating with the audience. Symbolist plays often seem to take place in a dream world, and their most important dramatic goal is not to tell a story but rather to evoke atmosphere and mood. Probably the most renowned symbolist authors were Maurice Maeterlinck (1862–1949) in Belgium and Paul Claudel (1868–1955) in France.

The symbolists, like the realists, needed independently organized theatre companies to produce their plays. In France, two theatre companies were dedicated to antirealistic drama and production style. Théâtre d'Art was organized by Paul Fort (1872–1960) in 1890. Three years later, Théâtre de l'Oeuvre was established by Aurélien-Marie Lugné-Poë (1869–1940). (Possibly the most notorious of Lugné-Poë's presentations was not a symbolist work but a play by Alfred Jarry [1873–1907] called **Ubu the King** [1896], a takeoff in comic-book style on Shakespeare—in particular, on **Julius Caesar**, *Macbeth,* and the history plays. In addition to farce and satire, it employed a number of scatological references.) In Ireland, the Abbey Theatre and the poet William Butler Yeats (1865–1939), who was also a playwright, were associated with early symbolist drama.

Expressionism

Expressionism Movement in Germany at about the time of World War I, characterized by an attempt to dramatize subjective states through distortion; striking, often grotesque images; and lyric, unrealistic dialogue.

Expressionism, which flourished in Germany at the time of World War I, was a movement in art and literature in which the representation of reality was distorted in order to communicate inner feelings. In a painting of a man, for example, the lines in his face would be twisted to indicate the turmoil he feels inside.

Expressionism in drama has well-defined characteristics. Expressionist plays are often highly subjective and the dramatic action is seen through the eyes of the protagonist and therefore frequently seems distorted or dreamlike. The protagonist

Part 4   Global Theatres: Past and Present

in a typical expressionist play is a Christlike figure who journeys through a series of incidents that may be causally unrelated. Characters are representative types, often given titles—such as Man, Woman, or Clerk—rather than names. The language of the plays is often telegraphic, with most speeches consisting of one or two lines, but these speeches alternate with long lyrical passages. Many expressionist playwrights were politically motivated, supporting socialist and pacifist causes, though some were apolitical.

The major German expressionist playwrights were Georg Kaiser (1878–1945) and Ernst Toller (1893–1939). Shortly after expressionism flourished in Europe, its influence was felt in the United States, for example, in some of Eugene O'Neill's plays, including **The Emperor Jones** (1922), as well as in **The Adding Machine** (1923), by Elmer Rice (1892–1967).

ELMER RICE'S *THE ADDING MACHINE*
This play, like many dramas of the early 1920s, uses expressionistic techniques. The audience sees the drama through the eyes of the protagonist, Mr. Zero, an accountant who is to be replaced by an Adding Machine. Shown here are Joel Hatch, left, as Mr. Zero and Joe Farrell as Shrdlu in a musical adaptation of *The Adding Machine* at the Minetta Lane Theater in New York, in a production that originated in Chicago. (©Sara Krulwich/The New York Times/Redux)

Futurism and Surrealism

Futurism originated in Italy around 1909. Unlike the expressionists, the futurists idealized war and the machine age. They attacked artistic ideals of the past, ridiculing them as "museum art" and arguing that new forms had to be created for new eras. They also believed that audiences should be confronted and antagonized.

Surrealism began in 1924. One of its major exponents was André Breton (1896–1966), and its center was France. Surrealists argued that the subconscious is the highest plane of reality and attempted to re-create its workings dramatically. Many of their plays seem to be set in a dream world, mixing recognizable and fantastic events.

Futurism Art movement, begun in Italy about 1909, which idealized mechanization and machinery.

Surrealism Departure from realism that attempted to present dramatically the working of the subconscious.

Unique Voices

Throughout the modern period there have been playwrights who presented a unique voice, a voice that does not fit neatly into one of the categories we have been discussing. Examples are the Italian playwright Pirandello and two French dramatists, Jean Giraudoux and Jean Anouilh. Luigi Pirandello (1867–1936), in **Six Characters in Search of an Author** (1921), has six characters from an unfinished play existing in a playwright's mind enter a theatre and interrupt a rehearsal, in the hope that the troupe will act out their unfinished story. In the course of the action—as in several of his other plays—Pirandello deals very theatrically with questions of appearance versus reality and art versus life.

Two significant French playwrights of the period between World War I and World War II were Jean Giraudoux (1882–1944) and Jean Anouilh (1910–1987). Giraudoux believed in the primacy of the word, and his language was usually eloquent as well as witty. He also stressed contradictions, ironies, and antitheses in working out the themes of his plays. Among his better-known works are *Amphitryon 38* (1929) and *The Trojan War Will Not Take Place* (1935). As can be seen from their titles, many of his plays were based on classic themes or plots.

A LANDMARK PLAY

Alfred Jarry's *Ubu Roi,* written in 1896, is often cited as a forerunner of many avant-garde movements of the twentieth century. It is an insane takeoff of *King Oedipus* and a number of Shakespeare's histories and tragedies. Shown here, with Denis Lavant as the King, is a production at the Théâtre de Gennevilliers in France. (©Jean-Paul Lozouet)

Unit set Single setting that can represent a variety of locales with the simple addition of properties or scenic elements.

Jean Anouilh also used a classic source for his best-known play, *Antigone* (1943), a reworking of the Greek classic that spoke to the situation in Nazi-occupied France.

How Were Departures from Realism Staged?

There were many artists who experimented with production techniques to stage the nonrealistic dramas of the era. Among them were key designers and directors.

Designers: Appia and Craig Scene designers also contributed to the departure from realistically based representations of life. Adolphe Appia (1862–1928) and Edward Gordon Craig (1872–1966), in particular, were able to present many of the symbolists' theories visually. Appia (who was born in Switzerland) and Craig (who was English) both argued against photographic reproduction as a basic goal of scene design; rather, they believed that a setting should suggest a locale but should not reproduce it. Both employed levels and platforms to design spaces that would be functional for the performer, and both took full advantage of the introduction of electricity and used light as an integral visual element. Appia and Craig influenced many of the leading twentieth-century American designers; for example, devices such as Craig's *unit set*—a single setting that can represent various locales— have been especially important.

Russian Theatricalism: Meyerhold

The reaction against realism also influenced a number of Russian artists. Possibly the most influential was the director Vsevolod Meyerhold (1874–1940), who was the leading Russian antirealist between 1905 and 1939 and frequently experimented with *theatricalism*. Theatricalists liked to expose the devices of theatre, such as the way stage machinery works, to make the audience conscious of watching a performance; they also borrowed techniques from the circus, the music hall, and similar entertainments.

The list of Meyerhold's innovations and experiments is astounding, and much of what was called avant-garde in the second half of the twentieth century can be traced back to his experiments early in the century. Meyerhold's theatre was a director's theatre: He was literally the author of his productions, and he frequently restructured or rewrote classics. He searched for suitable environments for his

APPIA'S DESIGN FOR *IPHIGENIA IN AULIS*
Appia's ideas of lighting and scenery were revolutionary. He moved from realistic settings to the use of shapes and levels that would serve as acting areas. He was also among the first to realize the vast possibilities of modern lighting techniques.
(©Billy Rose Theatre Collection, New York Public Library for the Performing Arts/Art Resource)

presentations, arguing for the use of found spaces; that is, spaces (such as streets, factories, and schools) not originally meant for theatre. He experimented with, and theorized about, multimedia in stage productions.

Meyerhold also attempted to train his performers physically by using techniques of commedia dell'arte, the circus, and vaudeville. He devised an acting system known as ***biomechanics***, which emphasized external, physical training; the implication of biomechanics was that the performer's body could be trained to operate like a machine. Meyerhold's sets, known as ***constructivist*** settings, provided machines for his performers to work on; these settings consisted of skeletal frames, ramps, stairways, and platforms and often looked like huge Tinkertoys.

Artaud and Brecht: The Theatre of Cruelty and Epic Theatre

The two most influential theatrical theorists in Europe between the world wars were Bertolt Brecht and Antonin Artaud. Both reacted vehemently against the principles and the aesthetics of realistic theatre. Antonin Artaud (1896–1948), who was French and who had originally been associated with the surrealists, proposed a ***theatre of cruelty*** in the 1930s. Artaud did not literally mean that theatre artists should be cruel to their audiences or physically brutalize them—although some avant-garde theatre artists in the 1960s interpreted cruelty as actual physical confrontation with spectators. He felt, instead, that the viewers' senses should be bombarded. (A contemporary example of such sensory involvement

Theatricalism Exposing the elements of theatre to make the audience members aware that they are watching theatre.

Biomechanics Meyerhold's theory that a performer's body should be machinelike and that emotion could be represented externally.

Constructivism Post–World War I scene-design movement in which sets—frequently composed of ramps, platforms, and levels—were nonrealistic and were intended to provide greater opportunities for physical action.

Theatre of cruelty Antonin Artaud's visionary concept of a theatre based on magic and ritual, which would liberate deep, violent, and erotic impulses.

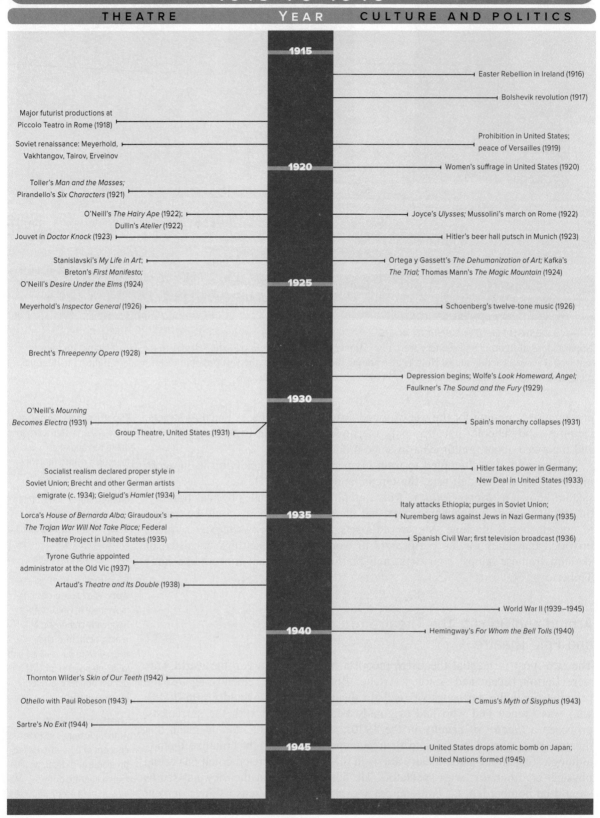

1915

Easter Rebellion in Ireland (1916)

Bolshevik revolution (1917)

Major futurist productions at
Piccolo Teatro in Rome (1918)

Soviet renaissance: Meyerhold,
Vakhtangov, Tairov, Erveinov

Prohibition in United States;
peace of Versailles (1919)

1920

Women's suffrage in United States (1920)

Toller's *Man and the Masses;*
Pirandello's *Six Characters* (1921)

O'Neill's *The Hairy Ape* (1922);
Dullin's *Atelier* (1922)

Joyce's *Ulysses;* Mussolini's march on Rome (1922)

Jouvet in *Doctor Knock* (1923)

Hitler's beer hall putsch in Munich (1923)

Stanislavski's *My Life in Art;*
Breton's *First Manifesto;*
O'Neill's *Desire Under the Elms* (1924)

Ortega y Gassett's *The Dehumanization of Art;* Kafka's
The Trial; Thomas Mann's *The Magic Mountain* (1924)

1925

Meyerhold's *Inspector General* (1926)

Schoenberg's twelve-tone music (1926)

Brecht's *Threepenny Opera* (1928)

Depression begins; Wolfe's *Look Homeward, Angel;*
Faulkner's *The Sound and the Fury* (1929)

1930

O'Neill's *Mourning
Becomes Electra* (1931)

Group Theatre, United States (1931)

Spain's monarchy collapses (1931)

Socialist realism declared proper style in
Soviet Union; Brecht and other German artists
emigrate (c. 1934); Gielgud's *Hamlet* (1934)

Hitler takes power in Germany;
New Deal in United States (1933)

Lorca's *House of Bernarda Alba;* Giraudoux's
The Trojan War Will Not Take Place; Federal
Theatre Project in United States (1935)

Italy attacks Ethiopia; purges in Soviet Union;
Nuremberg laws against Jews in Nazi Germany (1935)

1935

Spanish Civil War; first television broadcast (1936)

Tyrone Guthrie appointed
administrator at the Old Vic (1937)

Artaud's *Theatre and Its Double* (1938)

World War II (1939–1945)

1940

Hemingway's *For Whom the Bell Tolls* (1940)

Thornton Wilder's *Skin of Our Teeth* (1942)

Othello with Paul Robeson (1943)

Camus's *Myth of Sisyphus* (1943)

Sartre's *No Exit* (1944)

1945

United States drops atomic bomb on Japan;
United Nations formed (1945)

would be a multimedia presentation or a sound and light show at a rock concert.)

He argued that Western theatre needed to be totally transformed because its literary tradition, which emphasized language, was antithetical to its ritualistic origins. Artaud believed that Western theatre artists should study the stylized Asian theatres. He also asserted that there were "no more masterpieces," by which he meant that the classics should be produced not for their historical significance but only if they were still relevant to contemporary audiences. For Artaud, a text was not sacred but could be reworked in order to point up its relevance. Artaud, like many of the antirealists who preceded him, wanted to reorganize the theatre space to make the audience the center of attention.

Bertolt Brecht (1898–1956), who was German, developed what he called *epic theatre*. Brecht's major plays—including *Mother Courage* (1937–1941), *The Good Person of Szechwan* (1938–1940), and *The Caucasian Chalk Circle* (1944–1945)—were written between 1933 and 1945, while he was in exile from Hitler's Germany. His theories, most of which were formulated in the 1930s but frequently revised, have influenced many contemporary playwrights and directors. As the term *epic theatre* implies, Brecht's plays are epic in scope. They are, accordingly, episodic in structure: They cover a great deal of time, shift locale frequently, and have intricate plots and many characters. Brecht, an ardent socialist, believed that theatre could create an intellectual climate for social change, and the goal of his epic theatre is to instruct. He believed that a production should force the audience to remain emotionally detached—or *alienated*—from the dramatic action. To prevent emotional involvement, Brecht's works are highly theatrical; the audience is always made aware of being in a theatre. A narrator is frequently used to comment on the dramatic action, for example. To alienate the audience, Brecht also used a technique he referred to as historification. Many of his plays, such as *Mother Courage,* are set in the past, but it is apparent that he is really concerned with contemporary events paralleling the historic occurrences.

BERTOLT BRECHT

Brecht's epic theories and plays continue to be part of contemporary theatre; his concepts, including alienation and historification, continue to be debated and are still influential. Brecht's personal life has been no less controversial than his work: Recent scholarship suggests that some of his work was plagiarized and that his political stance was perhaps hypocritical. A prime example of Brecht's work is *Mother Courage and Her Children,* shown here with Meryl Streep as Courage and Frederick Weller as Eilif in a new version translated by Tony Kushner and directed by George C. Wolfe, at the Delacorte Theatre in Central Park. (©Michael Daniel)

Impact of Totalitarianism on Theatre

Before we discuss avant-garde theatre and departures from realism in the quarter century following World War II, we should briefly discuss how the rise of totalitarianism impacted the theatre and many of the artists. In totalitarian societies—particularly the Soviet Union under Stalin and Germany under Hitler—government-supported

Epic theatre Form of drama associated with Bertolt Brecht and aimed at the intellect rather than the emotions in order to effect social change.

IN FOCUS: EVALUATING TOTALITARIAN ART

How can we evaluate works created by artists who support dictatorial regimes? There were many playwrights, actors, directors, and designers who served Adolf Hitler by creating theatrical propaganda. There were many playwrights, as another example, who wrote plays in the "socialist realist" style supporting the totalitarian regime of Josef Stalin in Russia. How can we assess such works aesthetically? Can a work be classified as great art if it is politically unacceptable? Can we distinguish between an artist's politics and the aesthetic qualities of his or her works?

One debate of this nature is over the films of Leni Riefenstahl (1902–2003), a German director greatly admired by Hitler. Riefenstahl's films are documentaries that are formally beautiful and were significant advances in the art of documentary filmmaking. However, her films *The Triumph of the Will* (1935) and *Olympia* (1936–1938) glorify Nazism and paint a glowing picture of Hitler's Germany in the mid-1930s. Can we divorce the aesthetic qualities of these works from their politics? How should we discuss Riefenstahl's contributions to filmmaking?

Similar questions can be asked about the theatre artists who wrote and produced plays in Hitler's Germany, Mussolini's Italy, Franco's Spain, and Stalin's Russia. For example, the playwright Maxim Gorky (1868–1936) became a proponent of socialist realism. How can we evaluate his later works in light of the oppression of those artists who opposed the aesthetic control imposed by the totalitarian regime? How do we evaluate Luigi Pirandello who was an avid supporter of fascism and Mussolini and donated his Nobel Prize to the fascist Italian government? Does Pirandello's support of a fascist regime decrease the significance of his plays? How can we reconcile his politics with his aesthetics?

Similar questions have been raised about the plays of August Strindberg because of his misogynist and sexist beliefs. In more recent times, film actor and director Mel Gibson has made racist, sexist, and anti-Semitic comments. How then do we judge his Academy Award–winning film *Hacksaw Ridge* (2016)?

Such questions do not seem difficult when an artist's work is aesthetically not very good; but they become extremely difficult when the work is aesthetically accomplished and historically significant.

theatres became instruments of propaganda. Courageous artists attempted to attack these regimes, but for the most part experimentation and freedom of expression were suppressed. The totalitarian rulers saw realistic art as easier to manipulate and to use for propaganda and viewed individual experimentation as dangerous because it implied freedom. Therefore, the fascists and communists vigorously attacked many of the artists who experimented with forms that departed from realism.

In Spain, for example, the playwright Federico García Lorca (1898–1936)—author of **Blood Wedding** (1933), *Yerma* (1934), and **The House of Bernarda Alba** (1936)—was killed by Franco's forces during the Spanish civil war. Productions of García Lorca's works, which poetically dramatized the oppression of Spanish women, were not allowed in Spain until after Franco's death in 1975.

Numerous German theatre artists, because of their religion or politics, had to flee Germany after Adolf Hitler's takeover in 1933. They included the directors Max Reinhardt and Erwin Piscator (1893–1966) as well as the playwrights Brecht and Toller. Many artists who opposed the Third Reich but did not leave were interned in the Nazi concentration camps.

Still, theatrical artists did resist totalitarianism; the most vivid example of such resistance was the theatre organized by inmates of the Nazi concentration camps. In camps in conquered territories during World War II, such as Auschwitz, there were surreptitious entertainments in the barracks: These improvised

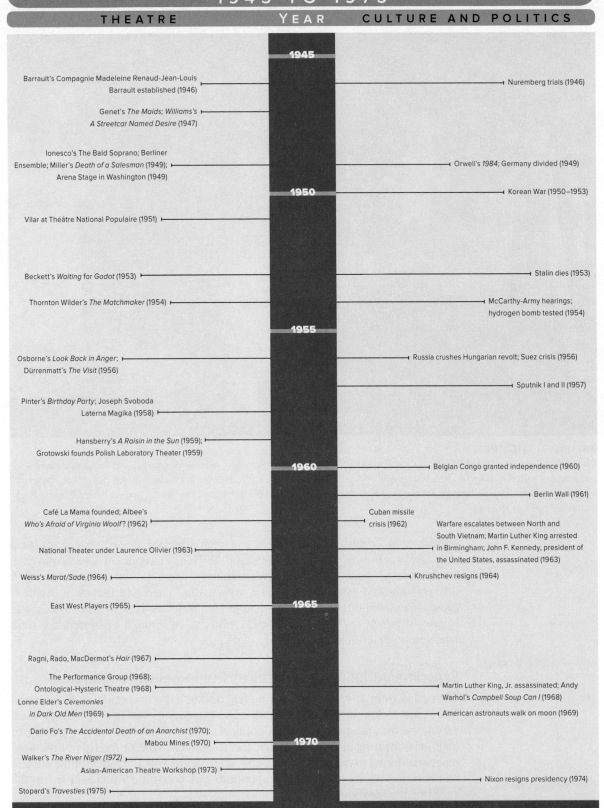

1945 TO 1975

| THEATRE | YEAR | CULTURE AND POLITICS |

1945

Barrault's Compagnie Madeleine Renaud-Jean-Louis Barrault established (1946) — Nuremberg trials (1946)

Genet's *The Maids*; Williams's *A Streetcar Named Desire* (1947)

Ionesco's The Bald Soprano; Berliner Ensemble; Miller's *Death of a Salesman* (1949); Arena Stage in Washington (1949) — Orwell's *1984*; Germany divided (1949)

1950 — Korean War (1950–1953)

Vilar at Théâtre National Populaire (1951)

Beckett's *Waiting* for *Godot* (1953) — Stalin dies (1953)

Thornton Wilder's *The Matchmaker* (1954) — McCarthy-Army hearings; hydrogen bomb tested (1954)

1955

Osborne's *Look Back in Anger*; Dürrenmatt's *The Visit* (1956) — Russia crushes Hungarian revolt; Suez crisis (1956)

— Sputnik I and II (1957)

Pinter's *Birthday Party*; Joseph Svoboda Laterna Magika (1958)

Hansberry's *A Raisin in the Sun* (1959); Grotowski founds Polish Laboratory Theater (1959)

1960 — Belgian Congo granted independence (1960)

— Berlin Wall (1961)

Café La Mama founded; Albee's *Who's Afraid of Virginia Woolf?* (1962) — Cuban missile crisis (1962) — Warfare escalates between North and South Vietnam; Martin Luther King arrested in Birmingham; John F. Kennedy, president of the United States, assassinated (1963)

National Theater under Laurence Olivier (1963)

Weiss's *Marat/Sade* (1964) — Khrushchev resigns (1964)

East West Players (1965) **1965**

Ragni, Rado, MacDermot's *Hair* (1967)

The Performance Group (1968); Ontological-Hysteric Theatre (1968) — Martin Luther King, Jr. assassinated; Andy Warhol's *Campbell Soup Can I* (1968)

Lonne Elder's *Ceremonies in Dark Old Men* (1969) — American astronauts walk on moon (1969)

Dario Fo's *The Accidental Death of an Anarchist* (1970); Mabou Mines (1970) **1970**

Walker's *The River Niger* (1972)

Asian-American Theatre Workshop (1973) — Nixon resigns presidency (1974)

Stopard's *Travesties* (1975)

Chapter 15 *The Modern Theatre Emerges*

ABSURDIST THEATRE
The period following World War II was particularly fertile for theatre. Among a number of nonrealistic forms of theatre was a movement called *absurdism,* which stressed illogical, random, inexplicable events and characters. An important playwright of absurdism was Eugène Ionesco, whose play *Exit the King* is shown here in a Broadway production starring Geoffrey Rush as the King. (©Joan Marcus)

presentations consisted of literature and drama recited from memory, satirical skits, and traditional songs. In the camp at Theresienstadt, in Czechoslovakia, satirical plays, operas, and cabaret entertainments were written and openly staged; this was allowed because the Nazis were using Theresienstadt as a "model" camp—they brought the Red Cross and foreign officials there in order to discredit rumors of atrocities. Most of the artists who passed through Theresienstadt were later sent to extermination centers.

Experimentation and Departures from Realism Continue

The period from 1945 to 1975 saw a great deal of experimentation with theatrical forms and techniques. Much of this experimentation was inspired by political unrest and by a desire to question political authority through the questioning of traditional theatrical practices, styles, and techniques. One of the first of the non-traditional forms to develop immediately after World War II, theatre of the absurd, was born out of the unanswerable questions this horrific conflict had left in the minds of the survivors.

Part 4   Global Theatres: Past and Present

Existentialism and Theatre of the Absurd *Existentialism* is a philosophy most clearly articulated by two Frenchmen, Jean-Paul Sartre (1905–1980) and Albert Camus (1913–1960), who were reacting, among other things, against World War II. Existentialists believe that existence has little meaning; that God does not exist; that humanity is alone in an irrational universe; and that the only significant thing an individual can do is accept responsibility for his or her own actions. Both Camus and Sartre wrote plays illustrating these beliefs. The best-known are Sartre's *The Flies* (1943), an adaptation of the Greek *Oresteia;* and *No Exit* (1944), in which hell is equated with other people.

In the early 1950s, a theatrical approach emerged that combined existentialist philosophy with revolutionary, avant-garde dramatic form. Although not an organized movement, it was called ***theatre of the absurd*** by the critic Martin Esslin (1918–2002). Esslin pointed out that the playwrights in this group have certain qualities in common: the notion that much of what happens in life is ridiculous or absurd and cannot be explained logically, and the belief that this ridiculousness or absurdity should be reflected in dramatic action. Among the writers taking this approach are Samuel Beckett (1906–1989), Jean Genet (1910–1986), Eugène Ionesco (1912–1994), Edward Albee, and Harold Pinter (1930–2008).

Absurdist playwrights present our existence, including human relationships and human language, as futile or nonsensical. To reinforce this theme, they use seemingly illogical dramatic techniques. Their plots do not have either traditional climactic structure or episodic structure. Frequently, nothing seems to happen: The plot moves in a circle, concluding in the same way it began. The characters are not realistic, and the settings are sometimes strange and unrecognizable. The language is often telegraphic and sparse; the characters fail to communicate.

Waiting for Godot (1953) by Samuel Beckett is probably the most famous of these enigmatic, nontraditional dramas. As in many absurdist dramas, the plot is cyclical: The action in Act II appears to start over, with nothing having changed since Act I. The two main characters, Vladimir and Estragon, spend their time waiting; they accomplish nothing and are unable to take control of their lives. The other two men, Lucky and Pozzo, also have no control over their destiny; fate reverses their roles, transforming one from master into servant and the other from servant into master. Beckett referred to *Waiting for Godot* as a "tragicomedy in two acts," a description that reveals his tragicomic view of the human condition.

After absurdism, there were further attempts to supersede traditional theatre practices. These experiments, carried out in Europe and the United States in the 1960s and 1970s, went in many directions—a reflection, no doubt, of the fragmentation of modern life. The experiments included happenings, multimedia, and environmental theatre.

Any discussion of departures from realism after World War II must also take into account new technology in scene and lighting design. The Czechoslovakian designer Josef Svoboda (1920–2002), for example, experimented with such elements as projections, multimedia, movable platforms, and new materials, including plastics. Computer technology as well has been incorporated into many modern theatre buildings and lighting systems.

Happenings were what the name suggests: unstructured events that occurred with a minimum of planning and organization. The idea—especially popular in the 1960s—was that art should not be restricted to museums, galleries, or concert halls but can and should happen anywhere: on a street corner, in a grocery store, at a bus stop.

Existentialism Term applied to plays illustrating a philosophy whose modern advocate was Jean-Paul Sartre and which holds that there are no longer any fixed standards or values.

Theatre of the absurd Term applied to the works of certain playwrights of the 1950s and 1960s who expressed a similar point of view regarding the absurdity of the human condition and believed that this should be reflected in the dramatic action.

Happening Nonliterary or unscripted theatrical event using a scenario that allows for chance occurrences.

1957, California The setting is San Quentin prison in California on November 19, 1957. In the prison's North Dining Hall, a stage is set up where a group from the Actors' Workshop will perform Samuel Beckett's *Waiting for Godot*. It will be the first performance at the prison in over forty years.

The Actors' Workshop is a theatre group dedicated to performing provocative, experimental, avant-garde works by both national and international playwrights. Its members have made a name for themselves not only in the San Francisco area but throughout the United States. When performing, they work closely together as an ensemble.

The performers today are nervous, not only because they are performing in a penitentiary, but also because of the play itself. *Waiting for Godot* is a drama without much action, and it is filled with literary and religious references. It has already baffled intellectuals in Europe and the United States; how, the actors wonder, will a group of restless prisoners react to it?

The setting is described simply as "A country road. A tree." In actuality, it is a barren plain. The two central characters, Vladimir and Estragon, who are also known as Didi and Gogo, are tramplike clowns who are waiting for the Godot figure. They have the vague expectation that somehow, if and when he comes, Godot will be able to help them. It is never stated who Godot is: He may be God, he may be

someone else, or he may not even exist. While they wait, they try to break the painful monotony of their boring lives with bickering and occasional vaudeville routines.

The difficulty of the play is compounded by the fact that the second act seems to be almost the same as the first act. In both acts, Vladimir and Estragon try to entertain themselves; they move between hope and despair; they engage in vaudeville routines and philosophical speculation.

Meanwhile, two other characters, Pozzo and Lucky, appear. Pozzo is an overbearing creature who treats Lucky as his slave. Lucky, who has been mute, toward the end of the first act suddenly makes a long speech filled with legal terms. In the second act, the roles of Pozzo and Lucky are somewhat reversed, as Pozzo has become blind.

There is not the usual progress or story line expected in a traditional play. There is no building of suspense, no careful development of characters, no sudden plot twist, no big payoff at the end. In short, the play defies most of the conventional notions of both the content and the structure of drama.

At the end of the play, Godot's identity still has not been revealed, nor has he ever appeared. Instead, a young messenger arrives at the close of the first and second acts and announces that while Godot will not come that day, he will no doubt come the next.

The members of the Actors' Workshop have been acting together for a long time; and when they approach a play, they take their time, exploring the text, becoming familiar with the characters, and engaging in improvisation as they develop a performance. Even with this background they are apprehensive as they approach the performance at San Quentin. These, after all, are prisoners, not a sophisticated, intellectual audience, and this material is difficult for even the most scholarly spectators.

With these difficulties in mind, the performers from the Actors' Workshop begin their presentation. Shortly after the performance is under way, they have an indication that the production will go over better and be more readily understood than they had anticipated. Within the first few minutes, the audience grows quiet. A group of men sitting on some steps who had planned to leave early become engrossed and stay.

To the surprise of the performers, the audience sits in rapt attention. The prisoners follow the play closely from beginning to end and seem to understand what is happening. After the performance is over, it is clear that the prisoners have understood much of what they have seen— perhaps more than other audiences might understand. These prisoners, waiting out their sentences in boredom and frustration, have intuitively connected with the men onstage who wait for the unknown Godot, who never comes.

Multimedia is a joining of theatre with other arts—particularly dance, film, and television. In work of this sort, which is still being produced, live performers interact with sequences on film or television. The idea here is to fuse the art forms or to incorporate new technology into a theatrical event. A current form that frequently combines theatre, dance, and media is called performance art.

The American director and teacher Richard Schechner (1934–) coined the term *environmental theatre* in the 1960s; many characteristics of environmental theatre, however, had developed out of the work and theories of earlier avant-garde artists, including Vsevolod Meyerhold and Antonin Artaud. Proponents of environmental theatre treat the entire theatre space as a performance area, suggesting that any division between performers and viewers is artificial. For every production, spatial arrangements are transformed. (See the discussion of created and found spaces in the chapter "Theatre Spaces.")

The major influence on Schechner's theories is the Polish director Jerzy Grotowski (1933–1999). Works staged by Grotowski with the Polish Laboratory Theatre from its founding in 1959 until 1970 had many characteristics of environmental theatre. For each production, the theatre space and the performer-audience relationship were arranged to conform to the play being presented. In his version of *Doctor Faustus,* for instance, the theatre space was filled with two large dining tables at which audience members sat as if attending a banquet given by Faustus. As is true of Schechner, for most of Grotowski's productions existing scripts were radically modified by the performers and director. The acting style was externally based, emphasizing body and voice rather than emotions. Grotowski called his theatre *poor theatre*, meaning poor in scenery and special effects. Rather, it relied on the performers for its impact.

ECLECTICS

Some theatre artists between 1875 and 1975 tried to bridge the gap between realism and antirealism. These practitioners—known as *eclectics*—were not doctrinaire; instead, they argued that each play should define its own form. It would be impossible to list every global eclectic during this time period. Early eclectic directors included the Austrian Max Reinhardt (1873–1943) and the Russian Yevgeny Vakhtangov (1883–1922).

The English director Peter Brook (1925–) is a well-known contemporary eclectic. In staging *Marat/Sade* (1964), Brook applied concepts borrowed from Artaud's theatre of cruelty. His production of Shakespeare's *A Midsummer Night's Dream* (1970) was clearly influenced by Meyerhold's experiments with biomechanics and circus arts; for example, the fairy gods appeared on trapezes. The eclectic director has also incorporated Asian theatrical conventions in some of his productions. Brook has tried to avoid what he calls "deadly" commercial theatre, which does not allow for experimentation, a theory he explained in his book *The Empty Space* (1968) and continues to experiment as a director; his most recent stage production was *Battlefield* (2015), created with long-time French collaborator, Marie-Hélène Estienne.

There have also been many directors on the European continent who have experimented with varied avant-garde theatre techniques. Some of these directors have worked only in alternative environments, but others have brought their experimental style of production into leading government-subsidized national theatres. Some have merged realistic and theatricalist techniques in their productions. They include Peter Stein (German, 1937–); Yuri Lyubimov

Multimedia Use of electronic or digital media, such as projections, films, video, or computer animation in live theatrical presentations.

Environmental theatre A type of theatre production in which the total environment—the stage space and the audience organization—is transformed in order to blur distinctions between performers and spectators.

Poor theatre Term coined by Jerzy Grotowski to describe his theatre, which was stripped to the bare essentials of actor and audience.

Eclecticism This strand of modern theatre combines various theatrical trends or works across the boundaries of different trends.

(Russian, 1917–2014); Tadeusz Kantor (Polish, 1915–1990); Peter Zadek (German, 1926–2009); and Ariane Mnouchkine (French, 1940–). Mnouchkine, who founded the avant-garde Théâtre du Soleil in Paris in 1964, is one of the most widely admired directors in Europe.

POPULAR THEATRE

Popular theatre is mainstream theatre. It does not aspire to be high art or to be philosophical. It is not interested in being experimental or "cutting edge" drama. Rather, it wishes primarily to engage its audience—to keep them on the edge of their seats at a suspense drama or to entertain them with music and laughter.

Popular theatre was widespread and immensely successful throughout the nineteenth century. Audiences flocked to plays as well as vaudeville, circuses, and musical revues. This continued into the twentieth century. In the 1927–28 season on Broadway an astounding 281 productions opened. That is more than two productions every three days. To accommodate these productions, there were 65 Broadway theatres. During the 1930s, the combination of the new talking movies

PETER BROOK: INNOVATIVE THEATRE DIRECTOR
In the last half of the twentieth century, a number of creative, innovative directors emerged on the European continent and in Britain. In England, Peter Brook distinguished himself, first with Shakespeare and then with far more experimental work at his theatre in Paris. Shown here is a rehearsal of Brook's recent production *Battlefield* at the Bouffes du Nord theater in Paris on August 31, 2015. The cast of global actors included: British actor Sean O'Callaghan (L), Rwandan actor Ery Nzaramba, Belgian actress Carole Karemera, and Jared McNeill. (©Bertrand Guay/AFP/Getty Images)

and the Depression cut the number of new productions sharply, but at mid-century, the number still remained higher than it is today.

Witty comedies were very much in evidence during the first four decades of the twentieth century and with writers like Neil Simon (1927–) well into the latter part of the 1900s. Rather than survey the entire field of popular theatre, melodrama, comedies, farces, and so forth, however, we will focus on a unique American contribution to popular theatre: the musical.

American Musical Theatre

The Appeal of Music and Dance   Before we look more closely at the history of musical theatre, it will be helpful to consider the special appeal that music and dance have as part of theatre.

It is not difficult to understand why singing and dancing frequently have been combined with dramatic productions. First, all three are performing arts, and so there is a natural affinity among them. Second, singing and dancing have wide popular appeal. People enjoy listening to music at home as well as in the theatre. Also, in today's world, through MP3 players, tablets, and smartphones, and the ability to instantaneously download music through such services as iTunes, people hear music everywhere—while they are walking, or riding in cars, planes, or buses. When hearing music, listeners respond to rhythms and to the emotional pull of a memorable melody, especially when performed by a singer with a captivating voice and personality. The grace and agility of a talented, expertly trained solo dancer or ensemble of dancers provide entertainment of a high order.

Beyond their value as entertainment, singing and dancing possess a powerful ability to capture the beauty of sound and movement to communicate a wide range of emotions. Some thoughts and feelings cannot be expressed adequately in everyday prose, and for these we turn to poetry. In the same way, there are expressions of beauty, anguish, spirituality and sheer joy that can best be conveyed in vocal and instrumental music and in dance.

Antecedents   A close relative and predecessor to musical theatre is opera. Opera can be defined as a drama set entirely to music. With rare exceptions, every part of the performance is sung, including not only the *arias*, long solo songs with orchestral accompaniment, but also the transitional sections between them, known as *recitatives*. Having begun in Florence, Italy, around 1600 as drama set to music, operas have been written to the present day in continental Europe, the United Kingdom and the United States.

In the nineteenth century, melodrama used music to accompany the action of plays. Singing and dancing also played a key role in other forms of nineteenth-century theatrical entertainment, such as vaudeville and burlesque. Another form that developed in the late nineteenth century was operetta—a romantic musical piece featuring melodic solos, duets, and choruses interspersed with spoken dialogue. Examples of operetta include the works from Great Britain of W. S. Gilbert (1836–1911) and Arthur Sullivan (1842–1900), such as *The Pirates of Penzance* (1879) and *The Mikado* (1885). The American composer Victor Herbert (1859–1924) also composed operettas, such as *Naughty Marietta* (1910).

In the early twentieth century, the musical shows of George M. Cohan (1878–1942), such as *Little Johnny Jones* (1904) and *Forty-Five Minutes from Broadway* (1906), had songs with an American flavor and more realistic dialogue and better plot development than earlier musicals. Cohan's shows moved

SHOWBOAT: LANDMARK MUSICAL

When *Show Boat* opened in 1927, it began a new chapter in the history of the American musical. The chorus line was eliminated, miscegenation (a romance between a white man and a black woman) was treated for the first time, and other problems facing African Americans were touched on. Also, it had a glorious score by Jerome Kern and Oscar Hammerstein. Shown here is a revival, staged by Harold Prince, at the Ahmanson Theatre in Los Angeles, in 1996. (©Anacleto Rapping/Getty Images)

Book Spoken (as opposed to sung) portion of the text of a musical play.

a step closer to today's "book" musicals—musicals that tell a story. (The dialogue and action of a musical are sometimes called the *book*, though the term libretto is also used.)

Around the time of World War I and in the period following, a truly native American musical began to emerge. It featured a story that was typically frivolous combined with enduring popular songs. Among the well-known composers of this period were Irving Berlin (1888–1989), Jerome Kern (1885–1945), George Gershwin (1898–1937), Cole Porter (1891–1964), and Richard Rodgers (1902–1979). Matching the inventiveness of the composers were the lyricists, including Ira Gershwin (1896–1983), who wrote lyrics for many of his brother's tunes; and Lorenz Hart (1895–1943), who teamed up with Richard Rodgers. Berlin and Porter wrote their own lyrics.

In 1927, Oscar Hammerstein II (1895–1960), who wrote the lyrics and libretto, and Jerome Kern, who composed the music, combined some of the best aspects of operetta and musical comedy to create *Show Boat*. The story was thoroughly American, rather than an exotic romantic fable, and it dealt with serious material—including the then-controversial love story of a black woman and a white man. It was also innovative in that the songs were integrated into the plot.

HIGH POINT OF AMERICAN MUSICALS
A classic American musical is *The King and I* by Richard Rodgers and Oscar Hammerstein II. While the score is revered, the plot line has been criticized for stereotypical representations of Asian characters, often played by Caucasian performers in early productions. In the 2015 revival at the Vivian Beaumont Theatre at Lincoln Center in New York, with Kelli O'Hara and Ken Watanabe, foreground, director Bartlett Sher cast Asian actors and attempted to be more accurate in the historic representation of Siam, which is today Thailand. (©Sara Krulwich/The New York Times/Redux)

Another milestone of musical theatre was Gershwin's *Porgy and Bess* (1935), with a book by DuBose Heyward (1885–1940). Set in the African American community of Charleston, South Carolina, it is even more realistic than *Show Boat;* and its score is so powerful that many people consider it an opera rather than a musical.

The High Point of American Musicals *Oklahoma!*—which was produced in 1943 and brought the team of Rodgers and Hammerstein together for the first time—heralded a significant era of the American *book musical. Oklahoma!* has been praised for seamlessly fitting together story, music, lyrics, and dances so that tone, mood, and intention became a unified whole. Its choreography, by Agnes deMille (1905–1993), included a ballet sequence that influenced many later choreographers, including Jerome Robbins (1918–1998) and Bob Fosse (1927–1987). Rodgers and Hammerstein went on to create other significant musicals such as *Carousel* (1945), *South Pacific* (1949), *The King and I* (1951), and *The Sound of Music* (1959).

Among other notable musicals during the 1940s and 1950s were Irving Berlin's *Annie Get Your Gun* (1946), based on the life of Annie Oakley; Cole Porter's musical version of *The Taming of the Shrew,* called *Kiss Me, Kate* (1948); *Guys and Dolls* (1950) by Frank Loesser (1910–1969); *My Fair Lady* (1956), by the librettist and lyricist Alan Jay Lerner (1918–1986) and the composer Frederick Loewe (1904–1988), based on George Bernard Shaw's *Pygmalion* (1913); and *West Side Story,* a modernization of *Romeo and Juliet* which was created by the composer Leonard Bernstein (1918–1990), the lyricist Stephen Sondheim (1930–), and the librettist Arthur Laurents (1918–2011).

Some commentators believe that *Fiddler on the Roof* (1964)—with music by Jerry Bock (1928–2010), lyrics by Sheldon Harnick (1924–), and book by Joseph Stein (1912–2010)—marks the end of this era of outstanding book musicals. *Fiddler on the Roof,* about a Jewish family whose father attempts to uphold tradition in a Russian village where the Jewish community faces persecution, was directed and choreographed by Jerome Robbins. One example of changes in the musical following *Fiddler on the Roof* was the rock musical *Hair* (1967), by Galt McDermot (1928–), James Rado (1932–) and Gerome Ragni (1935–1991), which had no actual story line and was a celebration of the anti-establishment lifestyle of the 1960s.

American Musicals after 1975   Although this chapter ends at the year 1975, with the musicals we are discussing it seems logical to continue tracing their development in this chapter rather than break off. We will, therefore, proceed at this point with our survey of American musicals.

After *Hair,* the musical scene became increasingly fragmented, with fewer and fewer book musicals being written. In place of book musicals, there were other approaches, one being the concept musical, in which a production is built around an idea rather than a story. Two examples, both composed by Stephen Sondheim (1930–) and directed by Harold Prince (1928–), are *Company* (1970) and *Follies* (1971). Two of Sondheim's other works, *Sunday in the Park with George* (1985) and *Into the Woods* (1988), can also be considered concept musicals.

Another significant development in musicals of the 1970s and 1980s was the ascendancy of the choreographer as the director of musicals. Jerome Robbins, director of *West Side Story* and *Fiddler on the Roof,* was generally recognized as the leading director-choreographer in the United States. Following him, *A Chorus Line* was developed by the director-choreographer Michael Bennett (1943–1987). Other significant director-choreographers were Gower Champion (1920–1980), responsible for *Hello Dolly!* (1964) and *42nd Street* (1980); Bob Fosse, who directed *Sweet Charity* (1966) and *Pippin* (1972); and Tommy Tune (1939–), who directed *Nine* (1982) and *Grand Hotel* (1989). Other contemporary director-choreographers are Susan Stroman (1954–), responsible for *Contact* (1999), *The Producers* (2001), and *Big Fish* (2013), and Kathleen Marshall (1962–), director of the Broadway revival of *Anything Goes* (2010).

Still another major development since 1965 has been the emergence of British composers and lyricists. The leading figure in this movement is the composer Andrew Lloyd Webber (1948–), who, with the lyricist Tim Rice (1944–), wrote

Jesus Christ Superstar (1971) and *Evita* (1979). Webber has also written *Cats* (1982), *The Phantom of the Opera* (1987), and *The School of Rock* (2015). Two other large-scale British musicals of the period were *Les Misérables* (1987), originally conceived in France, and *Miss Saigon* (1989), both of which have had successful recent revivals. In 2008 *Billy Elliott* and in 2013 *Matilda* arrived on Broadway from London. In 2014, the rock musician Sting's musical *The Last Ship* opened in New York.

Four additional trends are discernible in the contemporary musical theatre from 1990 to the present. One is the unprecedented number of major revivals of past musical successes. One reason for the increase in revivals has been the rising cost of producing musicals, which has led producers to present tried-and-true musical classics that are considered safe investments. At the same time, this is a clear indication that there has not been the same output of new work as in earlier years. On the positive side, the trend confirms that these outstanding musicals from the past form part of an important heritage and have lasting value.

A second trend has been musicals based on films. This list would include *The Producers, Monty Python's Spamalot* (2005), *Hairspray* (2003), *Young Frankenstein, Billy Elliott* (2005), *Once* (2011), *Kinky Boots* (2012), *Honeymoon in Vegas* (2015), *Waitress* (2015), and musicals presented by the Disney organization, such as *The Lion King* (1997), *Mary Poppins* (2004), *The Little Mermaid* (2007), and *Aladdin* (2011).

The third trend is the creation of productions out of the music of former popular music stars and groups, sometimes referred to as "jukebox musicals." The most successful of these has been *Mamma Mia!* (1999)—a story taking place in the Greek islands and based on the music of the group ABBA. The music of Billy Joel formed the basis of Twyla Tharp's dance musical *Moving Out.* In the years that followed, show after show was created by stringing together hits from one music group or another, good examples being *Jersey Boys* (2005), *Rock of Ages* (2008), and *Motown* (2013). *American Idiot* (2009) created a musical around the rock group Green Day's recordings and *Beautiful* (2014) used the music of Carole King to tell her life story.

A fourth trend—a refreshing counterpoint to the rush of revivals—has been the appearance of fresh, off-beat musicals, indicating that the genre remains full of vitality. For example, *Rent* (1996), about a group of anti-establishment young people, won numerous awards, including the Pulitzer Prize and the Tony Award for best musical of the year. Another example is *Avenue Q* (2003), a lively, iconoclastic musical featuring puppets operated by onstage characters.

Next to Normal, which was awarded the 2009 Tony Award, concerns a mother who is struggling with bipolar disorder and the effects her disease has on her family. As her condition worsens, other concerns surface—suicide, drug abuse, psychiatric ethics—none of which are typical subjects for a musical.

Some other original musicals during this time period mix elaborate spectacle with newly composed music; examples include: *Wicked* (2003) and *Spiderman: Turn off the Dark* (2011). There have also been successful new musicals with original music scores, often using pop and rock music, such as *Spring Awakening* (2006), *Memphis* (2009), and *The Book of Mormon* (2011).

A number of contemporary musical theatre composers combine the traditions of the golden era of the musical with the recent trends of the American musical, including Adam Guettel (1964–), Michael John LaChiusa (1961–), Andrew Lippa (1964–), and Jeanine Tesori (1961–), whose *Fun Home* (2013) deals with the coming out of its lesbian protagonist and was the first musical

MUSICAL REVIVALS
The twenty-first century in the American theatre, as well as other parts of the world, has seen many revivals of well-known American musicals from the past. A good example is the 2017 revival of *Hello Dolly,* starring Bette Midler. The musical has music and lyrics by Herry Herman and a book by Michael Steward. The revival was directed by Jerry Zaks. (©Sara Krulwich/ The New York Times/Redux)

to win Tonys for a female composer, and female author of the book, playwright Lisa Kron (1961–).

The contemporary composer who has made a major impact on the American musical is Lin-Manuel Miranda (1980–). His first major work *In the Heights,* winner of the 2008 Tony Award for Best Musical, covers three days in the lives of characters in the Dominican-American section of Washington Heights in Manhattan and features hip-hop, meringue, salsa, and soul music. Miranda's *Hamilton* (2015), which tells the story of the Founding Fathers by using multicultural, nontraditional casting and hip-hop music, is a theatrical phenomenon, with unprecedented demand for tickets in New York and in other cities.

It is clear that the musical theatre scene at the present time is a patchwork quilt, featuring old and new, revues and book musicals, imports and original material. All in all, the musical remains a mainstay of Broadway, and of those large

RECENT AMERICAN MUSICALS
The immensely popular new musical *Hamilton* by Lin-Manuel Miranda deals with the founding of the United States and combines history with rap music, anachronisms, and non-traditional casting. Seen here are Okieriete Onaodowan, Daveed Diggs, Anthony Ramos and Lin-Manuel Miranda at the Richard Rodgers Theater in New York on July 11, 2015. (©Sara Krulwich/The New York Times/Redux)

theatres across the United States that feature shows with music, dance, spectacular scenery, and well-known performers.

GLOBALIZATION AND THEATRE IN THE TWENTIETH CENTURY AND BEYOND

We said at the beginning of this chapter that globalization was one of the developments characteristic of twentieth-century theatre. ***Globalization*** is the exchange of ideas, money, goods and services, art works, and languages among nations and across cultures. Advances in technology, communication, and transportation systems made possible the rapid and relatively easy exchange among people around the world of ideas and techniques in all fields, including the arts.

Globalization   A strand of modern theatre that involves the mutual influences of theatre from around the world.

We have already seen, as just a small example, the impact on the American musical by artists from England and France. For that matter, the American musical has become a popular form throughout Europe as well as in Korea and China.

In what follows, we will take a look at the exchange between Asian and Western theatre as a particularly rich example of cultural exchange; we will discuss more fully theatrical globalization in the chapter "Today's Diverse Global Theatre."

KATHAKALI: INDIAN DANCE DRAMA

Much Asian theatre includes a large element of dance. A prime example is kathakali, a dramatic form found in southwestern India. In kathakali, stories of strong passions, the furies of gods, and the loves and hates of extraordinary human beings are told in dance and mime. Notice the makeup and stylized costumes and headdresses on these dancers in Kerala, India.
(©EyesWideOpen/Getty Images News/Getty Images)

Some Background on Asian Theatre

Before we come to this artistic exchange among nations from 1875 to 1975, however, as background we should address important events in Asian theatre that occurred prior to that time. In Japan, for example, the three ancient forms—nō, kabuki, and bunraku—were alive and well through the centuries and continued into the twentieth century.

In India, during the three centuries before 1900, an interesting form of dance drama, called ***kathakali***, had been prominent in the southwestern portion of the country. Kathakali is produced at night by torchlight, on a stage approximately sixteen feet square covered with a canopy of flowers. In subject matter it heightens certain elements of Sanskrit drama, presenting violence and death onstage in dance and pantomime. The stories revolve around clashes between good and evil, with good always winning. A language of 500 or more gestural signs has been developed to tell these stories.

In China, a nineteenth-century development was an immensely popular form known as ***Beijing opera***. Originally, it was called Peking opera, but when the name of the city was changed from Peking to Beijing, the newer name was

Kathakali Traditional dance drama of India.

Beijing opera A nineteenth-century popular theatre form in China which combines music, theatre, and dance with colorful conventions of makeup, costumes, movement, and voice production.

BEIJING (PEKING) OPERA
A highly formalized theatre, Beijing (or Peking) opera was developed in China in the nineteenth century. It is not like Western grand opera; rather, it is a popular entertainment filled with song, dance, and acrobatics. It makes wide use of symbols—with, for instance, a table standing for a mountain, or a blue fabric for the sea, as shown here—and is performed in highly colorful and stylized costumes like the ones we see in this performance. The production being enacted is *The Legend of the White Snake*. (©ArenaPAL/The Image Works)

assigned to the form. This form of theatre has recently been called by other Chinese names, jingju and xiqu being two of them. (Although mindful of the rationale for each of these, we will use the term Beijing opera.) In Beijing opera, elements of folk drama and other genres close to ordinary people form the basis of what is truly a popular theatre—one of the most colorful and striking theatrical forms now practiced in Asia.

Though it is called opera, Beijing opera combines music, theatre, and dance in its own unique way. Because of its origins in popular entertainment, it does not aspire to be a work of high literary merit or philosophical speculation. But it preserves long traditions of popular singing, acrobatics, and acting and thus provides insights into the high development of performance techniques in traditional Chinese theatre. Its plays or skits involve elaborate and colorful conventions of makeup, movement, and voice production. In staging, Beijing opera stresses symbolism. The furniture onstage usually consists only of a table and several chairs, but these few items are used with imagination. Depending on how they are arranged or referred to, they may represent a dining hall, a court of justice, or a throne room. The table may stand for a cloud, a mountain, or any other high place. A tripod on a table, holding incense, indicates a palace. When the script

IN FOCUS: TWO IMPORTANT GLOBAL DIRECTORS

Ariane Mnouchkine: Théâtre du Soleil

Since her founding of the avant-garde Théâtre du Soleil in Paris in 1964, the French director Ariane Mnouchkine (1939–) has become one of the most widely admired directors in Europe, and in fact, around the world. Although strongly influenced by Copeau, Brecht, Artaud, and Meyerhold, she is also known for her effective use of nonwestern dramatic techniques, especially those of Japan and India. She was born in a small town near Paris, France, and attended Oxford University in England, majoring in psychology. While there, she became involved with the Oxford University Drama Society and from that point on, her interest was theatre. In the early 1960s, Mnouchkine scraped together enough money to realize a lifelong dream of traveling to the far east. In Japan, Cambodia, and other parts of Asia, she found a beauty of form and a sense of ritual that she considered indispensable to theatre. When she returned to Paris in 1963, Mnouchkine and several of her friends established a "theatrical community" which was to become the Théâtre du Soleil (the Theatre of the Sun).

The company has produced everything from loose collections of improvised materials to acclaimed versions of Shakespeare's works to a powerful 10-hour staging of the *Oresteia,* the cycle of Greek tragedies about the house of Atreus. Mnouchkine is strongly in favor of the collaborative process in creating theatrical pieces. The director, she has stated, has become all powerful. Her goal, she says, "is to move beyond that situation by creating a form of theatre where it will be possible for everyone to collaborate without there being directors, technicians, and so on." She and her company use many techniques in developing their productions. These include improvisational exercises as well as styles such as commedia dell'arte and various Asian rituals.

Among the best-known collectively created productions of the Théâtre du Soleil are *1789* (1970), which environmentally dramatized the historical background of the French Revolution; *The Age of Gold* (1975); and *Les Atrides* (1991), the adaptation of the *Oresteia.* Among her most recent productions are *And Suddenly Sleepless Nights* (1997), which deals with the plight of illegal immigrants; the two-part, 6-hour *Le Dernier Caravansérail (Odysées) (The Last Caravan Stop)* (2003), which deals with the horrors of refugees. For this last piece, she and members of her troupe spent three years collecting poignant and tragic stories from refugees from all parts of the world which they wove into their drama. *Les Éphémères* (2009) consists of series of interwoven vignettes, chiefly about middle-class life in France.

Ariane Mnouchkine's *Le Dernier Caravanserail,* shown here, was based on interviews of refugees in camps and detention centers in many parts of the world. (©Martine Franck/Magnum Photos)

The Theatre of Julie Taymor

The American director and designer Julie Taymor (1952–) is known predominantly for her vibrant productions, which draw on theatrical traditions from across the globe. Her use of puppetry (adopted predominantly from Indonesia) and her costume designs mark her as a designer who uses eastern traditions.

Julie Taymor. (©Jerome Delay/AP Images)

Taymor has traveled to Sri Lanka, Indonesia, Japan, and India, and her travels have allowed her to encounter the very different theatrical forms of those countries. Her experiences of Japanese nō, bunraku, and avant-garde theatre, and Indonesian rod puppets (wayang golek) and shadow puppets (wayang kulit), were particularly influential in her later productions. In her early experiments with blending theatrical forms, she founded the theatrical company Teatr Loh, which included performers from Java, Bali, Sudan, and the west. This blending of eastern theatrical traditions has been continued through her many productions in the east and west.

Among Taymor's productions are an adaptation of a German novella set in India called *The Transposed Heads* (1984); a production of *Juan Darien* (1988, 1990), which drew on the puppet traditions of Indonesia and Japan and the music of Australia, South America, and Africa; and an opera adaptation of *Oedipus Rex* (1992), which drew on Greek sculpture and Japanese nō costumes. However, she is best known for her productions of *The King Stag* and the Disney musical *The Lion King.*

The King Stag was written in eighteenth-century Italy by Carlo Gozzi and tells of King Derramo and his evil prime minister, Tartaglia. In order to ensure that his daughter will marry the king, Tartaglia tricks the king into transferring his soul into the body of a stag, with the prime minister then taking control of the king's body. By her own count, Taymor identifies nine different countries whose theatrical traditions she drew from in creating *The King Stag.* She used masks from eighteenth-century Italian commedia dell'arte troupes, white ruffs from Elizabethan England, Japanese prints and colors, Taiwanese paper bird kites, Indonesian puppetry, Japanese bunraku, and ancient Chinese mirror stone techniques (through her use of Plexiglas puppets). The end result was an imaginative, colorful production that could not be defined by any one theatrical tradition.

Similarly, her Broadway production of *The Lion King* used elements of numerous theatrical cultures from across Asia, especially from Indonesia and Japan; also prominent was music from South Africa. Many of the scenes combine actors, masks, and puppets, illustrating once again her distinctive fusion of numerous theatrical forms. Taymor was also the original director and co-author of the musical *Spiderman: Turn off the Dark,* which proved to be her least successful venture. The show's spectacular theatricality, including characters flying over the audience, led to excessive budget overruns, delayed openings, and accidents. Taymor was eventually replaced prior to the official opening of the musical and it closed without recouping initial financial investments.

Owing to the wide range of sources, Julie Taymor's productions are not re-creations of any one theatrical source, but rather compositions drawn from global and historical theatrical traditions.

Prepared by Naomi Stubbs, Associate Professor LaGuardia College, CUNY.

PLAYING YOUR PART:
THINKING ABOUT THEATRE

1. Discuss why you believe a TV show or film that you have seen could be considered realistic.
2. Discuss why a TV show or film that you have seen could be considered a departure from realism.
3. Discuss how rock concerts use multimedia and environmental theatrical techniques.
4. Why do you think musical comedy has been more popular in theatre than in film?
5. Do you think absurdism continues to be relevant in today's theatre? Why? Why not?
6. Discuss how the theories of Artaud and Brecht influenced the theatre since 1945.

calls for a long journey, the performers walk in a circle about the stage. Later, this creative use of the stage impressed many Western dramatists. Well before the turn of the twentieth century, the vitality of Beijing opera had made it the most popular form of traditional theatre in China; and later its stars—including the great twentieth-century actor Mei Lanfang (1894–1961)—became performers of enormous reputation not only in China but also in the West.

Global Exchanges

The mention of Mei Lanfang introduces us to the exchanges in theatre between Asia and the West. Beginning in the early years of the twentieth century playwrights from China and Japan, for example, became aware of the ground-breaking work of Ibsen, Strindberg, and Chekhov in the West, and in some cases their work was influenced by their knowledge of these European playwrights. The East-West connection also worked in the other direction. In the feature box "In Focus: The Asian Influence on the playwrights Brecht and Wilder" in the chapter "Creating the Dramatic Script," we noted how two well-known playwrights, Thornton Wilder and Bertolt Brecht, had seen Mei Lanfang perform and become intimately acquainted with the symbolism, scenic approach, and story-telling techniques of Chinese theatre. We described how these authors began to incorporate the elements of Asian theatre into their own work.

As the new century progressed, the vigorous exchange among directors, playwrights, actors, and designers across the full range of theatrical ideas and concepts continued, interrupted only by World War II. In the late twentieth century, clear examples of East-West exchanges are seen in the works of Julie Taymor and Ariane Mnouchkine, two directors featured in the In Focus box, as well as Mary Zimmerman (1960–). Another example of an international artist is the Japanese director Tadashi Suzuki (1939–). After World War II, Suzuki worked frequently in the West and many American and other Western artists—actors, writers, directors—worked at his theatre in the mountains of Japan. Suzuki is discussed more fully in the next chapter.

It should be noted, too, that exchanges were not confined to East and West. South and Central America, South Africa, North Africa, Southeast Asia, Australia and New Zealand, Eastern and Western Europe, Canada: All these areas became acutely aware of what was occurring in other parts of the world, and consciously or unconsciously often incorporated it into their own work. We will discuss more fully many of these global theatres in the next chapter.

SUMMARY

1. Modern theatre in the West began in the late nineteenth century with the realistic plays of Henrik Ibsen, August Strindberg, and Anton Chekhov.

2. In realism, events onstage mirror observable reality in the outside world. The characters speak, move, dress, and behave as people do in real life; they are seen in familiar places such as living rooms, bedrooms, and kitchens.

3. One appeal of realism is that audiences can identify with and verify people and events onstage. One disadvantage of realism is that it excludes a number of traditional theatrical devices, such as poetry, music, ghosts, and special effects.

4. Despite this drawback, however, realism is so effective that it has been a dominant theatrical form of the past 100 years.

5. Because of its uncompromising presentation of life, realism was initially produced not commercially but by small independent theatres.

6. As it became more widely accepted, realism entered the mainstream of theatre. In the twentieth century, Synge and O'Casey in Ireland, O'Neill, Hellman, Miller, Williams, and Albee in the United States, and many other playwrights worldwide wrote powerful realistic drama.

7. From 1875 through 1975, there were also significant movements that departed from realism: These included symbolism, expressionism, futurism, surrealism, epic theatre, absurdism, and environmental theatre.

8. Among practitioners who attempted to move theatre away from realism were the designers Appia and Craig as well as the director Meyerhold.

9. Key theories arguing against realism are Artaud's theatre of cruelty and Brecht's epic theatre. Grotowski and Schechner were proponents of environmental staging.

10. There were many theatre companies and artists who produced new experimental works. In the United States, the off-Broadway, off-off-Broadway, and regional theatres nurtured new artists and forms.

11. Throughout this time period, there continued to be a strong tradition of popular theatre.

12. The American musical flourished between 1945 and 1975.

13. In Asian theatre, drama influenced by the West and avant-garde experimental theatre took its place alongside traditional forms, while writers, directors, actors, and designers in the West were strongly influenced by their Eastern counterparts.

16

TODAY'S DIVERSE GLOBAL THEATRE

In this chapter we will examine important trends in contemporary theatre. Four words that can characterize today's theatre are *global, diverse, multicultural,* and *eclectic:* global because of the extensive amount of theatre produced throughout the world as well as the interaction between national theatres; diverse and multicultural because the types of theatre available to audiences are so wide-ranging, and, as we noted in the chapter "Theatre is Everywhere," because the audiences themselves are so diverse and multicultural; and eclectic because contemporary theatre embraces such a wide variety of styles and types. Our ultimate goal in this chapter, however, will be to consider whether theatre as we know it will survive in the twenty-first century.

In order to understand our contemporary theatre, it must be viewed against the background of the complex, unsettled, often confusing political and social turmoil of the recent past.

THE DAWNING OF A NEW CENTURY

As we noted in the chapter "The Modern Theatre Emerges," social unrest and violence marked the second half of the twentieth century. Worldwide political, economic, and cultural turmoil continued as the century ended. Technological changes continued to make communication and personal and global interaction even more immediate.

Contemporary society was again confronted by genocide in Bosnia, Rwanda, and the Sudan, and by reports of torture of prisoners by American military or CIA personnel in the aftermath of the Iraq War, forcing us to question whether there have been any real changes in moral outlook since World War II. Although the fall of totalitarian communism was celebrated in Eastern Europe, the world has

◀ **TODAY'S DIVERSE THEATRE**
Immediate Family, *shown here and directed by Phylicia Rashad, reflects the diversity and multiculturalism of our contemporary theatre and drama. The comedy by Paul Oakley Stovall deals with a Chicago African American family's reaction to the gay relationship between one of the family members and a Caucasian Swedish photographer. The play was staged at the Goodman Theatre in Chicago and in Los Angeles at the Mark Taper Forum.* (©Craig Schwartz)

also been troubled by continued poverty, crime, and intolerance toward racial minorities. The unrest in the Ukraine in 2014, along with the internationally repudiated intervention by Russia, reflect the continued instability in Eastern Europe.

The American presidency, under Bill Clinton, was rocked by a number of scandals and impeachment hearings. George W. Bush, while losing the popular vote, was elected president in a highly contested election in 2000, and again in 2004 in another close election. Some suggest the United States had moved toward greater racial equality with the election of the nation's first African American president, Barack Obama, in 2008 and his reelection in 2012. However, in 2016, Donald Trump, a businessman with no previous political experience, was elected president after a contentious campaign in which he lost the popular vote by almost 2.9 million votes; because of his stated nationalistic policies, many questioned whether real advances had been made in gender, sexual orientation, and racial equality.

A significant economic recession affected the entire global economy, including the United States, in 2008 and its effects continue to be felt. The Occupy Wall Street protest, which spread to cities across the United States and the world in 2011, reflected the ongoing social unrest due to continuing economic disparities.

There has also been continuing violence in the Middle East. A horrific outcome of this instability was the terrorist attack on the United States on September 11, 2001. The United States proclaimed a war on terror and toppled the fundamentalist Islamic regime in Afghanistan. The United States and Great Britain also deposed the regime of Saddam Hussein in Iraq in 2003. The unrest in Afghanistan and Iraq continued, despite the death of 9/11 mastermind Osama bin Laden.

There remained unresolved conflicts between Israelis and Palestinians most recently culminating in the 2014 war in Gaza. And while there were demonstrations and revolts demanding democratic reform in Arab and African nations in recent years, fueled by the ability to communicate instantaneously and across the globe through the Internet on Facebook, Twitter, and YouTube, the outcomes of these protests remain unclear. The military incursions of the extremist group ISIS in Syria, caused in part by the civil war in that country, as well as in other parts of the Arab world, along with terrorist attacks in France, Belgium, and Germany, raised concerns in the Middle East and in the West.

TODAY'S THEATRE: GLOBAL, DIVERSE, MULTICULTURAL, AND ECLECTIC

As always, the arts have continued to reflect the world in which they are being created. Our theatre today is so complex because it mirrors the significant changes in our global society and the concerns of diverse and multicultural peoples who populate our world.

In this chapter, we will first turn our attention to two key types of the contemporary global theatre, which also reflect its eclecticism: performance art and postmodernism. We will then focus on examples of theatrical diversity and multiculturalism in the United States; in doing so, we will need to discuss early influences on these diverse contemporary theatres. We will then survey global theatres across our world, including those in England, Ireland, Australia, Canada, Asia, Latin America, and the Middle East; here, too, we will discuss earlier developments that shaped these societies' current theatres.

Finally we must always remember that it is not possible to survey all of our contemporary worldwide theatres and that these are just examples of today's vast range of global, diverse, multicultural, and eclectic theatrical activity.

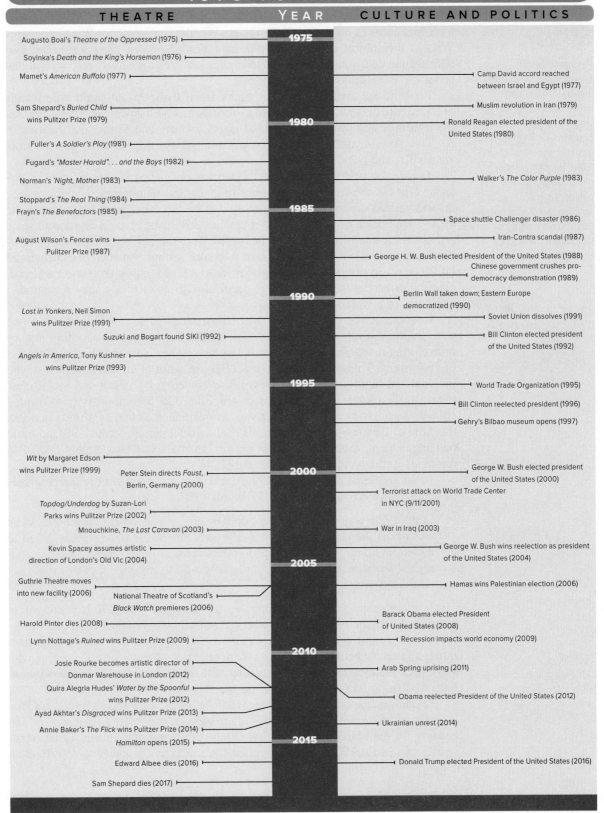

1975 TO PRESENT

THEATRE	YEAR	CULTURE AND POLITICS

Augusto Boal's *Theatre of the Oppressed* (1975)

1975

Soyinka's *Death and the King's Horseman* (1976)

Mamet's *American Buffalo* (1977)

Camp David accord reached between Israel and Egypt (1977)

Sam Shepard's *Buried Child* wins Pulitzer Prize (1979)

Muslim revolution in Iran (1979)

1980

Ronald Reagan elected president of the United States (1980)

Fuller's *A Soldier's Play* (1981)

Fugard's *"Master Harold"...and the Boys* (1982)

Norman's *'Night, Mother* (1983)

Walker's *The Color Purple* (1983)

Stoppard's *The Real Thing* (1984)

Frayn's *The Benefactors* (1985)

1985

Space shuttle Challenger disaster (1986)

Iran-Contra scandal (1987)

August Wilson's *Fences* wins Pulitzer Prize (1987)

George H. W. Bush elected President of the United States (1988)

Chinese government crushes pro-democracy demonstration (1989)

1990

Berlin Wall taken down; Eastern Europe democratized (1990)

Lost in Yonkers, Neil Simon wins Pulitzer Prize (1991)

Soviet Union dissolves (1991)

Suzuki and Bogart found SIKI (1992)

Bill Clinton elected president of the United States (1992)

Angels in America, Tony Kushner wins Pulitzer Prize (1993)

1995

World Trade Organization (1995)

Bill Clinton reelected president (1996)

Gehry's Bilbao museum opens (1997)

Wit by Margaret Edson wins Pulitzer Prize (1999)

Peter Stein directs *Faust*, Berlin, Germany (2000)

2000

George W. Bush elected president of the United States (2000)

Topdog/Underdog by Suzan-Lori Parks wins Pulitzer Prize (2002)

Terrorist attack on World Trade Center in NYC (9/11/2001)

Mnouchkine, *The Last Caravan* (2003)

War in Iraq (2003)

Kevin Spacey assumes artistic direction of London's Old Vic (2004)

George W. Bush wins reelection as president of the United States (2004)

2005

Guthrie Theatre moves into new facility (2006)

National Theatre of Scotland's *Black Watch* premieres (2006)

Hamas wins Palestinian election (2006)

Barack Obama elected President of United States (2008)

Harold Pinter dies (2008)

Lynn Nottage's *Ruined* wins Pulitzer Prize (2009)

Recession impacts world economy (2009)

2010

Josie Rourke becomes artistic director of Donmar Warehouse in London (2012)

Arab Spring uprising (2011)

Quira Alegria Hudes' *Water by the Spoonful* wins Pulitzer Prize (2012)

Obama reelected President of the United States (2012)

Ayad Akhtar's *Disgraced* wins Pulitzer Prize (2013)

Annie Baker's *The Flick* wins Pulitzer Prize (2014)

Ukrainian unrest (2014)

Hamilton opens (2015)

2015

Edward Albee dies (2016)

Donald Trump elected President of the United States (2016)

Sam Shepard dies (2017)

Performance Art

In the past three decades, a number of artists have experimented with forms that force audiences to confront certain issues: What is performance? What is theatre? What is the subject of theatrical representation? Some of these artists are also political-minded; some are not. ***Performance art*** is one relatively recent form that poses these questions and then some.

Performance art has important antecedents: earlier avant-garde experiments of the twentieth century, such as dada, surrealism, and happenings, which stressed the irrational and attacked traditional artistic values and forms; the theories of Antonin Artaud and Jerzy Grotowski; and popular forms, such as clowning, vaudeville, and stand-up comedy.

During the past three decades, the term performance art has referred to differing types of theatrical presentations. In its earliest manifestations, performance art was related on one hand to painting and on the other hand to dance. In the 1970s, one branch of performance art emphasized the body as an art object: Some artists suffered self-inflicted pain, and some went through daily routines (such as preparing a meal) in a museum or in a theatre setting. Another branch focused on site-specific or environmental pieces in which the setting or context was crucial: Performances were created for specific locations such as a subway station, a city park, or a waterfront pier.

In some of the earliest forms of performance art, story, character, and text were minimized or even eliminated. The emphasis was not on narrating a story or exploring recognizable characters but rather on the visual and ritualistic aspects of performing. This type of theatre was often the work of an individual artist who incorporated highly personal messages, and sometimes political and social messages, in the event. The overall effect was often like a continually transforming collage. As might be expected, there was, as mentioned earlier, an affinity between this kind of theatre—with its emphasis of the visual picture formed onstage—and painting. Often, stage movement in performance art was also closely related to dance, as in the work of Martha Clarke (1944–).

In an article in *Artsweek* in 1990, Jacki Apple explained how the emphasis in performance art shifted in the 1970s and 1980s:

> In the 1970s performance art was primarily a time-based visual art form in which text was at the service of image; by the early 80s performance art had shifted to movement-based work, with the performance artist as choreographer. Interdisciplinary collaboration and "spectacle," influenced by TV and other popular modes . . . set the tone for the new decade.[1]

In more recent years performance art has changed yet again. It is now often associated with individual artists who present autobiographical extended monologues or present one-person shows in which they portray various characters through interconnected monologues. There are also some performance artists who stage presentations that feature clowning and other popular slapstick techniques borrowed from the circus and other popular arts.

Several such artists—Karen Finley (1956–) is one of the most visible—became a center of controversy. These artists often support such causes as feminism and equality for the LGBTQ communities. Often nudity and other controversial representations of sexuality or sexual orientation are used to ask audiences to reflect on

---

Performance art
Experimental theatre that initially incorporated elements of dance and the visual arts. Since performance art often is based on the vision of an individual performer or director rather than a playwright, the autobiographical monologue has become a popular performance art form.

---

[1]Apple, Jacki, "Art at the Barricades," *Artsweek*, Vol. 21, May 3, 1990.

ASIAN AMERICAN THEATRE
Asian American playwrights and theatre companies have focused on works that accurately represent the experiences of Asian populations in the United States and provide opportunities for underrepresented Asian actors. This is a scene from *Charles Francis Chan Jr.'s Exotic Oriental Murder* by Lloyd Sur as staged by the National Asian American Theater Company at Walkedpace at Soho Rep in New York in 2015. The play, which deconstructs the racist representations of Asians in popular cutlure, was directed by Ed Sylavanus Iskandar. The actors are, from left, Jeffrey Omura, Peter Kim and Jeff Biehl. (©Hiroyuki Ito/Hulton Archive/Getty Images)

their biases. Such was the case in *Alice's Rape* (1989), in which Robbie McCauley performed nude as her great-great-grandmother, a slave on the auction block. These performance artists are continuing a trend begun by early realistic and antirealistic dramatists, whose works challenged the social status quo and were often banned.

Two artists who began performing solo pieces in alternative spaces but later received commercial productions are Spalding Gray (1941–2004) and Bill Irwin (1950–). Gray, a monologuist who discussed issues that ranged from his own personal concerns to politics, was reminiscent of ancient storytellers who created a theatrical environment single-handedly. Irwin's performances are mime-like, and he uses popular slapstick techniques to reflect on the contemporary human condition.

Anna Deavere Smith (1952–), an African American performance artist, won considerable acclaim in the early 1990s for pieces dealing with racial unrest. In her works, she portrays numerous real people she has met and interviewed. For example, her *Twilight: Los Angeles 1992* presented people affected by the uprising that followed the acquittals in the first trial of police officers charged with brutalizing Rodney King.

Other well-known monologuists are Eric Bogosian (1953–), Danny Hoch (1970–), John Leguizamo (1965–), who focuses on Latino-American issues, Mike

Daisey (1973–), Lisa Kron (1961–), and Sarah Jones (1973–). Ping Chong (1946–) is an Asian American performance artist who mixes multimedia into his works.

A number of spaces have become recognized for their presentation of performance artists. These include two in New York City: PS 122, a converted public school in the East Village in Manhattan; and the Kitchen, also located downtown. In addition, many museums throughout the United States are known for presenting series of performance artists, including the Walker Museum in Minneapolis and the Museum of Contemporary Art in Chicago. The fact that performance art is most often presented in converted, found spaces or museums, again reflects the eclectic nature of the form and its relationship to earlier avant-garde movements and the visual arts.

Along with those in the United States, there are also significant performance artists in most major cities around the world, such as Issei Ogata (1952–) in Japan.

Postmodernism

Contemporary global theatre, as can be seen from the examples of performance art above, is highly eclectic. Some works focus on political concerns; others on personal issues; still others focus on formal concerns. Many works mix techniques and styles. In contemporary theatre, many such complex works are often described by critics as postmodernist.

Postmodernism, a term used to categorize much of the experimentation in theatre in the past three decades, is difficult to define. According to A. O. Scott, film critic for the *New York Times*, **postmodernism** is characterized by the following attributes: "a cool, ironic affect; the overt pastiche of work from the past; the insouciant mixture of high and low styles."[2] However, we should note that some contemporary critics call into question the entire category of postmodernism and argue that each of the artists and works so categorized is unique. Still, postmodernism appears to have several characteristics.

Postmodernism questions the position of power in art and the idea of an accepted "canon" of classics: Postmodernists also ask why certain artists (such as playwrights) and certain groups (such as white males) should have held positions of power and privilege throughout theatre history.

Accordingly, postmodernists rebel against traditional readings of texts, arguing that theatre productions may have a variety of "authors," including directors and even individual audience members: They argue that each audience member creates his or her own unique reading. Postmodernist directors are noted for *deconstructing* classic dramas—that is, taking the original play apart, developing a new individual conceptualization, and trying to represent onstage the issues of power embedded in the text. When a classic is deconstructed in this way, it may serve simply as the scenario for a production rather than a strictly followed script.

Postmodernist artists question categorizations of works. The term postmodernism suggests that the "modernist" interest in realism, antirealism, and form is no longer central to theatre, that artists have now moved beyond being concerned with representing either reality or abstraction. Instead, postmodernists mix abstraction and realism, so that their works cannot be easily classified. Furthermore, the distinction between "high" art and popular art can no longer be clearly defined: Postmodernists mix popular concerns and techniques with those of high art.

For example, the Disney musical *The Lion King* directed by Julie Taymor, which was discussed in the previous chapter, breaks down the distinctions between

Postmodernism A contemporary concept suggesting that artists and audiences have gone beyond the modernist movements of realism and departures of realism.

[2]Scott, A.O., "Say 'Brian DiPalma.' Let the Fighting Start" *The New York Times*, September 17, 2006.

A POSTMODERN PRODUCTION

As a mark of postmodernism, theatre today is eclectic and widely diversified. Periods, styles, and theatrical intentions are often mixed or coexist side by side. One such mixture of styles and material was a staging of *Hamlet* by the Wooster Group, known for its experimental work. This Shakespearean tragedy was deconstructed by using the film of the 1964 stage production starring Richard Burton as its basis. Elizabeth LeCompte directed. (©Robbie Jack - Corbis/Getty Images)

popular art and high art, commercial and experimental theatre, and Asian and Western techniques.

Closely associated with the postmodernist approach to theatre is what is termed ***non-text-based theatre***, meaning that there is no text in a traditional sense, with dialogue written by a dramatist; rather, there is a scenario created by a director or an ensemble. The actors and the director then expand the scenario often through improvisation.

Among the most significant groups that have developed under the postmodernist banner are Mabou Mines, founded in 1970 under the artistic direction of Lee Breuer (1937–) and the Wooster Group. The Wooster Group is best known for its deconstruction of texts under the artistic direction of Elizabeth LeCompte (1944–). The film actor Willem Dafoe (1955–) began his acting career with this company and has frequently returned.

Another contemporary postmodernist company is New York's Elevator Repair Service, which was founded in 1991 and has toured throughout the United States and internationally. In 2005, it presented a reading of F. Scott Fitzgerald's novel *The Great Gatsby,* entitled *Gatz,* set in a dilapidated factory office; the entire novel is read and acted out by inhabitants of that office, and the performance takes more than six hours.

Non-text-based theatre
A term meaning that there is no text in a traditional sense, with dialogue written by a dramatist; rather, there is a scenario created by a director or an ensemble, which is then usually expanded through improvisation.

A postmodernist British company is Punchdrunk founded in 2000. Punchdrunk often uses abandoned spaces in which audience members follow performers to differing spaces to see sections of the productions staged. Audience members, therefore, do not see the same "production" each evening and are actively engaged in following the performance, which is usually a deconstructed version of a classic text.

Many other alternative theatres, playwrights, directors, and performance artists throughout the world can also be categorized as postmodernist. We will mention some of them later in this chapter.

DIVERSE AND MULTICULTURAL THEATRES IN THE UNITED STATES

We now turn our attention to the diverse and multicultural theatres found in the United States. First, we will look at the various types of alternative theatres in the United States. Alternative theatres were often organized to stage works that were noncommercial, too experimental or too controversial for mainstream commercial theatre, and continue to do so. The performance artists and postmodernist artists mentioned previously work in alternative theatre environments.

We will then survey the development of African American, Latino American, Asian American, Native American, feminist, and lesbian, gay, and transgender theatres and artists in the United States; many were part of the alternative theatre movement in the United States since their work reflected the expanding interest in ethnicity, gender, and sexual orientation, which was often too controversial for the mainstream, commercial theatre.

Alternatives to Commercial Theatre in the United States

A crucial development in American theatre in the second half of the twentieth century, which continues to impact the contemporary theatre, was the creation of important alternatives to traditional Broadway commercial theatre. These alternative theatres tended to be able to offer theatre for special audiences, as well as theatre that was often more daring, bold, and fresh, as well as experimental. Their offerings were often extremely eclectic in style and subject matter. Four manifestations were regional theatre, off-Broadway, off-off-Broadway, and alternative regional theatres.

Regional Theatre   An important development in the United States in the past half century has been the growth of major established regional theatres. (The phenomenon of important theatres established outside major cities is, again, a worldwide trend.) A number of significant regional theatres were founded in the 1950s and 1960s and began to flourish in large cities around the country. These are nonprofit rather than commercial theatres, but they employ professional performers, directors, and designers. They present the best dramas from the past as well as interesting new plays. In fact, in recent years nonprofit, regional theatres have been a chief source of new works in the United States. Among the best-known regional theatres are the Guthrie Theatre in Minneapolis, the Arena State in Washington, D.C., and the Goodman Theatre in Chicago.

Off-Broadway, Off-Off-Broadway, and Alternative Regional Theatres   In New York City, off-Broadway theatre began in the 1950s as an alternative to commercial Broadway, which was becoming increasingly costly. Off-Broadway theatres were smaller than Broadway theatres—most of them had fewer than 200 seats—and were located outside the Times Square neighborhood where the Broadway houses are situated. Because off-Broadway was less expensive than Broadway, it offered more opportunity for producing serious classics and experimental works.

In the past five decades, however, off-Broadway itself became more expensive and institutionalized. For example, in New York City, a group of off-Broadway theatres have become an important producing agency in the Broadway theatre district; among the best-known is Playwrights Horizons. Still, off-Broadway has and continues to present many significant playwrights and directors. Among the better-known dramatists are John Guare (1938–), Lanford Wilson (1937–2011), Marsha Norman (1947–), Wendy Wasserstein (1950–2006), as well as many of the playwrights of diverse backgrounds mentioned later.

As a result of off-Broadway's transformations, small independent producing groups had to develop another forum. The result was off-off-Broadway. Off-off-Broadway shows are produced wherever inexpensive space is available—in churches, lofts, warehouses, garages—and are characterized by low prices and a wide variety of offerings. It is in these theatres, too, that much experimentation takes place, including performance art and postmodernist works. One important off-off-Broadway theatre is Café LaMama; among the significant groups that have worked off-off-Broadway are the Living Theatre, the Open Theatre, the Performance Group, Mabou Mines, and the Wooster Group.

Two experimental directors whose works were also seen off-off-Broadway are Robert Wilson (1944–) and Richard Foreman (1937–). Their work is typically unified by a theme or point of view determined by the director, and their material is often organized into units analogous to frames in television or film. Stunning theatrical images containing the essence of the ideas that interest these directors are often the key to their work.

Counterparts of the off- and off-off-Broadway movements have also sprung up in other major cities across the United States—Washington, Atlanta, Chicago, Minneapolis, Los Angeles, San Francisco, Seattle, and others—where groups perform as alternatives to the larger, established regional theatres. Presentations by these alternative theatres include classics, new plays, and experimental works. Among the best-known are Steppenwolf Theatre Company and Lookingglass Theatre Company in Chicago. As these companies have become more established and mainstream, smaller nonequity (that is, nonunion affiliated) and equity storefront theatres (literally theatres established in former stores) have sprung up in Chicago and other cities.

Again, this trend of creating out-of-the-way alternative theatres outside the commercial centers of major cities is taking place worldwide. In London, for example, there is a long history of "fringe" theatres: theatres outside London's commercial West End, which were originally established to circumvent the English censorship laws and which present more experimental works.

Two American Playwrights with Roots in Alternative Theatre Two American playwrights whose work was first presented in small alternative, nonprofit theatres and who then became prominent in regional and off-Broadway theatres are Sam Shepard (1943–2017) and David Mamet (1947–). Like many of our contemporary playwrights, Shepard and Mamet mix concerns of high art—such as the plight of the American family and the demise of the American dream—with techniques borrowed from mass entertainments such as film, popular music, and melodrama. Also, they often blur the distinction between realism and abstraction. Many critics suggest that their work is, as discussed earlier, postmodernist.

REGIONAL AND OFF-BROADWAY PLAYWRIGHT
David Mamet is a playwright who came out of the alternative regional theatre scene in Chicago and off-Broadway movement of the late 1960s and the 1970s. Mamet is best-known for the plays he wrote in the late 1970s and early 1980s. One such play is *American Buffalo,* shown here in a 2015 production directed by Daniel Evans at London's Wyndham's Theatre, with John Goodman as Don Dubrow, Tom Sturridge as Bob and Damian Lewis as Walter Teach Cole. (©Nigel Norrington/Camera Press/Redux)

Sam Shepard first developed his playwriting skills off-off-Broadway with works that fused surreal and absurdist styles and abandoned traditional plot structure and development. His later dramas include *Buried Child* (for which he won a Pulitzer Prize in 1979), *True West* (1980), *Fool for Love* (1982), *A Lie of the Mind* (1985), *Heartless* (2012), and *A Particle of Dread (Oedipus Variations)* (2014). These plays deal with American mythology, the violence of American society, and the degeneration of the American family.

David Mamet came out of the Chicago theatre scene. His plays have naturalistic language and settings, but they do not provide the clear-cut exposition or dramatic resolutions of traditional realism. Like Shepard's, they attack many accepted ideals of American life. Among Mamet's best-known works are *American Buffalo* (1977), *Glengarry Glen Ross* (1983), *Oleanna* (1992), and *Race* (2009). Mamet has also written and directed a number of films.

Of course, there have been other significant contemporary playwrights whose careers were established in alternative theatres in New York, Chicago, and other cities. Among them are Tony Kushner (1956–), Neil LaBute (1963–), Bruce Norris (1960–), Tracy Letts (1965–), and many of the female, African American, Asian American, Latino/a American, and LGBTQ playwrights discussed later in this chapter.

We now turn our attention to the theatres and theatre artists who reflect the great diversity of the United States and whose works reflect the sociopolitical issues of our diverse populations.

African American Theatre

As we have noted previously, there are many theatres that appeal to diverse audiences with specific political viewpoints, concerns about gender, and sexual orientations. African American theatre—also referred to as Black theatre—is a prime example of a theatre that reflects the diversity of American culture and the contributions of a particular group to this culture. Since African American theatre has a long history, it will be helpful to trace its development from about 1900 on, so that we can better understand its significance and impact on our contemporary theatre.

African American Theatre from 1900 to 1950   At the turn of the twentieth century, the popular syncopated rhythms of ragtime had a strong influence on the emerging musical theatre and served as a bridge for a number of talented African Americans. Bob Cole (1864–1912) and William Johnson (1873–1954) conceived, wrote, produced, and directed the first Black musical comedy. The comedians Bert Williams (c. 1876–1922) and George Walker (1873–1911) and their wives joined composers and writers to produce musicals and operettas, in which Americans for the first time saw Blacks on the Broadway stage without burnt-cork makeup, speaking without dialect, and costumed in high fashion.

The early twentieth century also saw the formation of African American stock companies. The most significant was the Lafayette Players, founded in 1914 by Anita Bush (1883–1974), originally as the Anita Bush Players. By the time it closed in 1932, this company had presented over 250 productions and employed a number of Black stars.

Black performers and writers were also making inroads into commercial theatre in the 1920s. Twenty plays with Black themes were presented on Broadway in this decade, five of them written by African Americans. The decade also saw some Black performers achieve recognition in serious drama, among them Charles Gilpin (1878–1930), Paul Robeson, and Ethel Waters (1896–1977).

The Depression forced Black performers to find other ways of earning a living or to invent ingenious ways to create their own theatre. There were a few Broadway productions of plays by Blacks, such as the folk musical *Run Little Chillun* (1933) and *Mulatto* (1935) by Langston Hughes (1902–1967).

Possibly the most significant development for Black theatre during the 1930s was the Federal Theatre Project. This organization, discussed in the previous chapter, was meant to help theatre artists through the Depression; the Federal Theatre Project formed separate Black units in twenty-two cities, which mounted plays by Black and White authors and employed thousands of African American writers, performers, and technicians.

The 1940s saw a stage adaptation, in 1941, of the controversial novel *Native Son* by Richard Wright (1908–1960), directed by Orson Welles for his Mercury Theatre. Other important Broadway ventures included Paul Robeson's record run of 296 performances in *Othello* in 1943, and *Anna Lucasta* (1944), adapted by Abram Hill (1911–1986).

African American Theatre since 1950   The 1950s saw an explosion of Black theatre that would continue over the next five decades. *Take a Giant Step* by Louis

PLAYWRIGHT AUGUST WILSON

One of the most important playwrights of the past half century is the African American dramatist August Wilson. During the course of his career he wrote a monumental series of plays about the Black experience in America. There were ten in all, one for each decade of the twentieth century. Shown here are Viola Davis and Denzel Washington in *Fences,* recently revived on Broadway. (©Sara Krulwich/The New York Times/ Redux)

Patterson (1922–), a play about growing up in an integrated neighborhood, premiered in 1953. In 1954, the playwright-director Owen Dodson (1914–1983)—a significant figure in Black theatre since the 1930s—staged *Amen Corner* by James Baldwin (1924–1987) at Howard University.

Off-Broadway, the Greenwich Mews Theatre began casting plays without regard to race and also produced *Trouble in Mind* (1956) by Alice Childress (1920–1994)—the first play by an African American woman to receive a commercial production. Possibly the most important production of the postwar era was *A Raisin in the Sun* (1959) by Lorraine Hansberry (1930–1965). It is about a Black family in Chicago, held together by a God-fearing mother, who is planning to move into a predominantly White neighborhood where the family will be unwelcome. The son loses money in a get-rich-quick scheme but later assumes responsibility for the family.

Hansberry's play was directed by Lloyd Richards (1922–2006), the first Black director on Broadway. Richards later became head of the Yale School of Drama, where in the 1980s he nurtured the talents of the Black playwright August Wilson (1945–2005), author of a 10-play cycle, chronicling African American life in the twentieth century, including *Fences* (1985), *Joe Turner's Come and Gone* (1986), and *The Piano Lesson* (1990). In recent years, the Goodman Theatre and Court Theatre in Chicago have staged nationally recognized revivals of Wilson's plays.

From 1960 to the 1990s, there was an outpouring of African American theatre, much of it reflecting the struggle for civil rights. Amiri Baraka (1934–2014) came to theatregoers' attention in 1964 with *Dutchman,* a verbal and sexual showdown between an assimilated Black male and a White temptress, set in a New York subway. There were many other critically acclaimed African American dramas and playwrights during the 1960s and 1970s.

TODAY'S THEATRE: GLOBAL AND DIVERSE
The work of the playwright Lynn Nottage is an excellent example of theatrical diversity. *Sweat,* directed by Kate Whoriskey, was produced by the Oregon Shakespeare Festival, the Arena Stage in Washington, D.C., off-Broadway at the Public Theatre, and on Broadway. It is set in Reading, Pennsylvania and deals with the impact of the changing economy on blue collar workers of differing races. (©Sara Krulwich/The New York Times/Redux)

In 1970 the Black Theatre Alliance listed over 125 producing groups in the United States. While only a few of these survived the decade, many had a significant impact, including the Negro Ensemble Company, which was founded in 1967 and continues to produce today. One of the most notable in the contemporary theatre is Congo Square Theatre Company in Chicago, which was founded in 1999.

In addition to the emergence of these producing organizations, another major change in the 1970s was the presence of a larger Black audience at Broadway theatres, which accounted for a significant number of commercial African American productions, such as *Don't Bother Me, I Can't Cope* (1972); *The Wiz* (1975); and *Bubbling Brown Sugar* (1976).

African American artists continue to make an impact on commercial and noncommercial theatre. We mentioned August Wilson earlier. George C. Wolfe (1955–), author-director of *The Colored Museum* (1986), *Jelly's Last Jam* (1992), and *Bring in da' Noise, Bring in da' Funk* (1996), also directed both parts of the award-winning *Angels in America.* Wolfe was artistic director of the Public Theatre from 1993 to 2004. In 2013, he directed Tom Hanks in *Lucky Guy* on Broadway.

Another African American director, Kenny Leon (1955–), in 2002 founded the True Colors Theatre in Atlanta; and in 2004 and 2014 he directed revivals of *A Raisin in the Sun* and in 2010 *Fences* on Broadway. In 2011 Leon staged

A MILESTONE IN LATINO-LATINA THEATRE

A significant event in the emergence of Latino-Latina theatre was the 1978 production of *Zoot Suit* by Luis Valdez. It was a Brechtian-like musical based on a real event, but it was given a highly theatrical treatment. It originated in Los Angeles and moved to Broadway. Seen here is a 2017 revival at the Mark Taper Forum in Los Angeles directed by the author. (©Craig Schwartz Photography)

Actos Short agit-prop dramas about the lives of Chicano workers.

Agit-prop A term meaning agitation-propaganda, referring to plays with a strong social or political agenda.

two Broadway productions of plays by African American authors: *The Mountaintop,* by Katori Hall (1981–), and *Stick Fly,* by Lydia R. Diamond (1969–).

Suzan-Lori Parks (1964–), Pearl Cleage (1948–), and Cheryl West (1956–) are contemporary African American female playwrights whose works deal with issues of racism and feminism and have been produced in regional and alternative theatres. Two additional African American female dramatists whose works are politically charged are Kia Corthron (b. 1961) and Lynn Nottage (b. 1964). Nottage won the Pulitzer Prize for *Ruined* (2008) and *Sweat* in 2016.

Among the current generation of African American dramatists are Thomas Bradshaw (1980–) and Branden Jacobs-Jenkins (1985–), both of whose works have been staged in off-off-Broadway, off-Broadway, and regional theatres.

Latino-Latina Theatre

Contemporary Latino-Latina or Hispanic theatre in the United States can be divided into at least three groups: Chicano theatre, Cuban American theatre, and Puerto Rican or Nuyorican theatre. All three address the experiences of Hispanics living in the United States, and the plays are sometimes written in Spanish but are usually in English.

Chicano theatre, which originated primarily in the west and southwest, came to prominence during the time of the civil rights movements of the 1960s. The theatre troupe known as El Teatro Campesino ("farmworkers' theatre") grew out of the work of Luis Valdez (1940–), who joined César Chavez in organizing farmworkers in California. Valdez wrote ***actos***, short agit-prop pieces dramatizing the lives of workers. (The term ***agit-prop*** means "agitation propaganda"; it was applied in the 1930s to plays with a strong political or social agenda.)

El Teatro Campesino became the prototype for other Mexican and Latino theatre groups such as Teatro de la Gente ("people's theatre"), founded in 1967; and Teatro de la Esperanza ("theatre of hope"), begun in 1971 in Santa Barbara, California.

Valdez's play *Zoot Suit* (1978), about racial violence in Los Angeles in 1943, opened in Los Angeles to considerable acclaim; it later moved to Broadway. Other plays about the Chicano experience followed, one of the most notable being *Roosters* (1987) by Milcha Sanchez-Scott (1955–), in which cockfighting is a metaphor used to explore Chicano concerns and family conflicts. Luis Alfaro (1963–) is a Chicano performance artist, director, and playwright whose best known works are adaptations of *Oedipus the King, Oedipus el Rey* (2010) and of *Medea, Mojada* (2013).

Part 4   Global Theatres: Past and Present

Cuban American theatre developed chiefly in Florida. The Federal Theatre Project of the 1930s resulted in fourteen Cuban American productions in 1936 and 1937. A highly regarded Cuban American dramatist whose work began to be produced in the 1970s was Maria Irene Fornes (1930–). Another Cuban American playwright, Nilo Cruz (1960–), won the Pulitzer Prize in 2003 for *Anna in the Tropics.*

Nuyorican is a term that refers to Puerto Rican culture, mostly in New York, but elsewhere as well. Works by playwrights with a Puerto Rican background began to be produced in the 1960s and 1970s by groups such as the Teatro Repertorio Español, the Puerto Rican Traveling Theatre, and the New York Public Theatre founded by Joseph Papp (1922–1991). The Nuyorican Poets' Café presented plays by a number of Hispanic writers, including an ex-convict, Miguel Piñero (1947–1988), whose *Short Eyes,* a harshly realistic portrait of prison life, proved to be very successful and won a number of awards in the 1973–1974 season. Today many Puerto Rican playwrights have come to prominence. Quiara Alegreia Hudes (1978–) won the Pulitzer Prize in 2012 for *Water by the Spoonful,* which is part of a trilogy of plays, and also authored the book for the musical *In the Heights* (2007). Lin-Manuel Miranda (1980–), whose heritage is primarily Puerto Rican, is the composer of *In the Heights* as well as *Hamilton* (2015), for which he also wrote the book.

The vitality of Latino theatre is also reflected in the many companies that are dedicated to the presentation of works by Latino playwrights of various backgrounds. In 1971, a network of Latino theatres across the country was established. Current examples include two Chicago companies: Teatro Vista, established by two Cuban-born theatre artists, and Teatro Luna, organized by ten Latina women, including Mexican-born playwright Tanya Saracho (1980–).

Asian American Theatre

For most of the nineteenth century and the first half of the twentieth century, Asians appeared in dramatic offerings strictly as stereotypes. With the coming of cultural and ethnic awareness in the 1960s and 1970s, things began to change; Asian American theatre developed to represent Asian American identity on stage and to give Asian American artists opportunities not available in the mainstream theatre.

In 1965 several Asian American performers and directors founded the East West Players in Los Angeles. In 1973, two more groups were formed—the Asian Exclusion Act in Seattle and the Asian-American Theatre Workshop in San Francisco—and in 1977 the director-actor Tisa Chang (1945–) founded the Pan Asian Repertory Theatre in New York. These groups employed Asian American performers, produced dramas from the Asian cultural heritage, and emphasized new plays written by and for Asian Americans. More recent Asian American theatre groups include Ma-Yi Theatre Company, founded in New York in 1989; New York's National Asian American Theatre Company; Lodestone Theatre Ensemble, founded in Los Angeles in 1999; and Mu Performing Arts, founded in Minneapolis in 1992. Silk Road Theater Project, founded in Chicago in 2003, presents works by Asian, Middle Eastern, and Mediterranean playwrights with themes related to those peoples.

A number of plays by Asian American writers were produced in the 1970s and 1980s, including a memory play by Philip Kan Gotanda (1950–) called *Song for a Nisea Fisherman* (1980). A playwright who came to prominence in the

ASIAN AMERICAN THEATRE
The Vietnamese American playwright Qui Nguyen has had plays produced regionally and off-Broadway. Shown here is a scene from the New York City Center Stage's production of his best known work *Vietgone*, which depicts the relationship between two young, in love refugees from the Vietnam War (played by Paco Tolson and Jennifer Ikeda), while in a Middle American relocation camp. (©Emon Hassan/The New York Times/Redux)

1980s was David Henry Hwang (1957–), son of first-generation Americans who immigrated from China to California. Hwang wrote several plays that won wide recognition and in 1988, Hwang's *M. Butterfly* opened successfully on Broadway. Based on a true story, the play deals with a French diplomat who meets and falls in love with a Chinese opera singer who he thinks is a woman but turns out to be a man and a spy. Hwang has written many other works, including *Chinglish* (2011), which opened at the Goodman Theatre in Chicago and then transferred to Broadway, and *Kung Fu* (2014).

The newer generation of Asian American playwrights includes Diana Son (1965–), Chay Yew (1965–), who in 2011 became the artistic director of Chicago's Victory Gardens Theatre, Han Ong (1968–), and Young Jean Lee (1974–), who is also a director.

There has also been a movement to have more Asian Americans employed as performers in appropriate roles. Hwang and the actor B. D. Wong, who played the Chinese opera singer in the original production of *M. Butterfly,* led a vigorous protest against the hiring of an English actor to play the leading role in the musical *Miss Saigon.* That battle was lost; but by 1996, when a revival of *The King and I* opened on Broadway, it had a large proportion of Asian American performers.

However, there continues to be concerns regarding theatres not casting Asian actors. In 2012, the La Jolla Playhouse in San Diego cast a white actor as a Chinese emperor (and had only three Asian performers) in the workshop of the musical *The Nightingale.*

The Royal Shakespeare Company in London also created controversy in 2013 when Asian actors were cast only in minor roles in the classic Chinese play, *The Orphan of Zhao.*

Native American Theatre

Strictly speaking, there was no Native American theatre tradition; rather, there were spiritual and social traditions that had theatrical elements. These were found primarily in ancient rituals and communal celebrations, which were often infused with cosmic significance. Also, in these traditions, unlike traditional Western theatre, there was no audience as such: Those observing were considered participants just as much as the principal performers. Many of these ceremonies and the like were outlawed by the American government in the nineteenth century. Thus, the legacy of rituals and ceremonies, which had strong theatrical components—not to mention significant spiritual and cultural value—was forced to go "underground" if it continued at all.

The American Indian Religious Freedom Act of 1972 made it legal once again for certain ceremonies, such as the sun dance, to resume. This increased awareness of these rituals and celebrations contributed to the emergence of a Native American theatre. Two groups that led the way in the past three decades were the Native American Theatre Ensemble and Spiderwoman.

The Native American Theatre Ensemble, which was originally called the American Indian Theatre Ensemble, was founded by Hanay Geiogamah. (It is important to note that those familiar with Native American theatre invariably identify theatre companies and theatre artists not with the generic term Native American theatre, but in terms of their nations. Thus, Geiogamah is identified as Kiowa/Delaware.) Geiogamah's organization gave its premiere performance at La MaMa Theater in New York City in 1972, and later toured widely, not only in North America but also in Europe and elsewhere.

Spiderwoman Theatre comes under the headings of both Native American theatre and feminist theatre. Founded in 1975, it is the longest continually running women's theatre in North America, as well as a Native American theatre. Three of its founding members—Lisa Mayo, Gloria Miguel, and Muriel Miguel—draw on storytelling and other theatrical traditions to celebrate their identities as American Indian women and to comment on stereotypes of women in general.

NATIVE AMERICAN THEATRE
Native American theatre, also known as indigenous theatre, is written by and for Native Americans. The participants frequently attempt to recapture not only themes and subjects appropriate to Native American culture but also the production styles and approaches of the original theatrical presentations. The scene here is from a play by William S. Yellow Robe, Jr., *Grandchildren of the Buffalo Soldiers;* it dramatizes the visit of a man, Craig Robe (James Craven), who returns to his tribe after having lived elsewhere. In this scene he is with August Jackson (Maya Washington). The drama was coproduced by Penumbra Theatre Company and Trinity Repertory Company and directed by Lou Bellamy. (©Ann Marsden/Penumbra Theatre Company)

Another important Native American producing organization is Native Voices at the Autry. Randy Reinholz, a Native American, and his wife, Jean Bruce Scott, had developed a program presenting Native American drama at Illinois State University where they were on the faculty. In 2000, they were invited by the Autry Museum in Los Angeles to bring their project, Native Voices, to the Autry to become a full-time, professional producing organization. Since that beginning they have presented a series of readings, workshops, and full productions of a wide range of Native American dramatic writing. (Reinholz caused a stir in 2014 when he loudly booed an adaptation of *The Tempest* by the acclaimed avant-garde theatre company, The Wooster Group. Reinholz argued that the representations of Native Americans in the company's version of Shakespeare's play were racist.)

Native Voices productions include *Kino and Teresa* (2005), a retelling by James Lujan of the story of *Romeo and Juliet*. The play pits people from the Taos Pueblo against their Spanish conquerors. Other productions include *Super Indian* (2007) and *Stand-off at Highway #37* (2014) by Victoria Ramirez as well as an annual theatre festival of new plays.

What is important to note about Native American theatre today is that it is not primarily historical or ceremonial. Though elements of tribal traditions may be incorporated, the emphasis among playwrights and producers is really on contemporary work, fusing the problems and aspirations of today's Native Americans with their heritage. The challenges and preoccupations of young Native American playwrights are frequently similar to those addressed by their Euro-American counterparts.

Several Native American playwrights have recently published single-author anthologies of their works. These include William F. Yellow Robe, Jr. (Assiniboine), Diane Glancy (Cherokee), and E. Donald Two-Rivers (Anishinabe). Another important contemporary playwright is Bruce King (Turgle Clan, Hodenausaunee-Oneida). King and Yellow Robe are also directors who have founded their own companies and have taught playwriting and performance at the Institute of American Indian Arts in Santa Fe, New Mexico, an organization that nurtures the next generation of Native American theatre artists.

There are also many other Native American theatre organizations throughout the United States, including Thunderbird Theatre at Haskell Indian Nations University, founded in 1974; Red Earth Performing Arts, founded in Seattle in 1974; and the Tulsa Indian Actor's Workshop, founded in 1993. The American Indian Community House (ACH) in New York City uses its theatre space for Native American performing artists, hosting the Indian Summer Series, a month-long festival; ACH also keeps a database of native performers.

Additional Multicultural Theatres and Theatre Artists   While we have discussed many multicultural theatres in the United States, there are many other companies (and playwrights) that reflect the ever-expanding diversity of U.S. society.

For example, Noor Theatre in New York City, founded by three women of Middle Eastern descent, strives to present work from the growing Middle Eastern communities in the United States. Silk Road Rising is a Chicago theatre company that presents works relevant to the Asian American and Middle Eastern American experiences and says in its mission statement that it hopes to "advance a poly-cultural worldview."

Among the playwrights who reflect this diversity is Pakistani-American Ayad Akhtar (1970–), whose play *Disgraced* won the 2013 Pulitzer Prize; Stephen Karam (1980–), whose dramas include *Sons of the Prophet* (2011) and *The Humans* (2014);

and Rajiv Joseph (1974–), whose father immigrated from India and who authored *Bengal Tiger at the Baghdad Zoo* (2009) and *Guards at the Taj* (2015).

The impact of multicultural artists on U.S. theatre is also evident in the career of Palestinian American director Joseph Haj (1965–), directing at such theatres as the Oregon Shakespeare Festival, the Actors Theatre of Louisville, and the Folger Theatre in Washington, D.C.; serving as producing artistic director at the Playmakers Repertory Company in North Carolina; and then becoming the eighth artistic director of the Guthrie Theater in 2015, following the retirement of the Irish-born director Joe Dowling (1949–).

Feminist Theatre and Playwrights

Feminist theatre is another significant movement that began in the socially active atmosphere of the late 1960s and early 1970s. The movement is also international in scope and while we will focus on feminist theatre in the United States, there are similar companies and artists presenting feminist issues across the globe.

Feminist theatre developed alongside the more general feminist movement, which stressed consciousness raising to make people aware of the secondary position women had often been forced to occupy in social and political structures. Activists in this period attempted to revise cultural value systems and interpersonal relations in terms of an egalitarian ideology. In theatre this took the form of groups like the It's Alright to Be a Woman Theatre in New York, one of the first groups to translate consciousness raising into stage performances.

Feminist theatre developed in several directions. For one thing, there was an attempt to acknowledge women writers, past and present. Thus historical figures like Hrosvitha, a nun who wrote plays in her convent at Gandersheim in Germany in the tenth century, and the English playwrights Aphra Behn (1640–1689) and Susanna Centlivre (c. 1670–1723) were brought to the forefront. In addition, attention was paid to several women playwrights who had made their mark in the early and middle twentieth century. One significant artist from this time was the American playwright Rachel Crothers (1878–1958), who wrote and directed many successful plays from 1906 to 1937. All of Crothers's plays dealt with women's moral and social concerns, and most of them were set in urban high society. Crothers's plays are skillful, entertaining comedies, but she always focused on the issue of sexual equality. Other notable female playwrights earlier in the twentieth century were Susan Glaspell (1876–1948), Sophie Treadwell (1890–1970), and Lillian Hellman (1905–1984).

Another direction for feminist theatre was the active writing and production that emerged in the late 1960s, when many female playwrights questioned traditional gender roles and the place of women in U.S. society. Representative works include *Fefu and Her Friends* (1977) by Maria Irene Fornés, which offered insight into female friendship and the struggles women experience in a patriarchal culture; *Still Life* (1981) by Emily Mann (1952–); *Painting Churches* (1983) by Tina Howe (1937–); and three plays that won the Susan Smith Blackburn Award, an award given annually to a woman who writes in the English-language theatre, and later the Pulitzer Prize for Drama: *'Night, Mother* (1983) by Marsha Norman (1947–), *Crimes of the Heart* (1977) by Beth Henley (1952–), and *The Heidi Chronicles* (1988) by Wendy Wasserstein (1950–2006).

Although the women's movement weakened during the 1980s, women continued to write plays in increasing numbers. The playwrights who had broken new ground in the 1970s continued to write dramas, and now they were joined by

GENDER DIVERSITY: FEMINIST THEATRE
For some years now, a number of playwrights and theatre companies have treated contemporary issues and concerns confronting women. One of the most notable contemporary female dramatists is Sarah Ruhl. Shown here is a scene from her *The Clean House* at the Mitzi E. Newhouse Theater in New York in 2006, with John Dossett, and Concetta Tomei on the balcony; and below, Vanessa Aspillaga, left, and Blair Brown. (©Sara Krulwich/The New York Times/Redux)

other women's voices. *How I Learned to Drive* (1998) by Paula Vogel (1951–), about a girl's coming of age; and *Wit* (1998) by Margaret Edson (1962–), about a college professor who wrestles with a fatal illness, are examples of women's ongoing exploration of new subjects and new forms. Both plays won the Pulitzer Prize.

There are many contemporary U.S. female playwrights. Earlier in this chapter we mentioned four significant African American female playwrights: Suzan-Lori Parks, Pearl Cleage, Kia Corthron, and Lynn Nottage. We also noted that there are feminist Latina American, Asian American, and Native American playwrights.

Among other current female playwrights whose works deal with feminist and broader social issues are Sarah Ruhl (1974–), Theresa Rebeck (1958–), Rebecca Gilman (1965–), Carson Kreitzer, Amy Herzog (1979–), and Annie Baker (1981–).

Sarah Ruhl was awarded the Susan Smith Blackburn Prize in 2004 and was the recipient of a MacArthur "genius" grant. Ruhl's play *The Clean House*, a Pulitzer Prize finalist, concerns a Brazilian maid who turns out to be a comedian and who refuses to clean the messy house of her disorganized employers. Ruhl's *The Next Room* was presented on Broadway in 2009 and in 2014 her play *The Oldest Boy* premiered at Lincoln Center in New York. Among recent works by Herzog are *After the Revolution*, *4000 Miles*, and *Belleville*. In 2014, Annie Baker, author of *Circle Mirror Transformation* (2009) and *The Aliens* (2010), won the Pulitzer Prize for *The Flick*.

A successful writer for television, Theresa Rebeck in her play *The Scene* wrote a pointed satire about today's television industry. Her play *The Water's Edge* transplanted the Greek story of Agamemnon, the returning warrior, to modern times and developed a seriocomic drama that mixes a tragic situation with amusing observations. A more recent play by Rebeck is *Seminar*.

Carson Kreitzer has written several plays about women who are driven to kill. One of these plays—*Self-Defense, or Death of Some Salesmen*—was the story of Aileen Wuornos, a prostitute in Florida who became a serial killer. Kreitzer's *The Love Song of J. Robert Oppenheimer* concerns the soft-spoken man responsible for developing the atomic bomb.

Some scholars estimate that more than 100 feminist companies have been founded in the United States; these companies include At the Foot of the Mountain, Women's Experimental Theatre, and Omaha Magic Theatre, the latter founded by the playwright Megan Terry. One company, Split Britches, was started in 1981 by Lois Weaver (1949–), Peggy Shaw (1944–), and Deborah Margolin (1953–)

as an offshoot of Spiderwoman Theatre. Split Britches became well-known for its production of *Belle Reprieve* (1991), which made satiric references to Tennessee Williams's *A Streetcar Named Desire* and was created collaboratively with an English gay company, Bloolips.

Many of the feminist companies that were started in the 1970s and 1980s, at the height of the women's movement, have closed. But several still remain in operation, including Women's Project and Productions, which was founded in 1978 by Julia Miles. And new feminist companies have developed in recent years. Rivendell Theatre Ensemble, founded in Chicago in 1995, is, according to its mission statement, committed to presenting audiences with "artistically challenging, thought provoking plays that explore the female experience." Feminist theatre companies continue to urge audiences to reexamine their own gender biases and those of their society.

And as we noted, there are feminist companies and female playwrights across the globe. In England, for example, there are a number of significant female playwrights, including Caryl Churchill (discussed later), Timberlake Wertenbaker (1946–), Pam Gems (1925–2011), Nina Raine, Rebecca Lenkiewicz (1968–), the first living female dramatist to have her original work staged at London's National Theatre, and Lucy Prebble (1981–). In Austria, Nobel Prize-winner Elfried Jelinek (1946–) writes plays about current political issues, such as *On the Royal Road: The Burgher King* (2017), which satirizes President Donald Trump.

Gay, Lesbian, and Transgender Theatre

Lesbian theatre groups can be part of feminist theatre, but gay, lesbian, and transgender theatre is also a distinct movement. A number of plays and performers introduced gay, lesbian, and transgender themes into theatre before the 1960s. For example, in the nineteenth century and the early twentieth century there was a considerable amount of cross-dressing in performances: Men often appeared in "drag" and women in men's clothing, raising questions about sexual and gender roles. Also, plays included material on this subject; one example is Lillian Hellman's *The Children's Hour* (1934), in which a presumed lesbian relationship between two schoolteachers was presented.

However, the play that first brought gay life to the forefront was *The Boys in the Band* (1968), by Mart Crowley (1935–). Crowley depicted a group of men living an openly gay life. In 1969, the year after it opened, gay patrons of the Stonewall Inn in New York's Greenwich Village fought against police officers attempting to close the bar. This uprising, considered an early milestone of the modern gay rights movement, changed attitudes of gay activists, who now rejected what they considered a stereotype of homosexuals depicted in *The Boys in the Band*. However, successful New York revivals in 1998 and 2010 led to a reevaluation of the play's significance in the history of gay, lesbian, and transgender theatre in the United States.

In the years that followed, complex gay characters were presented unapologetically. Plays in the 1970s and 1980s included *The Ritz* (1975) by Terrence McNally (1939–) and *Torch Song Trilogy* (1983) by Harvey Fierstein (1954–), which was revived off-Broadway in 2017. Since then, more and more plays have dealt expressly with gay issues. In these dramas, not only are the daily lives of gays and lesbians presented forthrightly, but frequently gay or lesbian sociopolitical issues are also put forward. In addition to a general concern for gay, lesbian, and transgender issues, there was a sense of urgency engendered by the AIDS crisis. This has led to a number of significant dramas, including *The Normal Heart* (1985) by Larry Kramer (1935–), which was revived in a Tony award-winning production in 2011, *As Is* (1985) by William M. Hoffman (1939–2017), Tony Kushner's two-part play *Angels in America: A Gay Fantasia on National Themes* (1993–1994), and Terrence McNally's *Love! Valour! Compassion!* (1995).

Among the lesbian playwrights who paved the way for the current generation were many who also dealt with feminist and multicultural issues. They include Megan Terry, Maria Irene Fornes, and Paula Vogel, all of whom were mentioned earlier.

The twenty-first century continues to see plays tackling issues of gay, lesbian, and transgender identity and relationships. Commercially successful plays focusing on gay characters include *Take Me Out* (2003) by Richard Greenberg (1958–), *Next Fall* (2009) by Geoffrey Nauffts (1961–), and *Significant Other* (2015) by Joshua Harmon (1983–). The current generation of lesbian playwrights includes KS Stevens, author of *Butch Mamas!* (2009), solo artist Carolyn Gage (1952–), Elizabeth Whitney, creator of *Wonder Woman! A Cabaret of Heroic Proportions!* (2009), Meryl Cohen, author of *Reasons to Live* (2012), and Lisa Kron (1961–).

Taylor Mac (1973–), who in *Hir* (2015) dramatizes a family that includes a transgender sibling, Basil Kreimendehl, Jess Barbagallo, and MJ Kaufman, whose *Sagittarius Ponderosa* (2016) explores the transgender experience, are among the emerging twenty-first century transgender playwrights. In addition, Will Davis (1983–) is a transgender director, who has staged works off-Broadway and is the artistic director of Chicago's American Theatre Company. In 2017, he directed a production of William Inge's 1953 play *Picnic* with transgender performers playing the leads as well as other roles.

A series of Broadway musicals have reflected the growing awareness of gay, lesbian, and transgender concerns. In 1983, a Broadway musical version of *La Cage aux Folles* told the story of a gay couple who run a nightclub located in St. Tropez in the south of France and in which the male performers cross dress. Based on a play by Jean Poiret, it chronicles the comedic events of a dinner party in which two gay men pretend to be heterosexual in order to impress their son's ultra-conservative future in-laws. The book was written by Harvey Fierstein. *La Cage aux Folles* has had successful revivals, including on Broadway in 2010 and a tour of the United Kingdom in 2017.

In the following decade, *Hedwig and the Angry Inch* (1998), book by John Cameron Mitchell (1963–) and music and lyrics by Stephen Trask (1966–), opened off-Broadway. It tells the story of a transgender punk rock performer who emigrated from East Berlin and is following her former lover on his more successful tour. The 2014 musical *Kinky Boots*, which also deals with transgender issues and has a book by Fierstein and music by Cindy Lauper (1953–), tells the story of an encounter between a drag queen and a shoe factory.

As we noted in the previous chapter, the 2013 musical *Fun Home*, which moved to Broadway in 2015, was the first mainstream musical about a lesbian protagonist. Based on the graphic memoir of Alison Bechdel, the musical examines her childhood, her recognition of her sexual orientation, her coming out, and her relationship with her gay father. Lisa Kron, a successful lesbian playwright, performance artist, and founder of the theatre group Five Lesbian Brothers, whom we mentioned earlier, wrote the book and lyrics. Jeaaine Tesori (1961–) was the composer.

Groups that use cross-dressing to break stereotypes of gender and sexual orientation have also been extremely important in the past five decades. Among the early "gender-bender" groups were the Cockettes and the Angels of Light in San Francisco and Centola and Hot Peaches in New York. An important company in New York was the Theatre of the Ridiculous, founded by John Vaccaro, which developed an extraordinary writer and performer—Charles Ludlam (1943–1987).

IN FOCUS: UNDERREPRESENTATION AND MARGINALIZATION OF WOMEN AND AFRICAN AMERICANS IN U.S. THEATRE

At the opening of this chapter, we spoke of trends we would be discussing. One of those trends is a focus on multiculturalism and diversity, which examines theatre artists who are marginalized: women, peoples of color, and LGBTQ populations. We recognize certain theatre artists as pioneers because there have always been in the modern theatre (and in previous eras) a few members of underrepresented groups accepted into the mainstream. For example, there were many women in theatre in the 1920s, 30s, and 40s who were able, despite the inherent sexism of the times, to achieve recognition alongside their male counterparts.

Among these pioneering female theatre artists whom we have mentoned are director-performer Eva La Gallienne (1899–1991); the playwrights Rachel Crothers (1876–1958), Pulitzer Prize–winner Zona Gale (1874–1938), Sophie Treadwell (1885–1970), Susan Glaspell (1876–1948), and Lillian Hellman (1905–1984); the producer Cheryl Crawford (1902–1986); and the performer and renowned acting teacher Stella Adler (1901–1992).

While recognizing their accomplishments and fame, during a time of extreme marginalization of women, we must remember that the inherent sexism in society during this era meant that these women were only a tiny fraction of those who were lauded and achieved wide recognition in the theatre. It is this imbalance, which continues in our global theatre today, that in later decades has become the subject of increased concern and discussion worldwide.

As with women in theatre so, too, in the second, third, and fourth decades of the twentieth century certain African American individuals and theatre groups were recognized and were pioneers in bringing recognition to African American theatre.

Some of the groundbreaking artists we have noted are The Lafayette Players (1915–1932); the musical theatre composers Eubie Blake (1887–1983) and Noble Sissle (1889–1975); the actors Charles Gilpin (1878–1930), Ethel Waters (1896–1977), Paul Robeson (1898–1976), and Canada Lee (1907–1952); the playwrights Richard Wright (1908–1960) and Langston Hughes (1902–1967); as well as the choreographer Katherine Dunham (1909–2006).

Again, however, they represent a small, almost minuscule, minority of their white counterparts, and African American artists remained marginalized in the theatre in the United States.

And once again, as we discussed, in the years after World War II while more and more attention was given to this imbalance and louder pleas and demands were made for its correction, African American theatre artists remained underrepresented. The issue of underrepresentation and marginalization in the theater (and all performing arts as can be seen in the outrage over no African American actors being nominated for Academy Awards in 2015) continues to be unresolved in the twenty-first century. And this is also true for Latino/a American, Asian American, and Native American, as well as lesbian, gay, and transgender theatre artists.

Ludlam rewrote the classics to include a good deal of wild parody and frequent cross-dressing; he also created the long-lived Ridiculous Theatrical Company.

Another important group, mentioned earlier, was the Five Lesbian Brothers, a collective of five women, including the solo performance artist Lisa Kron, who were based in New York City(1876–1948) and staged plays parodying mainstream attitudes toward gender and sexuality. Chicago's About Face Theatre, founded in 1995, has as a mission: "to be Chicago's celebrated center for lesbian, gay, bisexual, transgender, queer and ally (LGBTQA) arts."

Though a number of groups have not survived, individual performers and playwrights in gay and lesbian theatre remain very much a focus of attention.

GAY AND LESBIAN THEATRE
Among the many alternative theatres that emerged in the last part of the twentieth century was theatre centering on the gay and lesbian experience. A recent drama in this category is *Significant Other* by Joshua Harmon, which focuses on a young gay man's quest for a romantic relationship. Seen here from left are: Lindsay Mendez, Carra Patterson and Gideon Glick in the 2015 production that moved from off-Broadway to Broadway. (©Sara Krulwich/The New York Times/Redux)

GLOBAL THEATRE

As we noted in the chapter "Theatre Is Everywhere," globalization has greatly affected the contemporary theatre. We can no longer very easily categorize theatre productions and artists by strictly delineated national boundaries. The fact that communication and travel are so easy makes it difficult to define national theatres and artists. As we also noted, globalization of theatre has led to interaction, collaboration, and adaptation of theatrical styles and techniques. So as we now survey some examples of global developments in England, Ireland, Australia, Canada, Asia, Latin America, and the Middle East, we must always remember that it is not possible to chronicle all of the global theatrical activity in the twenty-first century nor discuss all of the complex ways in which these theatres interact and collaborate. One intriguing example, however, is documentary drama.

A Continuing Global Trend: Documentary Drama

As we mentioned in the chapter "Theatres from the Restoration Through Romanticism" when discussing realism, certain theatrical trends and forms from past periods continue in our contemporary, global theatre. One such form is ***documentary drama*** (sometimes referred to as *theatre of fact*), which has roots in the classical Greek and Elizabethan theatres and in other theatres through the early twentieth century. Documentary drama reflects the diversity and eclecticism of our global theatre.

Documentary drama (or theatre of fact) Term encompassing different types of drama that presented material in the fashion of journalism or reporting. Drama that is supposedly based on factual occurrences and materials.

DOCUMENTARY DRAMA

A continuing trend in global theatre is documentary drama. This type of theatre is based on historical documents—papers, e-mails, recordings, television images—in order to give it the air of authenticity and historical reality. Some documentary presentations intersperse invented segments or dialogue, but others stick strictly to the public record. There are many documentary dramas dealing with the Iraq War. None has been more successful or more moving than *Black Watch,* the story of a 300-year-old Scottish regiment that saw combat in Iraq. A mixture of dramatic scenes, monologues, musical numbers, and horrific television footage of combat, it evoked the horror and sorrow of war. The production shown here, with Michael Nardone as Sergeant Munro, was created by the National Theatre of Scotland and first presented at the Edinburgh Festival. (©Geraint Lewis)

Documentary dramas are based on historical documents, which give an air of authenticity and historical reality. The goal of documentary drama is to convince audiences that they are watching history unfold, even when the dramatists have modified the documents for dramatic or political effect. One of the most famous documentary dramas is *The Investigation* (1965) by Peter Weiss (1916–1982), which dramatizes the war crimes trials of people who were guards at a Nazi extermination camp.

Documentary drama continues to be prevalent in the twenty-first century. Today, docudramas—as they are sometimes referred to—are also popular as made-for-television movies. Still, docudramas for the stage continue to be written. A good example is *Exonerated* (2002), a documentary about former death-row inmates who turn out to be innocent. There have also been numerous docudramas dealing with the war in Iraq, including *Black Watch* (2006), staged throughout the world by the National Theatre of Scotland. There are also examples of documentary drama from the contemporary African, Latin American, Asian, and Middle Eastern theatres. (Some of these will be noted later in this chapter.)

English and Irish Theatre

As we mentioned earlier, the diversity in today's theatre is worldwide. Alternative theatre companies and playwrights in the English and Irish theatres reflect this trend. In London, there are significant producing companies that support new playwrights and directors, some of which receive governmental support. These include the National Theatre, the Royal Shakespeare Company, the Old Vic, and the Royal Court Theatre.

There is also an alternative to commercial theatre known as *fringe theatre,* in which many contemporary political playwrights began their careers, though many then received productions at the subsidized and commercial theatres. These playwrights are in the postmodernist tradition, mixing reality with theatrical techniques and fusing concerns of high art with popular art. Some of the more recent fringe theatres, which also stage revivals of classical and popular works with unique contemporary approaches in addition to new dramas, and which have become internationally renowned, include the Royal Court, the Donmar Warehouse, the Almeida, and the Menier Chocolate Factory.

A good example of a playwright whose earliest work premiered at a fringe theatre is Caryl Churchill (1938–), the author of *Cloud Nine* (1979), *Top Girls* (1982), *Far Away* (2002), *A Number* (2004), and *Love and Information* (2012), whose work is also feminist.

There are many other significant playwrights in England whose works have been staged by fringe and governmentally supported theatres. Tom Stoppard (1937–) continues to write dramas emphasizing wordplay and intellectual concerns. A significant number of "angry" playwrights continue to attack traditional political, social, and economic institutions; among the best known are David Hare (1947–) and Howard Brenton (1942–). More contemporary socio-politically oriented British playwrights include Patrick Marber (1964–), Jez Butterworth (1969–), Sarah Kane (1971–1999), and Simon Stephens (1971–). There is also a new generation of young Irish playwrights who dramatize social, political, and historical issues. Martin McDonagh (1970–) and Conor McPherson (1971–) have gained international attention.

Key contemporary English directors have also begun their work in fringe theatres and then moved on to the larger governmentally supported theatres. An English director who has used a more experimental style of production, along with reinterpretations of texts that focus on feminist, gender, and other sociopolitical issues, is Deborah Warner (1959–). Warner began her career with an alternative London troupe, the Kick Theatre Company, which she founded in 1980, when she was twenty-one. She has since directed unique interpretations of the classics for the Royal Shakespeare Company and the National Theatre in London. She is best-known for the many productions she has directed that star the actress Fiona Shaw (1959–). In 2016, Warner staged *King Lear* at the Old Vic with Glenda Jackson playing the lead.

Among the other successful female directors in England are Josie Rourke (1980–), who took over as artistic director of the Donmar Warehouse in 2012, Phyllida Lloyd (1957–), Vicky Featherstone (1967–), the first female artistic director of the Royal Court, and Emma Rice (1967–), the artistic director of The Globe from 2016 to 2018.

Canada and Australia

Before World War II, Canadian and Australian theatres developed commercially, presenting popular forms of entertainments that also reflected national identity. Two Australian examples are *The Squatter's Daughter,* or, *The Land of the Wattle*

THE IRISH PLAYWRIGHT MARTIN MCDONAGH
British and Irish playwrights come from a long line of well-known predecessors. In the case of the Irish, there is a strong tradition going back over a century. Among the prominent younger Irish dramatists is Martin McDonagh. Often mixing comedy and cruelty and continuing the strong oral tradition of Irish writing, McDonagh includes gruesome details and creates vivid scenes and characters. The scene here is from his play *Hangmen*, directed by Matthew Dunster, with David Morrissey as Harry and Reece Shearsmith as Syd, which opened at London's The Royal Court Jerwood Theatre Downstairs in 2015. (©Geraint Lewis/Alamy Stock Photo)

(1907), which focused on the Australian outlaw known as the bushranger; and the pantomime *The Bunyip,* or *The Enchantment of Fairy Princess Wattle Blossom* (1916), which included a mythological Aboriginal character.

During the same period, Australia and Canada developed "little theatres"— some professional and some amateur—that presented noncommercial, and often politically charged, works. In Australia, three such companies were Sydney's New Theatre League, established in 1936; Melbourne's New Theatre Club, founded in 1937; and Brisbane's Unity Theatre, which also opened in 1937. Hart House Theatre, founded on the campus of the University of Toronto in 1919, was one example of the Canadian "little theatre" movement. It presented many of Canada's most important theatre artists in the two decades before World War II. After World War II, the Hart House became a venue for university productions, reflecting the vitality of university theatre across Canada.

Since World War II, the theatres of Canada and Australia have seen developments that parallel the complexity of international theatre. For example, in Canada in the 1950s and 1960s, many regional theatres were established. One of the most famous is the Stratford Shakespeare Festival in Stratford, Ontario. This festival, established in 1952 under the artistic direction of Tyrone Guthrie, continues to

BRITISH WOMEN COLLABORATORS
The director Deborah Warner has created several unusual and memorable theatre pieces. A good example is her production of *King Lear,* casting Glenda Jackson in the lead role as the monarch. The production was staged at the Old Vic in 2016. (©Geraint Lewis/Alamy Stock Photo)

produce classics, musicals, and contemporary works, in multiple venues. The Shaw Festival, established in 1962, stages works by Shaw, his contemporaries, and works set during his lifetime. Australia also saw the development of theatres across the nation from the 1950s through the 1970s.

Both Australia and Canada, from the late 1960s through the present, saw the development of theatre companies dedicated to new works, experimentation, and innovative revivals of classics. In 1967, Betty Burstall (1926–2013) established Melbourne's La Mama theatre, based on New York's famous experimental theatre. La Mama continues to function as does Company B, which was established in Sydney in 1985, and is known for presenting contemporary works and unique readings of classics. Among the stars who have recently appeared with the company are the film actors Geoffrey Rush (1951–) and Cate Blanchett (1969–). At the Sydney Theatre Company, founded in 1979, Blanchett was the co-artistic director from 2008 to 2013.

Playwrights and theatre artists have dealt with the issues related to these countries' diverse populations. In Canada and Australia, there are theatres that focus on native peoples and people of African descent. For example, the Australian musical *Bran Nue Dae* (1990) dealt with Aboriginal life. Playwrights have also dramatized issues of gender and sexual orientation in these countries. Michel Tremblay (1942–), who was born in Montreal, focuses on working-class Canadians and gay issues. Wadi Mouawad (b. 1968) was born in Lebanon and has written plays about his displaced community in Canada. Canadian Hannah Moscovitch (b. 1978) has dealt with feminist and Jewish issues in her work. The theatre company Buddies in Bad Times, established in 1979, is committed to gay and lesbian theatre. In the 1980s, feminist theatres in Australia included Home Cooking Theatre (1981) and Vital Statistix (1984).

There are also Canadian and Australian artists who present performance art, discussed earlier in this chapter, and multimedia works. The French-Canadian

Robert Lepage (1957–) is a well-known director, creator of theatrical and operatic productions, and actor. In 1993, he founded Ex Machina, a multimedia performance center in Quebec City. Lepage is probably best-known for *KÁ*, the Cirque du Soleil production he staged in Las Vegas in 2005, and the Metropolitan Opera production of Wagner's epic *Der Ring des Nibelungen* in 2012.

Australia also has many contemporary performance artists, such as Mike Parr (1945–) as well as companies that experiment with technology, site-specific spaces, and unique interactions with audience members. One Step at a Time Like This, a Melbourne company, tours individual audience members through city spaces connecting those spaces to theatrical interactions with individual performers along the way. Two of their works, *En Route* and *Since I Suppose* toured to Chicago in 2011 and 2014. Some critics have referred to this type of theatre, which we discussed earlier, as total immersion.

Asia, Africa, and Latin America

Theatres in India, China, and Japan As we noted in the previous chapter, the period at the end of the nineteenth century and the beginning of the twentieth saw increasing interchange between Asian and other theatres. Particularly, Western theatre had a growing influence on the modern theatres of India, China, and Japan. However, in the past four decades, there has been a unique return of traditional forms blended into the sociopolitical sensibilities of Asian theatre artists. This return to traditional forms, in itself, is a rejection of colonial and postcolonial Western intrusions into the continent.

In India several changes occurred a few decades into the twentieth century, an important one being the advent of cinema. In India, film became extremely popular, from the standpoint of both producers and consumers. Films began to be produced in great numbers, and audiences flocked to them. At mid-century, this trend, plus World War II, led to a great dropping off of professional theatre in many parts of India.

The theatre that emerged in the latter half of the twentieth century was primarily an amateur theatre. It is estimated that Calcutta has as many as 3,000 registered amateur theatre groups; Mumbai, formerly called Bombay, has perhaps as many as 500; and Madras has at least 50. These theatres keep alive plays written by Indian playwrights, past and present, as well as plays from other nations. There has also

JAPANESE SHAKESPEARE

A Japanese director known for presenting Western classics in a distinctly Japanese style is Yukio Ninagawa. Ninagawa has directed not only Shakespeare but also the Greek classics and modern works. In every case he creates his own, Japanese, version of the play. Shown here are Kayoko Shiraishi (Titania) and Goro Daimon (Bottom) in a production of Shakespeare's *A Midsummer Night's Dream* by the Ninagawa Company at the Mermaid Theatre, London. (©Donald Cooper/Photostage)

been a strain of experimental theatre in India led by such figures as Bidal Sircar (1925–2011), whose plays reflect the experience of urban life in India.

In China after the civil war and Mao Zedong's rise to power following World War II in 1949, spoken drama continued, but additional emphasis was given to traditional forms of popular theatre. These traditional forms were familiar in the countryside and became a medium for carrying messages of the government to remote corners of the nation. During the cultural revolution, which began in 1966, theatrical activity—particularly spoken drama—was more restricted; increasing emphasis was placed on a few dance-dramas, elaborately staged and performed, that had very heavy ideological or propagandistic content. For the most part, theatre artists, along with intellectuals, were seen as subversive and suffered greatly during this era in Chinese history.

Since the death of Mao, and the opening up of China to the West in the late 1970s, there has been cross-fertilization between the Chinese traditions and Western drama. Theatre artists from the United States and Europe have visited and performed in China. Arthur Miller, for example, directed a production of *Death of a Salesman* in Beijing in 1983. In addition, popular traditional forms, such as Beijing (Peking) opera and other forms of classic music-drama, which were demeaned during Mao's rule, are becoming popular again. Although much of the drama still remains socialist in point of view and realistic in style, there are a number of artists who push the boundaries of subject matter and style, fusing classical traditions with contemporary forms and issues; Yu Rongjun (1971–) is one of the best known.

Since the end of World War II, contemporary theatre in Japan has been in a healthy condition. A number of truly gifted playwrights emerged after the War, chief among them Kinoshita Junji, whose work combines social concerns with humor and, when appropriate, elements from Japanese folk tradition.

Japan, from the second half of the twentieth century to the present, has maintained three main branches of theatre. One is traditional theatre—nō, bunraku, and kabuki—of which the most active is kabuki. It is remarkable that these three ancient theatre traditions in Japan have remained so vital and active in the present day.

Shingeki Contemporary Japanese theatre that incorporated Western ideas about playwriting and theatre production.

A second branch consists of various manifestations of ***shingeki***, a word that means "new theatre." Shingeki began in the late nineteenth century and in one form or another continued throughout the twentieth century. Broadly speaking, it was a modern theatre, in contrast to the traditional classic theatres. It was more realistic than the traditional theatres and banished the gods and the fantastic from theatre, partly because they had played such a large role in classic theatre. Later, after World War II, nonrealistic elements were admitted to shingeki dramas. Overall, shingeki remains a theatre in which the playwright is a central figure; in recent years it has included female playwrights, who were almost nonexistent in earlier times. Among Japan's contemporary playwrights are Shoji Kokami (1958–), whose plays have been staged in England; Noda Hideki (1955–); and Keralino Sandorovich (born Kazumi Kobayashi in 1963).

The third strain of modern Japanese theatre has been avant-garde or experimental theatre. A good example of this movement is the work of Tadashi Suzuki (1939–), who began his work at Waseda University in Tokyo and then developed a theatre community in the mountains at Toga. Following the models of men such as Jerzy Grotowski and Peter Brook, Suzuki led a director-centered theatre that was international in its ideas and its reach. In his theatre, there was an emphasis on ensemble playing, on physical movement, and on combining the old and the new, the traditional and the experimental.

IN FOCUS: TADASHI SUZUKI, GLOBAL THEATRE ARTIST

Among important international theatre artists, a key figure is Tadashi Suzuki, a director, writer, and teacher who calls Japan his home but has worked with and influenced artists around the world. Suzuki first attracted attention as a part of Japan's *shōgekijō undō,* or "little theatre movement" in the 1960s and 70s. *Shōgekijō* was a response to what was seen as the restrictive realism and limited point-of-view of *shingeki.* Like proponents of "little theatre" and avant-garde movements in the West, *shōgekijō* artists largely rejected mainstream success, preferring smaller, more adventurous audiences who were willing to engage with provocative, experimental material. Other directors who were a part of this movement included Shūji Terayama (1935–1983), Shogo Ohta (1939–2007), and Yukio Ninagawa (1935–2016).

Today, Tadashi Suzuki is among the world's most famous theatre directors. His Suzuki Company of Toga, in the mountains of Japan, is well-known for combining stories and traditions from various cultures; this includes creating theatre pieces that remain distinctively Japanese while also entering into conversation with theatre across the globe. His work also frequently comments on international political situations. In addition to his own company in Japan, Suzuki co-founded the SITI company in 1992 with the prominent American director Anne Bogart.

An example of Suzuki's international work is his production of Euripides's *The Bacchae.* In 1981, Suzuki worked with students at the University of Wisconsin to develop a dual-language version of the play, which he had been working on in Japan for a number of years. In this production, the American actors spoke English and the Japanese actors spoke Japanese, the characters responding as if they understood each other. The production also emphasized the cyclical nature of violence and

A scene from Tadashi Suzuki's adaptation of Euripides's *Electra* at the King's Theatre at the Edinburgh Festival. (©Robbie Jack/Corbis/Getty Images)

power, suggesting that one tyrant dies only to be replaced by another.

Beginning in 1991, Suzuki introduced *Dionysus,* a new adaptation of the play that focused on the clash between religion and government. This production was widely interpreted as a comment on the escalating violence in the Middle East in general and the wars between the United States and Iraq more specifically.

Suzuki's actors are praised for their onstage presence and incredible athleticism. His actor-training system, the Suzuki method, combines elements of traditional Japanese theatre techniques with the experimental work that emerged from international theatre in the 1960s and 1970s. Actors spend a great deal of time focusing on their feet and the ground beneath them, building strength, flexibility, and balance through a physical connection to the earth. Many observers feel that Suzuki's most lasting impact on world theatre will be his work on actor training.

Prepared by Frank Episale

Another example is the performance artist Iseei Ogata (1952–). A comedian and film actor as well as theatre artist, Ogata has created popular stage pieces, including a very successful autobiographical work *Life Never Stops.*

Theatres in the Middle East   Although Islam has strong prohibitions against theatre, there have always been traditions of storytelling, folklore, and popular comedy, particularly in the Middle East. In Turkey and Egypt (which are not in the

THEATRE IN THE MIDDLE EAST
Syrian refugee women perform the play *The Syria Trojan Women* in Amman, Jordan on December 18, 2013. Syrian actress Nanda Mohammad trained Syrian refugee women for six weeks to reinterpret *The Trojan Women*, a tragedy by Greek playwright Euripides on the Greeks' treatment of Trojan women after the fall of Troy. *The Syria Trojan Women* traces the parallels between the fates of the women of Troy and Syrian women refugees fleeing the current violence in their country.
(©Reuters/Alamy Stock Photo)

Middle East but are Arabic nations), for example, religious stories were often brought to life with the use of shadow puppets. Professional storytellers would also relate tales of religious or historic events to audiences, often accompanied by musical instruments. It wasn't until the nineteenth century, however, that stage theatre was embraced as a popular means for conveying life in the Middle East.

As in Asia and Latin America, the close of the nineteenth century and the beginning of the twentieth century saw a rise in Western colonial influence on the theatres of the Middle East. The adaptation of historic events into plays became very popular. Three early playwrights are widely credited with the introduction of Western dramatic techniques into the Arab world: the Lebanese author Marun al-Naqqash (1817–1855), who combined drama with opera, such as his interpretation of Molière's *L'Avare*; Abu Khalil al-Qabbani (c. 1841–1902), a Syrian who came to Egypt after his theatre was closed in Damascus; and Ya'qub Sannu (1839–1912), a Jewish-Egyptian dramatist. Western influence was particularly prevalent in the years following World War I.

After World War II and through the 1970s, there was significant development of professional theatrical activity throughout the Middle Eastern region, including Egypt, Iran, Syria, Lebanon, and Iraq. The theatres of these countries continued to be influenced by Western practices and artists, and a good deal of theatrical cross-fertilization occurred. Iran, for example, hosted the Shiraz Arts Festival through the 1970s until the Islamic revolution in 1979. The festival featured works by such notable Western artists as Peter Brook, Jerzy Grotowski, and Robert Wilson, and many of these works clearly reflected the influence of Middle Eastern theatre and literature. However, the works of many Arab theatre artists were highly nationalistic during this era and returned to traditional folk materials.

With the rise of Islamic fundamentalism and totalitarianism in many of these countries, theatrical activities have been halted, significantly curtailed, or rigidly controlled by the state. For example, Iraq's war with Iran in the 1980s and economic hardships after the Persian Gulf War in the early 1990s severely damaged Iraq's theatrical infrastructure. The invasion and occupation of Iraq by the United States and Britain beginning in 2003 did not help matters. In Saudi Arabia, the state-sponsored Saudi Society for Culture and Arts, established in 1972, oversees much theatrical activity; however, there is great controversy over its support of theatrical art. There are currently a number of significant theatre artists who deal with the contemporary political turmoil of the Middle East, including the ongoing battles with Israel, particularly in Egypt and in the Palestinian territories. In Jordan, the Ministry of Culture has sponsored annual theatre festivals, and there have also been independent festivals that bring together theatre artists from many parts of the Arab world.

There has been Palestinian theatre since the 1850s, but historians have focused most on theatrical activities since the Israeli occupation in 1967. Many companies and playwrights have created theatrical works that express the Palestinian point of view toward Israel's control of the West Bank and, until recently, Gaza. A Palestinian company that is gaining international recognition from its visits to the Royal Court Theatre in London is Al-Kasaba Theatre, originally founded in Jerusalem in 1970 but now located in Ramallah in the occupied West Bank. In 2001, Al-Kasaba staged *Alive from Palestine: Stories behind the Headlines*, which consists of a series of monologues dealing with the intifada, the Palestinian uprising against Israel. The company's artistic director is George Ibrahim.

Two other productions that reflect the Palestinians' existence under Israeli occupation are *The Alley* (1992), a one-woman production written and performed by Samia Qazmouz al-Bakri, which focuses on the lives of Palestinian women since 1948; and *We Are the Children of the Camp* (2000) by al-Rowwad Theatre for Children in the Aida refugee camp near Bethlehem. This production, performed primarily by children, toured the United States in 2005. Among the other Palestinian theatre companies operating today are Ashtar Theatre and Freedom Theatre, founded in the Jenin Refugee camp in the West Bank.

With the recent political upheavals in many Arab Nations, known as the Arab Spring, which began in 2010, a number of young playwrights have dramatized emerging issues. They include Mohammad Al Attar (Syria), Kamal Khalladi (Morocco), Arzé Khodr (Lebanon), Laila Soliman (Egypt), and Elyes Labidi (Tunisia).

The civil war in Syria against the regime of President Bashar al-Assad, which began in 2011 and which has led to the strengthening of the terrorist organization ISIS and other opposition forces, also resulted in a significant number of Syrian refugees living in camps outside their country. In Jordan, the Syrian actor-director Nawar Bulbul (1973–), who founded Al-Khareef Theatre Troupe in Damascus, but was forced into exile in 2011, began creating theatre works in 2014 for young audiences in the Zaatari refugee camp. One of his works is an adaptation of *King Lear* in which he cast almost 100 young actors. An adaptation of the Greek tragedy *The Trojan Women*, entitled *Queens of Syria,* was performed by female refugees in 2013 in Amman, Jordan, and in 2016 in England.

heatre has developed since the founding of the state of Israel in 1948. Israeli drama has been influenced by the Eastern European origins of many of its founders as well as the Middle Eastern traditions of those Jews who left Arab nations to settle in the Jewish state.

One national theatre of Israel is the Habimah, which was established in Russia in the early twentieth century and settled in what was then British-controlled Palestine in 1931. The other large national theatre in Israel is the Tel Aviv Municipal Theatre, referred to as the Cameri, founded in 1944 by the director Yosef Milo (1916–). There are many other active Israeli theatres throughout the country—in Tel Aviv, Jerusalem, Haifa, and elsewhere. These theatres also reflect the diverse Jewish populations in Israel. For example, the Gesher Theatre, founded in Tel Aviv in 1991, consisted mostly of new Russian immigrants.

As in Europe and the United States, there are also smaller fringe theatrical groups, which experiment with avant-garde techniques, and performance artists. Most of the theatres in Israel receive some governmental subsidy. There are also alternative theatre groups and many are showcased in the annual Acco Festival for Alternative Theatre in Acre.

Early Israeli drama dealt with the establishment of the state and nationalism. More recent dramatic works explore the complexities of Middle Eastern politics, including Israel's relationship with the Palestinians. In the 1950s, Israel's best-known playwrights were Aharon Megged (1920–) and the poet Leah Goldberg (1915–1970). Nissim Aloni (1926–1998), in the 1950s and 1960s, was Israel's first author to focus exclusively on theatre. In the 1970s and 1980s, Hanoch Levin (1943–1999) was a prominent playwright and director, who focused on issues of hypocrisy and self-delusion in Israel society. The most internationally recognized Israeli dramatist is Joshua Sobol (1939–), whose play *Ghetto* (1984) was produced throughout the world. In the 1980s, Sobol served as an artistic director with the Municipal Theatre in Haifa, frequently combining Israeli and Palestinian actors in controversial productions. Among the other Israeli playwrights who have achieved productions across the world are Motti Lerner (1949–) and the female playwright Anat Gov (1954–2012). Currently, the Israel Playwrights Association, which requires the production of at least two plays in professional theatres for membership, has 50 members.

African Theatre and Drama   Early African societies had many traditional performances that were connected to ceremonies and rituals and used music, song, and dance. Colorful, exotic, and symbolic costumes were also a key element of many rituals and ceremonies. African theatre artists in the twentieth century used these traditional forms and subverted forms of popular Western theatre in order to create work that reflects anticolonial struggles as well as attacks against totalitarian regimes in the new independent African nations.

Contemporary African theatre and society are divided into English-speaking Africa, French-speaking Africa, Portuguese-speaking, and Arabic-speaking Africa. In all the African nations, which were originally defined by nineteenth-century colonial powers, there are also attempts to experiment with the indigenous languages of the peoples of Africa as well as with the precolonial theatrical traditions. In Portuguese-speaking Africa, which includes Angola, Cape Verde, Guinea-Bissau, Mozambique, and São Tomé and Principe, missionaries introduced religious drama in order to spread Catholicism. Before independence in 1975, much of the theatre of this part of Africa was somewhat like vaudeville, although some anticolonial dramas were written. After independence, there was a greater focus on theatre that would arouse social consciousness, and plays followed the model of agit-prop dramas. In Angola, for example, the National School of Theatre was founded in 1976 and staged works that focused on African liberation.

French-speaking (francophone) Africa includes areas south of the Sahara as well as nations in northern Africa. There is a vital theatre in the sub-Saharan nations, influenced by traditional forms of storytelling and music as well as by French theatre traditions. Many of the plays written in this part of French-speaking Africa have been produced in festivals organized in Paris. The plays of this region usually focus on historical chronicles, social concerns, and political circumstances. Theatre in French-speaking Africa also received international attention when such well-known contemporary directors as Roger Blin and Peter Brook employed actors from this region in some of their productions.

English-speaking (anglophone) Africa, which includes among other countries Nigeria, South Africa, Kenya, Uganda, and Zambia, has had a significant international impact. Anglophone theatre became more highly developed in the 1950s because of the influence of universities in this region. Universities encouraged the work of dramatists and also organized traveling theatre troupes.

Among the influences on the theatre of English-speaking Africa are traditional forms, popular theatre, and the indigenous languages of the peoples; in fact, there has been considerable debate over whether theatre should be created in the language of the African peoples or in English. Among the leading theatre artists from anglophone Africa are the Nigerians Hubert Ogunde (1916–1990), the playwright who is often cited as the founder of modern Nigerian theatre; Moses Olaiya Adejumo (1936–), an actor-manager; and Olu Obafemi (1951–), a playwright, director, and actor. Among the leading playwrights in Zimbabwe are S. J. Chifunyise (1948–), Ben Shibenke (1945–), and Thompson Tsodzo (1947–). In Kenya, the playwright Ngugi wa Thiong'o (1938–), who has created individual and collaborative works in Kenyan languages, was arrested by the oppressive government between 1977 and 1978 and then forced to live in exile. South Africa has produced many significant playwrights and theatre companies, including in the 1970s the Market Theatre, People's Space Theatre, and Junction Avenue Theatre Company; these companies frequently produced works that questioned South Africa's apartheid.

Following the end of apartheid, a vital theatre scene continues in South Africa today. Lara Font is a well-known playwright who is also artistic director of the Baxter Theatre Centre in Cape Town, known for producing new South African dramas.

Wole Soyinka and Athol Fugard   Concern for political and social equality is at the heart of the dramatic works of the South African Athol Fugard (1932–) and the Nigerian Wole Soyinka (1934–), and these two authors have become the most internationally renowned of all contemporary African playwrights. Fugard, who is White, attacked apartheid in such plays as *The Blood Knot* (1964), *Sizwe Banzi Is Dead* (1973), *Master Harold . . . and the Boys* (1982), and *A Lesson from Aloes* (1987). Soyinka, a Black playwright, is also a poet, essayist, and novelist, who began his career with the Royal Court Theatre in London in the late 1950s. His politically charged works led to his arrest in Nigeria in 1967, and to two years imprisonment. In 1973, he adapted Euripides's *The Bacchae* for the National

ATHOL FUGARD: A POLITICAL SOUTH AFRICAN PLAYWRIGHT

Master Harold and the Boys is among the South African writer Athol Fugard's most celebrated and popular plays. The play deals with the embedded racism in apartheid South African society and how it is reflected in a young boy's seemingly close relationship to two black South Africans. In this scene, from left are: Sahr Ngaujah, Noah Robbins and Leon Addison Brown in the Signature Theater's New York revival in 2016. (©Richard Termine/The New York Times/Redux pictures)

Theatre in England. Soyinka gained international recognition in 1986, when he received the Nobel Prize in literature. Among his best-known dramas are *The Swamp Dwellers* (1957), *The Road* (1965), *Death and the King's Horsemen* (1975), and *Play of Giants* (1985).

Latin American Theatre   In the twentieth century in Latin America, and continuing today, there has been a development of realistic drama, experimental theatre, radical sociopolitical drama, and popular forms, all existing side by side. Although there have been economic, political, and social problems, including periods of censorship and governmental repression (for example, in Chile during the dictatorship of Pinochet from 1973 to 1989), all the countries in Latin America have significant theatres and playwrights. Frequently these artists have responded to the political and social turmoil in their societies.

At the beginning of the twentieth century, for instance, many comedies were written throughout Latin America—and especially in Argentina—that dealt with the unique local customs of each of the Latin American nations. In the period between the world wars, the dramatists of Latin America were clearly influenced by such European styles as surrealism and expressionism but often touched on nationalistic issues.

Augusto Boal
(©Sucheta Das/AP Images)

If ever there was an international theatre figure in recent times it was Augusto Boal (1931–2009). Born in Brazil, Boal (pronounced Bo-AHL) attended Columbia University in the United States. Returning to Brazil, he began working in the Arena Theatre in São Paulo. At first he directed conventional dramatic works, but Boal was a man with a powerful social conscience. During his early years he began to develop his philosophy of theatre. He determined, for example, that mainstream theatre was used by the ruling class as a soporific, a means of sedating the audience and inoculating it from any impulse to act or revolt. In other words, conventional theatre was oppressive to ordinary citizens, especially the underprivileged.

Boal also became fascinated with the relationship of actors to audience members. He wished to establish a partnership between the two, and he felt strongly that spectators should participate in any theatre event, that a way must be found for them to become performers and a part of the action. In putting these theories into practice, he began to present agitprop plays, that is, plays with a strong political and social message. He experimented with several versions of such plays. One was the Invisible Theatre in which actors, seemingly spontaneously, presented a prepared scene in a public space such as a town square or a restaurant. Another was his Forum Theatre in which a play about a social problem became the basis of a discussion with audience members about solutions to the problem.

Considered an enemy of the authoritarian government in Brazil for his work in the 1960s, he was jailed in 1971 and tortured. Released after a few months, he was exiled from his native land. Following that he lived in various countries: Argentina, Portugal, and France. He decided along the way that his approach should be less didactic than it had been, that he would be more effective if he engaged the audience in the theatrical process rather than confronting them. This was the basis of his Theatre of the Oppressed, which became the cornerstone of his life's work from then on. He authored a book by that title which appeared in 1974.

In 1985 Boal returned to Brazil. From that point until his death, for the next quarter century, he traveled all over the world, directing, lecturing, and establishing centers furthering the Theatre of the Oppressed. He also authored other books that were widely read. Altogether, his approach to theatre found adherents in more than 40 countries. Wherever the Theatre of the Oppressed was established, its productions challenged injustice, especially in poor and disenfranchised communities where citizens are often without a voice or an advocate. In his later years he was looked upon by many as the most inspirational person of his time in propagating socially oriented theatre.

Following World War II, many Latin American dramatists began to focus on the unique national issues and concerns that confronted their individual countries. Some of Latin America's most developed and politically active playwrights and theatre companies can be found today in Argentina, Brazil, Chile, Mexico, and Peru. The theatre artists of these countries fused the popular styles of their peoples and the modernist styles of Western theatre, including realism, expressionism, and absurdism. Among the significant postwar Latin American dramatists are the Chilean Alejandro Sieveking (1935–), the Mexican Elena Garro (1920–1998), the Colombian Guillermo Maldonado (1945–), the Peruvian Mario Vargas Llosa (1936–), and the Brazilian Plinio Marcos (1935–1999).

One of the most renowned is the Brazilian playwright, director, and theorist Augusto Boal (1931–2009). Boal wrote many plays and in the 1960s created works about historical figures, theatrical and revolutionary. Because of his Marxist point of view, Boal was forced into exile.

In exile, Boal traveled throughout South America and other parts of the world, experimenting with different types of theatre. He created a documentary-like drama that focused on current political issues and an environmental style of theatre that presented performances in public spaces, catching spectators by surprise. Boal became internationally known for his theoretical work *Theatre of the Oppressed* (1975), which became a manifesto for revolutionary and socially conscious theatre. Until his death, Boal continued to teach, give workshops, and lecture throughout the world.

There are significant dramatists today throughout Latin America. Four young contemporary playwrights from Argentina are David Veronese (1955–), Lola Arias (1976–), Rafael Spregelburd (1970–), and Federica León (1970–). *Neva,* a play by Chilean playwright Guillermo Calderon (1971–), was produced at New York's Public Theatre. Contemporary Mexican theatre, according to a young playwright, Richard Viqueira (1976–), "wants to unburden itself from the influence of European theatrical models, and is seeking to forge its own voice. The move in new writing," he says, "more and more is away from the folkloric toward the more recognizably idiomatic."[3] Along with Viqueira, other recognized young Mexican playwrights include Javier Malpicak (1965–), Sabima Berman (1955–), Sylvia Pelaez (1965–), and Alberto Villarreal (1977–).

In Cuba, the country's communist government controls most theatres. Still, there are a number of theatre companies that have been able to present works by international playwrights and contemporary authors. These include Teatro Studio (founded in 1959), Compañia Teatral (founded 1962), Compañia Teatral Humbert de Blanck (founded 1992), Teatro El Publico (founded 1992), and Argos Teatro (founded 1996). In recent years, several Cuban companies have toured internationally. For example, Teatro Buendia, an independent theatre that was established in 1986 and that stages adaptations of historically significant texts using Cuban contexts and music, performed at the Goodman Theatre in Chicago as part of the 2010 and 2013 Latino Theatre Festivals.

TODAY AND TOMORROW: A LOOK AHEAD

In the twentieth century, theatre faced a series of unprecedented challenges. First came silent films, then radio, then sound films, then television. With each new challenge, it was assumed that theatre would suffer an irreversible setback. After all, each of these new media offered drama in a form that was less expensive and much more accessible than the traditional theatre setting. When sound film appeared, for example, it was argued that anyone who went out for entertainment would go to the movies rather than theatre: Film would be cheaper and would offer more glamorous stars. When television appeared, it was argued that people did not even need to leave their homes to see drama.

Inevitably, some changes in audiences' habits have resulted from new customs and from competition by films and television. For most of the eighteenth and nineteenth centuries, theatre was the main source of escapist dramatic entertainment—both comedies and suspense melodramas. Today, television, with its situation comedies,

[3]Richard Viqueira

PLAYING YOUR PART:
THINKING ABOUT THEATRE

1. Explain why some theorists might categorize a stand-up comedian as a performance artist.

2. Discuss why a film or television show you have seen might be categorized as postmodern.

3. Discuss key changes in communication that have had an impact on global theatre.

4. Discuss why a film or television show that you have seen might be categorized as a documentary drama.

5. How do you think theatre will be affected by new digital technologies? Explain your answer.

provides much of the light entertainment formerly offered by theatre, and film and streaming also provide much escapist entertainment.

Now in the twenty-first century, there is the additional concern that even newer technologies—such as 3-D blu-ray and television, interactive digital gaming, streaming of films, television shows, and even live theatre performances, as well as constantly evolving new computer, tablet, and smartphone entertainments and social media—will further erode interest in theatre.

But despite these new media, theatre has not suffered as predicted. Much to the surprise of the prophets of doom, there is probably more theatrical activity in the United States and worldwide today—as the discussions in this chapter and in the chapter "The Modern Theatre Emerges" suggest—than at any other time.

Why is this so? First, in spite of their similarities, there is a basic difference between theatre on the one hand and these technological entertainments on the other. As we pointed out in the chapter "The Audience," the difference is the presence in theatre of the live performer. All of these other technologies present images of people or animations, not the real thing. Human contact between audience and performers meets a profound, fundamental need that neither the large screens in movie theatres nor the small screens in our living rooms or on our computers, tablets, or smartphones can ever satisfy. The human electricity that flows back and forth between performers and audience—the laughter at comic moments and the hushed silence at serious moments—cannot be created in these other media. Even when a stage production is streamed into a movie theatre, the "live" quality of theatre is missing.

Second, there is the human impulse to create theatre. Earlier, we said that this universal impulse leads every society to create its own theatrical activity, unless such activity is expressly forbidden. The need and desire for theatre will continue into the future. The diverse theatres growing out of the diverse populations in our global society reflect the intense need by audiences for theatre that focuses on their issues and concerns as well as provides them with live entertainment.

When we turn from the theatre of today to the future, a question arises: Where will theatre go from here? It is impossible, of course, to answer with any certainty. We can assume, though, that the trends described in this chapter and in the chapter "The Modern Theatre Emerges" will continue. Theatre of the future will no doubt continue to present new works alongside a rich mixture of plays from the past. In both writing and production, theatre will draw on many sources. We cannot know whether or not new plays will attain the greatness of the past, but playwrights show no sign of abandoning theatre, despite the larger financial rewards offered by other media.

We can be sure that theatre will survive in a vigorous form, no matter what challenges it faces from electronic and digital media. At the same time, modern technology will play an important role in theatre: in lighting effects, with the use of computerized lighting boards; in the shifting of scenery; and in other ways. There will also, no doubt, continue to be multimedia experiments, fusing theatre with film, video, dance, and digitally generated media.

Theatre will, as we have noted, also find new ways of co-opting new technologies to reach out to audiences across the globe, such as digitally streaming live performances, seeking instantaneous feedback from spectators via Twitter, as well as interacting with potential and returning audience members by means of social media.

With all its innovations, however, theatre of the future will no doubt be an extension of theatre of the past. Theatre will continue to be enacted by women and men in person before an audience, and the plays they perform will deal primarily with the hopes, fears, agonies, and joys of the human race.

It is clear that the complexity of the global world will result in a heterogeneous theatre. Ongoing exploration of the diversity of contemporary society means that diverse theatres will continue to spring up. There is no question that in the twenty-first century, theatre will be as complex and fragmented as the world in which it exists. Yet from the start theatre has always focused on human concerns, and they will remain the source of its appeal as far ahead as we can see.

Evaluating a Production of a Contemporary or New Play

As a theatre audience member, you might be asked to attend a production of a contemporary play or possibly of one that is being staged for the first time. To help you better evaluate the production of a contemporary or new play, here are some questions you might ask yourself:

1. Has the contemporary play been staged at other theatres? If so, research those previous productions.
2. If the play is a new work, is there information available on the playwright? Is information available on her or his previous work(s)?
3. What type of play is it: realistic or a departure from realism? How did you arrive at that conclusion? Does the work seem to fit into any of the specific categories discussed in the previous two chapters (e.g., symbolism, expressionism, epic theatre, theatre of the absurd, selective realism, environmental theatre, performance art)?
4. Does the style of the play seem appropriate to the subject matter? Why or why not?
5. What is the intent of the playwright (e.g., entertainment, expressing a sociopolitical point of view, some combination)?
6. Can you identify the play's themes and what the playwright is hoping to communicate to the audience?
7. Why do you think the director chose this specific play? Has the director helped you better understand the intent of the playwright and the themes of the play? How?
8. Review all of the questions posed in the earlier chapters dealing with the elements of a stage production. All of those questions are relevant to your analysis of the success of a production of a contemporary or new play.

SUMMARY

1. Contemporary theatre is eclectic, combining styles and techniques from earlier periods as well as from other art forms.

2. Today's playwrights and directors draw from a wide range of sources.

3. Types of theatre available include realism and departures from realism (similar to the movements covered in the chapter "The Modern Theatre Emerges").

4. There are many forms of ethnic and political theatres such as African American theatre, Latino-Latina theatre, Native American theatre, feminist theatre, and gay and lesbian theatre.

5. All these exist side by side in numerous production settings, throughout the world: The rich storehouse of theatre available today is global in scope, with active theatres in Africa, Asia, Latin America, Canada, Australia, and the Middle East.

6. The vitality of today's theatre in the face of challenges by new technologies demonstrates the continuing appeal of live theatre and the performer-audience relationship.

7. If the present age is not one of great drama, it is a period of tremendous activity in writing and producing, in avant-garde experimental work, and in the revival of classics.

Design elements: Playing Your Part box (theatre seats): ©McGraw-Hill Education;
In Focus box (spotlight): ©d_gas/Getty Images

Plays That May Be Read Online

The following is a list of plays that are used as examples to highlight key concepts in *Theatre: The Lively Art,* 9th edition, and that can be read online. Any play in this edition that can be found on the Internet is highlighted in blue typeface. Should you want to read any of these plays, or if your teacher has assigned one, you can refer to this list and find an online version.

Abraham and Isaac http://www.wwnorton.com/college/english/nael/noa/pdf/13BromePlay_1_12.pdf
Adding Machine, The (Elmer Rice) http://www.scribd.com/doc/25952449/Elmer-Rice-The-Adding-Machine
Alchemist, The (Jonson, Ben) http://www.gutenberg.org/ebooks/4081
All For Love (Dryden, John) http://www.gutenberg.org/ebooks/2062
All's Well That Ends Well (Shakespeare, William) http://www.gutenberg.org/ebooks/1125
Anna Christie (O'Neill, Eugene) http://www.gutenberg.org/ebooks/4025
Antigone (Sophocles) http://classics.mit.edu/Sophocles/antigone.html
Antony and Cleopatra (Shakespeare, William) http://www.gutenberg.org/ebooks/2268
Arms and the Man (Shaw, George Bernard) http://www.gutenberg.org/ebooks/3618
Bacchae, The (Euripides) http://www.gutenberg.org/ebooks/35173
Beggar's Opera, The (Gay, John) http://www.gutenberg.org/files/25063/25063-h/25063-h.htm
Birds, The (Aristophanes) http://www.gutenberg.org/ebooks/3013
Blood Wedding (Lorca, Federico Garcia) http://www.poetryintranslation.com/klineasbloodwedding.htm
Brand (Ibsen, Henrik) http://archive.org/details/cu31924026309199
Busy Body, The (Centlivre, Susana) http://www.gutenberg.org/ebooks/16740
Caesar and Cleopatra (Shaw, George Bernard) http://www.gutenberg.org/ebooks/3329
Candida (Shaw, George Bernard) http://www.gutenberg.org/ebooks/4023
Chantecler (Rostand, Edmond) http://www.gutenberg.org/ebooks/10747
Cherry Orchard, The (Chekhov, Anton) http://www.gutenberg.org/ebooks/7986
Cid, The (Corneille, Pierre) http://www.gutenberg.org/ebooks/14954
Clouds, The (Aristophanes) http://www.gutenberg.org/ebooks/2562
Comedy of Errors, The (Shakespeare, William) http://www.gutenberg.org/ebooks/23046
Contrast, The (Tyler, Royall) http://www.gutenberg.org/ebooks/554
Country Wife, The (Wycherley, William) http://archive.org/details/countrywifecomed00wych
Cymbeline (Shakespeare, William) http://www.gutenberg.org/ebooks/1133
Cyrano de Bergerac (Rostand, Edmond) http://www.gutenberg.org/ebooks/1254
Desire Under the Elms (O'Neill, Eugene) http://gutenberg.net.au/ebooks04/0400081h.html
Doctor in Spite of Himself, The (Molière) http://archive.org/details/dramaticworksofm01moliiala
Doll's House, A (Ibsen, Henrik) http://www.gutenberg.org/ebooks/2542

Dream Play, A (Strindberg, August) www.archive.org/details/playsbyaugustst00bjgoog

Duchess of Malfi, The (Webster, John) http://www.gutenberg.org/ebooks/2232

Edward II (Marlowe, Christopher) http://www.gutenberg.org/ebooks/20288

Electra (Euripides) http://www.gutenberg.org/ebooks/14322

Electra (Sophocles) http://classics.mit.edu/Sophocles/electra.html

Emperor Jones, The (O'Neill, Eugene) http://archive.org/details/emperorjones00onegoog

Enemy of the People, An (Ibsen, Henrik) http://www.gutenberg.org/ebooks/2446

Eumenides, The (The Furies) (Aeschylus) http://www.gutenberg.org/ebooks/8604

Every Man in His Humour (Jonson, Ben) http://www.gutenberg.org/ebooks/3694

Every Man Out of His Humour (Jonson, Ben) http://www.gutenberg.org/ebooks/3695

Everyman http://archive.org/details/everyman00newy

Father, The (Strindberg, August) http://www.gutenberg.org/ebooks/8499

Faust (Goethe, Johann Wolfgang von) http://www.gutenberg.org/ebooks/14460

Frogs, The (Aristophanes) http://www.gutenberg.org/ebooks/7998

Ghost Sonata, The (Strindberg, August) http://www.gutenberg.org/ebooks/14347

Ghosts (Henrik Ibsen) http://www.gutenberg.org/ebooks/8121

Goetz von Berlichingen (Goethe, Johann Wolfgang von) http://www.gutenberg.org/ebooks/45145

Good Natur'd Man, The (Goldsmith, Oliver) https://archive.org/details/goodnaturdmanan01bakegoog

Government Inspector (The Inspector General) (Gogol, Nikolai) http://www.gutenberg.org/ebooks/8121

Great God Brown, The (O'Neill, Eugene) http://gutenberg.net.au/ebooks04/0400091h.html

Hairy Ape, The (O'Neill, Eugene) http://www.gutenberg.org/ebooks/4015

Hamlet (Shakespeare, William) http://www.gutenberg.org/ebooks/1524

Heartbreak House (Shaw, George Bernard) http://www.gutenberg.org/ebooks/3543

Hedda Gabler (Ibsen, Henrik) http://www.gutenberg.org/ebooks/4093

Henry IV, Pt. 1 (Shakespeare, William) http://www.gutenberg.org/ebooks/2251

Henry IV, Pt. 2 (Shakespeare, William) http://www.gutenberg.org/ebooks/1117

Henry V (Shakespeare, William) http://www.gutenberg.org/ebooks/1119

Hernani (Hugo, Victor) http://www.gutenberg.org/ebooks/9976

House of Bernarda Alba, The (Lorca, Federico Garcia) http://www.poetryintranslation.com/PITBR/Spanish/AlbaActI.htm

Imaginary Invalid, The (Molière) http://www.gutenberg.org/files/9070/9070-h/9070-h.htm

Importance of Being Earnest, The (Wilde, Oscar) http://www.gutenberg.org/ebooks/844

Julius Caesar (Shakespeare, William) http://www.gutenberg.org/ebooks/2263

King Lear (Shakespeare, William) http://www.gutenberg.org/ebooks/2266

King Stag, The (Gozzi, Carlo) http://www.epc-library.com/freeview/F_1814.pdf

Libation Bearers (Aeschylus) http://records.viu.ca/~johnstoi/aeschylus/libationbearers.htm

Life is a Dream (Calderon de la Barca, Pedro) http://www.gutenberg.org/ebooks/2587

Little Clay Cart, The (Sudraka) http://www.gutenberg.org/ebooks/21020

London Merchant, The (Lillo, George) http://archive.org/details/londonmerchanto00lillgoog

Love's Labours Lost (Shakespeare, William) http://www.gutenberg.org/ebooks/1109

Lysistrata (Aristophanes) http://www.gutenberg.org/ebooks/7700

Macbeth (Shakespeare, William) http://www.gutenberg.org/ebooks/1129

Major Barbara (Shaw, George Bernard) http://www.gutenberg.org/ebooks/3790

Marriage of Figaro, The (Beaumarchais, Pierre) http://oll.libertyfund.org/?option=com_staticxt&staticfile=show.php%3Ftitle=1563&Itemid=27

Master Builder, The (Ibsen, Henrik) http://www.gutenberg.org/ebooks/4070

Measure for Measure (Shakespeare, William) http://www.gutenberg.org/ebooks/1126

Medea (Euripides) http://www.gutenberg.org/ebooks/35451

Menaechmi, The (Plautus) http://www.perseus.tufts.edu/hopper/text?doc=Perseus:text:1999.02.0101

Merchant of Venice, The (Shakespeare, William) http://www.gutenberg.org/ebooks/2243

Merry Wives of Windsor (Shakespeare, William) http://shakespeare.mit.edu/merry_wives/full.html

Midsummer Night's Dream, A (Shakespeare, William) http://www.gutenberg.org/ebooks/1514

Misanthrope, The (Molière) http://archive.org/details/comedies00molirich

Miser, The (Molière) http://www.gutenberg.org/ebooks/6923

Miss Julie (Strindberg, August) www.gutenberg.org/ebooks/14347

Mrs. Warren's Profession (Shaw, George Bernard) http://www.gutenberg.org/ebooks/1097

Much Ado About Nothing (Shakespeare, William) http://www.gutenberg.org/ebooks/2240

No Exit (Sartre, Jean Paul) http://archive.org/stream/NoExit/NoExit_djvu.txt

Oedipus the King (*King Oedipus*) (Sophocles) http://classics.mit.edu/Sophocles/oedipus.html

Othello (Shakespeare, William) http://www.gutenberg.org/ebooks/1531

Peer Gynt (Ibsen, Henrik) http://archive.org/details/peergyntadramat01ibsegoog

Phaedra (*Phedre*) (Racine, Jean) http://www.gutenberg.org/ebooks/1977

Phormio (Terence) http://www.gutenberg.org/files/22188/22188-h/files/terence5_6.html#phormio

Pirates of Penzance, The (Gilbert, W.S. and Sullivan, Arthur) http://www.gutenberg.org/ebooks/808

Prometheus Bound (Aeschylus) http://www.gutenberg.org/ebooks/8714

Pygmalion (Shaw, George Bernard) http://www.gutenberg.org/ebooks/3825

Richard II (Shakespeare, William) http://www.gutenberg.org/ebooks/1111

Richard III (Shakespeare, William) http://www.gutenberg.org/ebooks/2257

Rivals, The (Sheridan, Richard Brinsley) http://www.gutenberg.org/ebooks/24761

Robbers, The (Schiller, Friedrich) http://www.gutenberg.org/ebooks/6782

Romeo and Juliet (Shakespeare, William) http://www.gutenberg.org/ebooks/1513

Rover, The (Behn, Aphra) http://www.gutenberg.org/files/21339/21339-h/files/rover.html

R.U.R. (Capek, Karel) http://ebooks.adelaide.edu.au/c/capek/karel/rur/

Saint Joan (Shaw, George Bernard) http://archive.org/details/SaintJoan

School for Scandal, The (Sheridan, Richard Brinsley) http://www.gutenberg.org/ebooks/1929

School for Wives, The (Molière) http://archive.org/details/comedies00molirich

Sea Gull, The (Chekhov, Anton) www.gutenberg.org/ebooks/1754

Second Shepherds' Play, The www.calvin.edu/academic/engl/215/ssp.htm

Servant of Two Masters, The (Goldoni, Carlo) http://gutenberg.ca/ebooks/goldonident-twomasters/goldonident-twomasters-00-h.html

Shakuntala (Kalidasa) http://www.sacred-texts.com/hin/sha/index.htm

She Stoops to Conquer (Goldsmith, Oliver) https://archive.org/details/goodnaturdmanan01bakegoog

Sheep Well, The or *Fuenteovejuna* (de Vega, Lope) https://archive.org/details/fuenteovejunacom00vega

Six Characters in Search of an Author (Pirandello, Luigi) http://www.ibiblio.org/eldritch/lp/six.htm

Sotoba Komachi (Zeami) http://etext.virginia.edu/toc/modeng/public/WalSoto.html

Spring's Awakening (Wedekind, Frank) http://www.gutenberg.org/ebooks/35242

Stolen Heiress, The (Centlivre, Susanna) http://gutenberg.readingroo.ms/3/6/2/3/36234/36234-h/36234-h.htm

Tamburlaine (Marlowe, Christopher) http://www.gutenberg.org/ebooks/1094

Taming of the Shrew, The (Shakespeare, William) http://shakespeare.mit.edu/taming_shrew/full.html

Tartuffe (Molière) http://www.gutenberg.org/ebooks/2027

Tempest, The (Shakespeare, William) http://www.gutenberg.org/ebooks/23042

Three Sisters, The (Chekhov, Anton) http://www.gutenberg.org/ebooks/7986

Tragical History of Dr. Faustus, The (Marlowe, Christopher) http://www.gutenberg.org/ebooks/779

Troilus and Cressida (Shakespeare, William) http://www.gutenberg.org/ebooks/1790

Twelfth Night (Shakespeare, William) http://www.gutenberg.org/ebooks/1526

Two Gentlemen of Verona (Shakespeare, William) http://www.gutenberg.org/ebooks/1108

Ubu the King (Jarry, Alfred) http://www.gutenberg.org/ebooks/16884

Uncle Vanya (Chekhov, Anton) http://www.gutenberg.org/ebooks/1756

Volpone (Jonson, Ben) http://www.gutenberg.org/ebooks/4039

Way of the World, The (Congreve, William) http://www.gutenberg.org/ebooks/1292

Widowers' Houses (Shaw, George Bernard) http://archive.org/stream/widowershousespl00shawuoft/widowershousespl00shawuoft_djvu.txt

Would-Be Gentleman, The (Molière) http://archive.org/details/comedies00molirich

Index